# THE EMPEROR AND THE ELEPHANT

# The Emperor and the Elephant

## CHRISTIANS AND MUSLIMS IN THE AGE OF CHARLEMAGNE

*Sam Ottewill-Soulsby*

PRINCETON UNIVERSITY PRESS
PRINCETON & OXFORD

Published by Princeton University Press
41 William Street, Princeton, New Jersey 08540
99 Banbury Road, Oxford OX2 6JX

press.princeton.edu


ISBN: 978-0-691-22796-2
ISBN (e-book): 978-0-691-22938-6

British Library Cataloging-in-Publication Data is available

Editorial: Ben Tate and Josh Drake
Production Editorial: Jenny Wolkowicki
Cover design: Chris Ferrante
Production: Danielle Amatucci
Publicity: William Pagdatoon

Jacket art: Indian elephant (*Elephas maximus indicus*), illustrated by Charles Dessalines d'Orbigny, from *Dictionnaire universel d'histoire naturelle*, 1892. Courtesy of Rawpixel.

This book has been composed in Miller

Printed on acid-free paper. ∞

Printed by CPI Group (UK) Ltd, Croydon CR0 4YY

10 9 8 7 6 5 4 3 2 1

To my parents, who understood that the animals were going to matter.

*There were at that time at Constantinople some elephants, whose conduct excited wonder and astonishment. Now it may easily happen that those who are given to ridicule will find only an occasion for derision in lighting upon a narrative of the acts of irrational animals in our histories: but we do not record it without reason. . . .*

—JOHN OF EPHESUS, *ECCLESIASTICAL HISTORY* II.48

CONTENTS

ILLUSTRATIONS

## *Maps*



## *Figures*

# ACKNOWLEDGEMENTS

MEDIEVAL AMBASSADORS DEPENDED upon support from allies at home, on the road, and in the courts they visited in order to carry out their mission. The composition of this book has been no different, although any envoy worth their salt would look askance at how long it has taken to complete this mission. I am indebted to John Osborne, whose generous financial support of my PhD via the Osborn Research Studentship made this book possible, and likewise to Sidney Sussex College, the British Spanish Society, and the Medieval Academy of America for their invaluable contributions.

I owe another deep debt to my doctoral supervisor, Rosamond McKitterick, whose infinite reserves of knowledge, energy, and kindness remain an inspiration to me. The advice of my doctoral examiners, Marios Costambeys and Jonathan Jarrett, has been immensely valuable, as has that of Andrew Wallace-Hadrill and the rest of the ERC-funded "Impact of the Ancient City" project. My deepest gratitude to Emma Brownlee for drawing the maps and to the Burgerbibliothek Bern, the Staatliche Kunstsammlungen Dresden, the Stiftung Museum Kunstpalast Düsseldorf, and the Maximilianeum in Munich for their kind permission to publish images. I am also grateful to my editor, Ben Tate, to my production editor, Jenny Wolkowicki, and to Princeton University Press for their support. Special gratitude to my copy editor, Jenn Backer, for making me look much cleverer than I deserve. My thanks also to the reviewer who advised a different press not to publish this book because "it is too well written." May I never have to read anything you write.

The work for this book took place within the community of scholars provided by the University of Cambridge, most notably the attendees of GEMS and CLANS. The final version was completed while I was a visiting fellow at the Eberhard Karls Universität Tübingen, participating in DFG-Kolleg-Forschungsgruppe 2496 "Migration und Mobilität in Spätantike und Frühmittelalter" under the generous guidance of Steffen Patzold. The support and camaraderie I experienced at both universities made the research and the writing a joy rather than a chore. I have benefitted from conversations and advice offered by colleagues seen and unseen, first thing in the morning at conferences, and late at night in the pub. I would like to thank Robert Evans, Ann Christys, Javier Martínez Jiménez, Fraser McNair, Vivien Prigent, Ingrid Rembold, Richard Sowerby, Graeme Ward, Philip Wood, and Edward Zychowicz-Coghill for their advice. Bob and Fraser went above and beyond the call of friendship in reading the drafts and asking the difficult questions.

This book is dedicated to my parents, who decided it was a clever idea to take their son to foreign lands and ancient ruins. This is clearly your fault.

# ABBREVIATIONS

| | |
|---|---|
| AA | *Auctores antiquissimi* |
| AB | *Annales Bertiniani* |
| AF | *Annales Fuldenses* |
| AL | *Annales Laureshamenses* |
| AMP | *Annales Mettenses priores* |
| ARF | *Annales regni Francorum* |
| AX | *Annales Xantenses* |
| Capit | *Capitularia regum Francorum* |
| CC | *Catalunya Carolíngia* |
| CCCM | *Corpus Christianorum Continuatio Medievalis* |
| CCSL | *Corpus Christianorum Series Latina* |
| Conc | *Concilia* |
| CSM | *Corpus scriptorum Muzarabicorum* |
| DD | *Diplomata* |
| Epp | *Epistolae* |
| Fontes Iuris | *Fontes iuris Germanici antiqui* |
| Formulae | *Formulae Merowingici et Karolini aevi* |
| MGH | *Monumenta Germaniae Historica* |
| Necr. | *Necrologia Germaniae* |
| PL | *Patrologia Latina* |
| Poet. | *Poetae Latini medii aevi* |
| SRG | *Scriptores rerum Germanicarum* |
| SRG NS | *Scriptores rerum Germanicarum, Nova series* |
| SRL | *Scriptores rerum Langobardicarum et Italicarum saec. VI–IX* |
| SRM | *Scriptores rerum Merovingicarum* |
| SS | *Scriptores* |

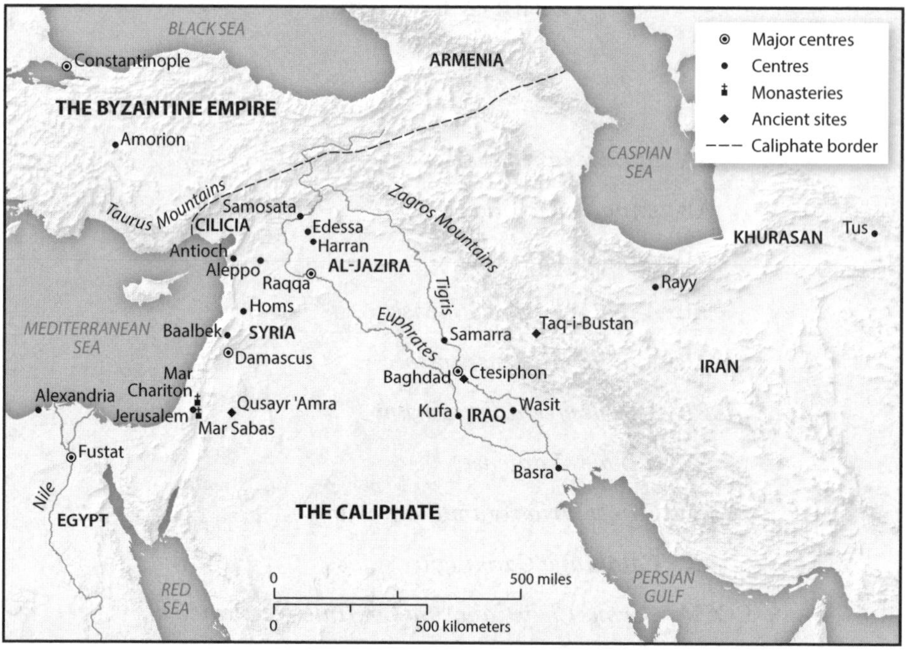


MAP 0.1. The Central Caliphate.

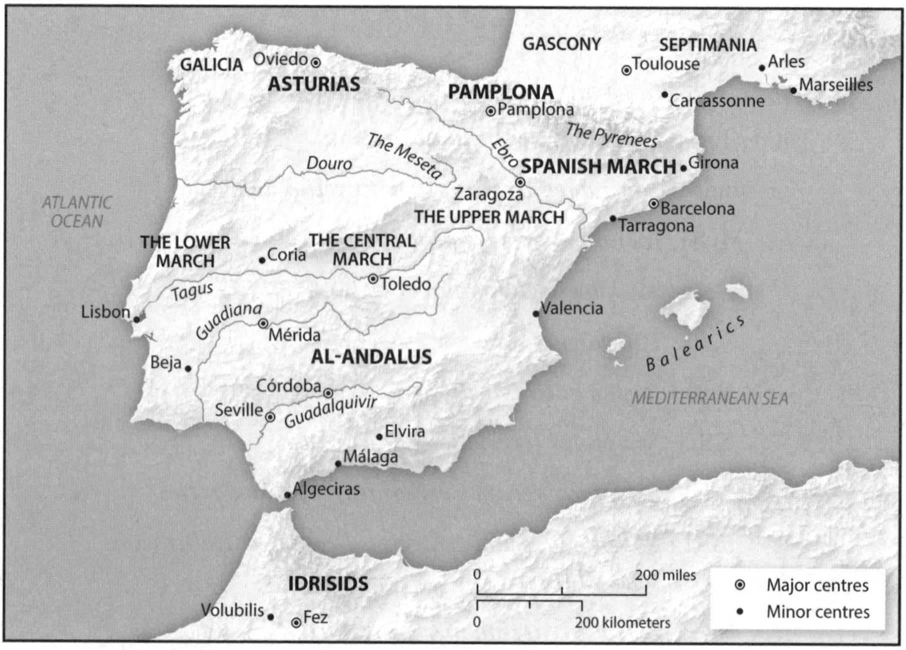


MAP 0.2. The Iberian Peninsula.

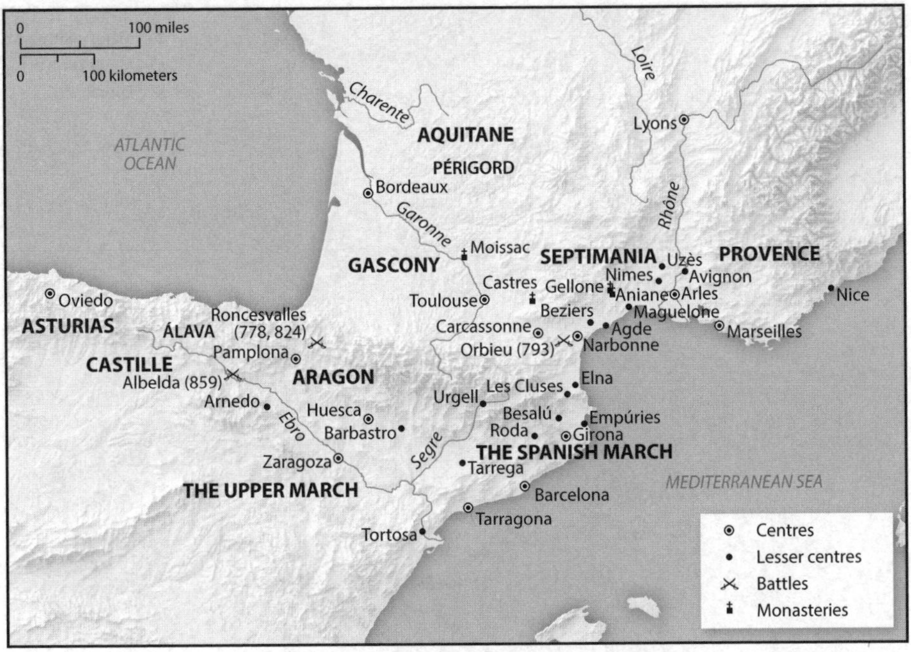


MAP 0.3. The Carolingian-Umayyad frontier.

MAP 0.4. The Italian Peninsula.

# THE EMPEROR AND THE ELEPHANT

CHAPTER ONE

# Introduction

CAROLINGIAN EMPERORS RARELY make an appearance in American electoral politics. In light of this scarcity, when in March 2016 "a white nationalist radio host" made a comparison between Charlemagne and then presidential candidate Donald Trump, a journalist writing for the *Washington Post* felt obliged to explain to their readers that the former was "the Holy Roman Emperor who tried to drive Muslims out of Europe."[1] While this interpretation of Charlemagne could hardly have been better designed to raise the blood pressure of historians of the Carolingian period, the depiction of the emperor as the dedicated enemy of Muslims is one with a pedigree that stretches all the way back to the high middle ages.[2] Epic poems of the eleventh century featured Charlemagne fighting Saracens in Spain and the Holy Land, teaching them with the sword that "pagans are wrong and Christians are right."[3] In 1190 the men gathered in Messina for the Third Crusade sang of Charlemagne "brave and strong and full of mettle" and of his wars in southern Italy against "Saracens, that race of vilest breed."[4]

It was romance of this sort that inspired Alfred Rethel, when commissioned to create a series of frescoes depicting the life of Charlemagne to ornament the newly restored Coronation Hall in the Rathaus of Aachen, to paint *The Battle of Cordoba* (fig. 1.1), which he completed in 1849/50.[5] In the fresco Charlemagne sweeps in from the left across a Spanish battlefield,

1. Miller, "Donald Trump Jr."

2. Morrissey, *Charlemagne and France*, 71–76; Stuckey, "Charlemagne as Crusader," 144, 147.

3. *Chanson de Roland*, "Paien unt tort e chrestïens unt dreit," line 1015, 151.

4. *The Song of Aspremont*, 16, 25; van Waard, *Études sur l'Origine*, 263.

5. Von Einem, "Die Tragödie."

FIGURE 1.1. Alfred Rethel, *The Battle of Cordoba*, oil on paper, on canvas, 61×71 cm, Kunstpalast, Düsseldorf, inv.-no. 4456, (c) Kunstpalast. Photo: Horst Kolberg.

leading his victorious army on a charging horse, while driving cringing Saracens before him in flight. Behind the king, a bishop raises a cross, while in the far corner a banner in black, red, and gold can be observed.

If this was all that was to be said about Charlemagne and Islam, then we could allow the depiction of Charlemagne as an uncomplicated foe of Muslims to stand unchallenged. Having performed copious research on the historical Charlemagne, Rethel was well aware that this was not the case. By his own admission he understood that in his depiction of *The Battle of Cordoba* he was "supplementing the fact with the legend."[6] Unlike the correspondent for the *Washington Post*, Rethel knew that Charlemagne the fighter of Muslims was only part of a much more complicated historical reality. Rethel's premature death in 1859 prevented him from completing

6. Ibid., "aus der Sage das Faktum ergänzt," 310.

FIGURE 1.2. Alfred Rethel, *Charlemagne Receives the Embassy of Hārūn al-Rashīd*, graphite, ink, white and gold highlights, 665×512 mm. SKD Kupferstich-Kabinett Dresden, C 1897–83. Photo: Herbert Boswank.

his Aachen fresco cycle. The surviving drafts for the remaining frescoes in the Staatliche Kunstsammlungen in Dresden show us the other subjects he intended to include. In one of the sketches (fig. 1.2) Charlemagne sits on the left of the composition, enthroned and crowned in his Aachen palace, while Arab ambassadors kneel before him in the centre.[7] The envoys came on the orders of the ʿAbbāsid caliph, Hārūn al-Rashīd. Included in the depiction is the extraordinary gift sent by the caliph, the elephant named Abū al-ʿAbbās, who arrived in Charlemagne's court in 802. Had they been finished, the full cycle of frescoes would have attested to the range of the Frankish ruler's dealings with the Islamic world.

Charlemagne's interactions with the Islamic world would loom large in the minds of many German rulers in the nineteenth century. The surviving oil paintings commissioned in 1852 for the Maximilianeum in Munich in honour of King Maximilian II of Bavaria include Julius Köckert's

7. Ibid., 311.

FIGURE 1.3. Julius Köckert, *Harun al Raschid Receives the Envoys of Charlemagne*, oil on canvas, 354×195 cm. Maximilianeum Munich.

depiction of Hārūn al-Rashīd receiving Charlemagne's envoys (fig. 1.3).[8] Arrayed with paintings on subjects such as the Battle of Salamis or the founding of Saint Petersburg, Köckert's work reflects the word-historical significance attributed to Frankish relations with the caliphate.[9]

By contrast, the painting of the envoys from al-Andalus who came to Paderborn in 777 on the walls of the Imperial Palace at Goslar fits this diplomatic activity into the story of the German nation. Hermann Wislicenus, commissioned to carry out the fresco cycle in 1877 on behalf of the fledgling Second Empire, perceived Charlemagne to have placed upon his people a duty of protecting and spreading the Christian faith to the world, a global task that had perhaps hindered the development of the Germans as a nation.[10] The Muslim ambassadors, complete with camels, reflected that mission. The old empire, much like the new one, was witnessed and watched by the world.[11]

Charlemagne was not the only Carolingian to communicate with the caliphs. His father, Pippin III, had done so before him and his son Louis the Pious would do so after him. Nor were these diplomatic relations confined to the ʿAbbāsids in the East. War against the neighbouring

8. Weigl, "Das Maximilianeum in München," 87–88.
9. *Verzeichniss der Gemälde*, 6.
10. Arndt, *Die Goslarer Kaiserpfalz*, 20–26, 33.
11. Pohlsander, *National Monuments*, 243.

Muslims of al-Andalus in the Iberian Peninsula was punctuated by peace, with envoys routinely crossing and re-crossing the Pyrenees. Never easy, diplomacy between the Carolingians and the Umayyads of Córdoba was nonetheless an indisputable fact of an early medieval reality alien to the imaginations of holy warriors, whether they belong to the twelfth century or the twenty-first.

This book is about the world revealed by Rethel's sketch. It is intended to examine the reasons why Charlemagne and his family sometimes made common cause with Muslim rulers and what the consequences of these dealings were. It is also intended to bring those Muslim rulers more fully into the foreground and understand their motivations for involving themselves with the Franks, to make them more than the supporting cast in the background of the story of Charlemagne. The chapters that follow will consider both the physical practicalities of this diplomacy and the mentalities of the people involved.

They must also reckon with the connection between Rethel's sketch of Aachen and his painting of Córdoba by examining the impact of warfare between Muslims and Franks in the period on their diplomacy. Although both parties could be fascinated by the culture of the other, these relations were not motivated by high ideals or by a deep commitment by the participants to respecting and celebrating diversity. In recent years, Carolingian diplomacy with the Islamic world has been employed as a counter to ideas of medieval narrowmindedness and intolerance. The construction of often misleading parallels between the Carolingian empire and the European Union means that conversations about Frankish contact with al-Andalus and the caliphate have been shaped by modern agendas.[12] The 2003 exhibition in Aachen which focussed on Abū al-ʿAbbās the elephant sought to present Charlemagne's regime, in the words of one commentator, as a "model of tolerance and multiculturalism."[13]

While appealing, this image has its own historical problems. To anyone familiar with the brutality of Charlemagne's campaigns in Saxony, or the intimate terror of the letters he wrote late in his life as he contemplated the fires of hell for his inability to ensure that all of his subjects were Christian, such a depiction of a tolerant empire seems risible at best and cynical at worst.[14] Carolingian relations with the Islamic world went hand in hand

12. McKitterick, *Charlemagne*, 1–7.

13. Wood, *The Modern Origins*, 318–319; see the exhibition catalogue, Dressen, Minkenberg and Oellers, *Ex Oriente*.

14. Rembold, *Conquest and Christianization*, 49–53, 75–84; Nelson, "The Voice of Charlemagne."

with conflict and violence, being normally dictated by pragmatism and opportunism. As the first chapter of this book will show, Franks and those Muslims they dealt with often viewed each other with suspicion and hostility. The people involved in these relations possessed that combination of practicality and imagination characteristic of successful politicians in any era. Many of the individuals we will encounter were noble in rank rather than in behaviour. Those amongst them who held themselves to higher standards frequently appal a modern reader most when they were acting at what they regarded as their most moral.

Carolingian diplomacy with the Islamic world has long been the subject of interest, beginning with the work of Jean Barbeyrac in 1739.[15] The past century saw an intensification of scholarly literature addressing the matter. Amongst the most important has been Francis W. Buckler's *Harunu'l-Rashid and Charles the Great*, published in 1931, which argued that Carolingian relations with the Islamic world could be understood as part of an alliance system between the four great powers of the Mediterranean at the time. In his view, realising that they shared common enemies in the Byzantines and the Umayyads of al-Andalus, the Carolingians and the ʿAbbāsids allied with each other against these opponents. Córdoba and Constantinople responded by coming to their own mutual arrangement, thus forming an alliance system. Although far from universally accepted, this argument was to be highly influential for subsequent scholars, providing a clear and satisfying answer to the problem of what interest Aachen and Baghdad could have had in each other.[16] We will return to this alliance system in due course.

Work on the Carolingians and the ʿAbbāsids did not cease with Buckler. Fruitful scholarship has linked their relationship with Frankish interest in the Patriarchate of Jerusalem and with Charlemagne's plans for his imperial coronation in 800.[17] The famous elephant sent by Hārūn al-Rashīd and arriving in Aachen in 802 has been the subject of much attention.[18] Nor have relations with the Umayyads been entirely neglected, with Abdurrahman Ali El-Hajji's monograph of 1970 providing useful discussion.[19]

15. Barbeyrac, *Histoire des anciens traitez*, 341–342. See Cobb, "*Coronidis Loco*," 53, 70.

16. For recent usage, see El-Hibri, "The Empire in Iraq," 281; Borgolte, "Experten der Fremde," 965; Nelson, *King and Emperor*, 89.

17. Schmid, "Aachen und Jerusalem"; Borgolte, *Der Gesandtenaustausch*; Grabois, "Charlemagne, Rome and Jerusalem"; Bieberstein, "Der Gesandtenaustausch."

18. Hodges, *Towns and Trade*, 35–38; Brubaker, "The Elephant and the Ark"; Dutton, *Charlemagne's Mustache*, 60, 189–190; Nees, "El Elefante de Carlomagno"; Hack, *Abul Abaz*; Albertoni, *L'elefante di Carlo Magno*; Cobb, "*Coronidis Loco*."

19. El-Hajji, *Andalusian Diplomatic Relations*.

Philippe Sénac has written multiple books and articles addressing both Carolingian diplomacy with the ʿAbbāsids and the Umayyads, while the year 2014 saw the publication of an enormous volume on Charlemagne and the Mediterranean.[20] The subject of early medieval diplomacy as a whole has also recently seen a revival.[21]

Given the apparent glut of scholarship, it is reasonable to ask why another volume on Carolingian diplomacy with the Islamic world is necessary. This book seeks to address two issues with existing approaches to the subject that have substantially hampered the ability of modern historians to understand exactly what was going on in this diplomatic activity. The first of these problems is the privileging of the Carolingian perspective; this is a consequence of the fact that the overwhelming majority of the source material that directly mentions diplomatic relations between the Carolingians and Muslims was produced in Latin by people connected to the Frankish world, with particular attention going to texts from the Carolingian court.[22] As a result relations have been understood via the narrative that the Carolingians wished to portray. It has also ensured that the vast majority of the modern academics to approach the subject have been specialists in the history of Western Europe. Most of the work done has considered very carefully the role of the Franks in these proceedings, trying to place these relations in the context of Carolingian affairs.[23]

Consequently, the roles and interests of Muslim rulers have taken a back seat in earlier discussion. Rather than engaging with the ʿAbbāsid caliphs or Umayyad emirs as historical actors operating within their own context, they have been treated as an inert fixture in the landscape. This is especially notable in depictions of the ʿAbbāsids, who acquire elements of the Oriental Despot, possessing absolute power in their eternal realms.[24] These Oriental states are apparently trapped outside historical processes

20. Sénac, *Musulmans et Sarrasins* and *Les Carolingiens et al-Andalus*; Segelken and Urban, *Kaiser und Kalifen*.

21. Shepard and Franklin, *Byzantine Diplomacy*; Barnwell, "War and Peace"; Gillett, *Envoys and Political Communication*; Drocourt, "Christian-Muslim Diplomatic Relations"; Hilsdale, *Byzantine Art*.

22. Drews, "Karl, Byzanz und die Mächte des Islam."

23. Grabois, "Charlemagne, Rome and Jerusalem"; Bieberstein, "Der Gesandtenaustausch," 159–169; Collins, *Charlemagne*, 152.

24. See, for example, Wittfogel, *Oriental Despotism*. For commentary, see Turner, *Weber and Islam* and *Marx and the End of Orientalism*; Mårtensson, "Discourse and Historical Analysis," 303; Lockman, *Contending Visions*, 14, 46–48. See also Valensi, *The Birth of the Despot*.

of change or contingency. While few modern historians would use the same terms, many of these assumptions on the nature of the ʿAbbāsid state remain present amongst Carolingianists. The caliphs in particular are presumed to be almighty potentates, with vast resources at their absolute command. The influence of the *Arabian Nights* and a series of somewhat literary biographies on Hārūn al-Rashīd can be detected here.[25] Few of the historians in question appear to have consulted any of the ʿAbbāsid histories.[26]

The reason for this neglect is that the Arabic sources very rarely refer to the Franks even in passing. This does not mean they cannot be employed to create a clearer view of their diplomatic relations. This book uses texts from the caliphate to build up a picture of the domestic political challenges faced by the Muslim monarchs who communicated with the Carolingians and the strategies with which they responded to them. The objective here is to comprehend both the environment and the patterns of behaviour that encouraged Muslim communications with the Carolingians, thereby providing a much fuller understanding of their practice of diplomacy as a whole.[27]

These sources also provide some of the tools necessary to address the second problem bedeviling the study of Muslim relations with the Carolingians, which is the lingering shadow of Buckler's alliance system. Recent scholarship rarely makes direct use of the thesis except to refer to it as a significant historiographical work.[28] Yet the impact of Buckler's book persists. The alliance system remains an important shorthand for Carolingianists who are not otherwise concerned with the subject, one that is frequently passed on to students. If nothing else this book seeks to make explicit in print the arguments against Buckler's hypothesis to lay it to rest once and for all.

Exorcising the lingering spectre of the alliance system opens possibilities that have not yet been fully appreciated. One of the consequences of Buckler's model is that it prioritised hard military realpolitik as the explanation for diplomatic relations between Muslims and Franks. The ʿAbbāsids and the Carolingians were hostile to or at war with Córdoba and Constantinople

25. Bosworth, "Translator's Foreword," xviii; El-Hibri, *Reinterpreting Islamic Historiography*, 19. Among the better specimens in English are Palmer, *Haroun Alraschid*; and Philby, *Harun al Rashid*.

26. But see the use made of these sources by Drews in his fascinating *Die Karolinger und die ʿAbbāsiden*.

27. On the importance of this, see Lebow, *A Cultural Theory*, 1–4.

28. Yet see El-Hibri, "The Empire in Iraq," 281; Borgolte, "Experten der Fremde," 965; Nelson, *King and Emperor*, 89.

at the same time. It was therefore assumed that it made sense for both to find a powerful ally who shared their geopolitical priorities in order to place additional military pressure on their common enemies. Removing the alliance system allows the consideration of other possible incentives for diplomatic relations beyond the geostrategic. Another advantage of fully moving past Buckler is that it makes it easier to understand Carolingian relations with the caliphate and Córdoba on their own terms. The Carolingians did not interact with the Umayyads in the same way or for the same reasons as they did with the ʿAbbāsids. Placing both as part of a shared alliance system flattens the dramatic differences in the dynamics between the different powers.

Further, by going beyond the alliance system, which prioritises political activity at a state or empire level, it becomes easier to consider the role of non-state actors. Powerful figures on the frontier between Francia and al-Andalus were frequently capable of acting autonomously. Marcher lords communicated with their peers on both sides of the frontier, waging war or making alliances as suited their interests. Some engaged with external rulers, as did other groups such as Christian populations in al-Andalus making contact with Carolingian monarchs. These relations could and often did set the pace for both Aachen and Córdoba, as the courts there sought to catch up with unfolding events.

A final benefit of rejecting the legacy of the alliance thesis is that it enables discussion of Carolingian relationships with other Muslim states at other times. Buckler's thesis was limited in its geography to the ʿAbbāsids and Umayyad al-Andalus and confined in its chronology to the late eighth and early ninth centuries. But there were other Islamic powers operating in the Mediterranean, most notably the Idrīsids and Aghlabids of western North Africa and the fledgling city-states established in southern Italy such as Bari and Taranto. Bringing them into our picture provides a much more complete understanding of the circumstances in which diplomacy between Muslims and Franks became desirable and when it did not.

It is this set of considerations that inspired the writing of this book and drives its fundamental argument and approach. Doing so involves working with an unusual range of material. The entire source base that directly refers to Carolingian diplomacy with the Islamic world is slender. To say that the Frankish material is the largest is to make a statement about how small the Arabic evidence is, rather than an indication that the Latin corpus is particularly copious. Excepting one or two lucky breaks, we lack the ambassadors' letters and reports, the complete formal treaties, and the bills for accommodation and feeding that are the bread and butter of people working on diplomacy in the modern or even the late medieval period. That one of the most detailed accounts of ʿAbbāsid diplomacy in the period is provided by Ibn Khurradādhbih concerning Caliph al-Wāthiq's embassy in 842 to the Gates of Alexander to check the state of the defences against Gog and Magog speaks volumes.[29] In his valuable monograph Philippe Sénac demonstrated the extent to which one can go with this source base.[30]

One of our strongest allies in responding to this problem is context. By understanding the circumstances in which rulers operated—the opportunities available to them, the limits to their resources, and the risks they faced—we can explain the otherwise apparently meaningless movement of ambassadors and armies. The sources may not tell us why envoys were sent to a distant court, but the wider picture they paint of both domestic and foreign issues provides the backdrop within which we can make sense of diplomatic behaviour. Such a method is hardly revolutionary, but it is worth being explicit about it. One of the consequences of this approach is that large sections of this book will be concerned with reconstructing the immediate context. In these passages diplomatic relations may appear to fade from view. A peripatetic approach is essential in order to establish the political and military background in which decisions were made.

Amongst the factors to be considered here are the internal politics of the states involved. On a basic level, the domestic situation of a polity shapes the resources available to its ruler, particularly those necessary to raise armies and maintain them in the field, as well as the time and energy the ruler can spare for each issue.[31] Instability within may incentivize a ruler to avoid external conflict with other powers, encouraging diplomatic activity in order to reduce the number of problems they face. Said division could also create more diplomatic actors, as rivals for the throne or border lords seeking stability reached out to their neighbours for aid. The internal geography of a polity also had an impact on the decisions made by rulers. Early medieval monarchs usually had a core area where the majority of their resources lay. In the case of the ʿAbbāsids, that area was the great river basins of Iraq, where the capital city of Baghdad was located.[32] While the centre of a Carolingian ruler's power shifted depending on the individual, generally the region between the Seine and the Rhine formed the heart of

29. Zichy, "Le voyage de Sallām"; van Donzel and Schmidt, *Gog and Magog*.

30. Sénac, *Les Carolingiens et al-Andalus*.

31. On the need to build domestic consensus for foreign policy, see Farnham, "Impact of the Political Context," 443.

32. Lassner, *The Shaping of ʿAbbāsid Rule*, 15–16; Berger, "Centres and Peripheries."

the Frankish realm and was bitterly contested by rival Carolingians.[33] The Umayyad core territory was the Guadalquivir river valley, the most fertile and densely populated part of the Iberian Peninsula, with good communications to North Africa.[34] Successful early medieval rulers prioritised securing and protecting these core regions over other challenges, including external invasion of more peripheral areas which could be recovered later with the resources of the centre.

This context is important to keep in mind, because it helps explain otherwise baffling decisions in the realm of foreign policy, in which rulers may appear to miss obvious external opportunities or dangers.[35] Examples of this tend to cluster around civil wars. Emir al-Ḥakam I of Córdoba (r. 796–822) allowed the Carolingians to take Barcelona in 801 because in the long run it was more important for him to defeat his uncles who were at that time leading armies in the Guadalquivir basin with the intention of overthrowing him.[36] From the 860s Charles the Bald (r. 840–877) was in a stronger position in dealing with his Umayyad counterparts than he had ever been before, but he concentrated on the renewed opportunities to acquire key Carolingian territories in Lotharingia and Italy from his family members instead.[37]

As a result of an investigation of the evidence following this approach, this book argues for a new vision of Carolingian relations with the Islamic world. First, Frankish monarchs did not deal with all Muslim rulers as part of a grand system. Rather, each power was engaged with on its own terms. Carolingian relations with the ʿAbbāsid Caliphate were motivated by very different concerns to that with Umayyad al-Andalus, which shaped their distinct characteristics.[38] Frankish interest in the ʿAbbāsids was driven primarily by domestic concerns and vice versa. That is to say, the most pressing reason for interaction between Aachen and the caliphate was to help the monarchs involved solve problems they were facing within their own territories and the key audience for this activity was a domestic one.

Engaging in foreign relations in response to challenges at home may seem like a slightly odd idea. To engage in foreign diplomacy for a domestic audience seems to confuse two distinct spheres of political activity.

33. Nelson, "Kingship and Royal Government," 385–386.

34. Collins, *Caliphs and Kings*, 37.

35. On the importance of the domestic context to foreign policy decisions, see Levy, "Domestic Politics and War"; Russett, "Processes of Dyadic Choice," 270.

36. See pp. 178–179.

37. Nelson, *Charles the Bald*, 220–251.

38. For another example of different types of diplomacy carried out with different partners, see Lee, "Treaty-Making," and Whitby, "Byzantine Diplomacy."

Further, it contradicts a long school of historical thought stretching back to Ranke that subordinates domestic to foreign politics.[39] It may be particularly unintuitive in this case because ʿAbbāsid-Carolingian diplomacy was immensely expensive in terms of the gifts sent and the lives of diplomats. Very few Frankish envoys returned alive from a trip to the caliphate.

However, this sort of behaviour is familiar in modern politics.[40] Political leaders facing trouble at home today seek to boost their authority with images of themselves engaged in major diplomacy with high-status world figures such as the president of the United States or the pope. Such displays communicate to a domestic audience that the individual in question is taken seriously by powerful global leaders and that they are fulfilling their function as the protector of their subjects' interests. Less quantifiably, it also separates and elevates leaders above their subjects or opponents by placing them beyond their audience's experience.

Early medieval rulers could not travel in the same way that their modern counterparts so readily do. Instead, they brought the glamour of far-off places and the admiration of their kings to their courts via elaborate gifts, delivered by foreign diplomats and displayed with grand ceremony. In doing so, they associated the magic of these evocative lands with themselves, while honouring the members of a court privileged enough to encounter distant wonders via the munificence of their monarch.[41] This book will show that the primary motivation for ʿAbbāsid-Carolingian diplomacy was the desire for caliphs and kings to secure their domestic position by accruing prestige through their dealings abroad. The diplomacy took place at times when the respective rulers had specific reason to want to bolster their status at home, and when they were engaged in similar contacts with other distant and wealthy neighbours. This is not to say that it was the only reason, with the Franks' genuine interest in Christians within the caliphate and especially Jerusalem playing a part, but that domestic considerations were the driving force for ʿAbbāsid-Carolingian diplomacy.

In order to distinguish this from other forms of diplomacy, we might call this "prestige diplomacy."[42] This type of diplomacy is defined by its purpose and its domestic audience. It is normally engaged in with rulers

39. Ranke, "Das politische Gespräch" and "Die grossen Mächte." For a historiographical review, see Simms, "The Return of the Primacy"; Otte, "The Inner Circle," 8–9. See also the essays in Mulligan and Simms, *The Primacy of Foreign Policy*.

40. For bibliography, see Fearon, "Domestic Politics," 290.

41. Helms, *Ulysses' Sail*.

42. Morgenthau, *Politics among Nations*, 83–96.

who are far away, to add to the impressiveness of the contact and to minimize any danger that this activity might jeopardize the political interests of the monarch involved. These rulers or the territories they oversee are familiar enough to the domestic audience in question to be meaningful but distant enough to avoid being controversial. They are also sufficiently wealthy to be able to send impressive gifts, which are the most tangible tokens of the exercise. This is an episodic form of diplomacy. While previous encounters might flavour future engagements, continuity is not essential. Provided both parties feel that they stand to gain through an association with the other, discussions are relatively free of content and therefore do not depend on regular interaction. Instead relationships can be revived periodically according to the interests of the participants. Prestige diplomacy can strengthen a shaky ruler or prepare the ground for a potentially controversial action. It will probably not save a regime in crisis on its own.[43] It will therefore not be a priority for a desperate monarch fighting for survival. Nor, given its expense in the early medieval period, is it likely to be indulged in by a regime that feels absolutely secure.

Carolingian diplomacy with Córdoba looked very different to that with the caliphate. Unlike the safely distant ʿAbbāsids, the Umayyads shared a long frontier with the Franks. This offered hope for Frankish territorial expansion, as the acquisition of cities like Girona and Barcelona demonstrates. On the other hand, the Carolingians found that making extended conquests in al-Andalus was unusually challenging, largely because of the heavily fortified nature of the cities of the Ebro river valley which defied easy capture. This meant that the Franks had to get used to permanently having a powerful neighbour on their southern border, one that could send armed forces to raid and cause serious damage over the frontier. The same considerations applied to the Umayyads, who faced an aggressive power to their north who could not be easily cowed or managed. Both parties had the clear capacity to harm each other. The situation was complicated by the participation of other actors, including powerful border lords, or interest groups such as Christians in al-Andalus, who were capable of conducting their own diplomatic relations with each other, or with Aachen and Córdoba.

There were times for Carolingian and Umayyad rulers when good relations with the other was desirable, generally because they were distracted

43. Cf. Koziol's enlightening comments on ritual: "ritual could not make a weak king strong or create a consensus where there was none . . . rituals could amplify currents; they could not create them" (*Begging Pardon and Favor*, 307).

by other matters, or because their position at that point in time was in some way weakened. This made diplomacy necessary in potentially being the difference between valuable peace and devastating invasion. Diplomacy offered channels by which unexpected clashes on the frontier could be smoothed over, and through which knowledge about the position and intentions of one's neighbour could be acquired and considered. These contacts might not always be effective, but they were always a potentially useful tool to be employed.

This form of diplomacy might be categorized as "frontier diplomacy." This is not to say that there is no overlap between these two categories. Rulers accrued prestige at home for successful frontier diplomacy. Elaborate gifts could also be exchanged in such relations. But frontier diplomacy works in very different ways to its prestige-based counterpart. It is directly concerned with managing relations with a formidable neighbour, with domestic audiences being an entirely secondary consideration. Often there is an ambiguous "frontier zone" between these neighbours, inhabited by powerful local figures through whom monarchs have to act but who have their own priorities and activities. Although the immediate importance of frontier diplomacy may wax and wane with the power and aggressiveness of the neighbour, the mechanisms that support it, including information gathering, tend to be continuous. The sending of envoys and messengers will be at least semi-regular. It will be engaged in by regimes that are concerned about their border regions. Rulers who feel secure in their frontier, or whose power and authority do not realistically stretch there, will be less invested in such activity.

It is from this distinction between Carolingian relations with Córdoba and the caliphate that the second major theme of this book emerges, which is the importance of the Carolingian-Umayyad relationship. Fundamentally, the ʿAbbāsids and the Carolingians were a sideshow to each other, an expensive means of acquiring political capital in times of uncertainty. Diplomacy with each other was occasionally useful but never a necessity. Relations between Aachen and Córdoba were a very different matter and this means that we have to pay considerably more attention to integrating the Iberian Peninsula into the wider history of early medieval Europe.

Early medieval al-Andalus has frequently been perceived as isolated from its neighbours across the Pyrenees, with 711 and all that serving to divide the Iberian Peninsula from Western Europe.[44] This in part reflects the complex array of new types of sources in a different language required

44. Burns, "Muslim-Christian Conflict," 238.

to approach Muslim Spain. These sources are often focused on Córdoba itself and not particularly interested in frontiers or foreign lands. The intricacies of Iberian historiography, shaped by debates generated by the unique history of the peninsula in the nineteenth and twentieth centuries, has also encouraged a certain insularity.[45] Much interest in Carolingian affairs in Spain has been based in Catalonia, where superb scholarship has been produced next to work designed to legitimate modern ideas of a long-standing Catalan identity.[46] This book aims to cross the Pyrenees by reintegrating the Carolingians and the Umayyads in each other's history. Umayyad policy in the northern peninsula was shaped by the presence of their Frankish neighbours. Precisely because of the danger they posed, Córdoba paid attention to the Carolingians in a way that they did not with the other Christian kings on their border.

Al-Andalus normally plays a relatively small part in histories of the Carolingian empire, often limited to a quick mention of Charlemagne's disastrous Roncesvalles campaign. Beyond that the Umayyads are generally an occasional menace at most. As this book will demonstrate, from the late eighth to the mid-ninth century, the Umayyads were in fact a crucial consideration for all rulers of the West Frankish kingdom. The capacity of Córdoba to cause trouble and undermine Carolingian rule by invading, or by supporting rebels in the Spanish March and Aquitaine, meant that Frankish monarchs always had to keep a watchful eye on their southern frontier. This does not mean that al-Andalus was always their highest priority but that the potential danger posed by the Umayyads ensured that they were a constant factor that needed to be taken into account in political calculations.

As the nature of the above discussion perhaps suggests, Carolingian relations with the Islamic world were complicated. The motivations that prompted it to take place and its characteristics differed depending on the actors involved and the context in which they operated. This is a much messier picture than the neat one provided by Buckler by necessity. Early medieval diplomacy, like all diplomacy, was intricate in its reality. Rulers, lords, and diplomats frequently had to improvise in the face of rapidly changing events.

Because of the importance of context for understanding these diplomatic relations, the majority of this book is arranged geographically and

45. Linehan, *History and the Historians*.

46. D'Abadal i de Vinyals, *Els Primers Comtes Catalans*, 3; Bisson, "The Rise of Catalonia," 128; Jarrett, *Rulers and Ruled*, 1–2; Chandler, *Carolingian Catalonia*.

within most of the chapters a rough chronology is observed. The first chapter is different, because it examines the mechanics of Carolingian diplomacy with the Islamic world. This involves investigating ambassadors, their retinues and routes, and the way they were received, but it also means being concerned with the ideas that the participants had of each other and the way that diplomacy with each other was perceived.

The following chapter moves east in order to deal with Carolingian diplomacy with the caliphate. Relations with the ʿAbbāsids have traditionally dominated scholarly work on Frankish contact with Muslim rulers. Drawing upon Arabic sources, the chapter begins by dismantling the idea of an alliance system pitting the ʿAbbāsids and the Carolingians against the Byzantines and the Umayyads. It then proceeds to characterize relations between Aachen and the caliphate as "prestige diplomacy," with special attention paid to the elephant Abū al-ʿAbbās. Finally, it considers the role played by Christians in the Holy Land in the framing of this relationship.

The importance of Umayyad relations with the Carolingians is indicated by the need for two chapters to do the subject justice. The first of these examines diplomacy between Córdoba and the Franks until 820, a period when the latter were normally more powerful than the former and thus generally, although not always, in possession of the political and military initiative. The expansion of both powers from the 770s brought them into close contact, prompting a greater engagement between them, although relations were often hostile. The challenges of diplomacy in the 810s receive particular attention.

The next chapter follows the changing patterns of Carolingian-Umayyad diplomacy after 820. The importance of Frankish dealings with al-Andalus are suggested by the disaster of 826–829 and its aftermath. Challenging internal politics weakened the ability of Carolingian rulers to be aggressive in the Iberian Peninsula. The consequences for relations with the Umayyads are discussed with reference to Charles the Bald. The chapter ends by considering the lack of contact between the Carolingians and the Umayyads in the tenth century, arguing that the weakened state of the West Frankish kings made them an irrelevance to Córdoba.

The fifth chapter shifts perspective to the Central Mediterranean in order to consider a theatre where the Carolingians came into close proximity with the Islamic world and yet little to no diplomacy took place. This helps illustrate the choices made by Frankish and Muslim rulers when they did decide to engage in diplomatic relations. The chapter begins by examining North Africa, where Charlemagne at the height of his power and Mediterranean ambition made contact with the rulers of Ifrīqiya.

While this demonstrates that Carolingian interests stretched further than often thought, it proved to be the product of an extremely brief moment, ending before the reign of Charlemagne did. A different set of dynamics pertained in Italy, where, in an environment characterized by complex relations, conditions combined to ensure no diplomacy took place between Louis II (r. 844–875) and the Muslim city-states of Bari and Taranto. Lacking the power of the Umayyads and posing a threat to Louis's interests, the city-states were instead the targets of the emperor's sustained hostility.

What follows in the remainder of the chapter is designed to provide the background necessary for the subsequent chapters to be fully understood. This begins with a brief discussion of the use of the term "diplomacy," the broad geopolitical context in which this diplomacy took place, introducing the principal states involved and the circumstances that brought them into contact. Finally, the chapter ends with an examination of the major categories of sources relied upon for the study, with a particular emphasis on the Arabic material.

## *Diplomacy*

In his celebrated *Diplomacy* (1939), the diplomat Harold Nicolson defined diplomacy as "the management of relations between independent states by the process of negotiation."[47] It follows from this description that diplomacy is a tool or technique employed to fulfil political objectives; as Nicolson commented, "not an end but a means; not a purpose but a method."[48] As this definition suggests, the study of diplomacy has traditionally focused on interactions between sovereign states, something that is problematic in the early medieval period, where autonomous political power was considerably more diffuse.[49] Relations between the Carolingians and Muslim border lords on the Spanish March surely constitute diplomacy, even if very few of the lords could plausibly be described as ruling a state.[50] In response to this difficulty, in his study on relations in the fifth century, Andrew Gillett preferred to refer to the "formalised management of relations among authorities."[51] In his book, he eschewed the

47. Nicolson, *Diplomacy*, 4–5.

48. Nicolson, *The Congress of Vienna*, 164–165.

49. Ruggie, "Continuity and Transformation," 274. On medieval states, see Reynolds, "The Historiography of the Medieval State"; Davies, "The Medieval State"; Reynolds, "There Were States."

50. On the participation of non-state actors in international diplomacy, see Osiander, "Sovereignty, International Relations."

51. Gillett, *Envoys and Political Communication*, 4.

employment of the word "diplomacy" as anachronistic, preferring "political communication," meaning by this "formal contact between parties of various levels of authority concerning public matters."[52]

Gillett was writing about a political environment in which many of the actors involved at least paid lip service to the overarching authority of the Roman emperor. Much of his book is concerned with embassies to rulers from their subjects. The landscape of the eighth and ninth centuries this book is concerned with was very different. This political communication is largely between powers who were not just de facto beyond each other's authority but understood to be independent and separate. For all the grandiose claims made by Frankish panegyrists for the respect felt by Hārūn al-Rashīd for Charlemagne, none could seriously propose the latter's sovereignty over the former. For all the capacity of the emir of Córdoba to raid his Frankish neighbours, at no point was he ever supposed to be their master. We are therefore examining relations between powers that were understood to be external to each other.[53] In this context, the word "diplomacy" is less misleading and indeed actively useful as a specific subset of political communication. For the purposes of this book, Nicolson's definition of diplomacy will be adapted to the management of relations between external autonomous powers by the process of negotiation.

Diplomacy is often misleadingly perceived as the opposite of military conflict.[54] In practice, in the relations discussed in this book, diplomacy was an adjunct to war and the most intense bouts of envoy sending tended to coincide with bursts of fighting.[55] As Clausewitz observed, the ambassador and the army were both tools to be employed by the ruler, frequently deployed in conjunction, and in order to explain the use of one, the reasons for not using the other need to be borne in mind.

## *Political Context*

The relations discussed in this book took place in a political context that was the result of a number of processes that began in the middle of the eighth century. The first was the ending of the political unity of the Islamic world.[56] The Umayyad caliphs had commanded an empire that

52. Ibid., 6.

53. Walker, *Inside/Outside*.

54. Berridge, *Diplomacy*, 1.

55. Barnwell, "War and Peace," 129; Padoa-Schioppa, "Profili del diritto internazionale," 34.

56. Nef and Tillier, "Les voies de l'innovation."

stretched from al-Andalus in the west to the Indus in the east and could plausibly claim to rule the entire Muslim community.[57] That political consensus was often questioned, with the Battle of Karbalāʾ in 680 being the climax of only the most famous challenge to their authority, but it was not until the mid-eighth century that the authority of Damascus started to permanently break down. In the west this began with the Great Berber Revolt of 739/740, which saw Berber soldiers in North Africa rebel against the caliph.[58] Although Ifrīqiya proper (modern Tunisia, eastern Algeria, and western coastal Libya) remained in Umayyad control after a series of battles in 742, the lands to the west stayed effectively independent from the reach of the caliph from then on. The turmoil in North Africa spread to al-Andalus, where news of the trouble prompted a coup overthrowing the governor in 741. This did not prevent Berbers in the peninsula from rebelling and raising armies. The ensuing civil war involved multiple factions, including a sizeable army of Syrians who arrived in al-Andalus fleeing defeat at the hands of the Berbers of North Africa. Although the details of this conflict are beyond the scope of this discussion, the result was an al-Andalus that was in practice beyond the rule of the caliphs from this point.

The lack of an effective response from Damascus to this crisis in the west can partly be explained by the political instability that began with the death of Caliph Hishām in 743. In 750 the Umayyads were overthrown by the ʿAbbāsids, who claimed to be the rightful leaders of the caliphate as the heirs of ʿAlī.[59] This claim was backed by an army built around the descendants of Arabs settled in Khurasan in the east.[60] Amongst the handful of Umayyad survivors was Hishām's grandson, ʿAbd al-Raḥmān b. Muʿāwiya, who fled to North Africa. After failing to gather support there, ʿAbd al-Raḥmān arrived in al-Andalus in 756, where he took advantage of the political chaos to proclaim himself emir of Córdoba. This was the beginning of a long and bloody process in which ʿAbd al-Raḥmān slowly took control of al-Andalus.[61] Unifying Muslim Spain around Córdoba was a difficult task, and large chunks of al-Andalus were willing and able to

57. Kennedy, *The Prophet and the Age of the Caliphates*, 82–122.

58. Manzano Moreno, "The Iberian Peninsula and North Africa," 590–593.

59. The literature on the ʿAbbāsid Revolution is enormous. For historiography, see Humphreys, *Islamic History*, 104–127; Shaban, *The ʿAbbāsid Revolution*; Lassner, *The Shaping of ʿAbbāsid Rule*; Kennedy, *The Early Abbasid Caliphate*; Sharon, *Black Banners*; Marín-Guzmán, *Popular Dimensions*.

60. Daniel, *The Political and Social History of Khurasan*.

61. Collins, *The Arab Conquest of Spain*, 174.

defy Umayyad power for long periods of time across the eighth and ninth centuries. Particularly relevant for our discussion is the extended Ebro river valley region in the northeast of the peninsula, which was dominated by Roman cities such as Zaragoza. The Muslim lords of these cities were frequently independent minded and capable of doing business with different Christian powers to the north of them.

The dramatic political events discussed above shaped Carolingian interaction with the Islamic world in a number of ways. First, the new ruling dynasty of the caliphate were the ʿAbbāsids, whose power base was Iraq rather than Syria.[62] This shifting of political weight meant that affairs in the Western Mediterranean received less attention than previously from the caliphs. In consequence, when ambassadors from the Franks first began arriving, they did so at a long remove from core ʿAbbāsid military or political concerns. Second, the division of the Islamic world prompted the development of new polities in North Africa. ʿAbd al-Raḥmān was not the only political fugitive to seek sanctuary amongst the Berbers of North Africa. More successful than the Umayyad was Idrīs b. ʿAbd Allāh, who fled the defeat of an ʿAlid revolt in 786. Settling in Volubilis in 788, he conquered most of what is now Morocco, founding a Shi'ite dynasty that would dominate the region throughout the ninth century.[63] Further east, from 800 the Aghlabid dynasty ruled Ifrīqiya.[64] In 827 they also began a protracted conquest of Sicily.[65] Muslim adventurers established short-lived emirates on mainland Italy at Taranto and Bari in the 840s.[66]

The Carolingians thus encountered a multipolar Islamic world. The immediate consequence of this was a shift in the balance of power between the Franks and al-Andalus. The invasion of the Iberian Peninsula in 711 had inaugurated a period where Muslim armies had been on the offensive in Francia, launching raids across the Pyrenees. Despite Charles Martel's famous victory at Tours in 732, two years later the governor of al-Andalus received the submission of Avignon and Arles.[67] The splintering that followed the Berber revolt ended any question of further Muslim expansion.[68] Isolated from support from the rest of the Islamic world and fighting for its political survival in al-Andalus, the new Umayyad Emirate faced the

62. Elad, "Aspects of the Transition."

63. Manzano Moreno, "The Iberian Peninsula and North Africa," 598–599.

64. Anderson, Fenwick, and Rosser-Owen, *The Aghlabids and Their Neighbors*.

65. Nef, "Reinterpreting the Aghlabids' Sicilian Policy."

66. Musca, *L'emirato di Bari*; Bondioli, "Islamic Bari."

67. *Chronicle of Moissac*, a.734 115.

68. Sénac and Ibrahim, *Los precintos de la conquista*.

Franks from a position of weakness that was to shape its interaction with the Carolingians for some time to come.[69]

The second political development of the eighth century of relevance to this discussion is the rise of the Carolingians to power in the Frankish world.[70] At their height the Merovingians, the previous dynasty to rule the Franks, had controlled an empire that stretched from the Pyrenees to across the Rhine.[71] By the early eighth century their influence was in serious decline. Peripheral regions such as Aquitaine and Bavaria were effectively independent under hereditary dukes.[72] Within the Frankish heartlands, the Merovingian kings were increasingly under the control of their Mayors of the Palace. Following a series of civil wars, this office was occupied by Charles Martel and his descendants, known to modern scholarship as the Carolingians.[73] The end of the Merovingian monarchy came in 751, when Martel's son, Pippin III, deposed Childeric III and had himself crowned king of the Franks.

The Carolingians were an expansionist power. Especially important for this book are the conquests of Septimania and Aquitaine, completed by Pippin and his son Charlemagne in 759 and 769, respectively, which took the Franks up to the border with al-Andalus.[74] The conquest of the kingdom of the Lombards in 774 brought the Carolingians permanently into Italy.[75] The defeat of the Lombard kings in northern Italy prompted the development of autonomous polities in the south of the peninsula, most notably the Principality of Benevento.[76] The Carolingians had a close relationship with the popes, offering them political and military backing in exchange for spiritual aid and legitimacy.[77] This bond was strengthened when Pope Leo III crowned Charlemagne emperor on Christmas Day in the year 800.

Frankish relations with the Islamic world were the result of these mid-eighth-century changes. An expanding Carolingian empire came into

69. Manzano Moreno, "The Settlement and Organisation," 95–104.

70. Costambeys, Innes, and MacLean, *The Carolingian World*.

71. Wood, *The Merovingian Kingdoms*.

72. Lewis, "The Dukes in the *Regnum Francorum*," 400–406; Rouche, *L'Aquitaine*, although see Bayard, "De la *Regio* au *Regnum*" and Bellarbre, "La 'nation' Aquitaine"; Jahn, *Ducatus Baiuvariorum*.

73. McKitterick, *The Frankish Kingdoms*, 16–40; Fouracre, "Frankish Gaul to 814," 85–90.

74. Bachrach, "Military Organisation"; Fournier, "Les campagnes de Pépin le Bref"; Kramer, "Franks, Romans, and Countrymen."

75. Costambeys, *Power and Patronage*, 273–352.

76. West, "Charlemagne's Involvement in Central and Southern Italy."

77. Noble, *The Republic of St. Peter*, 256–276.

contact with multiple polities ruled by Muslims in the Western Mediterranean. These encounters took place on the edges of Carolingian power in the Iberian Peninsula and southern Italy but also across the Mediterranean, as discussion of Charlemagne's interest in the Idrīsids and Ifrīqiya will show. While the caliphate retained an interest in the Western Mediterranean, the eastward shift in its centre of gravity ensured that affairs in Iraq and Iran held a much higher priority than al-Andalus, Africa, or even Egypt and Syria.

The importance of this geopolitical configuration is demonstrated by the way Carolingian relations with the Islamic world withered when it vanished. The late ninth century saw all the major powers involved hit by political crisis.[78] In the years between 861 and 870 four successive ʿAbbāsid caliphs were held prisoner by their own Turkish slave soldiers in a period known as the Anarchy at Samarra.[79] Although the ʿAbbāsids succeeded in restoring their control over Iraq after 870, the rest of the caliphate had been divided between a number of independent dynasties, including the Ṣaffārids in eastern Iran and the Ṭūlūnids in Egypt and Syria, removing any lingering interest the caliphs may have had in Carolingian affairs.[80] In al-Andalus, a breakdown in political order in the last years of Emir Muḥammad I worsened during the reign of ʿAbd Allāh (r. 888–912), whose power was frequently confined to the Guadalquivir valley, ensuring that he had little or no time for Frankish dealings.[81]

The overthrow of Emperor Charles the Fat in 887 by his illegitimate nephew Arnulf marked the end of the Carolingian monopoly on royal status in the Frankish world.[82] In the West Frankish kingdom it brought the non-Carolingian Odo (r. 888–898) to the throne.[83] The reign of his successor, the Carolingian Charles the Simple (r. 898–922), was characterised by struggle against overmighty subjects, as well as by the acquisition of Lotharingia.[84] Later Carolingians were also concerned with restoring their power within the West Frankish kingdom. In particular, Aquitaine and Septimania were generally beyond the rule of the Carolingians in

78. Pohl, "The Emergence of New Polities," 44.

79. Kennedy, "The Decline and Fall"; Gordon, *The Breaking of a Thousand Swords*, 90–104.

80. Bonner, "The Waning of Empire"; Brett, "Egypt"; Bosworth, *The History of the Saffarids*, 9–16.

81. Collins, *Caliphs and Kings*, 45–47.

82. Keller, "Zum Sturz Karls III"; MacLean, *Kingship and Politics*, 191–198.

83. Nelson, "The Frankish Kingdoms," 138–141.

84. McNair, "After Soissons"; Lößlein, *Royal Power*.

this period.[85] The shrinking size of the territory over which the Carolingians and ʿAbbāsids effectively controlled also shrank the distance of their diplomatic ambitions. As a consequence, the revived Umayyad state in al-Andalus under ʿAbd al-Raḥmān III (r. 912–961) found itself with very little need to engage with the politically distant Carolingians.

## *Sources*

The early medieval world often seems curiously devoid of diplomacy. Earlier historians, noting a gap in references to envoys in the historical narratives following the sixth century, have perceived a hiatus in diplomacy in Western Europe.[86] An important insight into this problem was provided by Paul Barnwell, who argued that diplomatic relations in the period were only recorded when they had specific relevance to the interests of particular chroniclers.[87] This was further demonstrated by Gillett with reference to Late Antiquity.[88] This observation has multiple implications. Not only does this suggest that the silence of contemporary political narratives does not necessarily prove the absence of diplomacy; it also implies the value of looking at texts which were not written with the purpose of talking about the subject but which contain hints hiding between the lines. Another important consideration in dealing with these sources is that most of them were composed by people with a closer connection to one party involved in the diplomacy than the other, which raises possible issues both of perspective and of bias.[89] As a consequence, understanding the nature of the sources being employed, the purpose for which they were compiled, and the context in which this took place is crucial to reconstructing early medieval diplomacy.

By the standards of the early medieval world, the Carolingians are represented by an unusually rich source base. Their worlds can be approached through a large corpus of royal biographies, charters, poems, and formularies.[90] The narrative spine for an examination of the politics

85. McNair, "Political Culture," 2–5.

86. Ewig, *Die Merowinger*, 40–47.

87. Barnwell, "War and Peace," 132.

88. Gillett, *Envoys and Political Communication*, 10.

89. Drocourt, "Christian-Muslim Diplomatic Relations," 54.

90. On relevant royal biographies, see Einhard, *Vita Karoli Magni*; see Innes and McKitterick, "The Writing of History," 204–208 and McKitterick, *Charlemagne*, 18–22; Löwe, "Die Entstehungszeit"; Tischler, *Einharts "Vita Karoli"*; Patzold, "Einhards erste Leser"; Thegan, *Gesta Hludowici imperatoris* and Astronomer, *Vita Hludowici*; on charters, Foot, "Reading Anglo-Saxon Charters," 41; McKitterick, *Charlemagne*, 188–204; Koziol,

of the dynasty is provided by the annals compiled in the period.[91] These annals are histories with information organized by year in ostensibly neutral, often terse, apparently disjointed sentences, providing a surface impression of objectivity which hides their true complexity as carefully constructed political texts.[92] Entries in the annals are normally short and frequently appear unconnected to each other. Some of the annals were updated year by year, with material being composed shortly after the events they describe. Others were clearly written in more extended chunks, or edited with the benefit of hindsight, a prime example being the *Annales regni Francorum* (ARF), which in turn has a later Revised variant which covers material until 812.[93]

Many of the annals can be tightly connected to the Carolingian dynasty. The *Continuations* to the *Chronicle of Fredegar*, which are very important for Frankish history in the eighth century, appear to have been overseen by Charles Martel's brother and nephew.[94] Unsurprisingly, they are strongly pro-Carolingian, presenting the dynasty's rise to power in a positive light. Likewise, the *Annales regni Francorum* contain a sophisticated justification for Carolingian rule and seem to have been kept and maintained at court.[95] Other annals were more distant. The West Frankish *Annals of St-Bertin* were produced from about 830 until 861 by Bishop Prudentius of Troyes away from the court.[96] Prudentius was of Iberian origin, which may explain the interest in Spanish affairs exhibited in the text.[97] The *Annals of Moissac* and *Aniane* represent a valuable southern history-writing tradition. Deriving from a now lost common source, they were redacted in c. 818 and c. 840, respectively.[98] Composed in Septimania, they frequently provide a closer perspective on events in the

---

*The Politics of Memory*; Chandler, *Carolingian Catalonia*, 18; on poems, Godman, "Louis 'the Pious' and His Poets" and *Poets and Emperors*; Depreux, "Poètes et historiens"; on formularies, Rio, *Legal Practice*, 81–100.

91. McKitterick, *Perceptions of the Past*, 66.

92. Innes and McKitterick, "The Writing of History," 211–213; Nelson, "History-writing," 438; McKitterick, *History and Memory*, 131; Foot, "Finding the Meaning of Form."

93. On the Reviser, see Collins, "The 'Reviser' Revisited" and McKitterick, *Charlemagne*, 27–31.

94. Collins, "Deception and Misrepresentation" and *Die Fredegar-Chroniken*, 89–96; "The Continuations of the Chronicle of Fredegar," 300; but see the doubts of McKitterick, "Political Ideology," 166, "Die Anfänge des karolingischen Königtums," 155–156, and *History and Memory*, 138.

95. McKitterick, "Constructing the Past," 115.

96. Nelson, "The "Annals of St. Bertin,'" 34–35.

97. AB 7.

98. D'Abadal i de Vinyals, "El Paso de Septimania," 17n9; Bisson, "Unheroed Pasts," 283–284; Buc, "Ritual and Interpretation," 201–207; Kramer, "A Crowning Achievement."

Spanish March than elsewhere, displaying detailed knowledge of Andalusian affairs.[99]

This Frankish material is immensely useful and is frequently the only contemporary source to directly refer to relations between the Carolingians and the Islamic world. They are nonetheless partial, being normally written by people who were generally sympathetic to the Carolingians and with only the broadest understanding of the politics on the Muslim side of the border. In order to counterbalance these defects, we must consider sources from the Islamic world. However, these are if anything more challenging than the Frankish evidence. As in the case of Carolingian history writing, much of the source base was composed close to and in support of dynastic rulers. They suffer the additional disadvantage of not being strictly contemporary.

The sources for the history of the early ʿAbbāsid Caliphate were compiled considerably later than the period with which they are concerned. By far and away the most important narrative account of the early ʿAbbāsid caliphs is that provided in the universal *History of the Prophets and Kings* of Muḥammad b. Jarīr al-Ṭabarī (839–923), which has been the linchpin of all subsequent scholarship. This work was completed in 915, almost a century after the last contact between a caliph and a Carolingian, but al-Ṭabarī was the heir to a considerably older historical tradition. A case in point is one of al-Ṭabarī's chief sources, the writer Ibn Isḥāq (d. 767), who was commissioned by al-Manṣūr (r. 754–775) to compose a universal history for the education of the caliph's son, the future al-Mahdī (r. 775–785).[100] Ibn Isḥāq complied but his history now only survives in fragments. That Ibn Isḥāq's knowledge was transmitted was due to the work of his students. As Gregor Schoeler observed, the most prestigious mechanism for learning in the period was listening to the lectures of teachers.[101] Teachers kept notes as mnemonic aids, while students took notes of lessons, both of which could circulate and be copied by others.[102] Similar mechanisms made the work of other key figures available to al-Ṭabarī, including al-Wāqidī (d. 822), al-Haytham b. ʿAdī (d. c. 822), and al-Madāʾinī (752–843), who were all patronised by the ʿAbbāsid regime.[103]

99. Buc, "Ritual and Interpretation," 189–191 and "Political Rituals," 197–198.

100. Schoeler, "The Transmission of the Sciences," 34, orig. published as "Die Frage der schriftlichen."

101. Schoeler, *The Genesis of Literature*, 24; Cook, "The Opponents of the Writing of Tradition."

102. Schoeler, "The Transmission of the Sciences," 34.

103. Schoeler, *The Genesis of Literature*, 7; Lindstedt, "The Role of al-Madāʾinī's Students," 295–340. For a list of al-Ṭabarī's teachers, see Gilliot, "La formation intellectuelle."

It is important to note that al-Ṭabarī assembled a large body of material that was previously circulating without a definite fixed shape transmitted by teachers or notes.[104] The scholars of the early ʿAbbāsid period had long careers in which they updated their notes and changed their lectures.[105] Different students took different records, and the chain of transmission across the ninth century offered opportunities for misunderstanding or distortion. Nonetheless, there is good reason to believe that the basic narrative of his material genuinely derives from the work of historians who were active in the time of the early ʿAbbāsids.

Writing history in the early ʿAbbāsid Caliphate could be a controversial business. The ʿAbbāsids were not the only possible dynasty that could have replaced the Umayyads as caliphs. Many would have preferred one of the descendants of ʿAlī b. Abī Ṭālib (r. 656–661), the fourth caliph and the Prophet's son-in-law, amongst them the historian al-Yaʿqūbī (d. 897).[106] Key events such as the civil war between Hārūn al-Rashīd's sons, Muḥammad al-Amīn (r. 809–813) and ʿAbd Allāh al-Maʾmūn (r. 813–833), proved to be extremely divisive.[107] Much of the surviving historical material served to legitimise the victors in these struggles.[108]

That said, the same narrative emerges in sources composed by historians with very different views. The account of the pro-ʿAlid al-Yaʿqūbī is essentially that of al-Ṭabarī, generally sympathetic to the ʿAbbāsids, "with added curses."[109] Further, the patchwork compiled nature of the text militates against too streamlined a narrative, with al-Ṭabarī frequently including contradictory material and leaving it to the reader to decide between them.[110] In the event that his history should offend or seem implausible, al-Ṭabarī defended himself by saying it is "the fault of someone who transmitted it to us. We have merely repeated it as it was repeated to us."[111] This is not to say that al-Ṭabarī had no agenda but that it is possible to observe discordant voices. Even al-Ṭabarī's contemporaries had difficulty divining his beliefs, with him being falsely accused of ʿAlid sympathies by his enemies.[112]

104. Schoeler, *The Genesis of Literature*, 75, 112.

105. Schoeler, "The Transmission of the Sciences," 33.

106. Millward, "Al-Yaʿqūbī's Sources." On the ʿAlids, see Bernheimer, *The ʿAlids*.

107. Yücesoy, *Messianic Beliefs*.

108. El-Hibri, *Reinterpreting Islamic Historiography*, 11–13.

109. Crone, *Slaves on Horses*, 11. See the reservations of Daniel, "Al-Yaʿqūbī and Shiʾism Reconsidered."

110. Robinson, "Islamic Historical Writing," 246.

111. Al-Ṭabarī, *The History of al-Ṭabarī, Vol. 1*, 170.

112. Mårtensson, "Discourse and Historical Analysis," 303.

Al-Ṭabarī's complete history comes to around 7,800 manuscript pages, stretching from Adam to his own time.[113] The sections that deal with the caliphate are structured both by year and reign, with the annalistic pattern breaking on the death of each caliph to allow al-Ṭabarī to include anecdotes and statements about the ruler's character that he found hard to place chronologically. References to a chain of authorities for a piece of information become fewer in number in al-Ṭabarī's history after 815, with none after 884. This may suggest that al-Ṭabarī was increasingly composing from his own knowledge rather than compiling earlier material as the history got closer to his lifetime.[114] The history bears witness to its creator's interests, with approximately a third of the material devoted to the time of Muḥammad and the Rāshidūn Caliphate, and much attention paid to Iran and the central caliphate. The treatment of regions such as Egypt and Ifrīqiya is much more cursory.[115] Al-Andalus is the subject of a handful of notices.[116] Given this, that al-Ṭabarī did not mention the Franks is to be expected. Nonetheless, by illustrating the other concerns and priorities of the ʿAbbāsid caliphs, he provides an essential guide to the changing circumstances that motivated and shaped their contact with the Carolingians.

The source base for al-Andalus in the eighth and ninth centuries resembles those for the caliphate in style and genre, being written by people who followed Eastern fashions in the writing of history.[117] It is therefore unsurprising that similar problems arise in handling it. The earliest surviving works concerning the history of al-Andalus are not only late, they are dependent on Egyptian material, suggesting a lack of a native tradition.[118] The tenth century saw a major increase in historical writing connected to the Umayyad court. These histories were intended to legitimise the rulers of Córdoba and, in particular, to support the adoption of the title of caliph by ʿAbd al-Raḥmān III in 929 in the face of competition

113. Leder, "The Literary Use of the *Khabar*," 277.

114. Shoshan, *Poetics of Islamic Historiography*, xxxii–xxxiii.

115. Kennedy, *The Early Abbasid Caliphate*, 216; Fenwick, *Early Islamic North Africa*, 7–8.

116. Al-Ṭabarī, *The History of al-Ṭabarī, Vol. 23*, 164, 182, 201, 215, 219; Al-Ṭabarī, *The History of al-Ṭabarī, Vol. 29*, 247–248; Al-Ṭabarī, *The History of al-Ṭabarī, Vol. 32*, 164–165; König, *Arabic-Islamic Views of the Latin West*, 78.

117. Manzano Moreno, "Oriental "Topoi.'"

118. Makkī, "Egypt and the Origin of Arabic Spanish Historiography." On the transmission of early material, see Marín, "La transmisión del saber"; Fierro, "The Introduction of Ḥadīth," 75.

from the ʿAbbāsids and Fāṭimids.[119] Their narratives celebrate the Umayyad dynasty, portraying ʿAbd al-Raḥmān as the worthy inheritor and saviour of a prestigious and divinely blessed line.[120] They concentrate on affairs in Córdoba and the court apparatus.[121] Of particular interest to them was the initial conquest period in the early eighth century, which provided opportunities to compare the caliph to his famous namesake and the founder of the emirate.[122]

Two of the most important accounts survive in a single late fourteenth-early fifteenth-century manuscript, Paris BNF Arabe MS 1867.[123] This manuscript contains the vivid if anecdotal history of Ibn al-Qūṭīya, who, as his name suggests, was a tenth-century Muslim of Gothic ancestry, and the more mysterious anonymous *Akhbār Majmūʿa* (Collected Accounts).[124] The latter has prompted historiographical debate that is fierce even by the heated standards of Iberian scholarship but is probably a tenth-century compilation assembled as part of efforts to legitimise the new Umayyad Caliphate.[125]

The core of most subsequent Andalusi history writing was the annals compiled by the al-Rāzī family, court historians to ʿAbd al-Raḥmān III and al-Ḥakam II (r. 961–976).[126] Their work was well-regarded enough by later medieval historians writing in Arabic to form the basis of their accounts. The coherence and level of agreement between the later sources are due to their shared dependence on the al-Rāzīs. It is no longer extant in full, only surviving abbreviated in an early fourteenth-century

119. Manzano Moreno, "El medio cordobés"; Safran, *The Second Umayyad Caliphate*, 111–116.

120. On the legitimisation efforts of the Umayyad Caliphate, see Safran, "Ceremony and Submission."

121. Manzano Moreno, *La Frontera de al-Andalus*, 14.

122. Martinez-Gros, *L'idéologie omeyyade*, 81–105; Manzano Moreno, "Las fuentes árabes," 431.

123. Fierro, "La Obra Histórica."

124. Christys, *Christians in al-Andalus*, 175–183; Clarke, *The Muslim Conquest of Iberia*, 67.

125. Arguing for a late composition: Chalmeta, "Una historia discontinua"; Molina, "Los Ajbār Maŷmūʾa" and "Un relato de la conquista"; for an eighth-century origin, Ribera, *Historia de la conquista*, xii–xix; Sánchez-Albornoz, *El "Ajbār maŷmūʾa"*; Oliver, "Los autores del *Ajbār Maŷmūʾa*" and "El *Ajbār Maŷmūʾa*"; for a tenth-century date, Martinez-Gros, *L'idéologie omeyyade*, 52; Chalmeta, *Invasión e Islamización*, 50; Safran, *The Second Umayyad Caliphate*, 120–134.

126. Manzano Moreno, *La organización fronteriza*, 101; Lévi-Provençal, "Sur l'installation des Rāzī en Espagne," 230; Pellat, "The Origin and Development," 119. On the Umayyad Secretariat, see Soravia, "Entre bureaucratie et *littérature*."

Portuguese version, which in turn is only preserved in a garbled fifteenth-century Spanish translation.[127]

The final end of the Umayyad Caliphate in 1031 loomed over all subsequent writers, turning their narratives into tragedies and encouraging the mourning of lost glories, often exaggerated.[128] The bedrock of modern histories of Umayyad Spain is the narrative of Abū Marwān b. Khalaf b. Ḥayyān (987–1075), the *Muqtabas*. Ibn Ḥayyān began his career as an official in the last days of the caliphate and deplored its fall.[129] His history is generally considered to be the most reliable of the surviving corpus, being almost entirely based on the al-Rāzī chronicle. María Luisa Ávila convincingly argued that the *Muqtabas* were composed after 1069.[130] Unfortunately it survives in fragmentary form in a handful of damaged manuscripts, with only the material for 796–880 (almost illegible from 847), 912–942, and 971–975 remaining. His history was used by most subsequent writers.[131] Amongst the writers who preserve material from Ibn Ḥayyān, the most important are ʿAlī b. al-Athīr (d. 1233), who wrote in Mosul and used it for his universal history, and Ibn ʿIdhārī, who included it as part of his history of the wider Maghrib, writing in c. 1312.[132]

Standing a little outside this tradition is the *muwallad* historian and geographer al-ʿUdhrī (d. 1085). Unlike most of the other historians discussed here, he was not based in southern Spain but spent much of his career at the *ṭāʾifa* kingdom of Zaragoza, which was one of the polities that emerged from the collapse of the caliphate of Córdoba.[133] Accordingly his *Tarṣī al-akhbār* is concerned with the history of Zaragoza and the Upper March and contains different perspectives on the exercise of Umayyad authority from Córdoba. As well as drawing upon the Córdoban al-Rāzī material, al-ʿUdhrī includes information that appears to be from sources local to the Upper March. His work is a geography, structured around accounts of the histories of different towns in the Upper March, of which only about a tenth survives.[134]

127. Collins, *Caliphs and Kings*, 19.

128. García Gómez, "Algunas precisions."

129. Chalmeta, "Historiografía," 379.

130. On the debate over the dating, see Chalmeta, "Historiografía," 390; Molina, "Sobre la Historia de al-Rāzī," 441; Ávila, "La fecha de redacción del *Muqtabis*."

131. Molina, "Técnicas de *amplificatio*."

132. Clarke, *The Muslim Conquest of Iberia*, 122; Molina, "Sobre la Historia de al-Rāzī," 435; Martos Quesada, "La labor historiográfica"; Sánchez-Albornoz, "Some Remarks on *Fatḥ al-Andalus*," 158.

133. Al-ʿUdhrī, "La Marca Superior."

134. Lorenzo Jiménez, *La dawla de los Banū Qasī*, 47.

It is with these slim traces that the history of the Islamic world's dealings with the Carolingians will be written. Doing so requires both close reading and wide comparison, bound together by inference. Just as a diplomat must try to draw an accurate picture of those they do business with and their motivations based on limited information, so too must the early medieval historian. Nonetheless, with regards to the subject at hand, we have material from all of the major powers involved, all of which can be connected, albeit often at second- or third-hand, to the period in question, and to the political actors involved, which provides an essential advantage in pursuing this question.

This book seeks to advance scholarly understanding of Carolingian diplomacy with the Islamic world by placing the activity within its wider political context. As discussed above, the extant Arabic sources can be used to build up a sophisticated picture of the Muslim polities with which the Carolingians interacted and the changing pressures and circumstances their rulers found themselves in. It was these factors that shaped their engagement with the Franks and without which their relationships cannot be fully understood. This diplomatic activity also needs to be placed within the context of Frankish politics, with similar attention being paid to the dangers and incentives faced by the Carolingians. This approach allows the field to move away from straightforward models of a grand alliance system and instead examine the way specific conditions defined different diplomatic moments. This brings the differences between Carolingian diplomacy with the ʿAbbāsids, here characterised as "prestige-based," and relations with the Umayyads, referred to as "frontier diplomacy," to the forefront. It also widens the scope of investigation by drawing Muslim states in North Africa and Italy into focus, and reopening questions about why the Carolingians engaged in diplomacy in some times and places, and not in others.

CHAPTER TWO

# Perception and Practice in Carolingian Diplomacy with the Islamic World

## *Problems of Perspective*

In the abbey of St Gall in the 880s, the monk Notker the Stammerer wrote in one of his stories about Charlemagne that the envoys sent by Hārūn al-Rashīd to the emperor "did not know where Francia lay."[1] They sought guidance en route from

> the bishops of Campania or Tuscany, Emilia or Liguria, Burgundy or Gaul, and to the abbots and counts; but they were either deceived by them or driven off, so that a whole year had gone round before, weary and worn out by their long journey, they reached Aachen at last and met Charles, most famous for his virtues.[2]

Fortunately, as always with Notker, justice was done, and Charlemagne punished the unkind nobles and clerics. Notker wrote long after events and his purposes were moralistic and didactic, portraying how a king ought to behave.[3] His means to achieve this, and the heart of the enduring

1. Notker, *Gesta Karoli Magni*, II.8 "Qui situm Francię nescientes," 59.

2. Ibid., "Cumque episcopis Campanie vel Tusciae, Emiliae vel Liguriae Burgundieque sive Galliae simul et abbatibus vel comitibus causam adventus sui indicassent dissimulanterque ab eisdem suscepti vel expulsi fuissent, tandem post anni revolutum circulum apud Aquasgrani famosissimum virtutibus Karolum defessi et nimio defecti reppererunt circuitu," 59.

3. Innes, "Memory, Orality and Literacy," 13; MacLean, *Kingship and Politics*, 199–229.

pleasure that reading him provides, was to focus on affairs at a human level.[4] Rather than considering the politics of the ʿAbbāsid embassy, the monk of St Gall preferred to think in terms of the practicalities of diplomacy, as the above story indicates.

The majority of this book is concerned with understanding and contextualising the politics of Carolingian diplomacy with the Islamic world, paying attention to its purpose and results. It tracks diplomats across Europe and the Mediterranean from on high in the gods, taking the means by which this diplomacy took place largely for granted. This chapter will follow Notker and take a different approach, by focusing on a more human perspective, thinking about the mechanics of this diplomatic activity.[5] This requires considering the identities of the envoys themselves, how they reached their destination, how they were received, and how they returned. But it also needs to reckon with the way Franks and Muslims thought about each other, and the way they coped with peaceful diplomacy with people of different faiths. Most of the misery suffered by the envoys in Notker's story came at the hands of prejudiced Franks rather than the challenges of the journey. Ideas and practicalities go hand in hand in understanding how diplomacy between the Carolingians and the Islamic world was made possible.

This is not a new subject. The history of foreign relations is arguably the oldest branch of historical enquiry, and historians have been interested in its practicalities for a not inconsiderable time.[6] As François Louis Ganshof put it in his magisterial study, "an account, even if summary, of the history of international relations would be very incomplete if a few pages were not devoted to the technical aspects of these relations."[7] Investigation of the mechanics of medieval diplomacy has long been hampered by nineteenth-century conceptions of what diplomatic activity looked like.[8] The absence of clearly defined states with permanent professional ambassadors made the medieval world appear unpromising for a study of the

4. Ganz, "Humour as History."

5. Otte, "The Inner Circle," 15.

6. Herodotus, *The Histories*, "Here are presented the results of the enquiry carried out by Herodotus of Halicarnassus. The purpose is to prevent the traces of human events from being erased by time, and to preserve the fame of the important and remarkable achievements produced by both Greeks and non-Greeks; among the matters covered is, in particular, the cause of the hostilities between Greeks and non-Greeks," 3.

7. Ganshof, *Histoire des Relations Internationales*, "un exposé, même sommaire, de l'histoire des relations internationales serait fort incomplete si l'on n'y consacrait quelques pages à l'aspect technique de ces relations," 36.

8. Nicolson, *Diplomacy*, 12.

practice of diplomacy.[9] To the extent that historians of international relations did venture into the murk of the pre-modern world, it was to find and retrieve the origins of the institutions they recognised, most notably from the city-states of late medieval Italy.[10]

In recent years, scholars have moved beyond this, seeking to understand the workings of medieval diplomacy on its own terms, as a set of practices sufficient for the requirements of the political and social systems that fostered them. Much excellent work has been done on the later middle ages, where researchers have benefitted from the far more extensive surviving documentation.[11] The practice of diplomacy in Late Antiquity and in the Byzantine world has also received considerable attention.[12] The Islamic world in this period has not been entirely ignored. Historians of the Crusades and al-Andalus after the fall of the caliphate in Córdoba have drawn upon the evidence available to them, while the ʿAbbāsid Caliphate has benefitted to some extent from work done on Byzantine diplomacy.[13] For the mechanics of Carolingian diplomacy, the essential reference work remains Ganshof's article.[14] This is not solely a testament to neglect, for Ganshof's scholarship was meticulous and comprehensive, but it does attest to the lack of attention the subject has received.

## CONSIDERING THE OTHER

Communication between different states is affected by a wide variety of factors, not the least of which is the participants' perceptions of each other.[15] These considerations are most obviously important when political actors are deciding whether or not to initiate contact, but the unstated and often unconscious assumptions and opinions held by both parties

9. Watkins, "Toward a New Diplomatic History," 2.

10. Mattingley, "The First Resident Ambassadors" and *Renaissance Diplomacy*; Queller, *The Office of Ambassador*. More recently, see Anderson, *The Rise of Modern Diplomacy*.

11. Berg, Kintzinger, and Monnet, *Auswärtige Politik*; Plöger, *England and the Avignon Popes*; Ebben and Sicking, *Beyond Ambassadors*.

12. Shepard and Franklin, *Byzantine Diplomacy*; McCormick, "Diplomacy and the Carolingian Encounter"; Hilsdale, *Byzantine Art*.

13. Holt, "The Treaties of the Early Mamluk Sultans"; Wansbrough, "Diplomatica Siciliana"; Burns, "A Unique Bilingual Surrender Treaty"; Anderson, "Islamic Spaces and Diplomacy"; Takayama, "Frederick II's Crusade"; Kohler, *Alliances and Treaties*; Behrens-Abouseif, *Practising Diplomacy*; Brett, "The Diplomacy of Empire," 149–159.

14. Ganshof, "The Frankish Monarchy," originally published as "Les relations extérieures."

15. On the importance of *Verstellungsgeschichte*, see Goetz, "The Perception of Other Religions."

can shape the way diplomacy is carried out.[16] One Carolingian example is the rapid change in Louis the Pious's behaviour towards the Rus travellers introduced to him in 839.[17] Their initially friendly reception rapidly turned hostile the moment the emperor realized the Rus had a Scandinavian background, information that transmuted the visitors from honoured guests to dangerous spies.

Historians have long observed a relative lack of interest of early medieval Western Europeans and Muslims in each other.[18] Richard Southern famously described this period of Christian-Muslim relations as "the Age of Ignorance."[19] The distribution of the sources does not help. The majority of both Frankish and Muslim commentators on the matter wrote a long way from the frontier, from a poor vantage point. Proximity mattered, as Bade observed, and goes a long way to explaining the difference between the relatively benign views of Regino (d. 915), safe in Prüm, to the more hostile views of his contemporary Ado (d. 874), exposed to Muslim attacks in Vienne.[20]

Early medieval Western European thought on the subject generally described the Arab conquests in ethnic terms, with frequent use of the word "Saracen."[21] This is the case in the *Chronicle of Fredegar*, one of the earliest Christian sources to mention the rapid expansion of the caliphate.[22] Many early accounts seem to have been somewhat confused about the religion of the Saracens, as witnessed in Arculf's description of Caliph Muʿāwiya I in around 680 praying to "Christ, the Saviour of the World."[23] Otherwise, information about Muslim religious beliefs was scarce. The earliest Western Latin *Lives* of Muḥammad appeared in Spain only in the ninth century.[24] Charlemagne may have been interested in Islam as a religion

16. Wendt, "Anarchy Is What States Make of It"; Lendon, "Primitivism and Ancient Foreign Relations." For a sceptical overview of arguments about the role of culture in international relations, see Desch, "Culture Clash."

17. Shepard, "The Rhos Guests."

18. Daniel, *Islam and the West* and *The Arabs and Medieval Europe*; Sénac, *L'image de l'autre*, 13–17.

19. Southern, *Western Views of Islam*, 14; Lewis, *The Muslim Discovery*. For a brief historiographical account, see Blanks, "Western Views of Islam." See also Kedar, *Crusade and Mission*; Rotter, *Abendland und Sarazenen*; d'Alverny, "La connaissance de l'Islam."

20. Bade, "Muslims in the Christian World Order."

21. Wolf, "Christian Views of Islam"; Tolan, "Réactions chrétiennes aux conquêtes" and *Saracens*, 42–46; Clarke, *The Muslim Conquest of Iberia*, 8–17; Valenzuela, "The Faith of the Saracens."

22. "The Chronicle of Fredegar," 232–234; Fischer, "Rewriting History."

23. Adomnán, *De locis sanctis*, "Christus mundi Saluator," 193.

24. Wolf, "The Earliest Latin Lives of Muḥammad."

because he asked Alcuin for a copy of a *disputatio* written by Bishop Felix of Urgell against the faith of the Saracens.[25] Alcuin's reply to the king, that he had once seen a debate with a Jew, implies that he placed both Jews and Saracens in the same category, perhaps implying a sense that were related to each other.[26] That these hints of knowledge of Islam are linked to the Iberian Peninsula suggests the role of al-Andalus as a zone for Christian-Muslim contact.[27]

Christian writers turned to scripture and late antique biblical commentary for further information. In his letter to the Byzantine emperor Basil I (r. 867–886), Louis II cited Psalm 71 to argue that the ruler of the Arabs was a king.[28] Biblical knowledge was mediated by the writings of Jerome, who had a major influence on early medieval thought on the Saracens in the Latin West.[29] Jerome's translation of Eusebius's *Universal Chronicle* popularized the idea of the Saracens as the descendants of Ishmael, Abraham's son by his slave Hagar, a concept developed by Josephus.[30] He returned to this theme in his *Commentary on Genesis*, declaring Ishmael's line "refers to the Saracens who wander with no fixed home and invade all the nations who border on the desert; and they are attacked by all."[31] In his *Commentary on Ezekiel*, Jerome said that the Agarenes, the descendants of Hagar, "now call themselves Saracens, falsely usurping the name of Sarah, thus appearing to be born of a free lady."[32]

In his *Etymologies* Isidore repeated this point, noting that the Ishmaelites were also called Agarenes, but "they perversely call themselves Saracens because they pride themselves in being descended from Sarah."[33] Bede's

25. Alcuin, *Epistolae* no. 172, 284–285.

26. Kedar, *Crusade and Mission*, 25; see also Aurast, "What Did Christian Authors Know."

27. Sénac, *L'image de l'autre*, 27; König, "Charlemagne's *Jihād* Revisited," 18–27.

28. Louis II, *Epistola ad Basilium I*, 388.

29. Scarfe Beckett, *Anglo-Saxon Perceptions*, 21–22. What follows is indebted to Tolan, "'A wild man, whose hand will be against all.'"

30. Eusebius-Jerome, *Die Chronik des Hieronymus*, 24a. On Josephus, see Millar, "Hagar, Ishmael, Josephus" and "The Theodosian Empire (408–450) and the Arabs," 299–302.

31. Jerome, *Liber quaestionum*, "id est sarracenos uagos incertis que sedibus, qui uniuersas gentes, quibus desertus ex latere iungitur, incursant, et impugnantur ab omnibus," 20.

32. Jerome, *Commentarii in Ezechielem*, "nunc saraceni appellantur, assumentes sibi falso nomen sarae quo scilicet de ingenua et domina uideantur esse generate," 335.

33. Isidore of Seville, *Etymologies* IX.ii.57, "perverso nomine Saraceni vocantur, quia ex Sarra se genitos gloriantur."

*Commentary on Genesis* quotes the description of Saracens in Jerome's commentary, before updating it for the eighth century by observing:

> But this was long ago. Now, however, his hand is against all, and all hands are against him [Genesis 16:12], so that the Saracens hold the whole length of Africa in their sway, and they also hold the greatest part of Asia and some part of Europe.[34]

Bede's debt to Jerome is also demonstrated by his repetition of the latter's description of Saracens as worshippers of the morning star.[35]

Another possible source for Frankish views on Saracens are the *Revelations* of Pseudo-Methodios.[36] Composed in Syriac in the late seventh century, this apocalyptic text blamed the Arab dominance on the sins of the conquered Christians, portraying the Saracens as violent oppressors.[37] The *Revelations* were translated into Latin before 727 but enjoyed only a limited circulation in the Frankish world.[38] An epitome of the *Revelations* composed in around 732 did rather better, with a large number of ninth-century manuscripts.[39] Although the savagery of the Arabs is toned down in the epitome, they are still described as brutal towards Christians.[40] The idea of Muslim expansion as a punishment for Christian failure spread. Boniface explained to King Æthelbald of Mercia in the 740s that the people of Spain, Provence, and Burgundy had brought down Saracen attacks upon themselves with their godlessness and fornication.[41]

Even if Latin writers had no understanding of Islam, they very clearly conceived of Saracens as non-Christians. When he wrote to Boniface in 745, Pope Zacharias classed Saracens with the pagan "Saxons and Frisians."[42] Haimo of Auxerre included them in a list of pagan peoples

34. Bede, *Commentary on Genesis*, "Sed haec antiquitus. Nunc autem in tantum manus eius contra omnes, et manus sunt omnium contra eum, ut africam totam in longitudine sua ditione premant, sed et asiae maximam partem, et europae nonnullam," 200–201, translated by Kendall, *Bede: On Genesis*, 279.

35. Jerome, *Commentarii in Amos*, 296; Bede, *Commentary on Acts*, 36.

36. Pseudo-Methodios, "Revelations."

37. Brock, "Syriac Views of Emergent Islam," 18–19; Reinink, "Ps.-Methodius," 176–186.

38. Pseudo-Methodios, "Revelations," ix–x; Alexander, "The Diffusion of Byzantine Apocalypses," 65–67.

39. Prinz, "Eine frühe abendländische Aktualisierung."

40. Pollard, "One Other on Another," 33–35.

41. Boniface, *Epistolae* no. 73, 146–155, 151.

42. Zacharias I, *Epistolae* no. 60, "Saxonum vel Fresonum," 123.

in his *Commentary on Ezekiel*.[43] Alcuin and Agobard compared them to Jews.[44] The language used by the sources, "infidel," "heretic," is that of the religious other.[45] Nor was this other sympathetic to Christendom. In his *Commentary on Genesis*, Bede described Saracens as "inimical and full of hate towards everybody" and as "enemies of the church" in his *Commentary on Samuel*.[46] Willibald claimed that the Saracens wanted to destroy the Church.[47] Paul the Deacon called Saracens "an infidel people and enemies of God."[48]

The Saracens could appear to be a dark, mocking mirror of the Christian world. Bishop George of Ostia wrote to Pope Hadrian I in 786 to inform him of an Anglo-Saxon synod that condemned the eating of food in secret as "Saracen."[49] This was a point taken up by Alcuin, who labelled clerics who did so "hypocrites and Saracens."[50] Some of these discussions of Saracens perverting Christianity reveal a growing appreciation that Islam could be related to Christianity. Haimo of Auxerre claimed that "Saracens baptise their children in the name of the Father, and the Son and the Holy Spirit" in order to protect them from demons.[51] As this was not done "out of faith" it was ineffective.[52] Where Haimo might have acquired this information is unstated, but Johannes Heil has argued that he was of Iberian origin.[53] Paschasius Radbertus reached for a Satanic explanation in his

43. Haimo of Auxerre, *Commentary on Ezekiel*, BNF Lat. 12302, fol. 71v, "Quicumque enim extra aecclesiam hanc sunt, munus quod Domino sit acceptum non offerunt neque Normannus scilicet, neque Sarracenus, neque Sclauus aut quilibet infidelis," quoted in Contreni, "Haimo of Auxerre's Commentary on Ezechiel," 241n22, and "'By Lions, Bishops Are Meant; by Wolves, Priests,'" 35n28.

44. Agobard of Lyons, *De iudaicis superstitionibus*, 215–216.

45. CC 2.ii, "ipse super ereticos sive Sarracenos infidels," 310.

46. Bede, *Commentary on Genesis*, "omnibus exosi et contrarii teneant," 201; Bede, *Commentary on Samuel*, "aduersarios ecclesiae," 231.

47. Hygeburg, *Vita Willibaldi*, "Illam aecclesiam christiani homines sepe conparabant ad paganis Sarracinis, qui illi volebant eam destruere," 95.

48. Paul the Deacon, *Historia Langobardorum*, VI.10, "gens infidelis et Deo inimica," 168.

49. George of Ostia, *Epistola ad Hadrianum*, 22.

50. Alcuin, *Epistolae* no. 3, 19–29, "hypocrisis et Saracenorum est," 22.

51. Haimo of Auxerre, *Commentary on Ezekiel*, fols. 51 r–v, "baptizant Sarraceni filios suos in nominee Patris, et Filii, et Spiritus Sancti"; Contreni, "Haimo of Auxerre's Commentary on Ezechiel," 233.

52. Haimo of Auxerre, *Commentary on Ezekiel*, fols. 51 r–v, "non ex fide"; Contreni, "'By Lions, Bishops Are Meant; by Wolves, Priests,'" 33.

53. Heil, *Kompilation oder Konstruktion*, 206, 279–280, and "Theodulf, Haimo, and Jewish Traditions."

*Commentary on Matthew*, probably composed in the 850s. According to this, the Saracens

> were wickedly seduced by some pseudo-apostles, disciples of Nicholas so to speak, and composed for themselves a law from the Old as well as the New Testament, and so perverted everything under the cult of one god, unwilling to agree with us or the Jews in any regard.[54]

Such contagion could spread. Pope Nicholas I (r. 858–867) advised Boris I of the Bulgars (r. 852–889) that "the profane books that you have taken from the Saracens" should be burned "for, as it is written [1 Cor. 15:33], Evil conversation corrupts good behaviour."[55]

The different terms that could be used to refer to Saracens, including Arab, Ishmaelite, Moor, and Hagarene, could occasion confusion. Isidore seems to have viewed the Saracens and Arabs as different peoples.[56] The *Annales regni Francorum* and the *Annals of St-Bertin* often distinguish between the king of the Saracens in Spain and the king of the Persians in the East, although Hārūn al-Rashīd is named by both titles.[57] Nonetheless, awareness of a commonality between the Muslims of al-Andalus and those of the caliphate existed. After discussing Saracens in Spain, Alcuin noted that "those same cursed Saracens, who are also Agarenes, exercise total dominion over the greatest part of Africa and Asia."[58] Descriptions of the Holy Land refer to Saracens often enough to indicate that most Frankish commentators could perceive Muslim inhabitants of the Islamic world as part of one group.[59]

These Latin perceptions of Muslims could have consequences for Carolingian diplomacy. The emphasis on their lack of Christian faith and distant origins served to put them in a different category to the mostly

54. Paschasius Radbertus, *Commentary on Matthew*, in Kedar, *Crusade and Mission*, 31, "sed male seducti a quibusdam pseudoapostolis, ut ita loquar Nicholai discipulis, propriam sibi tarn ex veteri testamento quam et ex novo condiderunt legem, ac si sub unius Dei cultu, nee tamen nobiscum nee cum Iudeis quippiam sentire volentes, omnia perverterunt," 205.

55. Nicholas I, *Epistolae* no. 99, "De libris profanis, quos a Sarracenis vos abstulisse . . . 'Corrumpunt' enim, sicut scriptum est, 'mores bonos colloquia mala,'" 599.

56. Tolan, *Saracens*, 11.

57. ARF, al-Ḥakam I and ʿAbd al-Raḥmān II as "rex Sarracenorum," a.812 137, a.815–816 143–145, a.826 170, a.827 172; Hārūn al-Rashīd as "regis Persarum," a.801 114, a.801–802 116–117, a.806–807 122–123, and as "rex Sarracenorum," a.810 131; AB, ʿAbd al-Raḥmān II and Muḥammad I as "rex Sarracenorum," a.847 53, a.863 104, 114; al-Maʿmūn as "de Perside," a.831 4.

58. Alcuin, *Epistolae* no. 7, "idem maledicti Saraceni (qui et Agareni) tota dominantur Africa et Asia majore maxima ex parte," 32.

59. Scarfe Beckett, *Anglo-Saxon Perceptions*, 69.

Christian neighbours the Franks otherwise had dealings with, who could be communicated with in terms of religious fellowship. Their association with the persecution of Christians added to the complications of entering bargains with Saracens, opening up those who did so to charges of complicity with this oppression. Further, the idea of Muslims as the instruments of divine wrath raised the stakes of warfare with them as defeat at their hands became an ominous message from the heavens.

Scholarship on Muslim perceptions of Latin Europe in the early medieval period has been heated. Older studies emphasised the general lack of interest of the Islamic world, evidenced by both the paltry material on Western Europe and the ignorance displayed in those writings that exist.[60] Eliyahu Ashtor believed this was because of the poverty of Western Europe, whereas Karl Jahn explained this due to religious intransigence.[61] Bernard Lewis controversially attributed it to Muslim arrogance and complacency.[62] Work done since then, most notably Daniel König's recent monograph, has sought to add nuance to that assessment.[63] König's observation of the wide variety of opinions expressed by early medieval Muslim writers, and the non-religious ways in which Western Europeans could be perceived, represents important progress on the subject.[64]

Many Muslims in the period would have seen themselves as superior to those outside the *dār al-islām*. On the one hand, for them the emergence of Islam marked a break with the ignorance, *jāhilīya*, of the past; on the other, educated individuals within the caliphate claimed to be the true inheritors of the wisdom of ancient learning and culture.[65] This latter manifested itself in the adoption of Greek ideas of classifying the populations of the world by the climatic regions they inhabited, with an ideal climate zone centred on Iraq which created the best people.[66] In this schema, Western Europe lay within a zone with a bleak climate, which doomed their peoples to stupidity and savagery, enlivened only by their brutish aggression.[67]

Many medieval Arabic descriptions of Europe are notable for their simplicity, with limited attention paid to the different peoples and languages

60. Miquel, "L'Europe vue par les Arabes"; Watt, *Muslim-Christian Encounters*; Waardenburg, *Muslim Perceptions of Other Religions* and *Muslims and Others*.

61. Ashtor, "Che cosa sapevano"; Jahn, "Das christliche Abendland."

62. Lewis, *The Muslim Discovery*.

63. Bennison, "The Peoples of the North"; König, *Arabic-Islamic Views of the Latin West*.

64. König, *Arabic-Islamic Views of the Latin West*, 325–328.

65. Bennison, "The Peoples of the North," 158.

66. Maqbul Ahmad, "Djughrāfiyā," 576–578.

67. Al-Azmeh, "Barbarians in Arab Eyes," 6–7; Abdullah, "Arab Views of Northern Europeans."

of the continent and a general assumption of the political supremacy of either the Byzantine emperor or the pope.[68] The tenth-century Persian explorer Ibn Rustah declared that the Byzantine empire stretched all the way to Britain.[69] Ibn Khaldūn (1332–1406) noted that early Muslim writers

> did not know the Franks. In Syria, they had only fought the Byzantines (*al-Rūm*). Because of this, they believed that they [the Byzantines] ruled over all Christian peoples and that Heraclius was the ruler over the entire Christian world. Consequently, they imposed the name *al-Rūm* on all Christian peoples.[70]

One striking exception to this rule is the detailed discussion of the Franks that was produced by the Baghdad-born historian and geographer al-Masʿūdī (d. 956). Unusually amongst his peers, al-Masʿūdī travelled widely, basing his claim to authority on personal observation or conversation with eyewitnesses.[71] In his monumental geography *The Meadows of Gold and Mines of Gems*, al-Masʿūdī commented at length on the difference between Franks, Lombards, Galicians, and Slavs.[72] He was very positive about the Franks, calling them "the most invincible and the most equipped" of Europeans, "the most disciplined, the most acquiescent and obedient to their kings."[73] His account included an incomplete king list of the Franks from Clovis I to Louis IV.[74] He acquired this list in Egypt in 947 from a document composed by the Bishop of Girona for the heir of ʿAbd al-Raḥmān III.[75]

Al-Masʿūdī was not alone in emphasising the warlike nature of the Franks. The Andalusi Ibn Ḥabīb (d. 853), while generally vague on the Franks, had Mūsā b. Nuṣayr describe them as "characterized by great numbers, equipment, endurance, strength, courage and intrepidity."[76] Ibn ʿAbd al-Ḥakam (d. 871) named the Franks "the fiercest enemies of al-Andalus" in his description of the Battle of Tours.[77] Writers in al-Andalus, closer to

68. Samarrai, "Some Geographical and Political Information," 305; König, "The Christianisation of Latin Europe" and *Arabic-Islamic Views of the Latin West*, 89.

69. König, "Arabic-Islamic Historiography," 434.

70. König, *Arabic-Islamic Views of the Latin West*, 189; Ibn Khaldūn, *Histoire des Berbères*, 208.

71. Khalidi, *Islamic Historiography*, 2–5; Touati, *Islam and Travel*, 119–126.

72. Al-Masʿūdī, *Les Prairies d'Or*, 2, 344.

73. Ibid.

74. Hermes, *The [European] Other*, 53.

75. Shboul, *Al-Mas'udi and His World*, 191.

76. Ibn Ḥabīb, *Kitāb al-Tārīkh*, 122, quoted in König, *Arabic-Islamic Views of the Latin West*, 193.

77. Ibn ʿAbd al-Ḥakam, *Conquête de l'Afrique du Nord*, 121.

the Frankish world, seem to have been fairly precise when they identified someone as a Frank, as opposed to a Galician.[78] As Amira Bennison has noted, Arabic writers in Spain prior to the tenth century were largely neutral in their discussion of Franks.[79] These perceptions were relevant for diplomacy insofar as they primed Muslim rulers, their courts, and their subjects to view the Franks as a powerful, aggressive, and potentially dangerous people. This could prompt caution in handling them and a respect not afforded to other Western Europeans. It might also make bringing them to the negotiating table a more impressive feat than other peoples.[80]

As this brief survey indicates, the vast majority of literary descriptions by both Muslims and Franks of each other in this period generally suggest some mutual lack of understanding. It should be stressed that the views expressed by early medieval writers were often highly varied. The sheer multitude of possible depictions is demonstrated by the writings of Bede, who portrayed the same groups of people in radically different ways.[81] Similarly, despite al-Masʿūdī's positive depiction of the Franks in *The Meadows of Gold*, in his later abridgement, *The Book of Admonition and Revision*, they appear as barbaric savages.[82]

Another important point is that many of these accounts depended less on fresh information than on the repetition of pre-existing materials. The writers of Latin Europe were heavily dependent on authorities such as Jerome and Isidore, who predated or were contemporaries of the first emergence of Islam. Those of the Islamic world were frequently constrained by the conventions of genre in the way they presented Europeans.[83] Nonetheless, Carolingian diplomacy with the Islamic world needs to be viewed within the context of these perceptions, which coloured the minds of its participants.

## CHRIST AND BELIAL

Given this potential for hostility, monarchs in this period sometimes needed to justify peaceful engagement with rulers from a cultural and religious background that could be interpreted as directly antithetical to

78. König, *Arabic-Islamic Views of the Latin West*, 216; Clément, "Nommer l'autre."

79. Bennison, "The Peoples of the North," 168.

80. I discuss this point further in Ottewill-Soulsby, "ʿAbbāsid-Carolingian Diplomacy," 225, 230.

81. Wallace-Hadrill, *Bede and His World*, 1:71–85; Scarfe Beckett, *Anglo-Saxon Perceptions*, 137.

82. König, *Arabic-Islamic Views of the Latin West*, 102.

83. Ibid., 324–325.

their own. The demonstrable fact that Christians and Muslims did engage in diplomacy with each other is of course the most eloquent testimony to the possibility of doing so. Ideological statements surrounding this diplomacy can seem redundant ornamentation, there to disguise or make palatable the ugly appearance and bitter taste of the real substance of medieval power politics.[84] The most important resources for understanding the practice of early medieval diplomacy are descriptions of it in action. Nonetheless, contemporary ideas about diplomacy need to be taken into account. These concepts provided the intellectual hinterland in which monarchs and diplomats operated, influencing their perceptions, their thoughts, and, potentially, their decisions. They played a key role in defining the limits of the possible, making some options seem less plausible to participants than others and shaping how diplomatic developments were conceptualized or justified.

The second half of the eighth and the first half of the ninth centuries saw the beginnings of what would become the four *madhāhib* or schools of Islamic law.[85] This was part of a process of codification, as the previously largely oral teaching of Muslim law was written down and regularized into a corpus.[86] Amongst the subjects addressed by these developments were foreign relations, named *siyar*.[87] In the view of contemporary Islamic jurisprudence, the world could be divided into two, the *dār al-islām* (the House of Submission), the lands ruled by Muslims, and the *dār al-ḥarb* (the House of War), everywhere else.[88] By virtue of not being ranked amongst the faithful, members of the *dār al-ḥarb* were deemed legally incapable, hindering any possibility of making agreements.[89] Shāfiʿīte jurists argued for a third division, the *dār al-sulḥ* or *dār al-ʿahd* (the House of Truce), although this was not accepted by all other schools.[90] The Qurʿānic imperative to fight the unbelievers until they converted or submitted made a permanent peace between a Muslim ruler and an independent non-Muslim problematic.[91]

84. For the realist perspective, see Fischer, "Feudal Europe, 800–1300."

85. Melchert, *The Formation of the Sunni Schools*.

86. Fowden, *Before and After Muḥammad*, 190–194. On the development of Islamic law, see Schacht, *The Origins of Muhammadan Jurisprudence* and *An Introduction to Islamic Law*.

87. Khadduri, *The Islamic Law of Nations*, 38–45; Istanbuli, *Diplomacy and Diplomatic Practice*, 110.

88. Crone, *Medieval Islamic Political Thought*, 359–362.

89. Khadduri, *The Islamic Law of Nations*, 12.

90. Ibid.

91. Ibid., 170.

Despite this rather uncompromising division, some scope for diplomacy was possible in the view of the jurists. The Prophet Muḥammad had after all entered into treaties with his enemies during his lifetime.[92] Al-Shāfiʿī (d. 820) cited the Qurʾān 9:3–4:

> Give those who disbelieve news of a painful punishment, except those idolaters with whom you have made a treaty, (and who) since then have not failed you in anything and have not supported anyone against you. Fulfil their treaty with them until their term.[93]

In his *Book of the Messengers of Kings* (*Kitāb Rusul al-mulūk*), Ibn al-Farrāʾ, probably writing in al-Andalus in the second half of the tenth century, argued that diplomacy was a religious act. As well as discussing the ways in which Muḥammad made use of diplomacy, Ibn al-Farrāʾ identified messengers with both prophets and angels, arguing that "God preferred the messengers amongst His prophets."[94]

Treaties (*muhādana*) could be made if fighting would inevitably lead to Muslim defeat, although only for a limited time, normally ten years.[95] Abū Yūsuf (d. 798), in his *Kitāb al-Kharāj*, summarized Ḥanafī thought, noting that if

> the Muslims fear for their lives and do not possess sufficient power to face the enemy, there is no harm to enter an agreement of peace with them and can offer to them property as ransom to save their lives.[96]

He warns that "if the Muslims have power over their enemy, it is not lawful for them to accept any of the above terms."[97] Al-Shaybānī (d. 805) agreed, saying that peace with the inhabitants of the *dār al-ḥarb* was permissible if "the inhabitants of the *dār al-ḥarb* are too strong for the Muslims to prevail against them and it would be better for the Muslims to make peace with them."[98] The model here was the treaty of Ḥudaybiya agreed between Muḥammad and the Quraysh of Mecca for ten years in 628, as preserved in Ibn Hishām's (d. 828/833) edition of Ibn Isḥāq's *Life of the Prophet*.[99] If need be the truce could be renewed, but only if the

92. Al-Ṭabarī, *Book of Jihād*, 77.
93. Ibid., 79.
94. Ibn al-Farrāʾ, *Diplomacy in the Early Islamic World*, 62.
95. Holmes, "Treaties between Byzantium and the Islamic World," 141.
96. Abū Yūsuf, *Kitab-ul-Kharaj*, 410.
97. Ibid., 411.
98. Al-Shaybānī, *The Islamic Law of Nations*, 154.
99. Ibn Hishām, *The Life of Muḥammad*, 504; Abū Yūsuf, *Kitab-ul-Kharaj*, 412–424; Iqbal, *Diplomacy in Islam*, 25–36.

Muslims still remained at a serious military disadvantage. This meant that any agreement between the caliph and a non-Muslim ruler could only be justified by desperate expedience and was to be strictly temporary in nature.[100]

The caliph could also make peace with the infidel if they had reason to believe that doing so would encourage them to convert.[101] Likewise, the sending and receiving of diplomats and gifts was respected in their opinion of the law and therefore would not fall foul of the strictures against alliances or permanent agreements. Arguments over the strict purpose of *jihād* offered further room for manoeuvre. Al-Shāfiʿī identified the disbelief of the unbeliever as the reason for the necessity of *jihād.* [102] Other jurists argued that *jihād* was only required against those who fought against Islam and the Muslim community. [103] This theoretically allowed the caliph to coexist with a non-Muslim neighbour so long as no official agreement was made.[104]

Despite these considerations, the opinions of the jurists establish an incredibly narrow set of parameters for diplomacy between the faithful and the faithless. The extent to which these rulings influenced actual practice is unclear. Jurists were connected to contemporary rulers. Abū Yūsuf's *Kitāb al-Kharāj* was commissioned by Hārūn al-Rashīd, who appointed Abū Yūsuf and al-Shaybānī to be the *qāḍī* of Baghdad and Raqqa, respectively.[105] Although relations between the caliph and al-Shaybānī became strained, the latter's book on *siyar*, *Kitāb al-Siyar al-Kabīr*, which does not survive, was recommended by Hārūn as a text to be taught to his sons.[106] The early ninth century saw the Mālikī school become dominant in al-Andalus, with ʿAbd al-Raḥmān II (r. 822–852) being a keen supporter.[107] Its founder, Mālik b. Anas (d. 796), had little to say about *siyar*, but his disciples tended to follow Ḥanafī opinions on the matter.[108]

100. Khadduri, *War and Peace*, 170.

101. Abū Yūsuf, *Kitab-ul-Kharaj*, 411.

102. Ibrahim, "Translator's Introduction," 20–21.

103. Al-Ṭabarī, *Book of Jihād*, 69–72.

104. Al-Shaybānī, *The Islamic Law of Nations*, 14.

105. Abū Yūsuf, *Kitab-ul-Kharaj*, 1; Al-Shaybānī, *The Islamic Law of Nations*, 29–34. On Abū Yūsuf and al-Shaybānī as judges, see Tillier, *Les Cadis d'Iraq*, 44–46, 139–141, 152–155, 177–180, 377–379.

106. Al-Shaybānī, *The Islamic Law of Nations*, 42–45.

107. Fierro, "El derecho Mālikí en al-Andalus," 128–130; Wilk, "Le malikisme et les Omeyyades."

108. Al-Shaybānī, *The Islamic Law of Nations*, 23.

While the jurists sought to establish norms, they also described a preexisting set of practices, much of it based on precedent.[109] Justifications of the paying of tribute to infidels for peace appear to originate in the reigns of Muʿāwiya I (r. 661–680) and ʿAbd al-Malik (r. 685–705), both monarchs who were at times forced to buy off the Byzantines.[110] The pattern of war and peace on the Byzantine frontier during the life of Hārūn al-Rashīd with campaigning being broken up by short, strictly chronologically limited truces fits the model of the jurists reasonably well. In 782, for example, Hārūn made an agreement on his father's behalf for a three-year truce with Irene in exchange for annual tribute.[111] Al-Ṭabarī expresses outrage in his entry for 785 at "the treason of the Romans" for breaking the truce after thirty-two months.[112]

The repeated offers by Idrīsid diplomats of truces lasting ten years to the Byzantine governor of Sicily echo comments about the maximum allowed duration of a peace.[113] As the Idrīsids were not Sunni, too close a connection with the specific rulings of the jurists discussed above cannot be accepted, but it might reflect a general principle. [114] The behaviour of the Umayyads of al-Andalus in the ninth century, with brief moments of expedient peace alternating with aggressive raiding, bears some resemblance to the ideal picture of the jurists. That part of the reason the governor of Ifrīqiya, Muḥammad al-ʿAkkī, was overthrown was that he was too friendly with Charlemagne suggests the potential penalties Muslim leaders could face for ignoring the jurists.[115]

Nonetheless, in their dealings with the Carolingians most Muslim leaders seem to have been willing to play hard and fast with the strict rules. Long-term arrangements between Frankish kings and Muslim lords in the Iberian Peninsula can be observed. Likewise, the Arabic chroniclers of al-Andalus make no mention of potential legal issues when discussing alliances and agreements between Muslims and Christians. Although a ruler like Hārūn al-Rashīd might have had the admonitions of Abū Yūsuf in the back of his mind when he negotiated with Christians, the evidence

109. Ibid., 19.

110. Khadduri, *War and Peace*, 215. On the payment of tribute, see Howard-Johnston, *Witnesses to a World Crisis*, 496–501; Humphreys, "The 'War of Images' Revisited."

111. Al-Ṭabarī, *The History of al-Ṭabarī, Vol. 29*, 221.

112. Ibid., 240.

113. Leo III, *Epistolae* no. 6, 97–99.

114. On ninth-century Zaydī views of Christians, see Freidenreich, "The Implications of Unbelief," 70.

115. Al-Tamīmī, *Kitāb al-Miḥan*, 427–429. See pp. 259–261.

is generally one of flexibility, with the law of necessity taking precedent over that of God.

The Carolingian world did not elaborate anywhere near as complex a theoretical framework for understanding diplomacy with those of different faiths as the *siyar* of Arabic scholars. That it was a problem that intellectuals in the Frankish empire grappled with is nonetheless clear. As the majority of the available material was produced by writers close to a ruling dynasty publicly engaged in diplomacy with the ʿAbbāsids and Umayyads, gauging the true opinions of Frankish elites towards Carolingian relations with Saracens is hard. For the most part there seems to have been a pragmatic acceptance of the necessity of diplomacy with non-Christians. Where opposition can be identified, it can generally be understood within a specific context.

Those opposed to diplomacy with non-Christians could find support in Paul's question in 2 Corinthians 6:15, "what concord hath Christ with Belial?" With these words Agobard and Florus of Lyons condemned agreements between Christians and Jews.[116] They were also employed by Pope Stephen III (r. 768–772) in his efforts to forestall a marriage alliance between the Frankish monarchs and the Lombards.[117] Pope John VIII (r. 872–882) turned to the passage to persuade the rulers of Italy to break their agreements with the Saracens, as did Louis II in his angry letter to the Byzantine emperor Basil I in 871 concerning the refuge provided to Muslim warriors in Naples.[118] Both John and Louis had staked much of their political credibility on opposing Saracens in Italy and it is therefore unsurprising that they might have a more hard-line approach to the matter than their contemporaries.[119]

A more sophisticated reading of this passage was provided by Pope Nicholas I for the newly Christian Boris I of the Bulgars in 866. The pope observed that "some of the saints and faithful made pacts and treaties of friendship with foreigners and infidels."[120] Elsewhere, he gave a

116. Agobard of Lyons, *Epistolae* no. 8, 191; Florus of Lyons, *De iniusta vexatione ecclesiae Lugdunensis*, no. 27, 557.

117. Stephen III, *Epistolae* no. 45, 560–563; Pohl, "Why Not to Marry a Foreign Woman."

118. John VIII, *Epistolae* nos. 41–42, 39–41, 39, 40; Louis II, *Epistola ad Basilium I*, 393.

119. Engreen, "Pope John the Eighth and the Arabs"; Gantner, "New Visions of Community in Ninth-Century Rome."

120. Nicholas I, *Epistolae* no. 99, "qui nullam communionem luci ad tenebras . . . nonnulli sanctorum et fidelium cum alienigenis et infidelibus pacta et amicitiae foedera contraxisse diversa," 594.

clear message to Louis II, stating that it was permitted to "enter into a pact with foreign men for the aid and security of the Christians" in order to pacify their "wild savagery."[121] In support of this, he pointed to the precedent of Solomon, "who made pacts with foreign peoples," and to Charlemagne, who worked for "the aid and comfort of the Christians."[122]

Despite this, alliances with non-Christians could be politically damaging. The Continuator of the *Fredegar Chronicle* condemns Duke Eudo of Aquitaine by falsely claiming that he and his men collaborated with the Muslim invasion of 732.[123] In its description of Pippin II of Aquitaine's time spent living with a Viking army in 864, the *Annals of St-Bertin* claims that he "kept their rites."[124] It should be noted that these accounts were written by those hostile to the accused. Eudo was presented as not just in communication with Muslim rulers but in cahoots with a direct attack on Christendom.[125] Pippin was deemed to have lost both his Christian and Frankish identity by joining the Vikings. The Continuator and the *Annals of St-Bertin* present diplomacy between more favoured Frankish leaders and Saracens in a positive or neutral light.[126]

Accusations of an unseemly alliance with non-Christians could be turned against the accuser, being used as an indication of the iniquity of Frankish enemies. Listing the crimes of Lothar I (r. 817–855), Nithard (d. 844), who was a partisan of Charles the Bald, wrote "worst of all, he had made war on his brother and drove him to seek the aid of the pagans," in this case Scandinavians.[127] The *Annals of Fulda* describe the pleas of Abbot Adalhard of St Bertin and Count Odo of Troyes to Louis the German (r. 817–876) that he march west against Charles the Bald in 858, or else "they would have to seek protection from the pagans with great danger to the Christian religion, since they could not get it from their lawful and orthodox lords."[128]

121. Ibid., no. 54, "cum exteris quibusque pro remediis et securitate Christianorum placitum inieritis . . . fera saevicia," 351–352.

122. Ibid., "cum exteris gentibus placitum confirmet . . . nonnisi ad remedium et solatium Christianorum," 352.

123. "The Continuations of the Chronicle of Fredegar," a.732 284; Rouche, "Les Aquitains ont-ils avant la bataille de Poitiers?"; Collins, "Deception and Misrepresentation," 239.

124. AB a.863 "et ritum eorum seruat," 105.

125. Kramer, "Franks, Romans, and Countrymen," 268.

126. "The Continuations of the Chronicle of Fredegar," 320; AB a.847 53; AB a.863 104; AB a.865 124.

127. Nithard, *Histoire*, II.8, "quod maximum est, in fratrem hostiliter irruit nec non et suffragium a paganis illum quaerere compulit," 72–74, translated by Scholz, 150.

128. AF a.858 "a paganis cum periculo christianitatis quaerere deberent defensionem, quam a legitimis et orthodoxis dominis invenire non possent," 51, translated by Reuter, 42.

Diplomacy with non-Christians could also be made into a glorious revelation of the power and mercy of a ruler. The sources for the later years of Charlemagne's reign are particularly concerned to depict the emperor graciously receiving the submission of foreign peoples.[129] Ermold the Black portrayed Louis the Pious demonstrating Christian kingship:

> The cares of the pious king extended in every direction, and the faith of the Franks grew right up to the sky. Nations and peoples flowed together from everywhere to see Caesar's Christian faith.[130]

Contact was framed as an aid to missionary work. Ermold's description of the dealings of Louis the Pious with Harald Klak centre around the Dane's conversion.[131] In his advice to Boris, Pope Nicholas pointed to the prohibition of divorce in a marriage between a Christian and a non-Christian in 1 Corinthians 7:12–13 to argue that:

> if the faithful has made a pact with the infidel with this purpose, that he be able to attract him to the worship of the true God, this is not forbidden.[132]

This does not seem to have been a concern with diplomacy with the Islamic world, as there is no evidence for any efforts being made to convert Saracens to Christ.[133] However, it did provide another space within which to justify Christian communication with non-Christians.

As Paul Kershaw has observed, much of Charlemagne's image as a great ruler amongst the Franks during his reign and in the reigns of his son and grandsons relates to his reputation as a monarch capable of enforcing peace within and beyond his borders, even if it was a peace brought about by the sword.[134] Concepts of "peaceful kingship" were pervasive in the courts of Louis the Pious and Charles the Bald, providing a context in which peace with non-Christians could be presented as triumphant.[135]

129. McKitterick, *Charlemagne*, 288. See also Latowsky, *Emperor of the World*, 19–58.

130. Ermold the Black, *In honorem Hludovici*, Bk. 4, "cura pii passim gliscebat denique regis Francorumque fides creverat usque polos; Undique collectim gentes populique fluebant Cernere christicolam Caesaris atque fidem," 144, translated by Noble, 170.

131. Ibid., 166–172.

132. Nicholas I, *Epistolae* no. 99, "si eo fidelis animo pactum cum infideli constituit, ut eum ad cultum veri Dei possit attrahere, non est prohibendum," 594.

133. Kedar, *Crusade and Mission*, 4–5; Tieszen, "From Invitation to Provocation," 24.

134. Kershaw, *Peaceful Kings*, 136, 142, 170–173.

135. Ibid., 175–240.

In 798, Alcuin advised Charlemagne that in dealing with an opponent who could not be beaten with arms or trickery, "the hatred of enemies should be destroyed by counsel of peace."[136] Sedulius Scottus censured the Roman emperor Julian for turning down efforts made by the king of Persia to achieve peace, thereby "anticipating victory with a false hope."[137] They suggest an environment in which diplomacy with the other was legitimate if it brought about positive consequences. Similar sentiments are expressed by the *Annals of Fulda*, when in 849 "quarrelsome" elements of the Frankish army rejected an offer of peace from the Bohemians and suffered a crushing defeat.[138] It is with these ideas in mind that Carolingian diplomacy with the Islamic world needs to be considered.

## *Envoys*

The information available on the envoys involved in this diplomacy is slim. Only one of the diplomats sent to the Franks by the ʿAbbāsids is named, ʿAbd Allāh, who led the embassy that arrived in 806.[139] Although the name ʿAbd Allāh is fairly ubiquitous, it does at least suggest that the leader of the mission was Muslim. Christians could also be selected as ambassadors, with the embassy of 831 being led by two Muslims and one Christian.[140] In addition to the advantages of sending the Franks a co-religionist as a diplomat, al-Maʿmūn may have had particular reason to send a prominent Christian in that year. The civil war that had brought him to power had been accompanied by the persecution of Christians, something of which the Carolingians were aware.[141] The caliph may have been attempting a show of good faith.

Choosing the right ambassador was of key importance, for it was agreed that "the messenger's flaw dishonours the sender, even if he is virtuous."[142] Al-Jāḥiẓ (d. 868/869) was highly concerned with the selection of envoys. In his *Kitāb al-Tāj* he goes into this in great detail, illustrating the subject

136. Alcuin, *Epistolae* no. 149, "tunc pacis consilio inimicitiarum odia esse delenda videntur," 242.

137. Sedulius Scottus, *De rectoribus Christianis*, "falsa spe victoriam praesumens," 170. Staubach argues that it was written for Charles the Bald in *Rex Christianus* 2, 105–112; Stone, *Morality and Masculinity*, 92–93.

138. AF a.849 "discordium," 39.

139. ARF a.806 122.

140. Astronomer, *Vita Hludowici*, c.46 466.

141. *Annales Laurissenses minores*, 38.

142. Ibn al-Farrāʾ, *Diplomacy in the Early Islamic World*, 73.

with Persian stories featuring Alexander the Great and the Sasanian monarchs.[143] Al-Jāḥiẓ advises the caliph that the good envoy is one

> who is of robust constitution and temperament, gifted with eloquence and ease in his manner of expression, able to grasp the subtleties of language and reply promptly, to transmit the letter and the spirit of the message of the King; he must have a sincere tone, and not be inclined to ambition or to vice, and remember well his instructions.[144]

Ibn al-Farrāʾ quoted al-Jāḥiẓ, while also referring to al-Balkhī's words on the qualities of an envoy:

> the one whom you send for the mission should be of a loud and clear voice, of handsome appearance and looks, good characteristics, eloquent, good with words, and should remember precisely what he should convey.[145]

According to Ibn al-Farrāʾ, Muḥammad also highlighted the physical requirements of an envoy, declaring "If you send me a messenger, he should be good-looking."[146] A bad envoy was one who was "a hasty person or talkative or boastful or one who is addicted to wine."[147]

It seems probable that many ʿAbbāsid diplomats were *mawālī* (non-Arab Muslims).[148] The administration had long been dependent on *mawālī* clients to the caliph, a phenomenon which intensified following the ʿAbbāsid Revolution.[149] Caliph al-Amīn is reported by al-Ṭabarī to have appointed ʿAlī b. Ṣāliḥ in charge of his *dīwān al-rasāʾil* (correspondence bureau).[150] Nothing is known of ʿAlī b. Ṣāliḥ except that he was also the keeper of al-Amīn's prayer rug. This is the earliest reference to this office, which otherwise only appears later in the sources and may be an anachronism on al-Ṭabarī's part.[151]

The embassy sent by Caliph al-Muqtadir in 921 to the Volga Bulgars, in which Ibn Faḍlān participated, seems to have contained people from the lands to be traversed who could act as interpreters.[152] This included

143. Al-Jāḥiẓ, *Le Livre de la Couronne*, 141–144.
144. Ibid., 141.
145. Ibn al-Farrāʾ, *Diplomacy in the Early Islamic World*, 67.
146. Ibid., 69.
147. Ibid., 79.
148. Ragheb, "La transmission des nouvelles," 41; Crone, "Mawlā," 880.
149. Crone, *Slaves on Horses*, 67–68; Lassner, *The Shaping of ʿAbbāsid Rule*, 101.
150. Al-Ṭabarī, *The History of al-Ṭabarī, Vol. 31*, 45.
151. Kennedy, *The Early Abbasid Caliphate*, 33.
152. Hermes, *The [European] Other*, 82.

the head of the embassy, the eunuch Sawsān al-Rassī, a former slave whose name suggests an origin in the Aras river basin.[153] Ibn Faḍlān himself was a *faqīh* (legal expert) who may have been an Arab, and whose responsibility it was to read al-Muqtadir's letter and present the gifts.[154]

Information on diplomats from Umayyad Spain is also parlous. A chance reference in Ibn al-Qūṭīya mentions that one al-Quṣbī was "sent on a mission by ʿAbd al-Raḥmān II to the king of the Franks and to the Byzantine emperor."[155] Whether this means specifically the Carolingians is unclear, for there are no details concerning the embassy he led. As most of Ibn al-Qūṭīya's account of al-Quṣbī concerns the inheritance of his estate (which included 3,000 silver dinars) after his death, it can be assumed that he was resident in Córdoba and a man of some wealth, possibly necessary to finance his diplomatic expeditions.[156] The son of the judge of Córdoba was accused of embezzling the money from al-Quṣbī's orphans, prompting a moral outcry, and Emir Muḥammad I felt compelled to intervene on behalf of the orphans "because of the relationship between him and their father, and his own father ʿAbd al-Raḥmān, before him."[157] As well as suggesting that al-Quṣbī's career had continued into the reign of Muḥammad, this indicates a close connection between the diplomat and the Umayyad court.

The other Umayyad ambassadors are anonymous. It seems plausible that amongst their retinues were Andalusi Christians. A century later the famous contact between Caliph ʿAbd al-Raḥmān III and Emperor Otto I began in 950, when the Umayyad sent an embassy to Otto consisting of a bishop and two priests bearing letters and gifts.[158] When Otto's envoy, John of Gorze, was imprisoned in Córdoba, the man sent to Frankfurt to fix the situation in 956 was Rabīʿ b. Zaīd, better known to later scholarship as Reccemund. Reccemund was a member of the palace staff "and exceptionally learned in both Arabic and Latin literature," being involved in the composition of an Arabic calendar of Christian Holy Days.[159] He acted as ambassador on several occasions, travelling to Constantinople and Jerusalem in the process, and was rewarded with the bishopric of Elvira.[160]

153. Ibn Faḍlān, *Ibn Fadlan and the Land of Darkness*, 3–4.

154. Ibid., 3.

155. Ibn al-Qūṭīya, *Early Islamic Spain*, 109.

156. Ibid.

157. Ibid., 110.

158. John of Saint-Arnoul, *La vie de Jean*, 142.

159. Ibid., "et litteris optime tam nostrorum quam ipsius inter quos versabatur linguae Arabicae institutus," 154; Reccemund, *Le Calendrier de Cordoue*, 73.

160. Christys, *Christians in al-Andalus*, 108–113.

Similarly, in 973 the Bishop of Toledo, ʿUbayd Allāh b. Qāsim, was sent to talk to King Ramiro III of León.[161]

The Carolingians may have had access to Arabic speakers. Spanish Christians were present in the Carolingian empire, including Bishop Theodulf of Orléans, Bishop Agobard of Lyons, and Bishop Prudentius of Troyes.[162] Whether any of them had any Arabic is unclear, although many of them were adults when they left the Iberian Peninsula or Septimania. Theodulf was a deacon when he arrived in Aquitaine.[163] He could recognize the "Arab tongue and script" on the gold coins with which people tried to bribe him.[164] Eulogius of Córdoba, who, despite his protestations to the contrary, appears to have had some familiarity with Arabic, had brothers at the court of Louis the German.[165] There are hints of a community of people from the Iberian Peninsula in Lyons.[166] Charlemagne was attended by Christian Syrians on his deathbed who helped him correct translations of the Gospels.[167] They could also have translated more prosaic messages.

Other possible translators included Francia's Jewish population. The role played by Jewish merchants was highlighted by twentieth-century economic historians, most notably Verlinden.[168] The history of Jews in the eighth and ninth centuries has often been written in the light of better-sourced, later centuries. The vast majority of Jews in this period were not merchants and vice versa.[169] Nor can it be assumed that all Jewish merchants were in communication with each other.[170] The temporal coincidence of Jewish financiers in Baghdad and Jewish communities in Marseilles or Narbonne does not prove some sort of commercial connection between the two.

Nonetheless, there is clear evidence to suggest that Jews could have been important to the functioning of Carolingian diplomacy with the Islamic world. This is most obvious when considering the caliphate. Charlemagne

161. El-Hajji, *Andalusian Diplomatic Relations*, 78–79, 88–93.

162. Fontaine, "Mozarabie Hispanique."

163. Freeman, "Theodulf of Orléans," 186; Freeman and Meyvaert, "The Meaning of Theodulf's Apse Mosaic," 137n7.

164. Theodulf of Orléans, *Contra iudices*, "Arabum sermo sive caracter," 498.

165. Eulogius, *Tertius epistolae*, 497.

166. Boshof, *Erzbischof Agobard von Lyon*, 168.

167. Thegan, *Gesta Hludowici imperatoris*, c.7 186.

168. For example, Verlinden, "A propos de la place des Juifs"; see also Verhulst, "Economic Organisation," 508.

169. Toch, *The Economic History of European Jews*, 177–191.

170. Menache, "Communication in the Jewish Diaspora."

employed Isaac the Jew to guide his envoys, Lantfrid and Sigimund, to the court of Hārūn al-Rashīd.[171] The extent to which Isaac's success (and survival) should be attributed to his faith is unclear. Jewish merchants seem to have been familiar on the Mediterranean.[172] Notker the Stammerer alludes to Jewish traders off Narbonne.[173] In one of his stories, Charlemagne employs a Jewish merchant "whose habit it was to go to the Promised Land and bring from there many precious and unknown things to the countries beyond the sea."[174]

Notker's near contemporary, Ibn Khurradādhbih, writing between 854 and 874, famously mentions the activities of the Rādhānite traders, supporting Notker's picture of Jewish merchants crossing the Mediterranean.[175] Ibn Khurradādhbih says they "speak Arabic and Persian and *Rūmī*, and *Ifranjī* and Andalusi and Slavic. They travel from east to west and from the west to the east, by land and by sea."[176] That these merchants were familiar with the rulers of the west is indicated by the line:

> sometimes they travel with it [their goods] to the king of *Firanja* and sell [them] there; and if they wish to transport their goods from *Firanja*, in the western sea, they go from Antioch and travel by land three *marḥalas* [days' journey] to al-Jābiya, and from there they sail the Euphrates to Baghdad.[177]

The exact significance of these traders is unclear, and Gil would argue that *Firanja* here means Italy rather than Francia.[178] Even if this is the case, the Rādhānites still represent an obvious line of communications between the Frankish world and the caliphate.

Jews can be observed at the Carolingian court. A small community was present in Aachen in 820, when a search was ordered of "the houses of all the merchants . . . Christians as well as Jews."[179] Over the subsequent decade, Louis the Pious took a number of prominent Jews into his

171. ARF, a.801 116.

172. Arenson, "Medieval Jewish Seafaring."

173. Notker, *Gesta Karoli Magni*, II.14, 77.

174. Ibid., "qui terram repromissionis sepius adire et inde ad cismarinas provintias multa preciosa et incognita solitus erat afferre," 19–21.

175. The Rādhānites have been the subject of long debate, summarised by Pellat, "al-Rādhāniyya"; Gil, *Jews in Islamic Countries*, 617–623.

176. Ibn Khurradādhbih, "Le Livre des Routes," 512.

177. Ibid., 512–514.

178. Gil, *Jews in Islamic Countries*, 627.

179. Louis the Pious, *Capitulare de disciplina palatii Aquisgranis*, no. 146, "par mansiones omnium negotiatorum . . . tam christianorum quam et Iudaeorum," 298.

patronage.[180] As well as stating Louis's protection of the individuals concerned, the wording of the orders recording this free them of a variety of tolls and taxes on the transport of goods, implying these Jews were involved in trade over some distance.[181] Of particular interest is the formula which concerns one "Abraham, inhabitant of the city of Zaragoza," who had come to Louis and sworn to "serve our palace faithfully."[182] While the content of the formula indicates that Abraham would spend a considerable amount of time in Francia, his Andalusian connections would have been valuable for Louis's diplomacy with the Umayyads.

In 839 Louis granted a charter to a Jewish family concerning land in the Spanish March on the road between Girona and Barcelona.[183] Their patron was Louis's half brother, Archchancellor Hugh. In her *Manual* Dhuoda offered her son, William of Septimania, advice in dealing with her Jewish creditors.[184] That Jews could link Carolingian kings with the Iberian Peninsula is indicated by a letter sent in 876 by Charles the Bald to the "inhabitants of Barcelona," which was carried by "Judas the Hebrew."[185] Judas, or Judacot as he is alternatively named in the letter, was sent to Bishop Frodoin of Barcelona with "ten pounds of silver for the reparation of his church."[186]

This material helps support the more dubious evidence for Jews as agents between Francia and Spain. The writings of Agobard portray Jewish merchants running chain gangs of enslaved pagans across Frankish territory to the markets of al-Andalus.[187] The veracity of their account, fuelled as it is by obvious anti-Judaism, has recently been challenged.[188] Likewise, Prudentius's claim that in 852 "the Moors took Barcelona because the Jews betrayed it to them" should be treated with caution,

180. Louis's reign has been described as a "golden age" for Jews. On this, see Graetz, *Volkstümliche Geschichte*, 234; Bachrach, *Early Medieval Jewish Policy*, 65. See more generally Geisel, *Die Juden im Frankenreich*, 361–729.

181. Devroey and Brouwer, "La participation des Juifs."

182. Louis the Pious, *Formulae*, no. 52, "Abraham, habitans in civitate Caesaraugusta . . . palatii nostri fideliter deservire," 325.

183. Linder, *The Jews in the Legal Sources*, 365–367.

184. Dhuoda, *Liber manualis*, Bk. 10:4, 226.

185. CC 2.ii, "omnibus Barchinonensibus," 431–432.

186. CC 2.ii, "ad Frodoynum episcopum libras X. de argento ad suam ecclesiam reparare," 435.

187. Agobard of Lyons, *De insolentia Iudaeorum*; Boshof, *Erzbischof Agobard von Lyon*, 102–135; Heil, "Agobard, Amolo, das Kirchengut"; Constable, "Muslim Spain and Mediterranean Slavery," 265–267.

188. Toch, *The Economic History of European Jews*, 177–195. See, however, Freudenhammer, "Frühmittelalterlicher Karawanenhandel."

particularly given its resemblance to his claim that in 848 "some Jews betrayed Bordeaux to the Danes."[189] Nonetheless, for much of the Carolingian period there are signs of Jews who were both connected to Spain and in direct contact with the Carolingian court. It seems distinctly implausible to suppose that no information about affairs in al-Andalus reached Frankish kings through this route.

Despite this, it seems likely that the Umayyads had readier access to Latin speakers than the Carolingians had to people familiar with Arabic, and that an important part of any Umayyad embassy would have been Andalusi Christians capable of acting as translators. A sufficiently large proportion of the Andalusi Christian community, particularly among the clerical hierarchy, possessed Latin.[190] This was often employed for translating religious texts such as the noted rendering of the Psalms not only into Arabic but into the *rajaz* metre of high Arabic poetry by Ḥafṣ b. Albār al-Qūṭī in 889. Ḥafṣ was trying to present his religion in a register that a cultured Muslim would deem worthy of respect, criticising a previous Arabic translator of the Gospels, for "he ruined the meanings through his ignorance of the laws of language."[191]

The lot of a Carolingian ambassador to the caliphate was not normally a happy one. Of the named individuals who we know journeyed to Raqqa, only Isaac survived to come back, with Lantfrid, Sigimund, and Radbert all perishing on their mission.[192] The timing, location, and circumstances of their deaths are unknown. The continuation of positive relations between Aachen and Raqqa makes disease or misadventure the probable cause. If their deaths are mysterious, their lives are even more so. None of these individuals can be placed in any other context. Michael McCormick has identified Roculf who, together with Agamus, arrived in Italy in 808 following a mission to Palestine sent by Charlemagne.[193] A Count Roculf was sent as *missus* between Aachen and Liège with Adalhard of Corbie in spring 806.[194] He is probably the same as the "Richolfus" who was a witness to Charlemagne's will made in 811.[195] This Roculf was a senior figure, which may

189. AB a.852 "Mauri Barcinoniam, Iudaeis prodentibus, capiunt," 64; AB a.848 "Dani Burdegalam Aquitaniae, Iudaeis prodentibus," 55, translated by Nelson, *Annals of St-Bertin*, 74, 65.

190. See Kassis, "Arabic Speaking Christians"; Wasserstein, "The Language Situation in al-Andalus"; Penelas, "Linguistic Islamization"; Wright, "Language and Religion," 115–126.

191. Kassis, "The Arabicization and Islamization," 150.

192. ARF a.801 116; ARF a.807 123.

193. McCormick, *Charlemagne's Survey*, 166.

194. Charlemagne, *Capitula a missis dominicis ad comites directa*, no. 85, 183–184.

195. Einhard, *Vita Karoli Magni*, c.33 41.

suggest something of the nature of the people sent to Jerusalem, although there is no evidence that he had any direct contact with the ʿAbbāsids.

Like their Arabic counterparts, the Carolingian sources are vague about the identities of their envoys sent to Córdoba. One of the few who can be identified is Count Salomon of Urgell, Cerdanya, and Conflent, who arrived in Córdoba in 863 to negotiate with Emir Muḥammad I.[196] Salomon is poorly chronicled, with his extended appearance as a villain in the *Gesta comitum Barcinonensium* owing more to the dynastic purposes of the twelfth-century counts of Barcelona than to any reality.[197] He was probably a Goth and was given Urgell and Cerdanya in 848 following the death of Count Sunifred I, in the midst of a crisis caused by William of Septimania's seizing of Barcelona with Umayyad support.[198] His elevation was ratified at the assembly at Narbonne in October 849. From 860 he was count of Conflent. Ties in Aquitaine are indicated by his patronage of the monastery of Castres, in which he deposited the relics of St Vincent.[199]

The value of someone like Salomon, known on both sides of the border, is suggested by the analogous figure of Thachulf, *dux* of the Sorbian March.[200] The *Annals of Fulda* state that the Bohemians "trusted him above all others as one who was knowledgeable in the laws and customs of the Slavic people."[201] Salomon fits within the wider context of other Carolingian diplomats, many of whom were also counts.[202] Senior church figures such as abbots and bishops are also well attested, with examples including Archbishop Amalarius of Trier, sent to Constantinople in 813.[203] It was common for envoys to be sent in pairs, frequently matching a secular and an ecclesiastical figure.[204] This is noted by Notker the Stammerer talking about the embassy of Bishop Haito of Basel and Count Hugh of Tours to Constantinople in 811, and the *Formulary of Marculf* contains letters that

196. Aimoin, *Historia translationis* 1018.

197. *Gesta comitum Barcinonensium*, 4–5, 24; Salrach, *El Procés de Formació Nacional*, 2:38.

198. Salomon's family connections have been a matter of some debate, see d'Abadal i de Vinyals, *Els Primers Comtes Catalans*, 30–39; Lewis, *The Development of Southern French*, 109.

199. Aimoin, *Historia translationis* 1018.

200. See also Shepard, "Trouble-Shooters and Men-on-the-Spot."

201. AF a.849 "cui prae ceteris credebant quasi scienti leges et consuetudines Sclavicae gentis," 40, translated by Reuter, *Annals of Fulda*, 29.

202. The best discussion of the demographics of Carolingian diplomats is McCormick, "From One Center of Power to Another." On Carolingian *missi*, see Davis, "Inventing the *Missi*."

203. ARF a.813 137; Amalarius of Trier, *Versus Marini*, 426–428.

204. For this phenomenon in a different context, Louis the Pious, *Capitulare missorum*, no. 141, 291. This seems to have been common practice from the fifth century: Gillett, *Envoys and Political Communication*, 237.

assume an embassy is led by an "apostolic man as well as [an] illustrious man."[205]

The role of religious figures as diplomats is particularly significant. The many reasons men of the Church might have for travelling offered opportunities for discrete communication. The journey of the monks Usuard and Odilard to al-Andalus in 857, ostensibly to retrieve relics but also concerned with contacting the martyrs of Córdoba, can be fitted into a wider tradition.[206] A decade later Hincmar of Rheims reports communicating with Pope Nicholas I "using as carriers clerics of his disguised as pilgrims to avoid the snares set by his enemies."[207] According to Nithard, Louis the Pious sent a monk named Guntbald, ostensibly on religious business, to talk secretly with Pippin I of Aquitaine and Louis the German.[208]

How heavily these diplomats were briefed is unclear. To be effective they would have needed knowledge of their own monarch's needs and desires and the situation they would encounter when they arrived. Instructions from Charlemagne for *missi* on what to say to Pope Hadrian I in 785 survive.[209] As well as including a summary of the contents of the letter they were to bear, the memorandum includes a precise script for the presenting of both it and the gifts.[210] Charlemagne's letter to Angilbert in 796, shortly before the courtier and poet was due to lead an embassy to Pope Leo III, does likewise.[211]

The extent to which ambassadors could be briefed was of course affected by the amount of information available to rulers.[212] From the time of Charlemagne in particular, Carolingian courts were defined by a drive to gather information.[213] The *De ordine palatii*, composed by Hincmar of Rheims for Carloman II in 882, offers an indication of this.[214] Claiming to have used as his basis a similar text by Adalhard of Corbie for Charlemagne, Hincmar presents the Frankish king interviewing people from

205. Notker, *Gesta Karoli Magni*, II.6, 55; Marculf, *Formulæ Marculfinæ*, I.11, "apostolico vero illo necnon et inluster vero," 49.

206. Aimoin, *De translatione* 939–960.

207. AB a.867 "quam per clericos suos sub peregrinorum habitu propter contrariorum vitandas insidias," 138, translated by Nelson, *Annals of St-Bertin*, 140.

208. Nithard, *Histoire des fils*, I.3, 14.

209. Charlemagne, *Memoratorium missis*, no. 111, 225.

210. Nelson, "The Settings of the Gift," 129–132. For another example of a letter with strict presentation notes, see Scior, "Stimme, Schrift und Performanz."

211. Charlemagne, *Epistolae* no. 92, 135–136.

212. This is a subject that has been addressed more thoroughly by specialists in Late Antiquity; see Lee, *Information and Frontiers*; Gillett, *Envoys and Political Communication* and "Communication in Late Antiquity"; Sotinel, "How Were Bishops Informed?"

213. Davis, *Charlemagne's Practice of Empire*, 304.

214. On the *De ordine palatii*, see Kasten, *Adalhard von Corbie*, 76–79.

all over his realm, with his agents being under strict instructions actively to collect information, including on foreign affairs.[215] Rumours could play an important role in spreading information.[216] Given the long distances and occasionally irregular communications, rapidly changing political situations could easily be misread, and actors frequently had to make decisions based on incomplete knowledge.

Pope Stephen III's letter to both Charlemagne and his brother Carloman is a case in point. As emerges in the letter, Stephen knew that one of these Carolingian kings was in talks to marry a Lombard princess, but not which one.[217] More confusing still was the summer of 874 at the court of Charles the Bald, where Hincmar of Rheims describes "various doubtful reports had been arriving about Salomon leader of the Bretons, some saying that he was ill, some that he was dead."[218] The death of Emperor Louis II was announced in 871, prompting Louis the German to order an invasion of Italy. These movements had to be reversed when it was revealed "that the Emperor Louis was alive and healthy in body."[219] Rulers in the early middle ages made important decisions with limited information.

## *Travel*

In addition to the lead envoys, early medieval embassies normally travelled with large retinues. This was not just to provide support staff such as translators and servants but to impress those by whom they would be received. A large group of companions also offered some protection on potentially dangerous roads.[220] Some sense of the scale of these retinues is suggested by a catalogue of goods listed in a formula connected to Louis the Pious, which orders nobles to provide his agents with the following:

> Twenty loaves of bread, two *friscingas*, one pig or lamb, two chickens, ten eggs, a *modius* of drink, salt, herbs, enough wood for forty-four days, two *sextarii* of vegetables, fish, depending on what can be found, and for their horses four *modii* of corn and two *modii* of hay.[221]

215. Hincmar of Rheims, *De ordine palatii*, c.36 94–96.

216. Gravel, *Distances, rencontres, communications*, 97–108.

217. Stephen III, *Epistolae* no. 45, 560–563.

218. AB a.874 "Salomon dux Brittonum, qui nuntiabatur interea dubiis nunciis quandoquidem infirmus quandoquidem mortuus," 196, translated by Nelson, *Annals of St-Bertin*, 186.

219. AB a.871 "quod ipse imperator Hludowicus viveret et sanus corpore esset," 183.

220. Reuter, "The Insecurity of Travel," reprinted in *Medieval Politics*, 38–71.

221. Louis the Pious, *Formulae*, no. 7, "panes 20, friscingas duas, porcellum sive agnum unum, pullos duos, ova 10, de potu modium unum, sal, herbola ortolanas, ligna sufficienter

This formula and others like it indicate that diplomats could rely on some support from their rulers.[222] In Francia they could use the network already existing for other royal agents.[223] That the Hispani lords settled in Septimania were expected to supply both Carolingian *missi* and "legates from the lands of Spain that have been sent to us" as they travelled is demonstrated by the instructions in a charter issued by Charlemagne before 801, repeated word for word in a grant of Charles the Bald in 844.[224] Charlemagne's *Capitulare de villis* orders that:

> the count in his district, or the men whose traditional custom it has been to look after our *missi* and their retinues, shall continue, as they have done in the past, to provide them with pack-horses and other necessities, so that they might travel to and from the palace with ease and dignity.[225]

That this was not a popular duty may be hinted by the repetition of this point in the *Capitulare missorum generale*.[226] Early in his imperial reign, Louis the Pious legislated against those who disrespected foreign envoys when they were escorted by his *missi*.[227] In the *Admonitio ad omnes regni ordines*, Louis condemned those who "poorly received" embassies and ordered the stewarding of "the roads and manors of our fathers and ours as ordained by the capitularies."[228]

A similar mobilization of agents of the state can be observed in the east. The writings of Abū Yūsuf suggest that foreign diplomats bearing letters from their ruler could secure an escort from local commanders to help them reach the caliph.[229] The eighth and ninth centuries saw the introduction of the *funduq* in the Islamic world.[230] Often founded or owned by Muslim rulers, these hostels for travelling merchants could be used to host

---

et intra quadragesimam cotidie formaticos quattuor, legumina sextaria duo, pisces, iuxta quod invenire possunt, et ad caballos eorum de annona cotidie modios quatuor et inter ambos de feno karradam," 292.

222. Marculf, *Formulæ Marculfinæ* I.11, 49.

223. Ganshof, "La tractoria."

224. CC 2.ii, "legatis qui de partibus Hyspanie ad nos transmissi fuerint," 416, 423.

225. Charlemagne, *Capitulare de villis*, no. 32, "Et comes de suo ministerio vel homines illi qui antiquitus consueti fuerunt missos aut legationes soniare, ita et modo inantea et de parveridis et omnia eis necessaria solitomore soniare faciant, qualiter bene et honorifice ad palatium venire vel redire possint," 85.

226. Charlemagne, *Capitulare missorum generale*, no. 40, 116.

227. Louis the Pious, *Capitula legibus addenda*, no. 139, 284.

228. Louis the Pious, *Admonitio ad omnes regni ordines*, no. 150, 306.

229. Abū Yūsuf, *Kitab-ul-Kharaj*, 382.

230. Constable, *Housing the Stranger*, 39.

officials and envoys.[231] This infrastructure probably made travelling in the caliphate easier for Christians than vice versa.[232]

As the formula from Marculf indicates, provisioning envoys and their retinue could be a major strain on a lord's resources. Einhard describes the large number of travellers received by Charlemagne as "burdensome."[233] The ability to demand supplies for diplomats was a display of royal authority in the peripheries of the Carolingian empire and a statement to visiting envoys. Despite these provisions, diplomacy was an expensive business for those who participated in it. Notker informs us that Haito and Hugh "spent a great deal on their ship and expenses" when travelling to Constantinople.[234] This explains the importance of monarchs giving gifts to foreign envoys, which might help defray these costs. Thegan and the Astronomer record that upon the death of his father in 814, Louis the Pious received the embassies that had come to see Charlemagne and gave them gifts.[235] When he sent back the envoy of Muḥammad I in 863, Charles the Bald "endowed him with many large gifts."[236]

The long time spent away could inconvenience the type of prominent men normally selected for diplomatic missions in other ways. Counts, bishops and abbots were central figures of their local communities and a prolonged absence to foreign lands disrupted the management of their affairs.[237] Some recognition of this fact is demonstrated in a different entry from Marculf's *Formulary*, which takes the form of a letter sent to a local notable informing them that as

> we presently ordered the apostolic man A—or: the illustrious man A—to travel to this place in our service, we therefore order that, while he is detained in these parts, all his legal cases and those of his friends and retainers, or of anyone for whom he is legitimately answerable, should remain on hold.[238]

231. Ibid., 70.

232. Constable, *Housing the Stranger*, 110.

233. Einhard, *Vita Karoli Magni*, c.21 "onerosa," 26.

234. Notker, *Gesta Karoli Magni*, II.6 "ingenti penuria confecti ad conspectum illius venire cogerentur," 55.

235. Thegan, *Gesta Hludowici imperatoris*, c.9 "magnis honoribus decoravit eos," 190; Astronomer, *Vita Hludowici*, c.23 "sumptuose muneratos tu remisit," 352.

236. AB a.863 "cum magnis et multis muneribus," 104.

237. Innes, *State and Society*, 118–129, 192–194; West, *Reframing the Feudal Revolution*, 20–40; Davis, *Charlemagne's Practice of Empire*, 32.

238. Marculf, *Formulæ Marculfinæ* I.23, "dum et nos ad presens apostolico viro illo, aut inlustris viro, pro nostris utilitatibus ibi ambulare precipimus, ideo iubemus, ut, dum illis partibus fuerit demoratus, omnes causas suas suisque amicis aut gasindis, seu undecumque

A Frankish envoy could legitimately expect a year to pass between being sent out on an embassy to Córdoba and returning. In that intervening time they might be vulnerable to the machinations of rivals at court or at home. Among the unfortunate was the monk Witbold, who missed his opportunity to succeed his uncle Widolaic as abbot of Fontenelle while on a diplomatic mission to Constantinople in 787.[239]

There were rather more physical dangers to be faced as a diplomat. Bad weather delayed the return of a Frankish legation from Byzantium in 763, reducing Pippin III to asking the pope for word of their movements.[240] Even with a large retinue, ambassadors were vulnerable to attack. In his poem concerning his embassy to Constantinople in 813, Amalarius of Trier recalls his sea journey back being punctuated by the threat of pirates, which they escaped with the help of a gale.[241] Papal legates returning from Constantinople in 870 "encountered pirates and lost everything they possessed" off Durrës, being held captive for eight months.[242] While bandits may have been a problem, the elites through whose lands envoys travelled presented a more serious threat. In his capitularies, Louis the Pious refers to legates suffering "open violence" and robbery.[243] In 836, King Horik I of the Danes "complained about the killing of the envoys he had sent to the emperor. They had been massacred a short while before near Cologne through the unauthorised action of certain men."[244]

Early medieval rulers were expected to take the safety of their roads and their messengers seriously. Apart from the practical benefits of protecting their agents, safeguarding the interests of pilgrims, merchants, and other travellers was part of the role of kingship. In the *Capitulary of Herstal* issued in March 779, Charlemagne ordered that "concerning travellers continuing to the palace or somewhere else: that no one is to dare to attack

---

ipse legitimo redebit mitio., in suspenso debeant resedere," 57, translated by Rio, *The Formularies of Angers and Marculf*, 157.

239. "Gesta abbatum Fontenellensium," 134.

240. Paul I, *Epistolae* no. 29, 533–535; *Chronicle of Moissac*, a.762 118.

241. Amalarius of Trier, *Versus Marini*, 427. On piracy, see Horden and Purcell, *The Corrupting Sea*, 157.

242. Anastasius Bibliothecarius, *Interpretatio Synodi* "sed Exdavenorum piratas incurrentes, omnia quae possidere videbantur penitus amiserunt," 39; Hadrian II, *Epistolae* no. 41, 759.

243. Louis the Pious, *Admonitio ad omnes regni ordines*, "apertas violentias," 305.

244. AB a.836 "de suorum ad imperatorem missorum interfectione conquestus est, qui dudum circa Coloniam Agrippinam quorundam praesumptione necati fuerant," 20, translated by Nelson, *Annals of St-Bertin*, 35.

these with an armed band."[245] Prudentius approved of the response of Louis the Pious to the murder of Horik's ambassadors, as he "very rightly avenged the slaughter of these envoys, sending *missi* solely to see to this."[246] For Notker, one of the hallmarks of Charlemagne's greatness was that:

> Because of the most vigorous efforts of Charles, the messengers of Hārūn, whether youths, boys or old men, passed easily from Parthia into Germany and returned from Germany to Parthia and it was not only possible but easy for them to come and go.[247]

Escorts were provided for high-status travellers, such as those granted to Pope Stephen IV in 816 or to King Æthelwulf of Wessex in 855.[248] This could sometimes be extended to diplomats. According to Thegan, Louis the Pious "sent his own envoys ahead of [foreign diplomats] to prepare anything they needed for their work while they were in his kingdom."[249]

Despite this support, the journeys involved were challenging. Braudel described distance as "the first enemy," something which applied to the early medieval age as much as to the early modern.[250] The Astronomer presents the Pyrenees as imbued with menace:

> These mountains almost touch heaven with their summits, terrify with the sharpness of their peaks, turn everything dark with the denseness of their forests, and nearly prevent the passage, not only of an army but even of a few men with the narrowness of their passageways or rather mere paths.[251]

245. Charlemagne, *Capitulare Haristallense*, no. 20, "De iterantibus, qui ad palatium aut aliubi pergunt, ut eos cum collecta nemo sit ausus adsalire," 51.

246. AB a.836 "quorum necem etiam imperator, missis ad hoc solum legatis, iustissime ultus est," 20, translated by Nelson, *Annals of St-Bertin*, 35.

247. Notker, *Gesta Karoli Magni*, II.9 "Propter industriam vigorosis simi Karoli, exitum vel reditum missorum eius et profectionem vel reversionem legatorum Aaron de Parthia in Germaniam sive de Germania in Parthiam iuvenibus, pueris et senioribus non solum possibile sed et facillimum videretur omnino," 64.

248. ARF, a.816 144; AB a.855 70.

249. Thegan, *Gesta Hludowici imperatoris*, c.9 "et ante eos misit missos suos praeparare eis, quicquid desiderabant ad opus eorum, quousque fuissent in regno eius," 190, translated by Noble, *Charlemagne and Louis the Pious*, 199.

250. Braudel, *The Mediterranean*, 355. On the problems raised by distance, see Gravel, *Distances, rencontres, communications*, 48–51; Nelson, *King and Emperor*, 21–23.

251. Astronomer, *Vita Hludowici*, c.2 "Qui mons cum altitudine caelum pene contingat, asperitate cautium horreat, opacitate silvarum tenebrescat, angustia viae vel potius semite commeatum non modo tanto exercitui, sed paucis admodum pene intercludat," 286–288, translated by Noble, *Charlemagne and Louis the Pious*, 229.

Despite this, diplomats journeying between the Carolingians and al-Andalus preferred overland routes. In this, they were not alone. Eulogius of Córdoba intended to travel to Francia overland but was frustrated by the war between Charles the Bald and Pippin II, which blocked his route.[252] The choice of route probably reflects the dangerous nature of the Gulf of Lion, being particularly hazardous for sea travel.[253]

As McCormick noted, diplomats and merchants were likely to follow the same roads.[254] For Francia and al-Andalus this was definitely true in the tenth century, when Otto I's envoy, John of Gorze, joined a convoy of merchants at Verdun travelling to Córdoba.[255] Toll stations like the ones at Barcelona, Les Cluses, and Narbonne imply the movement of people and goods.[256] Theodulf reported people in the south of the empire attempting to bribe him with Arabic gold and goatskins in the style of Córdoba.[257] The latter seems to have been a commodity with which the Franks were familiar, as Ansegis budgeted for the purchase of forty during his time as abbot of Fontenelle.[258] The paths these items took could also be used by diplomats.

The best recorded journey is that of the monks Usuard and Odilard, who travelled from Paris to Uzès in order to consult with Humfrid, *marchio* of Gothia, before taking the *strata francisca* to Barcelona, where they met Count Sunifred I and Bishop Athaulf.[259] From there they made their way to Zaragoza, whose Muslim lord placed them on a caravan going to Córdoba. The two monks began their return the next year in the company of the Umayyad army as Muḥammad I was marching on a rebellious Toledo.[260] Usuard and Odilard arrived at Toledo before the host and continued on, reaching Zaragoza. They found the *strata francisca* closed on their return due to bandits and so had to make a longer crossing, before making their way to Paris. This itinerary supports Jonathan Conant's observation that

252. Eulogius, *Tertius epistolae*, 497–498.

253. Braudel, *The Mediterranean*, 250–253.

254. McCormick, *Origins of the European Economy*, 271.

255. John of Saint-Arnoul, *La vie de Jean*, 144.

256. McCormick, *Origins of the European Economy*, 642. On Carolingian tolls, see Ganshof, "A propos du tonlieu."

257. Theodulf of Orléans, *Contra iudices*, 498.

258. McCormick, *Origins of the European Economy*, 697.

259. Aimoin, *De translatione* 941–943. For other routes, see Rouche, "Les relations transpyrénéennes." See pp. 240–241, 249–250.

260. Christys, "St-Germain des-Prés," 210.

the Franks perceived the Iberian Peninsula as a network of cities, through which a diplomat could move from nodal point to nodal point, gathering advice and directions at each stop.[261]

Usuard and Odilard also present the clearest picture of the length of these expeditions. The two monks left Paris in 857, crossing the Pyrenees before the winter weather could block the passes.[262] They arrived in Córdoba on 19 March 858 and stayed there two months, before leaving in early May.[263] Aimoin records that the return journey took six months, placing them in Esmans in November, something confirmed by the *Annals of St-Bertin*, which puts the arrival of relics they fetched in Francia at the end of 858.[264] This might be a slightly slow journey, for Usuard and Odilard are reported to have paused in Uzès for some time, but it resembles the pattern of embassies between Muḥammad and Charles the Bald in the early 860s. An Umayyad delegation arrived at Verberie in late 863.[265] Charles's response was carried by diplomats who left Compiègne mid-864 and arrived in Córdoba at the end of the year.[266] Charles at Compiègne received a final embassy from Muḥammad in late 865.[267] This suggests that travelling from Neustria to Córdoba overland would take approximately half a year.

Inevitably the season complicated these arrangements. Getting in and out of Spain between mid-autumn and early spring was a difficult challenge whether by land or sea.[268] The vast majority of arrivals at Carolingian courts from the Iberian Peninsula made their appearance in the second half of the year, allowing them to cross the Pyrenees in better weather. Among those that can be determined are the Asturian envoys of 798, the messenger of Ḥassān in 799, and the Umayyad diplomats of 816, 846, 863, and 865.[269]

The details of how diplomats travelled between the Franks and the ʿAbbāsids are limited but they always required Mediterranean travel. The question of Mediterranean shipping in the early middle ages has long exercised the minds of many of the most celebrated specialists in the

261. Conant, "Louis the Pious and the Contours of Empire," 345–346.
262. Christys, "St-Germain-des-Prés," 203.
263. Aimoin, *De translatione* 946.
264. Ibid.; AB a.858 79.
265. AB a.863 104.
266. Ibid., a.864 114.
267. Ibid., a.865 124.
268. Braudel, *The Mediterranean*, 246–253.
269. ARF a.798 102, a.799 108–109, a.816 144; AB a.847 53, a.863 104, a.866 124.

period.[270] Pirenne famously placed it at the heart of understanding the end of Antiquity. In his *Mahomet et Charlemagne* Pirenne argued for a continuation of the economic patterns of the Roman Mediterranean until the seventh century, when the unity of the *Mare Nostrum* was shattered by the armies and navies of Islam, ending large-scale commercial activity.[271] Most archaeologists and historians working today would place the beginning of a perceptible decline in trade in the fourth or fifth century and few would emphasise the importance of Muslim expansion in that process.[272] Indeed, the very existence of Carolingian-ʿAbbāsid diplomacy serves to undermine the idea of a Mediterranean riven into a no-man's-land between uncommunicative blocs.

The eighth century has nonetheless been viewed as a low point in Mediterranean shipping, as summarised by the work of Richard Hodges among others.[273] Peregrine Horden and Nicholas Purcell take the extremely long view, regarding this dip in commerce as a blip, in which the fundamental structures of Mediterranean interconnectivity remained intact.[274] McCormick argues that an economic boom in the Islamic world prompted revival in eighth- and ninth-century Europe, with the rise of commercial entrepots such as Amalfi and Venice in response to demand from North Africa and Iraq.[275] It is in McCormick's Mediterranean, one of steadily increasing activity, albeit from a low base, and linked to developments in the Middle East, that Carolingian contact with the caliphate seems to fit most naturally. His suggested mid-eighth- to early ninth-century boom, with a peak around the turn of the ninth century, does perfectly match the period of observable Carolingian diplomacy with both the ʿAbbāsids (767–831) and interest in North Africa (c. 790–813).[276]

270. Morris, "Mediterraneanization"; Valérian, "The Medieval Mediterranean."

271. Pirenne, *Mahomet et Charlemagne*. The historiography on the Pirenne Thesis and Mediterranean commerce in Late Antiquity is formidable; see Dopsch, *Wirtschaftliche und soziale Grundlagen*; Sabbe, "Quelques types de marchands" and "L'importation des tissus orientaux"; Dennett, "Pirenne and Muhammad"; Havighurst, *The Pirenne Thesis*; Hodges and Whitehouse, *Mohammed, Charlemagne and the Origins of Europe*; Rubin, "The Mediterranean and the Dilemma of the Roman Empire"; Pryor, *Commerce, Shipping and Naval Warfare*; Hodges, *Towns and Trade*.

272. Loseby, "Marseille and the Pirenne Thesis I" and "Marseille and the Pirenne Thesis II."

273. Hodges and Whitehouse, *Mohammed, Charlemagne and the Origins of Europe*; Wickham, *Framing the Early Middle Ages*, 716, 758. For an extreme view of disruption, see Pryor, "The Mediterranean Breaks Up."

274. Horden and Purcell, *The Corrupting Sea*, 153–166.

275. McCormick, *Origins of the European Economy*.

276. A similar point is made by Wickham, "The Mediterranean around 800," 164.

Envoys seem to have used pre-existing shipping networks. Of these, the most important were probably the pilgrimage routes to the Holy Land.[277] Charlemagne's first set of ambassadors to Hārūn al-Rashīd travelled to Jerusalem in the company of relic collectors from Treviso.[278] These ships initially hugged the northern shores of the Mediterranean but increasingly took the southern route, following the North African coast.[279] A growing emphasis on Egypt reflected swelling commercial links.[280] Italian cities such as Venice cultivated an eastern luxury trade.[281] Idrīsid envoys to the governor of Sicily were carried in Venetian vessels from North Africa in 813.[282] Different types of people were to be found on the same ships, with pilgrims to Jerusalem such as Bernard the Monk travelling on vessels containing Christian captives destined for the slave markets.[283]

Although the ambassadors sent by al-Manṣūr arrived in Marseilles, subsequent ʿAbbāsid missions seem to have passed through Italy.[284] Charlemagne's first embassy left from Venice and landed in Porto Venere in Liguria on their return.[285] Hārūn al-Rashīd's second group of envoys arrived in Venice in 806 and departed from Italy in 807, probably from Venice again.[286] While this shift from Marseilles to Italy naturally reflects Charlemagne's conquest of the Lombard kingdom in 774 and the subsequent strengthening of Frankish interests in Italy, it may also be a sign of changes in maritime traffic patterns.

A wide variety of factors had an impact on the duration of a voyage.[287] In the 860s, it took Bernard thirty days to sail from Taranto to Alexandria.[288] Evidence from Antiquity and the high middle ages, where itineraries that are more detailed are available, present relatively consistent journey times.[289] Sulpicius Severus (d. c. 425) records a trip from Alexandria to Marseilles that took thirty days.[290] A document from the Cairo Geniza refers to a journey taking important news from Marseilles to Alexandria in

277. McCormick, "Les Pèlerins Occidentaux."
278. *Ex miraculi S. Genesii*, 169–172.
279. McCormick, *Origins of the European Economy*, 171–173.
280. Lewis, "Mediterranean Maritime Commerce," 498–499.
281. Wickham, "The Mediterranean around 800."
282. Leo III, *Epistolae* no. 6, 98.
283. McCormick, *Origins of the European Economy*, 274; Bernard, *Itinerarium*, 310.
284. "The Continuations of the Chronicle of Fredegar," 320.
285. *Ex miraculi S. Genesii*, 169–172; ARF a.801 116.
286. ARF a.806–807 122–124.
287. Casson, *Ships and Seamanship*, 281.
288. Bernard, *Itinerarium*, 311.
289. Udovitch, "Time, the Sea and Society," 505.
290. Severus Sulpicius, *Dialogue 1*, 185.

twenty-five days.[291] These are record-breaking examples that occasioned comment, suggesting that travellers in less haste would take more time. The more routine records of the Geniza indicate that in the eleventh and twelfth centuries it took three to four weeks to get from Alexandria to Tunisia.[292] The prevailing winds of the Mediterranean make going east slightly quicker than travelling west.[293] Merchant ships might have several stops to make on the way, and the experience of some pilgrims suggests that changing vessels may have been necessary, adding time to the journey.[294] That said, the priest Zacharias managed to travel to and from Jerusalem over the course of 800, arriving in Rome on 23 December.[295]

Diplomats generally followed the seasons, crossing the Mediterranean in the relatively calm months between mid-March and early November.[296] Al-Manṣūr's envoys arrived in Marseilles at the start of winter.[297] The envoys from Ibrāhīm b. al-Aghlab arrived in Pisa in late May or early June 801, having crossed the Tyrrhenian.[298] Charlemagne ensured the shipping of Abū al-ʿAbbās took place before October. He was concerned to make sure that the ʿAbbāsid legates who reached him in 806 returned to Italy in time for the 807 sailing season.[299] Even avoiding the dangerous winter months did not guarantee the safety of the journey, as the Idrīsid ambassadors of 813 could testify. The Venetian vessel they travelled in was attacked by Andalusi pirates.[300]

Sickness was a very real problem. The vulnerability of people undertaking journeys to disease was well-known in the caliphate and often attributed to the change in climate or food. Travellers were counselled to carry clay from their homeland to mix with water from foreign lands, thereby mitigating the potentially upsetting impact of introducing unfamiliar fluids into their bodies.[301] Numerous treatises were available offering health advice for those on the road. Among the most celebrated was that of the Galenist Christian Qusṭā b. Lūqā (c. 820–c. 912), whose essay for

291. Udovitch, "Time, the Sea and Society," 510. For an introduction to the Cairo Geniza, see Goitein, *A Mediterranean Society*, 1:1–28. See also Goldberg, *Trade and Institutions*.

292. Udovitch, "Time, the Sea and Society," 513.

293. Ibid., 514.

294. On the practice of cabotage, see Horden and Purcell, *The Corrupting Sea*, 140–143.

295. ARF a.800 108, 110.

296. Braudel, *The Mediterranean*, 232–246.

297. McCormick, "Pippin III, the Embassy of Caliph al Mansur," 235.

298. ARF a.801 114, 116.

299. ARF a.806 123.

300. Leo III, *Epistolae* no. 6, 98.

301. Touati, *Islam and Travel*, 245.

pilgrims travelling to Mecca provided comprehensive guidance on a wide range of issues including diet, fatigue, earache, sex, dust, water quality, and snakebite.[302] Such perils may help explain the high mortality rate suffered by Carolingian diplomats in the caliphate. Frankish Europe was no safer from disease and had its own equivalent travel literature which drew heavily upon the classical past. These included the handbook compiled by Galen for his friend Glaucon before the latter set off on a journey, and *Pliny's Medicine*, a text revised in Late Antiquity which offered guidance for the traveller who wanted to avoid fraudulent physicians on the road.[303] Certain regions had particularly insalubrious reputations. Egypt was known to be especially unhealthy, while Alcuin warned travellers to be wary of sickness in Italy.[304]

A key institution for transport within the caliphate was the postal network or *barīd*. Instituted by Muʿāwiya I, the *barīd* was expanded under the ʿAbbāsids.[305] According to Ibn Khurradādhbih, postmaster for the province of Jibal from 846/847 to 873/874, the *barīd* had 930 stations funded by the caliph.[306] Al-Jāḥiẓ reports that Hārūn al-Rashīd's envoy to Emperor Constantine VI (r. 780–797) boasted that the caliph owned "40,000 mules for the conveyance of letters and news from the centre of his kingdom to the outlying provinces."[307] As al-Jāḥiẓ noted, this was something of an exaggeration, but the ninth-century *barīd* appears to have been a formidable instrument for gathering and transmitting information.[308] Fresh horses were kept at stations to allow couriers to move quickly. Other officials, including governors travelling to their posts, also made use of this infrastructure.[309]

Frankish envoys could probably have expected an escort in the caliphate. The eleventh-century Seljuq vizier, Niẓām al-Mulk, advised that

> officers at the frontiers must be told that whenever anyone approaches their stations they should at once despatch a rider [to the capital] and report who it is that is coming, how many men there are with him,

302. Ibn Lūqā, *Qusṭā Ibn Lūqā's Medical Regime*, translated by Bos.

303. Leja, *Embodying the Soul*, 216; Segoloni, "Il prologus"; Doody, "Authority and Authorship."

304. Ibn Riḍwān, *Medieval Islamic Medicine*, vii; Alcuin, *Epistolae* no. 224, 367–368; no. 281, 439–440.

305. Silverstein, *Postal Systems*, 54, 61. See also Touati, *Islam and Travel.*

306. Ibn Khurradādhbih, "Le Livre des Routes," 512.

307. Silverstein, *Postal Systems*, 77.

308. Ibid., 53.

309. Ibid., 67.

> mounted and unmounted, how much baggage and equipment he has, and what is his business. A trustworthy person must be appointed to accompany them and conduct them to the nearest big city; there he will hand them over to another agent who will likewise go with them to the next city or district, and so on until they reach the court.[310]

Jerusalem was a natural starting point for Europeans travelling further east. Bernard the Monk refers to "*Amormominis* who rules over all the Saracens, living in *Bagada* [Baghdad] and *Axinarri* [Samarra], which are beyond Jerusalem."[311] Frankish diplomats arriving in Palestine would probably have taken the road from Jerusalem to Damascus.[312] The road was well maintained as a major artery for pilgrims on the *ḥajj* who gathered at Damascus.[313] From there they could travel east to Baghdad or north to Raqqa. Ibn Khurradādhbih indicates that a traveller journeying from Ramla in Palestine to Raqqa by going north via Baalbek and Homs and turning east at Aleppo would pass through seventy-five stages, with each stage corresponding to a day's journey, suggesting a trip of two to three months.[314] He also describes an alternative route leading northwest from Homs across the Syrian Desert, passing through the pilgrimage centre at Resafa.[315] A messenger changing on fresh horses at *barīd* stations could cover ground more quickly. Record-breaking efforts could move a postbag 300–360 kilometres a day.[316] A more regular rate of transportation is demonstrated by letters sent by merchants in Damascus, which reached Baghdad after three weeks.[317]

Most envoys from the caliphate arrived in Italy. Travel between Italy and Francia was routine. The normal time for a journey between Rome and the Carolingian heartlands seems to have been six to eight weeks.[318] The priest Liutolf complained when bad weather meant his trip from Mainz to Rome took ten weeks, and in 873 Pope John VIII thought two months entirely adequate time for the Archbishop of Cologne to travel from his see to meet him.[319] The volume of pilgrims travelling to Rome

310. Niẓām al-Mulk, *Siyāsatnāmeh*, XXI.1, 93–94.

311. Bernard, *Itinerarium*, "Amormominis qui imperat omnibus Sarracenis, habitans in Bagada et Axinarri, qui sunt ultra Ierusalem," 310.

312. Elad, "The Southern Golan in the Early Muslim Period," 78.

313. Lewis and Wensinck, "Ḥad̲j̲d̲j̲."

314. Ibn Khurradādhbih, "Le Livre des Routes," 486.

315. Ibid. On Resafa, see Fowden, *The Barbarian Plain*.

316. Silverstein, *Postal Systems*, 191.

317. Ibid., 119.

318. McCormick, *Origins of the European Economy*, 479.

319. Liutolf, *Vita et translatio S. Severi*, 290; John VIII, *Epistolae* no. 30, 290.

encouraged the establishment of charitable organisations, such as hospitals and *xenodochia*, for travellers.[320] The most imposing obstacle on this route was the Alps, but large numbers of pilgrims and merchants made the crossing regularly. In addition to the tollbooth at Chur, other such tolls were located in the Val de Susa for the Mont Cénis pass and in the Val d'Aosta for the Great Saint-Bernard pass.[321] These are the two most likely routes for ambassadors travelling to the Carolingians, with the Gotthard and Simplon passes being largely inaccessible before the thirteenth century.[322] The Frankish armies that invaded Italy in 755, 756, and 773 used the Mont Cénis pass.[323] John VIII travelled through it to crown Louis the Stammerer in 878. The Great Saint-Bernard pass is slightly more likely for travel north, allowing easier access to the Rhône and Rhine, and was probably the pass used by diplomats journeying to the Carolingian centre.[324] The hoard of coins buried in 825–840 at Hermenches on the road leading north from the Great Saint-Bernard pass attests to the movement of people and money.[325] The account of Einhard's *Translatio et Miracula Marcellini et Petri* suggests that the Great Saint-Bernard pass could be crossed fairly quickly.[326] The onset of snow did not necessarily end the travelling season, with urgent messages making it across the Alps in the middle of winter.[327] Nevertheless, most travellers preferred to wait until spring, a decision made even more sensible when faced with the necessity of imitating Hannibal by getting an elephant over the Alps. The Carthaginian general's choice to cross in late September/early October was probably about as late in the year as was feasible.[328]

## *Reception*

Both the Carolingians and the rulers of the Islamic world put great store by palaces to impress foreign envoys, as demonstrated by the appearance of similar stories in each tradition. In his biography of Charlemagne, Notker tells the tale of Byzantine envoys to Aachen who were led through a series of increasingly impressively rooms, each inhabited by progressively

320. Dey, "*Diaconiae, Xenodochia, Hospitalia* and Monasteries."
321. McCormick, *Origins of the European Economy*, 642.
322. Bergier, "Le trafic à travers les Alpes," 28.
323. Duparc, "Les Cluses et la Frontière des Alpes," 10.
324. Bergier, "Le trafic à travers les Alpes," 27.
325. McCormick, *Origins of the European Economy*, 685.
326. Einhard, *Translatio et miracula*, 243.
327. McCormick, *Origins of the European Economy*, 447.
328. Prevas, *Hannibal Crosses the Alps*, 174n37.

grander officials mistaken by the legates for Charlemagne, in order to overwhelm the visitors.[329] This sort of treatment seems to have been an occupational hazard for Byzantine ambassadors, for the delegation who arrived in Baghdad in 917 allegedly had a similar experience at the palace of Caliph al-Muqtadir.[330] Putting aside the possibility that envoys from Constantinople were simply easily impressed, this is a literary trope recognizable from other medieval descriptions of diplomacy. Córdoba could play the same game, according to Abū Bakr Muḥyī ad-Dīn b. ʿArābī, who says that a Frankish embassy to ʿAbd al-Raḥmān III had to run an identical gauntlet before being received by the plain-clad caliph in a simple chamber.[331] These stories illustrate to an extreme the intended effect of a grand palace, to overawe visitors, thereby helping with negotiation and ensuring that foreign monarchs heard of the host's power and magnificence.

Our knowledge of Baghdad in the age of al-Manṣūr is almost entirely dependent on literary sources. The caliph's brick Round City has long since been swallowed by subsequent development.[332] Fortunately, Baghdad's continued status as an intellectual hub ensured that it possessed a large number of scholars interested in writing about the history and geography of their city.[333] These geographies paid particular attention to the reign of al-Manṣūr and the founding of Baghdad. There is a good chance that Pippin III's envoys may have arrived while Baghdad was still a building site. The location was selected by the caliph in 762 and initial construction completed in 766/767, with al-Manṣūr having already moved in in 763/764.[334] While the exact significance of the city's shape is debated, it would have been an impressive demonstration of al-Manṣūr's power.[335] The envoys would have had to pass through the great iron gates brought from Wāsiṭ and a network of arcades and walls.[336]

Al-Khaṭīb (d. 1071), in his *History of Baghdad*, provides the most detailed description of al-Manṣūr's palace, known as al-Qaṣr Bāb al-Dhahab, the Palace of the Golden Gate, or al-Qubbat al-Khaḍrāʿ, the Green Dome.[337] This latter epithet was a reference to the green dome on top of the palace,

329. Notker, *Gesta Karoli Magni*, II.6, 56–57.
330. Hilāl al-Ṣābiʿ, *Rusūm Dār al-Khilāfah*, 16.
331. Sénac, "Note sur les Relations Diplomatiques," 92.
332. Northedge, "Remarks on Samarra," 120.
333. Creswell, *Early Muslim Architecture*, 5.
334. Ibid., 6–7.
335. Al-Azmeh, *Muslim Kingship*, 70.
336. Creswell, *Early Muslim Architecture*, 14.
337. Scheiner and Janos, "Baghdād," 3.

on which rested "the figure of a horseman holding a lance in his hand."[338] Two floors beneath the dome was the audience hall (*īwān*), which was "thirty by twenty cubits" in size.[339] It was in this hall that envoys would have been received. Frankish diplomats may also have encountered al-Manṣūr's mosque. Al-Khaṭīb notes that "the dimensions of al-Manṣūr's palace were 400 cubits by 400 cubits and those of the first mosque 200 cubits by 200 cubits."[340] This mosque was placed next to the palace and finished in 766.[341] The new, grand centre that greeted the Franks made clear al-Manṣūr's immense resources and ambition.

Less literary information survives for Hārūn al-Rashīd's capital at Raqqa. Archaeological investigations over the past century help compensate for some of these deficiencies, although much of the old city has been lost following Raqqa's rapid expansion in the 1980s.[342] Nor has Raqqa's role as the capital of ISIL in 2014–2017 helped matters. Al-Manṣūr founded a new city to the west of Raqqa named al-Rāfiqa "the Companion" in 772. This complex, surrounded by a large set of double walls in a horseshoe shape with a diameter of 1,300 metres, contained the new Great Mosque.[343] The remains of the Great Mosque suggest an enormous rectangular structure 92.9 by 108.10 metres.[344] Otherwise al-Rāfiqa seems to have been lightly occupied, dominated by official buildings and parks, with the majority of the population remaining in Raqqa.[345]

By the time Frankish envoys arrived, the site would have been impressive. There are signs of rapid expansion following Hārūn making the double city his capital in 796, with a population smaller than that of Baghdad but larger than Damascus and dwarfing the cities of the Carolingian empire. Fifteen enormous palace structures have been discovered in the ten-square-kilometre area north of al-Rāfiqa, dateable to Hārūn's reign, and it seems likely that the Franks were received in one of these buildings, built of mud brick and covered with white plaster, with recognizable audience chambers decorated in stucco with vine and leaf

338. Lassner, *The Topography of Baghdad*, 53.

339. Ibid., 52.

340. Ibid., 95.

341. Creswell, *Early Muslim Architecture*, 31.

342. Meinecke, "Raqqa on the Euphrates," 26.

343. On the walls, see al-Kalaf, "Die ʿabbāsidische Stadtmauer"; Meinecke, "Raqqa on the Euphrates," 20.

344. Creswell, *Early Muslim Architecture*, 45.

345. Challis et al., "Corona Remotely-Sensed Imagery"; Henderson et al., "Experiment and Innovation," 133.

imagery.[346] Whether approached by boat on the Euphrates or by the Damascus Road, Raqqa would have been recognizable from some distance because of the major glassworks located between the old city and al-Rāfiqa.[347] The amount of smoke produced by this district earned it the epithet Raqqa al-Muḥtariqa or "Burning Raqqa."

Little is known about official ʿAbbāsid audiences.[348] The caliphs often wore special clothes, with red shoes being reserved for their use.[349] The early ʿAbbāsids occasionally bore the cloak, staff, and ring of Muḥammad, investing themselves with the Prophet's authority.[350] Diplomats were to speak only when commanded by the caliph, an order relayed by the chamberlain or a page.[351] In this event, all speech was to be in low voices, with the envoys looking only at the caliph's face. For a more intimate conversation, diplomats could be beckoned to approach the caliph. When dismissed, al-Jāḥiẓ advised visitors to back away facing the caliph.[352] A key figure in these arrangements was the *ḥājib* or chamberlain, who managed access to the caliph.[353] As well as acting as master of ceremonies for the reception of diplomats, the *ḥājib*, like the vizier, seems to have met visiting envoys before the caliph did.[354]

Detailed accounts of the reception of foreign envoys in Umayyad Spain exist for the tenth century.[355] Ibn Ḥayyān and Ibn ʿIdhārī preserve several from the reigns of ʿAbd al-Raḥmān III and al-Ḥakam II. They describe ambassadors prostrating and kissing the floor before being allowed to enter the presence of the caliph.[356] In 945, Byzantine envoys were received by ʿAbd al-Raḥmān III, who had the future al-Ḥakam II sat next to him. Other sons and chamberlains were sat in the room while visitors from across the Umayyad state gathered in the room to witness what took place.

346. Heusch and Meinecke, "Grabungen im ʿabbāsidischen Palastreal"; Siegel, "Frühabbasidische Residenzbauten."

347. Meinecke, "Raqqa on the Euphrates," 17–18. On the glassworks, see Henderson, "Archaeological and Scientific Evidence"; Heidemann, "The History of the Industrial and Commercial Area."

348. What follows is indebted to Al-Azmeh, *Muslim Kingship*, 135–140. On the development of the ʿAbbāsid court, see El Cheikh, "The Institutionalisation."

349. Hilāl al-Ṣābiʾ, *Rusūm Dār al-Khilāfah*, 15–16; *Book of Gifts and Rarities*, 73.

350. Meri, *The Cult of Saints*, 108, and "Relics of Piety and Power," 112–115.

351. Al-Jāḥiẓ, *Le Livre de la Couronne*, 36.

352. Ibid.

353. This paragraph follows El Cheikh, "The Chamberlain."

354. Hilāl al-Ṣābiʾ, *Rusūm Dār al-Khilāfah*, 16.

355. Cardoso, "The Scenography of Power."

356. Ibn Ḥayyān, *Anales Palatinos*, 45, 70, 192.

The problem with this material for understanding Carolingian-Umayyad diplomacy is that the sources portray ceremonies and receptions that postdate ʿAbd al-Raḥmān III's claiming of the caliphate in 926.[357] To serve their new dignity better, he and his son radically changed the existing court ceremonial, making it grander.[358] This reflects a growing competition with the ʿAbbāsids in Baghdad and the Fāṭimids in al-Mahdīya.[359] New settings for diplomatic activity emerged, with the aristocratic suburban villas (*munya*) of Córdoba being increasingly used to host envoys.[360] The most spectacular manifestation of this tendency was Madīnat al-Zahrāʾ, the famous palace-city constructed by ʿAbd al-Raḥmān that served as a combined capital with Córdoba.[361]

The evidence for the eighth and ninth centuries is comparatively scant. What does survive suggests a clearer emphasis on Córdoba as the locus of diplomatic activity. Escorts seem to have been provided to ambassadors travelling through al-Andalus, with an eye to ensuring a grand entrance and procession down the main road of Córdoba.[362] The emiral complex, on the main road in the heart of the city, centred on the emir's palace (*qaṣr* later Alcazar), built on the site of the former Visigothic governor's palace, would have served as a spectacular stage for receiving envoys.[363] Its impact would have been even greater due to its close proximity to the Great Mosque on the other side of the road, which was expanded throughout the ninth century.[364]

This grouping of mosque with the seat of government conforms to a wider Umayyad pattern, following the model of capitals in Syria and Iraq, while also confirming the layout of the Visigothic city.[365] The *qaṣr* itself is described as a series of courtyards with fountains, culminating in the *majlis* or main hall, where the emir would have received visitors.[366] It was

357. Fierro, "Sobre la adopción del título califal."

358. Barceló, "El califa patente"; Fierro, "On Political Legitimacy," 139; Safran, "Ceremony and Submission" and *The Second Umayyad Caliphate*, 51–97.

359. Gabrieli, "Omayyades d'Espagne et Abbasides"; Fairchild Ruggles, "The Mirador"; Bennison, "The Necklace of al-Shifā."

360. Anderson, *The Islamic Villa*, 137–139.

361. Fairchild Ruggles, "Historiography" and *Gardens, Landscape, and Vision*; Mazzoli-Guintard, "Remarques sur le fonctionnement d'une capitale"; Vallejo Triano, "Madīnat az-Zahrāʾ."

362. Safran, *The Second Umayyad Caliphate*, 79.

363. Hillenbrand, "'The Ornament of the World,'" 113–114.

364. Khoury, "The Meaning of the Great Mosque," 83; Safran, *The Second Umayyad Caliphate*, 61.

365. Bacharach, "Administrative Complexes"; Bennison, "Power and the City," 67.

366. Brookshaw, "Palaces, Pavilions and Pleasure-Gardens"; Bennison, "Power and the City," 69.

expanded by both ʿAbd al-Raḥmān II and Muḥammad I.[367] The court of ʿAbd al-Raḥmān I seems to have been small and relatively informal. ʿAbd al-Raḥmān II is said to have increased the ceremony of court life, bringing with it a commensurate rise in scale and sophistication.[368]

The journey of a Frankish diplomat to the Umayyads was simplified by the virtue of having a clear destination. The emirs were firmly based in Córdoba and could be expected to be found there any time they were not on campaign. This had benefits for the Umayyads as well as for the envoys, providing them with permanent facilities with which to host the visiting delegates and a stable stage in order to both overawe foreign dignitaries and display them for maximum effect to their own court.[369] The less fixed courts of the Carolingians posed greater challenges, but here too diplomats were successfully received on a regular basis.[370] They would have been assisted by the tendency of the court to draw other petitioners, particularly those crowds seeking legal redress who were described thronging centres like Aachen.[371] Hincmar advised kings to leave a senior official permanently at the palace to take care of embassies who arrived when they were absent.[372]

The Carolingians favoured a small number of palace sites.[373] These were generally not in cities, with most of them clustered in the Carolingian heartlands between the Seine and the Rhine.[374] Different Carolingians focused on different places depending on changing political realities and personal preferences, and generalizing is difficult.[375] The best-studied Carolingian palaces are Aachen, itself an unusual type of residence given the special importance Charlemagne assigned it from 793, Paderborn, and Ingelheim, also noted by contemporary sources as being particularly grand structures.[376]

367. Creswell, *Early Muslim Architecture*, 140.

368. Safran, *The Second Umayyad Caliphate*, 71.

369. Airlie, "The Palace Complex," 275–280.

370. Gravel, *Distances, rencontres, communications*, 52.

371. Airlie, "The Palace of Memory," 3.

372. Hincmar of Rheims, *De ordine palatii*, c.25 78.

373. Falkenstein, "Charlemagne et Aix-la-Chapelle," 231; McKitterick, *Charlemagne*, 157–177; McKitterick, "A King on the Move."

374. Ewig, "Résidence et capitale," 54; Renoux, "Karolingische Pfalzen," 131; McKitterick, *Charlemagne*, 137–213; Gravel, *Distances, rencontres, communications*, 49.

375. Bullough, "*Aula Renovata*," 269; Zotz, "Pfalzen der Karolingerzeit"; McKitterick, *Charlemagne*, 165.

376. Lobbedey, "Carolingian Royal Palaces," 129. Aachen has a long historiography: Binding, "Die Aachener Pfalz"; Untermann, "'*opere mirabili constructa*'"; Nelson, "Aachen as a Place of Power"; Sot, "Le palais d'Aix"; Rollason, "Charlemagne's Palace." On Ingelheim, see Sage, "Die Ausgrabungen in der Pfalz"; Grewe, "Die Königspfalz zu Ingelheim."

These palaces were clearly meant to be impressive.[377] The poetry of the Carolingian Renaissance is filled with praise for the royal residences.[378] Carolingian rulers paid attention to building and improving existing palaces, not just for their own comfort but to inspire awe in those who came to visit them. Built out of mortared stone, the complexes at Aachen compare not unfavourably in size to their late Roman or later medieval equivalents.[379] Travellers could have observed echoes of Roman and Byzantine influence in the architecture, or in the decorations, including the statue of Theoderic acquired by Charlemagne, which seems to have caught the attention of visitors from Scandinavia.[380] Notker writes of ʿAbbāsid diplomats being invited up to the *solarium* of the chapel at Aachen so they could view Charlemagne's assembled clergy and army.[381] A centre like Aachen provided an opportunity for a ruler to communicate the power of his realm in microcosm to foreign visitors. Charles the Bald built an equivalent residence at Compiègne.[382]

How enthralled the ambassadors would have been is hard to judge. Anyone coming from the palaces of Baghdad might have been a little underwhelmed by Aachen. Envoys from Córdoba could have been more impressed, particularly in the ninth century, before the construction of the great tenth-century palaces of al-Andalus. Used to permanent capitals situated in important cities, they would have been startled by how rural these centres were. Aachen was not simply the palace complex, but Córdoba or Baghdad would still have dwarfed it.[383]

The grand *aula regia* could act as a venue for receiving diplomats. In addition to archaeological investigation, clues as to the interior of these great halls are provided by contemporary descriptions, such as that of Ermold about the wall paintings at Ingelheim.[384] When the legates had

377. Nelson, "Was Charlemagne's Court a Courtly Society?" 40.

378. Riché, "Les représentations du Palais," 163.

379. Samson, "Carolingian Palaces," 110.

380. Untermann, "'*opere mirabili constructa*,'" 158. Berschin questions how aware most of the court were of the specific meaning of these allusions, in "Die Ost-West-Gesandtschaften." On the possible Scandinavian reception of the statue, see Andrén, Jennbert, and Raudvere, "Old Norse Religion," 11.

381. Notker, *Gesta Karoli Magni*, II.8, 59. On the *solarium*, see De Jong, "Charlemagne's Balcony," 281.

382. Lohrmann, "Trois Palais Royaux," 124–129; Barbier, "Le système palatial franc," 295; Airlie, "The Palace of Memory," 16.

383. McKitterick, *Charlemagne*, 167–168; Feldbauer and Steffelbauer, "Die 'islamische' Stadt," 183.

384. Ermold the Black, *In honorem Hludovici*, Bk. 4, 162–164. On Carolingian era wall painting, see Preißler, "Fragmente einer verlorenen Kunst."

been and gone, something of the exotic glamour they had brought remained in the gifts displayed throughout the complex.[385] Animal parks where celebrities such as Abū al-ʿAbbās could be displayed are a case in point.[386]

In his biography of Louis the Pious, Thegan provides a quick hint of the nature of the receiving of important diplomats:

> When they arrived, they found the lord Louis sitting on his father's throne, just as the Lord had ordained. He received them graciously, accepted their gifts with grace, and held intimate discussions with them from time to time while they were with him.[387]

The receiving of diplomats often took place in conjunction with the great political assemblies that brought the Frankish elite together.[388] Correctly managed, these assemblies allowed kings to unify the most powerful members of the empire under their leadership, displaying themselves as rulers while also building a sense of community and shared experience.[389] They provided an opportunity to show off foreign envoys and their gifts before an audience much larger than the usual members of the court.[390] Just as the gathered luminaries could watch justice being dispensed and the issuing of capitularies and charters, so they could also witness the king receiving the compliments of distant rulers. The *De ordine palatii* also suggests that at smaller assemblies, genuine discussion about foreign policy was expected, making it particularly useful to have ambassadors at hand.[391]

Charlemagne probably intended such an effect when Sulaymān al-ʿArābī and his retinue came to Paderborn in 777.[392] Barring the rebellious Widukind and his supporters, the newly conquered Saxons were gathered there to be baptized and pledge fealty to Charlemagne. The presence of Saracens from al-Andalus, come to ask the aid of the Frankish king, would have added to the demonstration of Carolingian power. Louis the Pious

385. Airlie, "The Palace of Memory," 14.

386. Hauck, "Tiergärten im Pfalzbereich"; Fenske, "Jagd und Jäger im früheren Mittelalter," 29–93.

387. Thegan, *Gesta Hludowici imperatoris*, c.9 "Illi venientes, in solio patris collocatum domnum Hludouuicum invenerunt, quia sic Dominus ordinavit. Ille eos benigne suscipiens et dona eorum cum gratiarum actione suscepit et colloquium familiare interim, quousque cum eo erant, habebat," 190, translated by Noble, *Charlemagne and Louis the Pious*, 199.

388. Airlie, "Talking Heads," 34.

389. Nelson, "The Lord's Anointed and the People's Choice," 166–167.

390. Reuter, "Assembly Politics," 440; Steiger, *Die Ordnung der Welt*, 34–35.

391. Hincmar of Rheims, *De ordine palatii*, c.30 84.

392. ARF a.777 48. On the palace at Paderborn, see Hauck, "Karl als neuer Konstantin 777"; Gai, "Die Pfalzen in Paderborn."

redirected Umayyad ambassadors who arrived in Compiègne in 816 to Aachen so they could be dealt with at the same time as embassies from the Byzantines and Danes.[393] When he was king of Aquitaine, Muslim lords attended Louis's assemblies at Toulouse from the frontier.[394]

Who was competent to perform the royal role of receiving foreign envoys could be a contested matter. In his planned division of his empire in 817, Louis the Pious emphasised the junior status of his younger sons to Lothar:

> On legates, if they have been sent by foreign nations to make peace or declare war, or hand over cities or fortresses, or on any other important business, they shall on no account answer them or send them back without their eldest brother's knowledge. But if the *missi* are sent to him from any country and reach one of them first, he shall send them honourably with his own loyal *missi* to his brother's presence.[395]

A sign of Lothar's claims to authority over his father, Louis the Pious, in 833 came with the arrival of an embassy from the Byzantine emperor Theophilos (r. 829–842). The Astronomer condemned Lothar for having "received the legation even though it had been sent to his father."[396]

Carolingian diplomacy with the Islamic world was not entirely conducted by emperors and emirs. As king of Aquitaine, Louis the Pious seems to have managed relations with Muslim frontier warlords, receiving Abū Tawr and Bahlūl b. Marzūq at Toulouse.[397] Even here Charlemagne was kept informed. It is noticeable that lords who brought proposals for Frankish intervention or who arrived during the war with al-Ḥakam, such as Saʿdūn al-Ruʿaynī and Ḥassān of Huesca, were sent to Aachen.[398] The *Annales regni Francorum* record that the envoys received by Louis the Pious in 816 were sent "from Zaragoza," by the son of the then Emir al-Ḥakam, the future ʿAbd al-Raḥmān II.[399] ʿAbd al-Raḥmān was the

393. ARF a.816 144–145.

394. Astronomer, *Vita Hludowici*, c.5 298.

395. Louis the Pious, *Ordinatio imperii*, no. 136, "De legatis vero, si ab exteris nationibus vel propter pacem faciendam vel bellum suscipiendum vel civitates aut castella tradenda vel propter alias quaslibet maiores causas directi fuerint, nullatenus sine senioris fratris conscientia ei respondeant vel eos remittant. Si autem ad illum de quacumque parte missi directi fuerint, ad quemlibetillorum primo pervenerint, honorifice eos cum fidelibus missis usque ad eius praesentiam faciat pervenire," 272.

396. Astronomer, *Vita Hludowici*, c.49 "Quam ille, licet ad patrem missam, ad se tamen venientem suscepit," 480.

397. Ibid., c.5 298.

398. ARF a.797 100; ARF a.799 108–109.

399. ARF a.817 "de Caesaraugusta," 145.

governor of the Upper March at the time and may have been given responsibility for dealing with the Franks. If so, it appears to have been an unusual situation and in all other cases Carolingian diplomats seem to have negotiated with the reigning emir.

The *De ordine palatii* stresses the importance of managing the palace so that "legations of any sort which came to see the king or to submit to him might be appropriately received."[400] It seems that Andalusi diplomats did not generally stay long at Carolingian courts. Charles the Bald's decision to keep the embassy of Muḥammad I in 863 at Senlis until the next year was also unusual enough to warrant Hincmar's comment.[401] This implies that a short visit was normal. The Frankish ruler probably arranged accommodation. A capitulary of Louis II dating to 850 orders the restoration of a "public house" in Rome for "our needs and the embassies of foreign peoples."[402] The *De ordine palatii* includes reference to a palace *mansionarius*.[403]

Caution in restricting the movements of envoys made sense given the other major role played by diplomats, that of spy.[404] Muḥammad's successor, Abū Bakr (r. 632–634), admonished Yazīd b. Abī Sufyān, "If you receive envoys of your enemies, be hospitable to them, and make short their stay, so that they leave you with the least information regarding your dispositions."[405] He continued, "Let not the people about you converse with [enemy envoys], so that you alone conduct the discourse."[406] In 808 Pope Leo III complained to Charlemagne about his envoy, Bishop Jesse of Amiens, who had been keeping "secret councils."[407] Jesse was recalled but remained in favour, suggesting that Charlemagne was not unhappy about his bishop's inquisitiveness. Skullduggery in foreign courts was a popular pastime. After Gausfrid was caught having "forged a document" in 775, Hadrian I apologized to an angry Charlemagne for sending the Pisan to him.[408] The potential dangers are illustrated by an incident of

400. Hincmar of Rheims, *De ordine palatii*, c.25 "Et ut qualis cunque legatio, sive speculandi sive etiam subdendi gratia veniret, qualiter omnes quidem honeste suscipi potuissent," 78.

401. AB a.863 104.

402. Louis II, *Capitulare Papiense*, no. 213, "publicae domus . . . nostris usibus et externarum gentium legationibus," 87.

403. Hincmar of Rheims, *De ordine palatii*, c.16 76.

404. Drocourt, "Passing on Political Information."

405. Istanbuli, *Diplomacy and Diplomatic Practice*, 59.

406. Ibid.

407. Leo III, *Epistolae* no. 2, "secretum consilium," 91.

408. Hadrian I, *Epistolae* no. 51, 572.

900, when the Hungarians "deceitfully sent ambassadors to the Bavarians offering peace so they could view the land."[409] Niẓām al-Mulk took the information-gathering role of envoys as a simple part of diplomacy.[410] Despite these suspicions, it was unusual for diplomats to be kept confined at all times. There is evidence for envoys participating in the traditional activities of the elite. Notker's account of ʿAbbāsid ambassadors being invited on hunting trips seems plausible.[411] The Astronomer reports that Louis the Pious feasted the embassies that arrived in 814.[412]

The ceremonies with which ambassadors may have been greeted are difficult to reconstruct.[413] Their regularity means that details are often only available when something went wrong.[414] These events were subject to change in response to the exact circumstances, and their meaning could be contested.[415] Such evidence as there is suggests efforts at grand spectacle. Clothes would be adjusted to help create an aura of grandeur. In his biography, Einhard stresses Charlemagne's love of simplicity, noting his preference for simple garments, but the biographer does observe that "he sometimes used a jewelled sword, but only on particular feast days or when the envoys of foreign peoples came," suggesting a special costume.[416]

That the diplomats were expected to dress up is indicated by Notker's criticism of the Byzantine emperor for forcing Bishop Haito of Basel and Count Hugh of Tours to attend his court "in shameful clothes."[417] Charlemagne took revenge by tricking the next Byzantine envoys into appearing before him in rags.[418] Although Notker was never witness to diplomats being received, he had been present for the visit of Charles the Fat to the

409. AF, a.900 "Missos illorum sub dolo ad Baworios pacem obtando regionem illam ad explorandum transmiserunt," 134.

410. Niẓām al-Mulk, *Siyāsatnāmeh*, XXI.2, 94.

411. Notker, *Gesta Karoli Magni*, II.8, 60; Goldberg, "Louis the Pious and the Hunt," 641, and *In the Manner of the Franks*, 106, 111; see also his very intriguing piece, "Hunting for the Asiatic Onager."

412. Astronomer, *Vita Hludowici*, c.23 352.

413. McCormick, "Analyzing Imperial Ceremonies"; Pohl, "Ritualised Encounters."

414. Brühl, "Frankischer Königsbrauch," 274. For an example, see Dutton, *The Politics of Dreaming*, 216–219; MacLean, "Ritual, Misunderstanding and the Contest for Meaning."

415. For debate on this subject, see Buc, *The Dangers of Ritual*; Koziol, "The Dangers of Polemic"; Buc, "The Monster and the Critics."

416. Einhard, *Vita Karoli Magni*, c.23 "Aliquoties et gemmato ense utebatur, quod tamen nonnisi in praecipuis festivitatibus vel si quando exterarum gentium legati venissent," 28.

417. Notker, *Gesta Karoli Magni*, II.6 "indigne habiti," 55.

418. Ibid.

monastery of St-Gall in 883, giving him an idea of the garb appropriate for interacting with a Carolingian ruler.[419]

A strong performance was also important at these moments, even when not in a palace. The *dux* of the Sorbian March, Thachulf, had taken an arrow to the knee, but when he was visited by envoys from the Bohemians "he spoke with the legates who had been sent to him, sitting on a horse as if in good health, so that they might not discover his weakness."[420] In 870, shortly before he was due to hold talks with Charles the Bald concerning the partition of Lotharingia, Louis the German was injured when a gallery he was in collapsed. Nonetheless, when meeting his brother, "he pretended good health," although Hincmar's comments in the *Annals of St-Bertin* suggest that Charles was not fooled.[421]

A key part of this reception process was the giving of letters by the diplomats from their monarch. Ibn al-Farrāʿ noted that "the letter is a hand and the messenger is a tongue."[422] Hadrian I praises the "gleaming and honey-like letters" he received from Charlemagne.[423] Much of the effect of the letter came from its presentation, being "shown, touched, open, passed from hand to hand, read, listened to, read again, commented or discussed," as Martin Gravel puts it.[424] These letters could be highly formulaic, as indicated by the texts copied by Marculf.[425] The draft letters in Marculf indicate an interest in the health of the monarch, a concern reflected in other sources. Amalarius of Trier records that in his conversation with Leo V (r. 813–820), the Byzantine emperor took pains to inquire with him about the health of Charlemagne and his family.[426]

Relying on the evidence of Marculf alone might suggest that the letters were entirely ceremonial, with the real business conducted verbally. That this was far from the case is indicated by Hadrian I's message to Charlemagne in 775 about a letter he had received from the Frankish king, pronouncing himself "greatly saddened to find the seals on this same letter

419. Ibid., I.34, 47.

420. AF a.849 "cum legatis vero, qui ad eum missi fuerant, quo minus ab eis debilitas eius deprehenderetur, equo sedens simulata sanitate locutus est," 38, translated by Reuter, *Annals of Fulda*, 29.

421. AF a.870 "simulata sanitate," 71; AB a.870 175.

422. Ibn al-Farrāʿ, *Diplomacy in the Early Islamic World*, 63.

423. Hadrian I, *Epistolae* no. 81, "Praefulgidos atque nectareos regalis potentiae vestrae per Aruinum ducem suscepimus apices," 614.

424. Gravel, *Distances, rencontres, communications*, "montrée, touchée, ouverte, passée de main a main, lue, écoutée, relue, commentée ou débattue," 178.

425. Marculf, *Formulæ Marculfinæ* I.9, 48.

426. Amalarius, *Versus Marini*, 427.

tampered with."[427] He accused Archbishop Leo of Ravenna of having read the contents and disseminated the secret information, judging that "there is no doubt that those enemies have already been told everything by the archbishop."[428]

Treaties could be agreed at these meetings, as arranged by Umayyad envoys to Charles the Bald in 863.[429] Witnesses were of crucial importance. When Charles and Louis the German made a pact at Tusey in 864, both parties selected witnesses "so that if by chance the terms of the treaty were infringed by anyone, these might point it out and recall to mind what had been done before, so that peace could more easily be restored."[430] These treaties then needed to be confirmed on the other end, as in 811, when Charlemagne agreed to a peace with a Byzantine envoy before sending Haito and Hugh to ratify that peace in Constantinople.[431]

The safety of envoys was a widely respected convention.[432] Isidore of Seville (d. 636) classed it as part of the *ius gentium*.[433] Similar unwritten rules were followed in the Islamic world.[434] According to *ḥadīth*, Muḥammad had respected the inviolability of envoys. Ibn Hishām in his *Life of the Prophet* records that when the ambassadors sent by a rival prophet, Maslama, in 631/632 vexed Muḥammad, he declared, "By God, were it not that heralds are not to be killed I would behead the pair of you."[435] Niẓām al-Mulk advised:

> Whatever treatment is given to an ambassador whether good or bad, it is as if it were done to the very king who sent him; and kings have always shown the greatest respect to one another and treated envoys well, for by this their own dignity has been enhanced not diminished.[436]

Despite the protection this offered, things could go wrong when foreign envoys met monarchs.[437] Those unlucky enough to have taken part in

427. Hadrian I, *Epistolae* no. 54, "Itaque valde tristes effecti sumus, quoniam sifoniatas bullas eiusdem epistolae repperimus," 576.

428. Ibid., "et dubium non est, cuncta iam praelatis emulis ab eodem archiepiscopo esse adnuntiata," 577.

429. AB a.863 104.

430. AF a.864 "si forte ab aliquot eiusdem pacti iura laederentur, his admonentibus et gesta priora ad memoriam revocantibus facilius in pristinum statum reformari possent," 62–63, translated by Reuter, *Annals of Fulda*, 52.

431. ARF a.811 133.

432. Padoa-Schioppa, "Profili del diritto internazionale," 35–38.

433. Isidore of Seville, *Etymologies*, V.6.

434. Bassiouni, "Protection of Diplomats."

435. Ibn Hishām, *The Life of Muḥammad*, 649.

436. Niẓām al-Mulk, *Siyāsatnāmeh*, XXI.1, 94.

437. On unfortunate ambassadors, see Drocourt, "L'ambassadeur maltraité."

diplomacy between ʿAbd al-Raḥmān III and Otto I could have testified to this, when four out of five envoys spent time in captivity.[438]

In the more common event that no such diplomatic disaster took place, the diplomats would be dismissed. The language of the annals, "received, heard and dismissed," implies that this was a formal act.[439] The ambassadors would then return to their native land, to be debriefed. The *Annals of Fulda* offer an unusual glimpse of this process when Thioto, the abbot of Fulda, was sent by Louis the German to talk to Louis II and Pope Nicholas I in 859.[440] Thioto met his king at Lake Constance bearing a letter from the pope, and was only permitted to return to Fulda after "he had satisfied the king about all."[441]

## GIFTS

The importance of the gift has long been recognized, with historians using concepts derived from anthropology in order to analyse their role in past societies.[442] They were a crucial part of early medieval diplomacy.[443] Along with the messenger and the letter, gifts formed the essential trinity of diplomatic communication.[444] As well as being a concrete statement of goodwill, they could also act as an acceptable and face-saving means to bribe or pay tribute.[445] The economic worth of these gifts was sometimes enormous.[446] Rulers could redistribute gifts to their followers.[447] A poor gift could be as eloquent as a good one in demonstrating unhappiness and dissatisfaction.[448] These gifts formed such a regular part of diplomacy that their exact nature is often obscure.[449]

In 799, in addition to the keys of Huesca, Ḥassān gave Charlemagne "gifts" or "tribute" according to the *Annales regni Francorum*.[450] In the

438. John of Saint-Arnoul, *La vie de Jean*.

439. AF a.848 "suscepit, audivit et absolvit," 37.

440. AF a.859 53.

441. AF a.859 "sua regi omnia satisfecisset," 53–54.

442. Malinowski, "Kula"; Mauss, *Sociologie et Anthropologie*. On the ways medieval historians have engaged with the sociology of the gift, see Bijsterveld, "The Medieval Gift as Agent"; Geary, "Gift Exchange and Social Science Modeling"; Rosenwein, "Francia and Polynesia."

443. See the principles laid out by Hannig, "Ars donandi," 18.

444. Nelson, "The Role of the Gift"; Ghersetti, "The Rhetoric of Gifts," 130.

445. Engemann, "Diplomatische 'Geschenke.'"

446. Cutler, "Gifts and Gift Exchange," 247.

447. Curta, "Merovingian and Carolingian Gift Giving," 688.

448. For an example, see Nelson, "The Settings of the Gift," 135–138.

449. Cutler, "Gifts and Gift Exchange," 247.

450. ARF a.799 "muneribus," 108, "dona," 109.

account of the Astronomer, Abū Tawr and Bahlūl b. Marzūq presented Louis the Pious with gifts in 793 and 795, respectively.[451] Other anonymous "gifts" were awarded to William of Septimania and his men in Córdoba.[452] Charles the Bald received "great and multiple gifts" from Muḥammad I in 863 and reciprocated the following year with "many presents and great gifts."[453]

The presents most likely to be recorded in detail are the particularly spectacular ones. These rarities were a testament to the donors' munificence, wealth, and culture, while allowing the recipient to display them to their court to demonstrate the high esteem in which other rulers held them.[454] The lengths to which al-Jāḥiẓ went to defend al-Manṣūr from charges of meanness indicate the importance of generosity as an attribute of being caliph.[455] Gift giving could be a sign of dominance. Upon receiving a gift from a Byzantine emperor, al-Maʿmūn is alleged to have responded by saying, "Send him a gift a hundred times greater than his, so that he realizes the glory of Islam and the grace that Allāh bestowed on us through it."[456]

Exotic presents indicated a mastery of new worlds.[457] A record of gifts seems to have been kept by the ʿAbbāsids from the ninth century and in Constantinople from at least the tenth.[458] Particularly valuable for reconstructing gifts in the medieval Islamic world is *The Book of Gifts and Rarities*, a catalogue compiled in the late eleventh century by an anonymous Fāṭimid official using material from the ninth century on.[459] *The Book of Gifts and Rarities* is filled with implausibly vast numbers of extravagant gifts.[460] It does, however, give some indication as to what sort of items were associated with diplomacy in the contemporary cultural imagination of elites.

The gifts sent by Hārūn al-Rashīd to Charlemagne in 806, among them, a tent, scents, a clock, and candles, have parallels elsewhere.[461] In 894,

451. Astronomer, *Vita Hludowici*, c.6 "dona," 300, c.8 "dona," 306.

452. Ibn Ḥayyān, "Pasajes del 'Muqtabis,'" 337.

453. AB a.863 "cum magnis et multis muneribus," 104; AB a.864 "plurimis et maximis donis," 114.

454. Cutler, "Significant Gifts," 93.

455. Al-Jāḥiẓ, *Le Livre de la Couronne*, 160–161.

456. *Book of Gifts and Rarities*, 77.

457. Shalem, "Objects as Carriers."

458. Cutler, "Significant Gifts," 84.

459. *Book of Gifts and Rarities*, 5–13; Hamidullah, "Nouveaux documents." On gifts in Islam, see Rosenthal, "Hiba"; Bosworth, "Hiba"; Colin, "Hiba in the West."

460. Grabar, "The Shared Culture of Objects," 128.

461. On metal candlesticks, see Baer, *Metalwork in Medieval Islamic Art*, 26–34.

ʿAmr b. Layth (r. 879–901), the Ṣaffārid ruler of Khurasan and Eastern Iran, sent Caliph al-Muʿtadid (r. 892–902):

> a gift amounting to a million dirhams, a thousand pieces of cloth, seven oblong pieces of cloth, twenty *mann* of musk, a hundred *mann* of aloeswood, a thousand *mithqāls* of ambergris . . . one great tent, and fifteen gyrfalcons.[462]

As well as being beautiful and valuable, the tent was a symbol of power.[463] On his final journey, Hārūn held court in a large tent in Ṭus in 809.[464] Sayf al-Dawla, the tenth-century Ḥamdānid emir of Aleppo, "possessed a brocade tent that accommodated five hundred persons" in which he received Byzantine diplomats.[465]

The most detailed account of gifts in Carolingian-Umayyad diplomacy is that recorded in the *Annals of St-Bertin* in 865, when envoys arrived at Compiègne bearing "many gifts: camels carrying couches and canopies, fine cloth of various kinds and many perfumes."[466] Expensive perfumes were a staple of gift giving in the Islamic world. Perfume was among the tribute received by al-Manṣūr from the governor of Yemen in 760.[467] Hārūn al-Rashīd celebrated his wedding to Zubayda in 781 by distributing to the guests "containers of ambergris and strong costly mixed scents."[468] Upon his death, the chamberlain reported that the treasury contained musk, ambergris, aloeswood, "one thousand vessels of baked clay full of costly scents," and "many kinds of perfume."[469]

## *Eating the Fish*

Notker the Stammerer tells a story of a Frankish ambassador who was almost executed by an apologetic Byzantine emperor for eating the fish he was served in a manner that defied Greek dining etiquette.[470] Although there is no evidence that this particular problem was ever faced by the diplomats who made diplomacy between the Carolingian and Islamic

462. *Book of Gifts and Rarities*, 87.

463. On tents, see Mullett, "Experiencing the Byzantine Text."

464. Sourdel, "Questions de cérémonial ʿAbbāside," 128.

465. *Book of Gifts and Rarities*, 113.

466. AB a.865 124; on this incident, see Ottewill-Soulsby, "The Camels of Charles the Bald."

467. *Book of Gifts and Rarities*, 69.

468. Ibid., 121.

469. Ibid., 207.

470. Notker, *Gesta Karoli Magni*, II.6, 54.

worlds possible, this chapter has explored some of the other difficulties they encountered. As in the case of Notker's ambassador, that these legates often succeeded in carrying out their instructions owed much to their skills and those of their masters. Their talents enabled astonishing journeys across much of the known world, the Carolingian network of informers in Córdoba, and the procuring and transport of an elephant. Despite the impressive novelty of many of these accomplishments, Carolingian diplomacy with the Islamic world was also dependent upon the fact that it did not happen in a vacuum. Diplomats travelled on the same routes as merchants and pilgrims. People who had experience in communicating with foreign peoples sent them. International conventions concerning gifts and the duty to protect and aid envoys played an important role in helping communications. Diplomacy between the Carolingians and Muslim rulers was by no means inevitable or natural, but it did form part of a wider world in which people, objects, and ideas were already moving.

CHAPTER THREE

# Carolingian Diplomacy with the ʿAbbāsid Caliphate

IF WE ARE TO BELIEVE the *Annales Mettenses priores*, the earliest diplomatic encounter between a Carolingian and Muslims took place in the age of Pippin II (d. 714, not to be confused with the later king of Aquitaine). Although never made king, following his victory at the Battle of Tertry in 687, Pippin became the dominant force in Frankish politics. According to the annals, such was the extent of his ascendancy that embassies "of the nations living round about, that is, the Greeks, Romans, Lombards, Huns, Slavs and Saracens, poured in to him."[1] The passage is fascinating, a depiction of a ruler in contact with peoples from across the early medieval world. It is also, as Irene Haselbach observed, "vollkommen unhistorische."[2]

There are a number of compelling reasons to discount the idea of diplomacy between Pippin II and the Islamic world. The idea fails basic plausibility. The Umayyad caliphs of the period, ʿAbd al-Malik (r. 685–705) and his son al-Walīd I (r. 705–715), had no interest in the Franks. The Armenian Catholicos Elias I addressed the former as "conqueror of the universe," but for most of his reign ʿAbd al-Malik had other affairs to be concerned about.[3] Until the defeat of his rival for the caliphate, Ibn al-Zubayr, in 692 ʿAbd al-Malik was largely confined to Syria and Egypt,

1. AMP a.692 "eum circumsitarum gentium legationes, Grecorum scilicet et Romanorum, Langobardorum, Hunorum quoque et Sclavorum atque Sarracenorum," 15, translated by Gerberding and Fouracre, *Late Merovingian France*, 361.

2. Haselbach, *Aufstieg und Herrschaft*, 91.

3. Dasxuranc̣i, *The History of the Caucasian Albanians*, III.5, 191; Robinson, *ʿAbd al-Malik*, 69.

fighting for his political survival while attempting to buy off predatory Byzantine attention.[4] The final fall of Carthage to Muslim forces in 698 introduced Umayyad power into the Western Mediterranean, but the comparatively low priority of this theatre is suggested by the delay until 705 for the next push west in North Africa.[5] The invasion of the Visigothic kingdom in 711 brought the power of Damascus into somewhat closer proximity, but Pippin was dead by the time Muslim armies began probing north of the Pyrenees in 720 with the fall of Narbonne.[6]

For all the claims of the *Annales Mettenses priores*, it seems very unlikely that Pippin was powerful enough to have been of interest to the Umayyads. There is no evidence that he had any influence in regions like the Iberian Peninsula or Italy that might have brought him to the attention of Damascus. Aquitaine and Provence appear to have been largely independent of Pippin's control.[7] Even in the core Frankish territories of Austrasia and Neustria the work of Richard Gerberding and Paul Fouracre suggests severe limits to Pippin's dominance.[8] There is no compelling reason for the caliphs to have shown much interest in this one Western European warlord amongst many.

Despite the inherent interest of Saracen envoys, the *Annales Mettenses priores* are the only source to report their presence. While the *Liber Historiae Francorum* is admittedly hostile to Pippin, it is surprising that they do not appear in the *Continuations of Fredegar*.[9] Compiled in 806, the *Annales Mettenses priores* are intensely pro-Carolingian, with Pippin receiving particularly positive treatment.[10] While much of the political agenda of the compiler of the annals was achieved by discreetly leaving out embarrassing material, there are places where the writer can be identified actively inventing events.[11] Pippin is described as having "brought

4. Howard-Johnston, *Witnesses to a World Crisis*, 496–501. On the civil war, see Hawting, *The First Dynasty of Islam*, 46–67. On ʿAbd al-Malik's relations with Byzantium, see Humphreys, "The 'War of Images' Revisited."

5. Kaegi, *Muslim Expansion and Byzantine Collapse*, 14–15, 247–260.

6. "Chronicle of 754," c.69 242; Manzano Moreno, *Conquistadores, Emires y Califas*, 32–64; Bonch Reeves, *Visions of Unity*, 71–111. On Narbonne, see Riess, *Narbonne and Its Territory*.

7. Rouche, "Les Aquitains ont-ils avant la bataille de Poitiers?"; Werner, "Les principautés périphériques"; Fouracre, "Observations on the Outgrowth of Pippinid Influence," 8.

8. Fouracre, "Observations on the Outgrowth of Pippinid Influence," 3–13; Gerberding, *The Rise of the Carolingians*, 92–115; Fouracre, *The Age of Charles Martel*, 40–54.

9. Reimitz, *History, Frankish Identity*, 276.

10. Gerberding and Fouracre, *Late Merovingian France*, 332–349; Hen, "The Annals of Metz and the Merovingian Past."

11. Collins, "Deception and Misrepresentation."

under the yoke of his authority the Swabians, Bavarians, and Saxons, worn down by repeated attacks and frequent battles," despite no evidence that Pippin ever intervened in Bavaria.[12] Likewise, after Tertry Pippin is described as having reconquered "the various peoples who had once been subjected to the Franks," including "the Saxons, Frisians, Alemans, Bavarians, Aquitainians, Gascons and Bretons."[13] This passage, which resembles that concerned with the Saracen diplomats in being a long list of peoples doing honour to Pippin, is demonstrably false, particularly with regards to the last four peoples.

Given the above, the question of whether Pippin II received Muslim envoys can be fairly answered in the negative. This does not mean the passage is without interest. The reasons for the annalist inventing the incident deserve closer scrutiny. Properly examined, it provides valuable clues for the nature of real Carolingian diplomacy with the Islamic world. The *Annales Mettenses priores* were composed by someone very close to the Carolingian inner circle and supportive of Charlemagne's reign.[14] Rosamond McKitterick observed that the *Annales Mettenses priores* frequently used the lives of the earlier Carolingians "to provide a series of precedents for the actions and status of the Carolingian ruler in the author's own day."[15] As the annals were being composed in the time of Charlemagne, a ruler who had entered diplomatic relations with all of the peoples listed, it seems plausible that the entry in question has more to do with justifying Carolingian foreign policy in the first decade of the ninth century than in the age of Pippin II.

But if the composer of the annals was attempting to present Charlemagne's behaviour as part of a longer tradition, they were also seeking to build the reputation of Pippin and thus of the Carolingian dynasty as a whole for an audience of elite Franks.[16] As has been noted by other scholars, Pippin was explicitly presented in royal and imperial terms, with

12. AMP a.688 "Hinc Suavos et Baiowarios et Saxones crebris irruptionibus frequentibusque preliis contritos sue ditioni subiugavit," 5, translated by Gerberding and Fouracre, *Late Merovingian France*, 353, with comments on 335, 349.

13. AMP a.687 "quae quondam Francis subiectae fuerant, invicto principi certamen instabat, id est contra Saxones, Frisiones, Alemannos, Bawarios, Aquitanios, Wascones atque Brittones," 12–13, translated by Gerberding and Fouracre, *Late Merovingian France*, 359.

14. Nelson, "Gender and Genre," 156–160; McKitterick, *History and Memory*, 125; McKitterick, *Charlemagne*, 61–65; Hen, "The Annals of Metz and the Merovingian Past," 177.

15. McKitterick, *Charlemagne*, 64.

16. Reimitz, *History, Frankish Identity*, 369.

frequent references to his "regnum" and "imperium."[17] By downplaying the role of figures such as the Merovingian king of the time, Childebert III (r. 694–711), the annalist could create a history in which Pippin served as a heroic ancestor figure, confirming the legitimacy of his descendants as the leaders of the Franks.[18] Having died almost a century before the annals were compiled, Pippin was a particularly useful figure as the absence of living memory made it easier to invent convenient material.

The annalist constructs a set piece in which Pippin's reception of foreign envoys adds to his imperial aura:

> Delegations, however, of the nations living round about, that is, the Greeks, Romans, Lombards, Huns, Slavs and Saracens, poured in to him. And the fame of his victory and triumphs so went out among all peoples that, deservedly on account of his virtue and prudence, all the nations round about sought his friendship with great gifts and rewards. And, receiving them kindly, he rewarded them with even greater gifts and sent them home. And he, with no less speed, sending his own legates through the various regions at the right moment for the well-being of his realm, obtained peace and friendship from the surrounding peoples with the greatest goodwill.[19]

The passage in full does a number of things. The number and variety of envoys and the gifts that they bring testify to Pippin's reputation and power. The generous manner in which he receives and rewards the envoys is used to indicate his moral character and the vast resources at his command, that he can outdo all the other princes of the world with his presents. Pippin's shrewdness and the benefits this mastery of diplomacy can bring for the Franks as a whole are then shown by his ability to acquire "peace and friendship" by sending envoys "at the right moment."[20] In this way, Pippin became the link between the Franks and the outside world,

17. Gerberding and Fouracre, *Late Merovingian France*, 340.

18. Fouracre, "The Long Shadow of the Merovingians," 6–7, 10.

19. AMP "Confluebant autem ad eum circumsitarum gentium legationes, Grecorum scilicet et Romanorum, Langobardorum, Hunorum quo que et Sclavorum atque Sarracenorum. Exierat enim fama victoriae et triumphorum eius in omnes gentes, ut merito propter virtutem et prudentiam eius cunctae circumsitae nationes amicitiam illius magnis oblatis muneribus implorarent. Quos ille clementer suscipiens maioribus remuneratos donis ad propria dirigebat. Ipse quoque haud segnius oportuno tempore legatos suos pro utilitatibus imperii sui per diversas regiones dirigens pacem et amicitiam circumpositarum gentium cum maximo favore impetrabat," 15, translated by Gerberding and Fouracre, *Late Merovingian France*, 361.

20. On the importance of *amicitia*, see Steiger, *Die Ordnung der Welt*, 652–698.

protecting the interests of his subjects and generating respect, while also providing them access to far-flung wonders.

Taken on its own this passage may not seem of much importance at all. Few historians have ever been fooled by the idea that Pippin II might have done business with the caliphate. But the motivations driving the anonymous annalist and their powerful patrons to choose to fabricate this fictional diplomatic encounter offer useful perspective clues as to the reasons behind the very real relationship between Pippin's descendants and the ʿAbbāsid caliphs. The imagined contact between Pippin and the Islamic world served to elevate his stature above the ranks of competing Frankish warlords of the late seventh century. It is this chapter's contention not just that diplomacy between the Carolingians and the ʿAbbāsids was used to bolster the legitimacy of both parties in their respective domestic spheres but that this was the primary reason for this diplomacy taking place.

The beginning of this book introduced the concept of "prestige diplomacy," that is to say, diplomacy undertaken with the purpose of impressing third parties with the glamour and power of those participating in the diplomacy. This chapter will seek to demonstrate that diplomacy between the Carolingians and the ʿAbbāsids needs to be understood on those terms. It begins by addressing the rather important question of whether any diplomacy actually took place, followed by a summary of events. We will then consider two of the major suggested explanations for Carolingian-ʿAbbāsid diplomacy: respectively, an alliance against the Byzantines and the Umayyads of Córdoba; and Frankish interest in the Patriarchate of Jerusalem, demonstrating why both are ultimately unsatisfactory. Instead, both dynasties used their contact with the other as part of a wider range of strategies to legitimise themselves in the eyes of a domestic audience.

## *Existential Questions*

Scepticism concerning the reality of Carolingian diplomacy with the ʿAbbāsids has been expressed for almost as long as it has been the subject of scholarly attention. In 1833 a noted French Orientalist, who gloried in the name François-Charles-Hugues-Laurent Pouqueville, expressed the opinion that Charlemagne was duped by Isaac the Jew, who guided the first set of unfortunate envoys sent out by the Frankish king and was the sole survivor to return bringing news of the elephant sent by Hārūn, declaring that Isaac had never reached the caliph.[21] Pouqueville's case needs to be

21. Pouqueville, *Mémoire historique et diplomatique*, 529.

considered in the light of his antipathy towards Jews, whom he called "a filthy race," expressed in other works about his travels in Ottoman Greece in the early nineteenth century.[22] He was challenged on this point by Joseph Reinaud, who observed that Christians and Muslims frequently conducted diplomacy in the medieval period but had to acknowledge that no Arabic sources existed for Charlemagne's dealings with Hārūn al-Rashīd.[23] This absence prompted Vasily Barthold to also doubt the reality of this diplomacy in 1912, arguing that the Franks and the ʿAbbāsids had no reason to communicate with each other and suggesting that Abū al-ʿAbbās was actually meant to be a present for the Byzantine emperor instead.[24] In the process he questioned the authority of non-Orientalists to comment on the subject. The lack of sources continued to be a problem for later specialists such as Walther Björkman.[25]

Fortunately for this book, which would otherwise be considerably shorter, there is nonetheless very good reason to accept the reality of Carolingian diplomacy with the Islamic world. The most important are the Frankish histories. Unlike in the case of Pippin II and the *Annales Mettenses priores*, relations between the ʿAbbāsids and Pippin III, Charlemagne, and Louis the Pious are attested by contemporary Frankish sources composed by informed writers.[26] Diplomacy between Charlemagne and Hārūn al-Rashīd is mentioned in multiple accounts; in both annals composed near the court[27] and those in peripheral territories;[28] in Einhard's biography;[29] and in a range of sources in other genres of writing.[30] These sources generally include unnecessary detail which suggests truthfulness. Charlemagne's employment of Isaac fits with our knowledge of the existence of a mercantile, Mediterranean Jewish community.[31] The fact that diplomats from Ibrāhīm b. al-Aghlab, the autonomous ruler of Ifrīqiya, accompanied the embassy of 802 also suggests authenticity.[32]

22. Margaroni, "The Blood Libel," 187.

23. Reinaud, *Invasions des Sarrazins en France*, 115–117.

24. Barthold is summarized by Buckler in *Harunu'l-Rashid*, 43–47. On Barthold's work on international contact, see Bregel, "Barthold and Modern Oriental Studies," 386–388.

25. Björkman, "Karl und der Islam."

26. "The Continuations of the Chronicle of Fredegar," 320; AB a.831 4.

27. ARF a.801 114, 116; ARF a.806 122; AL a.802 39.

28. *Chronicle of Moissac*, a.802 141.

29. Einhard, *Vita Karoli Magni*, c.16 19.

30. *Ex miraculi S. Genesii*; Florus of Lyons, *Qualiter sanctorum martyrum*, 544–545, and *Ubi ossa sancti Cipriani*, 546; *Formulae Salzburgenses*, no. 62, 453–454.

31. See pp. 52–55.

32. Revised ARF, a.801 116. On the Aghlabids, see Anderson, Fenwick, and Rosser-Owen, *The Aghlabids and Their Neighbors*.

The presence of Abū al-ʿAbbās at Charlemagne's court from 802 to 810 also points to the veracity of the Frankish sources. It is generally something of an effort to ignore an elephant and Abū al-ʿAbbās attracted a lot of attention, with the Irish geographer Dicuil noting in 825 the excitement caused by the pachyderm fifteen years after the elephant's death.[33] Given the difficulties involved with procuring an elephant, the most parsimonious explanation for Isaac being able to supply Charlemagne with Abū al-ʿAbbās is that he actually reached the court of Hārūn al-Rashīd.[34]

Reference to contact between the ʿAbbāsids and the Carolingians is not confined to Latin sources. During the civil war that followed the death of Hārūn al-Rashīd, Christians in Syria or Mesopotamia adapted Arabic apocalypses attributed to a pagan Roman Sibyl. These texts mention that Hārūn received "gifts from the islands of the sea, and from the countries of the Franks," pointing to an awareness of the caliph's engagement with the Carolingians within the Arabic-speaking world.[35] That the major chronicles of the ʿAbbāsid period do not refer to the Franks is a product of the interests of their compilers rather than a sign that diplomacy did not take place.[36] The majority of them were based in Baghdad and from an Iranian background, which shaped the material they were inclined to include. The neglect of the Carolingians in their work is not unusual, or a sign of particular disrespect, as they make no reference to the diplomacy with China attested in Chinese sources.[37] Of the foreign powers that the caliphs dealt with, only the great rival Byzantium features regularly in the chronicles.[38]

A rough outline of ʿAbbāsid-Carolingian relations can be drawn from the Frankish sources. Diplomacy between the two empires began in the mid-eighth century, during the reigns of Caliph al-Manṣūr and King Pippin III. Envoys from the caliph arrived in Marseilles in the beginning of the winter of 767 in the company of returning legates sent by Pippin in 764/765. In spring the next year these envoys were escorted to Champtoceaux on the Loire, near Pippin's location in Nantes.[39] The ambassadors

33. Dicuil, *Liber de mensura Orbis terrae*, 82–83.

34. Nees, "El Elefante de Carlomagno," 38.

35. Schleifer, "Die Erzählung der Sibylle," 33; *Tiburtine Sybil Arab V*, edited by Ebied and Young, "An Unrecorded Arabic Version," 296–297; Ottewill-Soulsby, "ʿAbbāsid-Carolingian Diplomacy."

36. Kennedy, *The Early Abbasid Caliphate*, 216.

37. Hoyland, *Seeing Islam as Others Saw It*, 249–253; Bielenstein, *Diplomacy and Trade*, 359.

38. Canard, "La Prise d'Héraclée."

39. "The Continuations of the Chronicle of Fredegar," 320. On the dating, see McCormick, "Pippin III, the Embassy of Caliph al Mansur," 233–235.

were received and gifts were exchanged, before the envoys were guided back to Marseilles for the return journey.[40]

More detail is available for the next wave of diplomatic activity, which began in 797 when Pippin's son Charlemagne sent Counts Lantfrid and Sigimund to Hārūn al-Rashīd, the grandson of al-Manṣūr. To help them on their way, they were guided by the Pouqueville-maligned Isaac.[41] *The Miracles of St Genesius* indicate that they passed through Treviso, where they were joined by a mission sent by Count Gebhard to acquire relics from Elias III, Patriarch of Jerusalem.[42] Gebhard secured his information on eastern affairs from merchants who arrived at Venice. Given these connections, it seems probable that the party sailed out of Venice on one of the merchant ships. Crossing the Mediterranean, the group travelled to Jerusalem, the embassy pressing on while the relic questers remained.[43] Gebhard's monks seemed to have expected the Frankish envoys to return reasonably soon. The monks of Treviso waited an unspecified amount of time, perhaps until the start of the sailing season in 798, perhaps longer, before sorrowfully returning to Treviso via Rome without the diplomats.[44]

This suggests that the embassy took longer than anticipated. Several explanations could be adduced for this. The Frankish envoys may simply have been kept waiting. Hārūn al-Rashīd was carefully preparing the ground for his removal of the powerful Barmakid family in the last years of the eighth century and Charlemagne's embassy might have been a low priority for the caliph as a result.[45] The acquisition of an elephant could be expected to take some time, particularly as Hārūn's Indian provinces, where a new one could be most probably sourced, were in revolt until 800.[46] One plausible factor would be the difficulty of finding Hārūn. The caliph was not in Baghdad but in Raqqa.[47] As this was a recent development, with Raqqa being made the capital in 796, the change may have forced the Franks to alter their original travel plans once in ʿAbbāsid territory. Hārūn also led the pilgrimage to Mecca in that year, placing him in the

40. "The Continuations of the Chronicle of Fredegar," 320.

41. ARF a.797 116.

42. *Ex miraculi S. Genesii*, 169–172.

43. Ibid., 170.

44. Ibid.

45. Kennedy, *The Early Abbasid Caliphate*, 127.

46. Al-Yaʿqūbī, "The History," 1155–1156; Ottewill-Soulsby, "Charlemagne's Asian Elephant," 196, 201–203.

47. Heidemann and Becker, *Raqqa II*.

Ḥijāz from late 797 to early 798, which could have complicated the access the Carolingian envoys had to him.[48]

The embassy next appears in the historical record when diplomats sent by Hārūn and by Ibrāhīm I b. al-Aghlab arrived in Pisa in late May or early June 801.[49] Although the dynasty he founded was to rule Ifrīqiya throughout the ninth century, Ibrāhīm I was new to his position, having overthrown the previous governor Muḥammad al-ʿAkkī only the year before.[50] He had come to an arrangement with Hārūn al-Rashīd that saw him acknowledge the caliph's authority in exchange for autonomy.[51] His position remained uncertain for much of his reign, having to crush revolts in major cities such as Tunis and Kairouan and among the Berber tribes. The Aghlabid ruler may have seen an opportunity to strengthen his position with friendly relations with the Franks in Italy.

The envoys were received by Charlemagne as the court travelled from Vercelli to Ivrea (17 to 24 June). They had good and bad news for the emperor. "Lantfrid and Sigimund had both died," but Isaac was in Africa "with large presents" from the caliph.[52] As these gifts included the elephant, Abū al-ʿAbbās, large was putting it mildly. Charlemagne "sent Ercanbald the notary to Liguria to prepare a fleet on which the elephant and whatever else he brought along might be transported," an impressive logistical feat swiftly achieved. Isaac and the elephant landed in Porto Venere in Liguria in October, wintering in Vercelli.[53] They braved the Alps the following year, reaching Charlemagne at Aachen on 20 July. The later poetry of Florus of Lyons implies that Isaac and the elephant had travelled down the North African coastline by land.[54] Given that the ʿAbbāsid and Aghlabid ambassadors were ready to travel to Italy right at the start of the sailing season of 801, it would be unsurprising if the group arrived in Ifrīqiya in late 800.

The emperor's return embassy seems to have been sent off fairly shortly after the arrival of the elephant, in either 802 or 803, probably

48. Al-Ṭabarī, *The History of al-Ṭabarī, Vol. 30*, 166–167.

49. ARF a.801 114.

50. Kennedy, "The Origins of the Aghlabids."

51. See pp. 268–269, 271.

52. ARF a.801 "cum magnis muneribus . . . nam Lantfridus ac Sigimundus ambo defuncti erant," 116.

53. Ibid., "Tum ille misit Ercanbaldum notarium in Liguriam ad classem parandam, qua elefans et ea, quae cum eo deferebantur, subveherentur," 116, translated by Scholz, *Carolingian Chronicles*, 82. On Carolingian Liguria, see Balzaretti, *Dark Age Liguria*, 97–102.

54. Florus of Lyons, *Qualiter sanctorum martyrum* and *Ubi ossa sancti Cipriani*, 544.

with Hārūn's legate.[55] This embassy returned to the Carolingian world in some style in 806, running a Byzantine blockade set in the Adriatic by Nikephoros I (802–811) when they "travelled through the stations of the Greek ships and returned to the haven of the port of Treviso, without being noticed by one of the enemies."[56] This dramatic arrival did not interfere with the ability of Hārūn's envoy to impress on his master's behalf. Upon reaching Aachen, the ambassador, ʿAbd Allāh, proceeded to deliver a spectacular series of gifts. This no doubt eased the painful news that once again his envoy to the caliph, this time Radbert, had perished on the journey. ʿAbd Allāh was dismissed later that year and sent to winter in Italy until "it was time to sail."[57]

The next, and final, evidence for contact comes in 831. According to the *Annals of St-Bertin*, in the summer of that year Charlemagne's son and heir, the emperor Louis the Pious, held an assembly at Thionville and "envoys came from Amiralmumminin of Persia, seeking a peace. As soon as this was granted, they returned."[58] The annals' use of a clear echo of the caliphal title Amīr al-Muʿminīn, "Commander of the Faithful" indicates that the envoys came from ʿAbd Allāh al-Maʿmūn, Hārūn's son and second successor.

## *Motivations*

As discussed above, one of the problems that troubled those sceptical about the reality of Carolingian-ʿAbbāsid diplomacy was the question of what purpose this relationship might have been intended to serve. As Barthold asked, "What interests could the Western European emperor and his subjects have had in the East, or the caliph and his subjects in the West?"[59] The sources demonstrate that this diplomacy did take place, but they are terse and not particularly concerned to explain why it happened. Both sides invested considerable resources in their communication with each other. The gifts sent by Hārūn include an elephant, a magnificent curtained tent, and a marvellous mechanical clock.[60] Charlemagne scrambled to

55. ARF a.806 122.

56. Ibid., "per ipsas Grecarum navium stationes transvecti ad Tarvisiani portus receptaculum nullo adversariorum sentiente regressi sunt," 122.

57. ARF a.807 "ibi eos tempus navigationis," 123.

58. AB a.831 "ibique ad eum legati amiralmumminin de Perside venientes, pacem petiverunt. Quam mox impetrata, reversi sunt," 4.

59. Barthold in Buckler, *Harunu'l-Rashid*, 44.

60. ARF a.801 116; ARF a.807 123.

acquire gold and cloth to match the splendour of these presents.[61] Given how long it took for embassies to return, rulers were depriving themselves of useful agents and envoys for years. Many of the ambassadors failed to come back, but the deaths of Lantfrid and Sigimund did not prevent Charlemagne from sending a second embassy, whose head, Radbert, also perished on the trip.[62] The willingness of both parties to tolerate this expense in lives and wealth suggests that something important was afoot. What follows considers two major explanations for diplomatic relations between the Carolingians and the ʿAbbāsids: the alliance system developed by Buckler, and the desire to communicate with the Patriarch of Jerusalem, most fully explored by Borgolte.

## THE ALLIANCE SYSTEM

When Francis W. Buckler's *Harunu'l-Rashid and Charles the Great* was first published in 1931, it was not to universal acclaim. The eminent Carolingianist Ganshof condemned it in two reviews, declaring it to be a "fantasy" that he had read "avec stupeur."[63] Many contemporary reviewers were similarly sceptical, with some being willing to use the word "fanciful."[64] Einar Joransson commented that "a thesis resting on the assumption of unswerving adherence to theory seems precarious" and criticized Buckler's treatment of Umayyad Spain.[65] In his work on Carolingian contact with the ʿAbbāsids, Karl Schmid described the book as "excitable and sensationalist."[66]

Despite this unpromising reception, it is impossible to discuss Carolingian diplomacy with the caliphate without engaging with Buckler's work. The central argument of his book, that the ʿAbbāsids and Carolingians formed a political and military alliance against a rival axis of their shared enemies, the Umayyads of Córdoba and the Byzantine empire, has been extremely influential. Buckler used this alliance system to explain all Carolingian-ʿAbbāsid diplomacy. The alliance model remains part of academic consciousness, appearing in textbooks and on

61. *Formulae Salzburgenses*, 453. See also Bischoff, *Salzburger Formelbücher*, 34.

62. ARF a.801 116; ARF a.807 123.

63. Ganshof, "Harunu'l-Rashid and Charles the Great" and "Harunu'l-Rashid et Charlemagne."

64. Rosenthal, "Harunu'l-Rashid and Charles the Great"; Meyer, "Harunu'l Rashid and Charles the Great"; Runciman, "Charlemagne and Palestine," 606.

65. Joransson, "Review: Harunu'l-Rashid and Charles the Great."

66. Schmid, "Aachen und Jerusalem," 124.

Wikipedia.[67] Even Ganshof, although saying Buckler "deviated from the rules of a healthy [historical] method," described the hypothesis as "perfectly justified."[68]

Buckler's case proved compelling for several reasons. First, he answered the question of why this diplomacy took place. Military and political necessity provided a pleasingly "rational" explanation for diplomacy.[69] Second, he found a way to make sense of the often confusing pattern of Frankish dealings with the Umayyads by placing them within a wider context. Third, his training as an Orientalist, his major area of study being the Indian Rebellion of 1857, provided him with the necessary credentials among the medieval academic community to present a persuasive picture of the caliphs as the heirs of a Mesopotamian tradition of absolute royal power, a "Perso-Muslim polity," explaining the reluctance of the scribes of Baghdad to discuss his dealings with a minor king he considered his inferior.[70]

In order to discuss the problems with this alliance model it is helpful to address the diplomatic encounters in chronological order. This is particularly the case with regards to the dealings between Pippin III and al-Manṣūr, because this is the period when Buckler's thesis is most convincing. The Mediterranean of the 760s was a considerably different one to that of the close of the eighth century and needs to be examined in its own terms. As will be discussed, al-Manṣūr was much more concerned with al-Andalus than his successors would be. The empire ruled by Charlemagne and Louis the Pious was larger and more interested in the Eastern Mediterranean than that of Pippin III was.

To take the earlier period first, it is important to remember that Pippin initiated contact with al-Manṣūr. Although the caliph was interested enough to respond, the opening move came from the Frankish king. It is hard to see the two monarchs as being in league against Constantinople. There is no indication that the Frankish king ever contemplated war against Byzantium. Pippin maintained good relations with Constantine V (r. 741–775)

67. See Grabois, "Charlemagne, Rome and Jerusalem," 795; Collins, *Charlemagne*, 152; McCormick, "Pippin III, the Embassy of Caliph al Mansur," 237; El-Hibri, "The Empire in Iraq," 281; Nelson, *King and Emperor*, 89; "Abbasid-Carolingian Alliance."

68. Ganshof, "Harunu'l-Rashid et Charlemagne," 556.

69. On the problems with placing too much emphasis on modern notions of rationality, see Abulof, "The Malpractice of 'Rationality.'"

70. Buckler, *Harunu'l-Rashid*, 4, 32. Interestingly in his writings on the Indian Rebellion, for which see *Legitimacy and Symbols*, Buckler proposes a similar idea to Charlemagne's subordination to Hārūn, arguing that the East India Company was perceived as the vassal of the Mughal emperor.

despite the latter's iconoclasm.[71] The Frankish king sent envoys to Constantinople in 756, 763, and 767 and received Byzantine embassies in 757 and 766.[72] Serious discussions took place concerning the possible betrothal of Pippin's daughter Gisela to Constantine's son and heir, Leo IV (r. 775–780).[73] Nor is it obvious that Byzantium was a priority for al-Manṣūr. Constantine had profitably used the confusion of the 740s and 750s to go on the offensive in the caliphate.[74] Al-Manṣūr organised his own raids in response.[75] Nonetheless, war with the Byzantines does not appear to have been important in his reign and he seems to have been confident of his ability to manage attacks across that frontier, making peace with Constantine in 772.[76]

Al-Andalus is an initially more promising arena to consider a Frankish alliance.[77] Al-Manṣūr was interested in the peninsula and made several attempts to reassert the authority of the caliphs in Muslim Spain. In 755 he supported an uprising in Zaragoza against Yūsuf b. ʿAbd al-Raḥmān al-Fihrī, who had ruled al-Andalus from 747. In doing so he inadvertently provided the future emir ʿAbd al-Raḥmān I with an opportunity to cross from North Africa to Spain by distracting al-Fihrī, eventually resulting in the Umayyad conquest of al-Andalus.[78] Al-Manṣūr had reason to be hostile to ʿAbd al-Raḥmān I. Not only did the latter hold al-Andalus in defiance of his authority, but his status as a rare survivor of the Umayyad dynasty that al-Manṣūr had helped overthrow represented a potential danger as a rival source of legitimacy. As a result, the caliph made efforts to remove the emir. ʿAbd al-Raḥmān's most dangerous opponent in his wars

71. Auzépy, "Constantin V"; Goosmann, "Carolingian Kingship," 337–342. The nature of Byzantine iconoclasm has been the subject of debate opened by Brubaker and Haldon, *Byzantium in the Iconoclast Era*; responded to by, amongst others, Dal Santo, "Text, Image, and the 'Visionary' in Early Byzantine Hagiography"; Krausmüller, "Contextualizing Constantine V's Radical Religious Policies"; Meier, "The 'Justinianic Plague.'" On Carolingian engagement with Byzantine iconoclasm, see McCormick, "Textes, images et iconoclasme"; Noble, *Images, Iconoclasm and the Carolingians*, 140–145.

72. "The Continuations of the Chronicle of Fredegar," a.756 308, a.757 308; ARF a. 757 15, a.767 25; Paul I, *Epistolae* nos. 28, 36, 37, 532–533, 544–550; "Life of Stephen II," 452.

73. On the marriage alliance, see Stephen III, *Epistolae* no. 45, 562; McCormick, "Textes, images et iconoclasme," 130–131; Pohl, "Why Not to Marry a Foreign Woman."

74. Theophanes, *Chronicle*, 575, 584, 594, 596; Al-Ṭabarī, *The History of al-Ṭabarī, Vol. 28*, 48–49, 54–55; Haldon and Kennedy, "The Arab-Byzantine Frontier"; Brubaker and Haldon, *Byzantium in the Iconoclast Era*, 166–167.

75. Brooks, "Byzantines and Arabs," 731–732.

76. Al-Ṭabarī, *The History of al-Ṭabarī, Vol. 29*, 70.

77. Buckler, *Harunu'l-Rashid*, 4; McCormick, "Pippin III, the Embassy of Caliph al Mansur," 238.

78. Akhbār Majmūʿa, *A History of Early al-Andalus*, 73.

to control al-Andalus was al-ʿAlāʾ b. Mughīth, who came very close to killing the emir in battle in 763. Al-ʿAlāʾ "wore black," the ʿAbbāsid colour, "and called for loyalty to [al-Manṣūr], who sent him a black standard on a lance head."[79] Defeated opponents of the emir, such as the governor of Algeciras, al-Rumāḥus b. ʿAbd al-Azīz al-Kinānī, successfully sought refuge with al-Manṣūr.[80]

On the Frankish side, Pippin spent much of his first decade as king waging war on the Muslims of al-Andalus. In 752, Pippin acquired Nîmes, Maguelone, Beziers, and Agde in Septimania.[81] This was followed by the capture of Narbonne in 759.[82] Frankish warfare against the Muslims of Spain was celebrated in history writing associated with Pippin's court.[83] The *Continuations* of the *Chronicle of Fredegar*, whose composition was probably supervised by Pippin's uncle Childebrand before being presented to the king, present Pippin's father, Charles Martel, as a heroic figure for his victories over armies from al-Andalus and his temporary capture of Avignon in 737.[84]

Nonetheless, there are problems with the idea of Pippin and al-Manṣūr forming an alliance against al-Andalus. All of the Andalusian territory Pippin took was in Septimania, north of the Pyrenees and isolated from Córdoba. His conquests were dependent on strong support by local elites among the Goths of Septimania, led by Count Ansemund of Nîmes.[85] That there were to be no more easy pickings is demonstrated by the strength of the resistance displayed by Narbonne, which defied the Franks for seven years before yielding.[86] Pippin was conciliatory to the inhabitants of the conquered city, allowing the native Goths to retain their law. Narbonne was evidence that a war in the Iberian Peninsula would not be a quick endeavour.

The acquisition of Rousillon in 760 completed the conquest of Septimania and there is no indication that Pippin intended to push further

79. Ibid., 102.

80. Ibid., 107.

81. "Annals of Aniane," a.752 118; Salrach, *El Procés de Formació Nacional*, 5–7.

82. "Annals of Aniane," a.759 118.

83. Ottewill-Soulsby, "'Those same cursed Saracens,'" 412–414.

84. "The Continuations of the Chronicle of Fredegar," "Usque nunc inluster vir Childebrandus comes, avunculus praedictorege Pippino, hanc historiam vel gesta Francorum diligentissime scribere procuravit. Abhinc ab inlustre viro Nibelungo, filium ipsius Childebrando, itemque comite, succedat auctoritas," 300; Collins, "Deception and Misrepresentation"; Fouracre, *The Age of Charles Martel*, 7.

85. "Annals of Aniane," a.752 118.

86. Ibid., a.759 118.

south. The next years saw the Frankish king focused on fighting Duke Waifar of Aquitaine (r. 745–768), rather than planning adventures in the Iberian Peninsula. Indeed, the years 764–765, when Pippin sent his envoys, represent something of a caesura even in that endeavour, with the *Annales regni Francorum* noting the absence of any campaigning by the king in those two years.[87] Pippin's war with Waifar prohibited him from marching into the Iberian Peninsula, as doing so would have left him exposed to Aquitainian power. Carolingian conflict with the dukes of Aquitaine would last until 769, when Charlemagne captured Waifar's son, Hunald II.[88]

Nor did Pippin have much reason to be concerned about developments in al-Andalus. The last Muslim offensive into Gaul had taken place thirty years before Pippin's embassy to al-Manṣūr, when Charles Martel routed an army from Córdoba in 737 outside Narbonne.[89] The *Chronicle of 754* notes that in 740 the governor, ʿUqba b. al-Ḥajjāj al-Salūlī, travelled to Zaragoza intending to attack the Franks but had to turn back upon hearing news of the spread of the Great Berber Revolt to the Iberian Peninsula.[90] For most of Pippin's career, al-Andalus was divided between warring factions in the wake of this disruption.[91] The early 760s saw ʿAbd al-Raḥmān still fighting to control southern al-Andalus.[92] The new emir of Córdoba would not begin to look north of the Guadalquivir river basin until the 770s.[93] Given Pippin's unresolved conflict in Aquitaine and the lack of danger from al-Andalus it seems very unlikely that he sent his envoys to the caliphate in order to seek an alliance against either Byzantium or Córdoba.

Much the same can be said about al-Manṣūr. Although the caliph sought to overthrow Yūsuf al-Fihrī and ʿAbd al-Raḥmān I and replace them with an obedient governor, al-Andalus was not a major priority. Rather more important to the caliph was Ifrīqiya, which al-Manṣūr spent most of the 760s attempting to reconquer, a feat he only achieved in 772, when the caliph committed a vast army at enormous expense to the task, reported to have cost 63 million dirhams, almost five times the annual

87. ARF a.764, 765 22.

88. ARF a.769 28.

89. Sénac and Ibrahim, *Los precintos de la conquista*.

90. "Chronicle of 754," c.82 262.

91. Collins, *The Arab Conquest*, 105; Savage, *A Gateway to Hell*, 43–45; Blankinship, *The End of the Jihâd State*, 203–222.

92. Manzano Moreno, *Conquistadores, Emires y Califas*, 149–150.

93. Collins, *The Arab Conquest*, 176.

revenue raised by the province.[94] Without control of Ifrīqiya, ʿAbbāsid efforts in al-Andalus had to be indirect. Al-Manṣūr sought to take advantage of internal dissent, supporting the 755 revolt in Zaragoza which was inspired by dissatisfaction with the regime of Yūsuf al-Fihrī, and one in Beja prompted by ʿAbd al-Raḥmān I appointing a relative as governor of Seville to the ire of existing military elites.[95] In both cases, al-Manṣūr's backing was limited to the sending of his banner and documents appointing the leader of the rebellion as his governor in al-Andalus. ʿAbd al-Raḥmān posed little direct danger to al-Manṣūr's regime, as the putative emir of Córdoba spent most of his reign fighting for survival in the Iberian Peninsula.

The caliph's most involved attempt to unseat ʿAbd al-Raḥmān took place in the early 770s, when ʿAbd al-Raḥmān b. Ḥabīb al-Fihrī al-Ṣiqlabī landed in Valencia with a small force.[96] Even this invasion paled in insignificance in comparison with that of Ifrīqiya. Al-Ṣiqlabī (the Slav), so named for his height, pale skin, blue eyes, and blond hair, seems to have gambled on his Fihrīd connections to gather local support.[97] His army was defeated by Sulaymān b. Yaqẓān al-ʿArābī, the lord of Barcelona and Girona. As we shall see, Sulaymān was a formidable figure in Andalusi politics, but his victory over al-Ṣiqlabī hints that the latter's invasion force was not particularly large. While al-Manṣūr was interested in al-Andalus, the mid-760s, when he was in communication with Pippin, saw him in no position to project force into the Iberian Peninsula. Given that al-Manṣūr seems to have perceived al-Andalus as rightfully part of the caliphate, the idea that he would be happy to encourage a Christian king to conquer more of it also lacks a certain plausibility.

If there are difficulties in viewing al-Manṣūr and Pippin's dealings as aimed at al-Andalus, more serious problems emerge with any attempt to draw a political and military alliance between Charlemagne and Hārūn al-Rashīd. Hārūn possessed none of his grandfather's interest in al-Andalus. There is no evidence for serious hostilities between the ʿAbbāsids and the Umayyads after al-Manṣūr, beyond ʿAbd al-Raḥmān I and Caliph al-Mahdī (r. 775–785) engaging in an abusive correspondence.[98] Like al-

94. Al-Ṭabarī, *The History of al-Ṭabarī, Vol. 29*, 67, 69; Kennedy, "The Origins of the Aghlabids."

95. Akhbār Majmūʿa, *A History of Early al-Andalus*, 81; Kennedy, *Muslim Spain and Portugal*, 35.

96. Collins, *The Arab Conquest*, 174.

97. Akhbār Majmūʿa, *A History of Early al-Andalus*, 106.

98. Al-Ṭabarī, *The History of al-Ṭabarī, Vol. 29*, 247–248.

Manṣūr, Hārūn appears to have prioritised Ifrīqiya, pouring money and soldiers into the province in an effort to restore order there in the 790s. In July 800, during the period in which he was in contact with Charlemagne, Hārūn made a deal with Ibrāhīm b. al-Aghlab, the warlord who had managed to defeat all his rivals in the province, granting Ibrāhīm complete autonomy in exchange for token acknowledgement and regular tribute, saving Hārūn the necessity of sending his own army to intervene.[99] While this may not have been envisaged as being so permanent an arrangement as it became, Hārūn had effectively surrendered Africa beyond Egypt.[100] If Hārūn had decided to cut his losses in Ifrīqiya, it seems unlikely that he had any ambitions for the poorer and more distant lands of the Iberian Peninsula.

The Umayyads themselves were in no position to threaten ʿAbbāsid power. The successors of ʿAbd al-Raḥmān I often had difficulty asserting power outside their base in the Guadalquivir river valley.[101] In the reigns of Hishām I (r. 788–796) and al-Ḥakam I (r. 796–822), the frontier zones (*thughūr*) saw limited intervention from Córdoba as the Umayyads fought to rule cities like Mérida and Toledo, to cope with riots on the streets of their own capital, and to remove rival members of their family. Even under the greater stability and control achieved by ʿAbd al-Raḥmān II (r. 822–852), the Umayyads still lacked a fleet until attacks by Vikings prompted the construction of one in the 840s.[102] Any attempt to attack ʿAbbāsid territory would have required proceeding through hundreds of miles of North African coastline, fighting through the hostile Idrīsids of Morocco and the Aghlabids of Ifrīqiya.

These difficulties are best expressed in a letter sent by ʿAbd al-Raḥmān II to the Byzantine emperor Theophilos in 839/40, preserved by Ibn Ḥayyān.[103] The emperor was under pressure from the campaigns of the ʿAbbāsid caliph al-Muʿtaṣim (r. 833–842). Theophilos had suggested to the emir that, as well as doing something about the Andalusi pirates plaguing the Eastern Mediterranean, he return his family to the Middle East in order to reclaim the caliphate, promising Byzantine support.[104] ʿAbd al-Raḥmān's reply included

99. Al-Ṭabarī, *The History of al-Ṭabarī, Vol. 30*, 174; Talbi, *L'Émirat Aghlabide*, 109.

100. Kennedy, *The Early Abbasid Caliphate*, 195.

101. Collins, *Caliphs and Kings*, 37.

102. Lirola Delgado, *El poder naval*, 82; but see the doubts of Christys, *Vikings in the South*, 73.

103. Ibn Ḥayyān, *Crónica de los emires*, 294–298; Signes Codoñer, *The Emperor Theophilos*, 316–323.

104. Ibn Ḥayyān, *Crónica de los emires*, 294.

the observation that God would determine when his dynasty would be restored and that Theophilos, being in possession of a fleet, was in a rather better position to do something about the pirates than he was.[105] Theophilos seems to have been proposing something new when he suggested an alliance between Constantinople and Córdoba, as Ibn Ḥayyān notes:

> This Theophilos was the first Christian king to propose a bond between them and the sovereigns of al-Andalus, not caring about the dishonour of taking the initiative, which tyrants often avoid.[106]

The lack of reference to the Franks in any of their correspondence indicates that a consistent countercoalition to an ʿAbbāsid-Carolingian axis needs to be ruled out.[107]

Moving to the later diplomacy between Hārūn al-Rashīd and Charlemagne, it can be observed that Hārūn's relationship with Constantinople was rather more bellicose than his grandfather's. During the reign of his father, al-Mahdī, Hārūn had led two campaigns into Byzantine territory in 780 and 782. This conflict intensified following his accession to the throne, as annuals raids were launched on Hārūn's orders throughout his reign, with only a brief pause that began in 798 and ended in 802 in which the Byzantines paid tribute instead. The caliph personally led the expedition of 806. Hārūn was intensely interested in the Byzantines and in a state of near permanent conflict with them. However, to argue that the caliph wanted Carolingian support for his wars against the Byzantines is to miss their true purpose.

Throughout the eighth and ninth centuries, even the most pugnacious ʿAbbāsid demonstrated little interest in conquering Byzantine territory.[108] Captured cities such as Amorion in 838 were not held, but looted, before the ʿAbbāsid army returned to the no-man's-land of Cilicia.[109] The acquisition of booty and prisoners was a far more important goal.[110] Above all, the campaigning was about display. In order to retain effective power, the ʿAbbāsids needed to act in a manner befitting a deputy of God. Byzantium

105. Ibid., 296.

106. Ibid., "Este Teófilo fue el primer rey cristiano que propuso ese lazo entre ellos y los soberanos de al-Andalús, no importándole el desdoro de tomar él iniciativa, lo que suelen evitar los tiranos," 295.

107. For more on Constantinople and Córdoba, see Manzano Moreno, "Byzantium and al-Andalus."

108. Haldon and Kennedy, "The Arab-Byzantine Frontier," 113.

109. Al-Ṭabarī, *The History of al-Ṭabarī, Vol. 28*, 108–119.

110. Al-Ṭabarī, *The History of al-Ṭabarī, Vol. 29*, 206.

retained a special status in the imagination of many Muslims of the period as the great Christian opponent. This is echoed in the panegyrics which emerge in Hārūn's reign, such as that of Marwān b. Abī Ḥafsa from 797, "every monarch of Rome has paid tribute to him, unwillingly, out of hand constrainedly, in a state of humiliation."[111] By going on campaign against it, caliphs were elevated to the status of *ghāzī* (holy warrior).[112] The war against the Byzantines was a means of deflecting criticism from religious critics, as well as channelling pious enthusiasm towards the mountains of Cilicia rather than the streets of Baghdad.[113] For Hārūn, war in the west had the added benefit of establishing a powerbase and ensuring that at least one part of the standing military, the men stationed on the frontier, was loyal to him.

This relationship with the eastern empire did not require Carolingian interference. There is no evidence that any of the caliphs actually intended to conquer Byzantium, which would simply deprive the ʿAbbāsids of their most useful enemy. Although the Byzantines remained a formidable opponent, they posed little active danger to the caliphate, as they only went on the offensive against Hārūn once, in 805.[114] The caliph had no need for Frankish aid to deal with Constantinople. It consequently seems dubious that Carolingian diplomacy with the ʿAbbāsids was much concerned with an alliance against the Byzantines.

This political reality was if anything more pronounced in 831 when the envoys of al-Maʾmūn arrived at the court of Louis the Pious. Louis had been in conflict with the Umayyads, but now had more serious internal difficulties to deal with, having just survived a serious coup attempt by his sons in 830.[115] In this context war with either Córdoba or Constantinople was not something to be reasonably considered. For his part, al-Maʾmūn had even less interest in al-Andalus than his father except insofar as pirates exiled from the peninsula caused difficulties for him in the Eastern Mediterranean.[116] While the caliph's campaigns against the Byzantines were to suffer a reverse in 831 when Theophilos took the field against them, at the time al-Maʾmūn's envoys would have been sent the news was all good, with ʿAbbāsid armies sweeping across Anatolia.[117]

111. Al-Ṭabarī, *The History of al-Ṭabarī, Vol. 30*, 306.
112. Bonner, *Aristocratic Violence and Holy War*, 69.
113. Ibid., 146.
114. Al-Ṭabarī, *The History of al-Ṭabarī, Vol. 30*, 261–262.
115. AB a.830 2–3.
116. Guichard, "Les débuts de la piraterie," 66–68.
117. Signes Codoñer, *The Emperor Theophilos*, 215–224.

To conclude this discussion, there is very little evidence for any consistent alliance between the ʿAbbāsids and the Carolingians aimed against the Umayyads and the Byzantines. While relations between the Carolingians and Byzantium were certainly subject to strain, and could break out into open fighting, these moments of conflict rarely coincided with ʿAbbāsid warfare against the Byzantines. Hārūn al-Rashīd and his successors display no interest in Andalusian affairs, having to contend with challenges closer to their centre of power. Even the most plausible moment for such an entente, which was the exchange of embassies between Pippin and al-Manṣūr, took place at a moment when both parties had more important priorities, Aquitaine and Ifrīqiya, respectively. We must therefore rule out the idea of an alliance system.

## PATRIARCHS AND POLITICS

If Carolingian diplomacy with the ʿAbbāsids cannot be understood in terms of a political and military alliance, an alternative purpose must be found. Another explanation links Charlemagne's dealings with Hārūn al-Rashīd to his relationship with the Patriarchs of Jerusalem. The Frankish ruler's desire to protect and fund the Church in the Holy Land has been adduced as an explanation for his contact with Hārūn, in order to get the caliph's permission and support for Charlemagne's activities. This was most extensively developed by Michael Borgolte in his magisterial monograph of 1976, *Der Gesandtenaustausch der Karolinger mit den ʿAbbāsiden und mit den Patriarchen von Jerusalem.*[118]

Western Europeans had long been interested in the Holy Land, with pilgrims like Arculf and Willibald travelling in the seventh and eighth centuries to be closer to the sanctity of the sites and to acquire relics with which to bring some of the spiritual potency back home.[119] Many of these figures can be identified among the Frankish elite, such as Madalveus, the future Bishop of Verdun, who acquired relics from the Patriarch of Jerusalem around 750.[120] Other relic hunters who benefitted from the Patriarch's generosity included the monks sent by Count Gebhard of Treviso, who

118. Borgolte, *Der Gesandtenaustausch.* See also the work of Borgolte's supervisor, Schmid, "Aachen und Jerusalem."

119. Hen, "Holy Land Pilgrims." On the role of Jerusalem in early medieval Christian thought, see Prawer, "Jerusalem in the Christian and Jewish Perspectives"; Limor, "'Holy Journey.'"

120. *Vita Madalvei,* 196–199. For debates on pilgrimage in the Carolingian world, see Nelson, "Opposition to Pilgrimage."

received the remains of Saints Genesius and Eugenius in 797.[121] Carolingian monarchs also showed great interest in Jerusalem, but only at specific moments. Although Pippin III received a message from Patriarch Cosmas I of Alexandria via Pope Paul I, there is no other evidence for him paying much attention to Christian sees in the Islamic Eastern Mediterranean.[122] If the Patriarch did play an important role in Frankish diplomacy with the caliphate, it was only from the time of Charlemagne onwards.

At the core of the issue is the puzzling statement made by Einhard on the matter in his biography of Charlemagne:

> when [Charlemagne's] envoys, whom he had sent to visit with gifts the most Holy Sepulchre of our Lord and Saviour and the place of his resurrection presented themselves before him [Hārūn] and made known their lord's will, he not only allowed what was asked, but even gave him possession of that holy and healthful place.[123]

It is Hārūn's alleged gift that is the most problematic part of Einhard's statement, not helped by his vagueness as to what "that holy and healthy place" refers to. In his *Supplément au grand corps diplomatique*, published in 1739, Barbeyrac interpreted this to mean that Hārūn granted Charlemagne control of Palestine, an idea developed by Couret and Riant to a background of French colonial interest in Syria.[124] The "Protectorate" thesis was most fully developed and defended by Bréhier in 1919 and 1928.[125] It was firmly discredited by Arthur Kleinclausz and Einar Joransson as an anachronism, and needs no revival.[126] That Einhard did not mean that Palestine became part of the Carolingian realm is indicated by the lack of reference to the Holy Land in the list of territories ruled by Charlemagne that he includes in his biography.[127]

Given the historiographical debate this passage has prompted, it is worth examining closely to check what Einhard says. He specifies that this

121. *Ex miraculi S. Genesii*, 169–172.

122. Paul I, *Epistolae* no. 40, 552–553.

123. Einhard, *Vita Karoli Magni*, c.16 "Ac proinde, cum legati eius, quos cum donariis ad sacratissimum Domini ac salvatoris nostri sepulchrum locumque resurrectionis miserat, ad eum venissent et ei domini sui voluntatem indicassent, non solum quae petebantur fieri permisit, sed etiam sacrum illum et salutarem locum, ut illius potestati adscriberetur, concessit," 19.

124. Couret, *La Palestine*, 273; Riant, "Inventaire critique," 10, and "La donation de Hugues," 153.

125. Bréhier, "Les origines des rapports" and "Charlemagne et la Palestine."

126. Kleinclausz, "La légende du Protectorat"; Joransson, "The Alleged Frankish Protectorate."

127. Einhard, *Vita Karoli Magni*, c.15 17–18.

took place during the second embassy, that of Radbert, which dates the event to between 802/803 and 806, most probably 804–805 in order to allow for travelling time.[128] From late 804 Hārūn was on the move, leading the pilgrimage to Mecca. Early the next year he travelled to Rayy in Iran, arriving there in April and staying for four months, then returning to Baghdad, which he reached in November, before returning to Raqqa.[129] This formidable pace suggests that the most likely year for Einhard's scene is 804. Einhard also indicates that contact with Hārūn was not the main target of the embassy, which was instead visiting Jerusalem.[130]

It is significant that it was Charlemagne's second embassy to Hārūn, rather than his first, that raised the issue of Jerusalem with the caliph. This suggests that the Frankish monarch did not initiate contact with the ʿAbbāsids with the Holy Land in mind. On their journey in 797, Charlemagne's first set of legates to the caliphate did stop off on Jerusalem, but this can be attributed to a combination of piety and the fact that they were travelling with monks who were seeking relics in Palestine. The account of the *Ex miraculi S. Genesii* suggests that Lantfrid, Sigimund, and company did not linger in Jerusalem but pressed on with their mission.[131]

While the envoys might have received useful directions from the Patriarch, it seems unlikely that he was otherwise in any position to help them at the ʿAbbāsid court. That the Chalcedonian Melkite Patriarchs could be used by the ʿAbbāsids to communicate with Christian rulers is indicated by events in the following century. ʿAlī b. ʿĪsā, the vizier of Caliph al-Muqtadir (r. 912–932), had the bishops of Jerusalem and Antioch send envoys to Byzantium in order to secure better treatment for Muslim prisoners being held there.[132] Confirmation of this embassy can be found in a letter written by the Patriarch of Constantinople, Nicholas I Mystikos.[133] This initiative seems to have been fairly extraordinary. That it was not a permanent partnership is suggested by the threats made by ʿAlī to the Melkite sees if the emperor refused, threats which were apparently realised if Nicholas's letter is to believed.

128. ARF a.806 122.

129. Al-Ṭabarī, *The History of al-Ṭabarī, Vol. 30*, 248–256.

130. On the Christian community in the caliphate, see Fiey, *Chrétiens Syriaques*; Kennedy, "The Melkite Church"; Schick, *The Christian Communities of Palestine*; Eddé, Micheau, and Picard, *Communautés Chrétiennes en pays d'islam*; Griffith, "The Church of Jerusalem and the 'Melkites'" and *The Church in the Shadow of the Mosque*.

131. *Ex miraculi S. Genesii*, 170.

132. Jenkins, "The Emperor Alexander," 389–393; Vasiliev, *Byzance et les Arabes Vol. II*, 217–218, n.4.

133. Nicholas I, *Letters* no. 102, 373–383.

As evidence against the Patriarchs having much in the way of connections with Hārūn al-Rashīd, we can point first to the general neglect of Palestine under the ʿAbbāsids. Jerusalem seems to have been less important for the new dynasty based in Iraq than it had been for the Umayyads of Damascus.[134] This is particularly the case for Hārūn who, unlike his grandfather and father, never visited the city during his reign.[135] This lack of attention may have facilitated the increase of violence in the region in the last decades of the eighth century. Local Christian accounts report attacks on monasteries, most notably the sack of Mar Chariton in 788 and the massacre of twenty monks at Mar Sabas in March 797.[136] While there is a strong hint of polemic to these stories, the unrest is confirmed by Muslim sources such as al-Ṭabarī.[137] Hārūn displayed no particular interest in the Patriarch of Jerusalem and did little to protect him. It seems unlikely that the Patriarch was acting as an intermediary between Hārūn and Charlemagne.

That Charlemagne was to become an important benefactor of the Holy Land was largely the result of the Patriarch's own initiative. In 799 a messenger from Patriarch George (797–807) arrived bringing "blessings and relics of the Lord's Sepulchre" to Charlemagne, who responded by sending a priest named Zacharias to the Patriarch the next year with his own gifts.[138] The timing of this exchange strongly suggests that George had been inspired by the arrival of the first Carolingian embassy to Hārūn. He found a receptive audience in Aachen. Alcuin sent a letter to George, congratulating him on his patience in the face of persecution.[139] Zacharias's mission went well enough that he returned to the Frankish court in December of that same year with more envoys from Jerusalem in time for Charlemagne's coronation as emperor in Rome, bearing "the keys of the Lord's Sepulchre and of Calvary, also the keys of the city and of Mount Zion with a banner."[140] The excitement that this caused at Charlemagne's court is expressed by Alcuin in a letter sent in 801 to the emperor's

134. Gil, *A History of Palestine*, 279.

135. Ibid., 297–298.

136. Griffith, "Byzantium and the Christians," 233. On Mar Sabas, see Patrich, *The Sabaite Heritage*.

137. Gil, *A History of Palestine*, 282–284.

138. ARF a.799 "veniens benedictionem et reliquias de sepulchre Domini," 108; ARF a.800 110.

139. Alcuin, *Epistolae* no. 210, 350–351.

140. ARF a.800 "claves sepulchri Dominici ac loci calvariae, claves etiam civitatis et montis cum vexillo," 112, translated by Scholz, *Carolingian Chronicles*, 81.

daughter, Abbess Gisela of Chelles.[141] The importance of this connection was confirmed by the next Patriarch, Thomas I (807–820), sending the monks George and Felix as envoys in 807, with further being received in 809.[142]

The primary purpose of the Patriarchs making contact with Charlemagne was to help them raise funds for their see. The Patriarch's need for money to support its ecclesiastical infrastructure, pay taxes, and occasionally repair buildings encouraged several fundraising efforts in the ninth century.[143] This included appeals to Constantinople and to the papacy.[144] The *Life of Michael Synkellos*, composed in the mid-ninth century, states that the eponymous Michael left the monastery of Mar Sabas in 812/813 because he was tasked with raising money from the pope in response to "a certain heavy fine [that] was imposed by the impious Hagarenes."[145] Charlemagne was to be extremely generous in his material investment in the holy sites of the region. The survey of the ecclesiastical establishment in the see of Jerusalem commissioned by the emperor and completed around 808 has recently been investigated by Michael McCormick and stands as a testament to his seriousness about supporting the Christian faith in the Holy Land.[146] A thorough investigation of the monasteries both within and without the city of Jerusalem and an accounting of the Patriarch's expenditures, Charlemagne's survey indicates that he was determined to be effective in his aid. Record survives of a meeting in 810 between Charlemagne and his advisers in order to discuss "the alms that had to be sent to Jerusalem for the restoration of the churches of God."[147]

In his *De administrando imperio*, Emperor Constantine VII Porphyrogenitus (r. 913–959) praised Charlemagne because "he sent much money and abundant treasure to Palestine and built a very large number of monasteries."[148] Among foundations that can be connected to Charlemagne's philanthropy is the convent of the Holy Sepulchre, of

141. Alcuin, *Epistolae* no. 214, 357–358.

142. ARF a.807 123–124; ARF a.809 129; *Monumenta negrologica*, 12.

143. On the Patriarch's finances, see McCormick, *Charlemagne's Survey*, 14–21.

144. Griffith, "Byzantium and the Christians."

145. *The Life of Michael the Synkellos*, c.6 57–59; Sode, *Jerusalem, Konstantinopel, Rom*, 146.

146. McCormick, *Charlemagne's Survey*, 175.

147. Charlemagne, *Capitulare missorum Aquisgranense* no. 64, "De elemosina mittenda ad Hierusalem propter aecclesias Dei restaurandas," 154; McCormick, *Charlemagne's Survey*, 163.

148. Constantine Porphyrogenitus, *De administrando imperio*, 109.

which seventeen of the twenty-five resident nuns were from "the empire of Lord Charles."[149] If the Latin community on the Mount of Olives was not founded by the emperor, it was certainly generously patronised by him.[150] In the account of his pilgrimage to the Holy Land in the 860s, Bernard the Monk makes reference to a hostel in Jerusalem for Latin pilgrims that was supported by lands bought by Charlemagne, connected to a church with a splendid Bible.[151] Towards the end of the ninth century, Christian of Stavelot mentions this institution in his *Commentary on Matthew*, although he notes that with the loss of its land the hostel was in dire straits.[152]

Carolingian contact with the Patriarch of Jerusalem should therefore be seen as an unexpected by-product of diplomacy with the ʿAbbāsids, insofar as it provided Patriarch George with evidence that the king of the Franks was interested in the East. By 802 at least two embassies from Jerusalem had been received by Charlemagne, time enough for him to have been introduced to the financial difficulties of the Patriarchate.[153] This information then shaped Charlemagne's second mission to Hārūn al-Rashīd, sent in either 802 or 803. This is indicated by Einhard's statement that these envoys discussed the Holy Land with the caliph and supported by the fact that the envoys returned home in the company of "monks from Jerusalem, who served as an embassy from the Patriarch Thomas," indicating that they had returned via Jerusalem.[154]

This still leaves the problem of what Einhard was referring to when he linked Charlemagne's interest in Jerusalem with a gift from Hārūn. The simplest and most straightforward way to understand Einhard's mention "of that holy and blessed place" is to read it as the caliph granting his permission for Charlemagne's establishing and support of Christian institutions in Jerusalem. If we accept a chronology wherein Charlemagne's major patronage of institutions in Palestine follows an agreement with Hārūn that he received back in 807 certain other details then make sense. The surveying of the Church in the Holy Land carried out in 808 becomes the beginning of a new phase in Carolingian involvement in the region, determining what needs doing in systematic fashion, something further

149. McCormick, *Charlemagne's Survey*, "de imperio domni Karoli," 207.

150. Ibid.

151. Bernard, *Itinerarium*, 316.

152. Christian of Stavelot, *Expositio super librum generationis*, 95–96.

153. ARF a.799 108; ARF a.800 110.

154. ARF a.807 "cum monachis de Hierusalem, qui legatione Thomae patriarchae fungebantur," 123.

developed at the meeting of 810, where Charlemagne and his advisers discussed work to be done in the Holy Land.[155]

The earliest evidence for the convent of the Holy Sepulchre comes from the *Survey of the Holy Land*.[156] The hostel is first mentioned by Bernard the Monk, travelling decades later.[157] Charlemagne's backing for both could postdate 807. More complex is the monastery on the Mount of Olives. The monastery clearly existed in 800, when one of its monks arrived in Rome.[158] The Mount of Olives community probably predates Charlemagne, with the Frankish monarch merely expanding it.[159] This is not to argue that all of Charlemagne's financial involvement needs to be placed after 807, but that an expansion in his investment can be observed after this point that would be explained by some sort of agreement with Hārūn dating to after this time.

This consent would have been very useful. The exact status of churches in the Islamic world was still a subject of debate in the late eighth and early ninth centuries. The text of the Pact of ʿUmar (*Shurūṭ ʿUmar*) which forbade any building or repairing of churches does not seem to have stabilized until later.[160] The *Muṣannaf* of ʿAbd al-Razzāq (d. 827), one of the earliest collections of *ḥadīth*, preserves traditions both in favour of and opposed to the destruction of churches. In his *Kitāb al-Kharāj*, Abū Yūsuf wrote Hārūn about "how the churches and the synagogues were left undestroyed when the Muslims captured those cities."[161] He explained that this was due to agreements made at the time of the conquest but that no new churches could be permitted to be built. Another Ḥanafī jurist, al-Shaybānī, summarized his views on the matter:

> [The *dhimmīs*] should be permitted to build neither a synagogue nor a church nor a fire temple in a Muslim city in the lands of the Muslims. But if they have retained a synagogue or a church or a fire temple in cities . . . conceded to them under peace agreement, they may keep it, and if it should be destroyed they should be permitted to rebuild it.[162]

155. McCormick, *Charlemagne's Survey*, xviii; Charlemagne, *Capitulare missorum Aquisgranense primum*, 152–154.

156. McCormick, *Charlemagne's Survey*, 207.

157. Bernard, *Itinerarium*, 312.

158. ARF a.800 112.

159. McCormick, *Charlemagne's Survey*, 77.

160. Levy-Rubin, "*Shurūṭ ʿUmar*."

161. Abū Yūsuf, *Kitab-ul-Kharaj*, 277.

162. Al-Shaybānī, *The Islamic Law of Nations*, 278.

Al-Shāfiʿī (d. 820) stated that churches in communities who were conquered by treaty (*ṣulḥ*) were safe and that in some cases new churches could be built if permitted by the original treaty.[163] Abū ʿUbayd (d. 838/839) used Jerusalem as an example of a city where churches were protected by treaty.[164]

How this worked in practice is even less clear, but some hostility to the building and repair of churches seems to have been present, even when not enforced by the authorities. The *Syriac Chronicle of 1234* states that ʿAbd Allāh b. Ṭāhir, governor of the Jazīra in the 820s, was asked to demolish new churches in Harran, Edessa, and Samosata but refused.[165] Patriarch Thomas I got into trouble with the authorities in Jerusalem for his ostentatious restoration of the roof of the Church of the Holy Sepulchre, presumably with Carolingian money.[166] Elias III's (878–907) letter to the Frankish bishops in 881 indicates the importance of having a sympathetic governor in order to be allowed to repair churches and monasteries.[167]

Something of the state's involvement with Christians in Palestine is demonstrated by pilgrimage to Jerusalem. Caliphal officials interacted with Christian pilgrims to the Holy Land, as attested by the misadventures of Willibald and his companions, arrested on suspicion of being spies in 724.[168] Similarly unfortunate was the group that included Bernard the Monk in the 860s who, despite taking the precaution of acquiring letters of safe-conduct from Sawdān, the emir of Bari, were forced to pay fees in Alexandria and Babylon Fortress for more letters.[169] Given this context, some sort of support from Raqqa would have been crucial, even if only in the form of turning a blind eye to building, and protecting the Patriarch from local backlash.

While Charlemagne seems to have sought Hārūn's permission to intervene in the Holy Land, his successors did not. In 826, Abbot Dominic of the Mount of Olives, "from the land beyond the sea," attended the court of Louis the Pious.[170] According to Notker the Stammerer, Louis the German paid regular support money to Jerusalem.[171] Among the martyrs of Córdoba killed in 852 was George of Bethlehem, a monk of Mar Sabas,

163. Levy-Rubin, "*Shurūṭ ʿUmar*," 178.
164. Ibid., 177.
165. Ibid., 190.
166. Kennedy, "The Melkite Church," 330.
167. Elias III, *Spicilegium*, 363.
168. Hygeburg, *Vita Willibaldi*, 94.
169. Bernard, *Itinerarium*, 310.
170. ARF a.826 "de partibus transmarini," 169.
171. Notker, *Gesta Karoli Magni*, II.9, 65.

originally on a fundraising expedition to Francia.[172] In 879 Pope John VIII apologised to Patriarch Theodosius II (862–878) for the poor gifts he was sending him.[173] As mentioned above, the final decade of Carolingian Europe saw a call from Patriarch Elias III for money from the bishops of Francia in 881, reporting an opportunity to rebuild the churches of Jerusalem under a friendly governor.[174] This continued financial and spiritual relationship seems to have proceeded without any reference to the caliphs.

Carolingian patronage of Jerusalem developed as a result of Charlemagne's diplomacy with Hārūn al-Rashīd. It was clearly an important part of the emperor's second embassy to the caliph, but not his first. It can therefore only be a partial explanation for diplomacy between the Carolingians and the ʿAbbāsids. There is no indication that it inspired Pippin III's interest in al-Manṣūr or was much of a factor in al-Maʾmūn's communication with Louis the Pious.

## PRESTIGE DIPLOMACY

Help in understanding Carolingian relations with the caliphate can be drawn from other disciplines. Using a range of modern and historical case studies, in 1988 the anthropologist Mary Helms argued that engagement with the external world could be a means for kings and specialists to acquire authority within their own political community:

> The capacity to cope ably with foreigners, their realms, and their powers . . . [could] be a measure of the power of a leader, and as such can be actively sought as an expression of leadership abilities.[175]

Whether by travelling far distances or by hosting and communicating with those who had, such individuals could demonstrate a knowledge of the wider world that placed them above others in their community. Access to rare and impressive items showed that the possessor had horizons beyond those of their peers, in addition to wealth. The coming of envoys from half-remembered lands indicated the status of a leader on a much grander scale than more localised elites as foreign kings signalled their respect to the recipient. In this way, such a leader became the point through which the wider community accessed distant lands.[176] Helms

172. Eulogius, *Memoriale sanctorum*, 426–430.
173. John VIII, *Epistolae* no. 178, 143.
174. Elias III, *Spicilegium*, 363.
175. Helms, *Ulysses' Sail*, 152.
176. Ibid., 163–164.

mentioned Charlemagne in her book, albeit primarily in the context of relations with the pope, but this idea can be applied to early medieval diplomacy more broadly.[177]

The political culture of both the Frankish world and the caliphate was one in which diplomacy with powerful, distant rulers was highly prestigious. In part this reflected the shadows of empires gone. Charlemagne's coronation as emperor in 800 is one of the clearest examples of the influence of the Roman past.[178] Poets proclaimed Charlemagne to be the new Augustus and Constantine.[179] Paintings of Augustus, Constantine, and Theodosius gazed down upon the revellers in Louis the Pious's palace at Ingelheim.[180] This reverence was paralleled in the Islamic world by an interest in Sasanian Iran, which served as an analogous model for imperial power.[181] There were ambiguities in this relationship. Efforts were made to demolish the remains of Sasanian palaces in Ctesiphon.[182] But the very proximity of Baghdad to the former heart of the Persian power speaks to the lingering fascination of the imperial past. Al-Jāḥiẓ and al-Yaʿqūbī wrote of al-Manṣūr that he sought to imitate the Persian kings of old.[183] In his Mirror for Princes, which was heavily dependent upon Sasanian material, al-Thaʿlabī (d. 864) noted the importance of Persian precedent to ʿAbbāsid court life "for they were the first in that and we took from them the regulations on kingship and kingdom."[184] This was a tendency reinforced by the relocation of the political centre of the caliphate to Iraq and by the increasing importance of Iranians to the administration and cultural life of the empire.[185]

Present among both these models was the idea of a ruler's power being displayed by the reception of dignitaries from distant lands. Anne Latowsky has pointed to the long history of the "foreign embassy topos"

177. Ibid., 146–147; McKitterick, *Charlemagne*, 374.

178. Collins, "Charlemagne's Imperial Coronation"; Nelson, "Why Are There So Many Different Accounts," 21; Pohl, "Creating Cultural Resources."

179. Godman, *Poets and Emperors*, 58, 77; Nelson, "Translating Images of Authority."

180. Ermold the Black, *In honorem Hludovici*, Bk. 4, 162–164. On Carolingian era wall painting, see Preißler, "Fragmente einer verlorenen Kunst." On Ingelheim, see Sage, "Die Ausgrabungen in der Pfalz"; Grewe, "Die Königspfalz zu Ingelheim."

181. Tor, "The Long Shadow"; Vacca, *Non-Muslim Provinces*, 10–16.

182. Savant, "Forgetting Ctesiphon"; Johnson, "'Return to Origin Is Non-Existence,'" 267.

183. Al-Masʿūdī, *Les Prairies d'Or*, 326; al-Yaʿqūbī, "The Book of the Adaptation of Men," 45.

184. El Cheikh, "The Institutionalisation," 352.

185. Lassner, *The Shaping of ʿAbbāsid Rule*, 169–175; Vacca, *Non-Muslim Provinces*, 211–214.

that Frankish writers such as Einhard drew upon, particularly in Roman histories.[186] In his celebration of Augustus, Suetonius wrote:

> The reputation for prowess and moderation which he thus gained led even the Indians and the Scythians, nations known to us only by hearsay, to send envoys of their own free will and sue for his friendship and that of the Roman people.[187]

Augustus is shown bringing the farthest edges of the world to Rome by his reputation for military and moral virtue. The concept of people from the caliphate bearing presents had particular resonance for Carolingian rulers familiar with Psalm 71, dedicated to Solomon, promising that "the kings of the Arabians and of Saba shall bring gifts," creating associations of wise and divinely blessed biblical kingship.

Similar ideas circulated in Iran. The sixth-century *Letter of Tansar* portrayed the Sasanian monarchs as the heirs of Darius I, of whom it was said that "from China to the western lands of Rome, all kings were his ready slaves and sent to him tribute and gifts."[188] Later historians writing in Arabic celebrated the universal rule of the Shahanshah. Al-Ṭabarī said of Khusrow I Anushiruwān (r. 531–579) that "all the nations were in awe of him; and numerous delegations from the Turks, the Chinese, the Khazars, and similar nations thronged his courts."[189] Al-Masʿūdī made the same point at greater length:

> After his return to Iraq, he received ambassadors and presents from various kings as well as deputations from various kingdoms. One of these ambassadors was sent to him by the Emperor of Rome, Caesar, carrying gifts and kindness . . . Khāqān, king of the Turks, granted the hand of his daughter and the daughter of his brother to Anushiruwān. The kings of India, Sind, and all the countries of the North and the South concluded peace with the king of Persia. From everywhere he received presents and deputations, for fear of his impetuosity, the strength of

186. Latowsky, *Emperor of the World*, 7, 19–58.

187. Suetonius, *The Lives of the Caesars I*, Augustus 21 "Qua virtutis moderationisque fama Indos etiam ac Scythas auditu modo cognitos pellexit ad amicitiam suam populique Rom. ultro per legatos petendam," 152. On the particular significance of India, see Ottewill-Soulsby, "Charlemagne's Asian Elephant," 193–211.

188. *The Letter of Tansar*, 53 (adapted); for further discussion, see Payne, "Cosmology and the Expansion," 22–23.

189. Al-Ṭabarī, *The History of al-Ṭabarī, Vol. 5*, 160. On his interest in the Sasanians, see Zakeri, "Al-Ṭabarī on Sasanian History"; Rubin, "Al-Ṭabarī and the Age of the Sasanians."

his army, and the extent of his empire, the recollection of his rapid conquests, the fatal treatment he had inflicted on so many kings, and in recognition of his taste for justice.[190]

In both cases the power of a celebrated ruler was demonstrated by his ability to earn the respect of other monarchs, manifested by the presence of foreign diplomats, thereby raising themselves above all colleagues and stretching their influence across the world.[191]

These were potent ideas. That they were important for the Carolingians is demonstrated by the works of people close to the regime. Poets at court placed Charlemagne on a global stage, with Theodulf declaring to the Frankish ruler that "the entire world resounds in your praise, my king."[192] In his biography, Einhard remarked that the emperor "added to the glory of his kingdom by building friendship with several kings and nations."[193] Not to be outdone, Thegan said of Louis the Pious:

> Envoys came to him from all the kingdoms and provinces and from foreign nations . . . announcing that they would keep peace and faith with him, and without pressure they offered their obedience freely.[194]

The memory of the reception of legates from across the world could be used to evoke a more glorious past. In his *Lament on the Division of the Empire*, written in the 840s, Florus of Lyons mourned the breakdown of imperial unity:

> And so the Frankish race became celebrated throughout the world,
> and the fame of its achievements reached the ends of the earth,
> foreign kingdoms everywhere sent their embassies from afar,
> both barbarians and Greeks, to the Latin tribunal.[195]

190. Al-Masʿūdī, *Les Prairies d'Or*, 232–233.

191. Payne, "The Making of Turan" and "Iranian Cosmopolitanism."

192. Theodulf of Orléans, *Ad Carolum regem*, no. 25, "Te totus laudesque tuas, rex, personat orbis," 483, translated by Godman, *Poetry*, 151.

193. Einhard, *Vita Karoli Magni*, c.16 "Auxit etiam gloriam regni sui quibusdam regibus ac gentibus per amicitiam sibi conciliatis," 19.

194. Thegan, *Gesta Hludowici imperatoris*, c.9 "legati venerunt ad eum ex omnibus regnis et provinciis et exteris nationibus . . . nunciantes pacem et fidem erga eum observare et spontaneum obsequium non coacti obtulerunt su," 190, translated by Noble, *Charlemagne and Louis the Pious*, 199.

195. Florus of Lyons, *Querela de divisione imperii*, no. 28, "Claruit hinc nimium toto gens Francica mundo, Famaque virtutum fines penetravit ad imos; Legatos hinc inde suos procul extera regna, Barbara, Graeca simul Latium misere tribunal," 561, translated by Godman, *Poetry*, 269.

As Florus indicates, the esteem of far-flung sovereigns also elevated the ruler's subjects.

Nor was this an alien concept for Muslim monarchs, as demonstrated by the frescoes at Quṣayr ʿAmra, an eighth-century desert castle constructed for the Umayyad al-Walīd II (r. 743–744), where "six kings" including the Byzantine emperor, Sasanian shah, and the Ethiopian negus are depicted paying tribute to the caliph.[196] When al-Walīd was overthrown, his short-lived successor Yazīd III (r. 744) famously declared, "I am the son of Kisrā and Marwān is my father; Caesar was my grandfather; my grandfather was Khāqān," thus presenting himself as the heir of Sasanian, Umayyad, Byzantine, and Central Asian rulers, respectively, uniting all the world in his ancestry.[197] In his account of the reign of al-Mahdī, al-Yaʿqūbī lists at length the kings who had done him honour:

> Al-Mahdī sent messengers to the kings, calling on them to submit, and most of them submitted to him. Among them were the king of Kabul Shāh, whose name was Ḥanḥal; the king of Tabaristan, the Iṣbahbadh; the king of Soghdia, the Ikhshīd; the king of Tukharistan, Sharwīn; the king of Bamiyan, the Shīr; the king of Ferghana,——; the king of Usrushana, Afshīn; the king of the Kharlukhiyya, Jabghūya; the king of Sijistan, Zunbīl; the king of Turks, Ṭarkhān; the king of Tibet, Ḥ-h-wr-n; the king of Sind, al-Rāy; the king of China, Baghbūr; the king of India and Atraḥ, Wahūfūr; and the king of the Tughuz-ghuz, Khāqān.[198]

Divorced of context, and demonstrating only a dubious understanding of the polities of Asia, this recounting turned the rulers of the East into ornaments to the glory of the caliph.[199]

Spectacular gifts were a testament to the donors' munificence, wealth, and culture, while allowing the recipient to display them to their court to demonstrate the high esteem in which other rulers held them.[200] Cassiodorus, writing to Boethius on behalf of King Theoderic, gives perhaps the clearest explanation of the value of sending astonishing gifts. The Burgundian king Gundobad had requested a "time-piece," which Theoderic planned to send him so that "they will experience a wonder which to me

196. Fowden, *Quṣayr ʿAmra*, 197–225.
197. Al-Masʿūdī, *Les Prairies d'Or*, 909.
198. Al-Yaʿqūbī, "The History," 1139.
199. On the eastern frontier, see Haug, *The Eastern Frontier*, 11–26, 212–222.
200. Cutler, "Significant Gifts," 93.

is a common-place."[201] The overall message was that "sweetness and pleasure many times produce what weapons fail to do. . . . For it is for this reason I am looking for toys, to achieve a serious purpose by their means."[202]

The ʿAbbāsids were no strangers to the uses of diplomacy in handling complex domestic issues. A case in point is the grand reception of Byzantine ambassadors in June 917 ordered by Ibn al-Furāt, vizier to Caliph al-Muqtadir (r. 908–932). Vividly described in multiple accounts, the event was clearly a no-holds-barred extravaganza of exotic animals, massed soldiery and full courtly regalia, in which the envoys paraded through the centre of Baghdad under the eyes of the inhabitants of the city.[203] The Byzantine officials in question appear to have been slightly nonplussed by the spectacle, having been sent in order to negotiate a routine prisoner exchange.[204] The display was prompted by issues within Baghdad. Al-Muqtadir's regime had been troubled by financial issues and Ibn al-Furāt had only just been reappointed vizier, having been dismissed in 912 after being unable to fund a public ceremony.[205] The large public reception of the Byzantine ambassadors was an opportunity to build confidence in the caliph's finances and cement Ibn al-Furāt's position.

Ibn al-Furāt's vizierate was not particularly successful and he was removed in November 918. Al-Muqtadir's reign is generally considered to have been one of decline, hastening the takeover of effective power by military strongmen.[206] Nevertheless, the reception of the Byzantine ambassadors must be considered a propaganda triumph, being remembered and written about by all historians of the period as a statement of power. This testifies to the potential impact of foreign diplomacy as a means to build political support in a difficult domestic context.

As the above suggests, both the Carolingians and the ʿAbbāsids operated in a world where diplomacy was not just about managing relations with foreign leaders. Not only did rulers and their ministers keep an eye on the opinion of sensitive domestic groups, such as military elites, or the

201. Cassiodorus, *Variae*, I.45, "horologium," "quod nobis cottidianum, illis videatur esse miraculum," 40, translated by Barnish, *The Variae*, 20.

202. Ibid., "frequenter enim quod arma explere nequeunt, oblectamenta suavitatis imponunt, sit ergo pro re publica et cum ludere videmur, nam ideo voluptuosa quaerimus, ut peripsa seria compleamus," 39–40, translated by Barnish, *The Variae*, 20.

203. Ibn Miskawayh, *The Eclipse of the ʿAbbāsid Caliphate*, 56–60; Hilāl al-Ṣābiʿ, *Rusūm Dār al-Khilāfah*, 15–16; *Book of Gifts and Rarities*, 152.

204. Ibn Miskawayh, *The Eclipse of the ʿAbbāsid Caliphate*, 59.

205. Kennedy, "The Reign of al-Muqtadir," 32. On Ibn al-Furāt, see van Berkel, "The Vizier."

206. Waines, "The Pre-Būyid Amirate"; Kraemer, *Humanism*, 31–37.

urban population of the capital city, but foreign policy could be subordinated to the need to manage internal politics. It is with this in mind that we need to understand relations between them.

## *First Contact: Pippin III and al-Manṣūr (767–768)*

The reign of Pippin III was shaped by the nature of its beginning. His usurpation of the last Merovingian king in 751 was a dangerous undertaking. The very careful composition of annals such as the *Continuations* of Fredegar suggests an awareness of the importance of controlling the narrative about Pippin's ascension to the throne, as do the campaigns to destroy the reputation of the Merovingians.[207] The new king's earlier career as Mayor of the Palace had been characterised by the sidelining of his brothers, removing them and their children from the succession.[208] Pippin's embassy to al-Manṣūr was a strikingly imaginative measure. It was the first time a Carolingian deliberately made contact with an Islamic ruler, but it fit within Pippin's wider political activity. Pippin was very aware of the importance of establishing his own legitimacy and foreign relations were an important part of his strategies for doing so. The most famous example of this was Pippin's championing of Pope Stephen II (r. 752–757) against the Lombards, one of the results of which was Pippin and his sons being anointed as kings by the pontiff in 754.[209] Pope Stephen actively worked to promote Pippin's reputation, informing the Frankish king in 757 that "I have often told of these things you have done (through some miracle) to the nations arriving from all over the globe."[210] His successor and brother, Pope Paul I (r. 757–767), continued this policy, telling Pippin:

> All the peoples on the face of the earth without exception have learnt of your exertions in defence of God's holy church and praise you as a great and outstanding king. But we too constantly spread your good reputation far and wide.[211]

207. McKitterick, "The Illusion of Royal Power"; Fouracre, "The Long Shadow of the Merovingians."

208. Collins, "Pippin III as Mayor of the Palace," 75.

209. ARF a.754 12; "Life of Stephen II," 452. On Pippin's Italian interests, see Pohl, "Das Papsttum und die Langobarden."

210. Stephen II, *Epistolae* no. 11, "que per te mirabiliter facta sunt, sepe convenientibus ex universo orbe terrarum nationibus dicere," 504, translated by McKitterick, *Codex Epistolaris Carolinus*, 193.

211. Paul I, *Epistolae* no. 17, "omnes enim omnino gentes, quae super faciem universae terrae consistunt conpertum habent tuum certamen, quod ad defensionem sanctae Dei ecclesiae adhibuisti, et magnum te ac praecipuum regem laudabiliter asserunt. Sed et

The pope had an unusual authority, but the early Carolingians did not depend upon them to build their reputation with foreign leaders. Charles Martel had sent the young Pippin to King Liutprand of the Lombards to have his hair cut as part of becoming a man.[212]

Most strikingly, as king, Pippin engaged in extended diplomacy with the Byzantines, despite the iconoclasm of Emperor Constantine V.[213] It had been some time since a Frankish monarch had entered diplomatic relations with any Eastern ruler.[214] The embassy sent by Dagobert I (r. 623–639) to Heraclius (r. 610–641) in 629 is the last recorded from a Merovingian to Byzantium.[215] Pippin sent envoys to Constantinople in 756, 763, and 767 and received Byzantine embassies in 757 and 766.[216] Much of this contact was related to Pippin's alliance with the papacy, and the mission sent in 763 was a joint Frankish-papal affair.[217] A debate was staged at Gentilly in 767 between Byzantine theologians and Greek-speaking Romans.[218]

As Erik Goosmann has recently demonstrated, Pippin was interested in relations with the Byzantines as a means to garner prestige at home.[219] Italy and theological questions appear most prominent in sources linked to the pope such as papal letters and the *Liber Pontificalis*.[220] The Frankish sources indicate a diplomatic relationship characterised by display. Constantine's first embassy in 757 brought "King Pippin many gifts, among others an organ; which came to him at Compiègne, where at this time he had a general assembly of the people."[221] This sort of impressive, public

---

nos bonam tuam famam longe lateque protelare atque dilatare non desistimus in eo," 516, translated by McKitterick, *Codex Epistolaris Carolinus*, 217.

212. Paul the Deacon, *Historia Langobardorum*, VI.53, 183.

213. Auzépy, "Constantin V." See chapter 3, n. 71. On Carolingian engagement with Byzantine iconoclasm, see McCormick, "Textes, images et iconoclasme"; Noble, *Images, Iconoclasm and the Carolingians*, 140–145.

214. For earlier contact, see Goubert, *Byzance avant l'Islam II*.

215. "The Continuations of the Chronicle of Fredegar," 226.

216. Ibid., a.756 308, a.757 308; ARF a. 757 15, a.767 25; Paul I, *Epistolae* nos. 28, 36, 37, 532–533, 544–550; "Life of Stephen II," 452.

217. Paul I, *Epistolae* no. 28, 532–533.

218. ARF a.767 25; McCormick, "Textes, images et iconoclasme," 113–130; Noble, *Images, Iconoclasm and the Carolingians*, 141.

219. Goosmann, "Carolingian Kingship," 342–343.

220. Brandes, "Das Schweigen des *Liber pontificalis*"; McKitterick, *Rome and the Invention*.

221. ARF a.757 "Constantinus imperator misit Pippino regi multa munera, inter quae et organum; quae ad eum in Conpendio villa pervenerunt, ubi tunc populi sui generalem conventum habuit," 15.

indication of Pippin's authority was continued. The synod at Gentilly ten years later might have been concerned with theology, but it was also a major event in front of the gathered assembly, one at which the Byzantine envoys proposed a marriage between Constantine's son and heir Leo IV and Pippin's daughter Gisela.[222]

For a ruler who came from a dynasty new to the title of king the legitimacy bestowed by the most senior monarch in Christendom sending gifts and proposing marriage was immensely important. Pippin's embassy to al-Manṣūr follows this pattern. Rather than swiftly dealing with the ʿAbbāsid envoys, the king had the legates overwinter in Metz and then brought to his grand assembly at Champtoceaux, where gifts were exchanged in full view of the Frankish elite, who could witness the respect and esteem in which Pippin was held even by distant Saracens. That al-Manṣūr's currency if not his name carried weight in Christian Europe is hinted by a gold coin issued by King Offa of Mercia that copied a dinar issued by the caliph in 773/774.[223]

Al-Manṣūr's regime was also shaped by the need to consolidate power. He came to the throne four years after the ʿAbbāsid Revolution in 750. Al-Manṣūr's reign can be divided into two periods, roughly before and after 762.[224] In the earlier phase he had to face a series of dangerous political challenges.[225] Some of these came from other architects of the ʿAbbāsid Revolution, including his uncle ʿAbd Allāh b. ʿAlī, his nephew ʿĪsā b. Mūsā, and the general and fixer Abū Muslim.[226] Also threatening were ʿAlīd claimants to the caliphal title. By the later period these problems had been dealt with. Abū Muslim was manoeuvred out of his Khurasani power base and murdered while meeting the caliph.[227] Judging from the sources, few people entirely believed al-Manṣūr's protestations of innocence in the death of ʿAbd Allāh: "Am I to blame if the house collapsed on ʿAbd Allāh b. ʿAlī?"[228] Al-Manṣūr survived his greatest challenge during the rebellion of the ʿAlīd brothers Muḥammad al-Nafs al-Zakiyya and

222. On the marriage alliance, see Stephen III, *Epistolae* no. 45, 560–563, 562; McCormick, "Textes, images et iconoclasme," 130–131.

223. Blunt, "The Coinage of Offa," 50–51; Scarfe Beckett, *Anglo-Saxon Perceptions*, 58–59.

224. Kennedy, *The Prophet and the Age of the Caliphates*, 115.

225. Marsham, *Rituals of Islamic Monarchy*, 192.

226. Al-Ṭabarī, *The History of al-Ṭabarī, Vol. 28*, 4; Kennedy, *The Early Abbasid Caliphate*, 58.

227. Al-Ṭabarī, *The History of al-Ṭabarī, Vol. 28*, 18–44.

228. Al-Ṭabarī, *The History of al-Ṭabarī, Vol. 29*, 17; Lassner, *The Shaping of ʿAbbāsid Rule*, 19–38; Cobb, *White Banners*, 26–27.

Ibrāhīm.[229] The latter's death in battle while marching on Kufa in February 763 marked a new period of stability in al-Manṣūr's caliphate.[230]

During the second part of al-Manṣūr's reign he articulated a more ambitious vision of his position as caliph, which saw him as a more universal monarch. One manifestation of this was the foundation of Baghdad. The site was selected by the caliph in 762 and initial construction completed in 766/767, with al-Manṣūr having already moved in in 763/764.[231] The shape of the Round City and the gates pointing in cardinal directions served to make a claim for cosmological significance, putting himself at the centre of the world.[232] Al-Manṣūr was also interested in the far reaches of the world. As his position at the heart of the empire stabilised, he began a series of initiatives seeking to re-establish the power of the caliphate among its neighbours following the breakdown that had begun in the 740s. The early 760s saw al-Manṣūr arrange an ill-fated marriage alliance between his governor of the Caucasus and the daughter of the ruler of the Khazars.[233] An army was sent in 762 to retake Ifrīqiya from Khārijite Berbers, although the province was only conquered in 772.[234] The caliph extorted tribute from the king of Ferghana.[235] In 768 al-Manṣūr ordered raids on the kings of Sind.[236] A demand sent by the governor of Egypt in 758 that the ruler of the Nubian kingdom of Makuria fulfil his treaty commitments to send slaves to the caliph and protect Muslim merchants probably also fits in with this moment of increased focus on foreign relations.[237] There is also evidence throughout this period for contact with China, although claims that al-Manṣūr sent troops to support the emperor in the midst of the An Lushan rebellion need to be taken with a grain of salt.[238]

This is a wide range of different activities, which is unsurprising given the variations among the states al-Manṣūr was interacting with. The

229. Nagel, "Ein früher Bericht"; Elad, *The Rebellion of Muḥammad al-Nafs*; Munt, "Caliphal Imperialism," 13.

230. Kennedy, *The Early Abbasid Caliphate*, 69.

231. Al-Yaʿqūbī, "The History," 1115; Creswell, *Early Muslim Architecture*, 6–7.

232. Wendell, "Baghdâd: Imago Mundi"; Gutas, *Greek Thought, Arabic Culture*, 28–52.

233. Vacca, *Non-Muslim Provinces*, 99–100; Evans, "The Mobile Court."

234. Al-Ṭabarī, *The History of al-Ṭabarī, Vol. 29*, 67, 69; Kennedy, *The Early Abbasid Caliphate*, 76.

235. Al-Yaʿqūbī, "The History," 1122.

236. Al-Ṭabarī, *The History of al-Ṭabarī, Vol. 29*, 53–56; Wink, *Al-Hind*, 209–210.

237. Hinds and Sakkout, "A Letter from the Governor"; Spaulding, "Medieval Christian Nubia."

238. Chavannes, *Documents sur les Tou-kiue*, 85–86, 88–89, 93. See the doubts of Gibb, "Chinese Records," 618–619. The silence in the secondary literature on al-Manṣūr and An Lushan is probably revealing; see, for example, Beckwith, *The Tibetan Empire*.

Nubians, Khazars, and Franks each needed to be handled on the basis of existing conditions and previous relations. Taken in aggregate, however, they provide a picture of a caliph seeking to reset relations with much of Eurasia and North Africa. Al-Manṣūr's reply to Pippin in 767 took place at a time when the caliph was interested in managing his relations with monarchs beyond the edges of his empire in ways that were visible to his own subjects.

If Pippin and al-Manṣūr were essentially looking for a means to impress their own elites, it would also help explain the long break in Carolingian-ʿAbbāsid diplomacy that followed Pippin's death in 768. Diplomacy was probably not helped by the rivalry between Pippin's sons, Charlemagne and Carloman (r. 768–771).[239] Charlemagne began sending diplomats to the caliphate only in the 790s and al-Manṣūr seems to have made no effort to make contact with Pippin's heirs. The visit of ʿAbbāsid legates in 767 might have inspired Charlemagne's later embassies to Hārūn al-Rashīd, but otherwise the long-term consequences of this diplomacy were to be fairly limited. It even seems to have drifted out of Frankish memory. It is telling that only the *Continuation* to the *Chronicle of Fredegar* refers to the arrival of the ʿAbbāsid ambassadors, an event ignored in the *Annales regni Francorum* and in the *Annales Mettenses priores*, the latter of which is otherwise largely dependent on the *Continuations*.[240] The same cannot be said for the next bout of Carolingian-ʿAbbāsid diplomacy, which would be remembered for a very long time indeed.

## *Charlemagne and Hārūn al-Rashīd*

The first evidence for Charlemagne being interested in ʿAbbāsid affairs appears in a letter sent by Pope Hadrian I, probably in April 781, preserved in the *Codex epistolaris Carolinus*.[241] In it Hadrian draws the king's attention to a campaign by "the Persian nation" against Byzantium, led by "the uncle of the king of the Persians," which reached Amorion, taking a large amount of booty.[242] This is most likely a reference to an expedition sent by Caliph al-Mahdī in 779, which Theophanes reports as unsuccessfully

239. ARF a.768 26; Jarnut, "Ein Brüderkampf und seine Folgen"; Nelson, "Making a Difference."

240. Fouracre, *The Age of Charles Martel*, 78.

241. Hadrian I, *Epistolae* no. 74, 604–605. On the *Codex Epistolaris Carolinus*, see Hack, *Codex Carolinus*; van Espelo, "A Testimony of Carolingian Rule?"; McKitterick et al., *Codex Epistolaris Carolinus*.

242. Hadrian I, *Epistolae* no. 74, "gens Persarum . . . thius regis Persarum," 605.

besieging Amorion.[243] Although the leader of this campaign was Ḥasan b. Qaḥṭabah, the Armenian historian Łewond places al-Mahdī's uncle, the experienced frontier general al-ʿAbbās b. Muḥammad, among their number.[244] While this letter is an interesting indication that Hadrian thought Charlemagne would be interested in the caliphate at this point, it is more instructive as evidence for the limits of Baghdad in Frankish considerations.[245]

If the letter is correctly dated to 781, it suggests a remarkably slow movement of news. Hadrian also spectacularly garbles subsequent events:

> As rumour relates, the uncle of the king of the Persians was the leader and general of their wicked army. When he had returned from an evil victory, puffed up with pride, he betrayed his own nephew and by the same army was made king of Persians. And it is said that within Persia there was tumultuous civil war between supporters of the nephew and those of the uncle.[246]

The pope's sources had dramatically misread the situation in the caliphate, where no such attempted usurpation or civil war was taking place. Al-ʿAbbās b. Muḥammad appears to have remained loyal to his nephew throughout his reign. Hadrian's tone was unsurprisingly hostile towards the Muslim advance. Nothing in the letter suggests any thoughts about sending an embassy to the ʿAbbāsids. Between 781 and 797, when Charlemagne sent his first embassy to Hārūn, something took place in the king's thinking to bring the ʿAbbāsids onto his diplomatic horizons.

There is only one near contemporary source that explicitly provides a motivation for Charlemagne contacting Hārūn al-Rashīd. In the passage of his biography of Charlemagne concerned with foreign diplomacy, Einhard states that Charlemagne "asked him [Hārūn] to send an elephant."[247] Abū al-ʿAbbās's arrival at Aachen was not an example of caliphal whimsy, nor was it the organic result of years of friendly contact. In his very first embassy to Hārūn, the Frankish king deliberately asked for an elephant.

243. Theophanes, *Chronicle*, a.779 624; Brooks, "Byzantium and Arabs," 735n61.

244. Łewond, *History*, 141–142; Al-Ṭabarī, *The History of al-Ṭabarī, Vol. 29*, 206.

245. On the popes as a link between east and west, see Gantner, "The Eighth-Century Papacy."

246. Hadrian I, *Epistolae* no. 74, "Et, sicut audivimus atque fama fertur, thius regis Persarum princeps et dux exercitui nefandissimi ipsorum existebat; qui, dum reversus fuisset cum iniqua victoria, elatus in superbia mentitus est proprio nepto suo et ab eiusdem exercito factus est rex Persarum. Et infra Perse tumultuantes pugnare ad invicem pro nepote et thio dicuntur," 605.

247. Einhard, *Vita Karoli Magni*, c.16 "roganti mitteret elefantum," 19.

This indicates the centrality of public relations to the point of the mission. While unsolicited gifts may be purely a means of securing goodwill with a foreign state, the value of a specifically requested present like the elephant lies in its domestic reception.

Hārūn's distant power no doubt added to the glamour of receiving gifts from him. Charlemagne's decision not to rename Abū al-ʿAbbās speaks to the importance of maintaining his alien, exotic image.[248] It may not be a coincidence that at some point between 800 and 804, Alcuin sent Charlemagne a collection of letters purportedly exchanged between Alexander the Great and Dindimus, king of the Brahmins of India.[249] Although the text is actually a fifth-century composition, Alcuin and Charlemagne could have seen in the correspondence a parallel to the emperor's own communication with a mighty eastern monarch.[250] This would have placed Charlemagne in very exalted company. The Franks may have had particular reason to associate Hārūn's lands with wealth, as Theodulf's reference to "Baghdad loaded with Agarenian goods" suggests, but the prestigious items appear to have made the biggest impact.[251] The composer of the contemporary *Annals of Lorsch* makes no reference to ʿAbbāsid envoys, choosing instead to close an entry for 802 largely concerned with domestic administration and a synod at Aachen with the line "that year also an elephant was brought to Francia."[252]

The *Annals of Lorsch* are striking in their lack of interest in diplomacy, but even the compilers of the *Annales regni Francorum* appear to have been primarily interested in the reception of envoys as political theatre.[253] They are much less terse than the Lorsch Annals and explain the circumstances in which Abū al-ʿAbbās came to Aachen. But if the author of the *Annales regni Francorum* is more verbose, their loquacity is largely focused on the gifts brought by the ambassadors. Abū al-ʿAbbās was the headline act, but the next wave of presents that arrived from Hārūn in 807 were worthy successors, including:

248. Booker, "By Any Other Name?" 420.

249. Alcuin, *Carmen 81*, 300. For the text of the letters, see Steinmann, *Alexander der Grosse*, 126–188. On the gift, see Hen, "Alcuin, Seneca and the Brahmins." For an interesting epitome of Orosius that emphasises material about India, see Evans and McKitterick, "A Carolingian Epitome."

250. Steinmann, *Alexander der Grosse*, 51–81.

251. Theodulf, *De eo quod avarus*, "Bagatat Agarenis rebus onusta," 461, translated by Andersson, *Theodulf of Orléans*, no. 7, 39–40.

252. AL a.802 "Et eo anno pervenit elefans in Francia," 39. On the annal entry, see Innes, "Charlemagne, Justice and Written Law," 158.

253. McKitterick, *History and Memory*, 104.

> a tent and curtains for the canopy made of different colours and of wonderful size and beauty. They were all of the best linen, the curtains as well as the strings, and dyed in different colours. The presents of the king consisted besides of many precious silken robes, of perfumes, ointments, and balsam; also a brass clock, a marvellous mechanical device, in which the course of the twelve hours moved according to a water clock, with as many brazen little balls, which fall down on the hour and through their fall made a cymbal ring underneath. On this clock there were also twelve horsemen who at the end of each hour stepped out of twelve windows, closing the previously open windows by their movements. There were many other things on this clock which are too numerous to describe now. There were moreover, apart from these presents, two brass candlesticks of amazing size and height.[254]

This extract is worth quoting in full for the sheer breathless excitement in the normally taciturn and neutral style of the annalist. Elephant, perfumes, and balsam would all have signalled a world apart from the everyday, even for the Frankish elite. So great a ruler was the emperor of the Franks that he made the Mediterranean vanish, assembling all the treasures of the world under his mantle.

The notices of the *Annales regni Francorum* on diplomacy with the ʿAbbāsids are otherwise extremely brief. For 807, the short lines on the arrival of ʿAbd Allāh and his departure are dwarfed by the extended description of the valuables he brought with him.[255] Rather than deploring the annalist's myopia for ignoring the "real" business of Hārūn's envoy in favour of focussing on earthly trinkets, we should observe that for Charlemagne the gifts were the point.[256] They provided direct physical evidence not just for Charlemagne's prestige but for the esteem in which he was held by a great foreign ruler. It is no accident that Einhard stresses

254. ARF a.807 "id est papilionem et tentoria atrii vario colore facta mirae magnitudinis et pulchritudinis. Erant enim omnia bissina, tam tentoria quam et funes eorum, diversis tincta coloribus. Fuerunt praeterea munera praefati regis pallia sirica multa et preciosa et odores atque unguenta et balsamum; necnon et horologium ex auricalco arte mechanica mirifice conpositum, in quo duodecim horarum cursus ad clepsidram vertebatur, cum totidem aereis pilulis, quae ad completionem horarum decidebant et casu suo subiectum sibi cimbalum tinnire faciebant, additis in eodem eiusdem numeri equitibus, qui per duodecim fenestras completis horis exiebant et inpulsu egressionis suae totidem fenestras, quae prius erant apertae, claudebant; necnon et alia multa erant in ipso horologio, quae nunc enumerare longum est. Fuerunt praeterea inter praedicta munera candelabra duo ex auricalco mirae magnitudinis et proceritatis," 123, adapted from Scholz, *Carolingian Chronicle*, 87.

255. ARF a.807 123.

256. Nelson, "The Settings of the Gift."

the power of Hārūn, "who, excepting India, ruled over almost the whole of the East," or that he emphasized Hārūn's respect for Charlemagne, so that Hārūn "preferred [Charlemagne's] friendship to that of all the kings and princes of the whole world, and judged him alone to be worth decorating with honour and generosity."[257] This glamour and grandeur mattered and had an impact. Notker the Stammerer in the 880s was still illustrating the power and majesty of Charlemagne by telling how "Aaron, the strongest heir of that name, understood from small things the superior power of Charles."[258] During the reign of Arnulf (887–899) the anonymous Poeta Saxo followed suit, celebrating the gifts as the "wonderful spectacle of the kingdom of the Franks."[259]

Charlemagne's determination to be publicly perceived as the caliph's equal can be seen in his eagerness in 807 to respond with equally resplendent presents. In a letter to Arn, Archbishop of Salzburg, Charlemagne mentioned Hārūn's envoys "bringing us a tent, of wonderfully beautiful work."[260] He urged the archbishop to "send to us great gifts, that I may be able to repay" the caliph.[261] Fearing perhaps that Arn might be uncertain what sort of thing would be appropriate, Charlemagne specified, "Send gold, if you can, or cloth, because that seems to be very precious in their country."[262] By involving subordinates such as Arn, Charlemagne pulled them into his prestige diplomacy, making them participants in a spectacle stretching beyond the confines of their normal lives, under the direction of the emperor.

The acquisition of impressive gifts from Hārūn was part of a wider practice in the second half of Charlemagne's reign. As McKitterick has observed, the *Annales regni Francorum* in this period placed great emphasis

257. Einhard, *Vita Karoli Magni*, c.16 "qui excepta India totum poene tenebat orientem talem habuit in amicitia concordiam, ut is gratiam eius omnium, qui in toto orbe terrarum erant, regum ac principum amicitiae praeponeret solumque illum honore ac munificentia sibi colendum iudicaret," 19.

258. Notker, *Gesta Karoli Magni*, II.9 "Quo viso nominis sui fortissimus heres Aaron ex rebus minimis fortiorem Karolum deprehendens," 63.

259. Poeta Saxo, *Annales de gestis Caroli magni*, "mira spectacula regno Francorum," 48. On the Poeta Saxo, see McKitterick, *Charlemagne*, 22–27; Rembold, "The Poeta Saxo at Paderborn."

260. *Formulae Salzburgenses*, "ferentes nobis papilionem, mire pulchritudinis opere contextam," 453. See also Bischoff, *Salzburger Formelbücher*, 34.

261. *Formulae Salzburgenses*, no. 62, "ut nobis ex vestris magnis muneribus mittere dignemini, ut aliquid eos rependere valeamus," 453.

262. Ibid., "Aurum, si valetis, aut pallium mittite, quia in suis provintiis valde hoc pretiosum esse videtur," 453.

on the arrival of diplomats from abroad.[263] As Charlemagne stayed longer in Aachen and led fewer campaigns in person, so the world increasingly was portrayed as coming to him. Jennifer Davis has recently written about a change in Charlemagne's reign from around 790 with "a shift toward active governance."[264] This manifested itself in a new range of more ambitious legislation and a sequence of church synods but also in a new range of written activity plausibly connected to the court, including annals and theological treatises.[265] The Frankish realm was increasingly portrayed as a universal Christian empire in the 790s in this output.[266]

It has sometimes been suggested that Charlemagne's embassy to Hārūn was part of a buildup towards the imperial coronation of 800.[267] Instead it seems more helpful to think of both of them as products of this grander post-790 conception of Charlemagne's role in the reform and government of the peoples of his empire. This was a bold vision which required the participation and support of elites throughout Charlemagne's domains. By reaching out to the caliphate and in particular by acquiring an elephant, the king could make this moment of transformation tangible, a demonstration that something important was happening that would elevate those who participated in the shared project of empire.

One of the biggest challenges in understanding Charlemagne's diplomacy with Hārūn al-Rashīd is the participation of the caliph. Elephants were not common in the caliphate. Crowds formed when a small herd were brought to Basra in the early eighth century.[268] While ivory could be obtained from Africa, domesticated elephants had to be acquired from India.[269] Elephants could only be bred there, something that "foiled all attempts and disappointed all expectations" of courtiers seeking "to win royal favour," and the difficulty of taming them was legendary.[270] The kings of India were not generous with their elephants, and some of them, particularly the Gurjara-Pratīhāras, had reason to be suspicious of the

263. McKitterick, *Charlemagne*, 49–54. See also Nelson, *King and Emperor*, 457.

264. Davis, *Charlemagne's Practice of Empire*, 357.

265. Ibid., 347–373.

266. Phelan, *The Formation of Christian Europe*, 53–55, 79–80; O'Brien, "Empire, Ethnic Election and Exegesis," 107–108.

267. Grabois, "Charlemagne, Rome and Jerusalem." On the coronation, see Collins, "Charlemagne's Imperial Coronation"; Nelson, "Why Are There So Many Different Accounts."

268. Ruska, "*Fīl*," 892.

269. Al-Masʿūdī, *Les Prairies d'Or*, 323. On the medieval trade in elephants in India, see Digby, *War-Horse and Elephant*, 67–70.

270. Al-Masʿūdī, *Les Prairies d'Or*, 327; Trautmann, *Elephants and Kings*, 138–166.

caliphate.[271] While scholars have generally scoffed at Einhard's assertion that Hārūn al-Rashīd sent Charlemagne "the only [elephant] that he had," it is true that the caliphs do not seem to have had many elephants at their disposal.[272] Hārūn's son, al-Muʿtaṣim, seems to have possessed one elephant, a gift from an Indian king, used to parade a captured rebel in 838.[273] Upon the arrival of Byzantine ambassadors in Baghdad in 917/918, they were led past a display of one hundred lions, two giraffes, and four elephants.[274]

At the time that Charlemagne's envoys would have reached Hārūn's court, the caliph's access to any resources in India would have been particularly fragile. The province of Sind, which was the caliphate's window into India for military, diplomatic, or commercial purposes, was in the midst of a civil war. Sind had been settled by different Arab kin groups following the conquests, and their descendants were extremely powerful in the province. It is unclear exactly when, but at some point in the middle of the 790s fighting broke out between the Yemeni faction and the Nizāriyya.[275] Hārūn al-Rashīd sent a series of governors to restore order, but they failed and were defeated in battle by local armies.[276] In 800 a newly appointed governor, Dāwūd b. Yazīd b. Ḥātim al-Muhallabi, succeeded in crushing the Nizāriyya, which he did with the utmost brutality.[277] It took several months and the capture and sack of all the cities of Sind, including the capital, al-Manṣūra. Not only were elephants rare, but at the specific time that the Carolingian envoys arrived in 797 or 798, it was a very real question whether Hārūn would ever have control over Sind, and therefore easy access to India. This means that the caliph was parting with a very scarce resource indeed, one he might potentially never get access to again.

Thus, when Hārūn sent Abū al-ʿAbbās to Charlemagne he was not making a small gift. It therefore follows that contact with the Franks was important to him. As discussed above, there is no reason to suppose that he sought an ally against Córdoba or Constantinople. Instead, like

271. Kauṭilya, *King, Governance, and Law*, XII.1, 394; Wink, *Al-Hind*, 265–268; Ottewill-Soulsby, "Charlemagne's Asian Elephant," 194–196.

272. Einhard, *Vita Karoli Magni*, c.16 "quem tunc solum habebat," 19; Brubaker, "The Elephant and the Ark," 176.

273. Kennedy, "Caliphs and Their Chronicles," 20.

274. *Book of Gifts and Rarities*, 152.

275. Wink, *Al-Hind*, 210.

276. Al-Yaʿqūbī, "The History," 1155.

277. Ibid., 1156.

Charlemagne, the caliph was seeking to use his relations with a distant king to help manage a complex internal political situation by building his image as a strong ruler.

Historical memory has been kind to Hārūn al-Rashīd. Over subsequent centuries his reign was remembered as "the golden prime of good Haroun Alraschid."[278] He features as the generic caliph of the *Thousand and One Nights*, wandering the streets of Baghdad in disguise, righting wrongs (or according to Italo Calvino's reinterpretation, joining plots to assassinate himself).[279] This reading has filtered through to historians of the Carolingians, inclining them to see Hārūn as a powerful, stable ruler. The reality was very different. Hārūn al-Rashīd's position was frequently highly unstable and his regime always open to challenge.

The manner in which Hārūn came to the throne illustrates this point well.[280] Hārūn's father, Caliph Muḥammad al-Mahdī, was succeeded by Hārūn's brother, Mūsā al-Hādī, who seems to have had the support of the generals and most of the court in Baghdad. He reigned for only a year, dying in 786, probably from a stomach ulcer, although it was rumoured that he had been smothered to death by slave girls acting on the orders of his mother, the formidable al-Khayzurān.[281] While the narrative sources try to portray Hārūn's succession as natural, and Hārūn as al-Hādī's appointed heir, in fact, with the support of the army, "Mūsā al-Hādī had deprived al-Rashīd of the succession and had secured their allegiance to his own son Jaʿfar."[282] Hārūn's powerbase was in the west, having been appointed governor of "Armenia, Azerbaijan and the Maghrib" in 780 by al-Mahdī, but he spent much of al-Hādī's reign under arrest in Baghdad, where his only major supporters were his mother, the Barmakid clan of administrators, and some of the western generals.[283] Al-Hādī had begun to replace Hārūn's men in the western provinces before dying.[284]

Hārūn's succession depended on the luck of al-Hādī's early death and the speed and ruthlessness of his partisans in launching a takeover,

278. Tennyson, "Recollections of the Arabian Nights."

279. Gerhardt, *The Art of Story-Telling*, 419–470; Calvino, *If on a Winter's Night*, 251.

280. Kimber, "The Succession to the Caliph"; Marsham, *Rituals of Islamic Monarchy*, 216–219.

281. Al-Ṭabarī, *The History of al-Ṭabarī, Vol. 30*, 41; Al-Masʿūdī, *Les Prairies d'Or*, 51. On al-Khayzurān, see Abbott, *Two Queens of Baghdad*.

282. Al-Ṭabarī, *The History of al-Ṭabarī, Vol. 30*, 46, 96; Kimber, "The Succession to the Caliph," 440.

283. Al-Ṭabarī, *The History of al-Ṭabarī, Vol. 29*, 215; al-Ṭabarī, *The History of al-Ṭabarī, Vol. 30*, 44; al-Masʿūdī, *Les Prairies d'Or*, 62.

284. Bonner, "*Al-Khalīfa al-marḍī*," 88.

stage-managed by al-Khayzurān and Yaḥyā b. Khālid b. Barmak, the head of the Barmakid family. Al-Ṭabarī reports that Hārūn's supporters broke into the young Jaʿfar's rooms and forced him to surrender his claims to succession at sword point.[285] Letters were sent out that night to the provincial governors to announce a fait accompli. The next morning Hārūn al-Rashīd completed the coup by distributing large sums of money to the army in Baghdad.[286] Several of Hārūn's most serious difficulties appear in this story, including the uncertainty of his relationship with the military and his dependence upon the Barmakids for political support.

Hārūn had a troubled relationship with the military establishment throughout his reign. When the ʿAbbāsids seized power in their revolution of 750, their military base had been among Arab soldiers settled in the eastern province of Khurāsān.[287] These Khurāsānis were responsible for defeating the Umayyad armies and they and their descendants (the *abnāʾ*) had been settled in Iraq as a standing army.[288] They continued to be influential in politics, ensuring the succession of al-Manṣūr by defeating the Syrian army of ʿAbd Allāh b. ʿAlī in 754, but the sources indicate that Hārūn could not rely upon their support.[289] He had not been their choice of caliph, and frequently had to buy them off.[290] The generals of the *abnāʾ* had to be negotiated with.[291]

The period also saw frequent revolts and rebellions.[292] Syria was racked with factional strife from 790 to 796 and again in 803 and 807–808.[293] Khārijite revolts broke out in al-Jazīra in 794, 796, 800, and 803. The edges of the empire began to fray, as we have already seen in the case of Ifrīqiya. Hārūn was to die in 809 on campaign against a major rebellion in Khurāsān, which had once been a bulwark of ʿAbbāsid support but had seen uprisings in 795–797, 799–802, and again from 806.[294] His backing in the other major centre of his dynasty's power, Iraq, also appears to have been decidedly shaky, with rebellions in 806 and 807, hence his decision

285. Al-Ṭabarī, *The History of al-Ṭabarī, Vol. 30*, 96.

286. Ibid., 92–94.

287. Daniel, *The Political and Social History of Khurasan*, 157.

288. Lassner, *The Shaping of ʿAbbāsid Rule*, 15–16; Elad, "Aspects of the Transition," 98–99.

289. Omar, "Politics and the Problem of Succession," 68–71; Shaban, *Islamic History*, 30.

290. Kimber, "The Succession to the Caliph," 446.

291. Kennedy, *The Armies of the Caliph*, 99–104.

292. Munt, "Caliphal Imperialism," 17–18.

293. Cobb, *White Banners*.

294. Daniel, *The Political and Social History of Khurasan*, 170–174.

to spend very little time in Baghdad, which he found "intolerable," and to base himself in his later reign in the city of Raqqa.[295]

The caliph responded to the challenges of his reign with a variety of strategies. Patricia Crone characterised the early caliphate as "kingship of a universal type: half brutal power and half theatre."[296] In his responses to the challenges he faced, Hārūn al-Rashīd is better remembered for his use of the former, as demonstrated by his shocking breaking of the Barmakids in 803, or the time he dismembered the brother of a prominent rebel into "a pile of chopped-up limbs."[297] However, his reign can also be seen as a master class in the latter attribute. Hārūn seems to have responded to difficulties through a series of activities that we might call "politics of display," which emphasised the theatrical half of his kingship and were designed to affirm his legitimacy by demonstrating power and indicate his fulfilment of the religious duties of his office.[298] Much of this behaviour was not new to his reign but intensifications of existing practice.[299]

A prime example of this is Hārūn's leadership of the annual pilgrimage to Mecca (*ḥajj*), something he undertook nine times, more than any other caliph in history.[300] On years when Hārūn did not lead the *ḥajj*, one of his close relatives did so and Hārūn's participation seems to have been linked to political affairs. He travelled to Mecca in the year of his accession in 786.[301] In 802, having completed the *ḥajj*, Hārūn chose to unveil his potentially controversial plan for the succession in Mecca, as we shall discuss below.[302] Fighting against the Byzantines intensified under Hārūn.[303] This too played a crucial function for the reign. Unlike previous

295. Al-Ṭabarī, *The History of al-Ṭabarī, Vol. 30*, 103, 173. On Raqqa, see Heidemann and Becker, *Raqqa II*.

296. Crone, *Medieval Islamic Political Thought*, 163.

297. Al-Ṭabarī, *The History of al-Ṭabarī, Vol. 30*, 298.

298. On the role of the caliph, see Al-Azmeh, *Muslim Kingship*, 154–161; Crone, *Medieval Islamic Political Thought*, 12–31, 87–97; Marsham, *Rituals of Islamic Monarchy*, 209–210. For a discussion of the caliph as a figure of religious authority, see Crone and Hinds, *God's Caliph*, 80–96.

299. Blankinship, *The End of the Jihâd State*, 6–7; Bonner, *Aristocratic Violence and Holy War*, 69; Marsham, *Rituals of Islamic Monarchy*, 208.

300. Al-Ṭabarī, *The History of al-Ṭabarī, Vol. 30*, 99, 108, 110, 114, 140, 154, 166, 179, 249. On the *ḥajj*, see Peters, *The Hajj*, 69–71.

301. Al-Ṭabarī, *The History of al-Ṭabarī, Vol. 30*, 99.

302. On the succession, see Gabrieli, "La successione di Hārūn ar-Rašīd"; Kimber, "Hārūn al-Rashīd's Meccan Settlement."

303. For a summary of the raids on Byzantine territory, see Brooks, "Byzantines and Arabs in the Time of the Early Abbasids" and "Byzantines and Arabs in the Time of the Early Abbasids: II."

caliphs, Hārūn regularly commanded the annual summer raid on Byzantine territory or ensured that a close relative, normally a son, brother, or uncle, led it.[304] Among his first actions as caliph was to arrange an administrative reorganisation on the frontier, as he "detached the whole of the Byzantine marches from al-Jazīra and Qinnasrīn, and made them into a single region called *al-ʿawāṣim* (the frontier strongholds)."[305] One of Hārūn's reasons for basing himself in his new capital Raqqa was to be able to more closely supervise the area.[306] While this was partly in order to secure a powerbase outside of Iraq, there was a wider audience for this activity that stretched to the streets of Baghdad.

Hārūn seems to have styled himself as the first *ghāzī*-caliph, dressing while on the frontier as a religious volunteer engaging in *jihād*.[307] The holy frontier warrior-ascetic Muʿāwiya b. ʿAmr noted this with approval, saying "in diligence for warfare and perspicuity in *jihād*, we saw a magnificent thing in the Commander of the Faithful Hārūn."[308] Panegyrics dedicated to Hārūn focus on his exploits against the Rūmī. Marwān b. Abī Ḥafṣa celebrated Hārūn's expedition of 797 thus:

> Through Hārūn, the frontier gaps were closed up, and the rope strands
> Of the Muslim's affairs made secure through him.
> His banner has not ceased to be raised in victory;
> He has an army, from which other armies are shattered into splinters.
> Each of the kings of Rome has paid tribute to him,
> Unwillingly, out of hand constrainedly, in a state of humiliation.[309]

That both pilgrimage and holy war were seen as key parts of the role of the caliph is indicated by the poet Dāwūd b. Rāzin al-Wardī, who portrayed Hārūn as:

> A leader who has ordered his affairs through attention to God's requirements,
> And whose greatest concern is with raiding the infidels and the Pilgrimage.[310]

304. Al-Ṭabarī, *The History of al-Ṭabarī, Vol. 30*, 100, 165, 248, 257, 262.
305. Ibid., 99. See Bonner, "The Naming of the Frontier."
306. Kennedy, *The Early Abbasid Caliphate*, 120.
307. Bonner, *Aristocratic Violence and Holy War*, 99–106.
308. Ibid., 105. On the warrior-ascetics, see Bonner, "Some Observations."
309. Al-Ṭabarī, *The History of al-Ṭabarī, Vol. 30*, 306.
310. Ibid., 100.

Marwān and Dāwūd are representative of this unprecedented focus on the ceremonial aspects of the caliph's role. With these poems Hārūn was building an image designed to secure legitimation.[311]

His overseeing of the pilgrimage and his holy war against the Byzantines helped Hārūn cement an image of himself as a pious ruler and fearsome warrior. But Hārūn also used foreign relations as a means to manage his internal problems. During his reign we can see a wide range of diplomatic activity. The *Old Tang History*, completed in its current form in 945, records Muslim embassies to China.[312] After a flurry of envoys corresponding to the reign of al-Manṣūr nothing is recorded until Hārūn's caliphate, when diplomats arrived in China in 791 and 798.[313] These are the last references until 924, although it is possible the Chinese sources are here deficient. The embassies of the 790s have been linked to a potential ʿAbbāsid-Tang alliance against the Tibetan empire, but there is very little evidence for any military cooperation.[314] The unusual length of the entries in the *History* concerning Hārūn's embassies may indicate that they were particularly elaborate, especially for that of 798, where all three of the ʿAbbāsid envoys were appointed Generals of the Gentlemen-of-the-Household, positions of great honour and a rare distinction.[315]

Perhaps inevitably, Hārūn's most elaborate foreign dealings were with the Byzantines. Byzantium held a unique place in the imagination of the Arabic world, as the caliphate's great rival.[316] The conquest of Constantinople had messianic associations. It was through his diplomacy with the Byzantines that Hārūn acquired his epithet of al-Rashīd, "the Rightly Guided." This was bestowed upon him by his father, al-Mahdī, in 782, following his negotiations with the Empress Regent Irene which secured a truce and annual tribute.[317] This pattern of activity continued into Hārūn's reign. The narrative histories contain unusually lengthy accounts of the caliph's exchange of letters with Nikephoros I.[318]

Hārūn staged carefully managed rituals of power. Following his victory over the Byzantines in 806, Hārūn insisted that Emperor Nikephoros and

311. On ʿAbbāsid panegyric, see Sperl, "Islamic Kingship" and *Mannerism in Arabic Poetry*, 9–27.

312. Hoyland, *Seeing Islam as Others Saw It*, 249–253.

313. Bielenstein, *Diplomacy and Trade*, 359.

314. Beckwith, *The Tibetan Empire*, 152.

315. Bielenstein, *Diplomacy and Trade*, 359.

316. Omar, *Abbāsiyyāt*, 25.

317. Al-Ṭabarī, *The History of al-Ṭabarī, Vol. 29*, 221.

318. Ibid., 239–241.

his son Staurakios personally pay the *jizya* (a tax due from non-Muslims living in Muslim-ruled territory).[319] Writing about this incident, the Byzantine chronicler Theophanes records that the caliph "was pleased and overjoyed, more than he would have been had he received ten thousand talents, because he had subjugated the Roman empire."[320] While this was humiliating for the Byzantines, the true religious significance of this, echoing the Qurʿānic surah 9.29, which enjoins the Believer to fight the People of the Book, including Christians, until they paid *jizya*, was surely aimed at a domestic market.[321] Also celebrated were Hārūn's exchanges of captives with the Byzantines, such as that of 805, which was commemorated in verse.[322]

Throughout his reign, Hārūn took measures to communicate with elites all over the caliphate via public letters. During the brief reign of his brother, Hārūn seem to have sought wider support through the medium of letters distributed to major urban centres.[323] Hārūn is known to have announced his seizure of power in 786 and his succession plan of 802 through the medium of letters sent to provincial governors.[324] Al-Ṭabarī reproduces the letter of 802.[325] Its emphasis on the agreement of the entire Muslim community implies that it was intended for wider consumption than just the governors. The *barīd* postal system allowed for the "conveyance of letters and news from the centre of his kingdom to the outlying provinces."[326] In 838, on the orders of Caliph al-Muʿtaṣim, "*kutub* (letters or books) were written to the main cities" to publicise the capture of the rebel Bābak Khorramdin.[327] Letters like these would offer a mechanism by which Hārūn's diplomacy could be communicated to a wider audience than the court.

The sources suggest a political strategy designed to display Hārūn acting as caliph, with a particular emphasis on managing foreign peoples, either through holy war on specific antagonists or through an exhibition of dominance via exotic diplomacy. But Charlemagne's diplomats also

319. Theophanes, *Chronicle*, 662; al-Ṭabarī, *The History of al-Ṭabarī, Vol. 29*, 70, 221.
320. Theophanes, *Chronicle*, 662.
321. Bonner, *Aristocratic Violence and Holy War*, 68.
322. Al-Ṭabarī, *The History of al-Ṭabarī, Vol. 30*, 251.
323. Ibid., 5.
324. Ibid., 92.
325. Kimber, "Hārūn al-Rashīd's Meccan Settlement"; Marsham, *Rituals of Islamic Monarchy*, 224.
326. Silverstein, *Postal Systems*, 77.
327. Kennedy, "Caliphs and Their Chronicles," 20.

arrived at an opportune time for the caliph. A shift in Hārūn's political management began in 796.[328] The previously dominant Barmakids began to lose influence with members of the family being dismissed from governorships or disgraced.[329] Hārūn seems to have started to favour the generals who had opposed his accession.[330] It was also in 796 that Hārūn moved his residence to Raqqa.

In December 802 Hārūn al-Rashīd led the pilgrimage to Mecca.[331] He was accompanied by the most important figures in the caliphate, and by his sons Muḥammad al-Amīn and ʿAbd Allāh al-Maʾmūn. At Mecca Hārūn published a plan for the succession, in which al-Amīn would be his heir and would in turn be succeeded by al-Maʾmūn.[332] In addition, al-Maʾmūn was to be the governor of the important province of Khurasan, the heartland of ʿAbbāsid military power, protecting his brother's eastern flank. The two sons swore to uphold this in the Kaʿba. The following month, January 803, Hārūn broke with the Barmakids. This is one of the most discussed events in ʿAbbāsid history and quickly acquired almost mythical overtones.[333] Large numbers of stories were assembled to explain Hārūn's motivations for imprisoning and executing his most senior officials, venturing from the plausible—the Barmakids were too rich and powerful—to fanciful, elaborate stories of sex and jealousy.[334] In reality, the downfall of the Barmakids was probably linked to Hārūn's plans for the succession, as he sought to build support for what was an extremely controversial proclamation.

This period of two months was arguably the most important part of Hārūn's reign since his accession. By their very nature succession plans tend to cause trouble by disappointing potential candidates. Hārūn's was unusual in placing a large chunk of the empire within the sphere of someone who was not his first heir. Although the power of the Barmakids had been reduced, they still ran the administration and held several governorships and could cause problems if they were not entirely destroyed. Further in breaking them, Hārūn was removing the family that had been his strongest supporters. There are signs that Hārūn was carefully preparing

328. Kennedy, *The Early Abbasid Caliphate*, 122.

329. Shaban, *Islamic History*, 2:37.

330. Marsham, *Rituals of Islamic Monarchy*, 220.

331. Al-Ṭabarī, *The History of al-Ṭabarī, Vol. 30*, 179–200.

332. Gabrieli, "La successione di Hārūn ar-Rašīd"; Kimber, "Hārūn al-Rashīd's Meccan Settlement."

333. Kennedy, *The Early Abbasid Caliphate*, 127.

334. Al-Ṭabarī, *The History of al-Ṭabarī, Vol. 30*, 201–230.

for this moment. Announcing the succession at Mecca following the *ḥajj* bestowed an aura of sanctity and piety about the plan. Hārūn also readied for his final reckoning with the Barmakids by advancing the careers of their enemies, such as al-Faḍl b. al-Rabīʿ, ʿAlī b. ʿĪsā b. Māhān, and Yazīd b. Mazyan, in the years leading to 803.[335]

This is the context in which Carolingian envoys started coming to the caliphate. The first would have arrived in 797 or 798, just as Hārūn was establishing his new court at Raqqa and distancing himself from the Barmakids. Charlemagne's second embassy probably arrived in 803, shortly after the new succession plan and the downfall of the Barmakids. This was extremely fortuitous timing for Hārūn, providing him with an opportunity to develop Raqqa as a centre and demonstrate his power, wealth, and reputation abroad at a time when he was attempting to do something extremely politically fraught.

This interpretation of Hārūn's relations with Charlemagne gains strength from the only contemporary Arabic references to it.[336] Following Hārūn's death in 809, the precarious succession deal that he had ordained at Mecca in 802 quickly crumbled, leading to war between al-Amīn and al-Maʾmūn. This conflict inspired a large number of apocalyptic writings, among them Christian texts written in Arabic purporting to be the prophecies of an ancient pagan Sibyl.[337] They included a history of events leading up to the civil war, written in the future tense. On the reign of Hārūn al-Rashīd they state:

> Syria and the great city which lies in the east shall be laid waste. A king [Hārūn al-Rashīd] shall reign there for twenty-three years but shall not complete the twenty-fourth. There shall come thither gifts from the islands of the sea, and from the countries of the Franks, since none of these things mentioned will occur in those lands. In his days the country of Syria shall flourish, but shall be ruined upon his decease. He shall leave as his successors two sons, the name of one [al-Amīn] being the same as the name of the one who shall come from the south [Muḥammad].[338]

The geographic focus of the passage suggests a Syrian origin. The account is broadly positive about Hārūn, seeing his reign as a good time for Syria.

335. Kennedy, *The Early Abbasid Caliphate*, 122.

336. Ottewill-Soulsby, "ʿAbbāsid-Carolingian Diplomacy."

337. Madelung, "ʿAbd Allāh b. al-Zubayr and the Mahdī"; El-Hibri, *Reinterpreting Islamic Historiography*; Arjomand, "Islamic Apocalypticism," 248; Yücesoy, *Messianic Beliefs*, 74–78.

338. Schleifer, "Die Erzählung der Sibylle," 33; *Tiburtine Sybil Arab V*, edited by Ebied and Young, "An Unrecorded Arabic Version," 296–297.

The prominence and importance of Frankish gifts in this description are striking. The passage indicates a wider awareness of Hārūn's dealings with Charlemagne than the silence of other Arabic sources might suggest. The emphasis placed on the gifts, which echoes the weight placed upon ʿAbbāsid gifts by the *Annales regni Francorum*, strongly implies that for Hārūn, as for Charlemagne, they were the most significant part of their relations.

Given that these Sibyls were written by Christians in the west of the caliphate, they are not necessarily representative of the entire empire. Because of Charlemagne's support for the church in Palestine, they had particular reason to be aware of the generosity of the Franks. Charlemagne thus probably loomed larger in their imagination than in those of Muslims further east. Nonetheless, writing after Hārūn's death, the composers of the Sibyl in provincial Syria wished to evoke the lost power and splendour of the deceased caliph. That they chose to do so by talking about his relations with Charlemagne suggests that Hārūn's engagement with the Franks mattered for audiences in the caliphate.

## THE ELEPHANT IN THE ROOM

If both Hārūn and Charlemagne were primarily interested in impressing their own domestic elites, the most striking manifestation of their shared purpose was Abū al-ʿAbbās the elephant. It is worth examining his significance further as a case study for the meaning of the spectacular gifts being granted.[339] Elephants came with multiple connotations in both the caliphate and the Frankish world, and that shared import helps explain the role played by Abū al-ʿAbbās in diplomacy between both. Much of the significance of elephants was straightforwardly a product of their strength and size, and having tusks of precious ivory. Alcuin joked in a letter thanking Archbishop Riculf of Mainz for a comb in 794:

> As many thanks as the gift has teeth! It is a wonderful animal with its two heads and sixty teeth, not as large as an elephant but of beautiful ivory.[340]

Writing to Abbot Fardulf of Saint-Denis, Theodulf wryly declared, "When trivial things are to be said, they have a grand preface / Then, great elephant, you give birth to a small mouse."[341]

339. See also the excellent analysis of Cobb, "*Coronidis Loco*," 62–70.

340. Alcuin, *Epistolae* no. 26, "tot agens gratias quot dentes in dono numeravi. Mirum animal duo habens capita et dentes LX non elefantinae magnitudinis sed eburneae pulchritudinis," 67. On the letter and accompanying riddle, see Sorrell, "Alcuin's 'Comb' Riddle."

341. Theodulf of Orléans, *Delusa expectatio*, no. 33, "Grande habet initium cum res vilissima dictu, Tunc gignis murem, magne elephante, brevem," 525, translated by Andersson, *Theodulf of Orléans*, 118.

Mare mundus est. Naues scā eccla in quibus sunt
populi dī. hic aūt piscis diabolus est qui transfigu
rat se uelut in angelo lucis ut incautas animas
facilius possit decipere.
DE ELIFANTO ET MANDRACORA
Non est coitus concupiscentiae quando uoluerint
facere iunctionem ambulant sup flumen para
disi & inueniunt mandracoram qui & cū femina
discurrit. Accipiens uero femina mandracora
praestat masculo & ludit cum eo donec manduc&
Et cum manducauerit masculus conuenit cum

FIGURE 3.1. Bern Physiologus, *Elephant*, Burgerbibliothek Bern, Cod. 318, fol. 19r. Photo: Codices Electronici AG.

Elephants also had royal connotations for both rulers. Elephants featured on the monumental relics of the pre-Islamic royal past, including the enormous rock relief raised by Khusrow II (r. 590–628) at Taq-i Bustan showing the Shahanshah hunting boar with the aid of elephants.[342] Khusrow was a familiar figure in accounts of Persian history composed in the Islamic period. Although highly ambiguous, associated with false pride and preening arrogance, he was also redolent of the magnificence of the kings of old.[343] Al-Masʿūdī wrote that Khusrow "had a thousand elephants whiter than the snow, some of them twelve cubits high, which is very rare among elephants of war, for their tallest size varies between nine and ten cubits."[344] He adds that Khusrow preferred them to all other animals on account of their intelligence and training.[345] Elephants appear as kings in the *Kalīla wa-Dimna* of Ibn al-Muqaffaʿ (d. 756/759), a translation from Pahlavi of a collection of originally Sanskrit fables.[346] Although Ibn al-Muqaffaʿ was executed on the orders of al-Manṣūr, his stories remained popular and Hārūn al-Rashīd is known to have praised a versification of these fables.[347] Caliph al-Manṣūr is himself described as having possessed elephants "because the old kings made much of them, buying them, taking them to war and making an ornament of them in their ceremonies."[348]

The association between elephants and royalty was explored by al-Jāḥiẓ. In his *Kitāb al-Hayawān* (*Book of Animals*) he described the elephant's "reluctance to have as master a man of low condition, to be bought by ordinary people of little nobility, or to be sold cheaply."[349] To be able to control or manage an elephant was therefore a sign of the owner's exalted status. Al-Masʿūdī notes among the many virtues of the elephant its unique ability to "distinguish a king from his entourage."[350] Caliphal responsibility for the disposition of elephants is indicated by the story recounted by al-Balādhurī of the conquest of Ctesiphon, where the victorious Muslims wrote to Caliph ʿUmar I (r. 634–644) asking what to do with the elephant

342. Movassat, *The Large Vault at Taq-i Bustan*, 86–89; Canepa, *The Two Eyes of the Earth*, 157. On the wider significance of the elephant in Sasanian Iran, see Daryaee, "From Terror to Tactical Usage."

343. Anderson, *Cosmos and Community*, 22–25.

344. Al-Masʿūdī, *Les Prairies d'Or*, 243.

345. Ibid., 244.

346. London, "How to Do Things with Fables." On the Persian tradition of Mirrors for Princes, see Arjomand, "Perso-Islamicate Political Ethic"; Ibn al-Muqaffaʿ, *Kalila et Dimna*.

347. Bosworth, "The Persian Impact on Arabic Literature," 490.

348. Al-Masʿūdī, *Les Prairies d'Or*, 326.

349. Ibid., 327.

350. Ibid., 244.

they had captured.[351] Al-Ṭabarī has a similar account of the taking of Makran in Balochistan in 644, when the commanding general, al-Ḥakam b. ʿAmr, wrote to ʿUmar "asking instruction concerning the elephants" he had captured.[352]

The elephant as symbol of kingship would have been as familiar in Aachen as it was in Raqqa. Hrabanus Maurus offered a biblical precedent for kings receiving elephants in his *De rerum naturis*, saying that in "the Book of Kings, monkeys and elephants were brought to Solomon."[353] This is not strictly accurate, with the relevant Bible verse, 1 Kings 10:22, saying that Solomon received "ivory and apes." As Hrabanus was the author of a celebrated *Commentary on Kings*, given to Louis the Pious in 832, which makes much of the significance of the ivory, this discrepancy is interesting.[354] Hrabanus had been a pupil of Alcuin at Tours from 801 to 803, the time when Abū al-ʿAbbās arrived in Aachen. When Hrabanus wrote of Solomon receiving elephants from a great foreign ruler, he may have had Charlemagne in mind.[355] Over a decade earlier, Hrabanus's student Walahfrid Strabo (d. 849) had made a similar connection in his *De imagine Tetrici*, written for Louis the Pious in 829.[356] Walahfrid compared Louis to Solomon and declared that elephants would come to obey him. As this indicates Abū al-ʿAbbās was an explicitly royal gift, with connotations of ancient kingship. The elephant was the sort of animal that monarchs controlled, elevating them above the normal run of men.

The particular context of the civil war in Sind added extra meaning to the gift for Hārūn al-Rashīd. Elephants do not move all that quickly. Given that Abū al-ʿAbbās and company arrived in North Africa early in 801, that balance of probability is that Hārūn sent him before Sind was back under his control. His doing so might then be interpreted as a statement of confidence in his ability to reconquer Sind, because he was willing to give away an elephant he might not be able to replace. In the less likely possibility that Hārūn sent Abū al-ʿAbbās after the rebels had been crushed, he might have been a symbol of victory, possibly captured in

351. Al-Balādhurī, *The Origins of the Islamic State*, 1:446–447.

352. Al-Ṭabarī, *The History of al-Ṭabarī, Vol. 14*, 77.

353. Hrabanus Maurus, *De rerum naturis*, "Unde scriptum est in libro Regum, quod adducerentur ad Salomonem simiae et elephanti," col. 222.

354. Hrabanus Maurus, *Commentaria in libros IV Regum*, col. 196; de Jong, "Carolingian Political Discourse," 92.

355. On the importance of Solomon as a model for early medieval kingship, see Kershaw, *Peaceful Kings*.

356. Walahfrid Strabo, "The 'De imagine Tetrici,'" 126.

battle in Sind itself. In this way, the caliph communicated what happened to his enemies.

If Abū al-ʿAbbās was plunder from the defeated rebels in Sind, then Hārūn sending him to Charlemagne to impress upon the Frankish king the power of his military and the wide reach of his ambitions would make an interesting parallel with the Carolingian ruler's own activities. Charlemagne's destruction of the kingdom of the Avars had produced vast quantities of treasure, some of which he sent to the kings of Northumbria and Mercia in 796.[357] Gold from the Avar hoard may also have been among the gifts taken by the envoys he sent to the caliphate in 797.[358] It would point to the commonalities between Hārūn's and Charlemagne's styles of rulership if both sent booty from victories won in the east to overawe smaller polities to the west, while also reminding us of the much larger scale on which the ʿAbbāsid caliph operated.

It mattered that Abū al-ʿAbbās meant the same things to both Charlemagne and Hārūn. Zoological presents could be the cause of misunderstanding. Notker the Stammerer writes that Charlemagne sent Hārūn dogs of "unusual quickness and ferocity."[359] The caliph was impressed by the prowess of these hounds at hunting lions, speaking at length of Charlemagne's hunting skills as personified by the dogs. Notker's readers would have spotted the humour in this account, for in the story preceding this one Charlemagne was nearly killed charging an aurochs with a sword and had to be rescued by his retinue.[360] The gift of animals led to potential miscommunications, particularly between rulers from very different worlds.

Abū al-ʿAbbās offered no such difficulties. When Charlemagne sent an embassy to Hārūn al-Rashīd to ask for an elephant, he was bringing their empires together in many ways. This mission marked the resumption of contact between the Carolingians and the caliphate. But the elephant also represented a nexus of mutual understanding. Charlemagne and Hārūn ruled very different realms and came from very different cultural backgrounds. In Abū al-ʿAbbās they had a point of common meaning, an animal whose significance was understood by both participants.

357. Alcuin, *Epistolae* no. 100, 146, no. 101, 147; Story, *Carolingian Connections*, 101–104. On the Avars, see Pohl, *Die Awaren*. On booty in the Carolingian world, see Reuter, "Plunder and Tribute."

358. Charlemagne mentions the caliphate's fondness for gold in a letter to Arn of Salzburg in 807, *Formulae Salzburgenses*, no. 62, 453.

359. Notker, *Gesta Karoli Magni*, II.8 "quoque agilitate et ferocia singulares," 63.

360. Ibid., II.8 60; Ganz, "Humour as History."

## *The End of Carolingian Diplomacy with the ʿAbbāsid Caliphs (831)*

Charlemagne may have sent another embassy to Hārūn al-Rashīd following the return of his envoys in 807. The letter sent to Archbishop Arn of Salzburg in 807 in which the emperor discusses the presents sent to him by Hārūn with the second embassy indicates that Charlemagne was collecting gold and cloth to present to the caliph.[361] Charlemagne remained in contact with Jerusalem, with two envoys, Agamus and Roculf, being sent to Jerusalem in 808.[362] That their mission was not particularly successful is suggested by Leo III's letter to Charlemagne begging him to "show mercy" to his "faithful servants, Agamus and Roculf," although the exact details of what happened are not known.[363] It is not impossible that the unlucky pair were also meant to visit Hārūn al-Rashīd, although their primary purpose was Christological debate. This focus is made stronger if, as McCormick argues, it was indeed this expedition that put together the *Survey of the Holy Land* for Charlemagne.[364]

Whether or not Agamus and Roculf had been meant to go to Raqqa, the absence of any reference to further diplomacy in the Frankish annals suggests that any efforts made by Charlemagne to continue relations after 807 were unrewarded. Given the evidence for continued Frankish interest, this suggests that obstacles arose from the ʿAbbāsid side. Much would depend on the timing of any Carolingian embassy. The pattern of previous missions suggests that the envoys would probably have travelled at the same time as the returning ʿAbbāsid diplomats in 808.[365] If that is the case they might have struggled to reach Hārūn, who was concerned by a rebellion in Khurasan that year, travelling from Raqqa to Baghdad in February and then heading from Baghdad in June.[366] He never returned, dying in Ṭus in March 809. Any Frankish diplomats kicking their heels in the capital would then have become an irritating distraction in the subsequent political confusion, as the caliphate was divided between Hārūn's sons. If said hypothetical envoys were quickly sent packing without suitable

361. *Formulae Salzburgenses* no. 62, 453.

362. Leo III, *Epistolae* no. 8, 66–67.

363. Ibid., "fideles servientes vestri, Agamus videlicet et Roculphus . . . misericordiam facere," 67.

364. McCormick, *Charlemagne's Survey*, 171–175.

365. ARF a.807 123.

366. Al-Ṭabarī, *The History of al-Ṭabarī, Vol. 30*, 291, 297.

presents they would be unlikely to appear in the annals. This would also have discouraged Charlemagne from sending further envoys.

A long gap in communication between the Carolingians and the ʿAbbāsids followed the contact between Charlemagne and Hārūn. The next, and final, evidence for contact comes in 831, when envoys from Caliph al-Maʿmūn attended an assembly held by Louis the Pious at Thionville.[367] The long silence from the ʿAbbāsids is easily explained. Hārūn's death in 809 prompted a long civil war between his sons, the Fourth *fitna*. Although al-Maʿmūn had defeated his brother, Muḥammad al-Amīn, by 813, much of the caliphate remained in turmoil from the breakdown of ʿAbbāsid control, exacerbated by al-Maʿmūn's decision to try to rule from Marv in the east, taking up residence in Iraq only in 819.[368] His control was particularly precarious in the west, with Syria only being cleared of Umayyad pretenders and rebel tribal chiefs in 826 and Egypt needing campaigns in 825 and 832 to be made to acknowledge Baghdad's authority.[369] Sending envoys across the Mediterranean was probably not feasible prior to the early 830s.

The *Annals of St-Bertin* make it very clear that the initiative in the expedition of 831 originated from Baghdad. Al-Maʿmūn was probably inspired to revive ʿAbbāsid interest in Carolingian affairs in 831 by similar motivations to those of his father. Distinct similarities can be observed in al-Maʿmūn's style of rulership to that of Hārūn's, including intense raiding of Byzantine territory and diplomacy with foreign rulers such as the emperor of the Indian Pala empire, the kings of Tibet and Kabul, and the khan of the Volga Bulgars.[370] These communications were couched in missionary terms, echoing *ḥadīth* concerning the messages Muḥammad sent Heraclius and Khusrow II, calling on them to convert.[371] Al-Maʿmūn's embassy to Louis in 831 coincides with the revival of the grand annual summer expeditions against Byzantium in 830 for the first time since 807.[372]

Al-Maʿmūn's talent for caliphal theatre is indicated by his claiming credit for the Dome of the Rock, replacing the name of the Umayyad caliph responsible, ʿAbd al-Malik, with his own. In a further display of

367. AB a.831 "ibique ad eum legati amiralmumminin de Perside venientes, pacem petiverunt. Quam mox impetrata, reversi sunt," 4.

368. Al-Ṭabarī, *The History of al-Ṭabarī, Vol. 32*, 204. See Gabrieli, "La successione di Hārūn ar-Rašīd."

369. Al-Ṭabarī, *The History of al-Ṭabarī, Vol. 32*, 164–165, 175, 191; Cobb, *White Banners*.

370. Dunlop, "A Diplomatic Exchange"; Yücesoy, *Messianic Beliefs*, 107–110.

371. Fowden, *Quṣayr ʿAmra*, 225.

372. Al-Ṭabarī, *The History of al-Ṭabarī, Vol. 30*, 290.

universal rulership, he commissioned the earliest known Arabic map of the world, *al-ṣūrat al-maʿmūniyya*.[373] The map does not survive, but the accounts of those who saw it suggest that it represented a blending of Greek and Persian knowledge.[374] Like Hārūn al-Rashīd, al-Maʿmūn needed to legitimate his rule and seems to have done so in part through displays of contact with and dominance of foreign rulers. Following his death, the accession in 833 of his brother, Abū Isḥāq al-Muʿtaṣim, initiated a revolution in caliphal authority.[375] While elements of previous styles of governance remained, such as an emphasis on war with the Byzantines, al-Muʿtaṣim and his heirs seem to have engaged in much less foreign diplomacy, relying instead on a professional army of Turkish slave soldiers to secure power.[376] Part of the explanation for the absence of any further evidence for diplomacy with the Franks after 831 may therefore be the changed political strategies on the ʿAbbāsid end.

ʿAbbāsid-Carolingian contact can be understood as prestige diplomacy. While Carolingian interest in the Holy Land may have acted as an incentive, the most important explanation of these diplomatic relations is that it was done to enhance the standing of the participants. For both the caliphs and the Carolingians, the key purpose of the envoys they sent each other was to secure their position as ruler in the eyes of their elite subjects. This was achieved first by the opportunity this communication provided for the monarchs in question to perform their role as ruler in dispatching and receiving ambassadors to and from distant lands. This demonstrated the respect and renown of the prince and their court far overseas. Second, the receiving of expensive and exotic gifts further cemented the splendour of the ruler. In their communication, kings and caliphs could elevate themselves into a shared category apart from other men.

This made diplomacy between the Franks and the ʿAbbāsids an expensive luxury with a noted track record of being fatal to the envoys involved. This explains the short-lived nature of these relations. The Patriarch of Jerusalem played a much more important role in the Frankish imagination than the king of the Persians. Contact between Aachen and Raqqa was optional. The next chapters will consider a longer-lasting and more politically significant relationship between the Carolingians and a Muslim dynasty, one in which diplomatic engagement was a necessity rather than a choice.

373. Tibbetts, "The Beginnings of a Cartographic Tradition," 95.
374. Ahmad, "Kharīṭa," 1078.
375. Kennedy, *The Prophet and the Age of the Caliphates*, 136.
376. Gordon, *The Breaking of a Thousand Swords*.

CHAPTER FOUR

# Carolingian-Umayyad Diplomacy

## PART 1: 751–820

IN HIS *REBUS DE HISPANIE*, completed in the mid-thirteenth century, the Archbishop of Toledo Rodrigo Jiménez de Rada complained:

> Not a few performers bear fables of [Charlemagne] having conquered towns and castles in the kingdoms of Spain, and having vigorously fought many battles with the Arabs and having established the pilgrimage road on the best path from Germany and Gaul to Santiago.[1]

The stories alluded to here by the archbishop would have been familiar to European audiences from twelfth-century epics such as the *Chanson de Roland*, *Pseudo-Turpin*, and the *Rolandslied*.[2] In these immensely popular accounts Charlemagne defeated Saracen armies, liberated Compostela, and conquered all of Spain. As this suggests, their historical accuracy was not always equal to their literary quality, something that incensed Jiménez de Rada. The archbishop had participated in the hard-fought battle at Las Navas de Tolosa in 1212 and not unreasonably felt that the continued existence of Muslim states in the Iberian Peninsula in his own day rather argued against claims that Charlemagne had driven the Saracens

1. Jiménez de Rada, *De rebus Hispanie*, "Non nulli histrionum fabulis inherentes ferunt Carolum civitates plurimas, castea et oppida in Hispaniis acquisisse multaque prelia cum Arabibus strenue perpetrasse et stratam publicam a Gallis et Germania ad Sanctum Jacobum recto itinere direxisse," 128, translation from Dolan Gómez, "*Rex Parvus* and *Rex Nobilis*?" 103–104.

2. Stuckey, "Charlemagne as Crusader?"

from Spain.[3] Unlike those of Jiménez de Rada's day, modern scholars have not taken *Pseudo-Turpin* or the *Chansons de geste* seriously as historical sources for Charlemagne's campaigns for centuries, and rightly so.[4] These accounts were fantastical in nature and shaped by contemporary politics.[5] But by associating the Frankish ruler above all with the Iberian Peninsula, the twelfth-century writers and singers of epics did perceive something important, that both the Carolingian empire and Umayyad al-Andalus were shaped by their relationship with each other.

This is something that is not often recognised in modern scholarship.[6] The histories of Carolingian Europe and the Iberian Peninsula as they are currently written rarely impinge upon each other. With the exception of Charlemagne's disastrous invasion of 778, the two great powers of Western Europe in the eighth and ninth centuries are treated entirely separately.[7] Muslim Spain has generally been seen as exceptional.[8] In part this reflects the different languages and types of sources that start appearing after that magic 711 date. But it also reflects a state of mind among historians in which the Arab Conquest serves to detach the Iberian Peninsula from the rest of Europe.

Part of the difficulty is the nature of the sources. Umayyad interest in the Franks is hard to identify. The main Arabic chroniclers of al-Andalus were highly focussed on internal affairs in Córdoba, with the marches rarely receiving much attention, much less the lands beyond.[9] Frankish writers had more to say about foreign peoples but could be reticent about communicating bad news. The *Annales regni Francorum* make no mention of the ambush at Roncesvalles in 778, and it was left to the later Reviser to fill in details about the disaster.[10] The Astronomer only briefly alludes to the affair.[11] But the misadventure was a defining moment of Charlemagne's reign. The Astronomer observes that names of the fallen were still well known in his day.[12] The Revised *Annales regni Francorum* say that "to have suffered this wound shadowed the king's view of his

3. Jiménez de Rada, *De rebus Hispanie*, 130. On the particular representation of Charlemagne in medieval Spain, see Bailey and Giles, *Charlemagne and His Legend.*

4. Morrissey, *Charlemagne and France*, 112–117.

5. For a fine example, see Doolittle, "Charlemagne in Girona."

6. For a recent, very useful, exception, see Chandler, *Carolingian Catalonia.*

7. Burns, "Muslim-Christian Conflict," 238.

8. Linehan, *History and the Historians*, 4; Bonch Reeves, *Visions of Unity*, 37–41.

9. Manzano Moreno, *La Frontera de al-Andalus*, 14.

10. ARF, Revised ARF a.778 51.

11. Astronomer, *Vita Hludowici*, c.2 288.

12. Ibid.

success in Spain."[13] Einhard speaks of the lingering frustration suffered by the Franks because of their inability to avenge themselves on the Basques.[14] As this indicates, events that mattered greatly could be downplayed by our sources. Roncesvalles was a fiasco, but it did not end Charlemagne's involvement with Spain. Even as his court was adorned by Gothic scholars such as Theodulf of Orléans, the advent of Adoptionism among Iberian Christians prompted a major campaign by figures such as Alcuin to prevent the spread of the heresy in Carolingian territory.[15] Writers from the reign of Charlemagne's son, such as Ermold the Black and the Astronomer, placed great emphasis on Louis the Pious's time on the Spanish March as an important part of his career.[16]

It is the relationship between the Carolingians and the Muslims of Spain that the next two chapters will explore. They will argue that this was one of the most important diplomatic engagements that both dynasties involved themselves in, because it was one of the few that either participated in with a near equal. The Carolingians and the Umayyads were used to dominating their immediate neighbours. Following the destruction of the Avar Ring in 796 there were very few powers that could plausibly threaten or stand against the Franks. Even Constantinople treated Aachen with caution. The Franks found in Umayyad Spain a power that could not be swiftly conquered like the Lombards and Avars, or even slowly occupied like the Saxons. More alarmingly, the Muslims of al-Andalus could launch their own expeditions into Frankish territory if not carefully managed. Likewise, although it could not make its writ run throughout the entire peninsula, Córdoba was the dominant power in Iberia, with rivals such as the kingdom of Asturias existing on the margins. But in the Carolingians the Umayyads encountered a neighbour of a completely different fighting weight, one that could mobilise vast resources from across half a continent, with ambitions to expand into Spain.

The result was a century in which two great powers faced each other over the Pyrenees, representing to each other both an opportunity for expansion and plunder on the one hand and a very real danger on the other. This had important consequences for both the Carolingians and the

13. Revised ARF a.778 "Cuius vulneris accepti dolor magnam partem rerum feliciter in Hispania gestarum in corde regis obnubilavit," 51, translated by Scholz, *Carolingian Chronicles*, 56.

14. Einhard, *Vita Karoli Magni*, c.9 12–13.

15. Fontaine, "Mozarabie Hispanique"; Cavadini, *The Last Christology of the West*; Chandler, "Heresy and Empire"; Kramer, "Adopt, Adapt and Improve."

16. Ermold the Black, *In honorem Hludovici*, Bk. 1, 8–51; Astronomer, *Vita Hludowici*, cc.4–19 294–340.

Umayyads. No matter what other business was going on in their respective realms, the two dynasties had to keep a cautious eye on their most powerful neighbour.[17] Diplomacy was an essential tool for managing this crucial frontier and appeared in two forms. The first, which was between the monarchs in question, generally aimed to create conditions of peace, ending an ongoing war between the Franks and Andalusis or heading off hostilities when they were likely to break out. The second type of diplomacy was the building of relationships with enemies of the opposing dynasty. The Carolingians and the Umayyads were adept at making alliances with discontented figures in the other realm. Frequently these were border lords on either side of the frontier, embedded far from the heartlands of Carolingian and Umayyad power. Religious dissidents were also employed by both sides. In times of peace these arrangements could offer intelligence and undermine a dangerous neighbour. During wartime, frontier lords on the other side of the border could be induced to provide military support.

This was a very different sort of diplomatic relationship from the one between Aachen and Raqqa. While the Carolingians and the Umayyads undoubtedly did accrue domestic prestige as a result of diplomatic relations, this was not the primary purpose for these relations taking place. Managing these relations was not optional for either power and resulted in a more continuous form of contact, as both dynasties remained constantly alert for opportunities and threats.

Previous treatments of this diplomacy naturally focussed very tightly on the embassies and treaties themselves.[18] What follows seeks to place Carolingian relations with the Muslims of Spain within their wider context. This involves investigating the way that war shaped dealings between Franks and Andalusis. It is also necessary to examine how the nature of the frontier defined the actions of the great powers. Emperors and emirs often responded to headaches and opportunities that emerged from the sometimes volatile politics of the Carolingian Spanish March and the Umayyad Upper March, forcing monarchs to take action even if they did not want to. Events rarely lined up neatly for the rulers of either realm and their freedom of manoeuvre was often constrained by issues many miles away from the frontier. The true significance of diplomacy between al-Andalus and the Franks appears much more clearly on this larger canvas.

17. König, "Charlemagne's *Jihād* Revisited," 18–27.
18. See especially here Sénac, *Les Carolingiens et al-Andalus*.

The scale of this picture necessitates that it be split into two chapters. While the dynamics sketched above were constant throughout the century studied, two periods can be usefully identified, related to the rough balance of power between the Franks and Córdoba. The second of these begins in the 820s, when internal conflict, civil war, and the division of the Carolingian empire ensured that the equilibrium tilted in a manner which favoured the Umayyads. This chapter examines the period before that point; when despite disasters and defeats in Spain such as Roncesvalles in 778 and 824 and Orbieu in 793, the Carolingians generally held the initiative in both war and peace. The Franks nearly always began military conflicts, seeking to seize cities in Spain, forcing the Umayyads on the defensive. From 796, Carolingian armies launched the most intensive attempt to make major territorial gains in the Iberian Peninsula. The eventual failure of most of these efforts and growing difficulties in the Spanish March led to a fragile stalemate in the 810s, punctuated by repeated outbreaks of war. This period of Frankish expansion and ambition is the subject of what follows.

## *The Frontier*

Any treatment of relations between al-Andalus and the Franks demands that we consider the frontier. The region where the two polities met was a constantly shifting one, divided between the Carolingian Spanish March (*Marca Hispanica*) and the Umayyad Upper March (*al-thaghr al-aʿlā*).[19] At their maximum extent, between them they covered the territory between the Ebro river valley and the Pyrenees, but this was a neighbourhood resistant to firm lines. Despite the best efforts of Aachen and Córdoba to control policy, they were reliant on figures from the frontier zone for information and aid in communications. Emperors and emirs were frequently forced to play catch up to developments from this febrile region, which offered both chances and challenges. Powerful lords felt no hesitation in making their own deals with their opposite numbers, as well as conducting negotiations with monarchs on the other side of the frontier.

The concept of the frontier has been embraced by scholars of the medieval Iberian Peninsula with such fervour that any attempt to summarise it is doomed to fail.[20] The formidable body of work that has appeared

19. Bosch Vilá, "Considerations with Respect."

20. See amongst the most important, McCrank, "The Cistercians of Poblet"; Manzano Moreno, "Christian-Muslim Frontier in al-Andalus"; Power, "Frontiers: Terms, Concepts"; Linehan, "At the Spanish Frontier"; Christys, "Crossing the Frontier."

does make it necessary to clarify in what sense the area we are concerned with was a frontier. This was not a frontier in the Turnerian sense of an expanding zone transforming the landscape, although the cores of both al-Andalus and Francia were influenced by developments on the frontier.[21] Nor, although new people did settle in the region, was it an empty zone in need of repopulation like Sánchez-Albornoz's Douro valley.[22] Although it was a space where cultural contact took place, it was a frontier that acted to divide rather than connect. A pre-existing population of Basques and Goths found themselves separated by new borders, with their elites adapting to the political and cultural mores that pertained on their side.

The edges of the Carolingian world varied depending on where and when one looks. In some places it could be a clearly defined line, such as those attempted between Louis the Pious and the Bulgar Khan Omurtag (r. 814–831) between 825 and 826.[23] Elsewhere, natural features such as rivers could be fortified.[24] Carolingian rulers often sought to establish a circle of tribute paying client states to stabilise their frontiers, with Charlemagne moving the Abodrites to create a buffer against the Danish kingdom.[25] The idea of a march, as a militarised zone intended to control movement at the borders, appeared in Lombard Italy in the middle of the eighth century.[26] While much of the formal terminology of the march first showed up in Carolingian sources in the late eighth and early ninth centuries, there are hints that the concept was familiar earlier.[27] From the early 780s the Frankish king was organising the area that faced onto al-Andalus into a distinctive region that became the Spanish March.

The land borders of al-Andalus were somewhat less diverse. Stretching across the Iberian Peninsula from west to east, they consisted of the Lower March and the Central March, which were both between the Tagus and the Douro, and the Upper March.[28] This last March was distinctive in a number of ways. It was the northernmost of the marches, being based on the Ebro river valley, making it the most distant from Córdoba.[29] It was also much closer to a powerful and potentially hostile neighbour than the other marches, which meant that the classic Umayyad strategy of

21. Burns, "The Significance of the Frontier," 307.

22. Sánchez-Albornoz, *Despoblación y Repoblación.*

23. ARF a.825 167; ARF a.826 168.

24. Hardt, "Hesse, Elbe, Saale."

25. Smith, "Fines Imperii," 171; Melleno, "Between Borders."

26. Pohl, "Frontiers in Lombard Italy."

27. Wolfram, "The Creation of the Carolingian Frontier-System," 233–239.

28. Bosch Vilá, "Considerations with Respect," 380; Collins, *Caliphs and Kings*, 27.

29. Collins, *Arab Conquest of Spain*, 156.

controlling faraway territories by levelling walls and defortifying settlements had to be limited.[30]

The Upper March and the Spanish March resembled each other closely. Both acted as defensive zones and launchpads for military expeditions. The former was a prosperous region, centred on the fertile agricultural land of the Ebro river valley.[31] Although some ancient cities, such as Tarragona, had declined dramatically in size, it remained densely populated and urbanised, with considerable surviving Roman infrastructure.[32] The Spanish March was less wealthy and had fewer cities and people, although that slowly changed as the March expanded with the acquisition of cities such as Girona and Barcelona. Carolingian charters suggest the existence of wasteland that was being settled by migrants from elsewhere, most notably Hispani from the Iberian Peninsula.[33] The development of fortifications and monasteries suggests a landscape that was changing over the course of the late eighth and ninth centuries.[34] There is little evidence for a no-man's-land between the two marches. The centres of power in both were close to each other. Both were organised around walled cities and fortresses, creating a network of nodes that travellers moved between rather than a line that was crossed.

The two marches were also multiethnic zones. Goths and Basques were prominent across both marches.[35] To these were added settlers from the imperial core, including Franks, Arabs, and Berbers.[36] At different times in its history, the Spanish March included, among other places, Basque Pamplona in the west, the county of Aragon in the centre, and Girona and Barcelona in the east. Control over the latter two cities was normally assigned to one count, who could become the dominant figure in the coastal area. The Upper March was similarly complex. Among the powers in the land there were descendants of elite Arab settlers. These families were the dominant forces in the area before ʿAbd al-Raḥmān I conquered the region at the start of the 780s and it was from their ranks

30. Collins, *Caliphs and Kings*, 42.

31. Glick, *Islamic and Christian Spain*, 58.

32. Macias Solé, "Tarracona visigoda"; Pérez Martínez, *Tarraco en la Antigüedad Tardía*.

33. Chandler, "Between Court and Counts"; Jarrett, "Settling the King's Lands"; Haack and Kohl, "Teudefred and the King," 229–235.

34. Astronomer, *Vita Hludowici*, c.8; Ollich i Castanyer, Rocafiguera Espona, and Ocaña Subirana, "The Southern Carolingian Frontier"; Ollich i Castanyer, "Vic: La ciutat"; CC 2.ii, 260–262; CC 3, 20–35; Chandler, *Carolingian Catalonia*, 86–88.

35. Chandler, *Carolingian Catalonia*, 17, 56–57.

36. Zimmermann, "Western Francia," 425; Collins, *Arab Conquest of Spain*, 120.

that the envoys who invited Charlemagne to invade al-Andalus in 777 were drawn.[37] After the Umayyad takeover, Arab families such as the Banū Salama and the Banū Tujib retained considerable influence in the area. Muslim converts of Basque or Gothic extraction became increasingly important over the ninth century. Most famous were the Banū Qāsī, who claimed descent from a fictional Visigothic count.[38] These families were capable of raising armies on their own.

Controlling this landscape was hard. The Umayyads rarely had much of a direct presence in the Upper March, with the exception of the future ʿAbd al-Raḥmān II in 816.[39] Otherwise members of the dynasty only appeared in the Upper March intermittently and at the head of an army, to march into Christian territory or crush rebellion. At least in theory the area was managed by urban governors. A clue as to the operations of the governors is provided by correspondence between ʿAbd al-Raḥmān II and ʿUbayd Allāh b. Yaḥyā, governor of Tortosa in 850/851. ʿUbayd Allāh recruited his own troops from the local area, and they were mostly Muslims descended from Christian families. The governor collected and kept the poll tax, tithes, and other dues to pay his men, maintain the defences, and ransom captives.[40]

The Spanish March was attached to the neighbouring kingdom of Aquitaine. This was one of the biggest differences between the two marches. The Upper March was relatively isolated from the rest of al-Andalus, with communications having to run through a Toledo that was frequently in revolt. As a consequence, the March had a somewhat shallow hinterland. By contrast, the Spanish March's attachment to Aquitaine meant there was a much broader constituency in the wider Frankish world tied to the region. The exact nature of Aquitaine before the Carolingian conquest is debated.[41] From 781, it existed as a kingdom assigned to one of the throne-worthy sons of the dominant Carolingian in West Francia. It incorporated a diverse set of territories, from cities on the Loire such as Orléans and Tours, to the Basque population of Gascony, to the historically Gothic region of Septimania on the Mediterranean.[42]

37. Viguera Molíns, *Aragón musulmán*, 36–37.

38. Lorenzo Jiménez, *La dawla de los Banū Qasī*, 137–223. See also Fierro, "El Conde Casio"; Manzano Moreno, "A Vueltas con el Conde Casio."

39. ARF a.816 144.

40. Kennedy, *Muslim Spain and Portugal*, 59.

41. Bayard, "De la *Regio* au *Regnum*."

42. Bellarbre, "La 'nation' Aquitaine."

Among Aquitainian actors who became involved in the March, the most obvious was the king. Louis the Pious operated with considerable autonomy for much of his adult reign as king of Aquitaine, building support among key groups and acting as his father's agent and first responder in handling relations with Muslims of al-Andalus. Later kings, such as Pippin I (r. 817–832) and Louis the Stammerer (r. 866–877), seem to have had less independence, although Pippin managed to embed himself deeply enough that his namesake son continually received serious support for his bid for Aquitainian kingship.[43] Nor were kings the only important figures in the region. The count of Toulouse was frequently a leading actor in the March with authority over other magnates.[44] Other counts, particularly those of Provence, could also loom large in the area.[45] The old ducal line of Gascony kept producing leaders among the Gascons, acknowledged or otherwise by the Carolingians.[46] This deeper hinterland could make the Spanish March more resilient than the Upper March by providing an extra layer of powerful people invested in its security. But it also made the politics of the area more complicated, and division elsewhere in Aquitaine could spill out, with consequences for the March.

This complex landscape enabled relations between actors on the frontier, and with external monarchs. On the Carolingian side this ranged from border reavers seeking plunder to appointed officials desiring information and peace with their opposite numbers in the frontier to rebels looking for support from Córdoba. Nor were all these interventions made by secular lords. Monasteries in Aquitaine such as Conques and Castres interested in relics from the Iberian Peninsula sent their own representatives to al-Andalus.[47] While Carolingian rulers sought to manage these channels of diplomatic communication, and suppress those that might lead to major rebellion, fully controlling them was impossible. Indeed, these were the very channels through which they themselves communicated with and acquired information about the Iberian Peninsula. Direct Carolingian involvement in the March waxed and waned depending on the circumstances, but even at the heart of their realm they had to wield power by working with people on the ground. This applied even more so in distant regions such as the March. Likewise, within the Upper March, families

43. Collins, "Pippin I"; Martindale, "Charles the Bald."

44. Miro, "Les comtes de Toulouse."

45. D'Abadal i de Vinyals, "La Catalogne sous l'empire de Louis le Pieux," 253.

46. Collins, *The Basques*, 128–129.

47. Aimoin, *Historia translationis* 1013 and *De translatione* 942.

built connections across the frontier, most notably the Banū Qāsī marrying into the royal dynasty of Pamplona.[48] As a consequence, figures such as Mūsā b. Mūsā regularly had dealings with Franks, including kings such as Charles the Bald. Like the Carolingians, the Umayyads tended to rule in partnership with powerful families on the frontier. The ultimate downfall of the Banū Qāsī came at the hands of the Banū Tujib, who were backed by Córdoba.[49]

## *The Beginning of Carolingian Relations with the Umayyads, 751–793*

The year 712 saw Mūsā b. Nuṣayr triumphant. After decades of grinding counterinsurgency in the Atlas Mountains, the armies of God were once again on the march in the west. The Straits of Gibraltar had been crossed the previous year and the army of the Visigoths shattered in pitched battle, resulting in the death of their king.[50] Now as Mūsā raced north, the Iberian Peninsula fell into his hands. It was at this moment, according to the twelfth-century geographer al-Gharnāṭī, that Mūsā's mind turned to other prospects. Why should he be content with his victory when further prizes waited on the other side of the Pyrenees? Onwards he pushed into the mountain passes, intending to venture into the lands of the Franks. There he found:

> A statue of a man, with a copper tablet in his hand. On the tablet was written, "There is no way beyond. Turn back, and do not enter this land, or else you will be destroyed."

Sceptical of this warning, Mūsā sent a party of slaves forward. "From behind the trees, ants the size of ferocious lions dashed at them. They dismembered those men and their horses."[51] The chastened Mūsā returned south, before being summoned to Damascus in disgrace.

Al-Gharnāṭī's statue is of course fiction, with elements of the story being familiar from other Arabic traditions.[52] It does nonetheless reflect a

48. Manzano Moreno, "Christian-Muslim Frontier in al-Andalus," 93.

49. Al-ʿUdhrī, "La Marca Superior," 487, 503.

50. The best introduction to this remains Collins, *The Arab Conquest*, though see also Chalmeta, *Invasión e Islamización*.

51. Al-Gharnāṭī, "*Tuḥfat al-Albāb*," 64, translated in Clarke, *The Muslim Conquest of Iberia*, 77. On medieval ideas of giant ants, see Gerhardt, "The Ant-Lion"; Cesario, "Antlore in Anglo-Saxon England."

52. On fantastic geographies of al-Andalus, see Hernández Juberías, *La Peninsula Imaginaria*.

reality. Mūsā's successors were intermittently tempted to try their luck in the lands of the Franks, but the 730s saw the end of the great expeditions, and the first Umayyad emir of Córdoba, ʿAbd al-Raḥmān I, did not initially display much interest in the world of the Franks. Nor were the kings of the Franks much exercised by matters in Spain before 777. In any era that produced histories worth the name, this lack of interaction could be safely attributed to the aforementioned lion-sized ants, but in this fallen age we must instead find other explanations for the absence of contact in these years.

This period of Carolingian relations with al-Andalus is the most challenging to examine. The eighth century is the most poorly sourced in the history of Muslim Spain, and this is particularly the case for its second half. The histories of the conquest of Spain, such as those of Ibn ʿAbd al-Ḥakam and the *Fatḥ al-Andalus*, are much less informative for the post-conquest period.[53] The ending of the *Chronicle of 754* also leaves a gap in the historical record. The surviving fragments of the invaluable history of Ibn Ḥayyān begin with 796, leaving us dependent upon later writers such as Ibn al-Athīr and Ibn ʿIdhārī, who apparently based their accounts on Ibn Ḥayyān. The *Akhbār Majmūʿa* and the writings of Ibn al-Qūṭīya are also available but take the form of collections of anecdotes about famous events and people.[54] The surviving material is not only comparatively meagre and late even by the standards of Andalusi history but also frequently irreconcilable, with different narratives providing mutually exclusive accounts.[55] Even where the different sources agree, problems arise with the dating of events. The historians of the tenth century were attempting to arrange in chronological narrative a tradition largely composed of anecdotal material. While the order of their material is relatively certain, the exact year is not, and there is a noticeable tendency to place simultaneous occurrences sequentially. This is why Ibn al-Athīr dates Charlemagne's invasion to 781 rather than the correct 778.[56]

53. On Ibn ʿAbd al-Ḥakam, see Sánchez-Albornoz, *En torno a los orígenes*, 64–68; Clarke, *The Muslim Conquest of Iberia*, 25–26; Coghill, "How the West Was Won."

54. On Ibn al-Qūṭīya, see Fierro, "La Obra Histórica"; Christys argues that Ibn al-Qūṭīya's connection to the material is tenuous in *Christians in al-Andalus*, 179–183; Clarke, *The Muslim Conquest of Iberia*, 67–68. The *Akhbār Majmūʿa* is if anything more controversial; see Ribera, *Historia de la conquista de España*, xii–xix; Sánchez-Albornoz, *El "Ajbār maŷmūʿa,"* "La saña celosa de un arabista," and "Réplica al arabista Chalmeta"; Chalmeta, "Una historia discontinua"; Molina, "Los Ajbār Maŷmūʿa" and "Un relato de la conquista"; Oliver, "Los autores del *Ajbār Maŷmūʿa*" and "El *Ajbār Maŷmūʿa*."

55. Collins, *The Arab Conquest*, 25.

56. Ibn al-Athīr, *Annales*, 129; Collins, *The Arab Conquest*, 175–176.

Despite the problems with the sources, the reason for the lack of interest in the Franks displayed by al-Andalus in the decades after 737 can be identified as the political instability that threatened the control of Córdoba over the heartlands of the province. Beginning with the Berber uprisings in 740, the subsequent struggle between different Arab leaders, and then the fragile independent regime of Yūsuf b. ʿAbd al-Raḥmān al-Fihrī from 747, this was a period when the leading powers of al-Andalus were distracted by internal upheaval.

This prioritisation made sense within the historical geography. Much of the Iberian Peninsula is mountainous and arid.[57] Historically, people and prosperity have tended to concentrate on the coastline and along the great fertile and flat river valleys. The first governors of al-Andalus had made the major wealth of the Guadalquivir basin in the south their first priority.[58] They established their capitals in Seville and Córdoba and paid close attention to controlling the other cities of the area, while maintaining communications with North Africa. This prioritisation of the south of the peninsula meant that Frankish expansion into Septimania, including the conquest of Nîmes, Maguelone, Beziers, and Agde in 752, was a secondary problem for the rulers of al-Andalus. This was particularly the case after 753, when the governor of Narbonne, ʿAbd al-Raḥmān al-Lakhmī, rebelled against Yūsuf al-Fihrī, further reducing Córdoba's incentive to defend Septimania.

When ʿAbd al-Raḥmān b. Muʿāwiya arrived in al-Andalus in 756, the refugee Umayyad was one warlord among many. The Syrian general al-Ṣumayl, one of ʿAbd al-Raḥmān's most formidable opponents, predicted memorably of the newcomer, "he is from a band who, if one of them pissed in this land we would all . . . drown in his piss."[59] Al-Ṣumayl was prophetic in assuming that the tide of the Umayyads would eventually cover most of the peninsula, but the success of the future emir ʿAbd al-Raḥmān I was by no means assured at this point. His powerbase was restricted to Medina Elvira and Córdoba itself and his political survival was very much in question.[60] Most of the factions competing for control of al-Andalus at this time were considerably longer established than the newly arrived Umayyad.[61] The

57. On the geography of the Iberian Peninsula, see Wickham, *Framing the Early Middle Ages*, 37–41.

58. Collins, *Arab Conquest of Spain*, 205.

59. Akhbār Majmūʿa, *A History of Early al-Andalus*, 86; Cruz Hernández, "The Social Structure of al-Andalus," 64.

60. Kennedy, *Muslim Spain and Portugal*, 32.

61. Manzano Moreno, *Conquistadores, Emires y Califas*, 149–150.

northern part of the peninsula was thus somewhat beyond his area of concern. These circumstances also explain the concurrent long peace between Córdoba and the fledgling kingdom of Asturias.[62]

For their part, the Carolingians had their own challenges to attend to. They were rather more secure in their position, but both Pippin III and his son Charlemagne had to contend with rivals within their own family, as well as regional princes grown accustomed to considerable independence and disinclined to submit to a new dynasty.[63] Muslim Septimania was a potentially dangerous thorn in the side of the Carolingians. Former governors of Narbonne had played an important role in Frankish politics, including Yūsuf al-Fihrī, who had supported opponents of the Carolingians in Provence in 735, something that many of Pippin's nobles, including his uncle Childebrand, would have remembered.[64] By contrast, Córdoba itself represented much less of an immediate threat than the dukes of Aquitaine.[65] The dukes remained serious obstacles to Carolingian power in the region until Charlemagne's final defeat of Hunald II in 769.

Although possession of the full extent of the lands to which both ʿAbd al-Raḥmān and the Carolingians aspired might theoretically make them neighbours, in practice neither wielded complete authority in regions near to each other. This explains the lack of contact between Córdoba and the Franks until the 770s. When the Carolingians did intervene in the Iberian Peninsula, the results were to be dramatic enough to inspire the high medieval epic tradition that so irritated Jiménez de Rada.

## SULAYMĀN, CHARLEMAGNE, AND THE RONCESVALLES CAMPAIGN, 777–781

It is Charlemagne's misfortune that his most famous campaign was also one of his least successful. He might have predicted that the ignominy of his march on Zaragoza and subsequent ambush at Roncesvalles in 778 would loom large in the memory of the Frankish aristocracy.[66] The perspicacity required to foresee the subsequent immortalisation of the invasion

62. Collins, *Early Medieval Spain*, 184–186 and *The Arab Conquest of Spain*, 165.

63. Jarnut, "Ein Brüderkampf und seine Folgen"; Costambeys, Innes, and MacLean, *The Carolingian World*, 51–61.

64. *Chronicle of Moissac*, a.735 115; d'Abadal i de Vinyals, "El Paso de Septimania," 35–38; Geary, *Aristocracy in Provence*, 127–128.

65. Manzano Moreno, *La Frontera de al-Andalus*, 75–76.

66. On the lasting memory of the Roncesvalles disaster, see the references to the incident in Einhard, *Vita Karoli Magni*, c.9 12–13; Revised ARF a.778 51; AL a.778 31; Astronomer, *Vita Hludowici*, c.2 288.

was beyond even Notker the Stammerer's prophetic Charlemagne.[67] But the events of 778 were to have a legacy beyond providing subject matter for epic.[68] The disaster may have been the nadir of Charlemagne's military fortunes, but it also marks the beginning of Carolingian involvement in al-Andalus.

This intervention was the product not of deliberate planned policy on the part of Charlemagne but of developments within al-Andalus serving to provide an opportunity for the Frankish king. The initiative in the beginning of diplomacy was taken by political figures in al-Andalus. In 777, Sulaymān b. Yaqẓān al-ʿArābī, lord of Barcelona and Girona, sent an embassy to Charlemagne's court at Paderborn, asking for help, prompting Frankish intervention.[69] Sulaymān was a leading figure in the Ebro river valley in the northeastern part of the peninsula, which contained and supported cities such as Zaragoza, Tarragona, and Huesca, and on the nearby coast, Barcelona.[70] He was allied with al-Ḥusayn b. Yaḥyā al-Anṣārī of Zaragoza and Abū Tawr of Huesca. Both of the former were Arabs and appear to have been well established, because their sons were able to draw upon considerable reservoirs of local support after the deaths of their fathers.[71] Sulaymān had been powerful enough to defeat the army sent by the ʿAbbāsid caliph al-Manṣūr in 777 under al-Ṣiqlabī.[72] Al-Ḥusayn could claim descent from Saʿd b. ʿUbāda, one of Muḥammad's earliest followers, thereby granting him a high dignity in the Muslim world.[73]

There is reason to believe that the meeting at Paderborn was primarily the result of Sulaymān's initiative.[74] Charlemagne had shown no interest in al-Andalus previously and it would be some time after 778 before he next intervened militarily in the Iberian Peninsula. By contrast, Sulaymān and his allies had very pressing motives to be seeking outside help. Sulaymān's embassy was the result of recent events elsewhere in al-Andalus. The same year that they travelled to Paderborn saw the death of the Berber chieftain Shāqya b. ʿAbd al-Walīd al-Miknasī. Proclaiming himself to be the

67. Notker, *Gesta Karoli Magni*, II.14, 77–78.

68. See, for example, Morrissey, *Charlemagne and France*; Gabriele, *An Empire of Memory*.

69. Revised ARF a.777 48–49.

70. Dupré, "La place de la Vallée de l'Ebre," 133–138.

71. Ibn al-Athīr, *Annales*, 141; Collins, *The Arab Conquest*, 205.

72. Ibn al-Athīr, *Annales*, 126; Akhbār Majmūʿa, *A History of Early al-Andalus*, 106.

73. Akhbār Majmūʿa, *A History of Early al-Andalus*, 107; Al-ʿUdhrī, "La Marca Superior," 462.

74. Cf. Nelson, *King and Emperor*, 165, who suggests that Charlemagne may have initiated contact.

descendent of Muḥammad, Shāqya had dominated the hills and mountains of the central Meseta for the best part of a decade, preventing Emir ʿAbd al-Raḥmān I of Córdoba from expanding north.[75] It would be surprising if Charlemagne ever heard the name of Shāqya, but the end of the Berber's brief career was to have major consequences for him.

The cities of the Ebro were largely uninvolved in ʿAbd al-Raḥmān's wars to subdue the south, but events indicate that Sulaymān and his allies were paying close attention. The death of Shāqya did not just secure the centre of the peninsula for ʿAbd al-Raḥmān, it also ensured that the emir of Córdoba controlled the roads that led from Toledo to the Ebro, bringing with it the prospect of the projection of Umayyad power north, something that had worked out poorly for independent rulers elsewhere in al-Andalus.[76] ʿAbd al-Raḥmān had also recently defeated the final opposition from the Syrian *junds*, the last alternative source of military power in the south, by crushing the revolt of ʿAbd al-Ghaffār in 772 in Seville, leaving his hands free for expansion elsewhere.[77] ʿAbd al-Raḥmān's interest in the Ebro valley was demonstrated by the appointment of his close ally Badr as governor of the frontier in 774.[78] It was the growing possibility of an intervention by Córdoba that prompted Sulaymān's appeal.

This was not a gambit without precedent. In 731 the ruler of Cerdanya, a Berber named Munuza, had rebelled against the Umayyad governor and allied with Duke Eudo of Aquitaine, to the extent of marrying the duke's daughter.[79] Munuza's revolt had been quickly defeated and Córdoba's wrath was expressed in the campaign that ended in Charles Martel's famous victory at Tours.[80] Sulaymān may also have been inspired by previous figures in the region, including ʿĀmir al-ʿAbdarī, the besieger of al-Ṣumayl in Zaragoza in 754, who had sought support from the ʿAbbāsids.[81] Having scuppered an attempt by al-Manṣūr to reclaim al-Andalus he could expect no aid from that quarter, but Charlemagne might have served as an alternative.

75. Ibn al-Athīr, *Annales*, 118; Akhbār Majmūʿa, *A History of Early al-Andalus*, 104–106. On the dating of Shāqya's revolt, see Manzano Moreno, *La Frontera de al-Andalus*, 238–239; Aguadé, "Some Remarks about Sectarian Movements," 64–65; Fierro, *La Heterodoxia en al-Andalus*, 28–29.

76. Collins, *The Arab Conquest*, 176.

77. Manzano Moreno, "The Settlement and Organisation," 100.

78. Chalmeta, *Invasión e Islamización*, 368.

79. "Chronicle of 754," 254.

80. Deviosse, *Charles Martel*, 159–62.

81. Akhbār Majmūʿa, *A History of Early al-Andalus*, 81.

It is also possible that Sulaymān had been in contact with the Franks for considerably longer than the brief account in the *Annales regni Francorum* suggests. The *Annales Mettenses priores*, uniquely among the Latin sources, records that shortly after Pippin's conquest of Narbonne in 759, "Solinoan, who was a leader of the Saracens and ruled the cities of Barcelona and Girona, submitted all he had to the dominion of Pippin."[82] Solinoan looks like a Latin rendering of the name Sulaymān. Sénac suggested that this Sulaymān could be a border lord unnerved by Frankish success following the fall of Septimania, a disillusioned supporter of Yūsuf al-Fihrī or an ʿAbbāsid loyalist, before concluding that "it is impossible to choose between these hypotheses."[83]

If this would seem to miss the obvious identification between one Sulaymān described as the lord of Barcelona and Girona in the late 750s and another man with the same name and lands in the 770s, Sénac is not alone. The compilers of the *Annales Mettenses priores* also do not connect the two figures, referring to the man who approached Charlemagne in 777 as "Ibinalardi" or Ibn al-ʿArābī.[84] If Sulaymān al-ʿArābī had been in contact with Pippin in 759, this would explain not only his willingness to turn to Charlemagne but also the depth of his knowledge of Frankish affairs.

Sulaymān's early career is largely unknown. In most of the Arabic sources, focussed as they are on the rise of ʿAbd al-Raḥmān, he appears in the 770s as the emir turned his attention to the Ebro valley. Ibn al-Athīr says he was a prisoner in Córdoba until 773/774, when ʿAbd al-Raḥmān sent him to Zaragoza.[85] This account is somewhat confused and contradicts what Ibn al-Athīr says about Badr's appointment to the same post in the same year.[86] Even if true, time spent in Córdoba would not have prevented Sulaymān from having had an earlier career in Barcelona and Girona.

As we have seen there is reason to be sceptical of the Metz Annals. They are heavily dependent on the *Annales regni Francorum*, as in the case of their account of the events of 777 and 778, and on the *Continuation of the Chronicle of Fredegar*, neither of which mentions Sulaymān in 759.[87] The annalist has a track record of introducing Muslim envoys in unexpected and implausible places, as in the account of Pippin II receiving a Saracen

82. AMP a.759 "Solinoan quoque dux Sarracenorum, qui Barchilonam Gerundamque civitatem regebat, Pippini se cum omnibus quae habebat domination subdidit," 43–44.

83. Sénac, *Les Carolingiens et al-Andalus*, 41.

84. AMP a.777 66.

85. Ibn al-Athīr, *Annales*, 123; Chalmeta, *Invasión e Islamización*, 368.

86. Ibn al-Athīr, *Annales*, 123.

87. AMP a.777–778 66–67; ARF a.777–778 48–49.

delegation.[88] The reference in the Metz Annals may therefore be intended to set a precedent for Charlemagne's own dealings with Muslim border lords and probably should not be taken too seriously.

At some point in the mid-770s, ʿAbd al-Raḥmān decided he needed to deal with Sulaymān. The chronology of the Arabic sources is confused, but it appears that the emir sent an army north commanded by Thaʿlaba b. ʿUbayd. Thaʿlaba had achieved high favour with the emir after warning him of an assassination plot.[89] Sulaymān "attacked him, took him prisoner and handed him to the king of the Franks."[90] When Sulaymān gave Thaʿlaba to Charlemagne is also unclear. It may have been during the embassy to Paderborn in 777 or when the Frankish king was in Spain in 778. We have few details for the negotiations of Thaʿlaba's release but he retained sufficient status after his return to Córdoba to merit the future emir Hishām I attending his funeral.[91]

Importantly Sulaymān's embassy coincided with the Frankish king being in a position to intervene. The long competition between the Carolingians and the dukes of Aquitaine had only ended definitively in 769, when Duke Lupus of Gascony surrendered the fugitive Hunald II to Charlemagne and submitted to the Frankish king.[92] The taking of Aquitaine and Septimania placed the Carolingians on the border with Spain. The death of Carloman in 771 left his brother Charlemagne freer to involve himself in foreign adventures.[93] Frankish confidence was boosted by the conquest of the Lombard kingdom of Italy in 774.[94]

It is hard to discern exactly what Sulaymān offered the Frankish king. The Revised *Annales regni Francorum* claim that they "surrendered themselves and the cities the king of the Saracens had appointed them over."[95] The Reviser, who was writing three decades after the event, may have exaggerated the offer to point up Saracen perfidy and strengthen their claims on the Spanish frontier. Possibly Sulaymān calculated that a

88. AMP a.692 15. On this, see McKitterick, *Charlemagne*, 52–54, 64.

89. Akhbār Majmūʿa, *A History of Early al-Andalus*, 95.

90. Al-ʿUdhrī, "La Marca Superior," 462; Akhbār Majmūʿa, *A History of Early al-Andalus*, 108.

91. Ibn al-Qūṭīya, *Early Islamic Spain*, 82.

92. ARF a.769 28–29; Bachrach, "Military Organisation," 13.

93. ARF a.771 32–33. On Carloman, see Jarnut, "Ein Brüderkampf und seine Folgen"; Nelson, "Making a Difference"; McKitterick, *Charlemagne*, 78–87.

94. ARF a.773 34; ARF a.776 44, 46; Costambeys, Innes, and MacLean, *The Carolingian World*, 65–69.

95. Revised ARF a.777 "dedens se ac civitates quibus eum rex Sarracenorum praefecerat," 49.

Frankish overlord, far away and distracted, would have far less scope for control than one in Córdoba.

Sulaymān's envoys are difficult to identify. The *Annales regni Francorum* call them "Ibn al-ʿArābī and the son of Deiuzefi who in Latin is named Joseph, and likewise his son-in-law."[96] Recent historians have taken the presence of the patronymic Ibn to imply the embassy was led by a son of Sulaymān, possibly Aysūn or Maṭrūḥ.[97] This could then be reconciled with the *Annales Laureshamenses*, which describe one Abinlarbi being "brought back to Francia" in 778 as a prisoner, when Sulaymān's later career in Spain is well attested.[98] It is true that the *Chronicle of Moissac* uses *ibin* in this sense, referring correctly to ʿAbd al-Raḥmān I as Ibn Muʿāwiya.[99] But in the accounts of the *Annales regni Francorum*, its Revised variant, and the *Annales Laureshamenses*, Ibn al-ʿArābī is described acting as a ruler in his own right, giving hostages and submitting his lands.[100] The *Annales Laureshamenses* even name him "king."[101] If Ibn al-ʿArābī was a son acting for his father, we would expect reference to an al-ʿArābī somewhere in the narrative. The absence of such a figure and the behaviour of Ibn al-ʿArābī suggest that we should identify him with Sulaymān.

The *Annales Laureshamenses* are not alone in saying that Ibn al-ʿArābī was taken prisoner, but the other accounts that agree, the *Annales Mosellani* and the *Fragmentum Chesnianum*, share the same material before 785.[102] It is noteworthy that the well-informed compiler of the *Chronicle of Moissac* follows the narrative of the *Annales Laureshamenses* for 778 almost word for word but does not mention Ibn al-ʿArābī at all.[103] This suggests that the *Annales Laureshamenses* is mistaken and

96. ARF a.777 "hi sunt Ibin al-ʿArābī et filius Deiuzefi qui et latine Iuseph nominatur, similiter et gener eius," 48.

97. Collins, *The Arab Conquest*, 177–178.

98. AL a.778 "et ibi venit ad eum Abinlarbi alter rex Saracenorum quem et fecit adducere in Francia," 31.

99. *Chronicle of Moissac*, a.797 130.

100. ARF a.777–778 49–51; AL a.778 31.

101. AL a.778 31.

102. *Annales Mosellani*, a.778 496; *Fragmentum Chesnianum*, 34; Halphen, *Études critiques*, 26–36; Collins, "Charlemagne's Imperial Coronation," 54–64.

103. Compare AL a.778 "Fuit rex Carlus in Spania cum exercitu, et conquesivit civitatem Pampalonam; et Habitaurus Saracinorum rex venit ad eum, et tradidit civitates quas habuit, et dedit ei obsides fratrem suum et filium. Et inde perrexit domnus rex usque ad Caesaris-Augusta, et ibi venit ad eum Abinlarbi alter rex Saracenorum quem et fecit adducere in Francia. Et interim quod domnus rex illis partibus fuit," 31; with the *Chronicle of Moissac*, "Et in anno DCCLXXVIII, congregans Karolus rex exercitum magnum, ingressus

that *Annales regni Francorum* should be preferred, meaning that there is no contradiction to resolve between the Frankish and Arabic sources on Sulaymān's post-778 career, indicating that the lord of Barcelona led the embassy himself. This was presumably a gesture of good faith and lends credence to Frankish claims that Sulaymān was offering more than just an alliance. It also matches subsequent accounts of Muslim leaders coming directly to the Franks.[104]

The "son of Deiuzefi" is even more mysterious but could conceivably refer to a son of Yūsuf al-Fihrī, as suggested by Evariste Lévi-Provençal.[105] Yūsuf's fall had not ended Fihrīd claims to al-Andalus, and his sons, Abū al-ʿAṣwād Muḥammad and Qāsim, led a revolt in Toledo in 785.[106] Abū al-ʿAṣwād is known to have been in captivity in Córdoba in 777. It is possible that Qāsim or an unknown brother took refuge with Sulaymān and sought Charlemagne's aid in reclaiming Córdoba. Their father had been governor of Narbonne, which might have given them contacts across the Pyrenees. Some Frankish familiarity with Yūsuf b. ʿAbd al-Raḥmān al-Fihrī is suggested by his appearance in the *Chronicle of Moissac* as "Iusseph Ibin Abderraman."[107]

It is possible that Charlemagne's main objective in his invasion of Spain was to strengthen his hold on Gascony by bringing about the submission of the Basques. The *Annales regni Francorum* specifically mentions that Charlemagne "subjugated the Basques of Spain" and sacked Pamplona.[108] This might then explain the ambush by Basques in Roncesvalles Pass but is problematic. A war against the Basques would not require a march to Zaragoza. It also assumes that Basques on either side of the Pyrenees were in contact and inclined to support each other.[109] The best part of a decade separated the conquest of Aquitaine in 769 and the Iberian adventure, during which there are no references to campaigns in Aquitaine in the *Annales regni Francorum*.[110]

---

est in Spania et conquisivit civitatem Pampilonam et ibi Taurus, Sarracenorum rex, venit ad eum et tradidit civitates quas habuit et dedit ei obsides fratrem suum et filium. Et inde perrexit usque ad Caesaraugusta," 121.

104. ARF a.797 100; Revised ARF a.797 101.

105. Lévi-Provençal, *Histoire de l'Espagne musulmane*, 1:124; Chalmeta, *Invasión e Islamización*, 369, is more doubtful of this possibility.

106. Lévi-Provençal, *Histoire de l'Espagne musulmane*, 1:109–110; Manzano Moreno, *La Frontera de al-Andalus*, 272.

107. *Chronicle of Moissac*, a.751 118.

108. ARF a.778 "Hispani Wascones subiugatos," 50.

109. Collins, "The Basques in Aquitaine and Navarre," 8.

110. Rouche, *L'Aquitaine*, 129.

That the invasion was prompted by Sulaymān's appeal suggests that Charlemagne's primary motivation must have stretched beyond the Basques. Waging war on non-Christians may have appealed to the Frankish king.[111] The passages of Fredegar that concern Charles Martel's wars against Saracens celebrate him as a Christian hero and were probably composed by the 760s.[112] Charlemagne was concerned about Christian interaction with Muslims, voicing his disquiet in a letter of 776 to Pope Hadrian I about rumours that Christians were being sold to Saracens as slaves.[113]

A letter written by Pope Hadrian in April 778 to Charlemagne expresses "great tribulation and affliction" at the news from the Frankish king "that the nation of the Agarenes (may God frustrate them!) intends to invade your territory and conquer it."[114] The pope assured Charlemagne that:

> all our priests and devout monks, all the clergy and our entire people, are entreating the clemency of the Lord our God without cease that he may subject to you the unspeakable nation of the Agarenes and cast them beneath your feet, and that they utterly fail to prevail against you.[115]

The missive suggests that Charlemagne had told Hadrian that ʿAbd al-Raḥmān was about to invade Francia. This was in reality very improbable given that the emir had only just subdued the centre of the Iberian Peninsula. It is possible that Sulaymān might have misrepresented the situation in order to encourage Charlemagne to get involved by making him think he was at more immediate risk than he actually was. Alternatively, Hadrian might have misunderstood Charlemagne's letter to him. Despite this, it seems that neither king nor pontiff was thinking in terms of a defensive war against Saracen aggression. Having compared the Agarenes to the Egyptians of Exodus, Hadrian concluded his discussion of the subject by advising Charlemagne that "we entreat the majesty of the Lord before the *confessio* of the same apostle [Peter] of God that he may enlarge your

111. Ottewill-Soulsby, "'Those same cursed Saracens.'"

112. "The Continuations of the Chronicle of Fredegar," 286–290.

113. Hadrian I, *Epistolae* no. 62, 585.

114. Ibid., no. 61, "magna exinde tribulatione atque affliction," "Deo sibi contrario, Agarenorum gens cupiunt ad debellandum vestris introire finibus," 588.

115. Ibid., "incessanter pro vobis cum omnibus nostris sacerdotibus atque religiosis monachis et cunctum clerum vel universum populum nostrum domini Dei nostri deprecamus clementiam, ut ipsam necdicendam Agarenorum gentem vobis subiciat et vestri eam substernat pedibus, et minime prevalere adversus vos valeant," 588.

kingdom."[116] This implies that the pope foresaw Charlemagne conquering territory in Spain, rather than merely preventing an Arab attack.

Hadrian's letter should not be taken too far. Frankish accounts of the invasion of 778 are largely secular in tone and Charlemagne certainly had no objections to allying with the non-Christian Sulaymān.[117] His attack on al-Andalus should probably be seen as a straightforward acceptance of an opportunity to acquire plunder, influence, and territory. The Revised version of the *Annales regni Francorum* states that Charlemagne invaded with "the legitimate hope of capturing several cities in Spain."[118] The Frankish king may have anticipated a repeat of his Italian triumph, in which a powerful kingdom had been swallowed up comparatively quickly.[119]

That this did not happen was largely due to the breakdown of the agreement with Sulaymān and his allies. Unlike the relatively centralised Lombard kingdom, there was no central city or ruler in the area whose defeat and capture by Charlemagne would lead to widespread acceptance.[120] While the powers of the Ebro valley cooperated, they retained their independence of action. Abū Tawr of Huesca seems to have been willing to collaborate with the Franks, but al-Ḥusayn al-Anṣārī of Zaragoza shut his gates to them.[121] Al-Ḥusayn's motivations are unclear, but his later actions indicate that he thought he could bargain with ʿAbd al-Raḥmān. The walled cities of the Ebro valley were also a formidable challenge, as Charlemagne learned when he found himself besieging Zaragoza because of al-Ḥusayn's resistance. In Italy Charlemagne had trapped the Lombard king Desiderius by besieging him in his capital of Pavia over the winter.[122] For whatever reason, most probably the risk of trouble elsewhere, this was not an option at Zaragoza and the Frankish king was forced to retreat back across the Pyrenees, only for his rear-guard to be ambushed by Basques, granting Roland his meeting with immortality at Roncesvalles.[123]

116. Ibid., "ante confessionem eiusdem Dei apostoli Domini deprecamus maiestatem, ut vestrum dilatet regnum," 588.

117. Einhard, *Vita Karoli Magni*, c.9 12; AL a.778 31; Christys, "Crossing the Frontier," 42; Collins, *The Arab Conquest*, 215.

118. Revised ARF a.778 "spem capiendarum quarundam in Hispania civitatum haud frustra," 51.

119. ARF a.773 34; Bautier, "La campagne de Charlemagne," 10; McKitterick, *Charlemagne*, 133.

120. Collins, *Charlemagne*, 62; McKitterick, *Charlemagne*, 109.

121. *Annales Mosellani*, a.778 496; Akhbār Majmūʿa, *A History of Early al-Andalus*, 108.

122. ARF a.773 34.

123. Revised ARF a.778 51; Einhard, *Vita Karoli Magni*, c.9 12.

The consequences of this misadventure were numerous and significant. The first was to accelerate ʿAbd al-Raḥmān's expansion north. Charlemagne's army had neither encountered Umayyad forces nor entered territory effectively controlled by Córdoba, but the campaign may have alarmed ʿAbd al-Raḥmān, encouraging him to take the region in hand.[124] Ibn al-Athīr says that the emir postponed plans to invade Syria due to the need to deal with the lords of the Ebro.[125] In 781 al-Ḥusayn murdered Sulaymān while he was in Zaragoza. The *Akhbār Majmūʿa* claims this happened in the mosque on Friday, al-ʿUdhrī that this was on ʿAbd al-Raḥmān's orders.[126] Al-Ḥusayn tried to come to an agreement with the emir which ended when the latter killed him in 783/784.[127] Al-Ḥusayn's son, Saʿīd, gave ʿAbd al-Raḥmān some difficulties, but by 785 the Ebro valley was largely under Umayyad control.[128]

For Charlemagne's part, the campaign of 778 was a fiasco.[129] Although some scholars have suggested that the expedition was more successful than usually thought, this is at odds with what the Frankish sources tell us.[130] Despite the efforts of the *Annales regni Francorum* to downplay the scale of the defeat (Collins, "masterly to the point of mendacity"), Einhard makes clear the trauma of the defeat at Roncesvalles.[131] Had the adventure been a profitable success, we might expect further invasions in subsequent years. Instead, it was to be almost two decades until a Carolingian next led an army into the Iberian Peninsula, and then with much more modest ambitions. Having been hamstrung by the lack of cooperation from a presumed ally at Zaragoza, the campaign had been in trouble even before the ambush at Roncesvalles. Rather than checking Umayyad expansion and creating a buffer of friendly clients, the expedition had contributed to division between the lords of the Ebro river valley.

The Roncesvalles campaign encapsulated several characteristics of Carolingian involvement in al-Andalus that were to continue in later decades. Powerful Muslim allies already embedded in the political landscape were to remain central to Carolingian strategy and tended to play a key role in pulling the Franks into al-Andalus. These hint at an awareness

124. Chalmeta, *Invasión e Islamización*, 377.

125. Ibn al-Athīr, *Annales*, 128.

126. Akhbār Majmūʿa, *A History of Early al-Andalus*, 108; Al-ʿUdhrī, "La Marca Superior," 462.

127. Al-ʿUdhrī, "La Marca Superior," 462.

128. Ibn al-Athīr, *Annales*, 141.

129. Ganshof, "Une crise dans le règne."

130. Hägermann, *Karl der Grosse*, 157–161; Nelson, *King and Emperor*, 171.

131. Einhard, *Vita Karoli Magni*, c.9 12–13; Collins, *Charlemagne*, 67.

in Carolingian circles of developments within Muslim Spain, as the Franks attempted to respond to the growth of Umayyad power. The weaknesses of this strategy were also demonstrated in 778. Charlemagne's frustration outside the walls of Zaragoza was to be repeated elsewhere and the Franks struggled to take fortified cities in the Upper March that were held by determined defenders. Dissension among the Carolingians' Muslim allies was also to be a recurrent problem, with conflicts between the lords of the Upper March undermining efforts to fight the Umayyads.

Charlemagne retained an interest in Spain. Following the submission of Sulaymān and Abū Tawr, the territory north of the Ebro river was now Frankish in Carolingian eyes. Einhard described Charlemagne's empire as "stretching as far as the Ebro, which rises in Navarre, flows through the most fertile plains of Spain and then joins the Balearic Sea under the walls of the city of Tortosa."[132] Subsequent conquests were described as restorations.[133] Importantly, the Franks claimed the Christian city of Pamplona, whose walls Charlemagne had levelled.[134] This began an unhappy association between the restive city and the Carolingians, until the latter's pretensions to rule were ended once and for all by the uprising and defeat that was named the "Second Roncesvalles" in 824.[135]

Charlemagne began organising Septimania and neighbouring territory in Spain, encouraging settlement in the area from those fleeing "the unjust and cruel yoke of oppression, put on their shoulders by the Saracens" in a charter from around 780.[136] The charters demonstrate that the original conception of the "Spanish March" that came to be formed out of this was to be defensive in nature, established for "our protection and defence."[137] In 781, Charlemagne crowned his infant son Louis king of Aquitaine.[138] The sole survivor of the Ebro alliance, Abū Tawr of Huesca, seems to have

132. Einhard, *Vita Karoli Magni*, c.15 "ad Hiberum amnem, qui apud Navarros ortus et fertilissimos Hispaniae agros secans sub Dertosae civitatis moenia Balearico mari miscetur," 18.

133. ARF a.797 100.

134. Ibid., a.778 50.

135. Ibid., a.824 166.

136. CC 2.ii, "iniquam oppresionem et crudelissimum jugum, quod eorum cervicibus inimicissima christianitati gens Sarracenorum imposuit," 412. On the organisation of the Spanish March, see Chandler, *Carolingian Catalonia*, 60–87.

137. CC 2.ii, "subprotectione et defensione nostra," 412. On the Spanish March, see d'Abadal i de Vinyals, "Nota Sobre la locución 'Marca Hispánica'"; Werner, "Missus-Marchio-Comes," 211–221; Salrach, "Carlemany i Catalunya"; Wolfram, "The Creation of the Carolingian Frontier," 243.

138. ARF a.781 56; Astronomer, *Vita Hludowici*, c.4 294.

remained on good terms with the Franks, reappearing in the Astronomer's life of Louis, "seeking peace and sending royal gifts" to King Louis in 790.[139]

## AN UNUSUAL PROPOSITION

The most detailed description of relations between Charlemagne and ʿAbd al-Raḥmān I is contained in the history of al-Maqqarī, who states:

> Qāruluh, King of the Franks, and one of the most powerful sovereigns of that nation, after warring for a length of time with ʿAbd al-Raḥmān, sent him an embassy, and solicited an alliance with him by marriage; but the latter having met with an accident in the loins, which injured his virility, the alliance was abandoned. Qāruluh, however, sought his friendship and alliance, and again insisted on the marriage, but this was declined, although a peace was concluded between the two sovereigns.[140]

As a number of historians, generally Hispanicists and Arabists, have argued that this passage is genuine, it is worth considering in more detail.[141]

Al-Maqqarī, who worked in the seventeenth century, is the earliest recorder of this proposed marriage alliance.[142] Lévi-Provençal argued that al-Maqqarī drew upon Ibn Ḥayyān but provided no reasoning for this.[143] None of Ibn ʿIdhārī, Ibn al-Athīr, nor Ibn Khaldūn, who based their historical narratives on Ibn Ḥayyān, mentions this, leaving the attribution to Ibn Ḥayyān unlikely. The fourteenth- or fifteenth-century *Dhikr Bilād al-Andalus* (Description of the Country of al-Andalus) would seem to add credence to al-Maqqarī's account by declaring that the mother of Emir al-Ḥakam I, Zuhruf, was a concubine offered by Charlemagne.[144] This can be dismissed fairly simply. Al-Ḥakam is known to have come to the throne in 796 at the age of twenty-six, placing his birth in 770, long before the earliest contact between Charlemagne and ʿAbd al-Raḥmān I.

There are other reasons to treat this account with caution. The rulers of al-Andalus were willing to marry royal Christian women. The most

139. Astronomer, *Vita Hludowici*, c.5 "pacem petens et dona regia mittens," 298.

140. Al-Maqqarī, *The History of the Mohammedan Dynasties*, 85–86.

141. Rosenthal, "Der Plan eines Bündnisses," 441–445; El-Hajji, *Andalusian Diplomatic Relations*, 127.

142. On al-Maqqarī, see Duri, *The Rise of Historical Writing*, 40.

143. Lévi-Provençal, *Histoire de l'Espagne musulmane*, 1:120–121.

144. Sénac, *Les Carolingiens et al-Andalus*, 57.

famous of these marriages is that between ʿAbd al-ʿAzīz, the son of the conqueror Mūsā b. Nuṣayr, and Egilona, the widow of the last Visigothic king, who is said to have been incited by him to claim royal status, leading to disaster.[145] Diplomatic marriages with members of the royal houses of northern Spain also took place.[146] The Umayyad emir ʿAbd Allāh married Onneca, the daughter of King Fortún Garcés of Pamplona; their grandson would be ʿAbd Allāh's successor, ʿAbd al-Raḥmān III.[147] In 983 the strongman Abū ʿĀmir al-Manṣūr took Urraca, daughter of King Sancho II of Pamplona, as his wife; their son, nicknamed ʿAbd al-Raḥmān Sanchuelo after his maternal grandfather, briefly ruled in Córdoba (r. 1008–1009).[148] On a more local scale the ruling dynasty of Pamplona was thoroughly mixed with the Banū Qāsī, the most powerful Muslim family on the other side of the frontier.[149]

That ʿAbd al-Raḥmān I might have entertained a marriage alliance with Charlemagne is therefore not impossible. However, it is very unlikely that Charlemagne would have made any such offer.[150] In 770 Pope Stephen III sent an extremely aggressive letter to Charlemagne and his brother Carloman, vigorously condemning foreign marriages.[151] Despite his words, proposals for marriage alliances with foreign rulers were by no means unknown to the Carolingians. Charlemagne's daughter Rotrud was betrothed to the young Byzantine emperor Constantine VI in 782.[152] Carolingians occasionally, although rarely, married non-Christians. Pippin II's son, Grimoald II, married Theodelinda, the daughter of the pagan Frisian chief Radbod in 711.[153] Dudo of Saint-Quentin claims that Charles the Simple's daughter, Gisela, married the Norman leader Rollo.[154]

145. "Chronicle of 754," 35–36; Ibn al-Qūṭīya, *Early Islamic Spain*, 53; Barton, *Conquerors, Brides and Concubines*, 15–17.

146. El-Hajji, "Intermarriage between Andalusia."

147. Lacarra, "Textos navarros," 231; Fairchild Ruggles, "Mothers of a Hybrid Dynasty," 66–77.

148. *Una descripción anónima de al-Andalus, Vol.* 2, 198.

149. Manzano Moreno, "Christian-Muslim Frontier in al-Andalus," 93.

150. Le Jan, "Mariage et Relations Internationales," 204–207.

151. Stephen III, *Epistolae* no. 45, 560–563; Pohl, "Why Not to Marry a Foreign Woman."

152. *Annales Mosellani*, a.781 497. On Byzantine-Carolingian relations, see Lounghis, *Les ambassades byzantines en Occident*; McCormick, "Diplomacy and the Carolingian Encounter."

153. Costambeys, Innes, and MacLean, *The Carolingian World*, 41.

154. Dudo of Saint-Quentin, *De moribus*, 168–169. On the problems with this account, see Searle, *Predatory Kinship*, 43, 93; Nelson, "Normandy's Early History," 10.

In spite of this, according to Einhard, Charlemagne was in general opposed to his daughters marrying.[155] Rotrud's betrothal broke down in 788, with Constantine outraged at being "denied the king's daughter."[156] If the *Gesta abbatum Fontenellensium* is to be trusted, at around the same time King Offa of Mercia proposed that his son Ecgfrith be wed to Charlemagne's daughter Bertha.[157] This led to a diplomatic and commercial crisis, with English ships banned from Frankish ports.[158] None of Charlemagne's daughters married, although Rotrud and Bertha had children. Most of them became abbesses at important convents or remained at his court, where they played a crucial role in managing his palace and the elites who congregated there.[159] While a marriage proposal from Charlemagne was not impossible it should probably be deemed very implausible.

Simon Barton has convincingly argued that marriages between elite Muslim men and Christian women in early medieval al-Andalus were frequently, although not always, portrayed as statements of dominance, reflecting the power of the bridegroom to demand a bride.[160] In the case of al-Maqqarī's account, Charlemagne's offer of a marriage alliance could therefore be read as an indication of ʿAbd al-Raḥmān's superiority over the Frank for a later Arabic audience, albeit one comically undercut by the emir's impotence. The *Akhbār Majmūʿa* reports stories of ʿAbd al-Raḥmān refusing the daughter of Yūsuf al-Fihrī, preferring instead to purchase concubines.[161] This might suggest that al-Maqqarī's story is an embellishment of an earlier theme, with Charlemagne standing in for al-Fihrī. The story should therefore be dismissed as a later fiction rather than as a sign of anything that might have happened.

## MY GIRONA, 781–793

Following the Roncesvalles campaign and ʿAbd al-Raḥmān's securing of the Ebro valley, Carolingian involvement in al-Andalus becomes less obvious. The most important exception is recorded in the entry in the

155. Einhard, *Vita Karoli Magni*, c.19 23–24.

156. ARF a.788 83.

157. "Gesta abbatum Fontenellensium," 136. See the interesting if not entirely convincing discussion in Hammer, "Christmas Day 800," 9–11.

158. On this, see Story, *Carolingian Connections*, 184–188. McKitterick is sceptical, *Charlemagne*, 282–284.

159. Nelson, "Women at the Court of Charlemagne" and "Le Cour impériale de Charlemagne."

160. Barton, *Conquerors, Brides and Concubines*, 43.

161. Akhbār Majmūʿa, *A History of Early al-Andalus*, 90, 96; Marín, *Mujeres en al-Ándalus*, 552.

*Chronicle of Moissac* for 785, when "the men of Girona delivered the city of Girona to King Charles."[162] As in the case of Sulaymān, while Girona was quickly assimilated into the Spanish March, the initiative came from the southern side of the Pyrenees. This could possibly be interpreted as a reaction to increased Umayyad dominance in the region, with the death of Saʿīd b. al-Ḥusayn in that year marking the end of local efforts to challenge ʿAbd al-Raḥmān.[163] The inhabitants of Girona may also have taken advantage of a revolt in Toledo to turn to the Franks. The lack of reaction from Córdoba suggests that ʿAbd al-Raḥmān, having secured Toledo by the end of the following year, was disinclined to fight Charlemagne for a city far away from his heartlands and content that his possession of Zaragoza and Barcelona was sufficient to control the region.

That Charlemagne remained interested in Spain is suggested by his role in sending Egila to preach in al-Andalus around 780.[164] The original idea for this venture is attributed to Archbishop Wilcharius of Sens, and although Pope Hadrian was involved as sponsor, Charlemagne appears to have acted as an intermediary between Egila and Hadrian, intervening when papal letters failed to reach Egila.[165] The project imploded in the most embarrassing manner, as Hadrian discovered to his alarm that Egila had adopted the ideas of the heretic Migetius.[166] D'Abadal's argument that this was a bid by Charlemagne to take over the Visigothic church hierarchy is probably overstated, but the Egila fiasco points to continuous Carolingian engagement with the Iberian Peninsula.[167]

The peace between the Carolingians and al-Andalus, barring the possibility of some raiding, survived the death of ʿAbd al-Raḥmān I in 788. That year saw Charlemagne holding an assembly at Ingelheim which was the climax of growing tensions with Duke Tassilo III of Bavaria, which may have encouraged him to concentrate on matters beyond the Iberian Peninsula.[168] If so, his attention was brought back in 793, with the first invasion of Francia organised from Córdoba since the Battle of Tours sixty years earlier. An army led by ʿAbd al-Malik b. ʿAbd al-Wāḥid b. Mughīth sacked

162. *Chronicle of Moissac*, a.785 "Eodem anno Gerundenses homines Gerundam civitatem Carolo regi tradiderunt," 125. An event celebrated for a long time: Doolittle, "Charlemagne in Girona," 115–116.

163. Ibn al-Athīr, *Annales*, 141.

164. Hadrian I, *Epistolae* nos. 95–97, 636–648.

165. Ibid., no. 95, 637, no. 97, 648.

166. On the Migetian heresy, see Cavadini, *The Last Christology of the West*, 10–23.

167. D'Abadal i de Vinyals, *La batalla del adopcionismo*, 35–50; Innes, "'Immune from Heresy.'"

168. Becher, *Eid und Herrschaft*; Airlie, "Narratives of Triumph."

the outskirts of Narbonne and defeated Count William of Toulouse, in a battle in which they "killed many Franks and returned victorious."[169] The attack was unexpected, catching Charlemagne overseeing the construction of a canal between the Rhine and the Danube.[170] Louis, the young king of Aquitaine, was in Italy, campaigning with his brother Pippin in Benevento.[171] It was a bad year for William's family, as his father Theoderic was killed by a Saxon ambush on the other side of the empire.[172] Despite the success of the raid, it was not followed up. The timing of the attack was probably deliberate. The *Chronicle of Moissac* and the *Annales Laureshamenses* state that Hishām I chose to strike while the Avars "fought bravely" against Charlemagne, suggesting an impressive level of knowledge about Frankish affairs.[173]

The invasion can be explained not as the product of Frankish provocation or Umayyad territorial expansion but as the result of internal developments within al-Andalus. Following ʿAbd al-Raḥmān I's death civil war broke out between the emir's sons, with Hishām I emerging triumphant and exiling his brothers Sulaymān the Syrian and ʿAbd Allāh the Valencian to North Africa in 790.[174] From 791 the new emir had an aggressive relationship with his neighbours, launching attacks on Asturias in 791, 792, 794, and 795 which resembled that of 793 on the Franks.[175] As well as leading the expedition of 793, ʿAbd al-Malik was in command of the raids of 792 and 795. These incursions were intended to cement Hishām's authority after his contested succession, by accruing plunder and glory through military success.[176] The expeditionary armies also reminded the fractious frontier regions they passed through of Córdoba's power. The Arabic accounts portray the campaigns as *jihād*, part of Hishām's claim to be a holy warrior and therefore a legitimate ruler.[177] The *Akhbār Majmūʿa* commends Hishām for "protecting the Marches," claiming that in his reign not one Muslim female captive could be found in Christian lands "so well were the Marches guarded; so many captives did [Hishām] rescue; so

169. Revised ARF a.793 "multis Francorum interfectis victores ad sua regressi sunt," 95; AL a.793 35; *Chronicle of Moissac*, a.793 131.

170. Revised ARF a.793 95.

171. Astronomer, *Vita Hludowici*, c.6 302.

172. Revised ARF a.793, 93.

173. AL a.793 "fortiter dimicassent," 35; *Chronicle of Moissac*, a.793 131.

174. Ibn al-Athīr, *Annales*, 142; Manzano Moreno, *Conquistadores, Emires y Califas*, 195.

175. Collins, *Early Medieval Spain*, 196.

176. Collins, *The Arab Conquest*, 206.

177. Kennedy, *Muslim Spain and Portugal*, 39.

weak were the enemy."[178] Ibn al-Qūṭīya stresses Hishām's piety, incorrectly claiming that the emir used the plunder from the raid of 793 to build the Great Mosque of Córdoba.[179]

Septimania was invaded not because it belonged to the Franks but because it was Christian and vulnerable. The attack of 793 was to be the prologue for a series of hostilities that lasted more than twenty years. Whereas Charlemagne had ignored the civil war of 788–790, the Franks took full advantage of that which followed Hishām's death in 796. Increased Carolingian activity in Spain from the mid-790s took place for several reasons, but one of them was probably a new awareness of the potential danger posed by the Umayyads.

## 751–793 CONCLUSION

If the period from 751 to 793 was one of relatively little Carolingian-Andalusi interaction, punctuated with the odd explosion, several observations can be made. The first is that Charlemagne was generally reactive in his policy to Spain. His invasion of 778 and the acquisition of Girona in 785 were initiated by actors within al-Andalus. Establishing Louis in the region and encouraging settlement in the Spanish March were defensive actions, designed to secure gains already made rather than pushing further south. Faced with possibilities on other, more promising frontiers, Charlemagne seems to have been content to wait for opportunities to arise.

The second is that neither Charlemagne nor ʿAbd al-Raḥmān was interested in diplomacy for its own sake. Rather, their contact was restricted to straightforward problem solving, as in the case of the ransom of Thaʿlaba. This was less the case with the lords of the Upper March such as Abū Tawr, for whom keeping in regular positive contact with the Franks became steadily more important after 778. But the Carolingians and the Umayyads communicated because they were increasingly brought into closer proximity of the sort likely to lead to clashes unless properly handled.

Following on from these first two points, much of the shape of Carolingian-Umayyad interaction was determined by the internal politics of al-Andalus. The unstable nature of the Umayyad state, with its multiple regional powers and unclear laws of succession, would create

178. Akhbār Majmūʿa, *A History of Early al-Andalus*, 113–114. On the importance of such protection for the legitimacy of Islamic rulers, see Munt, "Caliphal Imperialism," 9–10.

179. Ibn al-Qūṭīya, *Early Islamic Spain*, 83. On the Great Mosque, see Creswell, *A Short Account*, 291–302; Dodds, "The Great Mosque of Córdoba"; Ocaña Jiménez, "The Basilica of San Vicente."

opportunities for Frankish intervention.[180] The priority placed by the emirs upon internal affairs, and in particular Córdoba and the Guadalquivir, meant that their engagement with the Carolingians was dependent upon what best suited their need to manage their central territories, rather than on affairs at the frontier. Hishām's campaigns of the early 790s, inexplicable in the light of Umayyad relations with Charlemagne, make sense as performances for a mostly Andalusi audience. The final thing to note is that this behaviour was not specific to the Carolingians and the Umayyads. From the 770s on, the political landscape increasingly mirrors that of the 720s and 730s, with the appeal of Sulaymān recalling that of Munuza, while Hishām's attack resembles those of the governors of Córdoba.[181] Once again there were two great powers more or less at the Pyrenees with semi-independent figures in the zone between them, capable of pulling them into contact.

## *The Franks on the Offensive, 796–812*

The attack of 793 was to be answered several times over. From 796 Carolingian forces, led primarily by Charlemagne's son, Louis the Pious, the king of Aquitaine, attacked Andalusi territory nearly annually until 812. Accompanying and supporting these offensives were alliances with other Iberian rulers, forming a loose coalition against Umayyad power. This period represented a radical increase in both Carolingian interest and military investment in al-Andalus, at odds with previous activity on the frontier.

In a letter of 790 written to Colcu in Northumbria, Alcuin celebrated "the leaders and captains of the most Christian king [who] took many parts of Spain from the Saracens."[182] Despite this impressive language, there is no evidence that anything more than skirmishing took place up to that point, and there seems to have been limited Carolingian pressure on the Muslims inhabiting the Upper March facing onto Frankish territory. Other hints of campaigning are difficult to find. In 795 Charlemagne granted an estate to the warrior John as a reward for having won "a great battle against the heretic or infidel Saracens in the country of Barcelona."[183] The lack of any reference to John's battle in the annals suggests that it was actually a relatively small-scale affair.

180. Cruz Hernández, "The Social Structure of al-Andalus," 67.

181. On the attacks of the 720s and 730s, see Chalmeta, *Invasión e Islamización*, 268–288; Manzano Moreno, *Conquistadores, Emires y Califas*, 82–84.

182. Alcuin, *Epistolae* no. 7, "Etiam et ejusdem Christianissimi regis duces et tribuni multam partem Hispaniae tulerunt a Saracenis," 32.

183. CC 2.ii, 310; Chandler, "Between Court and Counts," 29–33. On John's career, see Haack, *Die Krieger der Karolinger*, 156–171.

This sort of minor hostility is portrayed in the tale of Datus in Ermold the Black's *In honorem Hludovici*, which tells a story of raids across the frontier targeting single holdings.[184] Something of the contested nature of the Spanish March in this period can be suggested by the Reviser of the *Annales regni Francorum* in his comment that the city of Barcelona was "now alternating between Frankish dominion and that of the Saracens."[185] Charlemagne was certainly not uninterested in Spain, as his involvement in the Adoptionist controversy and the trial of Bishop Felix of Urgell indicates, but the Carolingians do not seem actively to have sought territorial expansion in the early 790s.[186]

The second half of the 790s saw a major increase in Carolingian activity in the Upper March, with a commensurate surge in communication with Muslim figures there, as new arrangements were made and old contacts used in new ways. This change in the status quo began in 796, three years after ʿAbd al-Malik defeated Count William. That summer, according to the *Annales Laureshamenses* and the *Chronicle of Moissac*, Charlemagne sent out an army "into the territories of the Saracens with his *missi* where . . . they devastated the land there" before returning to Aachen.[187] The Franks returned in force the following year when Louis led an army into the March for apparently the first time.[188] In tandem with this aggressive expansion, Louis sought to secure existing gains in 798:

> [He] set up an extremely strong defence for the boundaries all around Aquitaine. He fortified and repopulated the city of Vic, the fortress of Cardona, Casserres, and other towns that were once deserted, and he instituted Borrell as count with suitable forces to guard them.[189]

Carolingian armies were to campaign intensively in the Upper March until 812.

184. Ermold the Black, *In honorem Hludovici*, Bk. 1, 22–27.

185. Revised ARF a.797 "Barcinona civitas in limite Hispanici sita, quae alternante rerum eventu nunc Francorum nunc Sarracenorum dicioni subiciebatur," 101.

186. On the Adoptionist controversy, see Cavadini, *The Last Christology of the West*; Chandler, "Heresy and Empire."

187. AL a.796 "transmissit in fines Saracinorum cum missis suis . . . vastaverunt terram illam," 37; *Chronicle of Moissac*, a.796 "Et tercium exercitum in eadem estatem transmisit in Spania, in fines Sarracenorum cum missis suis, qui et ipsi fecerunt similiters," 135.

188. Revised ARF a.797 107.

189. Astronomer, *Vita Hludowici*, c.8 "Ordinavit autem illo in tempore in finibus Aquitanorum circumquaque firmissimam tutelam; nam civitatem Ausonam, castrum Cardonam, Castaserram et reliqua oppida olim deserta munivit, habitari fecit et Burrello a comiti cum congruis auxiliis tuenda commisit," 308, adapted from Noble, *Charlemagne and Louis the Pious*, 234–235.

This spurt of activity is hard to explain in terms of changes within the Frankish empire. Louis was now a young man with his own retinue, but he had been given arms already in 791 and had campaigned with his brother Pippin of Italy in Benevento and his father in Saxony, indicating that his age was not the crucial condition determining the timing of the invasions.[190] It has been suggested that Louis was attempting to placate the Iberian refugees at his Aquitainian court by waging war on the frontier, but, again, these figures had been present long before this wave of invasions.[191] In any case, the importance of Louis to this war should not be overstated.

Although Louis and his retinue played a key role, the first campaign in 796 was initiated by Charlemagne.[192] Louis and Charlemagne had regular meetings in the period. His older brother, Charles the Younger, was also sent to support the king of Aquitaine at the siege of Barcelona.[193] The conflict was in no sense Louis's private war. Nor was it an exercise in keeping the troops busy. The Carolingians were already engaged in campaigns on several fronts. The army sent to Spain in 796 was the third that year, as Pippin marched against the Avars while Charlemagne, Charles, and Louis waged war against the Saxons.[194] The Carolingians were to continue campaigning against the Saxons for the rest of the decade.[195]

If the Franks felt they were now in a position to go on the offensive in the Spanish March, the reason lies in the confusion on the other side of the frontier. The death of Emir Hishām I on 12 June 796 led to political chaos in al-Andalus, because the succession of the deceased emir's son, al-Ḥakam I, was challenged by two of his uncles, Sulaymān the Syrian and ʿAbd Allāh the Valencian.[196] After the death of Hishām I, Sulaymān left exile in North Africa to raise an army in the Guadalquivir river basin and march on Córdoba, thereby immediately becoming the new emir's first priority.[197] It would take several battles before Sulaymān was defeated, being handed over to his nephew by the governor of Mérida and executed in 800/801.[198] The ensuing civil war ensured that Córdoba was in no

190. Astronomer, *Vita Hludowici*, c.6 300. See Nelson, "The Siting of the Council at Frankfort," 159, and "Charlemagne—pater optimus?" 275–278.

191. Tremp, "Zwischen Paderborn und Barcelona."

192. AL a.796 37; *Chronicle of Moissac*, a.796 135.

193. Astronomer, *Vita Hludowici*, c.13 320.

194. ARF a.756 100; AL a.796 37.

195. On the Saxon wars, see now Rembold, *Conquest and Christianization*, 39–84.

196. Ibn Ḥayyān, *Crónica de los emires*, 15–19.

197. Collins, *Caliphs and Kings*, 29–30.

198. Ibn Ḥayyān, *Crónica de los emires*, 18.

position to intervene in the Upper March. Even had al-Ḥakam not been fighting for survival, a revolt in Toledo blocked his route to the Upper March, which was in political turmoil.[199] These circumstances provided the Carolingians with a way to divide the Umayyads, particularly when in 797 ʿAbd Allāh the Valencian visited Charlemagne looking for support.

The convenience of the civil war for the Franks is observed in the sources. Ibn Ḥayyān attributed the fall of Barcelona in 801 to "the period of agitation" saying that it "strengthened the Frankish enemy, may God break them."[200] The *Chronicle of Moissac* makes a similar link, as its account of the fall of Barcelona immediately follows a reference to the death of Hishām.[201] The excellence of the timing suggests that Charlemagne was keeping an eye on affairs in Córdoba. Given the impact of the Adoptionist controversy, which prompted Charlemagne to spend much of the early 790s concerned with religion in the Spanish March, it seems plausible that he would have had sources capable of informing him of the emir's death and an imminent civil war.[202]

For his sake it is to be hoped that Charlemagne's sources were better than those of the modern historian. The Frankish sources, which are the closest in time to the events, are confused in their chronology.[203] There is a fundamental disjunction between the fullest source, the anonymous *Vita* of Louis the Pious attributed to the Astronomer, and the *Annales regni Francorum*, even down to basic details like the year of the fall of Barcelona.[204] Josep Salrach has carefully untangled the chronology of the siege of Barcelona, proposing a campaign begun in 800 and ending with the fall of the city in April the following year. [205] The Arabic sources are generally jumbled in their chronology for this period, and Ibn Ḥayyān's misdating of the death of Charlemagne does not grant much confidence in even the more annalistic histories.[206]

An important part of Carolingian policy with al-Andalus was the cultivation of independent-minded Muslim frontier lords. Charlemagne's

199. Collins, *Caliphs and Kings*, 41.

200. Ibn Ḥayyān, *Crónica de los emires*, "el periodo de agitación," "se apoderó el enemigo franco, al que Dios quiebre," 36.

201. *Chronicle of Moissac*, a.803 142.

202. Charlemagne's interest is suggested by his request to Alcuin for Felix of Urgell's *Disputatio Felicis cum Sarraceno*; Alcuin, *Epistolae* no. 172, 284–285.

203. On the problems in the chronology, see Auzias, "Les Sièges de Barcelone"; Wolff, "Les Événements de Catalogne"; Bachrach, "Military Organisation," 14–28.

204. ARF a.801 116; Astronomer, *Vita Hludowici*, c.26 314.

205. Salrach, *El Procés de Formació Nacional*, 15–22.

206. Ibn Ḥayyān, *Crónica de los emires*, 47.

arrangement with Sulaymān al-ʿArābī may have ended in disaster but, as noted above, Abū Tawr of Huesca maintained his relationship with the Franks.[207] In 795 at Toulouse, Louis "received and dismissed the envoys of Bahlūl [b. Marzūq], leader of the Saracens, who ruled the mountainous land next to Aquitaine, asking for peace and bearing gifts."[208] These alliances were to proliferate and become increasingly important from 796.

One of the most important results of the civil war among the Umayyads was the encouragement it gave independent-minded regional powers to make their own bids for greater autonomy. In the Middle March, the cities of Toledo and Mérida rebelled.[209] Many of the lords of the Upper March did likewise and, to safeguard their position, some of these men turned to the Franks for help. The alliances forged by the Carolingians with these marcher lords played a key part in encouraging and supporting the Frankish offensive.

In the summer of 797, the governor of Barcelona, Saʿdūn al-Ruʿaynī, came to Aachen and "returned" the city to Charlemagne but was granted it back by the king.[210] Travelling further to talk to the Frankish king was ʿAbd Allāh the Valencian, who arrived at Aachen in the autumn of the same year, fresh from his North African exile.[211] ʿAbd Allāh was well received by Charlemagne and was escorted to the Spanish March by Louis in November, where he emerged in the same year allied to Bahlūl b. Marzūq, who had sent an envoy to Louis two years earlier.[212] Bahlūl rebelled in the same year against the Banū Salama in Huesca, taking that city and Zaragoza.[213] It seems plausible that it was the Franks who put ʿAbd Allāh in contact with him. Frankish support for ʿAbd Allāh seems to have been an attempt to destabilise al-Andalus, either by encouraging civil war or by putting a friendly ruler in power in Córdoba. Either end could be served by helping ʿAbd Allāh establish a powerbase in the Upper March.

Many people in the Iberian Peninsula were clearly looking toward the Franks for backing at this point. It is in the context of this upheaval in the Upper March that the brief report in the *Annales regni Francorum* that in 799 "Azan [probably Ḥassān] leader of the city which is called

207. Astronomer, *Vita Hludowici*, c.5 298.

208. Ibid., c.8 "Necnon et Bahaluc Sarracenorum ducis, qui locis montuosis Aquitaniae proximis principabatur, missos pacem petentes et dona ferentes suscepit et remisit," 306.

209. On Toledo in this period, see Christys, *Christians in al-Andalus*, 18–21.

210. ARF a.797 100; Revised ARF a.797 "reddita est," 101.

211. ARF a.797 100; Ibn Ḥayyān, *Crónica de los emires*, 17.

212. ARF a.797 102; Ibn Ḥayyān, *Crónica de los emires*, 20.

213. Al-ʿUhdrī, "La Marca Superior," 464; Ibn ʿIdhārī, in Millàs i Vallicrosa, *Textos dels historiadors*, 102; Ibn al-Athīr, *Annales*, 160.

Huesca, sent the keys of the city with his envoy with gifts" should be understood.[214] This Ḥassān is otherwise unknown, unless he was one of the Banū Salama, and his tenure in Huesca must have been brief. The appeal to the Franks was an indication of just how precarious his situation was and the city was to remain under Muslim control until 1096. The reference to presenting the city keys, a symbol of submission going back at least to the time of Justinian, need not be taken too seriously. Louis the Pious is reported to have sent Charlemagne the keys to Tortosa in 809 despite failing to take the city.[215]

It is beyond the scope of this chapter to do more than note that it was not just Muslims who saw this as a moment to ally with the Carolingians. King Alfonso II of Asturias (r. 791–842) seems to have coordinated his campaigns with Louis, sending envoys to the Franks with trophies of victory in 795 and before and after sacking Lisbon in 798.[216] The murky nature of the surviving evidence makes it hard to be certain, but the killing of the governor of Pamplona, Muṭarrif b. Mūsā, by the inhabitants of the city in 799 may also be a product of this moment, although the city only came under Carolingian influence again in 806, before decisively rejecting Frankish power in 824.[217]

By 797 the situation in the Upper March was highly promising for Charlemagne and Louis, with Córdoba distracted and a large number of potential allies ready to look for alternatives to Umayyad power. It was a situation that the Carolingians were to take full advantage of, and Charlemagne "sent his son Louis to besiege Huesca with an army in Spain," possibly in collaboration with Bahlūl.[218] Yet the results were disappointing for the Carolingians, with the only major success in subsequent years of campaigning being the fall of Barcelona in 801. Much of the reason for this failure lies in the breakdown of the alliances made by the Carolingians with the warlords of the Upper March. The collapse of these arrangements

214. ARF a.799 "Azan praefectus civitatis, quae dicitur Osca, claves urbis per legatum suum cum muneribus transmisit," 108; Viguera Molíns, *Aragón Musulmán*, 54.

215. McCormick, *Eternal Victory*, 377.

216. Astronomer, *Vita Hludowici*, c.8 306; ARF a.798 102, 104. On Alfonso II and Charlemagne, see Defourneaux, "Carlomagno y el Reino Asturiano"; Fernández Conde, "Relaciones políticas"; Escalona, "Family Memories," 226–231.

217. Ibn Ḥayyān, *Crónica de los emires*, 35; ARF a.806 122; ARF a.824 166; Lorenzo Jiménez, *La dawla de los Banū Qasī*, 120. The kingdom of Pamplona is poorly understood, but see Lacarra, "Textos navarros"; Pérez de Urbel, "Lo Viejo y lo Nuevo"; Sánchez-Albornoz, "Problemas de la historia Navarra"; Lacarra, *Historia Política*; Collins, *The Basques*, 133–163.

218. Revised ARF a.797 "filium suum Hludowicum ad obsidionem Oscae cum exercitu in Hispaniam misit," 101.

can be explained by the lack of trust and understanding between the Franks and their Muslim allies, and the lack of coordination between the rebel lords themselves.

The first problem was a product of the tension between the desire of the Muslim allies for greater autonomy and Carolingian pretensions to dominate the region. A case in point is the fate of Saʿdūn al-Ruʿaynī. The arrangement between the governor of Barcelona and the Carolingians seems to have collapsed rapidly as the participants did not agree on the meaning of their alliance. The language of the Frankish sources implies that Charlemagne thought he had a pliant subordinate, for the Reviser of the *Annales regni Francorum* portrays Saʿdūn being "entrusted with the city" of Barcelona.[219] Saʿdūn appears to have viewed his status as one with rather more personal autonomy. This came to a head when Charlemagne dispatched Louis to take advantage of this new opportunity in 797, but "as he was approaching Barcelona, Zaddo [Saʿdūn], leader of the city, met him as a subject, but did not give him the city."[220] This led to a breakdown in relations, and the eventual siege of Barcelona, starting in 800 and ending the following year. When the city fell in 801 Saʿdūn was sent to Charlemagne with the other spoils of war as part of the triumphal proceedings, before being "condemned to exile."[221] This was obviously a less than ideal situation for Saʿdūn, but it also forced the Carolingians to waste time in which al-Ḥakam could put his house in order.

The warlords of the Upper March did not necessarily form a natural bloc and each possessed their own interests, which hindered coordinated action against Córdoba. An example of this is the breakdown in the alliance between Bahlūl b. Marzūq and ʿAbd Allāh. The rebel Umayyad allied with another warlord, Abū ʿImrān, and the Banū Salama.[222] Before long the two sides were undermining each other, literally in the case of Bahlūl who, while besieging ʿAbd Allāh in Huesca in 800/801, is said to have caused the tower his erstwhile ally resided in to collapse by tunnelling beneath it.[223] ʿAbd Allāh escaped to Valencia. Bahlūl also seems to have alienated the initially sympathetic ʿAbd al-Malik b. ʿAbd al-Wāḥid (who had led the 793 invasion of Francia) and his brother ʿAbd al-Karīm,

219. Revised ARF a.797 "cum civitate commendavit," 101; Steiger, *Die Ordnung der Welt*, 456.

220. Astronomer, *Vita Hludowici*, c.10 "Cui Barcinnone adpropianti Zaddo dux eiusdem civitatis iamque subiectus occurrit, nec tamen civitatem dedidit," 310.

221. ARF a.801 "exilio damnati sunt," 116.

222. Ibn al-Athīr, *Annales*, 162.

223. Ibn Ḥayyān, *Crónica de los emires*, 23–24.

driving them into the arms of al-Ḥakam.[224] Frankish intervention in the Upper March was made possible by division between key figures in al-Andalus, but the fundamental disunity of the Upper March itself, as in the case of Sulaymān al-ʿArābī and al-Ḥusayn al-Anṣārī, served to frustrate Carolingian designs, ensuring that ʿAbd Allāh could not establish himself in the Ebro valley.

This working at cross-purposes gave al-Ḥakam the time necessary to deal with Sulaymān the Syrian and to regain control of Toledo. The instrument he employed for this latter task was ʿAmrūs b. Yūsuf the Basque, a man who first came to emiral attention by killing Maṭrūḥ, the rebellious son of Sulaymān al-ʿArābī and presenting his head to Hishām I.[225] ʿAmrūs was from Huesca in the Upper March. In the crisis year of 797 he was governor of Talavera, when he was sent by al-Ḥakam to bring the rebellious city of Toledo to heel.[226] Following success in that enterprise, he was made governor of the Upper March in 801.[227] By 802, ʿAmrūs had defeated Bahlūl b. Marzūq and secured his position in the Upper March by giving Huesca to his cousin Sabrīt, and Tudela to his son Yūsuf.[228] Bahlūl was killed by one of his own supporters, Khalaf b. Rashīd of Barbastro.[229] ʿAbd Allāh managed to make peace with his nephew al-Ḥakam in 803, being allowed to retain control of Valencia, which effectively ended the Umayyad civil war.[230]

As a final demonstration of the highly contingent nature of Carolingian expansion in al-Andalus, the later career of ʿAmrūs deserves some attention. According to the majority of the Arabic sources ʿAmrūs was a model governor. Al-ʿUhdrī says "he remained many years as *walī* of Zaragoza, following the path of loyalty."[231] In 809 he participated in the campaign led by the emir's son, ʿAbd al-Raḥmān, which frustrated Louis the Pious's attempt to take Tortosa, a city strategically located close to the mouth of the Ebro.[232] Ibn Ḥayyān, on the other hand, casts doubt on this positive interpretation, informing us that in the year 809 "things changed

224. Ibid., 37.

225. Al-ʿUhdrī, "La Marca Superior," 465; Ibn ʿIdhārī, *Textos dels historiadors*, 92.

226. Ibn al-Qūṭīya, *Early Islamic Spain*, 86–87; Manzano Moreno, *La organización fronteriza*, 516–525; Collins, *Caliphs and Kings*, 32.

227. Al-ʿUhdrī, "La Marca Superior," 465.

228. Ibn Ḥayyān, *Crónica de los emires*, 38–39.

229. Al-ʿUhdrī, "La Marca Superior," 465.

230. Ibn Ḥayyān, *Crónica de los emires*, 37.

231. Al-ʿUhdrī, "La Marca Superior," 467.

232. ARF a.809 127; Astronomer, *Vita Hludowici*, c.15 326; Ibn ʿIdhārī, *Textos dels historiadors*, 108; Manzano Moreno, *La Frontera de al-Andalus*, 81–83.

with ʿAmrūs b. Yūsuf, Governor of the Upper March, because of a dispute, manifested in the hostility and perversion of his behaviour."[233] After some fighting, the chamberlain ʿAbd al-Karīm b. ʿAbd al-Wāḥid succeeded in bringing ʿAmrūs to Córdoba in 811.[234]

The behavioural perversions alluded to by Ibn Ḥayyān are unclear, but some light on the matter is shed by the *Annales regni Francorum*. The year 809 saw the death of the otherwise unknown Count Aureolus "who resided on the border of Spain and Gaul, across the Pyrenees against Huesca and Zaragoza."[235] ʿAmrūs stepped into the power vacuum, seizing the area, and "invaded, placed garrisons in his castles, and sent an embassy to the emperor, promising that he was willing to submit to him with everything he had."[236] Charlemagne seems to have been prepared in principle to contemplate the exchanging of a Christian ally for a Muslim one, so long as ʿAmrūs showed himself willing to cooperate.[237]

ʿAmrūs appears again the following year, asking "for a meeting with the guards of the Spanish border."[238] The Frankish emperor granted his permission but complications, presumably linked to Andalusi campaigning, prevented this conference from happening. Despite this failure to meet, al-Ḥakam seems to have recognised the potential danger of Frankish intervention. He began negotiations with Charlemagne, culminating in peace in 810 and the return of "Count Haimric, who had been captured by the Saracens and whom al-Ḥakam returned."[239] Rather than seeking gains in the area, Charlemagne used ʿAmrūs to bargain with al-Ḥakam for peace and hostage return, suggesting that the Spanish March was not his greatest priority at this point.[240]

The fate of ʿAmrūs demonstrates the difference between his moment of rebellion and conditions a decade earlier. Al-Ḥakam was able to respond swiftly to the straying of his governor from the path of loyalty because

233. Ibn Ḥayyān, *Crónica de los emires*, "Se torcieron los cosas con ʿAmrūs b. Yūsuf, gobernador de la Marca Superior a causa de una desavenencia, haciéndose manifiesta su hostilidad y la perversión de su proceder," 49.

234. Ibid., 50.

235. ARF a.809 "qui in commercio Hispaniae atque Galliae trans Pirineum contra Oscam et Caesaraugustam residebat," 130.

236. Ibid., "eius invasit et in castellis illius praesidia disposuit missaque ad imperatorem legatione sese cum omnibus, quae habebat, in deditionem illi venire velle promisit," 130, adapted from Scholz, *Carolingian Chronicles*, 91.

237. Cf. Chandler, "Heresy and Empire," 519.

238. ARF a.809 "colloquium fieret inter ipsum et Hispanici limitis custodies," 130.

239. ARF a.810 "Haimricum comitem olim a Sarracenis captum Abulaz remittente recipit," 133.

240. ARF a.810 130–133; Smith, "Fines Imperii," 172.

he was no longer fighting for his regime's existence. Perhaps due to the failures of his previous Muslim allies, Charlemagne viewed ʿAmrūs as expendable. With the ending of the crisis that accompanied al-Ḥakam's accession came the close of the window of opportunity for the Carolingians. The beginning of the ninth century saw frequent Carolingian campaigns in the March, with attempts to take Tarragona in 805, Tortosa in 805, 809, and 810, and Huesca in 811 and 812.[241] Not one of these attempts was particularly successful, largely due to the armies sent out from Córdoba and the lack of support from within the Upper March.[242]

The wave of Carolingian campaigning in Spain depended on conditions within al-Andalus, namely the distraction in Córdoba caused by the Umayyad civil war and the willingness of Muslim border warlords to enter into agreements with the Franks. Charlemagne and Louis took advantage of this to seize Barcelona and establish a loose coalition of allies in the Upper March. The end of those conditions saw the end of Aachen's ability to dominate the region. Charlemagne and Louis seem to have been well informed about the internal politics of the Iberian Peninsula and to have responded to it opportunistically, taking advantage of openings as they appeared. The Upper March needs to be understood therefore, at least in part, in terms of its relationships with the Umayyad and Carolingian political centres, with the level of autonomy available to political actors based in the region being highly dependent on the status of these cores.

Many of these elements can be observed in Carolingian dealings with other neighbours. Charlemagne's support for ʿAbd Allāh the Valencian is reminiscent of the shelter he offered to Theodore, "a prince of Huns," in 805, and his backing of the deposed King Eardwulf of Northumbria in 808.[243] Charlemagne and Louis periodically involved themselves in the internal conflicts of the kings of Denmark.[244] Alliances with pagan Viking chiefs such as that between the emperor Lothar and Harald in 834, the arrangement between Pippin II and the Loire Vikings from 857 to 864, and the career of Rorik in Frisia provide an interesting comparison with the arrangements made with Muslim warlords on the Spanish frontier.[245] Relations between the East Frankish kingdom and the Moravians also

241. ARF a.809 127; Astronomer, *Vita Hludowici*, c.14 322, c.15 326, c.16 330, c.17 330–332; Salrach, *El Procés de Formació Nacional*, 1:29–33.

242. Ibn ʿIdhārī, *Textos dels historiadors*, 108.

243. ARF a.805 119–120, 126; Story, *Carolingian Connections*, 145–156.

244. On Danish royal politics in this period, see Maund, "'A Turmoil of Warring Princes.'"

245. Coupland, "From Poachers to Gamekeepers."

provide compelling similarities. The attempts by Louis the German and Karlmann to divide Duke Rastislav from his nephew Svatopluk show the same logic as that discussed above.[246] Likewise the role of figures such as Duke Pribina in Lower Pannonia as loosely associated subordinates based on the frontier, retaining considerable freedom of action but centred on Carolingian interests, is intriguing.[247]

Other examples could be assembled. Their contours are harder to trace due to a more limited source base but they suggest that the Spanish March was not entirely anomalous. Nonetheless, the importance of the specific context of each case must be stressed. The Carolingians may have had a repertoire of strategies and techniques but they approached each situation separately.[248] Muslim lords in the Upper March acting for their own political advantage often frustrated Carolingian plans. The emirs also had to pay attention to the sensibilities of these figures, which probably explains the gentle handling ʿAmrūs received. According to Ibn Ḥayyān, the time spent by ʿAmrūs and his family in Córdoba was fairly congenial, with al-Ḥakam treating them as honoured guests and deigning to play polo with them.[249] In 812 ʿAmrūs was restored to his former position, although al-Ḥakam kept his cousin Sabrīt hostage.[250] The governor died shortly afterwards in Zaragoza in 813/814. He may have appreciated the irony that he had done more than most to reassert the Umayyad power that eventually brought him down.

## USELESS PEACE, 810–820

In the study of Carolingian-Umayyad diplomacy, it is frequently the Frankish sources that are the most useful, because they are generally written closest to events. For the 810s, however, even the Carolingian sources start to become unclear, as they grow increasingly vague about relations with Córdoba. If this is frustrating for the modern historian, the text of the *Annales regni Francorum* suggests that the annalist was also experiencing a certain amount of irritation. The entry for the year 815 contains the following:

246. AF a.870 70; Althoff, "Zur Bedeutung der Bündnisse"; Goldberg, "Ludwig der Deutsche und Mähren"; Innes, "Franks and Slavs" provides a useful overview.

247. Štih, "Pribina"; Goldberg, *Struggle for Empire*, 83–85, 138–140, 265–267.

248. Smith, "Fines Imperii," 172.

249. Ibn Ḥayyān, *Crónica de los emires*, 50.

250. Ibid.

> Peace, which had been made with Abulaz [al-Ḥakam] king of the Saracens and had been kept for three years, was broken as useless and war was resumed against him.[251]

Another peace was made between al-Ḥakam and Louis the Pious in 817, but in 820, the annals announce:[252]

> The treaty between us and Abulaz, the king of Spain, which did not satisfy either party, was purposely broken, and war against him was resumed.[253]

These terse lines are not recording a decade of diplomatic success. Throughout the 810s, attempts at peace were made and promptly broken. The years 810 and 812 had also seen Charlemagne and al-Ḥakam making short-lived treaties.[254] As we have seen, the *Annales regni Francorum* are somewhat vague in their comments, noting that the peaces were not useful and deliberately broken.

Part of the problem with understanding the events of the 810s is the lack of clear information about the treaties being negotiated. The best way to assess what was agreed on these occasions is to observe what changed when they were broken in 815 and 820, respectively. In both cases the composer of the *Annales regni Francorum* comments that "war was resumed," so clearly at least part of the original agreement was the abeyance of military hostilities.[255] The end of the peace meant the entry into a state of war.[256] Theodulf of Orléans appears to have anticipated conflict with the Umayyads, as in a poem he wrote for Louis between 814 and 818 he included the lines "May you subdue Spain, as you yourself pursue wild beasts / As the wild boar yields to you, so may the Moor and Arab yield."[257] Despite this, there is no evidence of the Franks actively campaigning against Córdoba in these years. From 815 to 817, war was regarded as less

251. ARF a.815 "Pax, quae cum Abulaz rege Sarracenorum facta et per triennium servata erat, velut inutilis rupta et contra eum iterum bellum susceptum est," 143.

252. ARF a.817 145.

253. ARF a.820 "Foedus inter nos et Abulaz regem Hispaniae constitutum et neutrae parti satis proficuum consulto ruptum bellumque adversus eum susceptum est," 153, translated by Scholz, *Carolingian Chronicles*, 107.

254. ARF a.810 133; ARF a.812 137.

255. ARF a.815 "et contra eum iterum bellum susceptum est," 143; ARF a.820 "bellumque adversus eum susceptum est," 153.

256. On the ambiguity of peace in the early medieval world, see Lund, "Peace and Non-Peace in the Viking Age"; Wolfthal, "Introduction," xvi.

257. Theodulf of Orléans, *Eiusdem ad Hluduicum valedictio*, no. 39, "Hesperiam reprimas, ut premis ipse feras. Ut tibi cedit aper, Maurus tibi cedat Arabsque," 531.

useless than peace, and yet apparently absolutely nothing was done by the Carolingians to prosecute it.

This rather confusing record of phoney war and equally phoney peace raises two questions. Why was peace between the powers so hard to maintain and yet so apparently desirable? And why, despite the frequent declarations of war, is there limited reference to actual military activity? The diplomatic confusion of the 810s was a consequence of a shift in the balance of power in general between Aachen and Córdoba. Having defeated his domestic rivals, al-Ḥakam found himself in a considerably stronger position on the frontier. By contrast, Charlemagne and Louis the Pious faced serious difficulties in managing their frontier zone with al-Andalus, the Spanish March, and, particularly, Gascony.

There are a number of alternative explanations. One possibility is that the activity of Muslim pirates in the Western Mediterranean in this decade provoked Carolingian anger against Córdoba.[258] The early 810s saw heavy raiding by Muslim pirates in the Western Mediterranean, as recorded by the *Annales regni Francorum*. In 810, for example, "the Moors with a fleet of immense size, which had been gathered from the whole of Spain, landed first in Sardinia, then in Corsica."[259] Two years later the two islands were attacked again, as were Sicily and Lampedusa.[260] The following year Civitavecchia and Nice were sacked.[261] These depredations are unlikely to be a contributory factor for several reasons. There is little to connect the raids in this period to Córdoba. While it is true that the majority of the raiders were based in Spain, they seem to have operated out of the east coast, from the territory under the authority of al-Ḥakam's unruly uncle, ʿAbd Allāh.[262] According to the Arabic sources, they were for the most part criminals on the run from Umayyad justice.[263] Even if this was a distinction beyond most Franks, the record of the annals and papal letters demonstrate that Charlemagne was well aware that many of the raiders came from Africa.[264]

The timeline of raiding does not match the making and breaking of treaties. Records of raiding end in 813, with the exception of a reference

258. Lankila, "Saracen Maritime Raids," 190–192.

259. ARF a.810 "Mauri de tota Hispania maxima classe conparata primo Sardiniam, deinde Corsicam appulerunt," 130, translated by Scholz, *Carolingian Chronicles*, 91.

260. ARF a.812 137; Leo III, *Epistolae* no. 6, 7, 96–99.

261. ARF a.813 139.

262. Guichard, "Les débuts de la piraterie," 64.

263. Ibid., 82–83; Manzano Moreno, "Byzantium and al-Andalus," 216–217.

264. ARF a.812 137; Leo III, *Epistolae* no. 6, 7, 96–99.

to one attack on shipping in the Tyrrhenian in 820.[265] Al-Ḥakam cracked down on piracy in the mid-810s and a large fleet of Andalusi pirates appeared in the Eastern Mediterranean in 814/815, corresponding precisely to their vanishing in the Western Mediterranean.[266] Despite this apparent drop in piratical activity, peace was broken in 815 and only restored in 817, arguing against any connection between maritime raiding and Frankish dissatisfaction.

Another proposal for explaining at least part of the strange diplomacy in this period comes from the writings of Ibn Ḥayyān, who records the following:

> Peace was concluded between the Emir al-Ḥakam and Charles, son of Pippin, king of Francia, after an exchange of ambassadors. . . . This conclusion was motivated at this moment by the appearance of Idrīs b. ʿAbd Allāh al-Ḥasanī on the North African coast, to the dismay of the Franks.[267]

While it is plausible that he refers here to the peace made in 812 and broken in 815, Ibn Ḥayyān's chronology is confused, for he dates Charlemagne's death to 806 or 807.

The Idrīs Ibn Ḥayyān refers to, also known as Idrīs I (r. 789–791), was the founder of the Idrīsid dynasty that ruled much of modern Morocco in the ninth and tenth centuries.[268] The suggestion that he influenced Charlemagne to make peace runs into difficulty fairly quickly. Ibn Ḥayyān's order of events is somewhat shaky, but whether we opt for 807 or 812 as the date of this supposed agreement, the fact remains that Idrīs I was most definitely dead, having been assassinated in 791.[269] We might choose to let the matter lie here, if not for the fact that a letter from Pope Leo III sent to Charlemagne in 813 spends a lot of time discussing the Byzantine governor of Sicily's negotiations with Idrīs I's son and successor, Idrīs II

265. ARF a.820 153.

266. Lévi-Provençal, *Histoire de l'Espagne musulmane*, 1:170–173; Guichard, "Les débuts de la piraterie," 66.

267. Ibn Ḥayyān, *Crónica de los emires*, "Se concluyó la paz entre el emir Alḥakam y Carlos, hijo de Pipino, rey de Francia, tras un intercambio de embajadores, que duraba desde comienzos del reinado de Alḥakam, y laboriosas vicisitudes. Fue motivo de su conclusión en este momento la aparición en la costa norteafricana de Idrīs b. ʿAbdallāh Alḥasanī, entre la consternación de los francos," 47.

268. Abun-Nasr, *A History of the Maghrib*, 76–82; Laroui, *The History of the Maghrib*, 109–112; Fentress, "Idris I and the Berbers."

269. Manzano Moreno, "The Iberian Peninsula and North Africa," 599.

(r. 791–828).[270] This suggests that the pope had reason to believe that the Frankish emperor would be interested to hear news of Idrīsid diplomatic activity, the year after Charlemagne had made peace with al-Ḥakam.

Despite this letter, there is reason to doubt that Charlemagne's peace was linked to worry about potential Idrīsid pressure. This emerges in Leo's letter, in which the Idrīsid ambassadors explained raids on Byzantine territory by reference to Idrīs II's inability to control the pirates of the Moroccan coast.[271] Idrīs II had been born two months after his father's death and brought up under the care of a regent.[272] An analysis of the coins from the period suggests multiple political players operating at various levels of independence in the period and that Idrīs's power within Morocco, never mind beyond it, was strictly limited.[273] The main focus of Idrīsid attention seems to have been controlling the inland silver mines of Morocco and the trade routes of the Sahara.[274] While Ibn Ḥayyān may be presenting a dim reflection of Carolingian interest in Idrīsid affairs, it seems unlikely that Frankish diplomacy with the Umayyads was much influenced by Fez.

A more plausible explanation for this strange pattern of useless peace is to be found in the changing balance of power between Aachen and Córdoba. The Frankish annals frame relations between Córdoba and Aachen at this time as being driven by Frankish power. The *Chronicle of Moissac* presents Charlemagne generously granting al-Ḥakam peace in 812.[275] The *Annales regni Francorum* specifically states that peace was broken in 815 and 820 because it no longer served Frankish interests.[276] This depiction of the Carolingians as the aggressive party in the decade has persuaded scholars such as El-Hajji, who was convinced that the Umayyads were in favour of peace.[277] There are problems with such a view, including hints that the Frankish annals should not be taken at face value here. The

270. Talbi, *L'Émirat Aghlabide*, 396.

271. Leo III, *Epistolae* no. 7, 98.

272. Manzano Moreno, "The Iberian Peninsula and North Africa," 599.

273. Colin, "Monnaies de la Période Idrīsite"; Benchekroun, "Les Idrīssides," 175–180.

274. On the importance of Moroccan silver, see Rosenberger, "Les premières villes islamiques," 236, and Savage and Gordus, "Dirhams for the Empire." But see Eustache, "El-Baṣra, capitale Idrīssite."

275. *Chronicle of Moissac*, a.812 145.

276. ARF a.815 143; ARF a.820 153.

277. El-Hajji, *Andalusian Diplomatic Relations*: "In the Umayyad period, Andalusian policy in general was a policy of non-aggression—a policy which was continued after the establishment of [ʿAbd al-Raḥmān I]'s rule and throughout the Umayyad period . . . Cordoba, however, was always ready to bestow her friendship on those who desired it" (291–292).

chronicler at Moissac began their account of the diplomacy of 810 by writing that "al-Ḥakam, king of the Saracens, hearing from Spain reports and opinions of the virtues of the Lord Emperor Charles, sent his envoys to him."[278] This description is clearly meant to be flattering for Charlemagne, presenting him as a virtuous ruler whose inherent nobility is spoken of far beyond his realm. It tells us very little about diplomatic relations. The *Annales regni Francorum* offer an image in which Charlemagne and Louis the Pious are fundamentally in control, but behind the bland words, the rapid oscillation between peace and war suggests that something more complicated was happening.

More damaging for the Carolingian aggression hypothesis is the lack of any evidence for any Frankish campaigning in the period. Instead, it is the Umayyads who appear to have gone on the offensive. Ibn ʿIdhārī says that in 815, "a most famous and terrible expedition" was sent against Barcelona.[279] In the following year, al-Ḥakam I sent an army which attacked Pamplona.[280] The chronology of the Carolingian annals indicates that the peace between the Franks and al-Andalus was broken at some point between late July and September 815, which fits Ibn ʿIdhārī's account.[281] This suggests that Louis did not necessarily desire war at this point but was forced to declare it by Umayyad provocation. The strange diplomacy of the period is better explained by al-Ḥakam placing pressure on the frontier than by Frankish belligerence.

The Carolingian offensives before 810 worked as a reaction to Umayyad internal weakness. By the 810s the situation was rather different. Compared to the years of civil war, al-Ḥakam had considerably more control over al-Andalus.[282] Now that the emir was not actively fighting for survival, targeted strikes across the frontier could be a useful way of reaffirming his legitimacy. Ibn al-Qūṭīya praised the Umayyad emir al-Ḥakam I because "he believed in the righteous ways of doing things, and he prosecuted the holy war regularly."[283]

Ibn ʿIdhārī claims that the Muslim forces defeated a Christian army in 815 with divine help, before returning. This marks a return to the practice

278. *Chronicle of Moissac*, a. 812 "Abulaz, rex Sarracenorum, ex Espania audiens famam et opinionem virtutum domni Karoli imperatoris missus suos direxit," 145.

279. Ibn ʿIdhārī, *Textos dels historiadors*, 112.

280. Ibn Ḥayyān, *Crónica de los emires*, 54.

281. In the ARF, the breaking of the peace takes place after Louis's assembly at Paderborn on 1 July and his subsequent journey to Frankfurt but before reports of flooding in September; see ARF a.815 142–143.

282. Collins, *Caliphs and Kings*, 32.

283. Ibn al-Qūṭīya, *Early Islamic Spain*, 86.

of *ṣawā'if*, summer raids sent into Christian territory to plunder as a fulfilment of the Umayyad emir's duty to take part in *jihād*.[284] Under al-Ḥakam's father, Hishām I, they were an annual event, frequently with multiple armies in the field.[285] The civil war beginning in 796 curtailed these *ṣawā'if*. They started reappearing after the civil war, but they remained sporadic during al-Ḥakam's reign. The attack of 815 was the first on Carolingian territory since the expedition of 793.

This policy of raiding was particularly feasible as the crucial frontier region of the Upper March was more stable than it had been in decades. From the beginning of the Umayyad presence in the area, it had been a major centre of rebellion, particularly in the late 790s and early 800s.[286] Following Córdoba's crushing of the revolt of 'Amrūs b. Yūsuf in 810, the Upper March became very quiet.[287] Even as al-Ḥakam was fighting to retain control of Córdoba, his son, the future 'Abd al-Raḥmān II, seems to have had no trouble managing the Ebro river valley. The March was to remain peaceful until the 840s. This hindered the classic Carolingian strategy of making common cause with malcontents in the area.

When discussing the peace made between Charlemagne and al-Ḥakam, Ibn Ḥayyān notes:

> This peace did not last as the tyrant Charles died the following year, 191 [Nov 806–Nov 807], and was succeeded by his son Louis, son of Charles, breaking the peace and beginning the war with the Franks.[288]

As established above, Ibn Ḥayyān's account is fundamentally flawed, but the idea of a connection between the Umayyad attack on Barcelona and the accession of Louis in 814 seems plausible. Al-Ḥakam was probably probing for weakness, using the opportunity of the succession much in the same way that the Carolingians had started raiding his own territory following his assumption of power in 796.[289]

284. Manzano Moreno, "Christian-Muslim Frontier in al-Andalus," 88; Collins, *Caliphs and Kings*, 23. For the wider context, see Blankinship, *The End of the Jihâd State*, 6–7; Bonner, *Aristocratic Violence and Holy War*, 47.

285. Lévi-Provençal, *Histoire de l'Espagne musulmane*, 1:142–146.

286. Collins, *The Arab Conquest*, 131.

287. Ibn Ḥayyān, *Crónica de los emires*, 50.

288. Ibid., "pero esta paz no duró, pues el tirano Carlos murió al año siguiente, 191, siendo sucedido por su hijo Ludovico, hijo de Carlos, rompiéndose la paz y estallando la Guerra con los francos," 47.

289. AL a.796 37; *Chronicle of Moissac*, a.796 135; Ibn Ḥayyān, *Crónica de los emires*, 15–19, 36.

If any Carolingian had the training and experience to be able to handle Iberian affairs, it was Louis. King of Aquitaine from 781, Louis had grown up in the territory immediately abutting Umayyad land.[290] Many of his closest advisers were from Aquitaine.[291] Louis had engaged in extensive campaigning in al-Andalus and negotiated with Muslim lords on several occasions.[292] Louis's position was complicated by the issue of the succession to Charlemagne. The deaths of Charlemagne's other sons in 810 and 811, which wrecked the plan of succession, would seem to ensure that Louis would inherit the bulk of the empire. However, the sources hint at tensions underlying Louis's eventual assumption of power after Charlemagne's death.[293] While the domestic situation was not necessarily unstable, it was certainly complex and Louis was still consolidating his power in the face of potential opposition. This does not mean that Septimania and the March were neglected, as a number of charters for the region granted in 814 and 815 reveal his continued interest in key monastic institutions and churches.[294] But Louis could not be continually present in the area, and his dealings with Córdoba needed to be juggled as part of a wider set of problems.

One particular moment highlights the way Louis's internal concerns might have influenced his handling of diplomacy with Muslim Spain. While staying in Compiègne in the late autumn of 816, Louis received "the envoys of ʿAbd al-Raḥmān, son of King al-Ḥakam."[295] These envoys had been sent from Zaragoza "to ask for peace."[296] Rather than considering their case in Compiègne, Louis had them "travel ahead of him to Aachen," where he was to winter.[297] There, they were finally sent back, apparently in February 817. We are told "they had been kept waiting for three months and were beginning to despair of returning home."[298]

How do we explain this delay? Louis was clearly very busy at this point. At Aachen he received Byzantine envoys to discuss Dalmatia and

290. ARF a.781 56; Astronomer, *Vita Hludowici*, c.5 296.

291. Werner, "*Hludovicus Augustus*," 55.

292. Astronomer, *Vita Hludowici*, c.5 298, c.8 306.

293. Innes, "Charlemagne's Will"; De Jong, *The Penitential State*, 18.

294. Louis the Pious, *Urkunden*, no. 11 33–36; no. 12 36–37; no. 13 37–39; no. 35 91–94; no. 37 96–98; no. 44 114–116; no. 55 141–142; no. 61 154–155; no. 76 187–189; no. 77 189–192; no. 81 197–199.

295. ARF a.816 "legatos Abdirahman filii Abulaz regis," 144.

296. Ibid., "pacis petendae," 145.

297. Ibid., "Aquasgrani eum praecedere iussi sunt," 145.

298. ARF a.817 "Legati etiam Abdirahman, cum tribus mensibus detenti essent et iam de reditu desperare coepissent, remissi sunt," 145.

a Danish embassy asking for peace.[299] These negotiations seem to have been intense and may have required that the Umayyad envoys take a back seat. On the other hand, the matter of peace with al-Andalus was hardly a trivial affair, particularly after attacks on Carolingian territory in 815 and 816. Louis may have been deliberately intimidating the Andalusi ambassadors, reminding them of how vulnerable their position was and thus sending a message to ʿAbd al-Raḥmān about his confidence in his ability to control communication with the Umayyads. This was something all the more important to achieve given that the initiative in this war was clearly with Córdoba.

But the Umayyads were not the only audience for such a display of dominance. In August 817, Louis appointed Benedict of Aniane over a council of abbots in order to regularise the adoption and practice of Benedictine monasticism across the empire.[300] At the same time, Louis appointed his oldest son, Lothar, as his co-emperor and made Pippin and Louis the German kings of Aquitaine and Bavaria, respectively, in a succession plan that controversially cut out his nephew Bernard of Italy.[301] These were key parts of Louis's political programme, to which he might expect opposition. Bernard's subsequent rebellion, and his presentation in later Frankish sources, suggests that he was not without supporters within the empire.[302]

Louis had spent very little time in Aachen before becoming emperor. His first action upon arriving in Aachen was to initiate a purge as part of a moralising initiative, removing most of the previous power brokers, most notably his sisters and Charlemagne's cousin Wala, whom the Astronomer refers to as a potential threat.[303] The presence of ʿAbd al-Raḥmān's ambassadors, together with those from the Byzantine emperor Leo V and the Danish king Harald Klak at Aachen at the same point, would have been a formidable statement of Louis's authority. Because negotiations took place during winter, only the immediate circle at Aachen would have witnessed them, but this was precisely the audience that Louis most needed to win over.

299. ARF a.817 145.

300. On reform in the early years of Louis's reign, see Kramer, *Rethinking Authority*.

301. Louis the Pious, *Ordinatio imperii*, 271; ARF a.817 146; Ganshof, *The Carolingians*, 273–277; McKitterick, *History and Memory*, 265–269.

302. See Noble, "The Revolt of King Bernard"; Jarnut, "Kaiser Ludwig der Fromme und König Bernhard von Italien."

303. Astronomer, *Vita Hludowici*, c.21 346; Dutton, *The Politics of Dreaming*, 58–59, 68–74; Nelson, "Women at the Court of Charlemagne," 55–60; De Jong, *The Penitential State*, 190–191.

While Louis's domestic problems provide a context in which he might find it difficult to intervene fully in the Iberian Peninsula, it cannot explain the decade of useless peace as a whole. The most important reason for the unstable state of Carolingian-Umayyad diplomacy in this period is to be found away from Córdoba and Aachen, in the frontier regions of the Carolingian Spanish March. The sources for Louis's campaigns against the Umayyads prior to the 810s emphasise the coalition of forces he managed to coordinate in his wars, bringing Basques, Franks, and Goths into one unified fighting force.[304] The evidence for the 810s suggests a breakdown in this unity. A charter from 2 April 812 indicates that Charlemagne had to intervene in the March to protect settlers from the Iberian Peninsula from the depredations of his own counts.[305] There are records of fighting between marcher lords in 818.[306] In 820 Aznar Galíndez, Count of Aragon, who appears to have been appointed by Charlemagne, was driven out of Spain into Frankish exile by García Galíndez the Bad, who proved to be less loyal to the Carolingians.[307]

Particular attention in this case needs to be paid to the Basques. The sources for the Basques at this point are slim and difficult, but there are growing hints of trouble in Gascony in the 810s.[308] The Astronomer notes that in 810, Louis heard a rumour:

> That a certain group of the Basques, who had some time ago been received in surrender, were now plotting revolt and were rising in rebellion. The public welfare demanded for him to go and repress their stubbornness.[309]

In his capacity as king of Aquitaine, Louis gathered an army and plundered the city of Dax, receiving the submission of the rebels, pardoning them as they had "lost all."[310]

That this may not have endeared Louis to the inhabitants of the region is suggested by the *Annals of Aniane*, which says that in 815 "the Gascons

304. Ermold the Black, *In honorem Hludovici*, Bk. 1, 28.

305. CC 2.ii, 312–314; Chandler, "Between Court and Counts"; Davis, *Charlemagne's Practice of Empire*, 104–105.

306. ARF a.818 150.

307. Lacarra, "Textos navarros," 241; Sénac, "Estudio sobre los Primeros Condes," 1503.

308. See, for example, Lacarra, "Textos navarros."

309. Astronomer, *Vita Hludowici*, c.18 "quod quedam Uuasconum pars iam pridem in deditionem suscepta, nunc defectionem meditate in rebellionem adsurgeret, ad quorum reprimendam pervicatiam ire publica utilitas postularet," 332.

310. Ibid., "perditis omnibus," 334.

rebelled against the emperor."[311] Of the instigators of this revolt, we are told that "the rebel Basques chose García to be leader over them."[312] That trouble had been brewing for some time is indicated by the *Annales regni Francorum* in its entry for 816, which comments:

> The Basques, who live beyond the Garonne and around the mountains of the Pyrenees, because of the removal of their leader named Sigiwin, who was removed by the emperor on account of his arrogance and wicked ways, moved by their usual recklessness, conspired together and defected in revolt in every way. But in two campaigns they were beaten so thoroughly that surrender and petition for peace could not be carried out fast enough for them.[313]

The composer of the *Annales regni Francorum* let their enthusiasm get away from them. The *Annals of Aniane* observe that it was only in 818, after the killing of García, that the troubles died down.[314]

García's brother, Lupus Centulli, was exiled in the same year because:

> He had fought in battle that year with Counts Berengar of Toulouse and Warin of Auvergne, in which he lost his brother Garsand [García], a man of unmatched folly, and came near to death, but saved his life by flight.[315]

The name of the exile here is interesting. Lupus was a name borne by several individuals known as princes or dukes of the Basques.[316] Centullus is another unusual name, one employed by Count Aznar Galíndez of Aragon for his oldest son.[317] The name García was used frequently in the families

311. "Annals of Aniane" a.815 "Wascones revellant contra imperatore," 148.

312. Ibid., a.816 "Wascones autem rebelles, Garsiamuci super se in principem aelegunt," 148.

313. ARF a.816 "Wascones, qui trans Garonnam et circa Pirineum montem habitant, propter sublatum ducem suum nomine Sigiwinum, quem imperator ob nimiam eius insolentiam ac morum pravitatem inde sustulerat, solita levitate commoti coniuratione facta omnimoda defection desciverunt; sed duabas expeditionibus ita sunt edomiti, ut tarda eis deditio et pacis impetratio videretur," 144, adapted from Scholz, *Carolingian Chronicles*, 100–101.

314. "Annals of Aniane," a.818 150.

315. ARF a.819 "qui cum Berengario Tolosae et Warino Arverni comite eodem anno proelio conflixit,—in quo et fratrem Garsandum singularis amentiae hominem amisit et ipse, nisi sibi fugiendo consuleret, prope interitum fuit," 150.

316. On Lupus I of Gascony, see Julian of Toledo, *Historia Wambae regis*, c.28 524; for Lupus II of Gascony, see ARF, a.769 30–31; Astronomer, *Vita Hludowici*, c.2 286; for Lupus Sancho, see Einhard, *Vita Karoli Magni*, c.5 7.

317. On Centullus Aznarez, see Lacarra, "Textos navarros," c.18–19 240–241.

that ruled Pamplona and Aragon.[318] This suggests that Lupus and García were part of a well-established family in Gascony that may have had links across the Pyrenees.[319] Lupus "came before the emperor and was unable to purge himself of the treachery of which the mentioned counts [Berengar and Warin] accused him."[320] This was not the end of the matter, for in 819 Louis's son, Pippin, the recently appointed king of Aquitaine, "on his father's order entered Gascony with an army, removed the rebels, and so pacified the whole province."[321]

On the other side of the Pyrenees was the territory of the city of Pamplona. Pamplona seems to have entered the Carolingian orbit in 806, when the *Annales regni Francorum* note that "in Spain, the people of Navarre and Pamplona . . . were returned to loyalty."[322] They do not seem to have rested easy in this state and, following his 810 looting of Dax, Louis "descended upon Pamplona; and stayed in those places for as long as seemed right, to order things for the use of both public and private welfare."[323] He installed one Velasco as the lord of the city. That Louis did not feel particularly secure about these arrangements is evident in the account of his return journey "through the narrow straits of that mountain," where the king and his men had to "evade [the Basques] safely and cautiously."[324]

Repeated revolts in Gascony would have complicated any attempt to wage war on the Umayyads, forcing Louis to prioritise managing existing Carolingian territory. It may be significant that the Umayyads followed up their attack on Barcelona with a raid on Pamplona.[325] According to Ibn Ḥayyān, in 816 "took place the expedition of chamberlain ʿAbd al-Karīm b. ʿAbd al-Wāḥid b. Mugīth against the enemy of God, Velasco

318. Lacarra, "Textos navarros," c.1–2, c.9–12 229–230, 233–235.

319. Collins, *The Basques*, 129–130.

320. ARF a.818 "cum in conspectum imperatoris venisset ac de perfidia, cuius a memoratis comitibus inmane accusabatur, se purgare non potuisset," 150, translated by Scholz, *Carolingian Chronicle*, 105.

321. ARF a.819 "iussu patris Wasconiam cum exercitu ingressus sublatis ex ea seditiosis totam eam provinciam ita pacavit," 152; adapted from Scholz, *Carolingian Chronicles*, 106.

322. Ibn Ḥayyān, *Crónica de los emires*, 35; ARF a.806 "In Hispania vero Navarri et Pampilonenses . . . in fidem recepti sunt," 122.

323. Astronomer, *Vita Hludowici*, c.18 "Pampalonam descendit; et in illis quamdiu visum est moratus locis, ea que utilitati tam publicae quam private conducerent ordinavit," 334.

324. Ibid., "montis remeandum foret angustias . . . mox sunt prudenti astutia deprehensi, consilio cauti atque cautela vitati," 334.

325. Pérez de Urbel, "Lo Viejo y lo Nuevo," 6; Sánchez Albornoz, "Problemas de la historia Navarra," 15.

the Basque, lord of Pamplona."[326] Velasco was defeated and never heard of again. In the face of this onslaught, he received help from other rulers in northern Spain. Among those listed as fallen in the battle are a relative of King Alfonso II of Asturias and the mysterious "Ṣaltān, champion of the pagans."[327] Absent in this account is any reference to the Franks, presumably because they were busy campaigning in Gascony.

Basque rebels may even have been in contact with al-Ḥakam. Louis's caution in returning from Pamplona in 810 was well justified in 824, when an expedition sent to restore Carolingian control after the fall of Velasco ran into trouble:

> Counts Aeblus and Aznar. . . . were led into an ambush by the treachery of the mountain people, surrounded and captured. Those who had followed them were almost utterly destroyed.[328]

This battle was not a struggle between Franks and Basques. The two counts were leading Basque troops when they were ambushed and Aznar could presumably claim some Basque connection as "being a relative of them [he] was allowed to return home."[329] The unfortunate Aeblus, on the other hand, "was sent to Córdoba."[330] This not only marks the end of Carolingian pretensions to rule in Pamplona but also suggests Umayyad influence in the city.

This section began with two problems, trying to explain the strange pattern of Carolingian-Umayyad diplomacy in the 810s and the limited military activity despite the number of wars that were declared. Both questions can be answered by Carolingian weakness in the Spanish March, combined with increasing Umayyad confidence. The chaotic state of the Spanish March, with lords competing with each other, and in particular the rebellions in Gascony and Pamplona, forced Charlemagne and Louis

326. Ibn Ḥayyān, *Crónica de los emires*, "Tuvo lugar la expedición del chambelán ʿAbdalkarīm b. ʿAbdalwāḥid b. Muġīt contra el enemigo de Dios, Balašk Alǧalaškī, señor de Pamplona," 54.

327. Ibid., "Ṣaltān, paladín de los *maǧūs*," 54. On the problems in identifying the relative of Alfonso, see Collins, *Caliphs and Kings*, 207, and a possible solution in Martínez Díez, *El Condado de Castilla*, 102–103.

328. ARF a.824 "Aeblus et Asinarius comites . . . perfidia montanorum in insidias deducti ac circumventi capti sunt, et copiae, quas secum habuere, pene usque ad internicionem deletae," 166.

329. Ibid., "Asinarius vero misericordia eorum, qui eum ceperant, quasi qui consanguineus eorum esset, domum redire permissus est," 166. For an attempt to identify this Aznar, see Higounet, "Les Aznar," 6–9.

330. ARF a.824 "quidem Cordubam missus," 166.

the Pious to deal with internal matters. As the Umayyads reasserted their authority on the Upper March, peace with them became more desirable, hence the Peace of 812.

Carolingian internal difficulties allowed al-Ḥakam to be provocative, attacking Frankish territory and reigniting conflict in 815. The Umayyads seem to have been content with dislodging Pamplona from the Carolingian sphere in 816, prompting another peace in 817 which Louis's continued problems in the March forced him to accept, no matter how he might try to present it to an audience in Aachen. The lack of an aggressive Frankish response in this period was due to the need to manage Gascony. It was only after the Basque revolt had been crushed in 819 that Louis felt confident enough to declare war on the Umayyads. Carolingian armies went on the offensive in Spain in the 820s. In 822 "the counts of the Spanish March" launched a raid into al-Andalus.[331] Two years later, as discussed above, a Carolingian attempt to retake Pamplona went badly wrong.

Carolingian-Umayyad diplomacy in this period proved to be fairly cutthroat, with both sides willing to break truces for immediate gain. Neither the Umayyads nor the Carolingians were willing to settle for a long-term peace. In this decade, peace was just a momentary solution to a temporary imbalance of power. This decade of broken diplomacy had consequences. The first was the end of Carolingian expansion in the Iberian Peninsula. More importantly, the failure of the Carolingians effectively to manage the tensions within the Spanish March would have explosive results in 826. Those disaffected by the status quo in the March rebelled with Umayyad support, launching the crisis that would bring Louis the Pious to the brink of disaster in the early 830s and haunt the Carolingians for the rest of their time in power.[332]

## CONCLUSION

If this chapter has seemed as much concerned with Carolingian-Umayyad warfare as with diplomacy, it should be observed that the two were fundamentally linked. Both the Carolingians and the Umayyads had more incentive to make war than to keep the peace when conditions looked favourable for the success of their armies. Campaigning in Spain offered the Franks the prospect of plunder and conquest, whereas the emirs of Córdoba could aspire to the acquisition of loot, glory, and the opportunity

331. ARF a.822 158.
332. ARF a.826 171.

to fulfil their role as holy warriors. Both sides could also inflict serious damage on the other. While this meant both sides had to keep a wary eye on the other, it promoted a diplomacy that was highly practical if rather concerned with the short term. Carolingian diplomacy with the Muslims of Spain aimed to end conflicts that neither side felt they could win or to build coalitions in al-Andalus that could allow further successful war.

CHAPTER FIVE

# Carolingian-Umayyad Diplomacy

## PART 2: 820–864

IN THE YEAR 863, Count Salomon of Urgell, Cerdanya, and Conflent travelled to Córdoba to carry out a heist.[1] In place of a crack team, he had a silver tongue and a lot of silver coins. His objective, more precious than gold or rubies, was the holy body of St Vincent, a late antique martyr, which had spent more than six centuries resting in a tomb in Valencia. In 855, a monk had sought to spirit the saint back to his monastery of Conques in Aquitaine but had been intercepted on his return by Bishop Senior of Zaragoza, who confiscated the body.[2] Now Salomon was on a mission to claim the body. Rather than going to Zaragoza, he made for Córdoba and the true centre of power in al-Andalus, Emir Muḥammad I. With a combination of smooth talking and a hefty bribe of a hundred *solidi*, Salomon convinced the emir that the body was in fact that of his father, Sunyer. His outrage lubricated by cash, Muḥammad sent a letter ordering the governor of Zaragoza to force the bishop to hand over the body to Salomon. The count then took St Vincent to his new home, the monastery of Castres.

There are reasons to be sceptical about this story beyond the unlikely means by which Salomon persuaded Muḥammad to help him. Our source, the *Historia translationis sancti Vincentii* written by the monk Aimoin of Saint-Germain-des-Prés, is a contemporary one, composed by someone

1. Aimoin, *Historia translationis* 1018.
2. Ibid., 1013; Aimoin, *De translatione* 942.

who claimed to have talked to some of the participants. Nonetheless, as Ann Christys has observed, the narrative draws heavily upon the tropes of relic thefts.[3] Nor does it help that a number of institutions claimed to possess the body of St Vincent, most notably in Benevento.[4] Yet the story of Salomon and the saint is a valuable one for thinking about Carolingian diplomacy with the Umayyads of Córdoba from roughly 820 on. This is not just because Salomon was almost certainly sent by Charles the Bald to Muḥammad I in 863, as will be discussed below. The way in which the count sought to achieve his aims, with clever words and generous gifts, is symptomatic of the way in which relations between the Franks and al-Andalus had changed over the previous decades.

On the surface, the relationship between the Carolingians and the Umayyads in the mid-ninth century resembled that of the previous period. Both powers remained a potentially dangerous neighbour to each other. Their diplomatic relations continued to be an exercise in pragmatism aimed at ensuring the peace when it was in the different actors' interest to do so. What was different was the context in which this diplomacy took place. The balance of power increasingly shifted south of the Pyrenees, something indicated by the ending of campaigning by Frankish armies in the Iberian Peninsula. The causes of this shift will be considered below.

Umayyad control of al-Andalus was increasingly strong in the first half of the ninth century. This is not to say that the emirs faced no internal challenges. Cities such as Mérida and Toledo rebelled frequently, while religious riots took place on the streets of Córdoba, and these difficulties would be important for shaping how the Umayyads interacted with the Carolingians.[5] But in the ninety years between 796 and 886, al-Andalus had three emirs. The long reigns of al-Ḥakam I (r. 796–822), ʿAbd al-Raḥmān II (r. 822–852), and Muḥammad I (r. 852–886) helped build institutional continuity. Despite the rebellions, after al-Ḥakam had defeated his uncles in 803 the ruling emir rarely risked losing control of the core territories of the Guadalquivir valley. The resulting stability provided a strength and confidence which allowed Umayyad emirs to project force against the Frankish world with more frequency than previously.

A more important development was the changes taking place in the Carolingian world. The first chronologically, which shall be explored in

3. Christys, "St-Germain des-Prés," 212–214. The classic work on such narratives is Geary, *Furta Sacra*.

4. Aimoin, *De translatione* 942.

5. Collins, *Caliphs and Kings*, 38.

some detail in this chapter, was the collapse of political unity on the Spanish March from 820. As it became apparent that no further Carolingian expansion in al-Andalus was likely, increased competition within the March for lands and offices took place, which could be expressed in open violence. Losers in these struggles launched revolts, and appealed to Córdoba for support. This shift was localised to the Spanish March but could have dramatic ramifications. The first half of this chapter is concerned with the consequences of this change.

The second change was the end of political unity across the empire, starting with the political instability that began in 830, which was then made permanent by the civil war that followed the death of Louis the Pious in 840 and the division of the empire between his sons in 843. The result was a political landscape in which Charles the Bald, the king of the West Franks whose kingdom faced onto the Umayyad realm, had to deal with the emirs of al-Andalus with both a smaller resource base than his father and grandfather and the additional hazard of having to watch his back against the machinations of his family. The second half of this chapter will consider the challenges of Carolingian relations with Spain in this period.

## *Disaster on the Frontier, 820–830*

The wider significance of Carolingian-Umayyad relations is especially apparent in the late 820s. Military defeat in the Spanish March in 827 was to have enormous consequences. From 796 the Franks had generally been able to set the pace of relations. This had begun to shift in the 810s, but it was the events of 827 that ended this period of Carolingian initiative. No Frankish army ever marched into Umayyad territory after this turning point, while the Carolingians would thereafter have to bargain with Córdoba to end Andalusi raids. The ramifications of events on the March would stretch further, leading to a chain of events that would end with the Carolingian empire divided against itself and Louis a prisoner of his own sons.

This would have seemed an unlikely outcome before 827. For most of the decade, Louis's position was secure.[6] Following his penance at Attigny in 822 for blinding and killing his nephew, which represented a reboot of the reign after a troubled first few years, Louis had succeeded in uniting most of the senior figures of the empire under his regime.[7] His confidence

6. Semmler, "Renovatio regni Francorum."

7. De Jong, *The Penitential State*, 35–36.

is exemplified by an ambitious reforming agenda in these years.[8] Louis's power was also demonstrated by his apparent mastery over his neighbours, manifested by the "envoys of the barbarians which had either been ordered to come or had come of their own accord" at his assemblies.[9] Those foreign peoples who would not show their respect, such as the Bretons, received "iron and fire."[10] As Ermold declared in his poem in honour of Louis, "Kingdoms that your father's arms were unable to take by any contest offer themselves to you willingly."[11]

Despite Ermold's fine words, there were still one or two kingdoms of the earth that might resist the emperor's embrace, al-Andalus being among them. Even here, Frankish arms were not without success. In 822, "the counts of the Spanish March crossed the River Segre into Spain, laid waste the fields, burned down a number of villages and returned having taken no little plunder."[12] A run of grants in the early 820s may indicate Louis's renewed purpose in the region.[13] The raid of 822 had originally been planned in February 821, but its success may have had something to do with the death of Emir al-Ḥakam I in May 822.[14] This prompted ʿAbd Allāh the Valencian, a man who could never be accused of a lack of persistence, to contest the Umayyad succession for the third and final time. This challenge and a revolt in Córdoba kept the attention of the new emir, ʿAbd al-Raḥmān II, firmly away from the frontier.[15]

This was to change in the later years of the decade. In 826, the *Annales regni Francorum* report a rising in the region of Osona in the Spanish March against the Carolingians, multiple centres being taken and sacked. The rebels secured the backing of ʿAbd al-Raḥmān, who ordered an incursion the following year which caused considerable damage. An army sent by Louis failed to bring this force to battle before it returned to al-Andalus.

8. Louis the Pious, *Admonitio ad omnes regni ordines*, 303–307; Costambeys, Innes, and MacLean, *The Carolingian World*, 208.

9. ARF a.823 "barbarorum legationes, quae vel iussae vel sua sponte venerunt," 160, translated by Scholz, *Carolingian Chronicles*, 112.

10. ARF a.824 "ferro et igni," 165.

11. Ermold the Black, *In honorem Hludovici*, Bk. 4, "Arma patrum nullo quae non valuere duello, Sponte sua, capere, te modo regna petunt," 190, translated by Noble, *Charlemagne and Louis the Pious*, 183.

12. ARF a.822 "Comites marcae Hispanicae trans Sicorim fluvium in Hispania profecti vastatis agris et incensis compluribus villis et capta non modica praeda regressi sunt," 158, adapted from Scholz, *Carolingian Chronicles*, 111.

13. Louis the Pious, *Urkunden*, no. 173 428–430; no. 175 434–436; no. 185 458–460; no. 188 464–465; no. 200 493–497; no. 205 505–508; no. 206 509–511; no. 211 521–522.

14. ARF a.822 154.

15. Ibn Ḥayyān, *Crónica de los emires*, 271–272.

The leaders of this Frankish army, Counts Hugh of Tours and Matfrid of Orléans, were stripped of their prominent positions for this failure, while the hero of the crisis, Count Bernard of Barcelona, was elevated.[16] Although Córdoba did not continue to apply pressure, the Carolingians did not succeed in reclaiming the rebellious territories. The resulting blow to Louis's prestige following the attack and the resentments stoked by the recriminations afterwards were to prompt the rebellion that saw the emperor imprisoned by his own sons in 830.

In order to understand this complicated sequence of events, we can begin in mid-October 826, when Louis held an assembly at Salz. It was there, while dealing with a delegation from Naples, that he learned that one Aizo had fled to the Spanish March.[17] There Aizo had "fraudulently entered Osona, and treacherously deceived the people who received him. He destroyed the city of Roda."[18] The main settlement of the county of Osona, Vic, was also known as Vicus Ausona, and it was here that Aizo established his base. Roda was a natural defensive site on the routes from the Pyrenees to Barcelona, which lies directly south of Roda and Vic, and Girona, on the river Ter directly east. It had a long history of fortification and Louis had raised new walls on it and garrisoned it.[19] By destroying the city, Aizo had broken the Carolingian defensive lines on the river Ter, substantially weakened their grip on Osona, and threatened their communications with Barcelona. He may also have secured the backing of Vic by removing a rival settlement in the area.

Worse, Aizo "sent his brother to ʿAbd al-Raḥmān, king of the Saracens and asked and accepted that king's help against us," thus raising the stakes dramatically.[20] Louis's reaction appears to have been one of fury, but he opted to wait and seek counsel, perhaps not anticipating much in the way of escalation.[21] In 827 Aizo gathered allies from disaffected border lords, most notably Willemund, the son of Bera, a former count of Barcelona. They went on the offensive in Cerdanya, to the north of Osona, and in Vallès, the region in between Osona and Barcelona, attacking the

16. ARF a.826–828.

17. ARF a.826 170.

18. Ibid., "fraudulenter Ausonam ingressus, et a populo illo quem dolo deceperat receptus, Rotam civitatem destruxit," 170.

19. Ollich i Castanyer, Rocafiguera Espona, and Ocaña Subirana, "The Southern Carolingian Frontier."

20. ARF a.826 "missoque ad Abdiraman regem Sarracenorum fratre suo, auxilium quod petebat, iussu eiusdem regis contra nostros accepit," 170.

21. Ibid.

lords in the March with Muslim support, so that "by incessant raids he [Aizo] had wearied them so thoroughly that some of them deserted the castles which they were meant to protect and withdrew."[22] Accompanied by "Saracens and Moors," Aizo afflicted "Cerdanya and Vallès with daily robbing and burning."[23] Helisachar, who was Louis's former archchancellor and originally from the area, was sent by the emperor to attempt "to calm and appease the Goths and Hispani living in this territory," some of whom may have sympathised with Aizo.[24] Meanwhile, Bernard, the new Count of Barcelona, battled Aizo's forces. The description that Bernard faced "the ambushes of Aizo" suggests that Bernard may have been in territory seized by the rebels, trying to crush the revolt.[25]

Whatever troops Helisachar and Bernard could assemble were soon to be outmatched by the arrival of an army sent by ʿAbd al-Raḥmān from Córdoba, commanded by Abū Marwān ʿUbayd Allāh, the son of ʿAbd Allāh the Valencian (and therefore the emir's first cousin once removed).[26] In June 827, this army "invaded the country of the Franks," plundering, looting, and meeting no effective opposition.[27] Whereas Aizo and his allies had remained in the more marginal, but still important, territories of Osona and Cerdanya, Abū Marwān campaigned further east, threatening the two great centres of the March, Barcelona and Girona. Their count, Bernard, was distracted by Aizo and probably out of position to offer greater resistance to Abū Marwān. A Frankish force commanded by King Pippin of Aquitaine and Counts Hugh and Matfrid failed to reach the area in time to engage them before the Umayyad army returned to Zaragoza.[28] Something of the impact of Abū Marwān's attack is hinted at by a reference in a ninth-century Visigothic law manuscript (Paris BNF lat.4667), which notes that in the year 827 "[Abū] Marwān came to Girona on 10th October."[29]

This incident raises several questions, not the least of which concerns the identity of Aizo, a question guaranteed to unite specialists in

22. ARF a.827 "eosque adsiduis incursionibus in tantum fatigavit, ut quidam illorum, relictis quae tueri debebant castellis, recederent," 172.

23. Ibid., "Sarracenis ac Mauris Ceritaniam et Vallensem rapinis atque incendiis cotidie," 172.

24. Ibid., "ad sedandos ac mitigandos Gothorum atque Hispanorum," 172.

25. Ibid., "Aizonis insidiis," 172.

26. ARF a.827 172; Ibn Ḥayyān, *Crónica de los emires*, 286.

27. Ibn Ḥayyān, *Crónica de los emires*, "invadiendo el país de los francos," 286.

28. ARF a.827 173.

29. Alturo, "El *liber iudicum* manuscrito," "sic uenit marohane ad Ierunda VI° Idus hoctubres," 13.

the Spanish March in shared frustration.[30] The catalyst of the revolt that prompted the most serious assault on Carolingian territory by Umayyad forces of the ninth century, and led to the greatest crisis of Louis the Pious's entire reign, remains infuriatingly mysterious. He bursts onto the historical stage, escaping an unexplained captivity in an unidentified Carolingian palace, before fleeing to the March.[31] In 1903 Codera proposed that Aizo was ʿAysūn, the son of Sulaymān al-ʿArābī, a position that was strengthened by the publication of the writings of al-ʿUdhrī by de la Granja in 1967.[32] This history includes an account of ʿAysūn escaping Carolingian captivity that has convinced many of the validity of Codera's identification.[33] Such an identification might help explain Aizo's success in finding support from Córdoba, if ʿAbd al-Raḥmān were persuaded to help the son of an opponent against Umayyad authority.

Upon examination, problems arise with this solution, as Jonathan Jarrett has demonstrated.[34] None of the sources concerning Aizo provide any hint of Arab parentage. The only indication of Aizo's ethnicity is to be found in the *Annals of Fulda*, which call him a Goth, but the grounds for this statement are unclear.[35] ʿAysūn is known to have been active in 778. If he were still alive, by 826 he would have been pushing seventy, making a desperate escape and flight slightly implausible. Aizo sent his brother to negotiate with ʿAbd al-Raḥmān, but the only known brother of ʿAysūn, Maṭrūḥ, was murdered in 791, ironically by the same man whom al-ʿUdhrī claims rescued ʿAysūn.[36] Aizo's apparent lack of success in rallying support in the immediate environs of Barcelona and Girona, Sulaymān al-ʿArābī's old base, would also be surprising if Aizo were ʿAysūn.[37]

These issues have caused scholars to examine instead the only geographical locations with which Aizo can be firmly associated. His occupation of Osona in 826, which he "deceitfully entered," has suggested to Imma Ollich i Castanyer a local connection, indicating that he was an aristocrat from the vicinity.[38] Ollich i Castanyer argued that he was a prominent Goth. Ultimately the limited evidence available makes a definitive

30. Jarrett, "Rebel without a Pension"; Chandler, "The Mysterious Case of Aizo."

31. ARF a.826 170.

32. Codera y Zaidín, "El Godo o moro Aizón"; al-ʿUdhrī, "La Marca Superior."

33. Salrach, *El Procés de Formació Nacional*, 1:80–87; Aurell, "Pouvoir et Párenté," 470.

34. Jarrett, "Rebel without a Pension."

35. AF a.826 24; Chandler, "The Mysterious Case of Aizo."

36. Al-ʿUdhrī, "La Marca Superior," 465; Ibn ʿIdhārī, *Textos dels historiadors*, 92.

37. Jarrett, "Rebel without a Pension."

38. ARF a.826 "quomodo fraudulenter Ausonam ingressus," 170; Ollich i Castanyer, "Vic: La Ciutat."

statement almost impossible. However, a few observations may be relevant. Positioning Aizo as a prominent lord in Osona may underestimate his significance. There are a couple of hints toward Aizo's importance. His "treachery" in escaping implies that he was a hostage, indicating high status.[39] Far from indicating obscurity, the very lack of an explanation in the *Annals* as to who Aizo was may imply that the original compilers thought it so obvious that no more need be said. The narrowing of focus in the March to Osona may miss the wider expanse of events. Aizo's ally, Willemund, hailed from one of the most powerful families in the March.[40] Their raids stretched well beyond the confines of Osona, into Cerdanya and Vallès.[41] Aizo's ability to seize territory was limited not just to Osona but extended also to "the stronger castles of the country."[42] Between them, the two were able to cause enough trouble to keep the Count of Barcelona busy and to make sending a former archchancellor to calm the situation a sensible precaution.[43] That the crisis escalated beyond Aizo and Willemund is indicated by the way they vanish from the sources, but the absence of any reference to Osona suggests that they managed to retain control of the county in the midst of the confusion.[44]

Córdoba's involvement in the crisis can be understood in the context of Umayyad policy. ʿAbd al-Raḥmān had been following an aggressive strategy with his Christian neighbours for some years. One year after his accession in 822 he ordered the first Andalusi expedition against Asturias after a decade of peace, attacking Álava and Castile.[45] This was repeated in 824, and again in 825, which was the first led by Abū Marwān, who was to gain a reputation as a campaigner in the North, with another following in 826.[46] These operations are explicitly described as "summer expeditions" or *ṣāʿifah*, raids designed to punish the infidel and to accrue booty and glory for the emir as a warrior for God.[47] The attack of 827 fits into this pattern, with ʿAbd al-Raḥmān seizing the opportunity provided by Aizo. Although the emir was looking for Christian targets generally, there might

39. ARF a.826 "perfidia," 170; Kosto, "Hostages in the Carolingian World" and *Hostages in the Middle Ages*, 53–73.

40. ARF a.827 172.

41. Ibid.

42. ARF a.826 "castella eiusdem regionis quae firmiora," 170.

43. ARF a.827 172.

44. Chandler, *Carolingian Catalonia*, 101–102.

45. Ibn Ḥayyān, *Crónica de los emires*, 282.

46. Ibid., 283–284.

47. Collins, *Caliphs and Kings*, 23.

also be a hint of reprisal against the Frankish campaign of 822, seeking to reassert Umayyad prestige and dominance.

The deeper causes of the crisis, and the reason the Spanish March was left vulnerable and divided, lie within the Spanish March itself. Aizo's revolt has reasonably been understood as an anti-Carolingian movement. Aizo seized control of one city with a Carolingian garrison and destroyed another. Louis the Pious sent troops to fight him and rewarded those on the March who did so. Aizo and his comrades had clearly decided that their political interests were best served beyond Carolingian authority, as demonstrated by their appeal to the emir of Córdoba for help.

In another light the events of 826 appear to be a civil war between the leading families of the Spanish March. Aizo seems to have won support in Vic by playing on its rivalry with the upstart city of Roda. It was in this spirit that Carolingian agents first approached the situation. Louis the Pious sent Abbot Helisachar, a trusted adviser since Louis's days as king of Aquitaine and a former archchancellor, to conciliate and mediate.[48] This aspect of Aizo's revolt will be the focus of this discussion, which will argue that the rising of 826 marked a flashpoint in a much longer process of growing internal competition and breakdown within the Spanish March.

## LEADERS AND TRIBUNES

The core of the army that Louis led in the Iberian Peninsula when he was king of Aquitaine was formed out of a coalition of different aristocratic and military leaders based in or around the Spanish March. This martial assemblage is worth considering as one of the most tangible manifestations of loyalty and support to the Carolingians in the region. Examining it reveals not just the bases on which Frankish power on the Iberian frontier was built but also the conditions required for an aggressive foreign policy against al-Andalus. At an early stage, the linchpin was the count of Toulouse, who also acted as Louis's guardian. This role was played by William of Gellone from about 790, a cousin of Charlemagne and future saint.[49] The success of Louis and William in building and maintaining the campaigning coalition discussed below was crucial to Carolingian momentum in the Iberian Peninsula. Even after the end of regular campaigning in 810, the subsequent stability of the March was ensured by the continuation

48. AB 827 172. On Helisachar, see Depreux, *Prosopographie*, 235–240.

49. Astronomer, *Vita Hludowici*, c.5 298. On William, see Salrach, "Guillaume et Barcelone"; Dubreucq, "Guillaume de Toulouse."

of this wartime coalition, and the distribution of rewards, in the form of offices and lands.

From 796 Louis provisioned his captains using his own stores, bringing them closer to him.[50] One of the clearest glimpses of the coalition comes from Ermold the Black's poem *In honorem Hludovici*, written between 826 and 828 and thus just as Aizo's revolt was taking place.[51] Ermold presents the taking of Barcelona as a group effort. Louis presides and makes the key decisions; his companions are utterly loyal to him. But Ermold creates great set pieces out of Louis summoning to council "the well-known forces, that is, the select among the people, the heads of the realm, by whose counsels affairs were going to be organised."[52] His "prime men came swiftly, obeying willingly, each one followed by his own huge band."[53] Louis consults his men, who give long speeches, before determining the correct course of action.

Ermold also took pains to list some of Louis's chief men:

> For his part, Prince William set up his tents, as did Heribert, Liutard, and Bego, as well as Bera, Sannio, Leibulf, and Isembard, as well as many others whom it would take too long to name.[54]

These men were to be important not just during the campaign but also after. In 801 Bera and Liutard became counts of Barcelona and Fézensac, respectively, and the former was named as a witness of Charlemagne's will.[55] Bego was a great-grandson of Charles Martel. In 806 he succeeded William as count of Toulouse and counselled Louis shortly after Charlemagne's death. He was also probably married to Louis's illegitimate daughter Alpais.[56] Sannio is also known as Lupus Sancho, "Prince of the Basques," whose family had been dukes in Gascony for several generations.[57] Leibulf

50. Astronomer, *Vita Hludowici*, c.7 304.

51. Godman, *Poets and Emperors*, 111; Depreux, "Poètes et historiens."

52. Ermold the Black, *In honorem Hludovici*, Bk. 1, "Scilicet electos populi, seu culmina regni, Quorum consiliis res peragenda manet," 116, translated by Noble, *Charlemagne and Louis the Pious*, 131.

53. Ibid., "Occurrunt celeres primi parentque volendo, Quos sequitur propius vulgus inorme satis," 116, translated by Noble, *Charlemagne and Louis the Pious*, 131.

54. Ibid., "Parte sua princeps Vilhelm tentoria figit, Heripreth, Lihuthard, Bigoque sive Bero, Santio, Libulfus, Hilthibreth, atque Hisimbard, Sive alii plures, quos recitare mora est," 28, translated by Noble, *Charlemagne and Louis the Pious*, 134–135.

55. ARF a.801 152; Einhard, *Vita Karoli Magni*, c.33 41; Astronomer, *Vita Hludowici*, c.13 314.

56. Depreux, *Prosopographie*, 120–121.

57. Collins, *The Basques*, 128–129.

is attested as the count of Provence until his death in 828.[58] Many of these men also took part in subsequent campaigns.[59]

The poet was writing panegyric with an eye to being allowed to return from exile, raising questions about his reliability. But he had been part of the court circle of Louis's son Pippin I, king of Aquitaine from 817, and was probably familiar with many of the key players in the Spanish March. He had also accompanied Pippin on campaign in 824 against the Bretons.[60] His description has support from other sources. The Astronomer's account of the campaigns against the Umayyads emphasizes the role played by figures like Bera, Isembard, Heribert, and Liutard.[61]

Ermold chose to stress the various ethnic identities present in the army, describing "the young men camped all over the field: the Frank, the Gascon, the Goth, the troop of Aquitainians."[62] The *Chronicle of Moissac* makes a similar point about the siege of Barcelona, saying that Louis "assembled an army from Aquitaine, Gascony as well as from Burgundy, Provence and the Goths."[63] The picture Ermold presents is no doubt idealised, but the image of a group of young aristocratic men brought together by shared experience on campaign, forming bonds with each other and their king under the watchful eyes of the veteran William, is compelling. The communal experience of campaigning together annually for almost a decade was probably of immense importance for these men both politically and emotionally, with major consequences for the subsequent running of the March.

Alcuin alludes to the significance of Louis's "leaders and tribunes" in his letter to Colcu.[64] The men of the March were probably foremost among their ranks. The importance of the counts of the March only increased when Louis became emperor, forcing him to spend less time in Aquitaine and on the March.[65] Their value is indicated by the *Annales regni Francorum*, whose entry for 821 highlights the role of "the commanders of this

58. Depreux, *Prosopographie*, 292–293.

59. Astronomer, *Vita Hludowici*, c.14 322.

60. Ermold the Black, *In honorem Hludovici*, Bk. 2, 154.

61. Astronomer, *Vita Hludowici*, c.14 322, c.15 326, c.16–17 330.

62. Ermold the Black, *In honorem Hludovici*, Bk. 1, "Caetera per campos stabulat diffusa iuventus, Francus, Wasco, Getha, sive Aquitana cohors," 28, translated by Noble, *Charlemagne and Louis the Pious*, 135.

63. *Chronicle of Moissac*, a.803 "Qui congregato exercito ex Aquitania, Wasconiam, necnon de Burgundia, Provincia atque Gotia," 142.

64. Alcuin, *Epistolae* no. 7, "duces et tribuni," 32.

65. Louis came to Aquitaine in 818, 832, and 839. The first visit was largely confined to Tours and Anjou, while that of 832 was concerned with suppressing the rebellion of Pippin I. AB a.832 5; AB a.839 33; Astronomer, *Vita Hludowici*, c.31 388, c.47 470, c.61 538.

border [the Spanish March]."[66] The following year it is recorded that "the counts of the Spanish March crossed the River Segre into Spain."[67] As on other frontiers, the lords of the March were expected not simply to defend their territory but to act as Louis's agents in the area.[68] This shared sense of purpose also appeared in other areas. Charlemagne and Louis the Pious patronised monastic institutions in Aquitaine and the March.[69] Other great aristocrats in his circle did likewise. Count Bello of Carcassonne (790–810) granted land to the monastery of La Grassa near Narbonne, while Count Bego of Toulouse established the monastery of Alaó in Ribagorza in 806.[70]

The coalition of aristocratic interests established in the late 790s was a highly successful body of support for Louis, going to war for him repeatedly for over a decade. It also represents a high point for the internal stability of the Spanish March. Subsequent decades were to be defined by the fraying, although not the complete collapse, of this consensus, the most spectacular incidence of which was Aizo's revolt in 826. The previous chapter examined increasing problems with the Basques as a cause of difficulties in the 810s. If Louis's authority over the Basque world, and his relationships with the leaders of Gascony, was in trouble, a more significant process can be seen elsewhere on the borderlands with Spain. Here the issue was less local opposition to Carolingian rule and more competition between the major figures of the Spanish March, as tensions rose between the victors of Barcelona and their descendants. Much scholarship has sought to explain the tensions within the Spanish March through reference to animosity between "native" Goths and "foreign" Franks.[71] Subsequent work has complicated and undermined this picture.[72] As the following discussion should indicate, loyalties on the frontier were rather more complex than a struggle between ethnic groups.

Hints of problems first emerge in a charter of 812. Hispani who had been settled as refugees from al-Andalus in the Spanish March by Charlemagne complained to the emperor that they were being oppressed by

66. ARF a.821 "hoc illius limitis praefectis," 154.

67. ARF a.822 "Comites marcae Hispanicae trans Sicorim a fluvium in Hispania profecti," 158, translated by Scholz, *Carolingian Chronicles*, 111.

68. Werner, "Missus-Marchio-Comes," 211–221.

69. CC 2.ii, 260–262; CC 3, 20–35; Chandler, *Carolingian Catalonia*, 86–88.

70. Chandler, "Land and Social Networks," 18–19.

71. Auzias, *L'Aquitaine carolingienne*, 91–96; d'Abadal i de Vinyals, *Els Primers Comtes Catalans*, 229.

72. Salrach, *El Procés de Formació Nacional*, 1:88–90; Zimmermann, "Western Francia," 446.

the local counts.[73] Charlemagne sent instructions to Louis to summon the counts and correct their behaviour.[74] Four years later, the then emperor Louis promised to protect "the smaller and weaker" Hispani settlers from the depredations of "the more important and more powerful."[75] These incidents might simply be seen as the standard problems of managing a far-flung empire, but they are an early indication of the competition for resources that would soon break out among the counts of the March.[76]

Further signs of trouble can be detected in an account of a tribunal held in Narbonne on 11 September 833.[77] Here Teudefred, the son of the John who had been granted land for fighting Muslims near Barcelona in the 790s, successfully reclaimed those lands from one Dexter.[78] Teudefred brought witnesses who supported his right to the land, reporting that John had been unlawfully driven off them by Count Leibulf of Provence. Leibulf's death in 828 means that this dispossession happened during the period of breakdown being discussed in the 820s, most likely after the excitement caused by the Aizo affair but possibly in the years of tension before them.[79] What made this distinctive was not that magnates were trying to seize control of John's estates. John had been part of the delegation of Hispani who visited Aachen in 812, complaining to Charlemagne of comital oppression.[80] In 814 Count Adhemar of Narbonne had attempted to take the land from John.[81] What was different was that Leibulf succeeded. Charlemagne and Louis the Pious had protected Hispani like John. John won his case against Adhemar and in 815 Louis had reconfirmed his claim to the land.[82] That Leibulf could muscle John out and his family be unable to do anything about it for at least four years speaks to a change in Louis's involvement in the region. This environment undermined the unity within the areas on the front line with al-Andalus.

More dramatic was the downfall of Count Bera of Barcelona. Bera had been accused of treason by one Sanila and chose to defend himself

73. On this incident, see Chandler, "Between Court and Counts"; Davis, *Charlemagne's Practice of Empire*, 104–105.

74. CC 2.ii, no. 2, 313–314.

75. Louis the Pious, *Urkunden*, no. 88 214–217, "illos minores et infirmiores," "eos maiores et potentiores," 216.

76. Gravel, *Distances, rencontres, communications*, 105.

77. Haack and Kohl, "Teudefred and the King," 229–235.

78. Haack, *Die Krieger der Karolinger*, 156–171.

79. Depreux, *Prosopographie*, 292–293.

80. CC 2.ii, no. 2, 313–314.

81. Depreux, *Prosopographie*, 401–403.

82. Louis the Pious, *Urkunden*, no. 48 124–127.

through trial by combat.[83] The two men duelled on horseback with lances at Aachen in January 820, in front of the emperor and his court.[84] Bera lost the duel but had his death sentence commuted to life exile in Rouen. The exact nature of his crime is unclear. The *Annales regni Francorum* informs us only that "for a long time he had been accused by his neighbours of bad faith and treason."[85] It has in the past been argued that Bera was negotiating with Muslims across the border and that he had favoured a policy of peace with the Umayyads, but the grounds for this belief are unclear.[86]

Bera had been a frequent companion of Louis on campaign, serving with him in 804, 808, and 809.[87] The count's guilt is hard to establish. The nature of the ordeal, employed only when there was no other evidence either way, indicates that Bera's accusers had no very convincing proof.[88] As Bera was a Goth, the trial has been interpreted as evidence of Franco-Gothic hostility: the native elite rebelling against foreign rule, or Frankish nobles conniving to bring down an enemy Goth. [89] This is unconvincing, as d'Abadal demonstrated, for Sanila was also a Goth.[90] It is more likely that Bera was brought down by local rivals eager for the resources and offices he possessed. When Sanila was executed by supporters of Lothar I at Chalon-sur-Saône in 834, he was the lieutenant of Gaucelm, the count of Empúries and Roussillon, the son of William of Gellone, and the brother of Bernard.[91] This suggests that Bera's downfall was engineered by William's descendants.

It has been argued by Pierre Ponsich that Bera was the son of William of Gellone from a marriage predating that which produced Gaucelm and Bernard.[92] Ponsich's article has been widely adopted in mainland Europe.[93] Nonetheless, this hypothesis is problematic for a number of

83. Astronomer, *Vita Hludowici*, c.32 398. On trial by combat, see Bartlett, *Trial by Fire and Water*, 103.

84. ARF a.820 206.

85. Ibid., "qui iam diu fraudis et infidelitatis a vicinis suis insimulabatur," translated by Scholz, *Carolingian Chronicles*, 107.

86. Auzias, *L'Aquitaine carolingienne*, 88.

87. Depreux, *Prosopographie*, 129–130.

88. Colman, "Reason and Unreason," 583.

89. Astronomer, *Vita Hludowici*, c.33 398.

90. D'Abadal i de Vinyals, *Els Primers Comtes Catalans*, 222–230.

91. Nithard, *Histoire des fils*, I.5 24–26.

92. Ponsich, "Bera I," 52.

93. Within one volume alone, Le Jan, ed., *La royauté et les élites*, see Duhamel-Amado and Catafau, "Fidèles et aprisionaires" and Aurell, "Pouvoir et Párenté." See also Aurell, *Les Noces du Comte*, 35–37.

reasons. The text of Count William's will refers to a seemingly comprehensive list of relatives, including multiple wives, with no mention of a Bera.[94] It seems unlikely that William would make several wills, for the best chance of enforcing his wishes would be through the participation of all interested parties.

Bera and his family are frequently referred to as Goths; William and his known descendants are never so called.[95] Ethnicity is a complex construct, but it would be strange for half brothers to be of different ethnic status, particularly if they inherited their position through their Frankish father.[96] If there is one thing an acquaintance with Carolingian history brings, it is an appreciation that brothers do not always get on, but that not one of the narrative sources touching on Bera's downfall mentions that the man he fought in single combat was in the retinue of his half brother is hard to explain.

Ponsich bases his case on a foundation document for the Abbey of Alet, saying that in 817, Count Bera of Razès, son of William of Gellone, granted the abbey land.[97] There are problems with this source. There is no evidence to indicate that Bera of Barcelona was ever count of Razès, leading d'Abadal to hypothesise two different Beras.[98] As Ponsich concedes, the manuscript on which it is preserved is very late and predates any other evidence of the abbey's existence by more than a century, which is why it was previously considered a forgery.[99] It seems reasonable to suggest that this earlier assessment was correct. While it is strange that a later forger would want the name of a famous traitor on his foundation document, the descendants of Bera remained powerful in the region into the tenth century and might have remained useful.[100] The inclusion of the illustrious St William is easier to understand.

If the evidence suggests that William's children may have been behind Bera's disgrace, the count of Barcelona may not have been the only casualty of this moment. Ramon Ordeig notes that 820 also sees the unexplained vanishing of Count Borrell I of Cerdanya, Urgell, and Osona from the late 790s.[101] The trial of Lupus Centulli in 818 discussed above also bears a

94. William of Toulouse, "Testament."

95. ARF a.826 171; Astronomer, *Vita Hludowici*, c.13 320, c.33 398, Ermold the Black, *In honorem Hludovici*, Bk. 1, 32.

96. Pohl, "Introduction: Strategies of Distinction," 2–8.

97. Ponsich, "Bera I," 51.

98. Ibid., 52; d'Abadal i de Vinyals, *Els Primers Comtes Catalans*, 222–230.

99. Ponsich, "Bera I," 51.

100. Ibid., 57.

101. Ordeig i Mata, *Els Orígens Històrics*, 54.

certain similarity to that of Bera, in which a key figure on the March was removed after accusations of treason. The generation of captains who had served Louis when he was king of Aquitaine was vanishing. If the Williamids hoped the removal of Bera at their instigation would get them the county of Barcelona, they were to be disappointed. Louis appointed instead a Frankish aristocrat named Rampo, defusing tension by bringing in an outsider.[102] That Rampo was well-known to Louis and trusted by him is suggested by the fact that he was the man sent to inform Louis of the death of his father in 814.[103]

Rampo died in the winter of 825.[104] It was probably at an assembly of February 826 in Aachen that Louis appointed as his replacement Bernard of Septimania, son of William of Gellone and the brother of Gaucelm, Sanila's patron. Louis was clearly concerned about the state of the Spanish March. At this meeting, Louis's son, the current king of Aquitaine, Pippin I, "came with his magnates and the guards of the Spanish border . . . after consulting with them the emperor made his decision on the protection of the western frontier against the Saracens."[105] Gathering all the leaders of the March together for the assembly may have been Louis's attempt to sort out any resentment and reinforce his authority. If so, it failed miserably.

It is in this context that Aizo's revolt must be understood. The Frankish annals, which are our major sources for the events of 826 and 827, serve to occlude the importance of tensions in the March by focusing on Aizo. The role of Aizo's allies in the March ("Willemund, son of Bera, defected to him as did some others equally anxious for change") is downplayed.[106] The implication must be that Aizo had considerable backing from people unhappy with the status quo who felt that the only way to achieve change was to oppose the Carolingians.[107]

That the trigger for many of Aizo's allies was the new count of Barcelona can be inferred from a couple of details, chief among them being

102. CC 2.ii 2, 45–47; Salrach, *El Procés de Formació Nacional*, 1:47–48; Chandler, *Carolingian Catalonia*, 96–97.

103. Astronomer, *Vita Hludowici*, c.21 346.

104. Ordeig i Mata, *Els Orígens Històrics*, 54.

105. ARF a.826 "cum sius optimatibus et Hispanici limitis custodibus circa Kalendas Februarias Aquasgrani—nam ibi tunc imperator hiemaverat—venit, cum quibus cum de tuendis contra Sarracenos occidentalium partium finibus esset tractatum atque dispositum," 169, translated by Scholz, *Carolingian Chronicles*, 119.

106. ARF a.827 "Defecit ad eum et filius Berani, nomine Willemundus, nec non et alii conplures novarum rerum gentilicia levitate cupidi," 172, translated by Scholz, *Carolingian Chronicles*, 121.

107. Cf. Chandler, *Carolingian Catalonia*, 99.

Willemund's leading role in the revolt. Bernard was certainly in the thick of the action according to the *Annales regni Francorum*, for he "stubbornly resisted the ambushes of Aizo and the cunning and treacherous machinations of those who had defected to him."[108] The attention paid to Bernard's counties of Barcelona and Girona by the invading Umayyad army of 827 may also be significant.[109]

Whereas in 800 Louis could call upon a coalition of Basques, Franks, and Goths who represented the entirety of the aristocratic, secular elites in the region and use them as a united military force, a quarter of a century later that consensus had vanished. Following a series of revolts, the leaders of the Basques were either entirely independent (Pamplona) or de facto detached from Carolingian affairs (Gascony). Meanwhile, the families of the Spanish March proper were divided against each other in competition over Barcelona and Girona.

## LIGHTS IN THE SKY

The consequences of this development were important. First, it led directly both to the Umayyad invasion of 827 and to raids later in the century. ʿAbd al-Raḥmān II had shown no particular aggression towards the Franks before this and his behaviour before and after the attack strongly suggests that this was an opportunistic raid following Aizo's invitation. Bernard's son, William, would in turn look for ʿAbd al-Raḥmān's help as the struggle for Barcelona intensified in the mid-840s.[110] The collapse of the coalition of 800 did not destroy the ability of the local counts to protect the March. Bernard and his family seem to have been capable of raising considerable forces. Nonetheless, it made fending off Umayyad advances more difficult. Second, it prompted a rivalry for high position in the March that destabilised the area and would help fuel war between Pippin II and Charles the Bald for Aquitaine in the next generation, as rival factions picked opposing Carolingians.

The reasons why Louis's coalition collapsed are not immediately obvious. One possible factor was the changing leadership of the March. Louis had grown up in Aquitaine and until his father's death in 814 spent the

108. ARF a.827 "Bernhardus quoque, Barcinonae comes, Aizonis insidiis et eorum qui ad eum defecerant calliditati ac fraudulentis machinationibus pertinacissime resisteret," 172, translated by Scholz, *Carolingian Chronicles*, 121.

109. ARF a.827 172; al-Nuwayrī, *Textos dels historiadors*, 114.

110. Ibn Ḥayyān, "Pasajes del 'Muqtabis,'" 337.

majority of his time there.[111] His campaigns would have ensured tight, personal bonds with the leading aristocrats of the March, who were accustomed to regular access to a Carolingian king. Upon becoming emperor, Louis's priorities moved elsewhere and he never returned to the March. The absence of his experience and presence might have been important in the deterioration of his coalition.

On the other hand, Louis appointed his son Pippin as the new king of Aquitaine in 817.[112] While Louis's interference in Pippin's management of the kingdom might be seen as a sign of his doubts about his ability, there are no particular reasons to accuse Pippin of incompetence.[113] Figures such as Ermold the Black and Jonas of Orléans took Pippin seriously, the latter dedicating his *De institutione regia* to the king of Aquitaine.[114] Indeed, the longevity of his son's ability to oppose Charles the Bald would suggest that Pippin I embedded himself fairly strongly within Aquitaine.[115]

A hint may come from the fierce competition for Barcelona. As the count of Barcelona was normally granted Girona as well, following the loss of Pamplona it represented the major and arguably only gains made by the Carolingians in Spain after 785.[116] To follow the arguments made more generally by Timothy Reuter about the Carolingian empire as a whole, in the first decade of the ninth century the prospect of future acquisitions incentivised the lords of the March to cooperate.[117] Some of the opportunities available are suggested by the grant made by Charlemagne to a warrior named John in 795, who was rewarded for his service in battle with "an abandoned estate in the country of Narbonne."[118] The major lords of the March may have aspired to greater prizes, but a similar principle of warfare in Spain leading to increased wealth would have applied. The desultory phoney wars of the 810s appeared to mark the definitive end of hopes of expansion. In the absence of more pie, aristocrats may have turned on each other to secure a larger slice.

The role played by the sons of Count William is suggestive here. William's retirement to his foundation of Gellone in 806 took place when

111. Astronomer, *Vita Hludowici*, c.5 296; Böhmer, *Regesta Imperii*, 1:234–239.

112. Collins, "Pippin I."

113. Eiten, *Das Unterkönigtum*, 290–294.

114. For Ermold's letters to Pippin, see Ermold the Black, "Letters to Pippin I"; Jonas of Orléans, *Le Métier de Roi*, 170; Stone, *Morality and Masculinity*, 40.

115. Coupland, "The Coinages of Pippin I and II," 200.

116. D'Abadal i de Vinyals, *Els Primers Comtes Catalans*, 22.

117. Reuter, "Plunder and Tribute" and "The End of Carolingian Military Expansion." See the response of McKitterick, *Charlemagne*, 135–136.

118. CC 2.ii "in pago Narbonense villare eremum," 310.

Bernard and Gaucelm were too young to have been of political significance.[119] Their father's offices passed to others, with Toulouse going to Bego.[120] William's sons presumably inherited some lands in the March to explain their continued prominence and Gaucelm was the count of Empúries and Roussillon, but Bernard did not hold an office until receiving Barcelona in 826.[121] Frankish chroniclers were to blame Bernard of Septimania for many of the crises in the empire of the 830s, with Paschasius Radbertus describing him as "the author of all evils."[122] It seems plausible that the sons of William, who frequently acted together as a family, might have felt excluded from the post-806 settlement and sought to restore their father's primacy in the March, something Bernard achieved in 827.[123] This would explain much of the disruption of the 820s, as their bid for higher offices brought them into competition with other families, most notably that of Bera.

It was probably in response to this disruption that Louis adopted a new strategy for managing the Spanish March. Past efforts to balance and mediate between the magnates were abandoned in favour of consolidating offices under one group, the Williamids. Although based on the Spanish March, they continued to be tightly connected to the Carolingian dynasty. Bernard was Louis the Pious's godson, and his sister was married to Wala, an illegitimate cousin of Charlemagne and a key adviser to three generations of Carolingians.[124] By 828 Gaucelm was granted Conflent and Razès, while Bernard was given the estates of the recently deceased Count Leibulf of Provence, including Narbonne, Béziers, Agde, Melgueil, Nîmes, and possibly Uzès.[125]

Louis's plans for Bernard and his family were hardly confined to the March. A relative, Odo, was made count of Orléans and, most precipitously, Bernard was summoned to Louis's court to be his chamberlain.[126] In Bernard's absence, Gaucelm was to manage his territories on the March, effectively concentrating most of the territories that had been divided

119. Collins, "Pippin I," 376.

120. Laurenson-Rosaz, "Les Guillelmides," 56.

121. Gaucelm can be seen intervening with Louis the Pious on behalf of the monastery of Sureda in 823; CC 2.ii, 267–269.

122. Paschasius Radbertus, "*Epitaphium Arsenii*," II.9 "auctor totius malitiae," 72.

123. Bernard is an understudied figure, with the last major monograph being Calmette, *De Bernardo Sancti*.

124. Paschasius Radbertus, "*Epitaphium Arsenii*," II.8, 69; De Jong, *Epitaph for an Era*, 151–156.

125. Salrach, *El Procés de Formació Nacional*, 1:93.

126. Astronomer, *Vita Hludowici*, c.44 456.

between the lords who took Barcelona in 801.[127] Gaucelm's influence with Louis can be seen in an immunity granted by the emperor to the monastery of Amer near Girona in 829 or 830 at his request.[128] Louis did not entirely sideline the rest of the marcher lords, as the granting to Sunifred in October 829 of an estate held by his father, Count Borrell, indicates.[129] The effectiveness of this new approach went untested, as Bernard's swift disgrace and the subsequent civil war led to both Bernard and Gaucelm being deprived of their honours in 832.

Division within the March not only caused the crisis of 826 but also hindered efforts to fix the situation. The best demonstration of the seriousness of the military disasters of 826 and 827 is to be found in contemporary Frankish reactions.[130] Louis was initially calm about the situation in the Spanish March, with the *Annales regni Francorum* in 826 declaring:

> Although the news of this greatly enraged the emperor, he judged that nothing should be done without consideration and decided to wait for the rest of his counsellors.[131]

This sanguine attitude was short-lived. By 828 Louis was willing to commit not just "many Frankish troops" but also two of his sons, Pippin and Lothar, to the Spanish March.[132] The military disaster caused major disruption to Louis's customary rhythms. The "needs of the kingdom" prevented him from going hunting that year.[133] The standard grand summer assembly, at which all the chief men of the empire could gather, had to be cancelled, as Louis and Lothar explained in a letter sent to the *fideles* in the winter of 828, due to "the movements of our enemies."[134]

Also indicative of a major crisis was the precipitous fall of Matfrid and Hugh, two of the most powerful men in Louis's court.[135] Something

127. Salrach, *El Procés de Formació Nacional*, 1:94–97.

128. CC 2.ii, 10.

129. Louis the Pious, *Urkunden*, no. 283 705–706.

130. De Jong, *The Penitential State*, 148–184.

131. ARF a.826 "Sed imperator licet huius rei nuntium graviter ferret, nihil tamen inconsulte gerendum iudicans, consiliariorum suorum adventum statuit opperiri," 170.

132. ARF a.828 "cum magnis Francorum copiis," 175.

133. Ibid., "necessaria regni," 177. On the importance of hunting for the reign of Louis the Pious, see Goldberg, "Louis the Pious and the Hunt" and *In the Manner of the Franks*, 103–128.

134. Louis the Pious and Lothar I, *Hludowici et Hlotharii epistola generalis*, "commotio inimicorum," 599. On assemblies, see Reuter, "Assembly Politics"; Airlie, "Talking Heads."

135. Depreux, "Le comté Matfrid"; Vollner, "Die Etichonen," 163–165; Hummer, *Politics and Power*, 156–161.

of Matfrid's influence is demonstrated by Jonas of Orléans addressing his *De institutione laicali* to the count of Orléans.[136] Matfrid was not a stranger to the Spanish March, having intervened with Louis the Pious on behalf of the monastery of Senterada in 823.[137] Matfrid and Hugh appeared in positions of honour in Ermold the Black's poem celebrating Louis. The poet places them flanking the Empress Judith at the baptism of Harald Klak at Ingelheim in 826.[138] That luminaries of their calibre should be dispossessed of all titles and lands, as happened at an assembly in February 828, due to their failure to protect the March, was a political earthquake in the midst of the court.[139] No less symptomatic is the spectacular elevation of Bernard, the count of Barcelona, to chamberlain. As the only count to emerge from the disaster well some reward would have been expected, but Bernard's level of power and the speed of his rise made him highly controversial.[140] Bernard's instatement as chamberlain in 829 was directly connected to his performance on the March and is striking testimony to the way in which events in the Iberian Peninsula could translate into political power right at the centre of the empire.[141]

Although Hugh and Matfrid might have served as scapegoats, ninth-century observers were convinced that this disaster was a warning and punishment from God.[142] That many people saw catastrophe on the Spanish March as an indication of divine wrath is indicated by the description of portents in the narrative sources.[143] In its account of the Umayyad raid of the March, the *Annales regni Francorum* report that "people were sure they saw battle lines and shifting lights in the sky at night and that these marvels foreboded the Frankish defeat."[144] Writing later, the Astronomer elaborated upon these strange tidings, declaring that "just before this catastrophe, there appeared in the night sky terrible battle lines reddened

136. Jonas of Orléans, *Instruction des laïcs*, 44n1.

137. CC 2.ii, 259–262.

138. Ermold the Black, *In honorem Hludovici*, Bk. 4, 176.

139. ARF a.828 174. On the dispossession of counts, see Krah, *Absetzungsverfahren als Spiegelbild*, 40–82; Davis, *Charlemagne's Practice of Empire*, 90–127.

140. ARF a.827 172; De Jong, *Epitaph for an Era*, 151–157.

141. ARF a.829 177.

142. Louis and Lothar, *Hludowici et Hlotharii epistola generalis*, 600.

143. Dutton, *Charlemagne's Mustache*, 93–110.

144. ARF a.827 "Huius cladis praesagia credita sunt visae multoties in coelo acies, et ille terribilis nocturnae coruscationis in aere discursus," 173, translated by Scholz, *Carolingian Chronicles*, 122.

with human blood flashing with the colour of fire."[145] Paschasius Radbertus, in his polemical *Epitaphium Arsenii*, which looked back at events from the 850s, portrayed God sending daily "calamities and scourges" upon the people in response to their sin.[146]

In the absence of a general summer assembly, the emperor gathered an inner council in the winter of 828.[147] Following this meeting, Louis and Lothar issued a letter to the leading figures of empire, informing them of developments, where they attributed the disaster to divine wrath.[148] Specific reference to defeat at the hands of non-Christian enemies emerges in the following passage:

> For this also should be ascribed to our sins, that the enemies of Christ's name, who entered this kingdom, have committed robberies, set fire to churches, captured Christians and killed the servants of God, boldly and with impunity—indeed most cruelly.[149]

In addition to notifying their correspondents of a three-day fast from 24 May the following year, Louis and Lothar announced that episcopal councils would be held at Lyons, Mainz, Paris, and Toulouse to consider how best to placate divine wrath.[150]

These commentaries mention other calamities. Paschasius Radbertus lists "disasters, plagues, famines, irregular weather and even terrifying visions."[151] In their letter, Louis and Lothar provided a similarly grim itemization, with the realm tormented "by constant hunger, by the death of animals, by plagues among men, by the sterility of almost all fruit trees."[152] Nor was Aizo's rebellion the only defeat suffered by the Franks for

145. Astronomer, *Vita Hludowici*, c.41 "Precesserunt sane hanc cladem terribiles illę nocturno sub tempore acies humano rutilantes sanguine ignisque pallore flagrantes," 440, translated by Noble, *Charlemagne and Louis the Pious*, 271.

146. Paschasius Radbertus, "*Epitaphium Arsenii*," II.1 "calamitatibus et flagellis," 61. On the *Epitaphium Arsenii*, see Ganz, "The *Epitaphium Arsenii*"; De Jong, *Epitaph for an Era*.

147. Einhard, *Translatio et miracula*, 252.

148. On this letter, see De Jong, *The Penitential State*, 170–176.

149. Louis and Lothar, *Hludowici et Hlotharii epistola generalis*, "Nam et illud nihilominus peccatis nostris deputandum est, quod inimici Christi nominis praeterito anno in hoc regnum ingressi depraedationes, incendia ecclesiarum et captivationes Christianorum et interfectiones servorum Dei audenter et inpune, immo crudeliter fecerunt," 599–600.

150. Louis and Lothar, *Hludowici et Hlotharii epistola generalis*, 600–601.

151. Paschasius Radbertus, "*Epitaphium Arsenii*," "clades, pestilentias, fames, inaequalitates aerum, terroresque etiam visionum," 61.

152. Louis and Lothar, *Hludowici et Hlotharii epistola generalis*, "in fame continua, in mortalitate animalium, in pestilentia hominum, in sterilitate pene omnium frugum," 599.

827 had also seen the Bulgars ravage Friuli.[153] Baldric, the *dux* of Friuli, received the same treatment as Hugh and Matfrid.[154]

Grievous as these other problems were, the crisis on the March needs to be seen as the trigger of Frankish anxieties and Louis's efforts to win back divine favour. The most obvious reason is the timing. The account of the 820s found in the *Annales regni Francorum* is littered with portents and unnatural occurrences.[155] Louis's calm in 826 contrasts very sharply with his activity in 827 and particularly 828. While the other afflictions may have been worrisome, the Carolingian reaction directly followed the military disasters of 827. The importance of Spain over Friuli can be observed in the aftermath. The *Annales regni Francorum* stresses that the assembly held at Aachen in February 828 addressed "especially those things which had happened in the Spanish March."[156] Baldric was a minor player and his fall from power did not have the same political ramifications as that of Matfrid and Hugh.[157] Nor was anyone able to turn a respectable performance against the Bulgars into political office in a manner similar to Bernard.[158]

The attack of 827 was not the first big Umayyad onslaught on Frankish territory, being preceded by Hishām's raid into Septimania in 793.[159] This defeat, combined with a Saxon revolt, was clearly bad news, yet it prompted neither the soul searching that was to follow a third of a century later nor the grave political crisis. Count William of Toulouse, in command of the defeated army, retained his *honores* and his prominence. Several differences between the defeat of 793 and that of 827 can be observed. In the case of the former, there was no hint of treachery or division. That was clearly not the case in 827, where Aizo had found considerable support among the disaffected and invited ʿAbd al-Raḥmān's invasion. Further, while 793 may have been a bad year for Frankish military achievement, it occurred in a general context of triumph. A major victory was won over the Avars in 791, while the Saxons were to be defeated in 794 and 795.[160]

153. ARF a.826 168.

154. Ibid.

155. ARF: Rains, pestilence, and an eclipse in a.820; 154, rain and cold weather in a.821; 159, a whole series of miracles and bizarre meteorological phenomena in a.823 166–167; cold weather, an eclipse, and falling ice in a.824 167–168. On these, see McCormick, Dutton, and Mayewski, "Volcanoes and the Climate Forcing," 881–884.

156. ARF a.828 "tum praecipue de his, quae in marca Hispanica contigerunt," 174.

157. De Jong, *The Penitential State*, 39.

158. On the Bulgar invasion, see Gjuselav, "Bulgarisch-Fränkische Beziehungen," 30–31; Bowlus, *Franks, Moravians, and Magyars*, 91–98.

159. ARF a.793 95.

160. ARF a.791 88, a.794 94, a.795 96.

Charlemagne faced multiple challenges, not least the attempted coup of Pippin the Hunchback in 792, but Carolingian armies were winning battles and forcing enemies to submit with sufficient regularity to maintain confidence.[161]

The Iberian Peninsula and the March were of particular significance to Louis. Following his coronation as king of Aquitaine, the Spanish March had been his responsibility from infancy for a quarter of a century.[162] The importance of this period was recognised by the Astronomer, who devoted a large section of his biography to Louis's years before he became emperor.[163] Louis famously dressed in Basque clothes as a youth.[164] Many of his closest advisers and formative influences when young were connected to the March. Among them were Archchancellor Helisachar and most notably Benedict of Aniane, the son of the count of Maguelonne.[165] Louis's commitment to Benedictine monasticism was made apparent in Aquitaine, with a large number of institutions founded or reformed by him.[166] That Saracens should threaten them was a direct blow to Louis's achievements.

Spain was also the theatre of most of Louis's military successes. His greatest victory, the fall of Barcelona in 801, had been widely celebrated.[167] The Astronomer gives some sense of the ceremony with which the capture of the city was greeted, with Louis entering Barcelona in procession, "in majestic solemnity."[168] Tribute, plunder, and the defeated leader were sent to Charlemagne as a sign of the victory.[169] Ermold, writing to win Louis's favour shortly before 826, spent nearly a quarter of his panegyric on the siege of Barcelona, turning it into a clash of champions, a victory over worthy foes, and a triumph for Christendom and order over paganism and banditry.[170] When Abū Marwān "laid waste the fields and burned the villages around Barcelona and Girona," he was ravaging the landscape of Louis's past glory.[171] Louis's general lack of delegation to Pippin may have made him appear more responsible for Spanish matters. February 826 had

161. Hammer, "'Pipinus Rex.'"
162. ARF a.781 56.
163. Astronomer, *Vita Hludowici*, cc.3–20 292–342.
164. Ibid., c.4 296.
165. Depreux, *Prosopographie*, 123–129, 235–240; Ardo/Smaragdus, *Vita Benedicti*.
166. Noble, "The Monastic Ideal"; De Jong, "Carolingian Monasticism," 629–634.
167. ARF a.801 116.
168. Astronomer, *Vita Hludowici*, c.13 "cum sollemni apparatu," 318.
169. ARF a.801 116.
170. Ermold the Black, *In honorem Hludovici*, Bk. 1, 12–50.
171. ARF a.827 "ut Abumarvan, vastatis Barcinonensium ac Gerundensium agris villisque incensis," 173, translated by Scholz, *Carolingian Chronicles*, 121.

seen Louis consulting with Pippin and his magnates, before "the emperor made his decision on the protection of the western frontier against the Saracens."[172] Disaster had struck when the March was under Louis's dispositions, which could have added to the need for Louis to procure scapegoats at speed.

Having scrambled in response to the defeat of 827, Carolingian forces on the March were confronted with an anti-climax. The next year saw Lothar and Pippin gathering at Lyons with a large army, only to find "that the Saracens were afraid or unwilling to come to the March."[173] Following the recent ravaging of the March, this must have come as something of a relief, but it also meant that the ghosts of the past years were not exorcised. Nonetheless, while the political fallout from the disaster was still unfolding, the actual military crisis was at an end. That this was the case is largely due to Louis's response and internal problems within al-Andalus.

As the presence of Lothar and Pippin demonstrated, Louis had understood the scale of the potential danger and committed a major force to the frontier, which would have discouraged a repeat raid. As the *Annales regni Francorum* recounts, even in 827 Abū Marwān had been careful to avoid engaging the army of Hugh and Matfrid before he "retreated to Zaragoza with his army intact before our army caught sight of him."[174] The Umayyads made no effort to retake Girona or Barcelona, indicating an unwillingness to fight a battle, something confirmed by the Arabic sources, which stress that Abū Marwān plundered for two months before returning to Córdoba.[175] The unfortunate Matfrid and Hugh were punished for their "cowardice," not for actually being defeated.[176]

A change in mood can be found in Walahfrid Strabo's *De imagine Tetrici*, dedicated to Louis and composed in 829, which declares that:

> the Bulgar and cur of Sarah, bad guest of the Spaniards,
> The brutish Britton, shrewd Dane and dreadful African,
> Bow their necks in terror before your venerable hands.[177]

172. ARF a.826 "cum quibus cum de tuendis contra Sarracenos occidentalium partium finibus esset tractatum atque dispositum, Pippinus in Aquitaniam regressus, aestatem in deputato sibi loco transegit," 169, translated by Scholz, *Carolingian Chronicles*, 119.

173. ARF a.828 "quod Sarraceni ad marcam venire aut timerent aut nollent," 175.

174. ARF a.827 "cum incolomi exercitu Caesaraugustam se prius reciperet, quam a nostro exercitu vel videri potuisset," 173, translated by Scholz, *Carolingian Chronicles*, 121–122.

175. Ibn ʿIdhārī, *Textos dels historiadors*, 114; al-Nuwayrī, *Textos dels historiadors*, 114.

176. Astronomer, *Vita Hludowici*, c.42 "ignaviae," 444.

177. Walahfrid Strabo, *De imagine Tetrici*, "Sic Vulgar Sarraeque cynus, malus hospes Hiberis, Brutus Britto, Danus uersutus et horridus Afer," translated by Herren, "The 'De imagine Tetrici' of Walahfrid Strabo," 130, 139.

The "cur of Sarah" occupying Spain is an allusion to the Muslims of the Iberian Peninsula, playing on Frankish perceptions of Saracens as claiming to be descended from Abraham via his wife Sarah, while actually being of the line of Hagar, his slave.[178] This is panegyric, written by someone new to court and seeking favour, so should not be seen as an accurate description of foreign affairs.[179] Nonetheless, that Walahfrid could present this without it seeming like a bad joke suggests an increase in confidence in Louis's court.

Louis's response to the crisis was energetic and aggressive, as indicated by a remarkable letter he sent to the city of Mérida.[180] This letter, which Conant has convincingly dated to between December 829 and April 830, was dispatched to the city while it was in the midst of a revolt against ʿAbd al-Raḥmān.[181] Louis offered the rebels an alliance, "since as that very king [ʿAbd al-Raḥmān] is our most certain opponent and enemy as much as he is yours, we should fight his cruelty with shared resolve."[182] The emperor also proposed himself as an alternative ruler, presenting an implied comparison with "the savagery of King ʿAbd al-Raḥmān who has oppressed you constantly and violently with his greedy desire for your possessions, which he has attempted to steal from you."[183] Louis on the other hand would "grant you your ancient rights to the fullest extent, without any reduction . . . free of tax or tribute . . . [with] no other law than the one under which you wish to live."[184]

This proposal would have seemed grandiose under normal circumstances. Mérida lies roughly one thousand kilometres from Barcelona and no Carolingian army ever got past the defences of the Upper March,

178. Millar, "Hagar, Ishmael, Josephus."

179. On Walahfrid's hunting metaphor, see Goldberg, "Louis the Pious and the Hunt," 630.

180. Einhard, *Epistolae* no. 12, 115–16.

181. Conant, "Louis the Pious and the Contours of Empire," 353. On Mérida, see Christys, "Crossing the Frontier," 38–40.

182. Einhard, *Epistolae* no. 12, "Et quia idem rex certissimus adversarius et inimicus tam noster quam et vester est, communi consilio contra sevitiam eius dimicemus," 116, translated by Dutton, *Charlemagne's Courtier*, 149.

183. Ibid., "quas patimini per crudelitatem regis Abdiraman, qui vos per nimiam cupiditatem rerum vestrarum, quas vobis auferre conatus est, sepissime violenter oppressit," 115, translated by Dutton, *Charlemagne's Courtier*, 148.

184. Ibid., "antiqua libertate vestra plenissime et sine ulla diminutione vobis uti et absque censu vel tribute inmunes vos esse perinittimus et non aliam legem, nisi qua ipsi vivere volueritis, vos tenere iubemus, nec aliter erga vos agree volumus," 116, translated by Dutton, *Charlemagne's Courtier*, 149.

leading early editors to assume Mérida was a mistake for Zaragoza.[185] Scholars have debated the sincerity of Louis's offer, given that the Franks had been unable to protect the Spanish March.[186] Two things should be noted on this question. First, Louis was not promising a Frankish army outside the walls of Mérida. Instead he says that he intended

> to send our army next summer to our March, where it might set up camp and remain ready and waiting for you to send word that it should advance . . . we shall, in order to assist you, send this army against our common enemies living in our March, so that if ʿAbd al-Raḥmān or his army wants to proceed against you, they will be stopped by our army.[187]

This is a highly practical strategy of mutual military support, aimed to distract or split Umayyad forces. It also resembles Louis's campaigns of the 790s and 800s, relying upon Andalusi support to achieve victory.

It seems unlikely that Louis, the man who had unsuccessfully besieged Tortosa on the Ebro three times, seriously anticipated reaching Mérida.[188] As emperor, he had treated al-Andalus with care, supporting minor raids in marked contrast to the type of major expeditions led by his father against the Saxons, Lombards, and Avars. Rather, Louis probably wanted to exacerbate ʿAbd al-Raḥmān's domestic problems. Decrying his plans for their ambition is to miss the point. The emperor needed a major victory in al-Andalus to restore confidence and his reputation. What the letter to Mérida demonstrates was the extent to which he was attempting to manage circumstances to make that victory more likely. There was precedent for this sort of effort. The ignominy of defeat in 793 had quickly been redeemed by Frankish exploitation of Umayyad civil war to go on the attack from 796.[189] Louis was not to be given an opportunity to repeat this strategy because of the coup that came in 830.

185. Conant, "Louis the Pious and the Contours of Empire," 338.

186. Sénac, *Les Carolingiens et al-Andalus*, 94–96; Manzano Moreno, *Conquistadores, Emires y Califas*, 327–328.

187. Einhard, *Epistolae* no. 12, "proxima estate exercitum nostrum ad marcam nostram mittere, ut ibi preparatus sedeat et exspectet, donec vos mandetis, quando promovere debeat; si ita vobis bonum visum fuerit, ut propter vos adiuvandos eundem exercitum contra communes inimicos nostros, qui in marca nostra resident, dirigamus ad hoc, ut, si Abdiraman vel exercitus eius contra vos venire voluerit, isti per nostrum exercitum inpediantur," 116, translated by Dutton, *Charlemagne's Courtier*, 149.

188. ARF a.809 127; Astronomer, *Vita Hludowici*, c.16 330.

189. AL a.796 37.

Louis's communication with Mérida hints at another reason for ʿAbd al-Raḥmān's failure to follow up his success. The raid in 827 was the last summer expedition Córdoba sent to attack a Christian power for some time. The mid- to late 820s saw a flurry of revolts and disturbances. Mérida had been a problem for a while, with ʿAbd Allāh b. Kulayb b. Thaʿlaba al-Judhāmī being sent to suppress a revolt in 826.[190] The same year saw trouble in Algeciras.[191] While Lothar and Pippin were waiting in Lyons, ʿAbd al-Raḥmān had committed all his forces to crushing sedition in Tudmir.[192] By 829 Toledo and Mérida, the capitals of the Central and Lower Marches, respectively, were up in arms.[193] ʿAbd al-Raḥmān was forced to spend the next few years mounting campaigns against and besieging these two cities, taking Mérida in 835 and Toledo in 838.[194] This took priority over intervening in Frankish affairs, explaining the absence of Umayyad forces in the March during the Frankish political turbulence of the 830s. Indeed, the *Annales Xantenses* suggest that by 832 at the latest ʿAbd al-Raḥmān had decided that he needed peace with the Franks, reporting that in October of that year "envoys of the Saracens came to the emperor to strengthen the peace, and returned in peace."[195] The emir may have been aware of Louis's correspondence with the rebels in Mérida, pressuring him to come to the negotiating table.

By 830, Louis may have felt that he had successfully weathered the crisis. In fact, the most serious consequences of the panic caused by the Umayyad attack of 827 were only just coming into view. The humiliation of Hugh and Matfrid and the elevation of Bernard had prompted large-scale resentment. In the spring of 830, Pippin, accompanied by, among others, Helisachar, Matfrid, and Hugh, took his father prisoner, accusing the empress Judith of infidelity with Bernard.[196] This was the beginning of a series of struggles between different Carolingians.[197]

Of interest are the participants in this coup. Hugh and Matfrid had obvious reason to be dissatisfied. The motives of Pippin are much less

190. Ibn Ḥayyān, *Crónica de los emires*, 285.

191. Ibid., 286.

192. Ibid., 287.

193. Ibid., 287–288.

194. Ibid., 287–292.

195. AX a.832 "Legati Sarracenorum venerunt ad imperatorem pacem con firmandam et cum pace reversi sunt," 7–8.

196. Thegan, *Gesta Hludowici imperatoris*, c.36 222; Astronomer, *Vita Hludowici*, c.43 454; Ward, "Caesar's Wife," 225–227, and "Agobard of Lyons and Paschasius Radbertus."

197. Boshof, *Ludwig der Fromme*, 192–210.

clear.[198] The sources portray him as concerned by the supposed behaviour of Bernard.[199] It might be no coincidence, however, that the son who first moved against Louis was also the son whose kingdom had suffered the most serious attack in 827 and which was most undermined by one family accumulating power and offices in the Spanish March under the patronage of Louis. Among his supporters was Helisachar, one of the men best placed to witness the events on the March as they unfolded. This was not a revolt from the March.[200] Bernard was able to flee to Barcelona, where his family remained in power.[201] However, the revolt against Louis was led by men who might have been alienated by the events of 827, explicitly against the one person who had benefitted from them.

Nothing as complicated as the series of revolutions and counterrevolutions that began in 830 has a simple origin. Nevertheless, when Pippin and his men marched against the emperor, they did so as the result of the breakdown of the political consensus that had underpinned Louis's reign, a breakdown that was the product of Louis's efforts to respond to the greatest military disaster of his reign. The conflict between Louis and his sons played out in Septimania and the March. The bishops of Girona, Narbonne, and Elna were supporters of Lothar in the subsequent dispute.[202] Lothar can be seen making grants of land in Roussillon to vassals in 832, and of privileges to the cathedral of Elna and the monastery of Oveix in April 834.[203] In order to reassert his authority, Louis granted his own privileges to Elna in 836.[204] This competition probably did little for the unity of the Spanish March. This disaster was the consequence of a failure to successfully manage al-Andalus and the Spanish March in the 820s. Far away in Córdoba, ʿAbd al-Raḥmān had effectively thrown his most dangerous neighbour into disarray for the best part of a decade. That the emir could never have predicted this result when he gave ʿUbayd Allāh his orders would have been of scant comfort to Louis.

198. Collins, "Pippin I," 381.

199. Thegan, *Gesta Hludowici imperatoris*, c.36 222; Astronomer, *Vita Hludowici*, c.43 454.

200. Collins, "Pippin I," 383.

201. Nithard, *Histoire des fils*, I.3, 12.

202. Schäpers, *Lothar I*, 287.

203. CC 2.ii, 101–103, 327–328, 471–472.

204. CC 2.ii, 104–106; Chandler, *Carolingian Catalonia*, 106.

## *Charles the Bald and Umayyad Spain, 840–864*

The reign of Charles the Bald is unusual in the study of Carolingian-Umayyad diplomacy in that his engagement with Córdoba has received considerable attention. In addition to the work of El-Hajji and Sénac, who were directly concerned with Carolingian relations with the Islamic world, scholars coming from different perspectives such as Carolingian studies in the case of Janet Nelson, or Ann Christys from the vantage point of al-Andalus, or specialists in Aquitaine and the northern Christian lands of Spain (Auzias and d'Abadal, respectively) have brought their own approaches to the matter.[205] Their conclusions have tended to address specific moments within Charles's reign. This section will examine his relations with Córdoba as a whole, while also placing them in a wider context.

Talking about Charles the Bald's foreign policy objectives is a difficult task. The Carolingians were pragmatic opportunists, with no grand master plan, generally reacting to openings and problems as they emerged.[206] As we have seen, the political history of the Franks in the eighth and ninth centuries is best interpreted as a series of short-term measures in response to changing exigencies and chances.[207] The geopolitical context played a crucial role in determining what opportunities and dangers the king of the West Franks had to face. Like his father, Charles had to reckon with a powerful al-Andalus under capable management by emirs who were willing to take advantage of opportunities to invade. By the late 830s ʿAbd al-Raḥmān II had resecured his authority over most of the peninsula. Umayyad confidence is suggested by the resumption of attacks on the kingdom of Asturias in 838.[208] ʿAbd al-Raḥmān launched large raids on Carolingian territory in 842 and 848, a practice continued by his son Muḥammad I in 861.[209] This meant Charles could not rely on military force to intimidate Córdoba and achieve his aims. He had to keep a wary eye on his southern frontier to fend off invasions.

205. El-Hajji, *Andalusian Diplomatic Relations*, 131–133; Sénac, *Les Carolingiens et al-Andalus*, 101–107; Nelson, *Charles the Bald*, 136, 150–151; Nelson, "The Franks, the Martyrology of Usuard, and the Martyrs of Cordoba"; Christys, "St-Germain des-Prés"; Auzias, *L'Aquitaine carolingienne*, 183; d'Abadal i de Vinyals, *Els Primers Comtes Catalans*, 173–184.

206. Smith, "Fines Imperii," 172.

207. Costambeys, Innes, and MacLean, *The Carolingian World*, 386.

208. Collins, *Caliphs and Kings*, 41.

209. Ibn Ḥayyān, *Crónica de los emires*, 286, and "Pasajes del 'Muqtabis,'" 338; al-Nuwayrī, *Textos dels historiadors*, 126.

A powerful al-Andalus was the first of three political realities that shaped Charles's relations with the Umayyads. The second reality was the multitude of other external difficulties he had to deal with. In the west Charles had difficult relations with the Bretons and suffered several setbacks at their hands, most notably his defeat at Jengland in 851.[210] His most notorious problem was provided by Scandinavian raiders.[211] The 850s and 860s in particular saw Viking armies almost permanently based in the Seine and Loire river basins. Perhaps the most dangerous threat to Charles was his own family. The division of Louis the Pious's empire between his sons at Verdun in 843 had been the product of battle as well as negotiation. Subsequent decades saw Charles and his brothers seek to enlarge their share of their inheritance, most notably Louis the German's bid to displace Charles in 858.[212] As Gwyn Jones famously observed when discussing the Vikings, "It must have appeared to Charles as though he was a man with a wolf at his throat and a wasp in his hair, and in this menagerie of menace the Danes were the wasp."[213] Consequently, the Iberian Peninsula frequently took a low place in Charles's priorities as he coped with other crises.

The third reality was Charles's often loose control over the kingdom of Aquitaine and the adjacent Spanish March.[214] Here Charles faced stiff competition for authority, most markedly from his nephew Pippin II, the son of the former king of Aquitaine, Pippin I.[215] The second Pippin rejected being written out of the succession plan by Louis the Pious, who had granted Aquitaine to Charles, and he seized power in the south of the kingdom with the support of important local figures such as the Gascon count Sancho II Sánchez.[216] Pippin proved to be a serious contender until his death in 864. Even without Pippin, factions among the Aquitainian aristocracy were willing to oppose Charles, raising alternative candidates such as Louis the German's son Louis the Younger in 854.[217] The lords of

210. Nelson, *Charles the Bald*, 165–166. On the Bretons, see Davies, "On the Distribution of Political Power."

211. Coupland, "Charles the Bald and the Defence of the West Frankish Kingdom," "The Frankish Tribute Payments," and "The Carolingian Army"; Searle, "Frankish Rivalries and Norse Warriors"; Gillmor, "War on the Rivers"; Lund, "Allies of God or Man?"

212. AB a.858 78; AF a.858 50–51; Koziol, *The Politics of Memory*, 130–140.

213. Jones, *A History of the Vikings*, 213.

214. On Charles's rule of Aquitaine, see Auzias, *L'Aquitaine carolingienne*, 183–346; Martindale, "The Kingdom of Aquitaine" and "Charles the Bald."

215. Koziol, *The Politics of Memory*, 69–74, 119–128.

216. Bayard, "De la *Regio* au *Regnum*"; see Coupland, "The Coinages of Pippin I and II," for a useful narrative of Pippin II's career until 848.

217. AB a.854 68–69.

the Spanish March could be as fractious as those of Aquitaine. Masked beneath the Carolingian warring for the crown that dominates the sources lay a secondary level of conflict as local aristocratic families struggled for power and access to office, a continuation of battles begun under Louis the Pious. This competition often manifested itself in accusations of treason at the assemblies but could also break out into open warfare.[218]

An additional wrinkle came in the early 860s, which saw tensions emerge between Charles and his son Charles the Younger, appointed king of Aquitaine in 855.[219] Among the men who acted as *marchio* in the Spanish March during his reign, Count Bernard of Barcelona was executed for disloyalty in 844, Udalric was forced to flee to Louis the German in 858 or 859 under suspicion of conspiracy, Humfrid rebelled in 863 and had to be driven out of West Frankish territory the subsequent year, Bernard Plantapilosa was deposed in 864 following rumours of a plot to assassinate Charles, and Bernard of Gothia rebelled in 877.[220] Apart from raising important questions about the wisdom of trusting anyone named Bernard, the major point to be made is that for much of his reign, Charles's control over Aquitaine and the Spanish March was open to challenge.[221] Naturally this limited his capacity to project power into the Iberian Peninsula.

It should be noted that all three of these realities had a tendency to combine, particularly in the early decades of Charles's long reign.[222] While some of these were genuine alliances, such as that between the emperor Lothar and Pippin II, others seem to have been more opportunistic.[223] Signs of weakness encouraged predators to gather, so that Charles frequently had to deal with challenges from Spain, Brittany, Vikings, Aquitaine, and other Carolingians at the same time. His centre of power was the region around Paris and the Seine, which was accordingly prioritised. The entry in the *Annals of St-Bertin* for 854 is typical, noting that at the height of

218. AB a.862 92–93.

219. Nelson, *Charles the Bald*, 196–197; Goldberg, "'A Man of Notable Good Looks,'" 359–360.

220. AB a.844 45, a.863 97, a.868 151, a.877 216; Salrach, *El Procés de Formació Nacional*, 2:54; Collins, "Charles the Bald and Wilfred the Hairy," 177–179. On Bernard's career, see Ward, "Caesar's Wife," 205–222; Nelson, "The Last Years of Louis the Pious," 153–160.

221. On the problem of "the three Bernards," see Bouchard, *Those of My Blood*, 181–189.

222. Auzias, *L'Aquitaine carolingienne*, 183.

223. Nithard, *Histoire des fils*, II.1, 46, II.10, 80, III.3, 104–105; AB a.841 38; Koziol, *The Politics of Memory*, 69.

the crisis with Louis the Younger, Charles "returned from Aquitaine having achieved nothing," in order to deal with Lothar and Louis the German.[224]

Charles's relations with Córdoba were complicated by a fundamental disjuncture between his objectives and those of the Umayyads. Given the challenges Charles faced, there was no realistic prospect of him invading al-Andalus and acquiring plunder or territory. Therefore any conflict that took place between him and Córdoba would take the form of an Andalusi invasion or Umayyad support for his opponents, neither of which could be described as a good result for him. Charles therefore had no incentive to start wars with al-Andalus and every reason to maintain good relations.

Unfortunately for him, ʿAbd al-Raḥmān II and Muḥammad I had the reverse incentives. Despite El-Hajji's claims to the contrary, the emirs of Córdoba could be extremely aggressive in this period.[225] At no point did Umayyad armies attempt to conquer territory, not even cities like Barcelona that they had previously held.[226] The invasions served a different purpose, as suggested by Arabic accounts of the raid of 827. Al-Nuwayrī describes the campaign in celebratory terms: "repeated raids, looting, killing and capturing, there were enemies, but in a great victory, they defeated them and made a great slaughter."[227] These campaigns provided booty and demonstrated Andalusi power, but the primary audience for these attacks was a domestic one. It displayed Umayyad mastery of barbarian infidels, something celebrated in the sources. Ibn ʿIdhārī wrote of Muḥammad I that he "was given to campaign against the polytheists and the rebels. How often did he penetrate the land of the enemy for six months or more, burning and destroying?"[228]

The invasions were often identified as *ṣāʾifah* and thus explicitly characterised as *jihād* in which most of the participants were religious volunteers (*ghāzī*).[229] The summer campaigns bestowed religious legitimacy upon the Umayyads. They were generally led either by the emir or by a close member of his family, often a favoured son. Those emirs who launched a large number of raids, particularly Muḥammad I, were celebrated by historians as pious men as well as strong rulers.[230] Umayyad

224. AB a.854 "ab Aquitania nullo peracto negotio repedans," 69, translated by Nelson, *Annals of St-Bertin*, 79.

225. El-Hajji, *Andalusian Diplomatic Relations*, 291–292.

226. Collins, *Caliphs and Kings*, 23.

227. Al-Nuwayrī, *Textos dels historiadors*, 114.

228. Ibn ʿIdhārī, "El emirato de Muḥammad I," 239.

229. Chalmeta, "El Concepto de Tagr," 15.

230. Kennedy, *Muslim Spain and Portugal*, 65.

emirs were lauded for leading men into battle "to face God's enemies and defend His faith," winning victories in which "the sum of heads taken from the enemies of God was thousands, all thanks to divine favour."[231] This rhetoric was highly stylised, bearing more than a superficial resemblance to panegyric poems in honour of ʿAbbāsid caliphs.[232] It was on this mismatch that Charles the Bald's relations with the Umayyads turned. Charles faced too many other challenges to want to start fights with Córdoba. The emirs benefitted from encouraging political conflict within Charles's kingdom and stood to improve their own legitimacy by launching raids on Carolingian territory. This fundamental tension would characterise Carolingian-Umayyad relations throughout Charles's reign.[233]

In summary, Charles the Bald faced a potentially formidable opponent in the Umayyads, with numerous other pressures on his attention and limited capacity to marshal and project military force against them. This situation demanded defensive diplomatic aims. Charles had to prevent two things: a direct invasion by Umayyad forces, especially at a time when he was otherwise occupied, and indirect Umayyad backing for rebels within Aquitaine. In pursuit of this, Charles seems to have employed two diplomatic strategies. The first was the establishment of good relations with Córdoba. The second was to undermine the Umayyads by surreptitiously supporting their internal opponents.

## THE SON OF EVIL, 847–851

Two major clusters of diplomatic activity with Córdoba can be identified during the reign of Charles the Bald, the first in 847–851, the second in 863–864. As these two diplomatic moments can be associated with times of crisis in West Francia and particularly in the kingdom of Aquitaine, their being recorded in the Latin sources may be a reflection of the scale of the emergency. Both of these incidents have been studied before, sometimes in great detail.[234] What this section will do is use them as a lens to understand diplomacy between the Franks and al-Andalus and in particular to view them from the perspective of Córdoba.

Charles the Bald's struggle with his nephew Pippin II for control over Aquitaine was not always very successful. Pippin had considerable support

231. Ibn ʿIdhārī, "El emirato de Muḥammad I," 240–241.

232. Sperl, "Islamic Kingship," 33, and *Mannerism in Arabic Poetry*, 9–27; see p. 134–135.

233. For an analogous situation, see Abels, "Paying the Danegeld."

234. Nelson, *Charles the Bald*, 150–152; Calmette, "Le Siège de Toulouse"; Auzias, *L'Aquitaine carolingienne*, 304–327.

within the kingdom and without, particularly from the emperor Lothar. In 845 Charles had been forced to acknowledge his nephew's position:

> Permitting him lordship of all of Aquitaine, except for Poitou, Saintonge and Aunis. So all the Aquitainians who until then had been with Charles hastened forthwith to attach themselves instead to Pippin.[235]

By 848 the balance of power had shifted. Lothar and Louis the German were distracted, dealing with Muslim pirates in Italy and the Bohemians, respectively, while Viking attacks on Aquitaine had eroded Pippin's credibility.[236] Charles made the most of this opening. On 6 June 848:

> The Aquitainians were compelled by Pippin's laziness and sloth to turn to Charles. At Orléans nearly all the nobility, with the bishops and abbots, elected him their king.[237]

Charles went on the offensive in Aquitaine with some success, as no charters issued by Pippin survive from after this year.[238]

It is in the context of this gambit that we should understand Charles's diplomacy with Córdoba. In 847:

> Envoys of ʿAbd al-Raḥmān, king of the Saracens, came from Córdoba in Spain to Charles to seek a peace and draw up a formal treaty. [Charles] received them with fitting ceremony at Rheims, and later let them leave.[239]

Sánchez-Albornoz suggested that this be seen as an attempt by ʿAbd al-Raḥmān to break up a possible alliance between Charles and the rebellious lord of the frontier, Mūsā b. Mūsā, discussed below.[240] Charles was probably also trying to prepare the ground for his bid to retake Aquitaine by making sure the Umayyads would not intervene in the ensuing conflict. The annals imply that the meeting at Rheims was perceived as a success

235. AB a.845 "totius Aquitaniae dominatum ei permisit, praetor Pictavos, Sanctonas et Ecolinenses. Unde et omnes Aquitanici, qui eatenus cum Karolo fuerant, ad eundem Pippinum continuo sui conversionem efficere studuerunt," 50, adapted from Nelson, *Annals of St-Bertin*, 61.

236. AB a.848 55; AF a.848 37.

237. AB a.848 "Aquitani, desidia inertiaque Pippini coacti, Karolum petunt, atque in urbe Aurelianorum omnes penes nobiliores cum episcopis et abbatibus in regem eligunt," 55.

238. Coupland, "The Coinages of Pippin I and II," 202.

239. AB a.847 "Legati Abdirhaman regis Saracenorum a Corduba Hispaniae ad Karolum pacis petendae foederisque firmandi gratia veniunt. Quos apud Remorum Durocortorum decenter et suscepit et absolvit," 53, translated by Nelson, *Annals of St-Bertin*, 64.

240. Sánchez-Albornoz, "El Tercer Rey," 28–29; see pp. 243–247.

by Charles and that the Frankish king had reason to feel confident that his invasion of Aquitaine would not be complicated by Córdoba. If so, he was to be rudely disabused of this notion the following year.

There is reason to believe that the Andalusi diplomats were not negotiating entirely in good faith. The Arabic chronicler Ibn Ḥayyān informs us that in the same year that Umayyad envoys arrived at Rheims, "Gulyālim, son of Barbāṭ son of Gulyālim, one of the great counts of Francia, asked to make peace with the Emir ʿAbd al-Raḥmān, and left for Córdoba to meet with the emir."[241] This Gulyālim can be identified as William, the son of Count Bernard of Barcelona, the hero of 827, who had been executed by Charles in 844 for trying to play him off against Pippin.[242] Bernard's lands and titles were granted to Charles's supporters, with Count Sunifred of Urgell and Cerdanya being given Barcelona, Girona, and authority over the Spanish March as a whole.[243] Pippin I of Aquitaine had been the first to lead the rebellion against Bernard's regime as chamberlain. Paschasius Radbertus alleged that the latter sought the former's death on campaign in Brittany in 830, although this should be treated with caution.[244] Despite the hostility between their fathers, Bernard's son, William, allied himself with Pippin II, taking part in the battle in the Angoumois that forced Charles to make terms with Pippin.[245]

William was well received in Córdoba. ʿAbd al-Raḥmān II granted William "hospitality and showered him and the members of the delegation accompanying him with gifts," clearly seeing the potential uses of the Frank, before sending him "back to the March to fight the Frankish king."[246] Umayyad support took the form of "the help of the governors of the border," allowing William to "lead victorious incursions into the lands of the Franks."[247] Ibn Ḥayyān may be oversimplifying William's movements here. He may be the "Duke William" captured by the Viking

241. Ibn Ḥayyān, "Pasajes del 'Muqtabis,'" "Gulyālim, hijo de Barbāṭ hijo de Gulyālim, uno de los grandes condes (Qūmis) de Ifranŷa, pidió hacer las paces con el emir ʿAbd al-Raḥmān, e (incluso marchó) a Córdoba para entrevistarse," 337.

242. AB a.844 45; Nelson, *Charles the Bald*, 139–140.

243. On Sunifred, see Auzias, *L'Aquitaine carolingienne*, 188–190; Salrach, *El Procés de Formació Nacional*, 2:5–19.

244. Paschasius Radbertus, "*Epitaphium Arsenii*," II.9, 71–72.

245. On Bernard's family, see Bouchard, *Those of My Blood*, 59–64.

246. Ibn Ḥayyān, "Pasajes del 'Muqtabis,'" "ʿAbd al-Raḥmān le recibió con hospitalidad y le colmó de regalos a él y a los miembros de la delegación quele acompañada. Luego le mandó que volviese a la Marca para combatir al rey de los francos Ludrīq, hijo de Qārlu, hijo de Bibin," 337.

247. Ibid., "Con la ayuda de los gobernadores de la Frontera pudo Gulyālim dirigir victorioso incursiones en tierras francas castigando a los que," 337.

army of Oskar that took Bordeaux in 848.[248] In which case William would have travelled to Bordeaux from Córdoba in 847, because the Viking siege began late in that year. If William had to cope with these tribulations, this may explain why his campaign against Charles began later in 848 and why reinforcements from al-Andalus only began to arrive in 849.

However convoluted his route, William's assault seems to have had an effect on Charles's partisans. Salrach has suggested that the disappearance of Counts Sunifred, Sunyer I of Empúries, and Bera II of Conflent at this point could be a sign they were killed by William.[249] William "took Empúries and Barcelona by a trick," expelling Count Aleran "the guard of the city and the Spanish frontier" from the latter in 848.[250] Confirmation of William's cooperation with the Umayyads emerges in the letter of Eulogius of Córdoba to Bishop Wiliesind of Pamplona, written c. 850, in which he complains that his journey to Francia was thwarted by military conflict:

> The way was filled with brigands, and corpses for all of Gothia was disturbed by the attacks of William, who at that time opposed Charles, king of the Franks, relying on the help of ʿAbd al-Raḥmān, king of the Arabs, agent of tyranny, rendering all paths impassable and inaccessible.[251]

William seized control of the transport network in the area, sending ʿAbd al-Raḥmān progress reports, while the emir promised him support.[252] According to Ibn Ḥayyān, in 849 William's army was "reinforced by contingents of Muslims" and ʿAbd al-Raḥmān ordered the governors of Tortosa and Zaragoza "to provide Gulyālim all kind of support and reinforcement."[253]

Charles was able to control the situation militarily. In Aquitaine in 849 he "managed to subdue nearly everyone," receiving the submission of

248. *Annales Fontanellenses*, a.848 "Nortmanni Burdegalim urbem ceperunt et ducem eiusdem Guilhelmum noctu," 302. On this identification, see Levillain, "Les Nibelungen historiques," 14–15; Collins, *Early Medieval Spain*, 257. I am grateful to Stephen Lewis for suggesting this point to me.

249. Salrach, *El Procés de Formació Nacional*, 2:27.

250. AB a.848 "Impurium et Barcinonam dolo magis quam vi capit," 56; *Annales Fontanellenses*, a.849 "custode illius urbis et limitis Hispanici," 302.

251. Eulogius, *Tertius epistolae*, "quoniam stipata praedonibus via, et funeroso quondam Wilihelmi tota Gothia perturbata erat incursu, qui adversum Carolum regem Francorum eo tempore auxilio fretus Habdarraghmanis regis Arabum, tyrannidem agens, invia et inadibilia cuncta reddiderat," 497.

252. Ibn Ḥayyān, "Pasajes del 'Muqtabis,'" 338.

253. Ibid., "reforzado por contingentes musulmanes . . . proporcionaran a Gulyālim todo clase de ayudas y refuerzos," 338.

Toulouse, Narbonne, and Bordeaux.[254] This allowed Charles to turn his attention to the Spanish March, sending Aleran, the newly appointed count of Barcelona, Empúries, and Roussillon, and Isembard to deal with William.[255] William captured the two counts in 850 "through the treachery of a false peace."[256] But his luck was about to run out. He was defeated and harried to Barcelona, where he was executed, "and so the son of evil perished."[257] The eventual resolution of the crisis notwithstanding, ʿAbd al-Raḥmān's change of policy from seeking peace to war had worsened the conflict, led to the death of many loyal counts, and complicated Charles's efforts to manage events. Nor had the emir finished with taking advantage of the situation. In 852 a Muslim army attacked Barcelona where "they slew nearly all the Christians, laid waste the town, and went away unscathed."[258] Among the casualties was the unlucky Count Aleran.

## REBELS AND VIKINGS, 863–864

The next major flurry of traceable diplomatic activity began in 863 when Salomon, count of Urgell, Cerdanya, and Conflent, arrived in Córdoba and met Emir Muḥammad I, as discussed at the start of this chapter.[259] Our source, an account of the translation of the relics of St Vincent from Zaragoza to Castres written by the Frankish monk Aimoin, emphasises the religious aspect of this mission.[260] Salomon was there to ask the emir to force the Bishop of Zaragoza to surrender the relics to him, pretending that they were in fact the body of Salomon's father. It was recognised by d'Abadal that something more was being discussed at that meeting.[261] Later that year, on 25 October, Charles "received with customary ceremony the envoy of Muḥammad, king of the Saracens, who came with many large gifts and with letters speaking of peace and a treaty of friendship."[262] Charles sent the envoy back the next year, with an envoy of his own, who returned in

254. AB a.849 "pene omnes . . . conciliando subiugat," 58.

255. Chandler, *Carolingian Catalonia*, 120.

256. *Annales Fontanellenses*, a.850 "per dolum pacis fictae," 303.

257. Ibid., "sicque filius iniquitatis periit," 303.

258. AB a.852 "interfecitisque pene omnibus christianis et urbe vastata, impune redeunt," 64, translated by Nelson, *Annals of St-Bertin*, 74.

259. On Salomon's family connections, see d'Abadal i de Vinyals, *Els Primers Comtes Catalans*, 30–39; Lewis, *The Development of Southern French*, 109.

260. Aimoin, *Historia translationis* 1018.

261. D'Abadal i de Vinyals, *Els Primers Comtes Catalans*, 35.

262. AB a.863 "legatum Mahomot regis Sarracenorum cum magnis et multis muneribus ac litteris de pace et foedere amicali loquentibus sollemni more suscepit," 104, translated by Nelson, *Annals of St-Bertin*, 110.

865 "with many gifts: camels carrying couches and canopies, fine cloth of various kinds and many perfumes."[263]

Charles badly needed good relations with Córdoba at this time. He had appointed his son Charles the Younger king of Aquitaine in 855, but in the early 860s relations between father and son began to break down.[264] In 862 Charles the Younger married against his father's wishes.[265] The same year Humfrid, *marchio* of Septimania and one of the younger Charles's firmest supporters, was accused of treachery, although Charles the Bald kept the peace.[266] Charles's bid to calm the situation did not last long as 863 saw Humfrid rebel, seizing Toulouse in August, possibly with the knowledge of Charles the Younger.[267] The situation was exacerbated by a force of Vikings which moved down the Charente into the Angoumois, where they killed Count Turpio in battle.[268] Early in 864 this group sacked Clermont. From 857 Pippin II had been allied with a different Viking host, based on the Loire. He saw his opportunity and in late 863 entered the Gironde with his allies and besieged Humfrid in Toulouse in early 864.[269] Charles the Bald sent forces that year to crush Humfrid while reconciling himself with his son. These *missi* were largely ineffectual, and Charles the Younger suffered an accident which left him incapable of aiding his father.[270]

Things were to improve later in 864. After an unsuccessful siege of Toulouse Pippin and his allies returned to the Loire where, in May, he was captured by Count Ramnulf of Poitou.[271] He was presented to the king at a general assembly at Pîtres on 1 June 864, where he was condemned "by the leading men of the realm as a traitor to his fatherland, and to Christianity and then sentenced to death."[272] A possible plot by Bernard Plantapilosa, brother of William of Septimania, on Charles's life

263. AB a.865 "cum multis donis, camelis videlicet, lecta et papiliones gestantes, et cum diversi generis pannis et multis odoramentis," 124, translated by Nelson, *Annals of St-Bertin*, 129. On the camels, see Ottewill-Soulsby, "The Camels of Charles the Bald."

264. AB a.855 71.

265. AB a.862 90–91.

266. AB a.862 93. On Humfrid, see Calmette, "Les Marquis de Gothie"; Chaume, "Onfroi, Marquis de Gothie."

267. AB a.863 97.

268. Coupland, "Charles the Bald and the Defence of the West Frankish Kingdom," 62.

269. Ibid., 64.

270. AB a.864 105, 112; Goldberg, "'A Man of Notable Good Looks,'" 359–360.

271. *Continuation of the Chronicle of Ado of Vienne*, a.864 324.

272. AB a.864 "primum a regni primoribus ut patriae et christianitatis proditor et demum generaliter ab omnibus ad mortem diiudicatur," 113, translated by Nelson, *Annals of St-Bertin*, 119.

was exposed, and Bernard fled.[273] Meanwhile Charles sent a second army south, which succeeded in taking "the cities and fortresses" of Septimania from Humfrid.[274]

The link between the embassies to and from Muḥammad and Charles's Aquitainian difficulties has long been suggested.[275] An Umayyad army would only have complicated the crisis, featuring as it already did three Carolingians, two Viking armies, a renegade *marchio*, and a very busy year for Toulouse. The connection between this diplomacy and crisis in Aquitaine is clear from the timeline. Upon receiving the envoy of 863, Charles

> decided to wait at Senlis for a suitable time to send this envoy in dignified fashion back to his king with honour and due protection and all the help he needed.[276]

This "suitable time" proved to be 1 July 864, exactly a month after Pippin was condemned and Bernard's plot revealed, by which point Septimania was back under control.[277]

The reason that Charles's second wave of *missi* had more success in subduing the Spanish March seems to have been Humfrid's absence. According to the *Annals of St-Bertin*, "Humfrid left Toulouse and Gothia, and travelled through Provence to Italy; and Charles again sent other *missi* to Toulouse and into Gothia to receive the cities and castles," with the clear implication that the two actions were linked.[278] Why he fled his power base, having already successfully fended off one army from Charles the Bald and Pippin's Vikings, is unclear. It is plausible that Humfrid had realised that he was to get no help from Charles the Younger.

Another explanation for Humfrid's flight, which strengthens the importance of Charles the Bald's Córdoban diplomacy, lies with the *marchio*'s own Iberian connections. Humfrid played an important role in Aimoin of St-Germain's account of the journey of the Frankish monks Usuard and Odilard in 858 to Córdoba.[279] The *marchio*'s friendship with

273. AB a.864 113–114; Nelson, *Charles the Bald*, 211–212.

274. AB a.864 "civitates et castella," 105.

275. Nelson, *Charles the Bald*, 202.

276. AB a.863 "quem cum honore et debito salvamento ac subsidio necessario in Silvanectis civitate oportunum tempus, quo remitti honorifice ad regem suum posset, opperiri disposuit," 104, translated by Nelson, *Annals of St-Bertin*, 110.

277. AB a.864 114.

278. AB a.864 "et Huntfrido, dimissa Tholosa ac Gotia, per Provinciam in partes Itlaiae transeunte, iterum alios missos ad recipiendas civitates et castella Karolus ad Tholasam et in Gotiam mittit," 112.

279. Aimoin, *De translatione* 943.

the *walī* of Zaragoza ensured that the latter sheltered and guided the two monks on their way. Given Humfrid's access to al-Andalus, the major purpose of Salomon's embassy in 863 was probably to forestall an offer of Umayyad support to the rebel. Humfrid may have counted on backing from Muḥammad. Its absence possibly prompted him to flee to Italy.

This leaves the question of why Muḥammad did not choose to press his advantage as his father had done in the analogous situation of 848. This problem is complicated by the loss of the best source for Andalusi political history, the narrative of Ibn Ḥayyān. The manuscript in which Ibn Ḥayyān's text is preserved is damaged to the point of being unusable for the sections pertaining to Muḥammad's reign.[280] This leaves the historian with the anecdotal and gossipy stories of Ibn al-Qūṭīya and the later histories of Ibn ʿIdhārī and al-Nuwayrī.[281] This makes it hard to understand Muḥammad's position. Ibn ʿIdhārī says that Charles "appreciated greatly his [Muḥammad's] intelligence and sent him rich presents," which has been interpreted as a sign of mutual esteem.[282] It is in fact a depiction of a rather one-sided relationship, designed to elevate the status of the emir. The pattern of events suggests that Muḥammad was probably not particularly fond of Franks. Ibn ʿIdhārī reports an attack on Barcelona in 856, while al-Nuwayrī records a raid in 861.[283]

The Umayyads regularly raided their northern neighbours in these years. The region of Álava in Asturias was attacked repeatedly from 855 to 868 while Pamplona suffered in 861. The most obvious possible impediment to Umayyad raiding died with Mūsā b. Mūsā of the Banū Qāsī in 862, on whom see below.[284] The rebellious city of Toledo had been quiet, although still autonomous, from 857 and although the Lower and the Upper Marches were to go into sustained revolt, troubles there began in 869 and 872, respectively.[285]

Ibn ʿIdhārī does suggest a plausible explanation. He notes that unusually in 864 there was no campaign at all because of the previous year's campaign as it was necessary "to rest the army."[286] Instead, Muḥammad unveiled a series of building projects in Córdoba including a *maqṣūra*

280. Kennedy, *Muslim Spain and Portugal*, 64.

281. Collins, *Early Medieval Spain*, 151; Viguera Molíns, "The Muslim Settlement," 27.

282. Sénac, *Les Carolingiens et al-Andalus*, 106.

283. Ibn ʿIdhārī, "El emirato de Muḥammad I," 217, 220; al-Nuwayrī, *Textos dels historiadors*, 126.

284. Ibn ʿIdhārī, "El emirato de Muḥammad I," 220.

285. Ibid., 217, 224. On the Upper March, see Collins, "Spain: The Northern Kingdoms," 287.

286. Ibn ʿIdhārī, "El emirato de Muḥammad I," 221.

in the great mosque. The campaign of 863 had seen Muḥammad's son, ʿAbd al-Raḥmān, lead an army into Álava with the support of the lord of the Middle March, ʿAbd al-Malik b. al-ʿAbbās.[287] The raid had progressed well until the king of Asturias, Ordoño I (r. 850–866), succeeded in ambushing them at the head of a gorge. While there is no direct reference to this battle in the Asturian sources, their accounts of the reign of Ordoño are extremely brief, and the *Chronicle of Albelda* does note that "he often emerged victorious over the Saracens."[288] Ibn ʿIdhārī presents the outcome as a great victory for the Muslims, but subsequent events suggest a rather more contested result.

In addition to the break in 864 as Muḥammad rested his army, the pattern of subsequent invasions indicates that the battle in 863 had touched a nerve. In a highly unusual concentration of attention, Umayyad armies attacked Álava in 866, 867, and 868.[289] Whereas normally the privilege of campaigning was spread among Muḥammad's sons, the first two of these campaigns were led by ʿAbd al-Raḥmān. This suggests that Córdoba's image had been damaged and Muḥammad was reasserting Umayyad prestige in the region and at home in general, and ʿAbd al-Raḥmān's status in particular. Charles the Bald's diplomatic outreach to Córdoba certainly did not harm his purposes. But the lack of Umayyad intervention in Aquitaine in the early 860s almost certainly had less to do with Carolingian diplomacy and can instead be explained by reference to Muslim campaigning against Asturias. In the eyes of Muḥammad, taking advantage of Frankish weakness was less important than putting the kings of Oviedo in their place and restoring Umayyad prestige.

Examination of these two bursts of diplomatic activity suggests several conclusions. Charles the Bald's diplomacy with the Umayyads was somewhat spasmodic, peaking at moments of specific crisis. The connections with Córdoba possessed by prominent aristocrats in Aquitaine and the Spanish March were a potential problem for Charles, and he attempted to persuade the emirs not to support rebellions by these figures. Umayyad invasions were a very real possibility and one Charles sought to avoid, but the danger they posed was that they would undermine his authority rather than drive the Franks out of the March. As a means of forestalling these threats, direct diplomacy with Córdoba was of minimal utility. Umayyad foreign policy with the Franks was determined largely

287. Ibid.

288. "The Chronicle of Albelda," "super Sarracenos uictor sepius extitit," 175.

289. Ibn ʿIdhārī, "El emirato de Muḥammad I," 251, 252, 253.

by contingent expedience. Invasion in 864 was averted because it was not in Muḥammad's interests rather than because of brilliant diplomacy, whereas ʿAbd al-Raḥmān felt no compunction about breaking a peace and formal treaty when it suited him in 848.

## THE THIRD KING OF SPAIN

Given the limited benefits for Charles the Bald of directly negotiating with the Umayyads, the Frankish king seems to have sought other means of managing his dangerous neighbour. This included coming to agreements with Andalusi enemies of the emir. Charles was to make agreements with people on the edge of the Christian world several times throughout his career, most notably with a series of Viking chiefs including Godfrid Haraldsson in 853 and Bjørn in 858.[290] In 853 he bribed the Bulgars to attack his brother Louis the German.[291] It is therefore not surprising that he should have sought friends in al-Andalus.

In 859, four years before his ambush of Emir Muḥammad's son, King Ordoño I of Asturias won a battle against a powerful Muslim frontier lord, Mūsā b. Mūsā, at Albelda.[292] The interest of this engagement for this discussion comes from the account of the *Chronicle of Alfonso III*, which describes that when the victorious Asturians overran the defeated lord's baggage train, they found "gifts, which Charles, king of the Franks, had sent."[293] As the unusual contents of his baggage indicate, the beaten lord had had a striking career. Seeking no doubt to emphasise Ordoño's status, the *Chronicle* claims that Mūsā called himself "the Third King of Spain."[294] Explaining why Mūsā had Frankish items in his baggage is difficult. The last recorded raid by Mūsā on Carolingian territory was in 856, and the Chronicler is emphatic that these items were gifts. Auzias interpreted them as the ransom for two captured lords, but as Charles paid the ransom for them in 851 or 852 this seems unlikely.[295] A better explanation is some sort of alliance between the king of the West Franks and the Third King of Spain.

290. AB a.853 66; AB a.858 76–77; Coupland, "From Poachers to Gamekeepers," 94–95, 103.

291. AB a.853 68.

292. The dating and nature of this battle are contested; see, for example, Sánchez-Albornoz, "La auténtica batalla."

293. "Chronicle of Alfonso III," "munera, qua ei Carolus rex Francorum direxit," 146.

294. Ibid., "tertium regem in Spania," 146; Lorenzo Jiménez, *La dawla de los Banū Qasī*, 140–143.

295. Auzias, *L'Aquitaine carolingienne*, 265.

Mūsā was the head of the Banū Qāsī, the preeminent family in the Upper March, claiming descent from an almost certainly mythical Visigothic count Cassius.[296] Based in the fortress of Arnedo, Mūsā was able to act with considerable independence.[297] Among the reasons for the success of the Banū Qāsī were their alliances with the Christian rulers of Pamplona, the House of Íñiguez. These included a series of marriages with the result that King Íñigo Arista (r. 824–851/852) was Mūsā's half brother.[298] This proven partnership with a Christian king may have been a recommendation for Charles the Bald when he started looking for Andalusi allies and certainly indicates that Mūsā had no qualms about doing business with non-Muslim rulers.

Exactly when Charles the Bald and Mūsā b. Mūsā began talking to each other is unclear. Mūsā fell out with ʿAbd al-Raḥmān II in 841, when he rebelled against the emir of Córdoba.[299] Mūsā was to spend the rest of the 840s in semi-permanent revolt. Despite being defeated in 844, Córdoba was too remote from the Upper March to dislodge Mūsā from Arnedo, leaving him free to rebel again in 847.[300] The early 840s saw Charles embroiled in civil war with his brother Lothar and it would be surprising if he had been thinking much about Spain before the division of the empire at Verdun in August 843.

A suggestive date would be 847 given the diplomatic activity between Charles and Córdoba that year, which may have been aimed at dissuading the Frankish king from backing Mūsā, and would match ʿAbd al-Raḥmān's support for William of Septimania at the same time. Mūsā's revolt in 847 seems to have been in response to the appointment of the brothers ʿAmīr and ʿAbd Allāh b. Kulayb as governors of Zaragoza and Tudela the previous year.[301] The pair were the grandsons of the loyal if unlucky Thaʿlaba who had served ʿAbd al-Raḥmān I and been captured by Sulaymān al-ʿArābī in the 770s. A vendetta broke out between the two families, with the Banū Kulayb brothers attacking Mūsā's allies before they "demolished the mills of Mūsā b. Mūsā, and hamstrung his horses, allowing [their] men to be devoted to looting, they took his goods and cut

296. Lorenzo Jiménez, *La dawla de los Banū Qasī*, 137–223. See also Fierro, "El Conde Casio"; Manzano Moreno, "A Vueltas con el Conde Casio."

297. Lorenzo Jiménez, *La dawla de los Banū Qasī*, 219.

298. Manzano Moreno, "Christian-Muslim Frontier in al-Andalus," 93.

299. Lorenzo Jiménez, *La dawla de los Banū Qasī*, 170–178.

300. Ibn Ḥayyān, *Crónica de los emires*, 321.

301. Al-ʿUdhrī, "La Marca Superior," 469. On the dating, see Lorenzo Jiménez, *La dawla de los Banū Qasī*, 170–171.

down his fruit trees."[302] ʿAbd Allāh b. Kulayb also took the possessions of members of the Íñiguez family in the Upper March. One of William of Septimania's strongest supporters in 848 in the Upper March was ʿAbd Allāh b. Kulayb, which might have suggested a parallel arrangement as two sets of feuds combined.[303] Beyond that tentative dating the evidence cannot be stretched.

This same evidence suggests a fairly loose relationship, largely founded upon gifts from Charles to Mūsā in order to keep the border lord on his side. It was also not necessarily a permanent arrangement. Mūsā spent most of the 850s loyal to the emir.[304] As well as being generally at war with Asturias and travelling south to fight the odd band of particularly adventurous Vikings, Mūsā led at least one raid into Frankish territory in 856, which resulted in the sack of the Carolingian fort at Tarrega.[305] Any association between them would have been subject to continual renegotiation.

Much of the benefit this alliance brought to Charles came from Mūsā's ability to control access through the March. He could assist Frankish agents travelling into al-Andalus. As the ruler of Zaragoza in 857, Mūsā can be identified with the "Abdiluvar" of the same position who assisted Usuard and Odilard on their journey to Córdoba at the request of Humfrid. According to Aimoin, the governor of Zaragoza, "although a barbarian, faithfully obeyed his friend's commands."[306] Charles put the monks in contact with Humfrid. Humfrid himself was a newcomer to the frontier, his family were of Alemannic origin, his major holdings in West Francia were in Burgundy, and he acquired office in the Spanish March in 854 at the earliest, when he and his brother sought refuge with Charles, fleeing a failed rebellion against Louis the German in the East Frankish kingdom.[307] Given the short amount of time Humfrid had spent in the area, it seems likely that most of his contacts came from pre-existing networks established by Charles the Bald.

Mūsā could also help manage people travelling the other way. Most obviously, the lord of the Banū Qāsī could block or at least seriously hinder Umayyad forces attacking Francia. This was possible even before Mūsā and Charles had reached any formal arrangement. ʿAbd al-Raḥmān

302. Al-ʿUdhrī, "La Marca Superior," 469.

303. Ibn Ḥayyān, "Pasajes del 'Muqtabis,'" 338.

304. Lorenzo Jiménez, *La dawla de los Banū Qasī*, 205.

305. Ibn ʿIdhārī, "El emirato de Muḥammad I," 217.

306. Aimoin, *De translatione*, "quamuis barbarus, religiose amicis obedire mandatis," 943.

307. Nelson, "The Franks, the Martyrology of Usuard, and the Martyrs of Cordoba," 74.

sought to exploit the Carolingian civil war that broke out after Louis the Pious's death by sending an expedition led by his son, Muṭarrif, in 842.[308] The collapse of this campaign was entirely due to Mūsā's refusal to cooperate. By forcing ʿAbd al-Raḥmān and Muḥammad to expend resources repeatedly subduing the Upper March, Mūsā gave Charles valuable security. Most successful Umayyad raids in Charles's reign took place either when Mūsā was not in revolt or, in the case of the attack of 861, after he and his Pamplonan allies had suffered crippling defeats in 859 and 860, respectively.[309]

The Third King of Spain also intervened in Carolingian affairs to Charles's benefit. In 851 the Gascon count Sancho II Sánchez and his brother-in-law, Count Emenon of Périgord, were captured by Mūsā, "partly through battle, partly through treachery."[310] Both men were partisans of Pippin II. Emenon had led the Aquitainian nobles who had supported Pippin in 838.[311] Sancho had been particularly prominent in the fighting in the west, as Eulogius records in his letter to Wiliesind, "where Pamplona and Seburicos border Long-Haired Gaul, rears the faction of stiff-necked Count Sancho Sánchez to the destruction of the aforesaid Charles."[312] That their release from captivity was arranged by Charles should not be seen as a sign of the king's generosity is suggested by events in the next year. In 852, "Sancho count of Gascony captured Pippin son of Pippin, and kept him under close guard until he got him into Charles' presence," where Charles had his nephew tonsured and confined to a monastery in Soissons.[313]

As Auzias argued, Sancho's volte face can probably be attributed to his defeat and imprisonment by Mūsā.[314] There are no details as to how Mūsā captured the two counts, but given his past relationship with Charles and the king's swift and successful intervention it seems plausible that Mūsā was working with the Carolingian as part of their alliance and

308. Al-ʿUdhrī, "La Marca Superior," 469; d'Abadal i de Vinyals, *Els Primers Comtes Catalans*, 174.

309. "Chronicle of Alfonso III," 146; Lorenzo Jiménez, *La dawla de los Banū Qasī*, 209–210.

310. "Chronicle of Alfonso III," "partim prelio, partim fraude cepit," 146.

311. Lewis, *The Development of Southern French*, 97.

312. Eulogius, *Tertius epistolae*, "quae Pampilonem et Seburicos limitat Gallia Comata, in excidium praedicti Caroli contumaciores cervices factionibus comitis Sancii Sancionis erigens, contra ius praefati principis veniens," 497.

313. AB a.852 "Sancius comes Vasconiae Pippinum, Pippini filium, capit et usque ad praesentiam Karoli servat," 64, translated by Nelson, *Annals of St-Bertin*, 74.

314. Auzias, *L'Aquitaine carolingienne*, 265–267.

helping Charles gain control over Aquitaine. Charles's alliance with Mūsā, although not always the most stable of arrangements, does seem to have played an important role in protecting and steadying his territory against Umayyad pressure as well as undermining Córdoba's ability to project force against him by denying the emirs the support of one of their most formidable subordinates.

## THE MARTYRS OF CÓRDOBA

The Frankish monks Mūsā helped guide to Córdoba testify to another set of relationships that Charles cultivated within al-Andalus. Beginning in 851, a group of Christians based in Córdoba challenged the Umayyad state by publicly breaking religious laws such as blasphemy. In doing so, they deliberately provoked the Muslim authorities into killing them, thus making martyrs of them.[315] By 859, when the movement seems to have petered out, about forty-eight Christians had been killed in this way.[316] The emirs responded by increasing the pressure on the Christian population, reiterating and enforcing old laws concerning blasphemy, the dress and costume of Christians, and the rebuilding of churches, while purging the state hierarchy of Christian officials.[317] The Christian community was divided between the hard-line supporters of the martyrs and the moderate majority, led by Reccafred, the Bishop of Seville, who were appalled and sought to disassociate themselves from the movement, arresting dissenting priests.[318]

The martyrs of Córdoba have received a lot of attention.[319] Historians have focused on trying to understand and explain the martyrs within the context of the situation of the Christian community in al-Andalus, emphasising the unique development of the Spanish Church, in isolation from the wider Christian world.[320] This emphasis has been exaggerated.

315. Wolf, *Christian Martyrs in Muslim Spain*, 25.

316. On execution in the early Islamic world, see Marsham, "Public Execution in the Umayyad Period"; Anthony, *Crucifixion and Death as Spectacle*.

317. Eulogius, *Memoriale sanctorum*, 436.

318. Paul Alvar, *Vita Eulogii*, 332.

319. Dozy, *Histoire des musulmans d'Espagne*, 318; Pérez de Urbel, *San Eulogio*, 226–227; Franke, "Die freiwilligen Märtyrer"; Colbert, *The Martyrs of Córdoba*; Cutler, "The Ninth-Century Spanish Martyrs"; Waltz, "The Significance of the Voluntary Martyrs Movement," 143–159, 226–236; Daniel, *The Arabs and Medieval Europe*, 38; Christys, *Christians in al-Andalus*, 53–75; Tieszen, *Christian Identity amid Islam*; Sahner, *Christian Martyrs under Islam*.

320. Collins, *Early Medieval Spain*, 206; Cavadini, *The Last Christology of the West*, 2–3.

While the causes of the movement were no doubt internal, once it began outside actors very quickly became interested in its activities. The fact that one of the martyrs was a monk from Jerusalem suggests the international dimensions of the crisis.[321] Charles the Bald sought to support and use the martyrs to promote his own interests. Frankish intervention is not a new observation, as the work of Janet Nelson, who first identified the significance of Usuard's journey to Córdoba, and of Ann Christys demonstrates, but the depth of the Carolingian involvement with the actors connected to the movement has not been fully appreciated.[322]

The Carolingians had long been interested in the Christian population of the Iberian Peninsula. This awareness was no doubt stimulated by the movement of men and material. The "Carolingian Renaissance" that drew in men from across Europe and Spain was no exception.[323] Many of the key figures in the courts of the Franks, such as Theodulf, Bishop of Orléans, Agobard, Bishop of Lyons, and Prudentius, Bishop of Troyes, were Goths, with interests in the Iberian Peninsula.[324] Men of Christ did not have to be alive to cross into Frankish territory, as the relics of saints were acquired by prominent Franks such as the retrieval of the body of St Cucuphat by Abbot Fulrad of St Denis, a close counsellor of Pippin III.[325] Pilgrims from Asturias travelled to visit the relics of St Martin at Tours.[326]

Charlemagne paid a great deal of attention to the Spanish Church hierarchy. While the suggestion of d'Abadal that he was trying to take it over probably goes too far, he seems to have been interested in using it to make allies and build networks.[327] In part he was trying to combat the spread of the Adoptionist heresy by Bishop Felix of Urgell in the Frankish-controlled Spanish March by combatting it at the source.[328] To this end he supported Beatus of Liébana in Asturias against the Adoptionist archbishop Elipandus of Toledo. Both participants in this controversy corresponded with

321. Eulogius, *Memoriale sanctorum*, 426–430. For a broader geographical context, see Sahner, *Christian Martyrs under Islam*, 235–237; Bonch Reeves, *Visions of Unity*, 125–132.

322. Nelson, "The Franks, the Martyrology of Usuard, and the Martyrs of Cordoba"; Christys, in "St-Germain des-Prés," 210, is more cautious in her use of Aimoin, arguing that much of what he wrote was concerned with repairing the reputation of Humfrid.

323. Heil, "Theodulf, Haimo, and Jewish Traditions."

324. Fontaine, "Mozarabie Hispanique."

325. De Gaiffier, "Relationes religeuses de l'Espagne," 8; Smith, "Old Saints, New Cults," 318, 321.

326. Alcuin, "Letter to Beatus" in Levison, *England and the Continent*, 318.

327. D'Abadal i de Vinyals, *La batalla del adopcionismo*; Chandler, "Heresy and Empire," 507–508.

328. Cavadini, *The Last Christology of the West*, 71; Kramer, "Adopt, Adapt and Improve," 32–50.

Charlemagne and Alcuin.[329] Beatus and his allies, writing in Catholic Asturias, were far more confrontational, and scornful of the attempts by Christians in al-Andalus to come to a modus vivendi with Muslims.[330] With the emergence of the martyrs of Córdoba, the Carolingians again allied with the more antagonistic party in Spanish Christian politics.

The best-known example of Carolingian interest in the case of the martyrs is the journey of Usuard and Odilard, two Frankish monks of St-Germain in Paris, to Córdoba in 858 alluded to above. Their adventure is recorded in a *translatio* composed by Aimoin, also of St-Germain, around 866.[331] The narrative concerns itself with the acquisition by the two monks of the bodies of three of the martyrs from Córdoba and their transport to St-Germain. As Nelson and Christys both noted, it seems clear that there was more going on beneath the surface. The Frankish king appears to have been involved in the Iberian enterprise from the beginning, providing crucial support and contacts.[332]

While the initial mission of the expedition was to acquire the relics of St Vincent, that quickly fell by the wayside in response to the martyrs of Córdoba. Aimoin presents news of the crisis as coming as a surprise to the monks, but this is probably artistic license to throw into better relief the "benevolent" workings of the divine.[333] The martyrs' movement had been underway for seven years by this point, and while Charles had been slow to take advantage of it, it is unlikely that he, his advisers, and the monks were unaware that something was happening. Apart from acquiring relics, it is not entirely clear what Usuard's brief was for Córdoba, but it probably involved information gathering and above all making contact or reaffirming contact with Christians in the Umayyad capital.[334] Certainly, as Aimoin's account makes clear, Usuard seems to have met nearly all the major figures in the church hierarchy sympathetic to the martyrs, including Saul, the Bishop of Córdoba, the Córdoban priest Eulogius, who was the primary chronicler of the martyrs, and several others who will be discussed below.[335]

329. Alcuin, *Epistolae* no. 183, 208; Colbert, *The Martyrs of Córdoba*, 67.

330. Beatus of Liébana and Heterius of Osma, *Adversus Elipandum*, 38–39, 65–66, 70–71, 82–83.

331. Aimoin, *De translatione* 943.

332. Ibid., 941.

333. Ibid., 943.

334. Christys, "St-Germain des-Prés," suggests that Usuard may have had access to the first two books of Eulogius's *Memoriale sanctorum* (211).

335. Aimoin, *De translatione* 945.

Charles remained interested in the martyrs after the return of Usuard and Odilard. He sent an envoy named Mancio to Córdoba to "search out on the spot the truth of what had happened" and presumably also in the process to reinforce earlier ties.[336] This is probably the same Mancio who was at Charles's court in the 860s and later became a royal notary and Bishop of Châlons-sur-Marne in 893.[337] He witnessed the execution of two unnamed martyrs before returning to Charles. In 872 Hincmar of Rheims used the bishop and Christian community of Córdoba as examples of the faithful showing resilience despite pagan persecution.[338]

The interest was not one-way. Before being martyred himself in 857, Eulogius of Córdoba wrote extensively in support of the movement, articulating anger at the adoption of Arabic culture by Spanish Christians and a desire to re-establish the boundaries between Muslims and Latin Christians, founded on fear of conversion. There is reason to suppose that Usuard's visit was not the first time Eulogius had contact with Franks. In 848 or 850, Eulogius travelled to the Spanish March.[339] Two of his brothers had been exiled to the court of Louis the German for unknown reasons and Eulogius intended to find them. However, the chaos caused by Charles's war with Pippin made the roads impassable, so he contented himself with visiting monasteries in the region.[340] Jacques Fontaine suggested that Eulogius's brothers had plotted against the Umayyads, explaining their exile, but for the moment that cannot be proved.[341]

Eulogius very strongly condemned Charles's enemies, suggesting some sympathy for the Carolingian, although this may simply be the fury of the frustrated traveller.[342] While in his letter to Wiliesind Eulogius portrays a picture of improvised wandering, the text needs to be treated with some care. The letter was quite clearly a public document as Alvar exhorts those reading his *Life* of Eulogius to read it.[343] Moreover, it was a letter written while Eulogius was in prison in Córdoba for his support of the martyrs.[344]

336. Ibid., "nec est oblitus delegans Mancionem Cordubae huius facti veritatem ex loco requirere," 957–958.

337. Nelson, "The Franks, the Martyrology of Usuard, and the Martyrs of Cordoba," 75; *Vita Radbodi*, 569. See also McKitterick, "The Palace School," 329.

338. Hincmar of Rheims, *De translationibus episcoporum*, col. 228C. On the context for this, see Sommar, "Hincmar of Rheims."

339. Wolf, *Christian Martyrs in Muslim Spain*, 54.

340. Eulogius, *Tertius epistolae*, 497–498.

341. Fontaine, "Mozarabie Hispanique," 29n33.

342. Eulogius, *Tertius epistolae*, 498.

343. Paul Alvar, *Vita Eulogii*, 335–336.

344. Eulogius, *Tertius epistolae*, 500.

These seem strong grounds to suppose that the priest was not being entirely candid. As Christys has pointed out, for a spontaneous reaction to events, Eulogius's journey through Pamplona seems highly organized and thorough.[345]

Other hints that key figures hostile to Umayyad rule had been interested in the Franks before the martyrs appear in the letters exchanged between Paul Alvar and Bodo-Eleazar. Alvar was a layman and a close friend and ally of Eulogius, having received instruction with him under Abbot Speraindeo.[346] In 838, scandal hit the Carolingian empire when Bodo, the palace deacon of Louis the Pious, converted to Judaism and changed his name to Eleazar while on pilgrimage to Rome.[347] The following year he travelled to al-Andalus, where he appears to have advised ʿAbd al-Raḥmān II to wage a campaign of forced conversion on the Christian population.[348] Alvar began a correspondence with Eleazar in 840, in which both parties ostensibly sought to convert the other (although as only Alvar's letters survive in full it is hard to determine exactly what Eleazar was saying).[349] While Alvar had plenty of reason to want to combat Eleazar himself, if he and Eulogius were already thinking of making contact with the Carolingians it could not have gone unnoticed that Louis the Pious would have been pleased by a refutation of the renegade deacon.

The Franks remained in Alvar's mind. In his *Indiculus Luminosus* of 854, he described the caliphate as the last and most terrible kingdom that shall come before Judgement Day, prophesied in Daniel 7.[350] His list of the three kingdoms defeated by the Saracens includes the Byzantines, the Goths, and "the Franks, who thrive under the name of the Romans."[351] Alvar's depiction of the Franks as a defeated people is not necessarily very encouraging, but he saw them as powerful, and as the heirs to Rome, unlike the utterly conquered Goths.

The reasons for this sustained interest in the Franks on the part of the martyrs may have been for purposes of morale. For men like Eulogius and

345. Christys, *Christians in al-Andalus*, 58.

346. Cabaniss, "Paulus Albarus," 100–102; Alvar suffered the ignominy of having an Arabized son, Ḥafṣ, whose Arabic poetry was well received; van Koningsveld, "Christian Arabic Literature," 206–212.

347. AB a.838 27–28; Löwe, "Die Apostasie des Pfalzdiakons Bodo," 157.

348. Riess, "From Aachen to Al-Andalus," 157.

349. Waltz, "The Significance of the Voluntary Martyrs Movement," 157. For Alvar's correspondence with Eleazar, see CSM 1, 227–270.

350. Tieszen, *Christian Identity amid Islam*, 85–86.

351. Paul Alvar, *Alvaro de Córdoba*, c.21 "Francorum que sub nomine Romanorum uigebat," 294.

Alvar, who felt themselves part of a beleaguered Latin culture under threat from a tide of Arabic custom, contact with a wider Christian environment may have been a considerable boost to their confidence. This circle might also have hoped for more temporal support from the Frankish king, although they do not state this directly. The last years of ʿAbd al-Raḥmān and the years following the accession of Muḥammad saw large parts of the country slip beyond direct Umayyad political control, with cities such as Mérida and Toledo in permanent revolt. The revolt in Toledo had leaders from several faiths, but the Christian community played a large part.[352] Eulogius was well aware of this, commenting that these rebellions lessened the pressure on the Christians of Córdoba by drawing emiral attention elsewhere.[353] In fact the opposite seems to be the case, as Muḥammad cracked down on dissension in his base and his harsh enforcement of anti-Christian edicts seems to be as much tied to escalations outside the capital as within it.[354]

Nonetheless, Eulogius perceived events in Córdoba in connection to those occurring elsewhere in al-Andalus. He had particular reason to pay attention to Toledo as in 852 he was elected bishop of the city, a post he never assumed in person. Alvar explains this by saying "divine providence . . . placed obstacles in his path."[355] It is unclear whether this means Eulogius was too interested in affairs in Córdoba or that his more moderate opponents within the church hierarchy had decided to forestall the potentially explosive consequences of Eulogius being in a position of authority in a city in which a revolt supported by the Christian population was occurring. Alvar's comment on the affair that "all saints are bishops, but not all bishops are saints," may hint toward the latter explanation.[356]

Alvar predicted the coming end of Saracen rule in the Iberian Peninsula.[357] Something Eulogius and his associates would probably have been aware of was that the rebels in Toledo had made an alliance with King Ordoño I of Asturias, who in 854, the same year Alvar was writing, advanced an army into the region. The defeat of the Asturian-Toledan army by forces led by Muḥammad at Guadacelete in June was not a particularly good omen, although Toledo remained free.[358] However, the

352. On Toledo and the importance of its Christian population, see Manzano Moreno, *La Frontera de al-Andalus*, 261–272; Christys, *Christians in al-Andalus*, 18–21.

353. Eulogius, *Memoriale sanctorum*, 441.

354. Wolf, *Christian Martyrs in Muslim Spain*, 18.

355. Alvar, *Vita Eulogii*, "Sed dispositio divina . . . quibusdam repagulis obviavit," 336.

356. Ibid., "Omnes namque sancti episcopi, non tamen omnes episcopi sancti," 336.

357. Tolan, *Saracens*, 89–93; Bonch Reeves, *Visions of Unity*, 115.

358. Collins, *Caliphs and Kings*, 44.

anti-Mozarabic party in Córdoba may have hoped for similar support from the rather mightier Charles the Bald. That the Frankish king might be seen as a potential defender by the Christians of al-Andalus is suggested by the petition sent to Charles the Bald in 847 from "all the Christians in that realm" asking for protection from the oppression of ʿAbd al-Raḥmān II's advisers.[359]

If Eulogius and Alvar had hoped for a Frankish military intervention, they were to be disappointed. Such ideas were circulating in Charles's court as well. In 853 Audradus Modicus, a prophetic monk of Tours, attested to nocturnal visions in which St Martin of Tours helped Charles the Bald "to free Spain from the infidel."[360] Nonetheless, Charles was in no position to wage war on Córdoba in these years. His interest in the martyrs should be seen as an effort to focus Muḥammad's attention firmly at home by encouraging unrest in Córdoba. The other major benefit the Frankish king accrued from his association with those around the martyrs was information. Having eyes right at the centre of al-Andalus would have been very valuable in understanding affairs in the Iberian Peninsula, with a legacy that continued after the end of the martyrs' movement.

In 864 Abbot Samson of the Basilica of Saint Zoilus left Córdoba, fleeing his enemies in the church hierarchy.[361] He explained the circumstances of his flight in his *Apologeticus*, which he wrote at this time. The year before his flight, he had been employed by Muḥammad I to translate letters to be sent to Charles the Bald from Arabic to Latin, as he done before, but his enemies accused him of spying and sending confidential material to Charles.[362] There seems to have been sufficient suspicion that Samson thought it worth his while to deny the charges in a primarily theological work. Samson seems to have survived the accusation of spying. More serious were allegations that he had incited one of the martyrs of Córdoba.[363] This rise in pressure from his enemies prompted him to leave town. That the church council which expelled Samson was called by Muḥammad might indicate that the emir was not best pleased with his translator.[364]

359. AB a.847 "omnium illius regni christianorum," 54.

360. Audradus Modicus, *Book of Revelations*, no. 11, "Do tibi, Karole, ut Hispanias duce beato Martino principe [iterum] liberes ab infidelibus," 383, translated by Dutton, *Carolingian Civilization*, 355; Dutton, *The Politics of Dreaming*, 124–143.

361. Colbert, *The Martyrs of Córdoba*, 357.

362. Samson, *Apologeticus*, 554.

363. Ibid.

364. Ibid.

Whether or not Samson was actually guilty, the seriousness of the accusation implies it was considered plausible. It was not Samson's faith that made him vulnerable, as his accusers, Bishop Ostegesis of Málaga and Count Servandus of Córdoba, were, despite Samson's claims to the contrary in the *Apologeticus*, both Christians.[365] Rather, Samson had been in contact with both the Franks and the martyrs in the past. According to Aimoin, Samson played a crucial role in helping Usuard acquire the bodies of martyrs because at the time he was the abbot of Pinna Mellaria, the monastery where they were buried, and he persuaded his initially unwilling community to part with the relics.[366] Samson's connections to the martyrs are suggested in other ways. Like Eulogius and Alvar, he was a pupil of Speraindeo. The monastery at Pinna Mellaria had been founded by the parents of the martyr Pomposa, and the martyr Fandila had previously been an abbot there.[367] Eulogius had spent time at Saint Zoilus, as had at least three of the martyrs.[368] When Samson left Córdoba he went to Martos, the same town that the martyr Flora had fled to.[369]

Samson's major dispute with his enemies in the church hierarchy seems to have been linked to charges of heresy, which is what most of the *Apologeticus* is concerned with. This is accompanied by the accusation that Ostegesis and Servandus were too close to the Umayyad state, oppressing their fellow Christians and Arabizing with too much enthusiasm.[370] The resemblance to the arguments of Eulogius and Alvar, particularly the latter's *Indiculus Luminosus*, are unmistakable, if somewhat incongruous coming from the man who claimed to have loyally worked as the emir's translator.[371] That the *Apologeticus* was seen as part of an anti-Mozarabic tradition is suggested by its sole preservation in a ninth- or tenth-century manuscript where it is paired with a treatise written by Beatus of Liébana and Bishop Etherius of Osma against Elipandus.[372]

These connections seem to have been enough for Samson's enemies to question his loyalty to the emir. Whether or not Samson was actually guilty is unclear. If he was it is improbable that he would admit to it if he had any hopes of returning to Córdoba. It seems likely that some of the

365. Ibid., 551.
366. Aimoin, *De translatione* 945.
367. Eulogius, *Memoriale sanctorum*, 444.
368. Colbert, *The Martyrs of Córdoba*, 357.
369. Ibid.
370. Samson, *Apologeticus*, 551.
371. Colbert, *The Martyrs of Córdoba*, 168.
372. Ibid., 357.

contacts made by Usuard, most of whom were in positions of spiritual and political authority in Córdoba, continued to pass secret information on to Charles the Bald after the end of the martyrs' movement.

## *The End of Carolingian-Umayyad Diplomacy*

A combination of internal and external factors placed Charles the Bald at a disadvantage in his dealings with Córdoba between 840 and the mid-860s and this shaped the nature of Carolingian-Umayyad diplomacy in the period. This encouraged Charles to seek good relations with his southern neighbours. His ability to achieve this was hindered by the way in which the emirs solidified their legitimacy by campaigning against non-Muslims, which incentivized an aggressive political approach to the Franks. In practice, Charles lacked the power to enforce the truces made with the Umayyads, who would keep to agreements only when they suited its interests. On the other hand, Charles's contacts with the opponents of Córdoba within the Iberian Peninsula proved more fruitful, providing him with valuable information on the part of Christian dissidents and a potentially vital ally who could block Umayyad expeditions into Carolingian territory in Mūsā b. Mūsā.

We began this chapter with the story of Salomon's adventure in Córdoba. Unable to use coercion, the count had to employ trickery and a bag full of silver to get what he wanted. In doing so, he demonstrates the realities of Carolingian diplomacy with the Umayyads in this period, characterised by Frankish defensiveness, Umayyad military initiative, and relatively limited control exercised by both great powers over their respective marches. Ironically, this journey came at the close of that era, which came to an end not with the absolute triumph of one party over the other or an enduring diplomatic arrangement but with the change of political realities. The Humfrid crisis of 862–864 was to prove to be the end of the old system and from the mid-860s a change can be discerned.

The first of the political realities to shift was Charles's position in Aquitaine. With the death of Pippin II in 864, Charles's control of the kingdom seems to have stabilised. Although the *Annals of St-Bertin* notes that in 869 Charles was "not without concern" over the situation in Aquitaine, nothing seems to have come of those fears.[373] He exercised very tight supervision over his son Louis the Stammerer, appointed king of Aquitaine in

373. AB a.869 "non sine sollicitudine," 152.

866, interfering regularly in government.[374] After Humfrid's revolt, Charles avoided uniting too many of the territories of Septimania and the Spanish March in the hands of one man.[375] Aquitaine and the Spanish March remained quiet until Bernard of Gothia's rebellion in 877. Given that this rebellion was linked to Count Boso of Provence and the powerful Hugh the Abbot in response to Charles's Italian interests, it should probably be understood in extra-Aquitainian terms.[376]

The mid-860s can be associated with other changes in Charles's situation. His confidence is suggested by the impressive coin reform of 864, although some distinction between Aquitaine and the rest of his territories is demonstrated by the limited circulation of the new coinage in Aquitaine.[377] Charles's other external opponents were also far less of a danger for the Frankish king.[378] Although Viking attacks remained a problem, the Breton frontier calmed considerably following a pact with King Salomon of Brittany in 867.[379] The death of the emperor Lothar in 855 replaced a dangerous rival with three smaller polities as Lothar's lands were split between his sons.[380] As well as taking the pressure off Charles, it presented opportunities to interfere in his nephews' affairs to his potential advantage.[381] Faced with opportunity in Provence, Lotharingia, and Italy, Iberian affairs may have been a lower priority.

The most important alteration to the political context was a decline in the ability of the Umayyads to enforce their authority in al-Andalus in the 860s. As Roger Collins has noted, "by 866 Umayyad authority in the marches was weaker and less effective than it had been in 852."[382] Cities such as Toledo were functionally independent. From 868 ʿAbd al-Raḥmān b. Marwān al-Jillīqi had established himself in the Lower March, operating out of Badajoz with Asturian support in a manner reminiscent of Mūsā b. Mūsā.[383] Beginning in 870, a series of revolts led by the descendants of ʿAmrūs b. Yūsuf and Mūsā b. Mūsā broke out in the Upper March against

374. Martindale, "Charles the Bald and the Government," 131–132. On Louis the Stammerer, see McCarthy, "Power and Kingship."

375. Chandler, *Carolingian Catalonia*, 127–128.

376. Nelson, *Charles the Bald*, 251–252.

377. Coupland, "The Early Coinage of Charles," 155. See also Grierson, "The 'Gratia Dei Rex'"; Metcalf, "A Sketch of the Currency."

378. Nelson, *Charles the Bald*, 221–253.

379. Smith, *Province and Empire*, 107.

380. AB a.855 71.

381. Nelson, *Charles the Bald*, 221–253.

382. Collins, *Caliphs and Kings*, 47.

383. Ibid., 45–46.

Córdoba. Although the Umayyads responded with military expeditions, after 885 the March was beyond their control.[384]

The raid on Barcelona in 861 was to be the last on territory claiming Carolingian allegiance until the next century. Nor are there any signs of Umayyad support for rebels in Aquitaine after 864, a consequence of both Umayyad weakness and the relative stability of Charles's position in the kingdom. This combined with Charles's increasing interest in opportunities to his east acted to limit Charles's motivation to send envoys to Córdoba, for which there is also no evidence after 864, ending a diplomatic tradition that had lasted from the 770s. The Umayyad dynasty slipped into crisis after the death of Muḥammad in 886. His son al-Mundhir was killed after two years in power, dying while on campaign against the rebel ʿUmar b. Ḥafṣūn at Bobastro. Ibn Ḥafṣūn and his sons were to oppose the Umayyads in their heartlands in southern al-Andalus until 928 but were only the most famous of the independent rulers who established themselves.[385] It was only with the accession of ʿAbd al-Raḥmān III in 912 that the Umayyads began to reassert their control outside the Guadalquivir basin and campaigns against Christians in the north of the peninsula resumed in 920.[386]

384. Lorenzo Jiménez, *La dawla de los Banū Qasī*, 224–272.

385. Acién Almansa, *Entre el Feudalismo y el Islam* provides an invaluable summary of the historiography. See also the work of Marín-Guzmán, "Rebellions and Political Fragmentation," "The Causes of the Revolt," and "Political Turmoil in al-Andalus"; and Wasserstein, "Inventing Tradition and Constructing Identity."

386. Fierro, *Abd al-Rahman III*.

CHAPTER SIX

# The Central Mediterranean

## THE LIMITS OF CAROLINGIAN DIPLOMACY WITH THE ISLAMIC WORLD

THIS CHAPTER IS CONCERNED with absence. Based on the preceding chapters, the reader would be forgiven for assuming that the medieval Islamic world in western Eurasia was limited to al-Andalus and the core territories of the caliphate, with a large gap between the Iberian Peninsula and Egypt. This was of course very far from being the case.[1] The final fall of Carthage in 698 marked the assertion of caliphal power in the region known as Ifrīqiya.[2] Under Aghlabid rule (800–909) Ifrīqiya was an important part of the Maghrib, a crucial hub in the centre of the Mediterranean, connecting al-Andalus with Egypt.[3] The close proximity of Ifrīqiya to Sicily and mainland Italy made it a natural point for commerce, with merchants crossing from southern Italy to North Africa, and vice versa. Where merchants could go, so did pirates and warriors. Aghlabid forces landed in Sicily in 827, beginning a protracted conquest of the island.[4] From 835, Muslim bands were hired as mercenaries by cities in mainland Italy, participating in their conflicts.[5] Over the course of the following decades emirates were established in Bari, Taranto, and Amantea. This complicated ninth century prompted a great deal of diplomatic relations

1. On the wider historiographical issues, see Nef and Tillier, “Les voies de l’innovation”; Rosser-Owen, “Mediterraneanism.”

2. Anderson, Fenwick, and Rosser-Owen, “The Aghlabids and Their Neighbors,” 2.

3. Goitein, “Medieval Tunisia,” 309–310; Carrillo, “Architectural Exchanges”; Salinas and Montilla, “Material Culture Interactions.”

4. Prigent, “La carrière du toumarque Euphèmios”; Nef, “Guerroyer pour la Sicile.”

5. Kreutz, *Before the Normans*, 19–20.

between Muslim leaders and Christians, including Italian princes and Byzantine emperors. From Charlemagne's conquest of the Lombard kingdom in 774 the Carolingians were placed within this central Mediterranean arena. Unlike their relationship with the Umayyads this proximity did not prompt regular diplomatic contact between the Franks and the Muslim powers of the region.

Explaining this gap is the subject of this chapter. There is a natural tendency in the study of history to ask why things happened, rather than why they did not. The latter question threatens to derail inquiry by wandering into a thicket of increasingly unlikely hypotheticals. Nonetheless understanding why diplomacy was not a major concern for Franks and Muslims in the area is useful not just for the light it sheds on the central Mediterranean but also for the comparisons it allows for Carolingian diplomacy with the Umayyads and the ʿAbbāsids.[6] Unpacking the circumstances and the incentives that made diplomacy unattractive in Ifrīqiya and Italy helps reveal the factors that made it more attractive in al-Andalus and the caliphs in the East. This chapter will investigate the problem in two parts. The first section addresses the evidence for limited diplomacy between the Carolingians and Ifrīqiya in the closing years of the eighth century, considering why it happened and why it ended. This is followed by an examination of the Carolingians and the emirates of Italy and the reasons why this was an entirely hostile relationship.

## *The Second Part of the World: Charlemagne and North Africa*

In the 790s, Alcuin wrote a short treatise to an otherwise unknown Gallicellulus expounding on the significance of numbers. On reaching three, Alcuin advised his correspondent that "all the world is divided into three parts, Europe, Africa and India."[7] Carolingian interest in the second part of this continental trilogy has generally gone unnoticed, but the decade that Alcuin wrote saw Charlemagne in contact with Muḥammad b. Muqātil al-ʿAkkī, the governor of Ifrīqiya from 797 to 799.[8]

Preserved in a single manuscript, Cambridge UL Qq 235, the *Kitāb al-Miḥan* (loosely, the Book of Trials) is a *maqtal* or martyrology produced by the Kairouan-based Mālikī legal and religious scholar Abū al-ʿArab

6. For an interesting example, see Herbers, "Christen und Muslime im 9. Jahrhundert."

7. Alcuin, *Epistolae* no. 81, "Totus orbis in tres dividitur partes, Europam, Africam et Indiam," 124.

8. Ilisch, "Geldgeschichten."

Muḥammad b. Aḥmad b. Tamīm b. Tammām b. Tamīm al-Tamīmī (d. 945).[9] Like most *maqātil*, it lists the violent deaths of prominent pious individuals for the edification of the reader.[10] Unlike the majority of the genre, which generally supported ʿAlī and his descendants, the Mālikī al-Tamīmī displays few ʿAlid tendencies.[11] His material is arranged roughly, although not entirely, chronologically and starts at a universal level, with the murders of Caliphs ʿUmar I in 644 and ʿUthmān in 656.[12] It then becomes increasingly localized to North Africa. Among the stories told in the *Kitāb al-Miḥan* is that of Bahlūl b. Rashīd, who was flogged by the governor of Ifrīqiya, Muḥammad b. Muqātil al-ʿAkkī, in 799.[13] Bahlūl had protested against al-ʿAkkī's close relationship with a foreign "tyrant," in particular the governor's intention to give the tyrant a skilled female slave singer.[14] Outraged by this flogging and other acts of brutality, the Syrian troops that made up the armies of Ifrīqiya rose up and drove al-ʿAkkī out of Kairouan.

There are reasons to approach al-Tamīmī's text with some caution. His narrative reads much like a fairy tale. The account contains many of al-Tamīmī's most cherished themes. There is a simple moral message about the perils of contact with non-Muslims outside the *dār al-Islām*. The leadership of religious scholars, the *ʿulamā*, is elevated over that of secular rulers.[15] Despite these difficulties, al-Tamīmī was well positioned to know something of the truth of events. He was both a prominent intellectual, with access to Kairouan records, and the great-grandson of Tammām b. Tamīm al-Tamīmī, who had led the uprising against al-ʿAkkī. This has its own problems. As well as celebrating the deeds of an ancestor, al-Tamīmī was justifying his own political activities.[16] His grandfather had died fighting the Aghlabids in 848, his son perished in a Fāṭimid prison, and al-Tamīmī had continued the family tradition by taking part in a rebellion against the Fāṭimids in 944.[17] But as al-Tamīmī had the story from his father, it would seem to represent a well of family history.[18]

9. Al-Ageili, "A Critical Edition of Kitāb al-Miḥan," 9–12.

10. Kister, "The 'Kitāb al-Miḥan.'"

11. Günther, "*Maqâtil* Literature," 192–194.

12. Mandalā, "Political Martyrdom and Religious Censorship," 153.

13. Al-Tamīmī, *Kitāb al-Miḥan*, 427–429.

14. Ibid., 427; ʿAthamina, "How Did Islam Contribute."

15. Mansouri, "Les *ʿUlamā*' en Rupture."

16. Ibid., 571.

17. On the 944 rebellion, see Halm, *The Empire of the Mahdi*, 298–322; Brett, *The Rise of the Fatimids*, 165–175.

18. Al-Ageili, "A Critical Edition of Kitāb al-Miḥan," 23.

The identity of the mysterious tyrant al-ʿAkkī consorted with is not immediately obvious. The word used by al-Tamīmī, *ṭāghiya*, is associated with prideful and illegitimate rule, being applied to Pharoah in the Qurʿān.[19] In the East it was commonly used to depict the Byzantine emperor, but this is rarely the case in North African texts. Mohamed Talbi suggested that this ruler was the Byzantine governor of Sicily, on grounds of geographical proximity and plausibility.[20] However, a more arresting identification has been made by Lutz Ilisch, who argues that this tyrant is none other than Charlemagne.[21]

In support of this, Ilisch draws upon the available numismatic evidence. Not many coins minted in Ifrīqiya appear in the Carolingian empire.[22] North of the Alps, a small number of finds of North African coins dating to the Carolingian period have been made. A stray dirham was discovered near Moudon in Switzerland in 1825, while almost thirty were found in 1830 at Steckborn. A hoard of 133 coins located at Ilanz in 1903 proved to contain two North African dirhams, while a single dirham was identified in a cache of 48 coins uncovered in 1921 at Biebrich. Finally, a stray coin was found in Hyères, near Marseilles.[23]

With such a tiny surviving corpus, all conclusions must be treated cautiously. Nonetheless, the finds listed above can all be connected. First, in chronological terms they are all extremely close together. The earliest of the African coins north of the Alps was minted in 785/786, while the latest of the securely dateable dirhams was produced in 799/800, when Muḥammad al-ʿAkkī was governor. The stray find at Hyères is too heavily worn to be dated or to have its mint identified, but the epigraphy suggests Ifrīqiya between 785 and 806. Where they were found in hoards, none of the non-Arabic coins postdated 800, and numismatists have agreed their deposition probably occurred around this point. The large find at Steckborn is particularly interesting. The hoard's contents were poorly recorded before they were dispersed, which made exact description difficult. Of the 29 Arabic dirhams, only a third received proper examination. All of the coins thus inspected were minted in Ifrīqiya between 785 and 800, with the latest two, which were also the latest coins in the entire hoard, bearing the name of Muḥammad al-ʿAkkī.

19. Lewis, *The Political Language*, 97.

20. Talbi, *L'Émirat Aghlabide*, 396.

21. Ilisch, "Arabische Kupfermünzen" and "Geldgeschichten."

22. Arabic coins in early medieval Europe have a long and controversial historiography, on which see Prigent, "The Myth of the Mancus."

23. On Marseilles, see Loseby, "Marseille and the Pirenne Thesis II," 167–193.

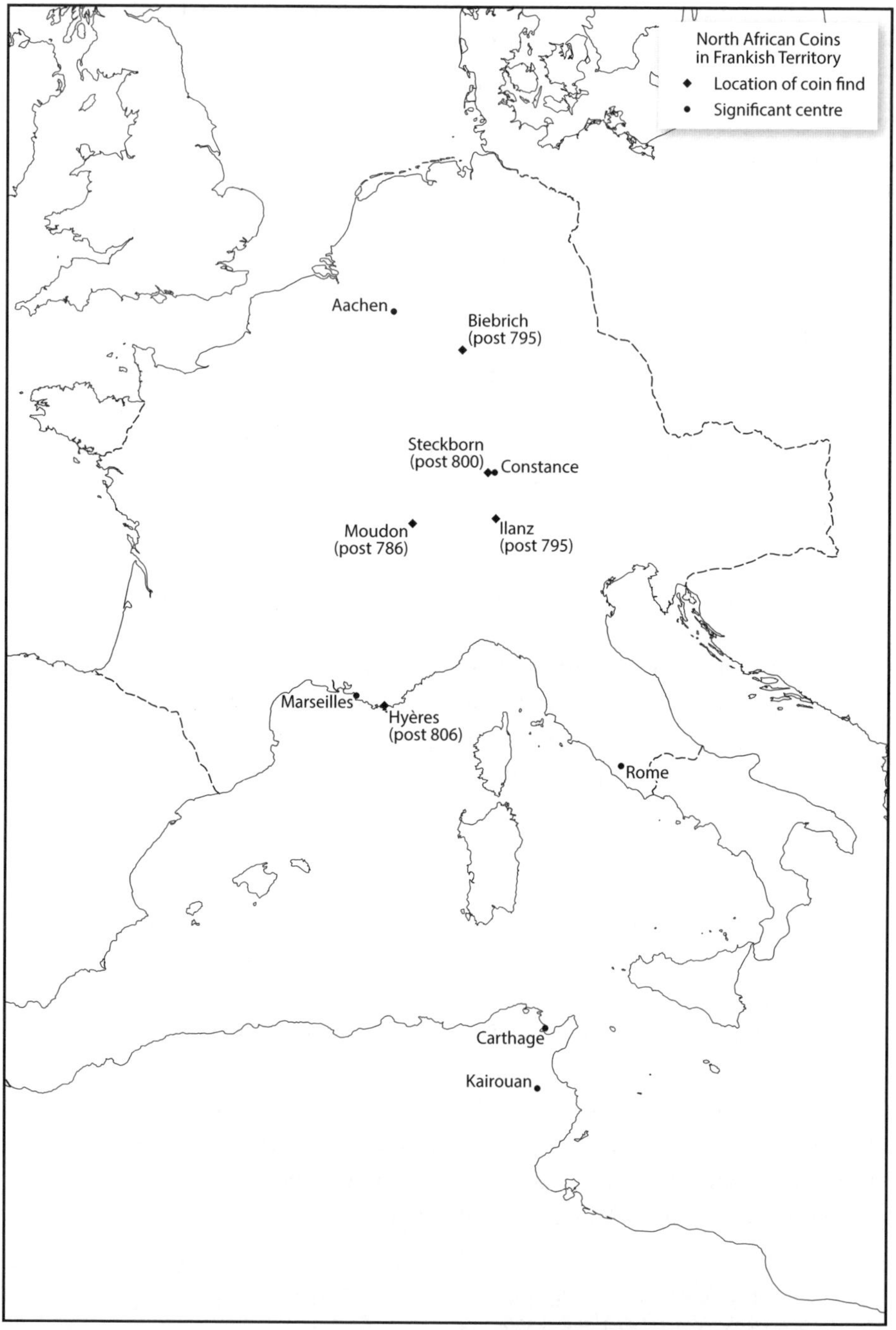


MAP 6.1. North African coins in Frankish territory.

That all of the coins minted in Ifrīqiya found in the Carolingian empire north of the Alps can be dated to the same fifteen years and appear to have been deposited in around 800 suggests a specific cause or moment in contact between Franks and North Africa. The geographical distribution of these hoards is also interesting. McCormick connects them all to a "corridor constituted by the Rhine and Meuse river basins," suggesting a commercial route.[24] Ilisch points to the close proximity of sites like Steckborn to major Carolingian centres such as Constance.[25] Charlemagne spent much of the years in which al-ʿAkkī was governor resident in Aachen, and McCormick's "Rhine corridor" would be a logical route from the Mediterranean to Aachen. The chronological and geographical concentration of these coin finds hints that something unusual was happening. That they completely vanish at the same time that al-ʿAkkī was overthrown, while appearing on a narrow route running from the Mediterranean to Charlemagne's palace centres on the Rhine, would match al-Tamīmī's account.

Another reason to take al-Tamīmī seriously is the existence of a clear and identifiable diplomatic link between Kairouan and Aachen at precisely that moment. According to the *Annales regni Francorum*, ʿAbd Allāh the Valencian, the son of the first Umayyad emir of Córdoba, ʿAbd al-Raḥmān I, arrived in Aachen in 797.[26] The death of his brother Hishām I afforded ʿAbd Allāh an opportunity to claim the emirate and he requested and received Frankish support in this enterprise. As the annalist notes, ʿAbd Allāh had been living in exile, in "Mauritania."[27] The Andalusi chronicler Ibn Ḥayyān is more precise, saying that ʿAbd Allāh had been living in Kairouan with the governor.[28] Ibn Ḥayyān's chronology is confused, as he identifies this governor as Ibrāhīm b. al-Aghlab, who only began to rule Kairouan in 800. The governor in 797, the year ʿAbd Allāh travelled to Aachen, was Muḥammad al-ʿAkkī. As well as demonstrating that travel between Kairouan and Aachen was possible, ʿAbd Allāh also provides a plausible link between Charlemagne and al-ʿAkkī.

With the exception of Ibrāhīm b. al-Aghlab's embassy to Charlemagne in 801, which will be discussed later in this chapter, the contact between Charlemagne and Muḥammad al-ʿAkkī represents the only known diplomacy between Ifrīqiya and the Carolingians. There is little evidence for

24. McCormick, *Origins of the European Economy*, 360.
25. Ilisch, "Geldgeschichten," 144.
26. ARF a.797 100.
27. Ibid.
28. Ibn Ḥayyān, *Crónica de los emires*, 17.

direct Frankish communication with Ifrīqiya prior to this moment. The governors of Ifrīqiya in the second half of the eighth century were preoccupied with managing Kharijite Berbers and the mutinous Syrian troops who had been sent to suppress the Berbers.[29] For most of his reign the Frankish king seems to have had little interest in the central Mediterranean, making only piecemeal attempts to stamp his authority over the princes of Benevento in southern Italy.[30] That the diplomacy took place at all is due to a confluence of two factors. From the late 790s Charlemagne was newly interested in projecting power across the Mediterranean, while al-ʿAkkī was a governor in an unusually vulnerable position with a particular need for political support.

The end of the last decade of the eighth century saw a shift in Charlemagne's attention.[31] Following an attack in 798 by Andalusi pirates, the inhabitants of the Balearic Islands are reported to have submitted to Charlemagne in exchange for protection.[32] This was duly provided and spoils from pirates defeated by the Balearics in 799 were presented to Charlemagne.[33] The Frankish king also appears to have been taking a closer interest in Byzantine Sicily at this time. In 799 he received envoys from Michael, the governor of Sicily.[34] Theophanes recorded in his *Chronicle* that in 800 there were fears in Constantinople that Charlemagne "intended to make a naval expedition against Sicily."[35] Al-ʿAkkī's tenure as governor of Ifrīqiya therefore coincided with a time when Charlemagne was interested in Mediterranean affairs.

Charlemagne may have been looking to extend his political influence to North Africa. The Carolingians often established friendly client regimes in territories neighbouring their empire.[36] The increasing confidence of the Carolingian navy in the Western Mediterranean indicates that this was a less implausible project than it might initially appear. The first decades of the ninth century saw Frankish fleets winning engagements against Muslim pirates at Corsica (807), Sardinia (812), and the Balearics (813).[37] In 815 Louis the Pious received tribute from Sardinia.[38] North Africa was

29. Kennedy, "The Origin of the Aghlabids," 34.
30. West, "Charlemagne's Involvement in Central and Southern Italy," 363–366.
31. On Charlemagne's later reign, see McKitterick, *Charlemagne*, 49–54.
32. ARF a.798 104. On the Balearics, see Jarrett, "Nests of Pirates?"
33. ARF a.799 108.
34. Ibid.; Nichanian and Prigent, "Les Stratèges de Sicile," 126–128.
35. Theophanes, *Chronicle* a.800 653.
36. Smith, "Fines Imperii," 172–173.
37. ARF a.807 124, a.812 137, a.813 139.
38. ARF a.815 143.

accessible to Frankish ships, as demonstrated in 801, when Charlemagne sent his notary Ercanbald to mobilise ships at short notice from Liguria to pick up his elephant.[39] The possibilities for Carolingian intervention in North Africa are also suggested by the adventure of Count Boniface II of Tuscany and Corsica in 828, when "he crossed over to Africa and landed between Utica and Carthage."[40] According to the *Annales regni Francorum*:

> He attacked a large number of the inhabitants who had suddenly gathered, fought a battle with them, and put them to flight after routing them at least five times. After slaying a great number of Africans and losing some of his own companions because of their daring, he retreated to his ships. This feat gave the Africans a great fear for them.[41]

Boniface's raid was an outlier but also stands as a salutary reminder of the power of the Carolingian navy and the widespread ambitions of the Frankish elite.[42]

These same years also saw the Frankish king paying increased attention to Christians in other lands. Christians still probably made up the majority of the population of Ifrīqiya in the early ninth century.[43] Their relations with Muslims seem to have been generally positive, and there is evidence for church building and the continued existence of bishops, even if they were in somewhat reduced circumstances.[44] Charlemagne's long-term ally Pope Hadrian I appears to have been concerned with the Christian population of the province to judge from his epitaph, which proclaims that "Africa, held captive for so many years, rejoices to have merited bishops by your prayers."[45] Papal contact with the bishops of Africa continued into the ninth century, even if it was not always friendly.

39. ARF a.801 116.

40. ARF a.828 "in Africam traiecit et inter Uticam atque Kartaginem egressus," 176, translated by Scholz, *Carolingian Chronicles*, 124.

41. ARF a.828 "innumeram incolarum multitudinem subito congregatam offendit; cum qua et proelium conseruit et quinquies vel eo amplius fusam fugatamque profligavit magnaque Afrorum multitudine prostrata, aliquantis etiam sociorum suorum per temeritatem amissis in naves suas se recepit atque hoc facto ingentem Afris timorem incussit," 176, translated by Scholz, *Carolingian Chronicles*, 124.

42. On the Carolingian navy, see Haywood, *Dark Age Naval Power*, 152–163.

43. Bulliet, *Conversion to Islam*, 102; Handley, "Disputing the End of African Christianity," summarises the debate. See also Marston Speight, "The Place of the Christians"; Talbi, "Le Christianisme maghrébin"; Valérian, "La permanence du christianisme au Maghreb."

44. Savage, *A Gateway to Hell*, 89–105; Conant, "Anxieties of Violence," 7–9.

45. *Epitaphia Hadriana Papae*, "Africa laetatur, multos captiva per annos, Pontifices precibus promeruisse tuis," 114.

In 854 Leo IV condemned Bishop Galerius of Tripoli for the immoral practices of his flock.[46]

That Charlemagne was in contact with the large Christian population of North Africa is attested by Einhard in his *Life*, who says that he gave alms

> across the sea in Syria and Egypt as well as Africa, Jerusalem, Alexandria and Carthage. Wherever he discovered that Christians were living in poverty, he sent them money regularly for their want. It was for this reason that he zealously sought the friendship of kings beyond the sea, so that some relief and comfort might result for the Christians living under their rule.[47]

That there was reality to Einhard's claim is suggested by the survey Charlemagne had assembled of the state of the Church in the Holy Land.[48] Charlemagne may have paid similar attention to his coreligionists in Africa.

North Africa was also a part of the Frankish Christian imagination. In his *Admonitio generalis*, Charlemagne referred to "the council of Africa" twice.[49] The Synod of Aachen in 816 repeatedly mentions African councils.[50] They also appear in the Pseudo-Isidorian Decretals, forged in the early ninth century.[51] African saints such as Cyprian of Carthage and Augustine of Hippo were revered in the Carolingian empire, the latter being a particular favourite of Charlemagne.[52] While they had previously had only a minimal presence in liturgical calendars in Gaul, the early ninth century saw a surge of interest in African saints, with hundreds appearing in Frankish martyrologies.[53] Ancient *Lives* of African saints were preserved in ninth-century copies.[54] North Africa was a place of pilgrimage. Between 855 and 863, Frotmund and his brother left the court of Lothar II (r. 855–869) to atone for an act of kin-slaughter. On their pilgrimage "they

46. Leo IV, *Epistolae* no. 26, 600.

47. Einhard, *Vita Karoli Magni*, c.27 "verum trans maria in Syriam et Aegyptum atque Africam, Hierosolimis, Alexandriae atque Cartagini, ubi Christianos in paupertate vivere conpererat, penuriae illorum conpatiens pecuniam mittere solebat; ob hoc maxime transmarinorum regum amicitias expetens, ut Christianis sub eorum dominatu degentibus refrigerium aliquod ac relevatio a proveniret," 31–32.

48. McCormick, *Charlemagne's Survey*.

49. Charlemagne, *Admonitio generalis*, "In concilio Africano," 55, 56–57.

50. *Concilium Aquisgranense*, no. 39 307–464.

51. *Concilia Africae*, v.

52. Einhard, *Vita Karoli Magni*, c.24 29.

53. Conant, "Europe and the African Cult of Saints," 24 and n. 94.

54. Ibid., 25.

turned their steps to Africa to visit the tomb of St. Cyprian."[55] The account of the *Gesta sanctorum Rotonensium* presents Carthage as part of a holy landscape, "where many great works and many great miracles are very often revealed by the Lord."[56]

On their return from Baghdad, the survivors among Charlemagne's embassy to Hārūn al-Rashīd acquired the remains of Cyprian and took them from Carthage. This moving was commemorated by Florus of Lyon, who claimed that Charlemagne granted the relics to Archbishop Leidrad of Lyon.[57] As this demonstrates, Africa was on travelling routes to the East. That Florus was particularly interested in Carthage may be suggested by his use of Orosius's description of the city in the collection of historical and geographical excerpts he gathered in the 840s.[58] Orosius's moralizing narrative on the evils of empire is ignored in favour of the geography.[59]

The expansionist Charlemagne would have found an unusually sympathetic partner in Muḥammad al-ʿAkkī, who was in a difficult political position. From the initial invasions by Arab forces in the 660s, Ifrīqiya was a challenging province to manage.[60] While the rich, urbanised region of coastal Tunisia could be occupied and taxed relatively easily, the Berber inhabitants of the mountainous interior proved to be tenacious and persistent opponents.[61] Conversion to Islam did not make them any more likely to respect the authority of Kairouan, with many groups embracing syncretic or Kharijite variants.[62] The power of the governors was based on an enormous army largely made up of Syrians, but the difficulties involved in paying these troops made mutiny a regular danger.[63]

55. "Gesta sanctorum Rotonensium," "ac exinde profecti direxerunt gressum ad Africam uisitare sepulchrum sancti Cypriani," 206–207.

56. Ibid., "ubi multae uirtutes et multa miracula a Domino saepius ostenduntur," 209.

57. Florus of Lyons, *Qualiter sanctorum martyrum* and *Ubi ossa sancti Cipriani*, 544. Courtois was sceptical in "Reliques carthaginoises"; but Ruggiero, *Atti dei martiri scilitani*, 53, and McCormick, *Origins of the European Economy*, 521, accept it.

58. BAV Vat.lat.3852 fol.42v; Orosius, *Historiae Adversum Paganos*, IV.22.4–6, vol. 2 71–73; Turcan-Verkerk, "Faut-il rendre à Tertullien"; Lozovsky, "Roman Geography and Ethnography," 328–329.

59. Merrills, *History and Geography*, 40–41.

60. Brett, "The Arab Conquest," 509; Kaegi, *Muslim Expansion and Byzantine Collapse*; Fenwick, "From Africa to Ifrīqiya," 9–33.

61. Fenwick, *Early Islamic North Africa*, 2, 33.

62. Brett, "The Arab Conquest," 518; Hagemann and Verkinderen, "Kharijism in the Umayyad Period," 497.

63. Kennedy, "Military Pay" and "The Origin of the Aghlabids," 37–38.

The early ʿAbbāsid caliphs solved the problem of Ifrīqiya by delegation. From 768 the province was governed by the Muhallabid family, loyal adherents of the caliphs who had taken part in the ʿAbbāsid Revolution, who were given major autonomy in running Ifrīqiya.[64] This proved highly successful, particularly under Yazīd b. Ḥātim al-Muhallabī, whose tenure as governor (771–787) saw the suppression of Kharijite rebels and an economic boom, with an enormous production of coins from Ifrīqiyan mints.[65] This period of stability ended in 794 when the last Muhallabid governor was killed by the Syrian troops. The rest of the decade saw repeated battles as Hārūn al-Rashīd attempted to control the province.[66]

In 797 the caliph appointed al-ʿAkkī as the new governor. Al-ʿAkkī was the son of a participant in the ʿAbbāsid Revolution and Hārūn's foster brother, as well as a friend of the powerful Jaʿfar b. Yaḥyā al-Barmakī.[67] Despite these connections at court, the new governor was extremely isolated in Ifrīqiya. While Hārūn had sent an army to restore order in 795, his attentions were fixed elsewhere in subsequent years, particularly from 797, preparing an extremely controversial plan of succession and the destruction of the Barmakid family.[68] The caliph was to be extremely unwilling to commit more resources to Ifrīqiya.[69] As al-Tamīmī reported in his story, al-ʿAkkī proved to be unpopular with the Syrian troops of Ifrīqiya, and he was eventually overthrown in 799. Lacking both local backing and support from Baghdad, al-ʿAkkī may have been looking for an alternative source of assistance. Had he sought this in Charlemagne, it would explain al-Tamīmī's account.

It is this combination of the Frankish monarchy at the zenith of its confidence and the governorate of Ifrīqiya at the nadir of its own that encouraged diplomatic contact. It did not do al-ʿAkkī much good, and if anything served as the trigger for his overthrowing. He was briefly restored to power in 800 with the support of the then governor of Zab, Ibrāhīm b. al-Aghlab. Ibrāhīm promptly dispensed with al-ʿAkkī, making a deal with Hārūn al-Rashīd that he would manage Ifrīqiya for the caliph in exchange for de facto independence. Ibrāhīm would acknowledge ʿAbbāsid authority

64. Djaīt, "La Wilāya D'Ifrīqiya," 97–98.

65. Noonan, "Early ʿAbbāsid Mint Output," 143–146; Brather, "Frühmittelalterliche Dirham-Schatzfunde," 109.

66. Talbi, *L'Émirat Aghlabide*, 77.

67. Ibid., 83–85.

68. Gabrieli, "La successione di Hārūn ar-Rašīd"; Kimber, "Hārūn al-Rashīd's Meccan Settlement"; Kennedy, *The Early Abbasid Caliphate*, 122.

69. Kennedy, *The Early Abbasid Caliphate*, 195.

and manage dangerous Kharijite and ʿAlid elements in the Maghrib while acting autonomously. Hārūn in turn would possess a faithful ally in North Africa without having to commit men and material to a political quagmire. The Aghlabids ruled as the emirs of Ifrīqiya for the next century.

Without an obvious partner in Ifrīqiya, Charlemagne's ability to intervene there waned, particularly as his position in southern Italy was not particularly strong.[70] Grimoald III (788–806) had become prince of Benevento in 788 having been Charlemagne's hostage.[71] By the early 790s he was acting as an independent ruler.[72] Rather than look across the sea, Charlemagne seems to have concentrated efforts on bringing Benevento to heel at the beginning of the ninth century, with only dubious success. His son Pippin of Italy (r. 781–810) led armies into Benevento in 800 and 801, while Ortona and Lucera were captured in 802.[73] Frankish momentum stalled as Grimoald recaptured Lucera the same year, taking Count Winigis of Spoleto prisoner.[74] Winigis was freed in 803 and the absence of any evidence for Carolingian campaigning subsequently suggests that Charlemagne had ended his efforts to conquer Benevento.[75] These difficulties may have discouraged any thoughts of Ifrīqiya.

That Charlemagne nonetheless remained interested in North Africa after the fall of al-ʿAkkī in 800 is indicated by a letter sent to him in 813 by Pope Leo III.[76] The letter contained a message intended for the Frankish emperor from Gregory, the Byzantine governor of Sicily, suggesting that Charlemagne had maintained his Sicilian contacts.[77] Gregory informed Charlemagne of recent negotiations he had held with "an envoy of the Saracens," who had come offering a peace treaty for ten years.[78] Gregory was sceptical, pointing to previous treaties that had been broken:

> To this the Saracen envoys responded, saying: "The father of this *Amiralmumin*, who now is seen to reign over us, died, and left this one a child. And he that was the slave was made free; and he who was free was a lord; and none gave thought to the king."[79]

70. West, "Charlemagne's Involvement in Central and Southern Italy," 363–366.
71. ARF a.788 82.
72. Erchempert, *Historia*, c.4 236; Meeder, "Monte Cassino and Carolingian Politics."
73. ARF a. 800 110, a.801 114, a.802 117.
74. ARF a. 802 117.
75. ARF a.803 118.
76. Leo III, *Epistolae* no. 6, 96–99.
77. Nichanian and Prigent, "Les Stratèges de Sicile," 129–131.
78. Leo III, *Epistolae* no. 6, "Sarracenorum missis," 97.
79. Ibid., "Ad haec respondebant ipsi Saracenorum missi, dicentes: 'Pater istius Amiralmumin, qui nunc apud nos regnare videtur, defunctus est, et iste relictus est parvulus.

This satisfied Gregory, and the treaty was made. From the information given, the sender of the envoys was probably Idrīs II, discussed above, then at the start of the long process of conquering most of Morocco.[80] That both Gregory and Leo III thought that Charlemagne would be interested in hearing this news about North African politics is intriguing, suggesting that information on the affairs of the Maghrib was generally passed north of the Alps.

The letter alludes to a reason for Charlemagne's ongoing attention. Leo mentions a pirate attack on Italy from Africa in 812, confirmed by the *Annales regni Francorum*, which refers to a fleet "from Africa as well as from Spain."[81] Leo included in the same letter an account of an African fleet that would have raided Sardinia but for divine intervention:

> The sea suddenly opened up and swallowed those hundred ships; and in great dread, the Saracens had shortly afterwards returned home and told the people in Africa what had happened and reported the news to the households of those who had been drowned; and there had been such grief as had never been known before.[82]

Seeking to confirm the truth of the story of the unfortunate African fleet, Leo's envoy in Sicily

> asked the notary who was looking after him whether what he had heard from the Saracens was true. And the notary told him that it was and that he had personally read out to the patrician a letter which a Christian friend of his had sent him from Africa and which contained the drowning of the aforesaid hundred ships.[83]

As this suggests, there remained means for Charlemagne to receive information about African affairs.

---

Et qui fuit servus, factus est liber; et qui liber fuit, effectus est dominus; et nullum se regem habere putabant,'" 98.

80. Abun-Nasr, *A History of the Maghrib*, 76–82; Laroui, *The History of the Maghrib*, 109–112; Manzano Moreno, "The Iberian Peninsula and North Africa," 599.

81. ARF a.812 "quae et de Africa u et de Hispania," 137.

82. Leo III, *Epistolae* no. 6, "subito aperta est maris et subgluttivit illa centum navigia; et postmodum sic cum magno timore reversi sunt ipsi Sarraceni; qui hoc dicebant in Africa et nuntiaverunt ad familiam de illis, qui submersi sunt, et talem luctum fecerunt, qualem nunquam ibidem fuit," 98.

83. Ibid., "interrogavit illum notarium, qui eum custodiebat, si veritas esset, quae ab illis Sarracenis audierat. Et dixit ipse notarius, quod ita esset, et ipse ore proprio legisset ad patricium illam epistolam, quam ei unus Christianus amicus suus ab Africa direxit, in qua de submersione de praedictis centum navigiis continebat," 98.

That Carolingian relations with Ifrīqiya went no further is probably due to an absence of enthusiasm not on Charlemagne's part but on that of the Aghlabids. Ibrāhīm I did not entirely neglect relations with Charlemagne, sending an envoy in 801. Talbi interpreted this as evidence of an alliance between the Aghlabids and the Carolingians against Byzantine Sicily.[84] Given that the trigger for al-ʿAkkī being overthrown had been unhappiness at a Frankish alliance, it seems unlikely that Ibrāhīm would be keen to replicate the experiment. The first Aghlabids needed to focus on dealing with internal difficulties and do not appear to have had any interest in Sicily.[85] Although not as desperate as al-ʿAkkī, Ibrāhīm had to face multiple challenges from Kharijites and the Syrian armies. It was not until the reign of his son Ziyādat Allāh I (r. 817–838) that the Aghlabids can be connected to raids on Sicily, reflecting a more settled political situation within Ifrīqiya.[86] When the dynasty did decide to reach across the sea, they characterised their conflict against the Byzantines in Sicily as holy war, legitimising their regime with its lustre, which complicated diplomacy with the Franks.[87]

In order to understand Ibrāhīm sending a legate in 801, it may be significant that the envoy arrived with one who came from Hārūn. The Aghlabids used their association with the ʿAbbāsid caliphs as a source of legitimation.[88] The name of the caliph was mentioned in Friday prayers, and when Ibrāhīm founded a new capital outside Kairouan, he named it in al-ʿAbbāsīya.[89] In the case of his embassy to Charlemagne, Ibrāhīm may have been associating himself with a piece of ʿAbbāsid prestige diplomacy, announcing his arrival on the political stage to the Carolingians. If Charlemagne had had a relationship with Ibrāhīm's predecessor, the sending of a diplomat with one of Hārūn's might also have signalled that the new emir of Ifrīqiya was aligned with the ʿAbbāsids and that Frankish efforts to build influence in North Africa would not be welcomed. Given that Ibrāhīm drew strength from his association with the caliph and also had concerns that drew his eyes away from the Mediterranean, it is not surprising that no further diplomacy took place with the Carolingians.

84. Talbi, *L'Émirat Aghlabide*, 401.

85. Chiarelli, *A History of Muslim Sicily*, 8–10.

86. Marazzi, "*Ita ut facta videatur Neapolis*," 168.

87. Nef, "Comment les Aghlabides," "Guerroyer pour la Sicile," and "Reinterpreting the Aghlabid Sicilian Policy."

88. Kennedy, "The Origin of the Aghlabids," 44.

89. Goodson, "Topographies of Power"; Fenina, "L'atelier monétaire."

Charlemagne was both interested in and well-informed about North African affairs. North Africa was an area of historical importance for his faith, the home of a large Christian population, and a source of pirates who attacked his territory. Nonetheless, as the above discussion indicates, evidence for Carolingian diplomacy with the rulers of North Africa is confined to a comparatively brief period in the later years of Charlemagne's reign. These years represent both the Carolingian empire at its most expansive in the Western Mediterranean and North African affairs in an unusual state of crisis between the Muhallabid and the Aghlabid regimes. Outside of this very specific combination of circumstances, the Carolingians appear to have had little opportunity to communicate with the rulers of Ifrīqiya.

## *All-Out War: The Emirates of Italy*

As the preceding discussion has hinted, North Africa served as a base for Muslim involvement in mainland Italy, referred to as "The Big Land" (*al-ʿarḍ al-kabīra*).[90] Pope Leo III informed Charlemagne of his fears for "our shores" in the face of the "infestation of pagans and our enemies" in 808.[91] In 813, Civitavecchia in Tuscany was attacked.[92] Although reports of raids decline from this point, the continuing threat was eloquently outlined by Bishop Claudius of Turin in a letter of 820:

> In the middle of spring, I go down armed with parchment and bearing weapons to the guard posts on the coast where I stay awake out of fear of the Agarenes and Moors.[93]

From 835 a more permanent Muslim military presence appeared in mainland Italy. In that year the city of Naples hired a company of Saracen mercenaries to defend it from Prince Sicard of Benevento (r. 832–839).[94] The next decade saw the capture of the cities of Taranto and Bari by Muslim forces.[95] While the emirate of Taranto may have been subject to the

90. Metcalfe, *The Muslims of Medieval Italy*, 16.

91. Leo III, *Epistolae* no. 1, "ab infestatione paganorum et inimicorum nostrorum," 88.

92. ARF a.817 139.

93. Claudius of Turin, *Epistolae* no. 6, "Post medium veris procedendo armatus pergameno pariter cum arma y ferens, pergo ad excubias maritimas cum timore excubando adversus Agarenos et Mauros," 601.

94. John the Deacon, *Gesta episcoporum*, c.57 431.

95. Erchempert, *Historia*, c.16 240; *Chronica Sancti Benedicti Casinensis*, c.11 474. On the dating, see Bondioli, "Islamic Bari," 472.

Aghlabids, that of Bari appears to have been independent, looking to the ʿAbbāsid caliphs for legitimacy.[96] These emirates lasted until 880 and 871, respectively.[97] There are also references to an emir of Amantea in 870.[98]

This expansion of activity narrowed the geographical distance between the Carolingians and Muslim polities in the central Mediterranean. The Carolingians had ruled northern Italy from Charlemagne's conquest of the kingdom of the Lombards in 774.[99] The Duke of Spoleto was at least theoretically under their authority and periodic efforts had been made by the Carolingians to intervene in the Principality of Benevento in the south.[100] As chapters 3 and 4 of this book have indicated, Italy was not the first Mediterranean peninsula to be occupied by both Franks and Muslims. Unlike Iberia, where this proximity brought communication and diplomacy as well as war, there is no evidence for diplomacy between the Carolingians and the emirs of Italy. Instead the rulers of Frankish Italy, Lothar I, king of Italy from 822, and his son Louis II, co-ruler from 844, proved to be unremittingly hostile to the new emirates.

In 849 Louis, represented by Duke Guy I of Spoleto, had brokered a treaty partitioning the Principality of Benevento between two warring claimants, Radelchis and Siconulf of Salerno.[101] Louis was in the area with a large army and was thus in an excellent position to dictate terms. Among the most interesting of these terms are those that refer to Saracens, which bear the unmistakable stamp of Louis's influence. While both Radelchis and Siconulf had employed Muslim mercenaries from 842, the treaty of 849 explicitly forbid anyone from seeking "the aid or friendship" of the Saracens.[102] More dramatically still, all Saracens were to be expelled from the Principality of Benevento, "excepting those who were Christian in the time of Lords Sico and Sicard [(817–839)], unless they have fallen into apostasy."[103] This was a dramatically uncompromising statement of Louis's policy. Not only would he no longer tolerate Saracen military companies

96. Bondioli, "Islamic Bari," 475–477. Cf. Marazzi, "*Ita ut facta videatur Neapolis*," 188.

97. Musca, *L'emirato di Bari*, is now superseded by Bondioli, "Islamic Bari."

98. Andreas of Bergamo, *Historia*, c.14 227–228.

99. ARF a.774 37. See Costambeys, *Power and Patronage*, 288–301.

100. West, "Charlemagne's Involvement in Central and Southern Italy"; Schieffer, "Die Politik der Karolinger."

101. *Radelgisi et Siginulfi*, 221–225. For the background to this, see Gantner, "A King in Training?"

102. *Chronica Sancti Benedicti Casinensis*, c.8 473; *Radelgisi et Siginulfi*, c.24 "adiutorium seu amicitiam," 224.

103. *Radelgisi et Siginulfi*, c.24 "praeter illos qui temporibus domni m Siconis et Sicardi fuerunt christiani, si magarizati non sunt," 224.

attacking Christians or intervening in Italian politics, there was to be no place in Italy for Muslims or suspected Muslims.

Louis fought repeated campaigns in the south of Italy against Muslims. His success rate was not particularly high, as the failed attempts to conquer the emirate of Bari in 852, 863, and 869 attest, but there could be no question of his commitment to the cause, particularly in the 860s.[104] This focus was demonstrated in 869, when he prioritised the siege of Bari over supporting his brother Lothar II in his attempts to divorce his wife.[105] When that same year Lothar died, leaving Lotharingia to his older brother, Louis's efforts to secure his inheritance were confined to ineffectual letters to his uncles, who promptly divided the kingdom between them.[106]

The complete absence of any diplomatic efforts is noticeable when compared to Carolingian relations everywhere else they encountered the Islamic world and needs explaining. There has been a tendency in the past to treat this conflict as natural, a straightforward product of the obvious antipathy between medieval Christendom and Islam.[107] The work of scholars of the last thirty years has done much to complicate this simple assessment of Christians and Muslims in this period.[108] What follows attempts to understand why diplomacy with Muslims was not an option for Lothar and Louis in a way that it had been for Louis the Pious or still was for Charles the Bald.

The sources for the Italian emirates are extremely slender, particularly for those of Taranto, and the shadowy polity based in Amantea.[109] The discussion will therefore focus on the best-documented emirate, that of Bari. The evidence that survives suggests that the emirate formed part of the wider political landscape of southern Italy. Throughout its brief existence it remained an aggressive state that regularly attacked its neighbours. But there are signs that other powers in the region were willing to come to arrangements with it. Indeed, the original conquerors of Bari appear to have positioned themselves as allies of Radelchis in his struggle with Siconulf.[110] After the Beneventan civil war, the *Chronicle of Salerno* reports that envoys from Bari were received in Salerno, being hosted in the

104. AB a.852 65; AB a.869 153; Erchempert, *Historia*, c.20 242.

105. AB a.869 153.

106. Ibid.; AF a.869 68; Hadrian II, *Epistolae* nos. 16, 21, 22, 24, 717–719, 724–727, 729–730.

107. Engreen, "Pope John the Eighth and the Arabs."

108. See, for example, Wolf, "Gli hypati di Gaeta."

109. Tonghi, "Gli Arabi ad Amantea."

110. Bondioli, "Islamic Bari," 477–479.

bishop's palace.[111] Count Hildebert of Camerino fled to Bari to escape the wrath of Louis II in 860.[112] In captivity after the fall of Bari, the last emir, Sawdān (r. 857–871), seems to have interacted with Christian elites easily, reportedly charming Louis and his family with his wit and learning.[113] This was not a tendency that was confined to politics. A case in point is the Frankish pilgrim Bernard, who visited Sawdān in order to get letters of safe passage for his journey to the Holy Land, a journey that began by taking a ship to Egypt from Taranto.[114]

Indeed, there are hints that many in southern Italy saw little distinction between Saracens and Franks.[115] Alliances with powerful Muslim leaders were common.[116] Naples was particularly well known for its Saracen alliances. In 871, Louis II accused Duke Sergius II of turning the city "into another Palermo, another Africa."[117] Infuriated by Sergius's Muslim alliances, in 877 Pope John VIII supported a successful coup against the duke by the Bishop of Naples, Athanasius II.[118] Three years later John had excommunicated Athanasius in turn for continuing the Muslim alliance, a policy that Athanasius maintained throughout his time as duke.[119] Contact is also implied by the awareness that some Italians had of the divisions between different Muslim groups. Radelchis is reported to have hired "Libyan Agarenes," while Siconulf recruited "Spanish Ishmaelites."[120] The *Chronicle of Salerno* says that Prince Guaifer of Salerno was warned of an impending Aghlabid siege in 871 by a friendly trader from North Africa.[121] This is not to say that either the emirates or the Saracen mercenaries were universally popular in southern Italy but rather to suggest that this was a context where a certain rough-and-ready pragmatism was possible. Predatory as they were, the emirs of Bari could be open to diplomatic contact. Other Italian states could and did send envoys to them. Not doing so was a deliberate choice rather than a necessity.

111. "The Chronicle of Salerno," 99–100.

112. *Chronica Sancti Benedicti Casinensis*, c.13 475; Delogu, "Strutture politiche e ideologia," 169.

113. Constantine Porphyrogenitus, *De administrando imperio*, c.29 129–135.

114. Bernard, *Itinerarium*, 310; *Chronica Sancti Benedicti Casinensis*, 481.

115. Loud, *The Age of Robert Guiscard*, 15; Kujawiński, "Le immagini dell' 'altro'"; Heath, "Third/Ninth-Century Violence," 31.

116. Citarella, "The Relations of Amalfi."

117. Louis II, *Epistola ad Basilium I*, "ita ut facta videatur Neapolis Panormus vel Africa," 393.

118. John VIII, *Epistolae* no. 76, 72–73.

119. Ibid., no. 279, 246–247.

120. Erchempert, *Historia*, c.17 "Agarenos . . . Libicos," "Hismaelitas Hispanos," 241.

121. "Chronicle of Salerno," 122–123.

Carolingian diplomacy with non-Christian neighbours took place in specific circumstances for specific reasons. As we have seen in the case of the Umayyads of Córdoba, it was commonly resorted to when the non-Christian state in question was dangerous enough to pose a potential threat to core Carolingian interests but too powerful to be easily defeated. This did not apply with the Muslim powers of southern Italy. Although they could threaten the pope and other Italian political actors, they lacked the resources to permanently invade Carolingian territory in the northern kingdom of Italy. Isolated in their cities, Louis had every reason to believe that the emirates could be successfully dislodged from their bases in a way that was unthinkable in al-Andalus.

Nor was there a rival in Italy the emirates could be usefully turned against. In the Iberian Peninsula the Carolingians were motivated to come to arrangements with figures such as Sulaymān al-ʿArābī or Mūsā b. Mūsā because they were potentially useful allies against the Umayyads of Córdoba. By contrast, in the mid-ninth century there were no other great powers in mainland Italy. The first evidence of serious Byzantine interest in mainland Italy following the disastrous sinking of the Venetian fleet in 841 comes in the last years of the 860s, when Basil I allied with Louis in opposition to Bari.[122] Byzantine armies began operating in mainland Italy in 873, with the arrival of Patrician Gregory at Otranto.[123] The Aghlabids appear to have been content to keep Taranto as a friendly base in order to disrupt Byzantine efforts to reinforce Sicily.[124] Their siege of Salerno in 871 marks a major escalation and seems to have been designed to fill the space vacated by the fall of Bari.[125] This offered Kairouan a chance to become the dominant Muslim force on the mainland. In the absence of a major opponent before this point, the Italian emirates were of limited usefulness to Lothar and Louis.

Another reason for entering diplomatic relations with a Muslim power was access to exotic objects and gifts. That was unlikely to happen with Bari, whose rulers were neither wealthy nor held in particularly high esteem across the Islamic world. The first Muslim ruler of Bari, Khalfūn (r. 840–844), was

122. John the Deacon, *Chronicon Venetum*, 17–18; Noyé, "Byzance et Italie méridionale"; Prigent, "Cutting Losses." See Hadrian II's letters to Basil I in 868 and 869, *Epistolae* no. 37, 747–748, no. 40, 754–758. On Louis II's relations with Byzantium, see Gantner, "'Our Common Enemies.'"

123. AB a.873 192; Bondioli, "From the Frontier Cities to the City."

124. Bondioli, "Islamic Bari," 476, but cf. Di Branco, "Strategie di penetrazione islamica."

125. Erchempert, *Historia*, c.35 247–248; "Chronicle of Salerno," 124–128.

an adventurer.[126] One of his successors, Mufarraj b. Sallām (r. 848–850), applied unsuccessfully to the ʿAbbāsid caliph al-Mutawakkil (r. 847–861) for recognition, something only achieved by Sawdān in 862 in the time of Caliph al-Mustaʿin (r. 862–866).[127] Even after this recognition, Sawdān's name carried little weight elsewhere as Bernard the Monk learned to his cost when his pass from the emir availed him little travelling in Egypt.[128]

If Lothar and Louis lacked the normal incentives to engage in diplomacy with Bari, there was also a very strong disincentive in the form of the threat Muslim pirates offered Christian institutions in Italy. The unique significance of the papacy and its importance to the self-fashioning of the image of Carolingian kingship created pressures and incentives that were not in play elsewhere. The Carolingians and the popes had enjoyed a "special relationship" since the mid-eighth century. In a letter to Leo III in 796, Charlemagne promised "to defend by force of arms the Holy Church of Christ in all places from the incursions of pagans and the ravages of infidels."[129] When Charlemagne planned the division of his empire in 806, he admonished his sons to "undertake in common the care and defence of the church of St Peter."[130] A defining moment was the attack on Rome in August 846 by Saracen pirates, which resulted in the sack of much of the city beyond the Aurelian Walls, including St Peter's on the Vatican Hill.[131] In October of that year Lothar issued a capitulary taking responsibility for the attack, promising to deal with the problem with measures ranging from penitential fasting across his lands to new walls for Rome.[132] Louis's campaign in Benevento that ended the civil war of Radelchis and Siconulf was one product of this new initiative.

Leaving aside questions of piety, a perceived failure to protect Rome could only damage Lothar and Louis.[133] The association between popes and imperial authority made them particularly important to Louis II,

126. *Chronica Sancti Benedicti Casinensis*, c.22 481; Al-Balādhurī, *The Origins of the Islamic State*, 371.

127. Al-Balādhurī, *The Origins of the Islamic State*, 372. On al-Mufarraj, see Di Branco, "Due notizie concernenti l'Italia meridionale."

128. Bernard, *Itinerarium*, 310; Halevi, "Bernard, Explorer of the Muslim Lake," 38–40.

129. Alcuin, *Epistolae* no. 93, "sanctam undique Christi ecclesiam ab incurs paganorum et ab infidelium devastation armis defendere foris," 137.

130. Charlemagne, *Divisio regnorum*, no. 45, "curam et defensionem ecclesiae sancti Petri suscipiant simul," 129.

131. "Life of Sergius II," 99; John the Deacon, *Gesta episcoporum*, c.60 432; *Chronica Sancti Benedicti Casinensis*, c.6 472; AB a.846 52–53; AF a.846 36; AX a.846 15–16.

132. Lothar I, "Francia Oktober 846," no. 12, 133–139.

133. On the relationship between the two, see Screen, "Carolingian Fathers and Sons."

who had to defend his claim to be the senior Carolingian after the death of his father in 855 in the face of opposition from his uncles. In his annals, Hincmar of Rheims gives Louis the derisive title of "so-called emperor of Italy."[134] The sort of censure Lothar and Louis could face is suggested by hostile Frankish annals from the other side of the Alps. Prudentius, writing in the *Annals of St-Bertin*, notes that in 847 "the Moors and Saracens attacked Benevento and laid waste Beneventan territory right up to where it bordered Rome's."[135] If criticism was implied in this entry, it was more explicit in Prudentius's comment that in 849 "the Moors and Saracens sacked the Italian city of Luni, and without meeting the least resistance ravaged the whole coast along to Provence."[136] More damning still were the reported complaints of the Romans in 853 about "the total neglect of their defence" by Lothar in the face of Saracen attacks.[137] Similar views were expressed in the *Annales Xantenses*. Writing in Lorsch, Gerward commented that in 850 "the Moors, however, devastated here [Rome] and then the coast towns in Italy."[138] His anonymous continuator at Cologne noted in a condemnation of Louis's dealings with Pope Nicholas II that in 869 Louis "did not drive the Moors from Benevento."[139] The potential threat posed by Muslim raiders to important Christian centres in Italy, most particularly the pope, placed major barriers to negotiation with Saracens in the peninsula. Lothar and Louis were under pressure from potential rivals outside their territory to perform or risk losing legitimacy and credibility. Acting to defend Rome also offered a way for Louis to secure his authority in the face of his detractors. By contrast, diplomatic negotiations potentially opened him to criticism.

On the other hand, unremitting opposition to the Italian emirates opened up political opportunities for the Carolingians in southern Italy. The year 870 saw Louis besieging Bari. This was to be the last siege of the city, which fell the following February. Writing seven years later, Andreas of Bergamo notes that Louis was approached by cities in Calabria that were under attack by the emir of Amantea. Louis sent a force under Count

134. AB a.863 "Italiae vocatus imperator," 96.

135. AB a.847 "Ea tempestate Mauri et Saraceni Beneventum invadunt et usque ad Romana confinia populantur," 55, translated by Nelson, *Annals of St-Bertin*, 65.

136. AB a.849 "Mauri et Saraceni Lunam Italiae civitatem ad redantes, nullo obsistente maritima omnia usque ad Provinciam devastant," 57, translated by Nelson, *Annals of St-Bertin*, 68.

137. AB a.853 "ob sui defensione omnino neglectam," 68, translated by Nelson, *Annals of St-Bertin*, 78.

138. AX a.850 "Mauri vero urbes maritimas in Italia hinc inde vastaverunt," 17.

139. AX a.869 "non Mauros de Beneventania expulit," 27.

Otto of Bergamo to deal with it.[140] This campaign, frequently lost amidst the drama of the siege of Bari, had important implications. Calabria had generally been beyond Frankish reach, residing in the Byzantine sphere of influence.[141] By fighting the Saracens in one part of Italy, Louis had become a natural source of aid for communities elsewhere.

For all the claims of Louis's predecessors, none was able to sustain power in southern Italy. Far away from the centres of Carolingian power, the Principality of Benevento was effectively independent in the early ninth century. The civil war and subsequent division of Benevento led to the creation of the Principality of Salerno and an autonomous Capua from 849. The result was a complex political landscape of small competing polities. It was in this environment that the emirates of Bari and Taranto thrived, as did other city-states such as Naples, Gaeta, and Amalfi. As Jules Gay noted long ago, the presence of Muslims provided Louis with a possible common enemy to rally the fractious and fiercely independent Christian polities of the region behind his authority.[142] It would also serve to separate the southern powers from access to the Muslim mercenaries with which they augmented their military capability.

This can be seen in Louis's careful coalition building in the 860s. Between 866 and 871 Louis and his wife and chief adviser Angilberga were permanently located in southern Italy, an unprecedented move.[143] While waging war against Bari, Louis was the first Carolingian to provide a sustained source of authority in southern Italy. In their first year they visited nearly every one of the local powers. Louis entered Capua and removed its ruler, Bishop Landulf.[144] He was more conciliatory when stopping in Salerno, Amalfi, and the vicinity of Naples, before basing himself in Benevento.[145] While this process of coalition building placed the political initiative with Louis, southern leaders could participate as well. Having come to power in a bloody coup in 861, Guaifer of Salerno in particular seems to have seen Louis as a useful source of legitimacy.[146]

That this policy failed to secure Frankish rule over southern Italy in the long term is clear. In August 871, six months after the capture of Bari by Frankish forces, Prince Adelchis of Benevento imprisoned Louis,

140. Andreas of Bergamo, *Historia*, c.14 227–228.

141. Di Gangi and Lebole, "La Calabria bizantina," 471–487.

142. Gay, *L'Italie méridionale*, 65; Cilento, *Italia meridionale longobarda*, 179; Albertoni, *L'Italia Carolingia*, 52.

143. On Angilberga, see La Rocca, "Angelberga, Louis's II Wife."

144. Erchempert, *Historia*, c.32 247.

145. Ibid.; *Chronica Sancti Benedicti Casinensis*, c.4 471.

146. *Codex Diplomaticus Cajetanus, Part I*, nos. 64–70; "Chronicle of Salerno," 105.

Angilberga, and their daughter Ermengard.[147] This move prompted rumours elsewhere that Louis and his family had been killed.[148] Their release, negotiated by the Bishop of Benevento, was conditional upon Louis swearing an oath never to return to Benevento and to seek no revenge upon the plotters.[149] In a sign that Louis had succeeded in unifying the region, but largely against himself, the plot was supported by Guaifer of Salerno and Sergius II of Naples.[150] The events of August 871 were clearly a serious blow for Louis's ambitions. The fall of Bari in 871, while a triumph for Louis, effectively ended much of his value for the rulers of southern Italy. He had been more militarily successful than was politically good for him. This impression is reinforced by the manner in which Louis subsequently reappeared in southern politics.

The late autumn of 871 saw a large Aghlabid army besiege Salerno.[151] Months after having been involved in driving Louis out, Guaifer of Salerno found himself in the invidious position of having to beg him to return to save him. Guaifer's embassy included not just the Prince of Salerno's son and heir, Guaimar, but also Bishops Landulf of Capua and Athanasius II of Naples, indicating widespread interest in Louis returning.[152] The siege of Salerno provided Louis with a perfect opportunity to return to southern Italy. A Frankish army sent by him and aided by Lombard contingents relieved Salerno in 872.[153] A policy of conflict with Muslim power in southern Italy seems to have consistently brought Louis his greatest gains. As a course of action it forced Louis into a path of total hostility to the Saracens, as any positive engagement with independent Muslims risked blurring his ideological message.

Louis's relationship, or lack thereof, with the Muslim states of mainland Italy thus makes sense when examined closely. The emperor had nothing to gain from diplomacy with the emirate of Bari, instead standing to suffer in prestige and credibility. Moreover, he could potentially benefit far more through hostility by potentially rallying southern Italy behind him. This case study helps us think in much wider terms about

147. Erchempert, *Historia*, c.34 247; Andreas of Bergamo, *Historia*, c.16 "Erant enim Franci separati per castellas vel civitates, fidentes absque ullo terrore, credentes fide Beneventanorum," 228–229. See Russo Mailler, "La politica meridionale"; Granier, "La captivité de l'empereur Louis II."

148. AB a.871 183.

149. Ibid.; "Chronicle of Salerno," 122.

150. John the Deacon, *Gesta episcoporum*, c.65 435.

151. Erchempert, *Historia*, c.35 247–248; "Chronicle of Salerno," 124–128.

152. Erchempert, *Historia*, c.36 248; *Vita Athanasii*, c.8 448; "Chronicle of Salerno," 123.

153. Erchempert, *Historia*, c.35 248.

Carolingian diplomacy. Louis was alive to the possibilities available to him, seeing opportunity in southern Italy through the impact of the emirates. But his options were also constrained by other considerations. His role as emperor placed demands upon his behaviour that limited his freedom for manoeuvre. Diplomatic relations with the Islamic world always took place within a much wider set of considerations and cannot be isolated from their political context.

## *Dogs in the Nighttime*

The late eighth and ninth centuries saw Muslim powers and the Carolingians in close proximity in the central Mediterranean. In a space where both engaged in diplomacy with other actors, the Carolingians with Byzantium, Bari with Benevento, they practised only very limited engagement with each other. This observation highlights the contingent nature of Carolingian contact with the Umayyads and ʿAbbāsids. Proximity did not make diplomacy automatic. North Africa and southern Italy demonstrate that both potential parties needed to feel that they would benefit from diplomatic relations for them to take place. Charlemagne showed signs of being actively interested in building contacts in North Africa. Nor are there any hints that the emirs of Bari would have rejected better relations with Louis II. The decision to engage in diplomatic relations was frequently taken not on the basis of the foreign power in question alone. Both Carolingians and Muslim rulers had to consider the impact such a step would have on both internal politics and their relations with other polities. Ibrāhīm I prioritised his efforts on managing his internal problems with his unruly standing army rather than making contact with Charlemagne. As the troubles faced by al-ʿAkkī showed, being associated with the Franks was a quick route to domestic opposition within Kairouan. Lothar I and Louis II faced pressure from other Carolingians to fight Saracens and protect the pope. From Louis's perspective, Bari was more useful as a goad to rally the Christian cities of southern Italy under his banner than as a potential diplomatic partner. All of these figures were navigating complicated situations, balancing opportunities in the face of difficulties and dangers. Similar considerations came into effect for ʿAbbāsid and Umayyad diplomacy with the Carolingians, but the circumstances there made diplomacy a more useful prospect.

CONCLUSION

# Death of an Elephant

IN THE YEAR 810 Abū al-ʿAbbās died.[1] The year of the elephant's passing was to be a busy one for Charlemagne, and filled with tragedy.[2] The annals record the eclipse of both the sun and the moon twice, the capture of Charlemagne's envoy by the Wilzi, a great plague wiping out the cattle herds of the empire, and the deaths of Charlemagne's son King Pippin of Italy and his daughter Rotrud.[3] It was also a year that displayed the full range of Charlemagne's interaction with the Islamic world. The same year that Charlemagne's largest souvenir from his ʿAbbāsid dealings perished saw Corsica attacked by Muslim pirates while the emperor negotiated peace with Emir al-Ḥakam I. In this book, the different types of Carolingian diplomacy with the Islamic world have been considered separately, but the annals provide a valuable reminder that all of these interactions could take place at the same time. The approach taken so far has been intended to untangle the distinct relations undertaken by Frankish leaders with the wide variety of Muslim powers they engaged with, which have been too often conflated in modern scholarship. The potential downside of doing so is that it can make it hard to see how these diplomatic entanglements fit into the wider activities of those who undertook them. This conclusion will attempt to redress that imbalance by bringing the strands of Carolingian relations with the Islamic world together.

To begin with a Frankish perspective, for Pippin III, after taking all the territory held by Muslims north of the Pyrenees, the Islamic world was a source of dynastic legitimacy, both through the stories told of the victories won by his father, Charles Martel, against invasions from al-Andalus

1. ARF a.810 131.
2. Hack, *Abul Abaz*, 38–41; Nelson, *King and Emperor*, 453–455.
3. ARF a.810 132–133.

and through the prestige diplomacy represented by the gifts and respect brought by the ambassadors sent by al-Manṣūr. By contrast, Charlemagne's relations with the Islamic world were more varied and involved. First, there was the potential for expansion, most notably in the Iberian Peninsula, but also across the Mediterranean. This promoted diplomacy in a number of ways. Charlemagne's wars with the Umayyads were not universally successful and often had to be ended by negotiation. But he also sought to extend his influence by allying with leading figures in the Upper March and in Ifrīqiya. The former helped him place pressure on Córdoba, while the latter formed part of a wider expansion of Carolingian power across the Mediterranean. Charlemagne's conquests in the Iberian Peninsula and in Italy brought his realms closer to the Islamic world. Such proximity had its perils. Raids, whether overland from al-Andalus or across the Mediterranean, were a problem that had to be dealt with, although here he preferred military means to diplomatic, building up fleets, reinforcing fortresses, and launching counterraids.

Like his father, for Charlemagne the caliphate ultimately offered a means to legitimise domestic political change through prestige diplomacy. His dealings with Hārūn al-Rashīd, and the extraordinary presents that the caliph sent, allowed him to bring a sense of wonder and scale to a regime that from the 790s had an increasingly ambitious agenda of legislative, religious, moral, and cultural reform. Following on from this was an interest in the well-being of Christians living across the Islamic world. Charlemagne sent money to his coreligionists in al-Andalus, North Africa, Egypt, Syria, and Jerusalem. Good relations with authorities in Ifrīqiya and the caliphate enabled this patronage, and Charlemagne's major investment in the Holy Land took place with Hārūn's blessing. The Frankish ruler's perception of the needs of the Christians of al-Andalus also shaped his relations with the Muslim powers of the Iberian Peninsula, by motivating him to send missionaries and other agents and providing him with friendly contacts who could offer information. If we are to believe his letter to Archbishop Elipandus, Charlemagne's desire to liberate the Christian community also inspired his wars with Córdoba.

As this indicates, Charlemagne engaged with Muslim powers for a wide variety of reasons. Often multiple motivations were at play in the same set of relations, as in the case of his embassies to Hārūn al-Rashīd, which could be both prestige diplomacy for a domestic audience and aimed at helping the Patriarch of Jerusalem, with the former taking precedence. These relations were not equally fruitful. Those with the ʿAbbāsids were broadly successful, even if they cost the lives of an absurdly high number of diplomats, because they brought Charlemagne prestige and enabled him to support Christians in the Holy Land. Elsewhere was more of a mixed bag. His friendly relations with the governor of Ifrīqiya were short-lived because his ally, Muḥammad al-ʿAkkī, was quickly overthrown, at least in part as a consequence of those relations. None of al-ʿAkkī's successors were willing to have as close a relationship with him. In al-Andalus, Charlemagne succeeded in building a coalition of Muslim allies among disaffected border lords and renegade Umayyad princes but was unable to turn this into more than minor gains. The emirs of Córdoba remained autonomous and dangerous neighbours, and the biggest prize won in decades of Carolingian warfare was Barcelona. Even Charlemagne's attempts to use diplomacy to end his wars with al-Ḥakam I in 810 and 812 seem to have been of limited success, with unwanted fighting soon breaking out again.

A further important observation is that this contact with the Islamic world was not evenly distributed throughout Charlemagne's reign. Barring the invasion of al-Andalus in 778, the overwhelming majority of Charlemagne's engagement with Muslim polities took place in the period after 790. In part this was a consequence of realities on the ground. The annual Frankish campaigning in al-Andalus that began in 796 was prompted by the outbreak of civil war that followed the accession of al-Ḥakam I, and sustained by the near permanent presence of a capable adult Carolingian captain in the form of Louis the Pious. But this wider chronology was also the result of the expansion of Carolingian power and ambition. The latter inspired prestige diplomacy with the caliphate, attempts to aid Christians in the Islamic world, and efforts to extend Carolingian influence in the Iberian Peninsula and the Western Mediterranean. All of these were enabled by the growth of Frankish power, which in turn brought the empire face-to-face with rival polities, such as the Umayyad emirate, or exposed them to raiders over land and sea, driving further conflict.

Louis the Pious scaled back this diplomatic activity. Although he received envoys from al-Maʾmūn in 831, there is no evidence that he initiated any contact or desired to deepen his relations with the caliph. Nor is there any hint that he shared his father's interest in North Africa. The stability of the empire in Louis's early reign suggests that we should read this as a deliberate choice on his part rather than a sign of weakness. By contrast, frontier diplomacy with the Umayyads was not optional, something that Louis, as a former king of Aquitaine, understood completely. The emperor engaged in frustrating relations with Córdoba, as his truces with first al-Ḥakam and then ʿAbd al-Raḥmān II were repeatedly broken by the Umayyads, who saw opportunity in the fraying coalition of Franks,

Basques, and Goths who had previously protected the Spanish March. Pamplona was effectively independent from 824.

This weakness was fully revealed by the crisis of 826–828. This was significant not only because an Andalusi army was able to pillage the Spanish March with impunity. The battle between Willemund and Aizo on one side and Bernard of Septimania on the other made clear the breakdown in unity on the March. It also marked the first time that Frankish lords made common cause with the Umayyad emirate. Others would follow their example. The disaster also established the conditions for the sequence of coups and countercoups that would pit Louis and his sons against each other for much of the 830s, distracting the emperor from his efforts to regain the upper hand in al-Andalus by allying with rebels in Mérida. This set a pattern for the early reign of Charles the Bald. Occupied with other threats, including his brothers, and having to battle his nephew Pippin II for authority in Aquitaine, Charles sought good relations with Córdoba but was in a weak position to enforce peace with the Umayyads. The different factions in Aquitaine sought help from al-Andalus, with Charles coming to an understanding with the mightiest of the border lords, Mūsā b. Mūsā, while allies of Pippin gained backing from ʿAbd al-Raḥmān and from Mūsā's local rivals. The situation stabilized for Charles by the mid-860s, following the death of Pippin and the end of civil war in Aquitaine, and the growing instability of Umayyad control over much of al-Andalus in the second half of the reign of Muḥammad I.

Interestingly, Charles chose to use this breathing space to focus his attention on affairs elsewhere in the Frankish world, so this period marks the end of Carolingian diplomacy with the Umayyads. Relations with the rest of the Islamic world appear to have effectively ended in 831. This is not to say that Muslims were unimportant for the Carolingians in the rest of the ninth century. In Italy, Lothar I and Louis II dedicated a huge amount of energy to battling Saracens, particularly after the sack of Rome in 846. This culminated in the latter's capture of Bari in 871. Neither Lothar nor Louis was interested in talking to the fledgling emirates of Italy, preferring to build coalitions among the Christian princes of the region instead or to ally with the Byzantines. The Muslims of Italy could offer them little, and presented both a possible danger to their legitimacy and an opportunity to unite the fractious cities of the south under Carolingian authority in an anti-Saracen league.

It is tempting to view diplomacy with Muslim powers as a manifestation of the growing and then shrinking confidence and ambition of the Carolingian family. There is something to such a perspective. The zenith of Carolingian relations with the Islamic world in around 794–831 surely speaks to a particular moment when Charlemagne and Louis the Pious were secure and powerful enough to reach out across long distances. Likewise, changes in the nature of relations with the Umayyads reflect the ebb and flow of the balance of power between the Carolingians and the emirate. That said, we should resist the urge to draw a simple narrative of decline from the death of Charlemagne.[4] The lack of diplomacy with the ʿAbbāsids after 831 was a choice. Charlemagne's grandsons regularly sent money to the Patriarch of Jerusalem and could presumably have dispatched envoys to Samarra had they so desired. Nor were Louis the Pious and Charles the Bald incompetent in their dealings with al-Andalus. Rather, both actively sought to build useful alliances in the Iberian Peninsula. Charles's interest in the Christians of al-Andalus, particularly in the martyrs of Córdoba, speaks against a straightforward narrative of the Frankish world under siege.

Understanding relations with the Islamic world purely as a manifestation of Carolingian greatness also removes the role played by the Muslim rulers who engaged with the Frankish world. On one level, the Umayyads of Córdoba did not get a choice in the matter. The same logic of frontier diplomacy that forced Carolingian rulers to keep a wary eye on al-Andalus was also at play in reverse. Given the level of Frankish aggression during the reign of Charlemagne, ʿAbd al-Raḥmān I and particularly Hishām I and al-Ḥakam I were if anything more incentivized than their northern counterpart to keep tabs on their powerful neighbour. Yet the strategy they employed was far from defensive. Umayyad armies raided Frankish territory for plunder, glory, and religious legitimation. In this, the emirs treated the Carolingian realm as a larger, more dangerous version of the other Christian polities of the Iberian Peninsula such as Asturias and later Galicia and Pamplona.

This was enabled by diplomatic means. Al-Ḥakam used treaties with Charlemagne and Louis the Pious to disarm and slow Frankish retribution, while breaking the peace whenever was opportune for him. As the unity of the Spanish March and Aquitaine frayed, ʿAbd al-Raḥmān II was able to ally with disgruntled figures such as Aizo and William of Septimania, which gave him further opportunities to raid and undermine Louis and Charles the Bald. This aggressive approach changed in the second half of Muḥammad I's reign, as growing domestic difficulties made holding onto the centre of al-Andalus a challenge. Under this pressure,

4. De Jong, "The Empire That Was Always Decaying."

a long-lasting peace with Charles became more desirable, culminating in the peace of 865 and the gift of camels.

Carolingian diplomacy with Córdoba was as much a product of Umayyad power as Frankish. The growing reach of ʿAbd al-Raḥmān I made the two polities neighbours from the 780s. The Umayyad capacity to raid incentivized Carolingian rulers to send embassies. From the 810s much of the rhythm of these relations was set by the emirs and their desire for war or peace, forcing Louis the Pious and Charles the Bald to respond to them. As a consequence, the domestic politics of al-Andalus became crucial in determining dealings with the Franks, with the Umayyads being motivated to impress their subjects in their piety and power, and to reassert their presence in the Upper March. As the capacity of Córdoba to control much beyond the Guadalquivir collapsed in the 860s and 870s, so too did their incentive or means to engage with the Franks.

ʿAbbāsid involvement in prestige diplomacy with the Carolingians was entirely voluntary. Although al-Manṣūr and Hārūn al-Rashīd were approached by Pippin III and Charlemagne, they chose to respond, while al-Maʿmūn sent an embassy to Louis the Pious entirely unprompted. These caliphs were actively interested in a relationship with the Franks. The contacts that ensued formed part of the wider political strategies being practiced at their courts. All three ʿAbbāsid rulers were engaged in expansive relations across Afro-Eurasia, with the cumulative consequence of placing the caliph at the centre of the world and impressing a domestic audience with the proof of the esteem in which they were held. While this made the Carolingians part of a grander menagerie, they were not the smallest beast in the enclosure. The reputation of the Franks for their disciplined ferocity and the quality of their weapons made gifts and tribute from them an impressive achievement, and one remarked on by Christian writers in the caliphate.

It is striking that in times of stress, ʿAbbāsid caliphs looked west. Al-Manṣūr did so while attempting to lay the basis of the ʿAbbāsid regime in peacetime. Hārūn was on the brink of implementing a radical new succession plan and removing his Barmakid advisers, when he received Charlemagne's envoys. Al-Maʿmūn sent his embassy shortly after returning the capital to Baghdad after decades of war and being based in the east. As a consequence, relations between the caliphate and the Carolingians trace the changing fortunes of the ʿAbbāsid dynasty. Diplomacy with the Franks represented the mix of confidence and uncertainty that characterized caliphal rule in the period, on the one hand ambitious enough to reach across continents, on the other in desperate need of the raw materials of glamour to impress and overawe challengers within their permanently restive empire.

Few of these relationships demonstrate more clearly the need for buy-in from Muslim rulers than Charlemagne's efforts to involve himself in North Africa. Despite the Frankish ruler's apparently continued interest in the region for multiple decades, he appears to have achieved sustained contact with a leader in Ifrīqiya once, in the form of Muḥammad al-ʿAkkī. The swift and unhappy fate of al-ʿAkkī helps illustrate why North African figures were unwilling to engage with Charlemagne. The risks were so great and the potential rewards so slim that only someone truly desperate would accept support from the Franks, and that was unlikely to be a lasting relationship even if Carolingian contact did not help undermine their North African ally. Ifrīqiya remained beyond regular Frankish diplomacy not because it was beyond Carolingian fleets or interest but because Muslim rulers in the region had no reciprocal interest in what Charlemagne had to offer.

All of this suggests that diplomacy between the Frankish and the Islamic worlds mattered for all parties. The importance of these contacts naturally varied. Diplomacy between the Carolingians and ʿAbbāsids was valuable not just for the gifts brought but as a statement of power and authority, a display of respect from a distant ruler which could be presented to overawe domestic audiences. Nonetheless, contact between the Franks and the caliphate paled in political significance in comparison to that with other Muslim powers. The stretch of Charlemagne's interests and zone of political involvement across the Mediterranean made him a factor to be considered by North African leaders, offering both opportunity and potential menace. More important was the diplomatic relationship between the Carolingians and al-Andalus. The two powers were each other's most formidable neighbour. They thus represented both the greatest danger and the greatest potential rewards.

Our understanding of the Carolingian empire frequently focuses upon the royal heartlands between the Seine and the Rhine. An examination of Carolingian relations with the Umayyads reveals much. Managing al-Andalus became increasingly important from the 820s. Failing to do so could lead to crisis, as in the case of the overrunning of the Spanish March in 848 and 849, or even disaster, as the fallout from the 827 expedition demonstrates. Likewise, Charlemagne's interest in North Africa is a prompt to reconsider the Carolingians as a Mediterranean power rather than as a purely European phenomenon. The "Carolingian South" mattered in the calculations of Aachen and Compiègne.

Despite how piecemeal and disjointed this diplomacy was, the rulers involved came to be defined by it. Posterity measured the emirs of Córdoba by their capacity to manage their northern neighbours. Hārūn al-Rashīd would be rendered recognizable even when anonymous in Arabic apocalypse by the gifts he received from the Franks. Such memory was strongest in the former Carolingian world. In 1843, King Frederick William IV of Prussia ordered the opening of the Karlsschrein in Aachen Cathedral containing Charlemagne's body.[5] Inside, the remains of the emperor were found wrapped in a splendid silk shroud dominated by images of elephants, probably woven in Constantinople in the eleventh century, now on display in the Aachen Cathedral Treasury. Exactly when the shroud reached Aachen is unclear, although the most plausible occasions would be the exhumation of Charlemagne's body by Frederick I Barbarossa on Christmas 1165 or the final placing of the remains in their current shrine by Frederick II in 1215.[6] Whatever the occasion, the design of the silk suggests the continued importance of Abū al-ʿAbbās to the memory of Charlemagne. Long after both elephant and emperor had passed away, the two remained bound together in death.

5. Tschacher, "Karl der Große," 33.
6. Latowsky, *Emperor of the World*, 183–185, 251–255.

# BIBLIOGRAPHY

## *Manuscripts*


Paris. Bibliothèque Nationale. Lat. 12302. Cited in John J. Contreni, "Haimo of Auxerre's Commentary on Ezechiel." In *L'École Carolingienne d'Auxerre: De Murethach à Remi*, edited by Dominique Iogna-Prat, Colette Jeudy, and Guy Lobrichon, 229–242. Paris: Beauchesne, 1991.

Vatican City. Biblioteca Apostolica. Vat.lat.3852. *Digital Vatican Library*. digi.vatlib.it/view/MSS_Vat.lat.3852.


## *Primary Sources*


Ibn ʿAbd al-Ḥakam. *Conquête de l'Afrique du Nord et de l'Espagne*. 2nd ed. Translated by Albert Gateau. Algiers: Carbonel, 1947.

Abū Yūsuf. *Kitab-ul-Kharaj*. Translated by Abid Ahmad Ali, revised by Abdul Hameed Siddiqui. Lahore: Islamic Book Centre, 1979.

Adomnán. *De locis sanctis*. Edited by Ludwig Bieler, 177–234. CCSL 175. Turnhout: Brepols, 1965.

Agobard of Lyons. *De insolentia Iudaeorum*. Edited by Lieven Van Acker, 189–195. CCCM 52. Turnhout: Brepols, 1981.

———. *De iudaicis superstitionibus et erroribus*. Edited by Lieven Van Acker, 197–221. CCCM 52. Turnhout: Brepols, 1981.

———. *Epistolae*. Edited by Ernst Dümmler, 150–239. *MGH Epp 5*. Berlin: Weidmann, 1899.

Aimoin. *De translatione SS. Martyrum Georgii Monachi, Aurelii et Nathaliae, ex Urbe Corduba Parisios*, 941–948. PL 115.

———. *Historia translationis sancti Vincentii levitae et martyris, ex Hispania in Castrense Galliae monasterium*, 1011–1026. PL 126.

Akhbār Majmūʿa. *A History of Early al-Andalus: The Akhbār Majmūʿa*. Translated by David James. London: Routledge, 2012.

Alcuin. *Carmen 81*. Edited by Ernst Dümmler, 300. *MGH Poet. 1*. Berlin: Weidmann, 1881.

———. *Epistolae*. Edited by Ernst Dümmler, 1–481. *MGH Epp 4.2*. Berlin: Weidmann, 1905.

———. "Letter to Beatus of Liebana." In *England and the Continent in the Eighth Century*, edited by Wilhelm Levison, 318. Oxford: Clarendon Press, 1946.

Amalarius of Trier. *Versus Marini*. Edited by Ernst Dümmler, 426–428. *MGH Poet. 1*. Berlin: Weidmann, 1881.

Anastasius Bibliothecarius. *Interpretatio Synodi VIII generali*, 9–196. PL 129.

Andreas of Bergamo. "The Annals of Aniane." In *Chronicon Moissiacense Maius: A Carolingian World Chronicle: From Creation until the First Years of Louis the*

*Pious*. 2 vols. Edited by Ir.J.M.J.G. Kats, prepared by David Claszen. Leiden: University of Leiden Research MA thesis, 2012.

———. *Historia*. Edited by Georg Waitz, 222–230. *MGH SRL*. Hannover: Hahn, 1878.

*Annales Bertiniani*. Translated by Félix Grat, Jeanne Vielliard, and Suzanne Clémencet. Edited by Léon Levillain. Paris: C. Klincksieck, 1964. *The Annals of St. Bertin: Ninth Century Histories, I*. Translated and annotated by Janet L. Nelson. Manchester: Manchester University Press, 1991.

*Annales Fontanellenses*. Edited by Georg Heinrich Pertz, 301–304. *MGH SS 2*. Hannover: Hahn, 1829.

*Annales Fuldenses*. Edited by Friedrich Kurze. *MGH SRG 7*. Hannover: Hahn, 1891.

*The Annals of Fulda: Ninth Century Histories, II*. Translated and annotated by Timothy Reuter. Manchester: Manchester University Press, 1992.

*Annales Laureshamenses*. Edited by Georg Heinrich Pertz, 22–39. *MGH SS 1*. Hannover: Hahn, 1826,

*Annales Laurissenses minores*. Edited by H. Schnorr von Carolsfeld. "Das Chronicon Laurissense breve." *Neues Archiv der Gesellschaft* 36 (1911): 15–39.

*Annales Mettenses priores*. Edited by Bernard von Simson. *MGH SRG 10*. Hannover: Hahn, 1905. Translated by Richard A. Gerberding and Paul Fouracre, 330–370. *Late Merovingian France: History and Hagiography, 640–720*. Manchester: Manchester University Press, 1996.

*Annales Mosellani*. Edited by J. M. Lappenberg, 491–499. *MGH SS 16*. Hannover: Hahn, 1859.

*Annales regni Francorum*. Edited by Friedrich Kurze. *MGH SRG 6*. Hannover: Hahn, 1895. Translated by Bernhard W. Scholz, 35–125. *Carolingian Chronicles*. Ann Arbor: University of Michigan Press, 1972.

*Annales Xantenses*. Edited by Bernhard de Simson, 1–39. *MGH SRG 12*. Hannover: Hahn, 1909.

Anonymous Description. *Una descripción anónima de al-Andalus, Vol. 2*. Edited and translated by Luis Molina. Madrid: Consejo Superior de Investigaciones Científicas, 1983.

Ardo/Smaragdus. *Vita Benedicti abb. Anianensis*. Edited by Georg Waitz, 200–220. *MGH SS 15*. Hannover: Hahn, 1887.

The Astronomer. *Vita Hludowici imperatoris*. Edited by Ernst Tremp, 279–555. *MGH SRG 64*. Hannover: Hahn, 1995. Translated by Thomas F. X. Noble, 219–302. *Charlemagne and Louis the Pious: The Lives by Einhard, Notker, Ermoldus, Thegan, and the Astronomer*. University Park: Pennsylvania State University Press, 2009.

Ibn al-Athīr. *Annales du Maghreb et de l'Espagne*. Translated by Edmond Fagnan. Algiers: A. Jourdan, 1898.

Audradus Modicus. *Book of Revelations*. Edited by Ludwig Traube. "O Roma nobilis: Philologische Untersuchungen aus dem Mittelalter." *Abhandlungen der Philosophisch-Philologischen Classe der Königlich Bayerischen Akademie der Wissenschaften* 19 (1891): 297–396.

Al-Balādhurī. *The Origins of the Islamic State*. Vol. 1. Translated by Philip K. Hitti. New York: Columbia University, 1916.

Beatus of Liébana and Heterius of Osma. *Adversus Elipandum libri II*. Edited by Bengt Löfstedt. CCCM 59. Turnhout: Brepols, 1984.

Bede. *Commentary on Acts*. Edited by Max L. W. Laistner, 3–99. CCSL 121. Turnhout, 1983.

——. *Commentary on Genesis*. Edited by Charles W. Jones. CCSL 118A. Turnhout: Brepols, 1967. Translated by Calvin B. Kendall. *Bede: On Genesis*. Liverpool: Liverpool University Press, 2008.

——. *Commentary on Samuel*. Edited by David Hurst, 5–287. CCSL 119. Turnhout: Brepols, 1962.

Bernard. *Itinerarium*. Edited by Titus Tobler and Auguste Molinier, 308–320. *Itinera Hierosolymitana et descriptiones Terrae Sanctae bellis sacris anteriora & latina lingua exarata* 1.2. Geneva: J. G. Frick, 1880.

Boniface. *Epistolae*. Edited by Michael Tangl. *MGH Ep. Sel. 1*. Berlin: Weidmann, 1916.

*Book of Gifts and Rarities*. Translated by Ghāda al Hijjāwī al-Qaddūmī. Cambridge, MA: Harvard University Press, 1996.

Cassiodorus. *Variae*. Edited by Theodor Mommsen. *MGH AA 12*. Berlin: Weidmann, 1894. Translated by S.J.B. Barnish. *The Variae of Magnus Aurelius Cassiodorus Senator*. Liverpool: Liverpool University Press, 1992.

*CC.2.ii*: *Els diplomes Carolingis a Catalunya*. Edited by Ramón d'Abadal i de Vinyals. Barcelona: Institut d'Estudis Catalans, 1952.

*CC.3*: *Els Comtats de Pallars i Ribagorça*. Edited by Ramón d'Abadal i de Vinyals. Barcelona: Institut d'Estudis Catalans, 1955.

*Chanson de Roland, The Song of Roland: The French Corpus*. Vol. 1. Edited by Joseph J. Duggan. Turnhout: Brepols, 2005.

Charlemagne. *Admonitio generalis*. Edited by Alfred Boretius, 52–62. *MGH Capit 1*, no. 22. Hannover: Hahn, 1883.

——. *Capitula a missis dominicis ad comites directa*. Edited by Alfred Boretius, 183–184. *MGH Capit 1*, no. 85. Hannover: Hahn, 1883.

——. *Capitulare de villis*. Edited by Alfred Boretius, 82–91. *MGH Capit 1*, no. 32. Hannover: Hahn, 1883.

——. *Capitulare Haristallense*. Edited by Alfred Boretius, 46–51. *MGH Capit 1*, no. 20. Hannover: Hahn, 1883.

——. *Capitulare missorum Aquisgranense primum*. Edited by Alfred Boretius, 152–154. *MGH Capit 1*, no. 64. Hannover: Hahn, 1883.

——. *Capitulare missorum generale*. Edited by Alfred Boretius, 114–116. *MGH Capit 1*, no. 40. Hannover: Hahn, 1883.

——. *Divisio regnorum*. Edited by Alfred Boretius, 126–130. *MGH Capit 1*, no. 45. Hannover: Hahn, 1883.

——. *Epistolae*. Edited by Ernst Dümmler. *MGH Epp 4.2*. Berlin: Weidmann, 1895.

——. *Memoratorium missis datum ad papam Adrianum legatis*. Edited by Alfred Boretius, 225. *MGH Capit 1*, no. 111. Hannover: Hahn, 1883.

Charles the Bald. *Recueil des actes de Charles II de Chauve, roi de France*, 2. Edited by Georges Tessier. Paris: Impr. Nationale, 1952.

Christian of Stavelot. *Expositio super librum generationis*. Edited by R.B.C. Huygens. CCCM 224. Turnhout: Brepols, 2008.

*Chronica Sancti Benedicti Casinensis*. Edited by Georg Waitz, 468–488. *MGH SS 15*. Hannover: Hahn, 1887.

"The Chronicle of Albelda." In *Crónicas asturianas: Crónica de Alfonso III (Rotense y "A Sebastián"): Crónica Albeldense (y "Profética")*, 151–188. Edited by Juan Gil Fernández and translated by José L. Moralejo and Juan I. Ruiz de la Peña. Oviedo: University of Oviedo, 1985.

"The Chronicle of Alfonso III." In *Crónicas asturianas: Crónica de Alfonso III (Rotense y "A Sebastián"): Crónica Albeldense (y "Profética")*, 113–149. Edited by Juan Gil Fernández and translated by José L. Moralejo and Juan I. Ruiz de la Peña. Oviedo: University of Oviedo, 1985.

"The Chronicle of Fredegar." In *Quellen zur Geschichte des 7. und 8. Jahrhunderts*, 44–271. Edited by Andreas Kusternig and Herbert Haupt. Darmstadt: Wissenschaftliche Buchgesellschaft, 1982.

*Chronicle of Moissac*. In *Chronicon Moissiacense Maius: A Carolingian World Chronicle: From Creation until the First Years of Louis the Pious*. 2 vols. Edited by Ir.J.M.J.G. Kats, prepared by David Claszen. Leiden: University of Leiden Research MA thesis, 2012.

"The Chronicle of Salerno." In *Chronicon Salernitanum: A Critical Edition with Studies on Literary and Historical Sources and on Language*. Edited by Ulla Westerbergh. Lund: Almquist & Wiksell, 1956.

"Chronicle of 754." In *Continuatio isidoriana hispana: Crónica Mozárabe de 754*. Edited and translated by J. Eduardo López Pereira. León: Centro de Estudios e Investigación San Isidoro, 2009.

Claudius of Turin. *Epistolae*. Edited by Ernst Dümmler, 600–602. *MGH Epp 4.4*, no. 6. Berlin: Weidmann, 1895.

*Codex Diplomaticus Cajetanus, Part I. Tabularium Casinense I*. Monte Cassino: Typis Archicoenobii Montis Cassino, 1969.

*Concilia Africae, a. 345–a. 525*. Edited by Charles Munier. CCSL 149. Turnhout: Brepols, 1974.

*Concilium Aquisgranense*. Edited by Albert Werminghoff, 307–464. *MGH Conc 2.1*, no. 39. Hannover: Hahn, 1906.

Constantine Porphyrogenitus. *De administrando imperio*. Edited by Gyula Moravcsik, translated by Romilly J. H. Jenkins. Washington, DC: Dumbarton Oaks, 1985.

*Continuation of the Chronicle of Ado of Vienne*. Edited by Georg Heinrich Pertz, 324–325. *MGH SS* 2. Hannover: Hahn, 1829.

"The Continuations of the Chronicle of Fredegar." In *Quellen zur Geschichte des 7. und 8. Jahrhunderts*, 272–324. Edited by Andreas Kusternig and Herbert Haupt. Darmstadt: Wissenschaftliche Buchgesellschaft, 1982.

Dhuoda. *Liber manualis*. Edited and translated by Marcelle Thiébaux. Cambridge: Cambridge University Press, 1998.

Dicuil. *Liber de mensura Orbis terrae*. Edited by James J. Tierney. Dublin: Scriptores Latini Hiberniae, 1967.

Dudo of Saint-Quentin. *De moribus et actis primorum Normanniae ducum*. Edited by Jules A. Lair. Caen: F. Le Blanc-Hardel, 1865.

Einhard. *Epistolae*. Edited by Karl Hampe, 105–145. *MGH Epp 5*. Berlin: Weidmann, 1899. Translated by Paul Edward Dutton. *Charlemagne's Courtier: The Complete Einhard*, 131–220. Peterborough, Ontario: Broadview Press, 1998.

——. *Translatio et miracula SS Marcellini et Petri*. Edited by Georg Waitz and Wilhelm Wattenbach, 238–264. *MGH SS 15*. Hannover: Hahn, 1888.

——. *Vita Karoli Magni*. Edited by Georg Heinrich Pertz and Georg Waitz. *MGH SRG 25*. Hannover: Hahn, 1911.

Elias III. Epistola. *Spicilegium sive collectio veterum aliquot scriptorum*. Vol. 3. Edited by Luc d'Achery, 363–364. Paris: Montalant, 1723.

*Epitaphia Hadriana Papae*. Edited by Ernst Dümmler, 113–114. *MGH Poet. 1*. Berlin: Weidmann, 1881.

Erchempert. *Historia Langobardorum Beneventi*. Edited by Georg Heinrich Pertz and Georg Waitz, 231–265. *MGH SRL*. Hannover: Hahn, 1878.

Ermold the Black. *In honorem Hludovici*. In *Poème sur Louis le Pieux et Épitres au roi Pépin*. Edited and translated by Edmond Faral, 1–201. Paris: Honore Champion, 1964. Translated by Thomas F. X. Noble, 119–186. *Charlemagne and Louis the Pious: The Lives by Einhard, Notker, Ermoldus, Thegan, and the Astronomer*. University Park: Pennsylvania State University Press, 2009.

——. "Letters to Pippin I." In *Poème sur Louis le Pieux et Épitres au roi Pépin*. Edited and translated by Edmond Faral, 202–232.

Eulogius. *Memoriale sanctorum*. Edited by Juan Gil, 365–459. *CSM 2*. Madrid: Instituto Antonio de Nebrija, 1973.

——. *Tertius epistolae ad Wiliesindum*. Edited by Juan Gil, 497–503. *CSM 2*. Madrid: Instituto Antonio de Nebrija, 1973.

Eusebius-Jerome. *Die Chronik des Hieronymus*. Edited by Rudolf Helm. Berlin: Akademie Verlag, 1956.

*Ex miraculi S. Genesii*. Edited by Georg Waitz, 169–172. *MGH SS 15.1*. Berlin: Weidmann, 1887.

Ibn Faḍlān. *Ibn Fadlan and the Land of Darkness: Arab Travellers in the Far North*. Translated by Paul Lunde and Caroline Stone, 3–58. London: Penguin, 2012.

Ibn al-Farrāʿ. *Diplomacy in the Early Islamic World: A Tenth-Century Treatise on Arab-Byzantine Relations*. Translated by Maria Vaiou. London: I. B. Tauris, 2009.

Florus of Lyons. *De iniusta vexatione ecclesiae Lugdunensis*. Edited by Ernst Dümmler, 555–559. *MGH Poet. 2*, no. 27. Berlin: Weidmann, 1884.

——. *Qualiter sanctorum martyrum Cypriani sperati Pantaleonis reliquiae Lugdunum advectae sint*. Edited by Ernst Dümmler, 544–546. *MGH Poet. 2*, no. 13. Berlin: Weidmann, 1884.

——. *Querela de divisione imperii*. Edited by Ernst Dümmler, 559–564. *MGH Poet. 2*, no. 28. Berlin: Weidmann, 1884.

——. *Ubi ossa sancti Cipriani Lugduni condita habentur*. Edited by Ernst Dümmler. *MGH Poet. 2*, no. 14. Berlin: Weidmann, 1884.

*Formulae Salzburgenses*. Edited by Karl Zeumer, 453–454. *MGH Formulae*, no. 62. Hannover: Hahn, 1886.

*Fragmentum Chesnianum*. Edited by Georg Heinrich Pertz, 34. *MGH SS 1*. Hannover: Hahn, 1826.

George of Ostia. *Epistola ad Hadrianum papam*. Edited by Ernst Dümmler, 19–29. *MGH Epp 4*. Berlin: Weidmann, 1905.

"Gesta abbatum Fontenellensium." In *Chronique des abbés de Fontenelle*, edited by Pascal Pradié, 1–194. Paris: Belles Lettres, 1999.

*Gesta comitum Barcinonensium: Textos llatí i catalá editats i anotats*. Edited by Louis Barrau-Dihigo and Jaime Massó Torrents. Barcelona: Impremta de la casa de caritat, 1925.

"Gesta sanctorum Rotonensium." In *The Monks of Redon: Gesta sanctorum Rotonensium and Vita Conuuoionis*. Edited and translated by Caroline Brett, 106–222. Woodbridge: Boydell Press, 1989.

Al-Gharnāṭī. "*Tuḥfat al-Albāb*." Edited by Gabriel Ferrand. *Journal Asiatique* 207 (1925): 32–148.

Ibn Ḥabīb. *Kitāb al-Tārīkh*. Edited by Jorge Aguadé. Madrid: Fuentes Arábico-Hispanas, 1991.

Hadrian I. *Epistolae*. Edited by Wilhelm Gundlach, 567–648. *MGH Epp 3*. Berlin: Weidmann, 1892.

Hadrian II. *Epistolae*. Edited by Ernst Perels, 691–765. *MGH Epp 6*. Berlin: Weidmann, 1925.

Haimo of Auxerre. *Commentary on Ezekiel*. Paris BNF Lat. 12302.

Ibn Ḥayyān. *Anales Palatinos del Califa de Córdoba al-Hakam II*. Translated by Emilio García Gómez. Madrid: Sociedad de Estudios y Publicaciones, 1967.

——. *Crónica de los emires Alḥakam I y ʿAbdarraḥmān II entre los años 796 y 847 (Almuqtabis II-1)*. Edited and translated by Maḥmūd ʿAlī Makkī and Federico Corriente. Zaragoza: Instituto de Estudios Islámicos y del Oriente Próximo, 2001.

——. "Pasajes del 'Muqtabis' de Ibn Ḥayyān de interes para la historia del siglo IX." Translated by Maḥmūd ʿAlī Makkī. *Cuadernos de Historia de España* 41–42 (1965): 336–339.

Herodotus. *The Histories*. Translated by Robin Waterfield. Oxford: Oxford University Press, 1998.

Hilāl al-Ṣābiʾ. *Rusūm Dār al-Khilāfah: The Rules and Regulations of the ʿAbbāsid Court*. Translated by Elie Abid Salem. Beirut: American University of Beirut, 1977.

Hincmar of Rheims. *De ordine palatii*. Edited by Thomas Gross and Rudolf Schieffer. *MGH Fontes Iuris* 3. Hannover: Hahn, 1980.

——. *De translationibus episcoporum, contra Actardum Namnetensem*. 210–230. PL 126.

Ibn Hishām. *The Life of Muḥammad*. Translated by Alfred Guillaume. Karachi: Oxford University Press, 1987.

Hrabanus Maurus. *Commentaria in libros IV Regum*. 9–290. PL 109.

——. *De rerum naturis*. 9–614. PL 111.

Hygeburg. *Vita Willibaldi episcopi Eichstetensis*. Edited by Oswald Holder-Egger, 86–106. *MGH SS 15.1*. Hannover: Hahn, 1887.

Ibn ʿIdhārī. "El emirato de Muḥammad I en el Bayān al-Mugrib de Ibn ʿIdārī." Translated by Juan Antonio Souto. *Anaquel de estudios árabes* 6 (1995): 209–247.

——. *Textos dels historiadors àrabs referents a la Catalunya carolíngia*. Translated by José María Millàs i Vallicrosa. Barcelona: Institut d'estudis catalans, 1987.

Isidore of Seville. *Etymologia, Isidori Hispalensis episcopi Etymologiarum sive originum libri XX*. Edited by W. M. Lindsay. Oxford: Clarendon Press, 1911.

Kauṭilya. *King, Governance, and Law in Ancient India: Kauṭilya's Arthaśāstra*. Translated by Patrick Olivelle. Oxford: Oxford University Press, 2013.

Ibn Khaldūn. *Histoire des Berbères: Et des dynasties musulmanes de l'Afrique Septentrionale*. Vol. 1. Translated by Baron William McGuckin de Slane. Paris: P. Geuthner, 1991.

Ibn Khurradādhbih. "Le Livre des Routes et des Provinces, par Ibn-Khordadbeh." Edited and translated by Charles Barbier de Meynard. *Journal Asiatique*, 6th ser., 5 (1865): 5–127, 227–295, 446–534.

Al-Jāḥiẓ. *Le Livre de la Couronne*. Translated by Charles Pellat. Paris: Les Belles Lettres, 1954.

Jerome. *Commentarii in Amos*. Edited by Marc Adriaen, 211–348. CCSL 76. Turnhout: Brepols, 1967.

———. *Commentarii in Ezechielem*. Edited by François Glorie. CCSL 75. Turnhout: Brepols, 1964.

———. *Liber quaestionum hebraicarum in Genesim*. Edited by Paul de Lagarde, 1–56. CCSL 72. Turnhout: Brepols, 1959.

Jiménez de Rada, Rodrigo. *De rebus Hispanie; sive, Historia Gothica*. Edited by Juan Fernández Valverde. CCCM 72. Turnhout: Brepols, 1988.

John VIII. *Epistolae*. Edited by E. Caspar & G. Lähr, 1–329. *MGH Epp 7*. Berlin: Weidmann, 1928.

John the Deacon (Naples). *Gesta episcoporum Neapolitanum*. Edited by Georg Waitz, 424–436. *MGH SRL*. Hannover: Hahn, 1878.

John the Deacon (Venice). *Chronicon Venetum*. Edited by Georg Heinrich Pertz, 4–47. *MGH SS 7*. Hannover: Hahn, 1846.

John of Saint-Arnoul. *La vie de Jean, abbé de Gorze*. Translated by Michel Parisse. Paris: Picard, 1999.

Jonas of Orléans. *Instruction des laïcs*. Edited by Odile Dubreucq. Paris: Editions du Cerf, 2012.

———. *Le Métier de Roi: De institutione regia*. Edited by Alain Dubreucq. Paris: Editions du Cerf, 1995.

Julian of Toledo. *Historia Wambae regis*. Edited by Wilhelm Levison, 486–535. *MGH SRM 5*. Hannover: Hahn, 1910.

Leo III. *Epistolae*. Edited by Karl Hampe. *MGH Epp 5*. Berlin: Weidmann, 1899.

Leo IV. *Epistolae*. Edited by Adolf de Hirsch-Gereuth, 585–612. *MGH Epp 5*. Berlin: Weidmann, 1899.

*The Letter of Tansar*. Translated by Mary Boyce. Rome: Istituto Italiano per il Medio ed Estremo Oriente, 1968.

Łewond. *History of Lewond: The Eminent Vardapet of the Armenians*. Translated by Zaven Arzoumanian. Wynnewood Penn: St. Sahag and St. Mesrob Armenian Church, 1982.

*The Life of Michael the Synkellos*. Edited and translated by Mary B. Cunningham. Belfast: Belfast Byzantine Enterprises, 1991.

"Life of Sergius II." In *Liber Pontificalis*. 2nd ed. Vol. 2. Edited by Louis Duchesne, 86–105. Paris: E. Thorin, 1892.

"Life of Stephen II." In *Liber Pontificalis*. 2nd ed. Vol. 1. Edited by Louis Duchesne, 440–462. Paris: E. Thorin, 1892.

Liutolf. *Vita et translatio S. Severi*. Edited by Lothar de Heinemann, 289–293. *MGH SS 15.1*. Hannover: Hahn, 1887.

Lothar I. "Francia Oktober 846." Edited by Wilfried Hartmann, 133–139. *MGH Conc. 3*. Hannover: Hahn, 1984.

Louis the Pious. *Admonitio ad omnes regni ordines*. Edited by Alfred Boretius, 303–307. *MGH Capit 1*, no. 150. Hannover: Hahn, 1883.

———. *Capitula legibus addenda*. Edited by Alfred Boretius, 280–285. *MGH Capit 1*, no. 139. Hannover: Hahn, 1883.

———. *Capitulare de disciplina palatii Aquisgranis*. Edited by Alfred Boretius, 297–298. *MGH Capit 1*, no. 146. Hannover: Hahn, 1883.

———. *Capitulare missorum*. Edited by Alfred Boretius, 288–291. *MGH Capit 1*, no. 141. Hannover: Hahn, 1883.

———. *Formulae Imperiales*. Edited by Karl Zeumer, 285–328. *MGH Formulae*. Hannover: Hahn, 1886.

———. *Ordinatio imperii*. Edited by Alfred Boretius, 270–273. *MGH Capit 1*, no. 136. Hannover: Hahn, 1883.

———. *Urkunden*. Edited by Theo Kölzer. *MGH DD 2*. Wiesbaden: Harrassowitz, 2016.

Louis the Pious and Lothar I. *Hludowici et Hlotharii epistola generalis*. Edited by Albert Werminghoff, 599–601. *MGH Conc 2.2*. Hannover: Hahn, 1908.

Louis II. *Capitulare Papiense*. Edited by Alfred Boretius and Victor Krause, 85–88. *MGH Capit 2*, no. 213. Hannover: Hahn, 1897.

———. *Epistola ad Basilium I*. Edited by Walter Henze, 385–394. *MGH Epp 7*. Berlin: Weidmann, 1928.

Ibn Lūqā, Qusṭā. *Qusṭā Ibn Lūqā's Medical Regime for the Pilgrims to Mecca: The* Risālā Fī Tadbīr Safar Al-ḥajj. Translated by Gerrit Bos. Leiden: Brill, 1992.

Al-Maqqarī. *The History of the Mohammedan Dynasties in Spain*. Translated by Pascual de Gayangos. London: W. H. Allen and Co., 1840–1843. Reprint, Routledge, 2002.

Marculf. *Formulæ Marculfinæ ævi Karolini*. Edited by Karl Zeumer, 32–129. *MGH Formulae*. Hannover: Hahn, 1886. Translated by Alice Rio. *The Formularies of Angers and Marculf: Two Merovingian Legal Handbooks*. Liverpool: Liverpool University Press, 2008.

Al-Masʿūdī. *Les Prairies d'Or*. Translated by Charles Barbier de Meynard and Abel Pavet de Courteille. Paris: Imprimerie Impériale, 1965.

Millàs i Vallicrosa, Josep Ma. *Textos dels historiadors àrabs referents a la Catalunya: Carolíngia*. Barcelona: Institut d'Estudis Catalans, 1987.

Ibn Miskawayh. *The Eclipse of the ʿAbbāsid Caliphate: Classical Writings of the Medieval Islamic World*. Vol. 1. Edited and translated by Henry Frederick Amedroz and David Samuel Margoliouth. London: I. B. Tauris, 2015.

Movsēs Dasxuranc̣i. *The History of the Caucasian Albanians*. Translated by C.J.F. Dowsett. London: Oxford University Press, 1961.

*Monumenta negrologica monasterii s. Petri Salisburgensis*. Edited by Sigmund Herzberg-Fränkel, 3–64. *MGH Necr. 2*. Berlin: Weidmann, 1914.

Ibn al-Muqaffaʿ. *Kalila et Dimna*. Translated by Genevève Rossignol. Beirut: Dar Albouraq, 2011.

Nicholas I (Patriarch). *Letters: Nicholas I, Patriarch of Constantinople*. Translated by Romilly J. H. Jenkins and Leendert G. Westerink. Washington, DC: Dumbarton Oaks, 1973.

Nicholas I (Pope). *Epistolae*. Edited by Ernst Perels, 257–690. *MGH Epp 6*. Berlin: Weidmann, 1925.

Nithard. *Histoire des fils de Louis le Pieux*. Edited and translated by Philippe Lauer, revised by Sophie Glansdorff. Paris: Les Belles Lettres, 2012. Translated by Bernhard W. Scholz, 127–174. *Carolingian Chronicles*. Ann Arbor: University of Michigan Press, 1972.

Niẓām al-Mulk. *Siyāsatnāmeh*. Translated by Hubert Darke. *The Book of Government, or, Rules for Kings: The* Siyar al-Muluk *or* Siyasat-nama *of Nizam al-Mulk*. 2nd ed. London: Routledge and Paul, 1978.

Notker the Stammerer. *Gesta Karoli Magni imperatori*. Edited by Hans F. Haefele, *MGH SRG NS 12*. Berlin: Weidmann, 1959.

Al-Nuwayrī. *Textos dels historiadors àrabs referents a la Catalunya carolíngia*. Translated by José María Millàs i Vallicrosa. Barcelona: Institut d'estudis catalans, 1987.

Orosius. *Historiae Adversum Paganos*. Edited by Marie-Pierre Arnaud-Lindet. Paris: Belles Lettres, 1990.

Paschasius Radbertus. "*Epitaphium Arsenii*." Edited by Ernst Dümmler, 1–98. *Abhandlungen der Königlichen Akademie der Wissenschaften zu Berlin*, Philosophische und historische Klasse 2. Berlin: Koniglichen Akademie der Wissenschaften, 1900.

Paul I. *Epistolae*. Edited by Wilhelm Gundlach, 507–558. *MGH Epp 3*. Berlin: Weidmann, 1892.

Paul Alvar. *Alvaro de Córdoba y la polémica contra el Islam: El Indiculus luminosus*. Edited by Feliciano Delgado León. Córdoba: Publicaciones Obra Social y Cultural Cajasur, 1996.

———. *Vita Eulogii*. Edited by Juan Gil, 330–343. *CSM 1*. Madrid: Instituto Antonio de Nebrija, 1973.

Paul the Deacon. *Historia Langobardorum*. Edited by Ludwig Bethmann and Georg Waitz, 45–187. *MGH SRL*. Hannover: Hahn, 1878.

Poeta Saxo. *Annales de gestis Caroli magni imperatoris libri quinque*. Edited by P. de Winterfeld, 1–71. *MGH Poetae 4.1*. Berlin: Weidmann, 1899.

Pseudo-Methodios. "Revelations." *Apocalypse of Pseudo-Methodius. An Alexandrian World Chronicle*. Edited and translated by Benjamin Garstad, 74–139. Cambridge, MA: Harvard University Press, 2012.

Ibn al-Qūṭīya. *Early Islamic Spain: The History of Ibn al-Qūṭīya*. Translated by David James. London: Routledge, 2009.

*Radelgisi et Siginulfi Divisio Ducatus Beneventani*. Edited by Georg Heinrich Pertz, 221–225. *MGH LL 4*. Hannover: Hahn, 1868.

Reccemund. *Le Calendrier de Cordoue de l'année 961: Texte arabe et ancienne traduction latine*. Edited and translated by Reinhart Dozy. Leiden: Brill, 1961.

Ribera, Julián, ed. *Historia de la conquista de España del abenalcotía el Cordobés seguida de fragmentos históricos de Abencotaiba*. Madrid: Revista de Archivos, 1926.

Ibn Riḍwān, ʿAlī. *Medieval Islamic Medicine: Ibn Riḍwān's Treatise "On the Prevention of Bodily Ills in Egypt."* Translated by Michael W. Dols. Berkeley: University of California Press, 1984.

Samson. *Samsonis Apologeticus contra perfidos*. Edited by Juan Gil, 506–658. *CSM 2*. Madrid: Instituto Antonio de Nebrija, 1973.

Sedulius Scottus. *De rectoribus Christianis*. Edited by R. W. Dyson. Woodbridge: Boydell, 2010.

Severus Sulpicius. *Dialogue 1*. 183–202. PL 20.

Al-Shaybānī. *The Islamic Law of Nations: Shaybānī's Siyar*. Translated by Majid Khadduri. Baltimore: Johns Hopkins Press, 1966.

*The Song of Aspremont*. Translated by Michael A. Newth. New York: Garland, 1989.

Stephen II. *Epistolae*. Edited by Wilhelm Gundlach, 487–507. *MGH Epp 3*. Berlin: Weidmann, 1892.

Stephen III. *Epistolae*. Edited by Wilhelm Gundlach, 558–567. *MGH Epp 3*. Berlin: Weidmann, 1892.

Suetonius. *The Lives of the Caesars I*. Edited by J. C. Rolfe. Rev. ed. Cambridge, MA: Harvard University Press, 1998.

Al-Ṭabarī. *Al-Ṭabarī's Book of Jihād*. Translated by Yasir S. Ibrahim. Lewiston, NY: Edwin Mellen Press, 2007.

———. *The History of al-Ṭabarī, Vol. 1, General Introduction, and, From the Creation to the Flood*. Translated by Franz Rosenthal. Albany: State University of New York Press, 1988.

———. *The History of al-Ṭabarī, Vol. 5: The Sāsānids, the Byzantines, the Lakhmids, and Yemen*. Translated by Clifford E. Bosworth. Albany: State University of New York Press, 1999.

———. *The History of al-Ṭabarī, Vol. 14: The Conquest of Iran, A.D. 641–643/A.H. 21–23*. Translated by G. Rex Smith. Albany: State University of New York Press, 1994.

———. *The History of al-Ṭabarī, Vol. 23: The Zenith of the Marwānid House: The Last Years of 'Abd al-Malik and the Caliphate of al-Walid A.D. 700–715/A.H. 81–96*. Translated by Martin Hinds. Albany: State University of New York Press, 1990.

———. *The History of al-Ṭabarī, Vol. 28: 'Abbāsid Authority Affirmed: The Early Years of al- Manṣūr A.D. 753–763/A.H. 136–145*. Translated by Jane Dammen McAuliffe. Albany: State University of New York Press, 1995.

———. *The History of al-Ṭabarī, Vol. 29: Al-Manṣūr and al-Mahdī A.D. 763–786/A.H. 146–169*. Translated by Hugh Kennedy. Albany: State University of New York Press, 1990.

———. *The History of al-Ṭabarī, Vol. 30: The 'Abbāsid Caliphate in Equilibrium: The Caliphates of Musa al-Hadi and Harun al-Rashid A.D. 785–809/A.H. 169–193*. Translated by Clifford E. Bosworth. Albany: State University of New York Press, 1989.

———. *The History of al-Ṭabarī, Vol. 31: The War between Brothers: The Caliphate of Muhammad al-Amin A.D. 809–813/A.H. 193–198*. Translated by Michael Fishbein. Albany: State University of New York Press, 1992.

———. *The History of al-Ṭabarī, Vol. 32: The Reunification of the 'Abbāsid Caliphate: The Caliphate of al-Ma'mun A.D. 813–833/A.H. 198–218*. Translated by Clifford E. Bosworth. Albany: State University of New York Press, 1987.

Al-Tamīmī. *Kitāb al-Miḥan*. Edited by Yaḥyá Wahīb al-Jubūrī. Beirut: Dār al-Gharb al-Islāmī, 1988.

Thegan. *Gesta Hludowici imperatoris*. Edited by Ernst Tremp, 167–278. *MGH SRG 64*. Hannover: Hahn, 1995. Translated by Thomas F. X. Noble, 187–218. *Charlemagne and Louis the Pious: The Lives by Einhard, Notker, Ermoldus, Thegan, and the Astronomer*. University Park: Pennsylvania State University Press, 2009.

Theodulf of Orléans. *Ad Carolum regem*. Edited by Ernst Dümmler, 483–489. *MGH Poet. 1*, no. 25. Berlin: Weidmann, 1881. Translated by Peter Godman, 150–163. *Poetry of the Carolingian Renaissance*. London: Duckworth, 1985.

———. *Contra iudices*. Edited by Ernst Dümmler, 493–517. *MGH Poet. 1*, no. 28. Berlin: Weidmann, 1881.

———. *Delusa expectatio*. Edited by Ernst Dümmler, 525–526. *MGH Poet. 1*, no. 33. Berlin: Weidmann, 1881.

———. *De eo quod avarus adglomeratis diversis opibus satiari nequit*. Edited by Ernst Dümmler, 460–462. *MGH Poet. 1*, no. 7. Berlin: Weidmann, 1881. Translated by Theodore M. Andersson, 39–40. *Theodulf of Orléans: The Verse*. Tempe: Arizona Center for Medieval and Renaissance Studies, 2014.

———. *Eiusdem ad Hluduicum valedictio*. Edited by Ernst Dümmler, 531. *MGH Poet. 1*, no. 39. Berlin: Weidmann, 1881.

Theophanes. *The Chronicle of Theophanes Confessor: Byzantine and Near Eastern History, AD 284–813*. Translated by Cyril Mango, Roger Scott, and Geoffrey Greatrex. Oxford: Clarendon Press, 1997.

*Tiburtine Sybil Arab IV*. Edited by R. Y. Ebied and M.J.L. Young. "A Newly-Discovered Version of the Arabic Sibylline Prophecy." *Oriens Christianus* 60 (1976): 83–94.

*Tiburtine Sybil Arab V*. Edited by R. Y. Ebied and M.J.L. Young. "An Unrecorded Arabic Version of a Sibylline Prophecy." *Orientalia Christiana Periodica* 43 (1977): 279–307.

Al-'Udhrī. Translated by Fernando de la Granja. "La Marca Superior en la Obra de Al-Udri." *Estudios de Edad Media de la Corona de Aragon* 8 (1967): 447–545.

*Vita Athanasii Episcopi Neapolitani*. Edited by Georg Heinrich Pertz and Georg Waitz, 439–449. *MGH SRL*. Hannover: Hahn, 1878.

*Vita Madalvei*. Edited by Joseph Van der Straeten, 191–201. *Manuscrits hagiographiques de Charleville, Verdun, et Saint-Mihiel*. Brussels: Société des bollandistea, 1974.

*Vita Radbodi Traiectensis episcopi*. Edited by Oswald Holder-Egger, 569–571. *MGH SS 15.1*. Hannover: Hahn, 1887.

Walahfrid Strabo. *De imagine Tetrici*. Edited by Michael W. Herren. "The 'De imagine Tetrici' of Walahfrid Strabo: Edition and Translation." *Journal of Medieval Latin* 1 (1991): 118–139.

William of Toulouse. "Testament de Guillaume, Comte de Toulouse." Edited by P. Alaus, L. Cassan, and É.J.M. Meynial, 144–146. *Cartulaires des abbayes d'Aniane et de Gellone publiés d'après les manuscrits originaux*, 1, CLX. Montpellier: J. Martel, 1898.

Al-Yaʿqūbī. "The Book of the Adaptation of Men to Their Time and Their Dominant Characteristics in Every Age." Edited and translated by Matthew S. Gordon, Chase F. Robinson, Everett K. Rowson, and Michael Fishbein, 29–60. *The Works of Ibn Wāḍiḥ al-Yaʿqūbī: An English Translation*. Vol. 1. Leiden: Brill, 2018.

———. "The History." Edited and translated by Matthew S. Gordon, Chase F. Robinson, Everett K. Rowson, and Michael Fishbein, 595–1293. *The Works of Ibn Wāḍiḥ al-Yaʿqūbī: An English Translation*. Vol. 3. Leiden: Brill, 2018.

Zacharias I. *Epistolae*. Edited by Michael Tangl, 120–125. *MGH Ep. Sel. 1*, no. 60. Berlin: Weidmann, 1916.

## *Secondary Literature*

D'Abadal i de Vinyals, Ramón. "El Paso de Septimania del dominio Godo al Franco." *Cuadernos de Historia de España* 19 (1953): 5–54.

——. *Els Primers Comtes Catalans*. Barcelona: Editorial Teide, 1958.

——. *La batalla del adopcionismo en la disentegración de la Iglesia visigodo*. Barcelona: Real Academia de Buenas Letras, 1939.

——. "La Catalogne sous l'Empire de Louis le Pieux." *Études Roussillonnaises: Revue d'histoire et d'archéologie méditerranéennes* 4 (1954–1955): 239–272; 5 (1956): 31–50, 147–177; 6 (1957): 267–295.

——. "Nota Sobre la locución 'Marca Hispánica.'" *Boletín de la Real Academia de Buenas Letras de Barcelona* 27 (1957–1958): 157–164.

"Abbasid-Carolingian Alliance." Wikipedia. en.wikipedia.org/wiki/Abbasid%E2%80%93Carolingian_alliance.

Abbott, Nabia. *Two Queens of Baghdad: Mother and Wife of Hārūn al-Rashīd*. Chicago: University of Chicago Press, 1946.

Abdullah, Thabit. "Arab Views of Northern Europeans in Medieval History and Geography." In *Images of the Other: Europe and the Muslim World before 1700*, edited by David R. Blanks, 73–80. Cairo: American University of Cairo Press, 1997.

Abels, Richard. "Paying the Danegeld: Anglo-Saxon Peacemaking with Vikings." In *War and Peace in Ancient and Medieval History*, edited by Philip de Souza and John France, 173–192. Cambridge: Cambridge University Press, 2008.

Abulof, Uriel. "The Malpractice of 'Rationality' in International Relations." *Rationality and Society* 27 (2015): 358–384.

Abun-Nasr, Jamil M. *A History of the Maghrib*. Cambridge: Cambridge University Press, 1971.

Acién Almansa, Manuel. *Entre el Feudalismo y el Islam: 'Umar ibn Ḥafṣūn en los Historiadores, en las Fuentes y en la Historia*. Jaén: Servicio de Publicaciones de la Universidad de Jaén, 1997.

al-Ageili, O. S. "A Critical Edition of Kitāb al-Miḥan by (Abū al-'Arab) M b. A. al-Tamīmi (d. 333/944)." PhD diss., University of Exeter, 1981.

Aguadé, Jordi. "Some Remarks about Sectarian Movements in al-Andalus." *Studia Islamica* 64 (1986): 53–77.

Ahmad, S. Maqbul. "Kharīṭa." *Encyclopedia of Islam*. 2nd ed. 4:1077–1083. Leiden: Brill, 1990.

Airlie, Stuart. "Narratives of Triumph and Rituals of Submission: Charlemagne's Mastering of Bavaria." *Transactions of the Royal Historical Society*, 6th ser., 9 (1999): 93–119.

——. "The Palace Complex." In *Diverging Paths?: The Shapes of Power and Institutions in Medieval Christendom and Islam*, edited by John Hudson and Ana Rodriguez, 255–290. Leiden: Brill, 2014.

——. "The Palace of Memory: The Carolingian Court as Political Centre." In *Courts and Regions in Medieval Europe*, edited by Sarah Rees Jones, Richard Marks, and A. J. Minnis, 1–20. Woodbridge: York Medieval Press, 2000.

——. "Private Bodies and the Body Politic in the Divorce Case of Lothar II." *Past and Present* 161 (1998): 3–38.

——. "Talking Heads: Assemblies in Early Medieval Germany." In *Political Assemblies in the Earlier Middle Ages*, edited by P. S. Barnwell and M. Mostert, 29–46. Turnhout: Brepols, 2003.

Albertoni, Giuseppe. *L'elefante di Carlo Magno*. Bologna: Mulino, 2020.

——. *L'Italia Carolingia*. Rome: NIS, 1997.

Alexander, Paul Julius. "The Diffusion of Byzantine Apocalypses in the Medieval West and the Beginnings of Joachimism." In *Prophecy and Millenarianism: Essays in Honour of Marjorie Reeves*, edited by Ann Williams, 57–71. Harlow: Longman, 1980.

——. "Medieval Apocalypses as Historical Sources." *American Historical Review* 73 (1968): 997–1018.

——. *The Oracle of Baalbek: The Tiburtine Sibyl in Greek Dress*. Washington, DC: Dumbarton Oaks, 1967.

Althoff, Gerd. "Zur Bedeutung der Bündnisse Svatopluks von Mähren mit Franken." In *Symposium Methodianum*, edited by Klaus Trost, Ekkehard Völkl, and Erwin Wedel, 13–22. Regensburg: Hieronymus Verlag, 1985.

Alturo, Jesús. "El *liber iudicum* manuscrito latino 4667 de la biblioteca nacional de Francia: Análisis Paleográfico." *Historia. Instituciones. Documentos* 30 (2003): 9–54.

d'Alverny, Marie-Thérèse. "La connaissance de l'Islam en Occident du IX^e au milieu du XII^e siècle." In *La connaissance de l'Islam dans l'Occident médieval*, edited by Charles Burnett, 577–602. Aldershot: Variorum, 1994.

Anderson, Benjamin. *Cosmos and Community in Early Medieval Art*. New Haven: Yale University Press, 2017.

Anderson, Glaire D. "Islamic Spaces and Diplomacy in Constantinople (Tenth to Thirteenth Centuries C.E.)." *Medieval Encounters* 15 (2009): 86–113.

——. *The Islamic Villa in Early Medieval Iberia: Architecture and Court Culture in Umayyad Córdoba*. Farnham: Ashgate, 2013.

Anderson, Glaire D., Corisande Fenwick, and Mariam Rosser-Owen. "The Aghlabids and Their Neighbors: An Introduction." In *The Aghlabids and Their Neighbors: Art and Material Culture in Ninth-Century North Africa*, edited by Glaire D. Anderson, Corisande Fenwick, and Mariam Rosser-Owen, 1–30. Leiden: Brill, 2018.

Anderson, M. S. *The Rise of Modern Diplomacy, 1450–1919*. London: Longman, 1993.

Andrén, Anders, Kristina Jennbert, and Catharina Raudvere. "Old Norse Religion: Some Problems and Prospects." In *Old Norse Religion in Long-term Perspectives: Origins, Changes, and Interactions*, edited by Anders Andrén, Kristina Jennbert, and Catharina Raudvere, 11–14. Lund: Nordic Academic Press, 2006.

Anthony, Sean W. *Crucifixion and Death as Spectacle: Umayyad Crucifixion in Its Late Antique Context*. New Haven: American Oriental Society, 2014.

Arenson, Sarah. "Medieval Jewish Seafaring between East and West." *Mediterranean Historical Review* 15 (2000): 33–46.

Arjomand, Saïd Amir. "Islamic Apocalypticism in the Classical Period." In *The Encyclopedia of Apocalypticism, Vol. 2, Apocalypticism in Western History and Culture*, edited by Bernard McGinn, 238–283. New York: Continuum, 2000.

——. "Perso-Islamicate Political Ethic in Relation to the Sources of Islamic Law." In *Mirror for the Muslim Prince: Islam and the Theory of Statecraft*, edited by Mehrzad Boroujerdi, 82–106. Syracuse, NY: Syracuse University Press, 2013.

Arndt, Monika. *Die Goslarer Kaiserpfalz als Nationaldenkmal: Eine ikonographische Untersuchung*. Hildesheim: Lax, 1976.

Ashtor, Eliyahu. "Che cosa sapevano i geografi arabi dell'Europa occidentale?" *Rivista storica italiana* 81 (1969): 453–479.

ʿAthamina, Khalil. "How Did Islam Contribute to Change the Legal Status of Women: The Case of the *Jawārī* or the Female Slaves." *al-Qanṭara* 28 (2007): 383–408.

Aurast, Anna. "What Did Christian Authors Know about Jews and Judaism? Some Remarks Based on Early Medieval Evidence." *Millennium* 10 (2013): 331–347.

Aurell, Martin. *Les noces du comte: Mariage et pouvoir en Catalogne (785–1213)*. Paris: Publications de la Sorbonne, 1995.

———. "Pouvoir et Párenté des Comtes de la Marche Hispanique (801–911)." In *La royauté et les élites dans l'Europe carolingienne (début IXe siècle aux environs de 920)*, edited by Régine Le Jan, 467–485. Lille: Centre d'histoire de l'Europe du Nord-Ouest, 1998.

Auzépy, Marie-France. "Constantin V, l'empereur isaurien et les Carolingiens." In *Les Assises du Pouvoir: Temps médiévaux, territoires africains*, edited by Odile Redon and Bernard Rosenberger, 49–65. Saint-Denis: Presses universitaires de Vincennes, 1994.

Auzias, Léonce. *L'Aquitaine carolingienne (778–987)*. Toulouse: Didier, 1937.

———. "Les Sièges de Barcelone, de Tortose et d'Huesca (801–811): Essai Chronologique." *Annales du Midi* 48 (1936): 5–28.

Ávila, María Luisa. "La fecha de redacción del *Muqtabis*." *al-Qanṭara* 5 (1984): 93–109.

al-Azmeh, Aziz. "Barbarians in Arab Eyes." *Past and Present* 134 (1992): 3–18.

———. *Muslim Kingship: Power and the Sacred in Muslim, Christian, and Pagan Polities*. London: I. B. Tauris, 1997.

Bacharach, Jere. "Administrative Complexes, Palaces and Citadels: Changes in the Loci of Medieval Muslim Rule." In *The Ottoman City and Its Parts: Urban Structure and Social Order*, edited by Irene A. Bierman, Rifaʿat Ali Abou-el-Haj, and Donald Preziosi, 111–128. New Rochelle: A. D. Caratzas, 1991.

Bachrach, Bernard S. *Early Carolingian Warfare: Prelude to Empire*. Philadelphia: University of Pennsylvania Press, 2001.

———. *Early Medieval Jewish Policy in Western Europe*. Minneapolis: University of Minnesota Press, 1977.

———. "Military Organisation in Aquitaine under the Early Carolingians." *Speculum* 49 (1974): 1–33.

Bade, Norman. "Muslims in the Christian World Order: Comprehension and Knowledge of the Saracens in Two Universal Histories of the Carolingian Empire." *Millennium* 10 (2013): 293–310.

Baer, Eva. *Metalwork in Medieval Islamic Art*. Albany: State University of New York Press, 1983.

Bailey, Matthew, and Ryan D. Giles, eds. *Charlemagne and His Legend in Early Spanish Literature and Historiography*. Cambridge: D. S. Brewer, 2016.

Balzaretti, Ross. *Dark Age Liguria: Regional Identity and Local Power, c. 400–1020*. London: Bloomsbury, 2013.

Barbeyrac, Jean. *Histoire des anciens traitez, ou recueil historique et chronologique des traitez répandus dans les Auteurs Grecs & Latins, & autres Monumens de l'Antiquité depuis le tems les plus reculez jusques à l'empereur Charlemagne.* Amsterdam: Chez les Janssons à Waesberge, Wetstein & Smith, 1739.

Barbier, Josiane. "Le système palatial franc: Genèse et fonctionnement dans le nord-ouest du *regnum.*" *Bibliothèque de l'École des Chartes* 148 (1990): 245–299.

Barceló, Miquel. "El califa patente: El ceremonial omeya de Córdoba o la escenificación del poder." In *Estructuras y Formas del Poder en la Historia: Ponencias*, edited by Reyna Pastor, Ian Kieniewicz, and Eduardo García Enterría, 51–71. Salamanca: Ediciones Universidad de Salamanca, 1990.

Barnwell, Paul S. "War and Peace: Historiography and Seventh-Century Embassies." *Early Medieval Europe* 6 (1997): 127–139.

Bartlett, Robert. *Trial by Fire and Water: The Medieval Judicial Ordeal.* Oxford: Clarendon Press, 1986.

Barton, Simon. *Conquerors, Brides and Concubines: Interfaith Relations and Social Power in Medieval Iberia.* Philadelphia: University of Pennsylvania Press, 2015.

Bassiouni, M. Cherif. "Protection of Diplomats under Islamic Law." *American Journal of International Law* 74 (1980): 609–633.

Baumer, Christoph. *The Church of the East: An Illustrated History of Assyrian Christianity.* London: I. B. Tauris, 2008.

Bautier, Robert-Henri. "La campagne de Charlemagne en Espagne (778): La réalité historique." In *Recherches sur l'histoire de la France médiévale*, 1–51. Aldershot: Variorum, 1991.

Bayard, Adrien. "De la *Regio* au *Regnum*: L'improbable 'nation des Aquitains' au premier Moyen Âge." *Revue de l'Institut Français d'Histoire en Allemagne* 6 (2014). https://journals.openedition.org/ifha/8032.

Becher, Matthias. *Eid und Herrschaft: Untersuchungen zum Herrscherethos Karls des Grossen.* Sigmaringen: Thorbecke, 1993.

Beckwith, Christopher I. *The Tibetan Empire in Central Asia: A History of the Struggle for Great Power among Tibetans, Turks, Arabs, and Chinese during the Early Middle Ages.* Princeton: Princeton University Press, 1987.

Behrens-Abouseif, Doris. *Practising Diplomacy in the Mamluk Sultanate: Gifts and Material Culture in the Medieval Islamic World.* London: I. B. Tauris, 2014.

Bellarbre, Julien. "La 'nation' aquitaine dans l'historiographie monastique du sud de la Loire (VIII^e^–XII^e^ siècles)." *Revue de l'Institut Français d'Histoire en Allemagne* 6 (2014).

Benchekroun, Chafik T. "Les Idrīssides: L'histoire contre son histoire." *Al-Masāq* 23 (2011): 171–188.

Bennison, Amira K. "The Necklace of al-Shifā: 'Abbāsid Borrowings in the Islamic West." *Oriens* 38 (2010): 249–273.

———. "The Peoples of the North in the Eyes of the Muslims of Umayyad al-Andalus (711–1031)." *Journal of Global History* 2 (2007): 157–174.

———. "Power and the City in the Islamic West from the Umayyads to the Almohads." In *Cities in the Pre-Modern Islamic World: The Urban Impact of Religion, State and Society*, edited by Amira K. Bennison and Alison L. Gascoigne, 65–95. London: Routledge, 2007.

Berg, Dieter, Martin Kintzinger, and Pierre Monnet, eds. *Auswärtige Politik und internationale Beziehungen im Mittelalter (13. bis 16. Jahrhundert).* Bochum: Winkler, 2002.

Berger, Lutz. "Centres and Peripheries in the Early Medieval Mediterranean." In *Southern Italy as Contact Area and Border Region during the Early Middle Ages: Religious-Cultural Heterogeneity and Competing Powers in Local, Transregional, and Universal Dimensions*, edited by Klaus Herbers and Kordula Wolf, 41–50. Cologne: Böhlau Verlag, 2018.

Bergier, Jean-François. "Le trafic à travers les Alpes et les liaisons transalpines du haut Moyen Âge au XVIIe siècle." In *Pour une histoire des Alpes, Moyen Âge et Temps modernes*, 1–72. Aldershot: Variorum, 1997.

van Berkel, Maaike. "The Vizier." In *Crisis and Continuity at the Abbasid Court: Formal and Informal Politics in the Caliphate of al-Muqtadir (295–320/908–32)*, edited by Maaike van Berkel, Nadia Maria El Cheikh, Hugh Kennedy, and Letizia Osti, 65–85. Leiden: Brill, 2013.

Bernheimer, Teresa. *The ʿAlids: The First Family of Islam, 750–1200*. Edinburgh: Edinburgh University Press, 2013.

Berridge, Geoff R. *Diplomacy: Theory and Practice*. 4th ed. New York: Palgrave Macmillan, 2010.

Berschin, Walter. "Die Ost-West-Gesandtschaften am Hof Karls des Grossen und Ludwig des Frommen (768–840)." In *Karl der Grosse und sein Nachwirken: 1200 Jahre Kultur und Wissenschaft in Europa*, edited by Paul Leo Butzer, Max Kerner, and Walter Oberschelp, 1:157–172. Turnhout: Brepols, 1997.

Bieberstein, Klaus. "Der Gesandtenaustausch zwischen Karl dem Großen und Hārūn ar-Rašīd und seine Bedeutung für die Kirchen Jerusalems." *Zeitschrift des Deutschen Palästina-Vereins* 109 (1993): 152–173.

Bielenstein, Hans. *Diplomacy and Trade in the Chinese World, 589–1276*. Leiden: Brill, 2005.

Bijsterveld, Arnoud-Jan. "The Medieval Gift as Agent of Social Bonding and Political Power." In *Medieval Transformations: Texts, Power, and Gifts in Context*, edited by Esther Cohen and Mayke de Jong, 123–156. Leiden: Brill, 2001.

Binding, Günther. "Die Aachener Pfalz Karls des Großen als archäologisch-baugeschichtlichen Problem." *Zeitschrift für Archäologie des Mittelalters* 25/26 (1997/1998): 63–86.

Bischoff, Bernhard. *Salzburger Formelbücher und Briefe aus Tassilonischer und Karolingischer Zeit*, II.2. Munich: Beck, 1973.

Bisson, Thomas N. "The Rise of Catalonia: Identity, Power and Ideology in a Twelfth-Century Society." In *Medieval France and Her Pyrenean Neighbours: Studies in Early Institutional History*, 125–152. London: Hambledon, 1989.

———. "Unheroed Pasts: History and Commemoration in South Frankland before the Albigensian Crusades." *Speculum* 65 (1990): 281–308.

Björkman, Walther. "Karl und der Islam." In *Karl der Grosse: Lebenswerk und Nachleben*, edited by Wolfgang Braunfels, 1:672–682. Düsseldorf: L. Schwann, 1965.

Blankinship, Khalid Yahya. *The End of the Jihâd State: The Reign of Hishām ibn ʿAbd al-Malik and the Collapse of the Umayyads*. Albany: State University of New York Press, 1994.

Blanks, David R. "Western Views of Islam in the Premodern Period: A Brief History of Past Approaches." In *Western Views of Islam in Medieval and Early Modern*

*Europe: Perception of the Other*, edited by Michael Frassetto and David R. Blanks, 10–53. Basingstoke: St. Martin's Press, 1999.

Blunt, Christopher E. "The Coinage of Offa." In *Anglo-Saxon Coins: Studies Presented to F. M. Stenton*, edited by D.H.M. Dolley, 39–62. London: Methuen, 1961.

Böhmer, Johann Friedrich. *Regesta Imperii*. Vol. 1. Tübingen: Akademie der Wissenschaften und der Literatur, 1833.

Bonch Reeves, Ksenia. *Visions of Unity after the Visigoths: Early Iberian Latin Chronicles and the Mediterranean World*. Turnhout: Brepols, 2016.

Bondioli, Lorenzo M. "From the Frontier Cities to the City, and Back? Reinterpreting Southern Italy in the *De administrando imperio*." In *From Constantinople to the Frontier: The City and the Cities*, edited by Nicholas S. M. Matheou, Theofili Kampianaki, and Lorenzo M. Bondioli, 365–384. Leiden: Brill, 2016.

———. "Islamic Bari between the Aghlabids and the Two Empires." In *The Aghlabids and Their Neighbors: Art and Material Culture in Ninth-Century North Africa*, edited by Glaire D. Anderson, Corisande Fenwick, and Mariam Rosser-Owen, 470–490. Leiden: Brill, 2018.

Bonner, Michael. "*Al-Khalīfa al-marḍī*: The Accession of Hārūn al-Rashīd." *Journal of the American Oriental Society* 108 (1988): 79–91.

———. *Aristocratic Violence and Holy War: Studies in the Jihad and the Arab-Byzantine Frontier*. New Haven: American Oriental Society, 1996.

———. "The Naming of the Frontier: *'Awāṣim, Thughūr* and the Arab Geographers." *Bulletin of the School of Oriental and African Studies* 57 (1994): 17–24.

———. "Some Observations Concerning the Early Development of Jihad on the Arab-Byzantine Frontier." *Studia Islamica* 75 (1992): 5–31.

———. "The Waning of Empire, 861–945." In *The New Cambridge History of Islam*, edited by Chase F. Robinson, 1:305–359. Cambridge: Cambridge University Press, 2010.

Booker, Courtney M. "By Any Other Name?: Charlemagne, Nomenclature, and Performativity." In *Charlemagne: Les temps, les espaces, les hommes: Construction et déconstruction d'un règne*, edited by Rolf Grosse and Michel Sot, 409–426. Turnhout: Brepols, 2018.

Borgolte, Michael. *Der Gesandtenaustausch der Karolinger mit den Abbasiden und mit den Patriarchen von Jerusalem*. Munich: Arbeo-Gesellschaft, 1976.

———. "Experten der Fremde Gesandte in interkulturellen Beziehungen des Frühen und Hohen Mittelalters." *Settimane di Studio* 58 (2011): 945–992.

Borrut, Antoine. *Entre mémoire et pouvoir: L'espace syrien sous les derniers Omeyyades et les premiers Abbassides (v. 72–193/692–809)*. Leiden: Brill, 2011.

Bosch Vilá, Jacinto. "Considerations with Respect to '*al-Thaghr* in al-Andalus' and the Political- Administrative Division of Muslim Spain." In *The Formation of al-Andalus: Part 1, History and Society*, edited by Manuela Marín, 378–387. Aldershot: Ashgate, 1988.

Boshof, Egon. *Erzbischof Agobard von Lyon: Leben und Werk*. Cologne: Böhlau, 1969.

———. *Ludwig der Fromme*. Darmstadt: Primus Verlag, 1996.

Bosworth, Clifford E. "Hiba: The Caliphate." *Encyclopedia of Islam*. 2nd ed. 3:344–346. Leiden: Brill, 1971.

——. *The History of the Saffarids of Sistan and the Maliks of Nimruz: (247/861 to 949/1542–3)*. Costa Mesa: Mazda, 1994.

——. "The Persian Impact on Arabic Literature." In *Arabic Literature to the End of the Umayyad Period*, edited by A.F.L. Beeston, 483–496. Cambridge: Cambridge University Press, 1983.

——. "Translator's Foreword." *The History of al-Ṭabarī, Vol. 30: The 'Abbāsid Caliphate in Equilibrium: The Caliphates of Musa al-Hadi and Harun al-Rashid A.D. 785–809/A.H. 169–193*, translated by Clifford E. Bosworth, xv–xxii. Albany: State University of New York Press, 1989.

Bouchard, Constance B. *Those of My Blood: Constructing Noble Families in Medieval Francia*. Philadelphia: University of Pennsylvania Press, 2001.

Bowlus, Charles R. *Franks, Moravians, and Magyars: The Struggle for the Middle Danube, 788-907*. Philadelphia: University of Pennsylvania Press, 1995.

Brandes, W. "Das Schweigen des *Liber pontificalis*: Die 'Enteignung' der päpstlichen Patrimonien Siziliens und Unteritaliens in den 50er Jahren des 8. Jahrhunderts." *Fontes minores* 12 (2014): 97–203.

Brather, Sebastian. "Frühmittelalterliche Dirham-Schatzfunde in Europa: Probleme ihrer Wirtschaftsgeschichtlichen Interpretationen aus Archäologische Perspektive." *Zeitschrift für Archäologie des Mittelalters* 23/24 (1995/1996): 73–153.

Braudel, Fernand. *The Mediterranean and the Mediterranean World in the Age of Philip II*. Vol. 1. Translated by Susan Reynolds. London: Collins, 1972.

Bregel, Yuri. "Barthold and Modern Oriental Studies." *International Journal of Middle East Studies* 12 (1980): 385–403.

Bréhier, Louis. "Charlemagne et la Palestine." *Revue historique* 157 (1928): 277–290.

——. "Les origines des rapports entre la France et la Syrie: Le protectorat de Charlemagne." *Congrès français de la Syrie à Marseille* (1919): 15–39.

Brett, Michael. "The Arab Conquest and the Rise of Islam in North Africa." In *The Cambridge History of Africa*, edited by J. D. Fage, 2:490–555. Cambridge: Cambridge University Press, 1979.

——. "The Diplomacy of Empire: Fatimids and Zirids, 990–1062." *Bulletin of the School of Oriental and African Studies* 78 (2015): 149–159.

——. "Egypt." In *The New Cambridge History of Islam*, edited by Chase F. Robinson, 1:541–580. Cambridge: Cambridge University Press, 2010.

——. *The Rise of the Fatimids: The World of the Mediterranean and the Middle East in the Fourth Century of the Hijra, Tenth Century CE*. Leiden: Brill, 2001.

Brock, Sebastian. "Syriac Views of Emergent Islam." In *Studies on the First Century of Islamic Society*, edited by G.H.A. Juynboll, 9–21. Carbondale: Southern Illinois University Press, 1982.

Brooks, E. W. "Byzantines and Arabs in the Time of the Early Abbasids." *English Historical Review* 15 (1900): 728–747.

——. "Byzantines and Arabs in the Time of the Early Abbasids: II: Extracts from Al Baladhuri." *English Historical Review* 16 (1901): 84–92.

Brookshaw, Dominic P. "Palaces, Pavilions and Pleasure-Gardens: The Context and Setting of the Medieval *Majlis*." *Middle Eastern Literatures* 6 (2003): 199–223.

Brubaker, Leslie. "The Elephant and the Ark: Cultural and Material Interchange across the Mediterranean in the Eighth and Ninth Centuries." *Dumbarton Oaks Papers* 58 (2004): 175–195.

Brubaker, Leslie, and John Haldon. *Byzantium in the Iconoclast Era c. 680–850: A History*. Cambridge: Cambridge University Press, 2011.

Brühl, Carlrichard. "Frankischer Königsbrauch und das Problem der *Festkrönungen*." *Historisches Zeitschrift* 194 (1962): 265–326.

Buc, Philippe. *The Dangers of Ritual: Between Early Medieval Texts and Social Scientific Theory*. Princeton: Princeton University Press, 2001.

———. "The Monster and the Critics: A Ritual Reply." *Early Medieval Europe* 15 (2007): 441–452.

———. "Political Rituals and Political Imagination in the Medieval West from the Fourth Century to the Eleventh." In *The Medieval World*, edited by Peter Linehan and Janet L. Nelson, 189–213. London: Routledge, 2001.

———. "Ritual and Interpretation: The Early Medieval Case." *Early Medieval Europe* 9 (2000): 183–209.

Buckler, Francis W. *Harunu'l-Rashid and Charles the Great*. Cambridge, MA: Mediaeval Academy of America, 1931.

———. *Legitimacy and Symbols: The South Asian Writings of F. W. Buckler*, ed. M. N. Pearson. Ann Arbor, MI: Center for South and Southeast Asian Studies, 1985.

Bulliet, Richard W. *Conversion to Islam in the Medieval Period: An Essay in Quantitative History*. Cambridge, MA: Harvard University Press, 1979.

Bullough, Donald. "*Aula Renovata*: The Carolingian Court before the Aachen Palace." *Proceedings of the British Academy* 71 (1985): 267–301.

Burns, Robert I. "Muslim-Christian Conflict and Contact in Medieval Spain: Context and Methodology." *Thought* 54 (1979): 238–252.

———. "The Significance of the Frontier in the Middle Ages." In *Medieval Frontier Societies*, edited by Robert Bartlett and Angus MacKay, 307–330. Oxford: Oxford University Press, 1989.

———. "A Unique Bilingual Surrender Treaty from Muslim-Crusader Spain." *The Historian* 62 (2000): 511–534.

Burridge, Claire. "Incense in Medicine: An Early Medieval Perspective." *Early Medieval Europe* 28 (2020): 219–255.

Cabaniss, Allen. "Paulus Albarus of Muslim Cordova." *Church History* 22 (1953): 99–112.

Calmette, Joseph. *De Bernardo Sancti Guillelmi filio: (?–844)*. Toulouse: Privat, 1902.

———. "Le Siège de Toulouse par les Normands en 864 et les circonstances qui s'y rattachment." *Annales du Midi* 29 (1917): 153–174.

———. "Les Marquis de Gothie sous Charles le Chauve." *Annales du Midi* 14 (1902): 185–196.

Calvino, Italo. *If on a Winter's Night a Traveller*. Translated by William Weaver. New York: Alfred A. Knopf, 1993.

Cañade Juste, Alberto. "El possible solar originario de los Banu Qasi." In *Homenaje a Don José María Lacarra de Miguel en su jubilación del profesorado: Estudios medievales*, 1:33–38. Zaragoza: Anubar, 1977.

———. "Los Banu Qasi (714–924)." *Principe de Viana* 41 (1980): 5–96.

Canard, Marius. "La Prise d'Héraclée et les Relations entre Hārūn ar-Rashīd et l'Empereur Nicéphore Ier." *Byzantion* 32 (1962): 345–379.

Canepa, Matthew P. *The Two Eyes of the Earth: Art and Ritual of Kingship between Rome and Sasanian Iran*. Berkeley: American Council of Learned Societies, 2009.

Cardoso, Elsa. "The Scenography of Power in al-Andalus and the Abbasid and Byzantine Ceremonial: Christian Ambassadorial Receptions in the Court of Cordoba in a Comparative Perspective." *Medieval Encounters* 24 (2018): 390–434.

Carrillo, Alicia. "Architectural Exchanges between North Africa and the Iberian Peninsula: Muqarnas in al-Andalus." *Journal of North African Studies* 19 (2014): 68–82.

Casson, Lionel. *Ships and Seamanship in the Ancient World*. Princeton: Princeton University Press, 1971.

Cavadini, John C. *The Last Christology of the West: Adoptionism in Spain and Gaul, 785–820*. Philadelphia: University of Pennsylvania Press, 1993.

Cesario, Marilina. "Ant-lore in Anglo-Saxon England." *Anglo-Saxon England* 40 (2011): 273–291.

Challis, Keith, et al. "Corona Remotely-Sensed Imagery in Dryland Archaeology: The Islamic City of al-Raqqa." *Journal of Field Archaeology* 29 (2004): 139–153.

Chalmeta, Pedro. "El Concepto de Tagr." In *La Marche Supérieure d'al-Andalus et l'Occident Chrétien*, edited by Philippe Sénac, 15–28. Madrid: Casa de Velázquez, 1991.

———. "Historiografía medieval hispania: Arabica." *al-Andalus* 37 (1972): 353–405.

———. *Invasión e Islamización: La sumisión de Hispania y la formación de al-Andalus*. Madrid: Editorial Mapfre, 1994.

———. "Una historia discontinua e intemporal (*jabar*)." *Hispanía* 33 (1973): 23–75.

Chandler, Cullen J. "Between Court and Counts: Carolingian Catalonia and the *Aprisio* Grant, 778–897." *Early Medieval Europe* 11 (2003): 19–44.

———. *Carolingian Catalonia: Politics, Culture, and Identity in the Imperial Province, 778–987*. Cambridge: Cambridge University Press, 2019.

———. "Heresy and Empire: The Role of the Adoptionist Controversy in Charlemagne's Conquest of the Spanish March." *International History Review* 24 (2002): 505–527.

———. "Land and Social Networks in the Carolingian Spanish March." *Studies in Medieval and Renaissance History*, 3rd ser., 6 (2009): 1–33.

———. "The Mysterious Case of Aizo." In *Mostly Medieval*, 7 August 2014. cullenjchandler.wordpress.com/2014/08/07/the-mysterious-case-of-aizo/.

Chaume, Maurice. "Onfroi, Marquis de Gothie: Ses origines et ses attaches familiales." *Annales du Midi* 52 (1940): 113–136.

Chavannes, Édouard. *Documents sur les Tou-kiue (Turcs) occidentaux: Recueillis et commentés, suivi de notes additionelles*. St. Petersburg: Adrien-Maisonneuve, 1903.

Chiarelli, Leonard C. *A History of Muslim Sicily*. Venera: Midsea Books, 2011.

Christys, Ann. *Christians in al-Andalus, 711–1000*. Richmond: Curzon, 2002.

———. "Crossing the Frontier of Ninth Century Hispania." In *Medieval Frontiers: Concepts and Practices*, edited by David Abulafia and Nora Berend, 35–53. Aldershot: Routledge, 2002.

———. "St-Germain des-Prés, St. Vincent and the Martyrs of Córdoba." *Early Medieval Europe* 7 (1998): 199–216.

———. *Vikings in the South: Voyages to Iberia and the Mediterranean*. London: Bloomsbury Academic, 2015.

Cilento, Nicola. *Italia meridionale longobarda*. Naples: R. Ricciardi, 1966.

Citarella, Armand O. "The Relations of Amalfi with the Arab World before the Crusades." *Speculum* 42 (1967): 299–312.

Clarke, Nicola. *The Muslim Conquest of Iberia: Medieval Arabic Narratives*. London: Routledge, 2012.

Clément, Francois. "Nommer l'autre: Qui sont les Ifranj des sources arabes du Moyen-Âge?" *Recherches 02. de mots en maux: Parcours hispano-arabe*, edited by Isabelle Reck and Edgard Weber, 89–105. Strasbourg: Service des publications de l'Université de Strasbourg, 2009.

Cobb, Paul M. "*Coronidis Loco*: On the Meaning of Elephants, from Baghdad to Aachen." In *Interfaith Relationships and Perceptions of the Other in the Medieval Mediterranean*, edited by Sarah Davis-Secord, Belen Vicens, and Robin Vose, 49–77. New York: Springer, 2021.

——. *White Banners: Contention in 'Abbāsid Syria, 750–880*. Albany: State University of New York Press, 2001.

Codera y Zaidín, Francisco. "El Godo o moro Aizón." In *Estudios críticos de historia Árabe Española, colección de estudios Árabes*, 7:201–224. Zaragoza: E. Maestre, 1903.

Coghill, Edward. "How the West Was Won: Unearthing the Umayyad History of the Conquest of the Maghrib." In *The Umayyad World*, edited by Andrew Marsham, 539–570. London: Routledge, 2020.

Colbert, E. P. *The Martyrs of Córdoba (850–859): A Study of the Sources*. Washington, DC: Catholic University of America Press, 1962.

Colin, Georges S. "Hiba in the West." *Encyclopedia of Islam*. 2nd ed. 3:346–347. Leiden: Brill, 1971.

——. "Monnaies de la Période Idrīsite trouvées a Volubilis." *Hesperis* 22 (1936): 113–125.

Collins, Roger. *The Arab Conquest of Spain, 711–797*. Oxford: Blackwell, 1994.

——. *The Basques*. 2nd ed. Oxford: Basil Blackwell, 1990.

——. "The Basques in Aquitaine and Navarre: Problems of Frontier Government." In *Law, Culture and Regionalism in Early Medieval Spain*, 3–17. Aldershot: Variorum, 1992.

——. *Caliphs and Kings: Spain, 796–1031*. Chichester: Wiley Blackwell, 2012.

——. *Charlemagne*. Basingstoke: Macmillan, 1998.

——. "Charlemagne's Imperial Coronation and the Annals of Lorsch." In *Charlemagne: Empire and Society*, edited by Joanna Story, 52–70. Manchester: Manchester University Press, 2005.

——. "Charles the Bald and Wilfred the Hairy." In *Charles the Bald: Court and Kingdom*. 2nd ed., edited by Margaret T. Gibson and Janet L. Nelson, 169–188. Aldershot: Variorum, 1990.

——. "Deception and Misrepresentation in Early Eighth Century Frankish Historiography: Two Case Studies." In *Karl Martell in seiner Zeit*, edited by Jörg Jarnut, Ulrich Nonn, and Michael Richter, 227–247. Sigmaringen: Thorbecke, 1994.

——. *Die Fredegar-Chroniken*. Hannover: Hahn, 2007.

——. *Early Medieval Spain: Unity in Diversity, 400–1000*. 2nd ed. Basingstoke: Macmillan, 1995.

——. "Pippin I and the Kingdom of Aquitaine." In *Charlemagne's Heir: New Perspectives on the Reign of Louis the Pious (814–840)*, edited by Peter Godman and Roger Collins, 363–389. Oxford: Clarendon Press, 1990.

——. "Pippin III as Mayor of the Palace: The Evidence." In *Der Dynastiewechsel von 751: Vorgeschichte, Legitimationsstrategien und Erinnerung*, edited by Matthias Becher and Jörg Jarnut, 75–91. Münster: Scriptorium, 2004.

——. "The 'Reviser' Revisited: Another Look at the Alternative Version of the *Annales regni Francorum*." In *After Rome's Fall: Narrators and Sources of Early Medieval History, Essays Presented to Walter Goffart*, edited by Alexander Callander Murray, 191–213. Toronto: University of Toronto Press, 1998.

——. "Spain: The Northern Kingdoms and the Basques, 711–910." In *The New Cambridge Medieval History*, vol. 2, edited by Rosamond McKitterick, 272–289. Cambridge: Cambridge University Press, 1995.

Colman, Rebecca V. "Reason and Unreason in Early Medieval Law." *Journal of Interdisciplinary History* 4 (1974): 571–591.

Conant, Jonathan P. "Anxieties of Violence: Christians and Muslims in Conflict in Aghlabid North Africa and the Central Mediterranean." *Al-Masāq* 27 (2015): 7–23.

——. "Europe and the African Cult of Saints, circa 350–900: An Essay in Mediterranean Communication." *Speculum* 85 (2010): 1–46.

——. "Louis the Pious and the Contours of Empire." *Early Medieval Europe* 22 (2014): 336–360.

Constable, Olivia Remie. *Housing the Stranger in the Mediterranean World: Lodging, Trade, and Travel in Late Antiquity and the Middle Ages*. Cambridge: Cambridge University Press, 2003.

——. "Muslim Spain and Mediterranean Slavery: The Medieval Slave Trade as an Aspect of Muslim-Christian Relations." In *Christendom and Its Discontents: Exclusion, Persecution and Rebellion, 1000–1500*, edited by Scott L. Waugh and Peter D. Diehl, 264–284. Cambridge: Cambridge University Press, 1996.

Contreni, John J. "'By Lions, Bishops Are Meant; by Wolves, Priests': History, Exegesis, and the Carolingian Church in Haimo of Auxerre's *Commentary on Ezechiel*." *Francia* 29 (2002): 29–56.

——. "Haimo of Auxerre's Commentary on Ezechiel." In *L'École Carolingienne d'Auxerre: De Murethach à Remi*, edited by Dominique Iogna-Prat, Colette Jeudy, and Guy Lobrichon, 229–242. Paris: Beauchesne, 1991.

Cook, Michael. "The Opponents of the Writing of Tradition in Early Islam." *Arabica* 44 (1997): 437–530.

Costambeys, Marios. *Power and Patronage in Early Medieval Italy: Local Society, Italian Politics and the Abbey of Farfa, c. 700–900*. Cambridge: Cambridge University Press, 2007.

Costambeys, Marios, Matthew Innes, and Simon MacLean. *The Carolingian World*. Cambridge: Cambridge University Press, 2011.

Coupland, Simon. "The Carolingian Army and the Struggle against the Vikings." *Viator* 35 (2004): 49–70.

——. "Charles the Bald and the Defence of the West Frankish Kingdom against the Viking Invasions, 840–877." PhD diss., University of Cambridge, 1987.

——. "The Coinages of Pippin I and II of Aquitaine." *Revue numismatique* 31 (1989): 194–222.

——. "The Early Coinage of Charles the Bald, 840–864." *Numismatic Chronicle* 151 (1991): 121–158.

———. "The Frankish Tribute Payments to the Vikings and Their Consequences." *Francia* 26 (1999): 57–75.

———. "From Poachers to Gamekeepers: Scandinavian Warlords and Carolingian Kings." *Early Medieval Europe* 7 (1998): 85–114.

Couret, Alphonse. *La Palestine sous les Empereurs Grecs, 326–636.* Grenoble: Imprimerie et lithographie de F. Allier, 1869.

Courtois, Christian. "Reliques carthaginoises et legend carolingienne." *Revue de l'histoire des religions* 129 (1945): 57–83.

Creswell, K.A.C. *Early Muslim Architecture: Umayyads, Early ʿAbbāsids & Ṭūlūnids.* Vol. 2. Oxford: Clarendon Press, 1932–1940.

———. *A Short Account of Early Muslim Architecture.* Aldershot: Scolar Press, 1989.

Crone, Patricia. "Mawlā: In Historical and Legal Usage." *Encyclopedia of Islam.* 2nd ed. 6:874–882. Leiden: Brill, 1991.

———. *Medieval Islamic Political Thought.* Edinburgh: Edinburgh University Press, 2005.

———. *Slaves on Horses: The Evolution of the Islamic Polity.* Cambridge: Cambridge University Press, 1980.

Crone, Patricia, and Martin Hinds. *God's Caliph: Religious Authority in the First Centuries of Islam.* 2nd ed. Cambridge: Cambridge University Press, 1986.

Cruz Hernández, Miguel. "The Social Structure of al-Andalus during the Muslim Occupation (711–53) and the Founding of the Umayyad Monarchy." In *The Formation of al-Andalus, Part 1: History and Sources*, edited by Manuela Marín, 51–83. Aldershot: Routledge, 1998.

Curta, Florin. "Merovingian and Carolingian Gift Giving." *Speculum* 81 (2006): 671–699.

Cutler, Anthony. "Gifts and Gift Exchange as Aspects of the Byzantine, Arab, and Related Economies." *Dumbarton Oaks Papers* 55 (2001): 247–278.

———. "The Ninth-Century Spanish Martyrs Movement and the Origins of Western Christian Missions to the Muslims." *Muslim World* 55 (1965): 321–339.

———. "Significant Gifts: Patterns of Exchange in Late Antique, Byzantine, and Early Islamic Diplomacy." *Journal of Medieval and Early Modern Studies* 38 (2008): 79–102.

Dal Santo, Matthew J. "Text, Image, and the 'Visionary' in Early Byzantine Hagiography: Incubation and the Rise of the Christian Image Cult." *Journal of Late Antiquity* 4 (2011): 31–54.

Daniel, Elton L. "Al-Yaʿqūbī and Shi'ism Reconsidered." In *ʿAbbāsid Studies*, edited by James E. Montgomery, 209–231. Leuven: Peeters, 2004.

———. "Arabs, Persians, and the Advent of the Abbasids Reconsidered." *Journal of the American Oriental Society* 117 (1997): 542–548.

———. *The Political and Social History of Khurasan under Abbasid Rule, 747–820.* Minneapolis: Bibliotheca Islamica, 1979.

Daniel, Norman. *The Arabs and Medieval Europe.* 2nd ed. London: Longman, 1979.

———. *Islam and the West: The Making of an Image.* Edinburgh: Edinburgh University Press, 1960.

Daryaee, Touraj. "From Terror to Tactical Usage: Elephants in the Partho-Sasanian Period." In *The Parthian and Early Sasanian Empires*, edited by Vesta Sarkhosh

Curtis, Elizabeth J. Pendleton, Michael Alram, and Touraj Daryaee, 36–41. Oxford: Oxbow, 2016.

Davies, Rees R. "The Medieval State, the Tyranny of a Concept?" *Journal of Historical Sociology* 16 (2003): 280–300.

Davies, Wendy. "On the Distribution of Political Power in Brittany in the Mid-Ninth Century." *Charles the Bald: Court and Kingdom*, edited by Margaret T. Gibson and Janet L. Nelson, 98–114. Aldershot: Variorum, 1990.

Davis, Jennifer R. *Charlemagne's Practice of Empire*. Cambridge: Cambridge University Press, 2015.

——. "Inventing the *Missi*: Delegating Power in the Late Eighth and Early Ninth Centuries." In *The ʿAbbasid and Carolingian Empires: Comparative Studies in Civilizational Formation*, edited by Deborah G. Tor, 13–51. Leiden: Brill, 2018.

Defourneaux, Maecelin. "Carlomagno y el Reino Asturiano." In *Estudios sobre la Monarquía Asturiana*, 90–114. Oviedo: Instituto de Estudios Asturianos, 1971.

Delogu, Paolo. "Strutture politiche e ideologia nel regno di Ludovico II (Ricerche sull'aristocrazia carolingia in Italia, II)." *Bullettino dell'Istituto Storico Italiano per il Medio Evo* 80 (1968): 137–189.

Dennett, Daniel C. "Pirenne and Muhammad." *Speculum* 23 (1948): 165–190.

Depreux, Philippe. "Le comté Matfrid d'Orléans (815–836)." *Bibliothèque de l'École des Chartes* 152 (1994): 331–374.

——. "Poètes et historiens au temps de l'empereur Louis le Pieux." *Le Moyen Age* 99 (1993): 311–332.

——. *Prosopographie de l'entourage de Louis le Pieux (781–840)*. Sigmaringen: Thorbecke, 1997.

Desch, Michael C. "Culture Clash: Assessing the Importance of Ideas in Security Studies." *International Security* 23 (1998): 141–170.

Deviosse, Jean. *Charles Martel*. Paris: Tallandier, 1978.

Devroey, Jean-Pierre, and Christian Brouwer. "La participation des Juifs au commerce dans le monde Franc (VI^e^–X^e^ siècles)." In *Voyages et Voyageurs à Byzance et en occident du VI^e^ au XI^e^ siècle*, edited by Alain Dierkens and Jean-Marie Sansterre, 339–374. Geneva: Dros, 2000.

Dey, Hendrik W. "*Diaconiae, xenodochia, hospitalia* and Monasteries: 'Social Security' and the Meaning of Monasteries in Early Medieval Rome." *Early Medieval Europe* 16 (2008): 398–422.

Di Branco, Marco. "Due notizie concernenti l'Italia meridionale dal *Kitāb al-ʿuyūn wa'l-ḥadaʾīqfīaḫbār al-ḥaqāʾiq*." *Archivio storico per la Calabria e la Lucania* 77 (2011): 5–13.

——. "Strategie di penetrazione islamica in Italia meridionale: Il caso dell'Emirato di Bari." In *Southern Italy as Contact Area and Border Region during the Early Middle Ages: Religious-Cultural Heterogeneity and Competing Powers in Local, Transregional, and Universal Dimensions*, edited by Klaus Herbers and Kordula Wolf, 149–164. Cologne: Böhlau Verlag, 2018.

Di Gangi, Giorgio, and Chiara Maria Lebole. "La Calabria bizantina (VI–XIV secolo): Un evento di lunga durata." *Histoire et culture dans l'Italie byzantine*, edited by André Jacob, Jean-Marie Martin, et al., 471–487. Rome: Ecole française de Rome, 2006.

Digby, Simon. *War-Horse and Elephant in the Delhi Sultanate: A Study of Military Supplies*. Oxford: Orient Monographs, 1971.

Djaït, Hichem. "La Wilāya D'Ifrīqiya au II$^{e}$/VIII$^{e}$ siècle: Étude institutionelle." *Studia Islamica* 27 (1967): 77–121.

Dodds, Jerrilynn D. "The Great Mosque of Córdoba." In *Al-Andalus: The Art of Islamic Spain*, edited by Jerrilynn D. Dodds, 11–25. New York: Metropolitan Museum of Art, 1992.

Doherty, Hugh. "The Maintenance of Royal Power and Prestige in the Carolingian Regnum of Aquitaine under Louis the Pious." MPhil thesis, University of Cambridge, 1997.

Dolan Gómez, Miguel. "*Rex Parvus* and *Rex Nobilis*? Charlemagne and the Politics of History (and Crusading) in Thirteenth-Century Iberia." In *The Charlemagne Legend in Medieval Latin Texts*, edited by William J. Purkis and Matthew Gabriele, 92–114. Cambridge: D. S. Brewer, 2016.

Donner, Fred M. *Narratives of Islamic Origins: The Beginnings of Islamic Historical Writing*. Princeton: Darwin Press, 1998.

Doody, Aude. "Authority and Authorship in the *Medicina Plinii*." In *Authorial Voices in Greco-Roman Technical Writing*, edited by Aude Doody and Liba Taub, 93–105. Trier: WVT, 2009.

Doolittle, Jeffrey. "Charlemagne in Girona: Liturgy, Legend and the Memory of Siege." In *The Charlemagne Legend in Medieval Latin Texts*, edited by William J. Purkis and Matthew Gabriele, 115–147. Cambridge: D. S. Brewer, 2016.

Dopsch, Alfons. *Wirtschaftliche und soziale Grundlagen der europäischen Kulturentwicklung von Cäsar bis auf Karl den Großen*. Vienna: L. W. Seidel, 1918–20.

Dozy, Reinhart. *Histoire des musulmans d'Espagne jusquà la conquéte de l'Andalousie par les almoravides*. Vol. 1, edited by Evariste Lévi-Provençal. Leiden: Brill, 1932.

Dressen, Wolfgang, Georg Minkenberg, and Adam C. Oellers, eds. *Ex Oriente: Isaak und der weisse Elefant: Bagdad-Jerusalem-Aachen: Eine Reise durch drei Kulturen um 800 und heute*. Mainz: Von Zabern, 2003.

Drews, Wolfram. *Die Karolinger und die ʿAbbāsiden von Bagdad: Legitimationsstrategien frühmittelalterlicher Herrscherdynastien im transkulturellen Vergleich*. Berlin: Akademie Verlag, 2009.

———. "Karl, Byzanz und die Mächte des Islam." In *Kaiser und Kalifen: Karl der Grosse und die Mächte am Mittelmeer um 800*, edited by Barbara Segelken and Tim Urban, 86–99. Darmstadt: Von Zabern, 2014.

Drocourt, Nicolas. "Christian-Muslim Diplomatic Relations: An Overview of the Main Sources and Themes of Encounter (600–1000)." In *Christian-Muslim Relations: A Bibliographical History*, edited by David Thomas and Alexander Mallett, 2:29–72. Leiden: Brill, 2010.

———. "L'ambassadeur maltraité: Autour de quelques cas de non-respect de l'immunité diplomatique entre Byzance et ses voisins (viii$^{e}$–xi$^{e}$ siècle)." In *Les relations diplomatiques au Moyen Âge*, 87–98. Paris: Publications de la Sorbonne, 2011.

———. "Passing on Political Information between Major Powers: The Key Role of Ambassadors between Byzantium and Some of Its Neighbours." *Al-Masāq* 24 (2012): 91–112.

Dubreucq, Alain. "Guillaume de Toulouse et la politique carolingienne en Aquitaine, d'apres les sources narratives." In *Entre histoire et épopée: Les Guillaume d'Orange (IX^e^-XIII^e^ siècles)*, edited by Laurent Macé, 183–205. Toulouse: Université de Toulouse-Le Mirail, 2006.

Duhamel-Amado, Claudie, and Aymat Catafau. "Fidèles et aprisionaires en réseaux dans la Gothie, des IX^e^ et X^e^ siècles: Le mariage et l'aprision au service de la noblesse méridionale." *La royauté et les élites dans l'Europe carolingienne (début IX^e^ siècle aux environs de 920)*, edited by Régine Le Jan, 438–465. Lille: Centre d'histoire de l'Europe du Nord-Ouest, 1998.

Dunlop, D. M. "A Diplomatic Exchange between al-Ma'mūn and an Indian King." In *Medieval and Middle Eastern Studies in Honor of Aziz Suryal Atiya*, edited by Sami A. Hanna, 133–143. Leiden: Brill, 1972.

Duparc, Pierre. "Les Cluses et la Frontière des Alpes." *Bibliothèque de l'École des Chartes* 109 (1951): 5–31.

Dupré, Nicole. "La place de la Vallée de l'Ebre dans l'Espagne romane." *Mélanges de la Casa Velázquez* 9 (1973): 133–175.

Duri, A. A. *The Rise of Historical Writing among the Arabs*. Edited and translated by Lawrence I. Conrad. Princeton: Princeton University Press, 1983.

Dutton, Paul Edward, ed. *Carolingian Civilization: A Reader*. 2nd ed. North York: University of Toronto Press, 2009.

——, trans. *Charlemagne's Courtier: The Complete Einhard*. North York, Ontario: Broadview Press, 2008.

——. *Charlemagne's Mustache and Other Cultural Clusters of a Dark Age*. New York: Palgrave Macmillan, 2009.

——. *The Politics of Dreaming in the Carolingian Empire*. Lincoln: University of Nebraska Press, 1994.

Ebben, Maurits, and Louis Sicking. *Beyond Ambassadors: Consuls, Missionaries, and Spies in Premodern Diplomacy*. Leiden: Brill, 2020.

Eddé, Anne-Marie, Françoise Micheau, and Christophe Picard. *Communautés Chrétiennes en pays d'islam: Du début du VII^e^ siècle au milieu du XI^e^ siècle*. Paris: SEDES, 1997.

Eickhoff, Ekkehard. *Seekrieg und Seepolitik zwischen Islam und Abendland*. Berlin: De Gruyter, 1966.

von Einem, Herbert. "Die Tragödie der Karlsfresken Alfred Rethels." In *Karl der Grosse: Lebenswerk und Nachleben*. Vol. 4, edited by Wolfgang Braunfels, 306–325. Düsseldorf: L. Schwann, 1965.

Eiten, Gustav. *Das Unterkönigtum im Reiche der Merovinger und Karolinger*. Heidelberg: C. Winter, 1907.

Elad, Amikam. "Aspects of the Transition from the Umayyad to the 'Abbāsid Caliphate." *Jerusalem Studies in Arabic and Islam* 19 (1995): 89–132.

——. *The Rebellion of Muḥammad al-Nafs al-Zakiyya in 145/762: Ṭālibīs and Early 'Abbāsīs in Conflict*. Leiden: Brill, 2015.

——. "The Southern Golan in the Early Muslim Period: The Significance of Two Newly Discovered Milestones of 'Abd al-Malik." *Der Islam* 76 (1999): 33–88.

El Cheikh, Nadia Maria. "The Chamberlain." In *Crisis and Continuity at the Abbasid Court: Formal and Informal Politics in the Caliphate of al-Muqtadir*

*(295–320/908–32)*, edited by Maaike van Berkel, Nadia Maria El Cheikh, Hugh Kennedy, and Letizia Osti, 145–163. Leiden: Brill, 2013.

———. "Courts and Courtiers: A Preliminary Investigation of Abbasid Terminology." In *Court Cultures in the Muslim World: Seventh to Nineteenth Centuries*, edited by Albrecht Fuess and Jan-Peter Hartung, 80–90. London: Routledge, 2011.

———. "The Institutionalisation of ʿAbbāsid Ceremonial." In *Diverging Paths?: The Shapes of Power and Institutions in Medieval Christendom and Islam*, edited by John Hudson and Ana Rodríguez, 351–370. Leiden: Brill, 2014.

El-Hajji, Abdurrahman Ali. *Andalusian Diplomatic Relations with Western Europe during the Umayyad Period: A. H. 138–366/A. D. 755–976, an Historical Survey.* Beirut: Dar al-Irshad, 1970.

———. "Intermarriage between Andalusia and Northern Spain in the Umayyad Period." *Islamic Quarterly* 11 (1967): 3–7.

El-Hibri, Tayeb. "The Empire in Iraq, 763–861." In *The New Cambridge History of Islam*. Vol. 1: *The Formation of the Islamic World, Sixth to Eleventh Centuries*, edited by Chase F. Robinson, 269–304. Cambridge: Cambridge University Press, 2010.

———. *Reinterpreting Islamic Historiography: Hārūn al-Rashīd and the Narrative of the ʿAbbāsid Caliphate*. Cambridge: Cambridge University Press, 1999.

Encuentra Ortega, Alfredo. "Luis el Piadoso, un Eneas Cristiano en el poema laudatorio de Ermoldo." *Latomus: Revue D'Études* 64 (2005): 445–455.

Engemann, Josef. "Diplomatische 'Geschenke'—Objekte aus der Spätantike?" *Mitteilungen zur Spätantiken Archäologie und Byzantinischen Kunstgeschichte* 4 (2005): 39–64.

Engreen, Fred E. "Pope John the Eighth and the Arabs." *Speculum* 20 (1945): 318–330.

Escalona, Julio. "Family Memories: Inventing Alfonso I of Asturias." *Building Legitimacy: Political Discourses and Forms of Legitimacy in Medieval Societies*, edited by Isabel Alfonso, Hugh Kennedy, and Julio Escalona, 223–262. Leiden: Brill, 2004.

Eustache, Daniel. "El-Baṣra, capitale Idrīssite, et son port." *Hesperis* 42 (1955): 217–238.

———. "Idrīs I." *Encyclopedia of Islam*. 2nd ed. 3:1031. Leiden: Brill, 1971.

Evans, Nicholas J. B. "The Mobile Court of a Khazar Royal Woman." In *Courts on the Move: Perspectives on the Global Middle Ages*, edited by Claudia Rapp, Ekaterini Mitsiou, Johannes Preiser-Kapeller, and Paraskevi Sykopetritou. Vienna: Vienna University Press (forthcoming).

Evans, Robert, and Rosamond McKitterick. "A Carolingian Epitome of Orosius from Tours: Leiden VLQ 20." In *Historiography and Identity III: Carolingian Approaches*, edited by Rutger Kramer, Helmut Reimitz, and Graeme Ward, 123–154. Turnhout: Brepols, 2021.

Ewig, Eugen. *Die Merowinger und das Imperium*. Opladen: Westdeutscher Verlag, 1983.

———. "Résidence et capitale pendant le haut Moyen Age." *Revue Historique* 230 (1963): 25–72.

Fairchild Ruggles, D. *Gardens, Landscape, and Vision in the Palaces of Islamic Spain*. University Park: Pennsylvania State University Press, 2000.

———. "Historiography and the Rediscovery of Madīnat al-Zahrāʾ." *Islamic Studies* 30 (1991): 129–140.

——. "The Mirador in Abbasid and Hispano-Umayyad Garden Typology." *Muqarnas* 7 (1989): 73–82.

——. "Mothers of a Hybrid Dynasty: Race, Genealogy and Acculturation in al-Andalus." *Journal of Medieval and Early Modern Studies* 34 (2004): 65–94.

Falkenstein, Ludwig. "Charlemagne et Aix-la-Chapelle." *Byzantion* 61 (1991): 231–289.

Farnham, Barbara. "Impact of the Political Context on Foreign Policy Decision-Making." *Political Psychology* 25 (2004): 441–463.

Fearon, James D. "Domestic Politics, Foreign Policy, and Theories of International Relations." *Annual Review of Political Science* 1 (1998): 289–313.

Feldbauer, Peter, and Ilja Steffelbauer. "Die 'islamische' Stadt." In *Kaiser und Kalifen: Karl der Grosse und die Mächte am Mittelmeer um 800*, edited by Barbara Segelken and Tim Urban, 182–201. Darmstadt: Von Zabern, 2014.

Felten, Franz J., ed. *Hrabanus Maurus: Gelehrter, Abt von Fulda und Erzbischof von Mainz*. Mainz: Kongress Mainz, 2006.

Fenina, Abdelhamid. "L'atelier monétaire d'al-'Abbassiyya: Du 'vieux château' (al-Qasr al-Qadim) à la ville princière aghlabide." In *The Aghlabids and Their Neighbors: Art and Material Culture in Ninth-Century North Africa*, edited by Glaire D. Anderson, Corisande Fenwick, and Mariam Rosser-Owen, 106–126. Leiden: Brill, 2018.

Fenske, Lutz. "Jagd und Jäger im früheren Mittelalter: Aspekte ihres Verhältnisses." In *Die Geschichte der Jagd: Kultur, Gesellschaft und Jagdwesen im Wandel der Zeit*, edited by Werner Rösener, 29–93. Düsseldorf: Artemis & Winkler, 2004.

Fentress, Elizabeth. "Idris I and the Berbers." In *The Aghlabids and Their Neighbors: Art and Material Culture in Ninth-Century North Africa*, edited by Glaire D. Anderson, Corisande Fenwick, and Mariam Rosser-Owen, 514–530. Leiden: Brill, 2018.

Fenwick, Corisande. *Early Islamic North Africa: A New Perspective*. London: Bloomsbury Academic, 2020.

——. "From Africa to Ifrīqiya: Settlement and Society in Early Medieval North Africa (650–800)." *Al-Masāq* 25 (2013): 9–33.

Fernández Conde, Francisco Javier. "Relaciones políticas y culturales de Alfonso II de Casto." In *Historia social, Pensamiento historiográfico y Edad Media*, edited by Isabel Loring García, 593–611. Madrid: Ediciones del Orto, 1997.

Fierro, María Isabel. *Abd al-Rahman III: The First Cordoban Caliph*. Oxford: Oneworld, 2005.

——. "El Conde Casio, los Banu Qasi y los Linajes Godos en al-Andalus." *Studia Historica: Historia Medieval* 27 (2009): 181–189.

——. "El derecho Mālikí en al-Andalus: Siglos II/VIII–V/XI." *al-Qanṭara* 12 (1991): 119–132.

——. "The Introduction of Ḥadīth in al-Andalus (2nd/8th–3rd/9th Centuries)." *Der Islam* 66 (1989): 68–93.

——. *La Heterodoxia en al-Andalus durante el periodo omeya*. Madrid: Instituto Hispano-Arabe de Cultura, 1987.

——. "La Obra Histórica de Ibn al-Qūṭiyya." *al-Qanṭara* 10 (1989): 485–512.

——. "On Political Legitimacy in al-Andalus." *Der Islam* 76 (1996): 138–150.

——. "Sobre la adopción del título califal por 'Abd al-Raḥmān III." *Sharq al-Andalus. Estudios Arabes* 6 (1989): 33–42.

Fiey, Jean Maurice. *Chrétiens Syriaques sous les Abbassides, surtout à Bagdad (749–1258)*. Louvain: Secrétariat du Corpus, 1980.

Fischer, Andreas. "Rewriting History: Fredegar's Perspectives on the Mediterranean." In *Western Perspectives on the Mediterranean: Cultural Transfer in Late Antiquity and the Early Middle Ages, 400–800 AD*, edited by Andreas Fischer and Ian Wood, 55–75. London: Bloomsbury Academic, 2014.

Fischer, Markus. "Feudal Europe, 800–1300: Communal Discourse and Conflictual Practices." *International Organizations* 46 (1992): 427–466.

Fontaine, Jacques. "Mozarabie Hispanique et Monde Carolingien." *Anuario de Estudios Medievales* 13 (1983): 17–46.

Foot, Sarah. "Finding the Meaning of Form: Narrative in Annals and Chronicles." In *Writing Medieval History*, edited by Nancy Partner, 89–102. London: Arnold, 2005.

———. "Reading Anglo-Saxon Charters: Memory, Record, or Story?" *Narrative and History in the Early Medieval West*, edited by Elizabeth Tyler and Ross Balzaretti, 39–65. Turnhout: Brepols, 2006.

Fouracre, Paul. *The Age of Charles Martel*. Harlow: Longman, 2000.

———. "Frankish Gaul to 814." In *The New Cambridge Medieval History*, vol. 2, edited by Rosamond McKitterick, 85–109. Cambridge: Cambridge University Press, 1995.

———. "The Long Shadow of the Merovingians." In *Charlemagne: Empire and Society*, edited by Joanna Story, 5–21. Manchester: Manchester University Press, 2005.

———. "Observations on the Outgrowth of Pippinid Influence in the 'Regnum Francorum' after the Battle of Tertry (687–715)." *Medieval Prosopography* 5 (1984): 1–31.

Fouracre, Paul, and Richard A. Gerberding. *Late Merovingian France: History and Hagiography, 640–720*. Manchester: Manchester University Press, 1996.

Fournier, Gabriel. "Les campagnes de Pépin le Bref en Auvergne et la question des fortifications rurales au VIII^e siècles." *Francia* 2 (1974): 123–135.

Fowden, Elizabeth Key. *The Barbarian Plain: Saint Sergius between Rome and Iran*. Berkeley: University of California Press, 1999.

Fowden, Garth. *Before and After Muḥammad: The First Millennium Refocused*. Princeton: Princeton University Press, 2014.

———. *Quṣayr ʿAmra: Art and the Umayyad Elite in Late Antique Syria*. Berkeley: University of California Press, 2004.

Franke, Franz Richard. "Die freiwilligen Märtyrer von Cordova und das Verhältnis der Mozaraber zum Islam." *Spanische Forschungen des Gorresgesellschaft* 13 (1953): 1–170.

Freeman, Ann. "Theodulf of Orléans: A Visigoth at Charlemagne's Court." In *L'Europe héritière de l'Espagne wisigothique*, edited by Jacques Fontaine and Christine Pellistrandi, 185–194. Madrid: Casa de Velázquez, 1992.

Freeman, Ann, and Paul Meyvaert. "The Meaning of Theodulf's Apse Mosaic at Germigny-des-Prés." *Gesta* 40 (2001): 125–139.

Freidenreich, David M. "The Implications of Unbelief: Tracing the Emergence of Distinctively Shi'i Notions Regarding the Food and Impurity of Non-Muslims." *Islamic Law and Society* 18 (2011): 53–84.

Freudenhammer, Thomas. "Frühmittelalterlicher Karawanenhandel zwischen dem Westfrankenreich und Al-Andalus." *Vierteljahresschrift fur Sozial und Wirtschaftsgeschichte* 105 (2018): 391–406.

Gabriele, Matthew. *An Empire of Memory: The Legend of Charlemagne, the Franks, and Jerusalem before the First Crusade*. Oxford: Oxford University Press, 2011.

Gabrieli, Francesco. "La successione di Hārūn ar-Rašīd e la guerra fra al-Amīn e al-Ma'mūn." *Rivisti degli Studi Orientali* 11 (1926–1928): 341–397.

——. "Omayyades d'Espagne et Abbasides." *Studia Islamica* 31 (1970): 93–100.

Gai, Sveva. "Die Pfalzen in Paderborn: Entweckung und Auswertung." In *799: Kunst und Kultur der Karolingerzeit: Karl der Grosse und Papst Leo III. in Paderborn*, edited by Christoph Stiegemann and Matthias Wemhoff, 183–196. Mainz: Von Zabern, 1999.

de Gaiffier, Baudouin. "Relations religieuses de l'Espagne avec le Nord de la France." *Recherches d'Hagiographie Latine*, 7–30. Brussels: Société des Bollandistes, 1971.

Ganshof, François Louis. "A propos du tonlieu a l'époque Carolingienne." *Settimane di Studio* 6 (1959): 485–508.

——. *The Carolingians and the Frankish Monarchy*. Translated by Janet Sondheimer. Ithaca: Cornell University Press, 1971.

——. "Harunu'l-Rashid and Charles the Great: Compte Rendu." *Revue Belge de Philologie et d'histoire* 11 (1932): 774–776.

——. "Harunu'l-Rashid et Charlemagne; une fantaise historique." *Byzantion* 7 (1932): 555–557.

——. *Histoire des Relations Internationales: Le Moyen Age*. Paris: Hachette, 1953.

——. "Les relations extérieures de la monarchie franque sous les premiers souverains carolingiens." *Annali di Storia del Dritto* 5–6 (1961–1962): 1–54.

——. "La tractoria: Contribution à l'étude des origines du droit de gîte." *Tijdschrift voor rechtsgeschiedenis* 8 (1928): 69–91.

——. "Une crise dans le règne de Charlemagne, les années 778 et 779." In *Mélanges d'histoire et de littérature offerts à Charles Gilliard*, edited by Louis Junod and Sven Stelling-Michaud, 133–145. Lausanne: F. Rouge, 1944.

Gantner, Clemens. "The Eighth-Century Papacy as Cultural Broker." In *The Resources of the Past in Early Medieval Europe*, edited by Clemens Gantner, Rosamond McKitterick, and Sven Meeder, 245–261. Cambridge: Cambridge University Press, 2015.

——. "A King in Training? Louis II of Italy and His Expedition to Rome in 844." In *After Charlemagne: Carolingian Italy and Its Rulers*, edited by Clemens Gantner and Walter Pohl, 164–182. Cambridge: Cambridge University Press, 2020.

——. "New Visions of Community in Ninth-Century Rome: The Impact of the Saracen Threat on the Papal World View." In *Visions of Community in the Post-Roman World: The West, Byzantium and the Islamic World, 300–1100*, edited by Walter Pohl, Clemens Gantner, and Richard Payne, 403–422. Farnham: Ashgate, 2012.

——. "'Our Common Enemies Shall Be Annihilated': How Louis II's Relations with the Byzantine Empire Shaped His Policy in Southern Italy." In *Southern Italy as Contact Area and Border Region during the Early Middle Ages: Religious-Cultural Heterogeneity and Competing Powers in Local, Transregional, and Universal Dimensions*, edited by Klaus Herbers and Kordula Wolf, 295–314. Cologne: Böhlau Verlag, 2018.

Ganz, David. "The *Epitaphium Arsenii* and Opposition to Louis the Pious." In *Charlemagne's Heir: New Perspectives on the Reign of Louis the Pious (814–840)*, edited by Peter Godman and Roger Collins, 537–550. Oxford: Clarendon Press, 1990.

——. "Humour as History in Notker's *Gesta Karoli magni*." In *Monks, Nuns, and Friars in Mediaeval Society*, edited by Edward B. King, Jacqueline T. Schaefer, and William B. Wadley, 171–183. Sewanee: Press of the University of the South, 1989.

García Gómez, Emilio. "Algunas precisiones sobre la ruina de la Córdoba omeya." *Al-Andalus* 12 (1947): 277–293.

García-Arenal, Mercedes, and Eduardo Manzano Moreno. "Légitimité et villes Idrīssides." In *Genèse de la ville islamique en al-Andalus et au Maghreb occidental*, edited by Patrice Cressier and Mercedes García-Arenal, 257–284. Madrid: Casa de Velázquez, 1998.

Garrison, Mary. "The Franks as the New Israel? Education for an Identity from Pippin to Charlemagne." In *The Uses of the Past in the Early Middle Ages*, edited by Yitzhak Hen and Matthew Innes, 114–161. Cambridge: Cambridge University Press, 2000.

Gay, Jules. *L'Italie méridionale et l'Empire byzantin depuis l'avènement de Basile Ier jusqu'à la prise de Bari par les Normands (867–1071)*. Paris: A. Fontemoing, 1904.

Geary, Patrick J. *Aristocracy in Provence: The Rhône Basin at the Dawn of the Carolingian Age*. Philadelphia: University of Pennsylvania Press, 1985.

———. *Furta Sacra: Thefts of Relics in the Central Middle Ages*. Rev. ed. Princeton: Princeton University Press, 1990.

———. "Gift Exchange and Social Science Modeling: The Limitations of a Construct." In *Negotiating the Gift: Pre-modern Figurations of Exchange*, edited by Gadi Algazi, Valentin Groebner, and Bernhard Jussen, 129–140. Göttingen: Vandenhoeck & Ruprecht, 2003.

Geisel, Christof. *Die Juden im Frankenreich: Von den Merowingern bis zum Tode Ludwigs des Frommen*. Frankfurt am Main: P. Lang, 1998.

Gemeinhardt, Peter. *Die Filioque-Kontroverse zwischen Ost- und Westkirche im Frühmittelalter*. Berlin: De Gruyter, 2002.

Gerberding, Richard A. *The Rise of the Carolingians and the* Liber Historiae Francorum. Oxford: Clarendon Press, 1987.

Gerhardt, Mia Irene. "The Ant-Lion: Nature Study and the Interpretation of a Biblical Text, from the Physiologus to Albert the Great." *Vivarium* 3 (1965): 1–23.

———. *The Art of Story-Telling: A Literary Study of the Thousand and One Nights*. Leiden: Brill, 1963.

Ghersetti, Antonella. "The Rhetoric of Gifts, or When Objects Talk." In *Abbasid Studies IV: Occasional Papers of the School of ʿAbbasid Studies Leuven, July 5–July 9, 2010*, edited by Monique Bernards, 130–141. Warminster: Gibb Memorial Trust, 2013.

Gibb, Hamilton A. R. "Chinese Records of the Arabs in Central Asia." *Bulletin of the School of Oriental and African Studies* 2 (1923): 613–622.

Gil, Moshe. *A History of Palestine, 634–1099*. 2nd ed. Cambridge: Cambridge University Press, 1992.

———. *Jews in Islamic Countries in the Middle Ages*. Translated by David Strassler. Leiden: Brill, 2004.

Gillett, Andrew. "Communication in Late Antiquity: Use and Reuse." In *The Oxford Handbook of Late Antiquity*, edited by Scott Fitzgerald Johnson, 815–846. Oxford: Oxford University Press, 2012.

———. *Envoys and Political Communication in the Late Antique West, 411–533*. Cambridge: Cambridge University Press, 2003.

Gilliot, Claude. "La formation intellectuelle de Tabari (224/5–310/839–923)." *La Société Asiatique* 176 (1988): 203–244.

Gillmor, Carroll. "War on the Rivers: Viking Numbers and Mobility on the Seine and Loire." *Viator* 19 (1988): 79–109.

Gjuselav, Vasil. "Bulgarisch-Fränkische Beziehungen in der ersten Häfte des IX.Jhs." *Byzantinoslavica* 2 (1966): 15–39.

Glick, Thomas. *Islamic and Christian Spain in the Early Middle Ages*. Leiden: Brill, 2005.

Godman, Peter. "Louis 'the Pious' and His Poets." *Frühmittelalterliche Studien* 19 (1985): 239–289.

——. *Poets and Emperors: Frankish Politics and Carolingian Poetry*. Oxford: Clarendon Press, 1987.

Goetz, Hans-Werner. "The Perception of Other Religions in the Earlier Middle Ages: Some Remarks on a Current Research Project. Introduction." *Millennium* 10 (2013): 275–280.

Goitein, Shelomo Dov. "Medieval Tunisia: The Hub of the Mediterranean." In *Studies in Islamic History and Institutions*, 308–328. Leiden: Brill, 1966. Originally *Etudes d'orientalisme dédiées à la mémoire de Lévi-Provençal*, 559–579. Paris: G.-P. Maisonneuve et Larose, 1962.

——. *A Mediterranean Society: The Jewish Communities of the Arab World as Portrayed in the Documents of the Cairo Geniza*. Vol. 1. Berkeley: University of California Press, 1967.

Goldberg, Eric J. "Hunting for the Asiatic Onager (*Equus hemionus*) in the ʿAbbasid, Byzantine, and Carolingian Worlds." In *The ʿAbbasid and Carolingian Empires: Comparative Studies in Civilizational Formation*, edited by Deborah G. Tor, 73–101. Leiden: Brill, 2018.

——. *In the Manner of the Franks: Hunting, Kingship, and Masculinity in Early Medieval Europe*. Philadelphia: University of Pennsylvania Press, 2020.

——. "Louis the Pious and the Hunt." *Speculum* 88 (2013): 613–644.

——. "Ludwig der Deutsche und Mähren: Eine Stucke zu Karolingische Grenzkriegen im Osten." In *Ludwig der Deutsche und seine Zeit*, edited by Wilfried Hartmann, 67–94. Darmstadt: Wissenschaftliche Buchgesellschaft, 2004.

——. "'A Man of Notable Good Looks Disfigured by a Cruel Wound': The Forest Misadventure of Charles the Young of Aquitaine (864) in History and Legend." In *Historiography and Identity III: Carolingian Approaches*, edited by Rutger Kramer, Helmut Reimitz, and Graeme Ward, 355–386. Turnhout: Brepols, 2021.

——. *Struggle for Empire: Kingship and Conflict under Louis the German, 817–876*. Ithaca: Cornell University Press, 2006.

Goldberg, Jessica L. *Trade and Institutions in the Medieval Mediterranean: The Geniza Merchants and Their Business World*. Cambridge: Cambridge University Press, 2012.

Goodson, Caroline. "Topographies of Power in Aghlabid-Era Kairouan." In *The Aghlabids and Their Neighbors: Art and Material Culture in Ninth-Century North Africa*, edited by Glaire D. Anderson, Corisande Fenwick, and Mariam Rosser-Owen, 88–105. Leiden: Brill, 2018.

Goosmann, Erik. "Carolingian Kingship, Apostolic Authority and Imperial Recognition: Pippin the Short's *Italienpolitik* and the Quest for Royal Legitimacy." In *East and West in the Early Middle Ages: The Merovingian Kingdoms in Mediterranean Perspective*, edited by Stefan Esders, Yaniv Fox, Yitzhak Hen, and Laury Sarti, 329–345. Cambridge: Cambridge University Press, 2019.

Gordon, Matthew S. *The Breaking of a Thousand Swords: A History of the Turkish Military of Samarra (A.H. 200–275/815–889 C.E.)*. Albany: State University of New York Press, 2001.

Goubert, Paul. *Byzance avant l'Islam II: Byzance et l'Occident sous les successeurs de Justinien, 2: Rome, Byzance et Carthage*. Paris: Picard, 1965.

Grabar, Oleg. "The Shared Culture of Objects." In *Byzantine Court Culture from 829 to 1204*, edited by Henry Maguire, 115–129. Washington, DC: Dumbarton Oaks, 1997.

Grabois, Aryeh. "Charlemagne, Rome and Jerusalem." *Revue Belge de Philologie et d'histoire* 59 (1981): 792–801.

Graetz, Heinrich. *Volkstümliche Geschichte der Juden*. Vienna: R. Löwit, 1909.

Granier, Thomas. "La captivité de l'empereur Louis II à Bénévent (13 août–17 septembre 871) dans les sources des IXe–Xe siècles: L'écriture de l'histoire, de la fausse nouvelle au récit exemplaire." In *Faire l'événement au Moyen Âge*, edited by Claude Carozzi and Huguette Taviani-Carozzi, 13–39. Aix-en-Provence: Publications de l'Université de Provence, 2007.

Gravel, Martin. *Distances, rencontres, communications: Réaliser l'empire sous Charlemagne et Louis le Pieux*. Turnhout: Brepols, 2012.

Grewe, Holger. "Die Königspfalz zu Ingelheim am Rhein 1960–1970." In *799: Kunst und Kultur der Karolingerzeit: Karl der Grosse und Papst Leo III. in Paderborn*, edited by Christoph Stiegemann and Matthias Wemhoff, 142–151. Mainz: Von Zabern, 1999.

Grierson, Philip. "The 'Gratia Dei Rex' Coinage of Charles the Bald." *Charles the Bald: Court and Kingdom*, edited by Margaret T. Gibson and Janet L. Nelson, 52–64. Aldershot: Variorum, 1990.

Griffith, Sidney H. "Byzantium and the Christians in the World of Islam: Constantinople and the Church in the Holy Land in the Ninth Century." *Medieval Encounters* 3 (1997): 231–265.

———. *The Church in the Shadow of the Mosque: Christians and Muslims in the World of Islam*. Princeton: Princeton University Press, 2010.

———. "The Church of Jerusalem and the 'Melkites': The Making of an 'Arab Orthodox' Christian Identity in the World of Islam (750–1050 CE)." In *Christians and Christianity in the Holy Land: From the Origins to the Latin Kingdoms*, edited by Ora Limor and Guy G. Stroumsa, 175–204. Turnhout: Brepols, 2006.

Guichard, Pierre. "Les débuts de la piraterie andalouse en Méditerranée occidentale (798–813)." *Revue de l'Occident Musulman et de la Méditerranée* 35 (1983): 55–76.

———. "Les relations diplomatiques des Omeyyades de Cordoue." *Oriente Moderno* 88 (2008): 229–247.

Günther, Sebastian. "*Maqâtil* Literature in Medieval Islam." *Journal of Arabic Literature* 25 (1994): 192–212.

Gutas, Dimitri. *Greek Thought, Arabic Culture: The Graeco-Arabic Translation Movement in Baghdad and Early 'Abbāsid Society (2nd–4th/8th–10th Centuries)*. London: Routledge, 1998.

Haack, Christoph. *Die Krieger der Karolinger: Kriegsdienste als Prozesse gemeinschaftlicher Organisation um 800*. Berlin: De Gruyter, 2020.

Haack, Christoph, and Thomas Kohl. "Teudefred and the King: On the Manuscript Carcassonne G 6 and the Intertwining of Localities and Centre in the Carolingian World." *Early Medieval Europe* 30 (2022): 209–235.

Hack, Achim Thomas. *Abul Abaz: Zur Biographie eines Elefanten*. Badenweiler: Badenweiler Wiss. Verl. Bachmann, 2011.

———. *Codex Carolinus: Päpstliche Epistolographie im 8. Jahrhundert*. Stuttgart: A. Hiersemann, 2006.

Hagemann, Hannah-Lena, and Peter Verkinderen. "Kharijism in the Umayyad Period." In *The Umayyad World*, edited by Andrew Marsham, 489–517. London: Routledge, 2020.

Hägermann, Dieter. *Karl der Grosse: Herrscher des Abendlandes*. Berlin: Propyläen, 2000.

Haldon, John F., and Hugh Kennedy. "The Arab-Byzantine Frontier in the Eighth and Ninth Centuries: Military Organisation and Society in the Borderlands." *Zbornik Radova Vizantoloshkog Institute* 19 (1980): 79–116.

Halevi, Levi. "Bernard, Explorer of the Muslim Lake: A Pilgrimage from Rome to Jerusalem, 867." *Medieval Encounters* 4 (1998): 24–50.

Halm, Heinz. *The Empire of the Mahdi: The Rise of the Fatimids*. Translated by Michael Bonner. Leiden: Brill, 1996.

Halphen, Louis. *Études critiques sur l'histoire de Charlemagne*. Paris: F. Alcan, 1921.

Hamidullah, Muhammad. "Nouveaux documents sur les rapports de l'Europe avec l'Orient Musulman au Moyen Âge." *Arabica* 7 (1960): 281–300.

Hammer, Carl I. "Christmas Day 800: Charles the Younger, Alcuin and the Frankish Royal Succession." *English Historical Review* 127 (2012): 1–23.

———. "'Pipinus Rex': Pippin's Plot of 792 and Bavaria." *Traditio* 63 (2008): 235–276.

Handley, Mark A. "Disputing the End of African Christianity." In *Vandals, Romans and Berbers: New Perspectives on Late Antique North Africa*, edited by Andrew H. Merrills, 291–310. Aldershot: Ashgate, 2004.

Hannig, Jürgen. "Ars donandi: Zur Ökonomie des Schenkens im frühen Mittelalter." In *Armut, Liebe, Ehre*, edited by Richard van Dülmen, 11–37. Frankfurt am Main: Fischer Taschenbuch Verlag, 1988.

Hardt, Matthias. "Hesse, Elbe, Saale and the Frontiers of the Carolingian Empire." In *The Transformation of Frontiers from Late Antiquity to the Carolingians*, edited by Walter Pohl, Ian Wood, and Helmut Reimitz, 219–232. Leiden: Brill, 2001.

Haselbach, Irene. *Aufstieg und Herrschaft der Karlinger in der Darstellung der sogenannten Annales Mettenses priores*. Lübeck: Matthiesen, 1970.

Hauck, Karl. "Karl als neuer Konstantin 777. Die archäologischen Entdeckung in Paderborn in historisches Sicht." *Frühmittelalterliche Studien* 20 (1986): 513–540.

———. "Tiergärten im Pfalzbereich." In *Deutsche Königspfalzen*, 1:30–74. Göttingen: Vandenhoeck & Ruprecht, 1963.

Haug, Robert. *The Eastern Frontier: Limits of Empire in Late Antique and Early Medieval Central Asia*. London: I. B. Tauris, 2019.

Havighurst, Alfred F., ed. *The Pirenne Thesis: Analysis, Criticism, and Revision*. Boston: D. C. Heath, 1958.

Hawting, Gerald R. *The First Dynasty of Islam: The Umayyad Caliphate, AD 661–750*. 2nd ed. London: Routledge, 2000.

Haywood, John. *Dark Age Naval Power: A Re-assessment of Frankish and Anglo-Saxon Seafaring Activity*. London: Routledge, 1991.

Heath, Christopher. "Third/Ninth-Century Violence: 'Saracens' and Sawdān in Erchempert's *Historia*." *Al-Masāq* 27 (2015): 24–40.

Heidemann, Stefan. "The History of the Industrial and Commercial Area of 'Abbāsid Al-Raqqa, Called Al-Raqqa Al-Muḥtariqa." *Bulletin of the School of Oriental and African Studies* 69 (2006): 33–52.

Heidemann, Stefan, and Andrea Becker. *Raqqa II: Die islamische Stadt*. Mainz: Von Zabern, 2003.

Heil, Johannes. "Agobard, Amolo, das Kirchengut und die Juden von Lyon." *Francia* 25 (1998): 39–76.

——. *Kompilation oder Konstruktion?: Die Juden in den Pauluskommentaren des 9. Jahrhunderts*. Hannover: Hahn, 1998.

——. "Theodulf, Haimo, and Jewish Traditions of Biblical Learning: Exploring Carolingian Culture's Lost Spanish Heritage." In *Discovery and Distinction in the Early Middle Ages*, edited by Cullen J. Chandler and Steven A. Stofferahn, 88–115. Kalamazoo, MI: Medieval Institute Publications, 2013.

Helms, Mary W. *Ulysses' Sail: An Ethnographic Odyssey of Power, Knowledge, and Geographical Distance*. Princeton: Princeton University Press, 1988.

Hen, Yitzhak. "Alcuin, Seneca and the Brahmins of India." In *Religious Franks: Religion and Power in the Frankish Kingdoms*, edited by Rob Meens et al., 148–161. Manchester: Manchester University Press, 2016.

——. "The Annals of Metz and the Merovingian Past." In *The Uses of the Past in the Early Middle Ages*, edited by Yitzhak Hen and Matthew Innes, 175–190. Cambridge: Cambridge University Press, 2000.

——. "Holy Land Pilgrims from Frankish Gaul." *Revue Belge de Philologie et d'histoire* 76 (1998): 291–306.

Henderson, Julian. "Archaeological and Scientific Evidence for the Production of Early Islamic Glass in al-Raqqa, Syria." *Levant* 31 (1999): 225–240.

Henderson, Julian, Keith Challis, et al. "Experiment and Innovation: Early Islamic Industry at al-Raqqa, Syria." *Antiquity* 79 (2005): 130–145.

Herbers, Klaus. "Christen und Muslime im 9. Jahrhundert in Italien und Spanien: Gewalt und Kontakt, Konzeptualisierung und Wahrnehmung." *Historische Zeitschrift* 301 (2015): 1–30.

Hermes, Nizar F. *The [European] Other in Medieval Arabic Literature and Culture, Ninth–Twelfth Century AD*. New York: Palgrave Macmillan, 2012.

Hernández Juberías, Julia. *La Peninsula Imaginaria: Mitos y Leyendas sobre Al-Andalus*. Madrid: Consejo Superior de Investigaciones Científicas, 1996.

Herren, Michael W. "The 'De imagine Tetrici' of Walahfrid Strabo: Edition and Translation." *Journal of Medieval Latin* 1 (1991): 118–139.

Heusch, Jan-Christoph, and Michael Meinecke. "Grabungen im 'abbāsidischen Palastreal von ar-Raqqa/ar-Rāfiqa 1982–1983." *Damaszener Mitteilungen* 2 (1985): 85–106.

Higounet, Charles. "Les Aznar: Une tentative de groupement de comtés Gascons et Pyrénéens au IX^e siècle." *Annales du Midi* 61 (1948): 5–14.

Hillenbrand, Carole. "'The Ornament of the World': Medieval Córdoba as a Cultural Centre." In *The Legacy of Muslim Spain*, edited by Salma Khadra Jayyusi, 112–135. Leiden: Brill, 1992.

Hilsdale, Cecily J. *Byzantine Art and Diplomacy in an Age of Decline*. New York: Cambridge University Press, 2014.

Hinds, Martin, and Hamdi Sakkout. "A Letter from the Governor of Egypt to the King of Nubia and Muqurra Concerning Egyptian-Nubian Relations in 141/758." In *Studia Arabica et Islamica 1*, edited by Wadād al-Qāḍī, 209–229. Beirut: American University of Beirut, 1981.

Hodges, Richard. *Towns and Trade in the Age of Charlemagne*. London: Duckworth, 2000.

Hodges, Richard, and David Whitehouse. *Mohammed, Charlemagne and the Origins of Europe: Archaeology and the Pirenne Thesis*. London: Duckworth, 1983.

Holdenried, Anke. *The Sibyl and Her Scribes: Manuscripts and Interpretation of the Latin "Sibylla Tiburtina" c. 1050–1500*. Aldershot: Ashgate, 2006.

Holmes, Catherine. "Treaties between Byzantium and the Islamic World." In *War and Peace in Ancient and Medieval History*, edited by Philip de Souza and John France, 141–157. Cambridge: Cambridge University Press, 2008.

Holt, Peter M. "The Treaties of the Early Mamluk Sultans with the Frankish States." *Bulletin of the School of Oriental and African Studies* 43 (1980): 67–76.

Horden, Peregrine, and Nicholas Purcell. *The Corrupting Sea: A Study of Mediterranean History*. Oxford: Blackwell, 2000.

Howard-Johnston, James. *Witnesses to a World Crisis: Historians and Histories of the Middle East in the Seventh Century*. Oxford: Oxford University Press, 2010.

Hoyland, Robert G. "History, Fiction and Authorship in the First Centuries of Islam." In *Writing and Representation in Medieval Islam: Muslim Horizons*, edited by Julia Bray, 16–46. London: Routledge, 2006.

———. *Seeing Islam as Others Saw It: A Survey and Evaluation of Christian, Jewish, and Zoroastrian Writings on Early Islam*. Princeton: Darwin Press, 1997.

Hummer, Hans J. *Politics and Power in Early Medieval Europe: Alsace and the Frankish Realm, 600–1000*. Cambridge: Cambridge University Press, 2005.

Humphreys, Michael. "The 'War of Images' Revisited: Justinian II's Coinage Reform and the Caliphate." *Numismatic Chronicle* 173 (2013): 229–244.

Humphreys, R. Stephen. *Islamic History: A Framework for Inquiry*. London: I. B. Tauris, 1991.

Ibrahim, Yasir S. "Translator's Introduction." In *Al-Ṭabarī's Book of Jihād*, 1–56. Lewiston, NY: Edwin Mellen Press, 2007.

Ilisch, Lutz. "Arabische Kupfermünzen an der Ostsee." *Numismatisches Nachrichten Blatt* 61 (2012): 296–302.

———. "Geldgeschichten: Handel zwischen islamischem und karolingischem Reich." In *Kaiser und Kalifen: Karl der Grosse und die Mächte am Mittelmeer um 800*, edited by Barbara Segelken and Tim Urban, 144–155. Darmstadt: Von Zabern, 2014.

Innes, Matthew. "Charlemagne, Justice and Written Law." In *Law, Custom, and Justice in Late Antiquity and the Early Middle Ages*, edited by Alice Rio, 155–203. London: Centre for Hellenic Studies, 2011.

———. "Charlemagne's Will: Piety, Politics and the Imperial Succession." *English Historical Review* 112 (1997): 833–853.

———. "Franks and Slavs c. 700–1000: The Problem of European Expansion before the Millennium." *Early Medieval Europe* 6 (1997): 201–216.

——. "'Immune from Heresy': Defining the Boundaries of Carolingian Christianity." In *Frankland: The Franks and the World of the Early Middle Ages*, edited by Paul Fouracre and David Ganz, 101–125. Manchester: Manchester University Press, 2008.

——. "Memory, Orality and Literacy in an Early Medieval Society." *Past and Present* 158 (1998): 3–36.

——. *State and Society in the Early Middle Ages: The Middle Rhine Valley, 400–1000*. Cambridge: Cambridge University Press, 2000.

Innes, Matthew, and Rosamond McKitterick. "The Writing of History." In *Carolingian Culture: Emulation and Innovation*, edited by Rosamond McKitterick, 193–220. Cambridge: Cambridge University Press, 1993.

Iqbal, Afzal. *Diplomacy in Islam: An Essay on the Art of Negotiations as Conceived and Developed by the Prophet of Islam*. Lahore: Institute of Islamic Culture, 1965.

Istanbuli, Yasin. *Diplomacy and Diplomatic Practice in the Early Islamic Era*. Oxford: Oxford University Press, 2001.

Jahn, Joachim. *Ducatus Baiuvariorum: Das bairische Herzogtum der Agilolfinger*. Stuttgart: Hiersemann, 1991.

Jahn, Karl. "Das christliche Abendland in der islamischen Geschichtsschreibung des Mittelalters." *Anzeiger der phil.-hist. Klasse der Österreichischen Akademie der Wissenschaften* 113 (1976): 1–19.

Le Jan, Régine. "Mariage et Relations Internationales: L'Amitié en Question?" *Settimane di Studio* 58 (2011): 189–222.

Jarnut, Jörg. "Ein Brüderkampf und seine Folgen: Die Krise des Frankenreiches (768–771)." In *Herrschaft, Kirche, Kultur: Beiträge zur Geschichte des Mittelalters*, edited by Georg Jenal and Stephanie Haarländer, 165–176. Stuttgart: Hiersemann, 1993.

——. "Kaiser Ludwig der Fromme und König Bernhard von Italien: Der Versuch einer Rehabilitierung." *Studi Medievali* 30 (1989): 637–648.

Jarrett, Jonathan. "Nests of Pirates? 'Islandness' in the Balearic Islands and La Garde-Freinet." *Al-Masāq* 3 (2019): 1–27.

——. "Rebel without a Pension: The Mystery of Aizó." In *A Corner of Tenth-Century Europe*, 25 June 2009. tenthmedieval.wordpress.com/2009/06/25/rebel-without-a-pension-the-mystery-of-aiz/.

——. *Rulers and Ruled in Frontier Catalonia, 880–1010: Pathways of Power*. Woodbridge: Boydell, 2010.

——. "Settling the King's Lands: Aprisio in Catalonia in Perspective." *Early Medieval Europe* 18 (2010): 320–342.

Jenkins, Romilly H. "The Emperor Alexander and the Saracen Prisoners." *Atti dell VIII Congresso Internationale di Studi Bizantini e Noelleniki* 7 (1953): 389–393.

Johnson, Sarah Cresap. "'Return to Origin Is Non-Existence': Al-Mada'in and Perceptions of Ruins in Abbasid Iraq." *International Journal of Islamic Architecture* 6 (2017): 257–283.

Jones, Gwyn. *A History of the Vikings*. 2nd ed. Oxford: Oxford University Press, 2001.

de Jong, Mayke. "Carolingian Monasticism: The Power of Prayer." In *The New Cambridge Medieval History*, vol. 2, edited by Rosamond McKitterick, 622–653. Cambridge: Cambridge University Press, 1995.

——. "Carolingian Political Discourse and the Biblical Past: Hraban, Dhuoda, Radbert." In *The Resources of the Past in Early Medieval Europe*, edited by Clemens Gantner, Rosamond McKitterick, and Sven Meeder, 87–102. Cambridge: Cambridge University Press, 2015.

——. "Charlemagne's Balcony: The *Solarium* in Ninth-Century Narratives." In *The Long Morning of Medieval Europe: New Directions in Early Medieval Studies*, edited by Jennifer R. Davis and Michael McCormick, 277–289. Aldershot: Ashgate, 2008.

——. "The Empire That Was Always Decaying: The Carolingians (800–888)." *Medieval Worlds* 2 (2015): 6–25.

——. *Epitaph for an Era: Politics and Rhetoric in the Carolingian World*. Cambridge: Cambridge University Press, 2019.

——. *The Penitential State: Authority and Atonement in the Age of Louis the Pious, 814–840*. Cambridge: Cambridge University Press, 2009.

Joransson, Einar. "The Alleged Frankish Protectorate in Palestine." *American Historical Review* 32 (1927): 241–261.

——. "Review: Harunu'l-Rashid and Charles the Great." *Speculum* 7 (1932): 116–121.

Kaegi, Walter Emil. *Muslim Expansion and Byzantine Collapse in North Africa*. Cambridge: Cambridge University Press, 2010.

Al-Kalaf, Murhaf. "Die ʿabbāsidische Stadtmauer von ar-Raqqa/ar-Rāfiqa." *Damaszener Mitteilungen* 2 (1985): 123–131.

Kassis, Hanna E. "Arabic Speaking Christians in Al-Andalus in an Age of Turmoil (fifth/eleventh century until A.H. 478/A.D. 1085)." *al-Qanṭara* 15 (1994): 401–422.

——. "The Arabicization and Islamization of the Christians of al-Andalus: Evidence of Their Scriptures." In *Languages of Power in Islamic Spain*, edited by Ross Brann, 136–155. Bethesda: CDL Press, 1997.

Kasten, Brigitte. *Adalhard von Corbie: Die Biographie eines karolingischen Politikers und Klostervorstehers*. Düsseldorf: Droste, 1986.

Kedar, Benjamin Z. *Crusade and Mission: European Approaches toward the Muslims*. Princeton: Princeton University Press, 1984.

Keller, Hagen. "Zum Sturz Karls III. Über die Rolle Liutwards von Vercelli und Liutberts von Mainz, Arnulfs von Kärnten und der ostfränkischen Großen bei der Absetzung des Kaisers." *Deutsches Archiv* 22 (1966): 333–384.

Kennedy, Hugh. *The Armies of the Caliph: Military and Society in the Early Islamic State*. London: Routledge, 2001.

——. "Caliphs and Their Chronicles in the Middle Abbāsid Period (Third/Ninth Century)." In *Texts, Documents and Artefacts: Islamic Studies in Honour of D. S. Richards*, edited by Chase F. Robinson, 17–35. Leiden: Brill, 2003.

——. "The Decline and Fall of the First Muslim Empire." *Der Islam* 81 (2004): 3–30.

——. *The Early Abbasid Caliphate: A Political History*. London: Croom Helm, 1981.

——. "The Melkite Church from the Islamic Conquest to the Crusades: Continuity and Adaptation in the Byzantine Legacy." In *The 17th International Byzantine Congress*, 325–343. New Rochelle: Caratzas, 1986.

——. "Military Pay and the Economy of the Early Islamic State." *Historical Research* 75 (2002): 155–169.

———. *Muslim Spain and Portugal: A Political History of al-Andalus*. London: Routledge, 1996.
———. "The Muslims in Europe." In *The New Cambridge Medieval History*, vol. 2, edited by Rosamond McKitterick, 249–271. Cambridge: Cambridge University Press, 1995.
———. "The Origins of the Aghlabids." In *The Aghlabids and Their Neighbors: Art and Material Culture in Ninth-Century North Africa*, edited by Glaire D. Anderson, Corisande Fenwick, and Mariam Rosser-Owen, 33–48. Leiden: Brill, 2018.
———. *The Prophet and the Age of the Caliphates: The Islamic Near East from the Sixth to the Eleventh Century*. 3rd ed. New York: Routledge, 2016.
———. "The Reign of al-Muqtadir (295–320/908–32): A History." In *Crisis and Continuity at the Abbasid Court: Formal and Informal Politics in the Caliphate of al-Muqtadir (295–320/908–32)*, edited by Maaike van Berkel, Nadia Maria El Cheikh, Hugh Kennedy, and Letizia Osti, 13–47. Leiden: Brill, 2013.
Kershaw, Paul J. E. *Peaceful Kings: Peace, Power and the Early Medieval Political Imagination*. Oxford: Oxford University Press, 2011.
Khadduri, Majid Khadduri. *The Islamic Law of Nations: Shaybānī's Siyar*. Baltimore: Johns Hopkins Press, 1966.
———. *War and Peace in the Law of Islam*. Baltimore: Johns Hopkins Press, 1955.
Khalidi, Tarif. *Islamic Historiography: The Histories of Mas'ūdī*. Albany: State University of New York Press, 1975.
Khoury, Nuha N. N. "The Meaning of the Great Mosque of Córdoba in the Tenth Century." *Muqarnas* 13 (1996) 80–98.
Kimber, Richard A. "Hārūn al-Rashīd's Meccan Settlement of AH 186/AD 802." In *Occasional Papers of the School of Abbasid Studies*, no. 1, 55–79. St. Andrews': School of Abbasid Studies, 1986.
———. "The Succession to the Caliph Mūsā al-Hādī." *Journal of the American Oriental Society* 121 (2001): 428–448.
Kister, M. J. "The 'Kitāb al-Miḥan': A Book on Muslim Martyrology." *Journal of Semitic Studies* 20 (1975): 210–218.
Kleinclausz, Arthur. "La légende du Protectorat de Charlemagne sur la Térre Sainte." *Syria* 7 (1926): 211–233.
Kohler, Michael A. *Alliances and Treaties between Frankish and Muslim Rulers in the Middle East: Cross-cultural Diplomacy in the Period of the Crusades*. Translated by Peter M. Holt, revised by Konrad Hirschler. Leiden: Brill, 2013.
König, Daniel G. "Arabic-Islamic Historiography on the Emergence of Latin-Christian Europe." In *Visions of Community in the Post-Roman World: The West, Byzantium and the Islamic World, 300–1100*, edited by Walter Pohl, Clemens Gantner, and Richard Payne, 427–445. Farnham: Ashgate, 2012.
———. *Arabic-Islamic Views of the Latin West: Tracing the Emergence of Medieval Europe*. Oxford: Oxford University Press, 2015.
———. "Charlemagne's *Jihād* Revisited: Debating the Islamic Contribution to an Epochal Change in the History of Christianisation." *Medieval Worlds* 3 (2016): 3–40.
———. "The Christianisation of Latin Europe as Seen by Medieval Arab-Islamic Historiography." *Medieval History Journal* 12 (2009): 431–472.

*Königssöhne und Königsherrschaft: Untersuchungen zur Teilhabe am Reich in der Merowinger- und Karolingerzeit*. Hannover: Hahn, 1997.

Kosto, Adam J. "Hostages in the Carolingian World (714–840)." *Early Medieval Europe* 11 (2002): 123–147.

———. *Hostages in the Middle Ages*. Oxford: Oxford University Press, 2012.

Koziol, Geoffrey. *Begging Pardon and Favor: Ritual and Political Order in Early Medieval France*. Ithaca: Cornell University Press, 1992.

———. "The Dangers of Polemic: Is Ritual Still an Interesting Topic of Historical Study?" *Early Medieval Europe* 11 (2002): 367–388.

———. *The Politics of Memory and Identity in Carolingian Royal Diplomas: The West Frankish Kingdom (840–987)*. Turnhout: Brepols, 2012.

Kraemer, Joel L. *Humanism in the Renaissance of Islam: The Cultural Revival during the Buyid Age*. 2nd ed. Leiden: Brill, 1992.

Krah, Adelheid. *Absetzungsverfahren als Spiegelbild von Königsmacht: Untersuchungen zum Kräfteverhältnis zwischen Königtum und Adel im Karolingerreich und seinen Nachfolgestaaten*. Aalen: Scientia, 1987.

Kramer, Rutger. "Adopt, Adapt and Improve: Dealing with the Adoptionist Controversy at the Court of Charlemagne." In *Religious Franks: Religion and Power in the Frankish Kingdoms*, edited by Rob Meens et al., 32–50. Manchester: Manchester University Press, 2016.

———. "A Crowning Achievement: Carolingian Imperial Identity in the *Chronicon Moissiacense*." In *Historiography and Identity III: Carolingian Approaches*, edited by Rutger Kramer, Helmut Reimitz, and Graeme Ward, 231–269. Turnhout: Brepols, 2021.

———. "Franks, Romans, and Countrymen: Imperial Interests, Local Identities, and the Carolingian Conquest of Aquitaine." In *Empires and Communities in the Post-Roman and Islamic World, c. 400–1000 CE*, edited by Rutger Kramer and Walter Pohl, 253–282. Oxford: Oxford University Press, 2021.

———. *Rethinking Authority in the Carolingian Empire*. Amsterdam: Amsterdam University Press, 2019.

Krausmüller, Dirk. "Contextualizing Constantine V's Radical Religious Policies: The Debate about the Intercession of the Saints and the 'Sleep of the Soul' in the Chalcedonian and Nestorian Churches." *Byzantine and Modern Greek Studies* 39 (2015): 25–49.

Kreutz, Barbara M. *Before the Normans: Southern Italy in the Ninth and Tenth Centuries*. Philadelphia: University of Pennsylvania Press, 1991.

Kujawiński, J. "Le immagini dell' 'altro' nella cronachista del Mezzogiorno Longobardo." *Rivista Storica Italiana* 118 (2006): 767–815.

Lacarra, José María. *Historia Política del reino de Navarra*. Vol. 1. Pamplona: Aranzadi, 1972.

———. "Textos navarros del Códice de Roda." *Estudios de Edad Media de la Corona de Aragon* 1 (1945): 194–283.

Lankila, Tommi P. "Saracen Maritime Raids in the Early Medieval Central Mediterranean and Their Impact in the South Italian Terraferma (650–1050)." PhD diss., Princeton University, 2017.

La Rocca, Cristina. "Angelberga, Louis's II Wife, and Her Will (877)." In *Ego Trouble: Authors and Their Identities in the Early Middle Ages*, edited by Richard Corradini et al., 221–226. Vienna: Verlag der Österreichischen Akademie der Wissenschaften, 2010.

Laroui, Abdallah. *The History of the Maghrib: An Interpretive Essay*. Translated by Ralph Manheim. Princeton: Princeton University Press, 1977.

Lassner, Jacob. *The Shaping of ʿAbbāsid Rule*. Princeton: Princeton University Press, 1980.

——. *The Topography of Baghdad in the Early Middle Ages*. Detroit: Wayne State University Press, 1970.

Latowsky, Anne A. *Emperor of the World: Charlemagne and the Construction of Imperial Authority, 800–1229*. Ithaca: Cornell University Press, 2013.

——. "Foreign Embassies and Roman Universality in Einhard's Life of Charlemagne." *Florilegium* 22 (2005): 25–57.

Laurenson-Rosaz, Christian. "Les Guillelmides: Une famille de l'aristocratie d'empire carolingienne dans le Midi de la Gaule (VIIIe–Xe siècles)." In *Entre histoire et épopée: Les Guillaume d'Orange (IXe–XIIIe siècles)*, edited by Laurent Macé, 45–81. Toulouse: Université de Toulouse-Le Mirail, 2006.

Lebow, Richard Ned. *A Cultural Theory of International Relations*. Cambridge: Cambridge University Press, 2008.

Leder, Stefan. "The Literary Use of the *Khabar*: A Basic Form of Historical Writing." In *The Byzantine and Early Islamic Near East*. Vol. 1: *Problems in the Literacy Source Material*, edited by Averil Cameron and Lawrence I. Conrad, 277–316. Princeton: Darwin Press, 1992.

Lee, A. D. *Information and Frontiers: Roman Foreign Relations in Late Antiquity*. Cambridge: Cambridge University Press, 1993.

——. "Treaty-Making in Late Antiquity." In *War and Peace in Ancient and Medieval History*, edited by Philip de Souza and John France, 107–119. Cambridge: Cambridge University Press, 2008.

Leja, Meg. *Embodying the Soul: Medicine and Religion in Carolingian Europe*. Philadelphia: University of Pennsylvania Press, 2022.

Lendon, J. E. "Primitivism and Ancient Foreign Relations." *Classical Journal* 97 (2002): 375–384.

Lévi-Provençal, Evariste. *Histoire de l'Espagne musulmane*. 2nd ed. Paris: G. P. Maisonneuve, 1950.

——. "Sur l'installation des Rāzī en Espagne." *Arabica* 2 (1955): 228–230.

Levillain, León. "Les Nibelungen historiques et leurs alliances de famille." *Annales du Midi* 50 (1938): 5–66.

Levy, Jack S. "Domestic Politics and War." In *The Origin and Prevention of Major Wars*, edited by Robert Rotberg and Theodore K. Rabb, 79–100. Cambridge: Cambridge University Press, 1989.

Levy-Rubin, Milka. "*Shurūṭ ʿUmar* and Its Alternates: The Legal Debate on the Status of the *Dhimmīs*." *Jerusalem Studies in Arabic and Islam* 30 (2005): 170–206.

Lewis, Archibald R. *The Development of Southern French and Catalan Society, 718–1050*. Austin: University of Texas Press, 1965.

——. "The Dukes in the *Regnum Francorum*, A.D. 550–751." *Speculum* 51 (1976): 381–410.

——. "Mediterranean Maritime Commerce: A.D. 300–1100 Shipping and Trade." *Settimane di Studio* 25 (1978): 480–501.

Lewis, Bernard. *The Muslim Discovery of Europe*. London: Weidenfeld and Nicolson, 1982.

——. *The Political Language of Islam*. Chicago: University of Chicago Press, 1988.

Lewis, Bernard, and Arent Jan Wensinck. "Ḥadjdj." *Encyclopedia of Islam*. 2nd ed. 3:31–38. Leiden: Brill, 1971.

Limor, Ora. "'Holy Journey': Pilgrimage and Christian Sacral Landscape." In *Christians and Christianity in the Holy Land: From the Origins to the Latin Kingdoms*, edited by Ora Limor and Guy G. Stroumsa, 321–353. Turnhout: Brepols, 2006.

Linder, Amnon. *The Jews in the Legal Sources of the Early Middle Ages*. Detroit: Wayne State University Press, 1997.

Lindstedt, Ilkka. "The Role of al-Madā'inī's Students in the Transmission of His Material." *Der Islam* 91 (2014): 295–340.

Linehan, Peter. "At the Spanish Frontier." In *The Medieval World*, edited by Peter Linehan and Janet L. Nelson, 37–59. London: Routledge, 2001.

——. *History and the Historians of Medieval Spain*. Oxford: Clarendon Press, 1993.

Lirola Delgado, Jorge. *El poder naval de Al-Andalus en la época del Califato Omeya*. Granada: Universidad de Granada, 1993.

Lobbedey, Uwe. "Carolingian Royal Palaces: The State of Research from an Architectural Historian's Viewpoint." In *Court Culture in the Early Middle Ages*, edited by Catherine Cubitt, 129–154. Turnhout: Brepols, 2003.

Lockman, Zachary. *Contending Visions of the Middle East: The History and Politics of Orientalism*. 2nd ed. Cambridge: Cambridge University Press, 2010.

Lohrmann, Dietrich. "Trois Palais Royaux de la Vallée de l'Oise d'après les travaux des érudits mauristes: Compiègne, Choisy-au-Bac et Quierzy." *Francia* 4 (1976): 121–139.

London, Jennifer. "How to Do Things with Fables: Ibn al-Muqaffa's Frank Speech from *Kalila Wa Dimna*." *History of Political Thought* 29 (2008): 189–212.

Lorenzo Jiménez, Jesús. *La dawla de los Banū Qasī: Origen, auge y caída de una dinastía muladí en la frontera superior de Al-Andalus*. Madrid: Consejo Superior de Investigaciones Cientificas, 2010.

Loseby, Simon. "Marseille and the Pirenne Thesis I." In *The Sixth Century: Production, Distribution and Demand*, edited by Richard Hodges and William Bowden, 203–229. Leiden: Brill, 1998.

——. "Marseille and the Pirenne Thesis II." In *The Long Eighth Century*, edited by Inge Lyse Hansen and Chris Wickham, 167–193. Leiden: Brill, 2000.

Lößlein, Horst. *Royal Power in the Late Carolingian Age: Charles III the Simple and His Predecessors*. Cologne: Modern Academic Publishing, 2019.

Loud, Graham A. *The Age of Robert Guiscard: Southern Italy and the Norman Conquest*. Harlow: Longman, 2000.

Lounghis, Télémaque C. *Les ambassades byzantines en Occident: Depuis la fondation des états barbares jusqu'aux Croisades (407–1096)*. Athens: T. C. Lounghis, 1980.

Löwe, Heinz. "Die Apostasie des Pfalzdiakons Bodo (838) und das Judentum der Chasaren." In *Person und Gemeinschaft im Mittelalter: Karl Schmid zum fünfundsechzigsten Geburtstag*, edited by Gerd Althoff, 157–169. Sigmaringen: Thorbecke, 1988.

———. "Die Entstehungszeit der Vita Karoli Einhards." *Deutsches Archiv fur Erforschung des Mittelalters* 39 (1983): 85–103.

Lozovsky, Natalia. "Roman Geography and Ethnography in the Carolingian Empire." *Speculum* 81 (2006): 325–364.

Lund, Niels. "Allies of God or Man? The Viking Expansion in a European Perspective." *Viator* 20 (1989): 45–59.

———. "Peace and Non-Peace in the Viking Age: Ottar in Biarmaland, the Rus in Byzantium, and Danes and Norwegians in England." In *Proceedings of the Tenth Viking Congress*, edited by James E. Knirk, 255–270. Oslo: Universitetets Oldsaksamling, 1987.

Macias Solé, Josep Maria. "Tarracona visigoda: Una ciudad en declive?" In *Recópolis y la ciudad en la época visigoda*, edited by Lauro Olmo Enciso, 293–301. Alcalá de Henares: Comunidad de Madrid, 2008.

MacLean, Simon. *Kingship and Politics in the Late Ninth Century: Charles the Fat and the End of the Carolingian Empire*. Cambridge: Cambridge University Press, 2003.

———. "Ritual, Misunderstanding and the Contest for Meaning: Representations of the Disrupted Royal Assembly at Frankfurt (873)." In *Representations of Power in Medieval Germany, c. 800–1500*, edited by Simon MacLean and Bjorn Weiler, 97–120. Turnhout: Brepols, 2006.

Madelung, Wilferd. "ʿAbd Allāh b. al-Zubayr and the Mahdī." *Journal of Near Eastern Studies* 40 (1981): 291–305.

Makkī, Maḥmūd ʿAlī. "Egypt and the Origin of Arabic Spanish Historiography: A Contribution to the Study of the Earliest Sources for the History of Islamic Spain." In *The Formation of al-Andalus, Part 2: Language, Religion, Culture and the Sciences*, edited by Maribel Fierro and Julio Samsó, 173–233. Aldershot: Ashgate, 1998.

Malinowski, Bronisław. "Kula: The Circulating Exchange of Valuables in the Archipelagoes of Eastern New Guinea." *Man* 20 (1920): 97–105.

Mandalā, Giuseppe. "Political Martyrdom and Religious Censorship in Islamic Sicily: A Case Study during the Age of Ibrāhīm II (261–289/875–902)." *al-Qanṭara* 35 (2014): 151–186.

Mansouri, Mohamed Tahar. "Les '*Ulamā*' en Rupture avec le pouvoir en Ifrīqiya d'après le *Kitāb al-Miḥan*." *Mélanges de l'École Française de Rome: Moyen Âge* 115 (2003): 565–580.

Manzano Moreno, Eduardo. "A Vueltas con el Conde Casio." *Studia Historica: Historia Medieval* 31 (2013): 255–266.

———. "Byzantium and al-Andalus in the Ninth Century." In *Byzantium in the Ninth Century: Dead or Alive?* edited by Leslie Brubaker, 215–227. Aldershot: Ashgate, 1998.

———. "Christian-Muslim Frontier in al-Andalus: Idea and Reality." In *The Arab Influence in Medieval Europe*, edited by Dionisius A. Agius and Richard Hitchcock, 83–99. Reading: Ithaca, 1994.

——. *Conquistadores, Emires y Califas: Los omeyas y la formación de Al-Andalus.* Barcelona: Crítica, 2006.

——. "El medio cordobés y la elaboración cronística en el al-Andalus bajo la dinastía de los Omeyas." In *Historia social, pensamiento historiográfico y Edad Media: Homenaje al prof. Abilio Barbero de Aguilera*, edited by María Isabel Loring García, 59–85. Madrid: Ediciones del Orte, 1997.

——. "The Iberian Peninsula and North Africa." In *The New Cambridge History of Islam*, vol. 1, edited by Chase F. Robinson, 581–622. Cambridge: Cambridge University Press, 2010.

——. *La Frontera de al-Andalus en época de los Omeyas.* Madrid: Consejo superior de investigaciones científicas, 1991.

——. "Las fuentes árabes sobre la conquista de Al-Ándalus: Una nueva interpretación." *Hispania* 59 (1999): 389–432.

——. *La organización fronteriza en al-Andalus durante la época Omeya: Aspectos militares y sociales (756–976/138–366 H.).* Madrid: Editorial de la Universidad Complutense de Madrid, 1989.

——. "La rebelión del año 754 en la Marca Superior y su tratamiento en las crónicas árabes." *Studia Historica: Historia Medieval* 4 (1986): 185–203.

——. "Oriental 'Topoi' in Andalusian Historical Sources." *Arabica* 39 (1992): 42–58.

——. "The Settlement and Organisation of the Syrian *Junds* in al-Andalus." In *The Formation of al-Andalus, Part 1: History and Sources*, edited by Manuela Marín, 85–114. Aldershot: Routledge, 1998.

Maqbul Ahmad, S. "Djughrāfiyā." *Encyclopedia of Islam.* 2nd ed. 2:575–587. Leiden: Brill, 1965.

Marazzi, Federico. "*Ita ut facta videatur Neapolis Panormus vel Africa*: Geopolitica della presenza islamica nei domini di Napoli, Gaeta, Salerno e Benevento nel IX secolo." *Schede Medievali* 45 (2007): 159–202.

Margaroni, Mary. "The Blood Libel on Greek Islands in the Nineteenth Century." In *Sites of European Antisemitism in the Age of Mass Politics, 1880–1918*, edited by Robert Nemes and Daniel Unowsky, 178–196. Waltham, MA: Brandeis University Press, 2014.

Marín, Manuela. "La transmisión del saber en al-Andalus (hasta 300/912)." *al-Qanṭara* 8 (1987): 87–98.

——. *Mujeres en al-Ándalus.* Madrid: Consejo Superior de Investigaciones Científicas, 2000.

Marín-Guzmán, Roberto. "The Causes of the Revolt of Umar ibn Hafsun in Al-Andalus 880–928: A Study in Medieval Islamic Social History." *Arabica* 17 (1995): 180–221.

——. "Political Turmoil in al-Andalus in the Time of the Amir 'Abd Allah (888–912): Study of the Revolt of Daysum ibn Ishaq, Lord of Murcia and Lorca and the Role of 'Umar ibn Hafsun." *Muslim World* 96 (2006): 145–174.

——. *Popular Dimensions of the 'Abbāsid Revolution.* Cambridge, MA: Fulbright-LAPSU, 1990.

——. "Rebellions and Political Fragmentation of al-Andalus: A Study of the Revolt of 'Umar ibn Hafsun in the Period of the Amir 'Abd Allah (888–912)." *Islamic Studies* 33 (1994): 419–473.

Marsham, Andrew. "Public Execution in the Umayyad Period: Early Islamic Punitive Practice and Its Late Antique Context." *Journal of Arabic and Islamic Studies* 11 (2011): 101–136.

———. *Rituals of Islamic Monarchy: Accession and Succession in the First Muslim Empire*. Edinburgh: Edinburgh University Press, 2009.

Marston Speight, R. "The Place of the Christians in Ninth-Century North Africa According to the Muslim Sources." *Islamochristiana* 4 (1978): 47–65.

Mårtensson, Ulrika. "Discourse and Historical Analysis: The Case of al-Ṭabarī's History of the Messengers and the Kings." *Journal of Islamic Studies* 16 (2005): 287–331.

Martindale, Jane. "Charles the Bald and the Government of the Kingdom of Aquitaine." In *Charles the Bald: Court and Kingdom*, edited by Margaret T. Gibson and Janet L. Nelson, 115–138. Aldershot: Variorum, 1990.

———. "The Kingdom of Aquitaine and the Dissolution of the Carolingian Fisc." *Francia* 11 (1985): 131–191.

Martínez Díez, Gonzalo. *El Condado de Castilla (711–1038): La historia frente a la leyenda*. Vol. 1. Valladolid: Junta de Castilla y León, Consejería de Cultura y Turismo, 2005.

Martinez-Gros, Gabriel. *L'idéologie omeyyade: La construction de la légitimité du Califat de Cordoue (Xe–XIe siècles)*. Madrid: Casa de Velázquez, 1992.

Martos Quesada, Juan. "La labor historiográfica de Ibn 'Idārī." *Anaquel de estudios árabes* 20 (2009): 117–130.

Mattingley, Garrett. "The First Resident Ambassadors: Medieval Italian Origins of Modern Diplomacy." *Speculum* 12 (1937): 423–439.

———. *Renaissance Diplomacy*. London: Cape, 1955.

Maund, K. L. "'A Turmoil of Warring Princes': Political Leadership in Ninth-Century Denmark." *Haskins Society Journal* 6 (1994): 29–47.

Mauss, Marcel. *Sociologie et Anthropologie*. 9th ed. Paris: Presses universitaires de France, 1985.

Mazzoli-Guintard, Christine. "Remarques sur le fonctionnement d'une capitale à double polarité: Madinat al-Zahra'-Cordoue." *al-Qanṭara* 18 (1997): 43–64.

McCarthy, Margaret J. "Power and Kingship under Louis II the Stammerer, 877–879." PhD diss., University of Cambridge, 2012.

McCormick, Michael. "Analyzing Imperial Ceremonies." *Jahrbuch der Österreichischen Byzantinistik* 35 (1985): 1–20.

———. "Byzantium and the Early Medieval West: Problems and Opportunities." In *Europa medievale e mondo bizantino: Contatti effettivi e possibilità di studi comparati*, edited by Girolamo Arnaldi and Guglielmo Cavallo, 1–17. Rome: Istituto storico italiano per il Medio Evo, 1997.

———. *Charlemagne's Survey of the Holy Land: Wealth, Personnel, and Buildings of a Mediterranean Church between Antiquity and the Middle Ages*. Washington, DC: Dumbarton Oaks, 2011.

———. "Diplomacy and the Carolingian Encounter with Byzantium down to the Accession of Charles the Bald." In *Eriugena: East and West*, edited by Bernard McGinn and Willemien Olten, 15–48. Notre Dame: University of Notre Dame Press, 1994.

———. *Eternal Victory: Triumphal Rulership in Late Antiquity, Byzantium and the Early Medieval West*. Cambridge: Cambridge University Press, 1986.

———. "From One Center of Power to Another: Comparing Byzantine and Carolingian Ambassadors." In *Deutsche Königspfalzen: Beiträge zu ihrer historischen und archäologischen Erforschung*. Vol. 8: *Places of Power, Orte der Herrschaft, Lieux*

*du pouvoir*, edited by Lutz Fenske, Jörg Jarnut, and Matthias Wemhoff, 45–72. Göttingen: Vandenhoeck & Ruprecht, 2007.
———. *Origins of the European Economy: Communications and Commerce, A.D. 300–900*. Cambridge: Cambridge University Press, 2001.
———. "Les Pèlerins Occidentaux à Jérusalem, VIII$^{e}$–IX$^{e}$ siècles." In *Voyages et voyageurs à Byzance et en occident du VI$^{e}$ au XI$^{e}$ siècle*, edited by Alain Dierkens and Jean-Marie Sansterre, 289–306. Geneva: Droz, 1999.
———. "Pippin III, the Embassy of Caliph al Mansur, and the Mediterranean World." In *Der Dynastiewechsel von 751: Vorgeschichte, Legitimationsstrategien und Erinnerung*, edited by Matthias Becher and Jörg Jarnut, 221–241. Münster: Scriptorium, 2004.
———. "Textes, images et iconoclasme dans le cadre des relations entre Byzance et l'Occident carolingien." *Settimane di studio* 41 (1994): 95–159.
McCormick, Michael, Paul Edward Dutton, and Paul A. Mayewski. "Volcanoes and the Climate Forcing of Carolingian Europe, A.D. 750–950." *Speculum* 82 (2007): 865–895.
McCrank, Lawrence. "The Cistercians of Poblet as Medieval Frontiersmen: An Historiographic Essay and Case Study." In *Estudios en homenaje a Don Claudio Sánchez-Albornoz en su 90 años*, 2:313–360. Buenos Aires: Universidad de Buenos Aires, 1983.
McKitterick, Rosamond. *The Carolingians and the Written Word*. Cambridge: Cambridge University Press, 1989.
———. *Charlemagne: The Formation of a European Identity*. Cambridge: Cambridge University Press, 2008.
———. "Constructing the Past in the Early Middle Ages: The Case of the Royal Frankish Annals." *Transactions of the Royal Historical Society*, 6th ser., 7 (1997): 101–129.
———. "Die Anfänge des karolingischen Königtums und die *Annales regni Francorum*." In *Integration und Herrschaft: Ethnische Identitäten und soziale Organisation im Frühmittelalter*, edited by Walter Pohl and Max Diesenberger, 151–168. Vienna: Verlag der Österreichischen Akademie der Wissenschaften, 2002.
———. *The Frankish Kingdoms under the Carolingians, 751–987*. London: Longman, 1983.
———. *History and Memory in the Carolingian World*. Cambridge: Cambridge University Press, 2004.
———. "The Illusion of Royal Power in the Carolingian Annals." *English Historical Review* 115 (2000): 1–20.
———. "A King on the Move: The Place of an Itinerant Court in Charlemagne's Government." In *Royal Courts in Dynastic States and Empires: A Global Perspective*, edited by Jeroen Duindam, Tülay Artan, and Metin Kunt, 145–169. Leiden: Brill, 2011.
———. "The Palace School of Charles the Bald." In *Charles the Bald: Court and Kingdom*, edited by Margaret T. Gibson and Janet L. Nelson, 326–339. Aldershot: Variorum, 1990.
———. *Perceptions of the Past in the Early Middle Ages*. Notre Dame: University of Notre Dame Press, 2006.
———. "Political Ideology in Carolingian Historiography." In *The Uses of the Past in the Early Middle Ages*, edited by Yitzhak Hen and Matthew Innes, 162–174. Cambridge: Cambridge University Press, 2000.

——. *Rome and the Invention of the Papacy: The* Liber Pontificalis. Cambridge: Cambridge University Press, 2020.

McKitterick, Rosamond, Dorine van Espelo, Richard Pollard, and Richard Price, eds. *Codex Epistolaris Carolinus: Letters from the Popes to the Frankish Rulers, 739–791*. Liverpool: Liverpool University Press, 2021.

McNair, Fraser Alexander. "After Soissons: The Last Years of Charles the Simple (923–929)." *Reti Medievali Rivista* 18 (2017): 29–48.

——. "Political Culture and Ducal Authority in Aquitaine, c. 900–1040." *History Compass* 18 (2020): 1–10.

Meeder, Sven. "Monte Cassino and Carolingian Politics around 800." In *Religious Franks: Religion and Power in the Frankish Kingdoms*, edited by Rob Meens et al., 279–295. Manchester: Manchester University Press, 2016.

Meier, Mischa. "The 'Justinianic Plague': The Economic Consequences of the Pandemic in the Eastern Roman Empire and Its Cultural and Religious Effects." *Early Medieval Europe* 24 (2016): 267–292.

Meinecke, Michael. "Raqqa on the Euphrates: Recent Excavations at the Residence of Hārūn er-Rashīd." In *The Near East in Antiquity: German Contributions to the Archaeology of Jordan, Palestine, Syria, Lebanon, and Egypt*, vol. 2, edited by Susanne Kerner, 17–32. Amman: Al-Kutba Publishers, 1991.

Melchert, Christopher. *The Formation of the Sunni Schools of Law, 9th–10th Centuries C.E.* Leiden: Brill, 1997.

Melleno, Daniel. "Between Borders: Franks, Danes, and Abodrites in the Trans-Elben World up to 827." *Early Medieval Europe* 25 (2017): 359–385.

Menache, Sophia. "Communication in the Jewish Diaspora." In *Communication in the Jewish Diaspora: The Pre-modern World*, edited by Sophia Menache, 15–58. Leiden: Brill, 1996.

Meri, Josef W. *The Cult of Saints among Muslims and Jews in Medieval Syria*. Oxford: Oxford University Press, 2002.

——. "Relics of Piety and Power in Medieval Islam." *Past and Present* 206 (2010): 97–120.

Merrills, Andrew H. *History and Geography in Late Antiquity*. Cambridge: Cambridge University Press, 2005.

Metcalf, D. M. "A Sketch of the Currency in the Time of Charles the Bald." In *Charles the Bald: Court and Kingdom*. 2nd ed. Edited by Margaret T. Gibson and Janet L. Nelson, 65–97. Aldershot: Variorum, 1990.

Metcalfe, Andrew. *The Muslims of Medieval Italy*. Edinburgh: Edinburgh University Press, 2009.

Meyer, O. "Harunu'l Rashid and Charles the Great." *Neues Archiv der Gesellschaft* 49 (1932): 575.

Millar, Fergus. "Hagar, Ishmael, Josephus and the Origins of Islam." *Journal of Jewish Studies* 44 (1993): 23–45.

——. "The Theodosian Empire (408–450) and the Arabs: Saracens or Ishmaelites?" In *Cultural Borrowings and Ethnic Appropriations in Antiquity*, edited by Erich S. Gruen, 297–314. Stuttgart: F. Steiner, 2005.

Miller, Michael E. "Donald Trump Jr. Stumbles out of Father's Shadow and into the Spotlight with White Nationalist Interview." *Washington Post*, 4 March 2016. www.washingtonpost.com/news/morning-mix/wp/2016/03/04/donald-trump-jr

-stumbles-out-of-fathers-shadow-and-into-the-spotlight-with-white-nationalist-interview/?hpid=hp_no-name_morning-mix-story-c%3Ahomepage%2Fstory.

Millward, William G. "Al-Yaʿqūbī's Sources and the Question of Shīʿa Partiality." *Abī-Nahrain* 12 (1971–1972): 47–74.

Miquel, André. "Iḳlīm." In *Encyclopedia of Islam*. 2nd ed. 3:1076–1078. Leiden: Brill, 1971.

———. "L'Europe vue par les Arabes jusqu'à l'an Mil." In *Lumières arabes sur l'Occident médiéval*, edited by Henri Loucel, André Miquel, and Toufic Fahd, 65–81. Paris, 1978.

Miro, Annick. "Les comtes de Toulouse en Pallars et Ribagorce au IXᵉ siècle: Princes souverains ou agents du prince?" *Territorio, Sociedad, y Poder* 6 (2011): 23–52.

Molina, Luis. "Los Ajbār Maŷmū'a y la Historiografía Árabe sobre el periodo omeya en al-Andalus." *al-Qanṭara* 10 (1989): 513–542.

———. "Sobre la Historia de al-Rāzī: Nuevos datos en el 'Muqtabis' de Ibn Ḥayyān." *al-Qanṭara* 1 (1980): 435–443.

———. "Técnicas de *amplificatio* en el *Muqtabis* de Ibn Ḥayyān." *Talia Dixit* 1 (2006): 55–79.

———. "Un relato de la conquista de al-Andalus." *al-Qanṭara* 19 (1998): 27–45.

Morgenthau, Hans Joachim. *Politics among Nations: The Struggle for Power and Peace*. 7th ed. Maidenhead: McGraw-Hill Education, 2005.

Morris, Ian. "Mediterraneanization." *Mediterranean Historical Review* 18 (2003): 30–55.

Morrissey, Robert. *Charlemagne and France: A Thousand Years of Mythology*. Translated by Catherine Tihanyi. Notre Dame: University of Notre Dame Press, 2003.

Movassat, Johanna Domela. *The Large Vault at Taq-i Bustan: A Study in Late Sasanian Royal Art*. Lewiston, NY: Edwin Mellen Press, 2005.

Mullett, Margaret. "Experiencing the Byzantine Text, Experiencing the Byzantine Tent." In *Experiencing Byzantium: Papers from the 44th Spring Symposium of Byzantine Studies, Newcastle and Durham, April 2011*, edited by Claire Nesbitt and Mark Jackson, 269–291. London: Routledge, 2016.

Mulligan, William, and Brendan Simms, eds. *The Primacy of Foreign Policy in British History, 1660–2000: How Strategic Concerns Shaped Modern Britain*. Basingstoke: Palgrave Macmillan, 2010.

Munt, Harry. "Caliphal Imperialism and Ḥijāzī Elites in the Second/Eighth Century." *Al-Masāq* 38 (2016): 6–21.

Musca, Giosuè. *Carlo Magno ed Harun al Rashid*. Bari: Dedalo litostampa, 1963.

———. *L'emirato di Bari, 847–871*. Bari: Dedalo litostampa, 1964.

Nagel, Tilman. "Ein früher Bericht über den Aufstand von Muḥammad b. ʿAbdallāh im Jahre 145 h." *Der Islam* 46 (1970): 227–262.

Nees, Lawrence. "El Elefante de Carlomagno." *Quintana* 5 (2005): 13–49.

Nef, Annliese. "Comment les Aghlabides ont décidé de conquérir la Sicile . . ." *Annales Islamologiques* 45 (2011): 191–211.

———. "Guerroyer pour la Sicile (827–902)." In *La Sicilia del IX secolo tra bizantini e musulmani: Atti del IX Convegno di studi*, edited by Simona Modeo, Marina Congiu, and Luigi Santagati, 13–40. Caltanissetta: S. Sciascia, 2013.

———. "Reinterpreting the Aghlabids' Sicilian Policy (827–910)." In *The Aghlabids and Their Neighbors: Art and Material Culture in Ninth-Century North Africa*, edited by Glaire D. Anderson, Corisande Fenwick, and Mariam Rosser-Owen, 76–87. Leiden: Brill, 2018.

Nef, Annliese, and Mathieu Tillier. "Les voies de l'innovation dans un empire islamique polycentrique." *Annales Islamologiques* 45 (2011): 1–19.

Nelson, Janet L. "Aachen as a Place of Power." In *Topographies of Power in the Early Middle Ages*, edited by Mayke de Jong and Frans Theuws, 217–242. Leiden: Brill, 2001.

———. "The 'Annals of St. Bertin.'" In *Charles the Bald: Court and Kingdom*. 2nd ed. Edited by Margaret T. Gibson and Janet L. Nelson, 23–40. Aldershot: Variorum, 1990.

———. "Charlemagne—pater optimus?" In *Am Vorabend der Kaiserkrönung: Das Epos "Karolus Magnus et Leo Papa" und der Papstbesuch in Paderborn 799*, edited by Peter Godman, Jörg Jarnut, and Peter Johanek, 269–281. Berlin: Berlin Akademie Verlag, 2002.

———. *Charles the Bald*. London: Longman, 1992.

———. "The Frankish Kingdoms, 814–898: The West." In *The New Cambridge Medieval History*, vol. 2, edited by Rosamond McKitterick, 110–141. Cambridge: Cambridge University Press, 1995.

———. "The Franks, the Martyrology of Usuard, and the Martyrs of Cordoba." *Studies in Church History* 30 (1993): 67–80.

———. "Gender and Genre in Women Historians of the Early Middle Ages." *L'Historiographie médiévale en Europe*, edited by Jean-Philippe Genêt, 149–163. Paris: Éditions du Centre national de la recherche scientifique, 1991.

———. "History-writing at the Courts of Louis the Pious and Charles the Bald." In *Historiographie im frühen Mittelalter*, edited by Anton Scharer and Georg Scheibelreiter, 435–442. Vienna: Oldenbourg, 1994.

———. *King and Emperor: A New Life of Charlemagne*. London: Allen Lane, 2019.

———. "Kingship and Royal Government." In *The New Cambridge Medieval History*, vol. 2, edited by Rosamond McKitterick, 381–430. Cambridge: Cambridge University Press, 1995.

———. "The Last Years of Louis the Pious." In *Charlemagne's Heir: New Perspectives on the Reign of Louis the Pious (814–840)*, edited by Peter Godman and Roger Collins, 147–160. Oxford: Clarendon Press, 1990.

———."Le Cour impériale de Charlemagne." In *La royauté et les élites dans l'Europe carolingienne (début IX^e^ siècle aux environs de 920)*, edited by Régine Le Jan, 177–191. Lille: Centre d'histoire de l'Europe du Nord-Ouest, 1998.

———. "The Lord's Anointed and the People's Choice: Carolingian Royal Ritual." In *Rituals of Royalty: Power and Ceremonial in Traditional Societies*, edited by David Cannadine and Simon Price, 137–180. Cambridge: Cambridge University Press, 1987.

———. "Making a Difference in Eighth-Century Politics: The Daughters of Desiderius." In *After Rome's Fall: Narrators and Sources of Early Medieval History, Essays Presented to Walter Goffart*, edited by Alexander Callander Murray, 171–190. Toronto: University of Toronto Press, 1998.

———. "Normandy's Early History since *Normandy before 1066*." In *Normandy and Its Neighbours, 900–1250: Essays for David Bates*, edited by David Crouch and Kathleen Thompson, 3–16. Turnhout: Brepols, 2011.

——. "Opposition to Pilgrimage in the Reign of Charlemagne?" In *Rome and Religion in the Medieval World*, edited by Valerie L. Garver and Owen M. Phelan, 65–82. Farnham: Ashgate, 2014.

——. "The Role of the Gift in Early Medieval Diplomatic Relations." *Settimane di Studio* 58 (2011): 225–248.

——. "The Settings of the Gift in the Reign of Charlemagne." In *The Languages of Gift in the Early Middle Ages*, edited by Wendy Davies and Paul Fouracre, 116–148. Cambridge: Cambridge University Press, 2010.

——. "The Siting of the Council at Frankfort: Some Reflections on Family and Politics." *Das Frankfurter Konzil von 794: Kristallisationspunkt karolingischer Kultur*, edited by Rainer Berndt, 149–165. Mainz: Selbstverlag der Gesellschaft für Mittelrheinische Kirchengeschichte, 1997.

——. "Translating Images of Authority: The Christian Roman Emperors in the Carolingian World." In *Images of Authority: Papers Presented to Joyce Reynolds on the Occasion of Her Seventieth Birthday*, edited by Mary Margaret Mackenzie and Charlotte Roueché, 194–205. Cambridge: Oxbow, 1989.

——. "The Voice of Charlemagne." In *Courts, Elites, and Gendered Power in the Early Middle Ages: Charlemagne and Others*, 76–88. Aldershot: Variorum, 2007.

——. "Was Charlemagne's Court a Courtly Society?" In *Court Culture in the Early Middle Ages*, edited by Catherine Cubitt, 39–57. Turnhout: Brepols, 2003.

——. "Women at the Court of Charlemagne: A Case of the Monstrous Regiment?" In *Medieval Queenship*, edited by John Carmi Parsons, 43–61. Stroud: Alan Sutton, 1993.

——. "Why Are There So Many Different Accounts of Charlemagne's Imperial Coronation?" In *Courts, Elites, and Gendered Power in the Early Middle Ages: Charlemagne and Others*, 1–27. Aldershot: Variorum, 2007.

Nichanian, Mikaël, and Vivien Prigent. "Les Stratèges de Sicile: De la naissance du thème au règne de Léon V." *Revue des Études Byzantines* 61 (2003): 97–141.

Nicolson, Harold. *The Congress of Vienna: A Study in Allied Unity, 1812–1822*. London: Constable, 1946.

——. *Diplomacy*. 3rd ed. London: Oxford University Press, 1963.

Noble, Thomas F. X. *Charlemagne and Louis the Pious: The Lives by Einhard, Notker, Ermoldus, Thegan, and the Astronomer*. University Park: Pennsylvania State University Press, 2009.

——. *Images, Iconoclasm and the Carolingians*. Philadelphia: University of Pennsylvania Press, 2009.

——. "The Monastic Ideal as a Model for Empire: The Case of Louis the Pious." *Revue Bénédictine* 86 (1976): 235–250.

——. *The Republic of St. Peter: The Birth of the Papal State, 680–825*. Philadelphia: University of Pennsylvania Press, 1984.

——. "The Revolt of King Bernard of Italy in 817: Its Causes and Consequences." *Studi Medievali* 15 (1974): 315–326.

Noonan, Thomas S. "Early 'Abbāsid Mint Output." *Journal of the Economic and Social History of the Orient* 29 (1986): 113–175.

Northedge, Alastair. "Remarks on Samarra and the Archaeology of Large Cities." *Antiquity* 79 (2005): 119–129.

Noyé, Ghislaine. "Byzance et Italie méridionale." In *Byzantium in the Ninth Century: Dead or Alive?* edited by Leslie Brubaker, 229–244. Aldershot: Ashgate, 1998.

O'Brien, Conor. "Empire, Ethnic Election and Exegesis in the *Opus Caroli* (*Libri Carolini*)." *Studies in Church History* 54 (2018): 96–108.

Ocaña Jiménez, Manuel. "The Basilica of San Vicente and the Great Mosque of Córdoba: A New Look at the Sources." In *The Formation of al-Andalus, Part 2: Language, Religion, Culture and the Sciences*, edited by Maribel Fierro and Julio Samsó, 257–273. Aldershot: Ashgate, 1998.

Oliver, Dolores. "El *Ajbār Maŷmūʿa*: Una obra pólemica." *Qurṭuba* 6 (2001): 77–108.

——. "Los autores del *Ajbār Maŷmūʿa*: Los Tammām ibn ʿAlqama?" *Anaquel de Estudios Árabes* 12 (2001): 514–554.

Ollich i Castanyer, Imma. "Vic: La ciutat a l'època carolíngia." In *Catalunya a l'època carolíngia: Art i cultura abans del romànic (segles IX i X)*, edited by Jordi Camps Soria, 89–94. Barcelona: Diputació de Barcelona, 1999. Translated as "Vic: The Town in the Carolingian Age," ibid., 464–466.

Ollich i Castanyer, I., Montserrat de Rocafiguera Espona, and Maria Ocaña Subirana. "The Southern Carolingian Frontier in Marca Hispanica along the River Ter: *Roda Civitas* and the Archaeological Site of L'Esquerda (Catalonia)." In *Fortified Settlements in Early Medieval Europe: Defended Communities of the 8th–10th Centuries*, edited by Hajnalka Herold and Neil Christie, 205–217. Oxford: Oxbow, 2016.

Omar, Farouk. *Abbāsiyyāt: Studies in the History of the Early ʿAbbasids*. Baghdad: University of Baghdad, 1976.

——. "Politics and the Problem of Succession in the Early ʿAbbasid Caliphate, 132/750–158/775." *Islamic Quarterly* 18 (1974): 61–75.

Ordeig i Mata, Ramon. *Els Orígens Històrics de Vic: (segles VIII–X)*. Vic: Publicacions del Patronat d'Estudis Ausonencs, 1983.

Osiander, Andreas. "Sovereignty, International Relations, and the Westphalian Myth." *International Organisation* 55 (2001): 251–287.

Otte, T. G. "The Inner Circle: What Is Diplomatic History? (And Why We Should Study It): An Inaugural Lecture." *History* 105 (2020): 5–27.

Ottewill-Soulsby, Sam. "ʿAbbāsid-Carolingian Diplomacy in Early Medieval Arabic Apocalypse." *Millennium* 16 (2019): 213–232.

——. "The Camels of Charles the Bald." *Medieval Encounters* 25 (2019): 263–292.

——. "Charlemagne's Asian Elephant: India in Carolingian-ʿAbbāsid Relations." In *Levant, Cradle of Abrahamic Religions*, edited by Catalin-Stefan Popa, 187–211. Münster: LIT Verlag, 2022.

——. "'Those same cursed Saracens': Charlemagne's Campaigns in the Iberian Peninsula as Religious Warfare." *Journal of Medieval History* 42 (2016): 405–428.

Padoa-Schioppa, Antonio. "Profili del diritto internazionale nell'alto medioevo." *Settimane di Studio* 58 (2011): 1–78.

Palmer, Edward Henry. *Haroun Alraschid: Caliph of Bagdad*. London: Marcus Ward, 1881.

Patrich, Joseph, ed. *The Sabaite Heritage in the Orthodox Church from the Fifth Century to the Present*. Leuven: Peeters, 2001.

Patzold, Steffen. "Einhards erste Leser: Zu Kontext und Darstellungsabsicht der 'Vita Karoli.'" *Viator Multilingual* 42 (2011): 33–55.

Payne, Richard E. "Cosmology and the Expansion of the Iranian Empire, 502–628." *Past and Present* 220 (2013): 3–33.

———. "Iranian Cosmopolitanism: World Religion at the Sasanian Court." In *Cosmopolitanism and Empire: Universal Rulers, Local Elites, and Cultural Integration in the Ancient Near East and Mediterranean*, edited by Myles Lavan, Richard E. Payne, and John Weisweiler, 209–230. New York: Oxford University Press, 2016.

———. "The Making of Turan: The Fall and Transformation of the Iranian East in Late Antiquity." *Journal of Late Antiquity* 9 (2016): 4–41.

Pellat, Charles. "al-Rādhāniyya." *Encyclopedia of Islam*. 2nd ed. 8:363–367. Leiden: Brill, 1995.

———. "The Origin and Development of Historiography in Muslim Spain." In *Historians of the Middle East*, edited by Bernard Lewis and Peter M. Holt, 118–125. London: University of Oxford Press, 1964.

Penelas, Mayte. "Linguistic Islamization of the 'Mozarabs' as Attested in a Late Ninth-Century Chronicle." In *Language of Religion, Language of the People: Medieval Judaism, Christianity and Islam*, edited by Ernst Bremer, Jörg Jarnut, Michael Richter, and David Wasserstein, 103–114. Munich: Wilhelm Fink Verlag, 2006.

Pérez Martínez, Meritxell. *Tarraco en la Antigüedad Tardía: Cristianización y Organización Eclesiástica (III a VIII siglos)*. Tarragona: Arola Editors, 2012.

Pérez de Urbel, Justo. "Lo Viejo y lo Nuevo sobre el Origen del Reino de Pamplona." *Al-Andalus* 19 (1954): 1–42.

———. *San Eulogio de Córdoba*. Madrid: Ediciones FAX, 1942.

Peters, Francis E. *The Hajj: The Muslim Pilgrimage to Mecca and the Holy Places*. Princeton: Princeton University Press, 1994.

Phelan, Owen M. *The Formation of Christian Europe: The Carolingians, Baptism, and the* Imperium Christianum. Oxford: Oxford University Press, 2014.

Philby, Harry St. John Bridger. *Harun al Rashid*. London: Peter Davies Limited, 1933.

Picard, Christophe. *La Mer et les Musulmans d'Occident au Moyen Age: VIII^e–XIII^e siècle*. Paris: Presses universitaires de France, 1997.

Pirenne, Henri. *Mahomet et Charlemagne*. 3rd ed. Paris: Félix Alcan, 1937.

Plöger, Karsten. *England and the Avignon Popes: The Practice of Diplomacy in Late Medieval Europe*. London: Legenda/Modern Humanities Research Association and Maney, 2005.

Pohl, Walter. "Creating Cultural Resources for Carolingian Rule: Historians of the Christian Empire." In *The Resources of the Past in Early Medieval Europe*, edited by Clemens Gantner, Rosamond McKitterick, and Sven Meeder, 15–33. Cambridge: Cambridge University Press, 2015.

———. "Das Papsttum und die Langobarden." In *Der Dynastiewechsel von 751: Vorgeschichte, Legitimationsstrategien und Erinnerung*, edited by Matthias Becher and Jörg Jarnut, 145–161. Münster: Scriptorium, 2004.

———. *Die Awaren: Ein Steppenvolk in Mitteleuropa 567–822 n. Chr.* Munich: Beck, 1988.

———. "The Emergence of New Polities in the Breakup of the Western Roman Empire." In *Empires and Communities in the Post-Roman and Islamic World, c. 400–1000 CE*, edited by Rutger Kramer and Walter Pohl, 28–63. Oxford: Oxford University Press, 2021.

———. "Frontiers in Lombard Italy: The Laws of Ratchis and Aistulf." In *The Transformation of Frontiers from Late Antiquity to the Carolingians*, edited by Walter Pohl, Ian Wood, and Helmut Reimitz, 117–141. Leiden: Brill, 2001.

———. "Introduction: Strategies of Distinction." In *Strategies of Distinction: The Construction of Ethnic Communities, 300–800*, edited by Walter Pohl and Helmut Reimitz, 1–15. Leiden: Brill, 1998.

———. "Ritualised Encounters: Late Roman Diplomacy and the Barbarians, Fifth–Sixth Century." In *Court Ceremonies and Rituals of Power in Byzantium and the Medieval Mediterranean: Comparative Perspectives*, edited by Alexander Daniel Beihammer, Stavroula Constantinou, and Maria Parani, 67–86. Leiden: Brill, 2013.

———. "Why Not to Marry a Foreign Woman: Stephen III's Letter to Charlemagne." In *Rome and Religion in the Medieval World*, edited by Valerie L. Garver and Owen M. Phelan, 47–63. Farnham: Ashgate, 2014.

Pohlsander, Hans A. *National Monuments and Nationalism in 19th-Century Germany*. Oxford: Lang, 2008.

Pollard, Richard M. "One Other on Another: Petrus Monachus' *Revelations* and Islam." In *Difference and Identity in Francia and Medieval France*, edited by Meredith Cohen and Justine Firnhaber-Baker, 25–42. Farnham: Ashgate, 2010.

Ponsich, Pierre. "Bera I, Comte de Barcelone et ses descendants: Le Problème de Leur Juridiction Comtale." In *Conflent, Vallespir et Montagnes Catalanes: Congreso de la Federacion Historica del Languedoc Mediterraneo y del Roussillon*. LI, 51–69. Montpellier: CNRS, 1980.

Pouqueville, François-Charles-Hugues-Laurent. *Mémoire historique et diplomatique sur le commerce et les établissements français au Levant, depuis l'an 500 de J.C. jusqu'à la fin du XVII^e^ siècle*. Paris: Académie Royale des Inscriptions et Belles-Lettres, 1833.

Power, Daniel. "Frontiers: Terms, Concepts, and the Historians of Medieval and Early Modern Europe." In *Frontiers in Question: Eurasian Borderlands, 700–1700*, edited by Daniel Power and Naomi Standen, 1–12. Basingstoke: St. Martin's Press, 1999.

Prawer, Joshua. "Jerusalem in the Christian and Jewish Perspectives of the Early Middle Ages." *Settimane di Studio* 26 (1980): 739–795.

Preißler, Matthias. "Fragmente einer verlorenen Kunst: Die Paderborner Wandmalerei." In *799: Kunst und Kultur der Karolingerzeit: Karl der Grosse und Papst Leo III. in Paderborn*, edited by Christoph Stiegemann and Matthias Wemhoff, 197–206. Mainz: Von Zabern, 1999.

Prevas, John. *Hannibal Crosses the Alps: The Enigma Re-examined*. Staplehurst: Spellmount, 1998.

Prigent, Vivien. "Cutting Losses: The Unraveling of Byzantine Sicily." In *Southern Italy as Contact Area and Border Region during the Early Middle Ages: Religious-Cultural Heterogeneity and Competing Powers in Local, Transregional, and Universal Dimensions*, edited by Klaus Herbers and Kordula Wolf, 79–100. Cologne: Böhlau Verlag, 2018.

———. "La carrière du toumarque Euphèmios, *basileus* des Romains." In *Histoire et culture dans l'Italie byzantine*, edited by André Jacob, Jean-Marie Martin, et al., 279–317. Rome: Ecole française de Rome, 2006.

——. "The Myth of the Mancus and the Origins of the European Economy." *Revue Numismatique* 171 (2014): 701–728.

Prinz, Otto. "Eine frühe abendländische Aktualisierung der lateinischen Übersetzung des Pseudo-Methodios." *Deutsches Archiv für Erforschung des Mittelalters* 41 (1985): 1–23.

Pryor, John H. *Commerce, Shipping and Naval Warfare in the Medieval Mediterranean*. London: Variorum, 1987.

——. "The Mediterranean Breaks Up: 500–1000." In *The Mediterranean in History*, edited by David Abulafia, 155–181. London: Thames & Hudson, 2003.

Queller, Donald E. *The Office of Ambassador in the Middle Ages*. Princeton: Princeton University Press, 1967.

Ragheb, Youssef. "La transmission des nouvelles en Terre d'Islam: Les modes de transmission." *Publications de l'École Française de Rome* 190 (1994): 37–48.

Ranke, Leopold von. "Das politische Gespräch." In *Das politische Gespräch und andere Schriftchen zur Wissenschaftslehre*, 10–36. Halle: Niemeyer, 1925.

——. "Die grossen Mächte." In *Völker und Staaten in der neueren Geschichte*, edited by Leonhard von Muralt, 44–88. Zürich: Eugen Rentsch, 1945.

Reimitz, Helmut. *History, Frankish Identity and the Framing of Western Ethnicity, 550–850*. Cambridge: Cambridge University Press, 2015.

Reinaud, Joseph Touissant. *Invasions des Sarrazins en France, et de France en Savoie, en Piémont et dans la Suisse, pendant les 8e, 9e et 10e siècles de notre ère, d'après les auteurs chrétiens et mahométans*. Paris: Dandey-Dupré, 1836.

Reinink, Gerritt J. "Ps.-Methodius: A Concept of History in Response to the Rise of Islam." In *The Byzantine and Early Islamic Near East*. Vol. 1: *Problems in the Literacy Source Material*, edited by Averil Cameron and Lawrence I. Conrad, 149–187. Princeton: Darwin Press, 1992.

Rembold, Ingrid. *Conquest and Christianization: Saxony and the Carolingian World, 772–888*. Cambridge: Cambridge University Press, 2018.

——. "The Poeta Saxo at Paderborn: Episcopal Authority and Carolingian Rule in Late Ninth-Century Saxony." *Early Medieval Europe* 21 (2013): 169–196.

Renoux, Annie. "Karolingische Pfalzen in Nordfrankreich (751–987)." In *799: Kunst und Kultur der Karolingerzeit: Karl der Grosse und Papst Leo III. in Paderborn*, edited by Christoph Stiegemann and Matthias Wemhoff, 130–137. Mainz: Von Zabern, 1999.

Reuter, Timothy. "Assembly Politics in Western Europe from the Eighth Century to the Twelfth." In *The Medieval World*, edited by Peter Linehan and Janet L. Nelson, 432–450. London: Routledge, 2001.

——. "The End of Carolingian Military Expansion." In *Charlemagne's Heir: New Perspectives on the Reign of Louis the Pious (814–840)*, edited by Peter Godman and Roger Collins, 391–405. Oxford: Clarendon Press, 1990.

——. "The Insecurity of Travel in the Early and High Middle Ages: Criminals, Victims and Their Medieval and Modern Observers." In *Träger und Instrumentarien des Friedens im Hohen und Späten Mittelalter*, edited by Johannes Fried, 169–201. Sigmaringen: Thorbecke, 1998. Reprinted in *Medieval Politics and Modern Mentalities*, edited by Janet L. Nelson, 38–71. Cambridge: Cambridge University Press, 2006.

——. "Plunder and Tribute in the Carolingian Empire." *Transactions of the Royal Historical Society*, 5th ser., 35 (1985): 75–94.

Reynolds, Susan. "The Historiography of the Medieval State." In *A Companion to Historiography*, edited by Michael Bentley, 117–138. London: Routledge, 1997.

——. "There Were States in Medieval Europe: A Response to Rees Davies." *Journal of Historical Sociology* 16 (2003): 550–555.

Riant, Paul. "Inventaire critique des lettres historiques des Croisades." *Archives de l'Orient Latin* 1 (1881): 1–224.

——."La donation de Hugues, marquis de Toscane, au Saint-Sépulchre et les établissements latins de Jérusalem." *Mémoirs de l'Institut National de France* 31 (1884): 151–195.

Riché, Pierre. "Les représentations du Palais dans les textes littéraires du Haut Moyen Age." *Francia* 4 (1976): 161–171.

Riess, Frank. "From Aachen to Al-Andalus: The Journey of Deacon Bodo (823–876)." *Early Medieval Europe* 13 (2005): 131–157.

——. *Narbonne and Its Territory in Late Antiquity: From the Visigoths to the Arabs.* Farnham: Ashgate, 2013.

Rio, Alice. *Legal Practice and the Written Word in the Early Middle Ages: Frankish Formulae, c. 500–1000.* Cambridge: Cambridge University Press, 2009.

Robinson, Chase F. *ʿAbd al-Malik.* Oxford: Oneworld, 2005.

——. "Islamic Historical Writing, Eighth through the Tenth Centuries." In *The Oxford History of Historical Writing.* Vol. 2: *400–1400*, edited by Sarah Foot and Chase F. Robinson, 238–266. Oxford: Oxford University Press, 2011.

Rollason, David. "Charlemagne's Palace." *Archaeological Journal* 172 (2015): 443–448.

Rosenberger, Bernard. "Les premières villes islamiques du Maroc: Géographie et fonctions." In *Genèse de la ville islamique en al-Andalus et au Maghreb occidental*, edited by Patrice Cressier and Mercedes García-Arenal, 229–255. Madrid: Casa de Velázquez, 1998.

Rosenthal, Erwin. "Der Plan eines Bündnisses zwischen Karl dem Großen und ʿAbdurrahmān in der arabischen Überlieferung." *Neues Archiv* 48 (1930): 441–445.

——. "Harunu'l Rashid and Charles the Great Review." *Historische Zeitschrift* 145 (1931): 630–631.

Rosenthal, Franz. "Hiba." *Encyclopedia of Islam.* 2nd ed. 3:342–344. Leiden: Brill, 1971.

Rosenwein, Barbara H. "Francia and Polynesia: Rethinking Anthropological Approaches." In *Negotiating the Gift: Pre-modern Figurations of Exchange*, edited by Gadi Algazi, Valentin Groebner, and Bernhard Jussen, 361–379. Göttingen: Vandenhoeck & Ruprecht, 2003.

Rosser-Owen, Mariam. "Mediterraneanism: How to Incorporate Islamic Art into an Emerging Field." *Journal of Art Historiography* 6 (2012): 1–33.

Rotter, Ekkehart. *Abendland und Sarazenen: Das okzidentale Araberbild undseine Entstehung im Frühmittelalter.* Berlin: De Gruyter, 1986.

Rouche, Michel. *L'Aquitaine, des Wisigoths aux Arabes, 418–781: Naissance d'une region.* Paris: École des hautes études en sciences sociales, 1979.

——. "Les Aquitains ont-ils avant la bataille de Poitiers?" *Le Môyen Age* 1 (1968): 5–28.

——. "Les relations transpyrénéennes du Ve au VIIIe siècle." In *Les Communications dans la Péninsule Ibérique au Moyen-Age*, edited by Pierre Tucoo-Chala, 13–20. Paris: Editions du Centre national de la recherche scientifique, 1981.

Rubin, Zeev. "Al-Ṭabarī and the Age of the Sasanians." In *Al-Ṭabarī: A Medieval Muslim Historian and His Work*, edited by Hugh Kennedy, 41–71. Princeton: Princeton University Press, 2008.

——. "The Mediterranean and the Dilemma of the Roman Empire in Late Antiquity." *Mediterranean History Review* 1 (1986): 13–62.

Ruggie, J. G. "Continuity and Transformation in the World Polity: Toward a Neorealist Synthesis." *World Politics* 35 (1983): 261–285.

Ruggiero, Fabio. *Atti dei martiri scilitani: Introduzione, testo, traduzione, testimonianze e comment*. Rome: Accademia nazionale dei Lincei, 1991.

Runciman, Steven. "Charlemagne and Palestine." *English Historical Review* 50 (1935): 606–619.

Ruska, J. "*Fīl*." *Encyclopedia of Islam*. 2nd ed. 2:892–893. Leiden, 1965.

Russett, Bruce. "Processes of Dyadic Choice for War and Peace." *World Politics* 47 (1995): 268–282.

Russo Mailler, Carmela. "La politica meridionale di Ludovico II e il 'Rythmus de captivitate Ludovici imperatoris.'" *Quaderni Medievali* 14 (1982): 6–27.

Sabbe, Étienne. "L'importation des tissus orientaux en Europe occidentale au Haut Moyen Age, IX$^{e}$ et X$^{e}$ siècles." *Revue Belge de Philologie et d'Histoire* 14 (1935): 1261–1288.

——. "Quelques types de marchands des IX$^{e}$ et X$^{e}$ siècles." *Revue Belge de Philologie et d'Histoire* 13 (1934): 176–187.

Safran, Janina M. "Ceremony and Submission: The Symbolic Representation and Recognition of Legitimacy in Tenth-Century al-Andalus." *Journal of Near Eastern Studies* 58 (1999): 191–201.

——. *The Second Umayyad Caliphate: The Articulation of Caliphal Legitimacy in al-Andalus*. Cambridge, MA: Harvard University Press, 2000.

Sage, Walter. "Die Ausgrabungen in der Pfalz zu Ingelheim am Rhein." *Francia* 4 (1976): 141–160.

Sahner, Christian C. *Christian Martyrs under Islam: Religious Violence and the Making of the Muslim World*. Princeton: Princeton University Press, 2018.

Salinas, Elena, and Irene Montilla. "Material Culture Interactions between al-Andalus and the Aghlabids." In *The Aghlabids and Their Neighbors: Art and Material Culture in Ninth-Century North Africa*, edited by Glaire D. Anderson, Corisande Fenwick, and Mariam Rosser-Owen, 429–447. Leiden: Brill, 2018.

Salrach, Josep M. "Carlemany i Catalunya en el marc de l'Europa carolíngia." In *Catalunya a l'època carolíngia: Art i cultura abans del romànic (segles IX i X)*, edited by Jordi Camps Soria, 19–27. Barcelona: Diputació de Barcelona, 1999.

——. *El Procés de Formació Nacional de Catalunya (segles VIII–IX)*. Barcelona: Edicions 62, 1978.

——. "Guillaume et Barcelone: La formation de la Marche Hispanique." In *Entre histoire et épopée: Les Guillaume d'Orange (IX$^{e}$–XIII$^{e}$ siècles)*, edited by Laurent Macé, 25–44. Toulouse: Université de Toulouse-Le Mirail, 2006.

Samarrai, Alauddin. "Some Geographical and Political Information on Western Europe in the Medieval Arabic Sources." *Muslim World* 62 (1972): 304–322.

Samson, Ross. "Carolingian Palaces and the Poverty of Ideology." In *Meaningful Architecture: Social Interpretations of Buildings*, edited by Martin Locock, 99–131. Aldershot: Avebury, 1994.

Sánchez-Albornoz, Claudio. *Despoblación y Repoblación del Valle del Duero*. Buenos Aires: Universidad de Buenos Aires, 1966.
——. *El "Ajbār maŷmū'a": Cuestiones historiográficas que suscita*. Buenos Aires: Facultad de filosofía y letras, 1944.
——. "El Tercer Rey de España." *Cuadernos de Historia de España* 49–50 (1969): 5–49.
——. *En torno a los orígenes del feudalism*. Vol. 2. Mendoza: Universidad Nacional de Cuyo, 1942.
——. "La auténtica batalla de Clavijo." *Cuadernos de Historia de España* 9 (1948): 94–139.
——. "La saña celosa de un arabista." *Cuadernos de la Historia de España* 27 (1958): 5–42.
——. "Problemas de la historia Navarra del siglo IX." *Príncipe de Viana* 20 (1959): 5–62.
——. "Réplica al arabista Chalmeta." *Cuadernos de la Historia de España* 59 (1976): 425–434.
——. "Some Remarks on *Fatḥ al-Andalus*." In *The Formation of al-Andalus, Part 2: Language, Religion, Culture and the Sciences*, edited by Maribel Fierro and Julio Samsó, 151–172. Aldershot: Ashgate, 1998.
Savage, Elizabeth. *A Gateway to Hell, a Gateway to Paradise: The North African Response to the Arab Conquest*. Princeton: Darwin Press, 1997.
Savage, Elizabeth, and Adon A. Gordus. "Dirhams for the Empire." In *Genèse de la ville islamique en al-Andalus et au Maghreb occidental*, edited by Patrice Cressier and Mercedes García-Arenal, 377–402. Madrid: Casa de Velázquez, 1998.
Savant, Sarah Bowen. "Forgetting Ctesiphon: Iran's Pre-Islamic Past, c. 800–1100." In *History and Identity in the Late Antique Near East*, edited by Philip Wood, 169–186. Oxford: Oxford University Press, 2013.
Scarfe Beckett, Katharine. *Anglo-Saxon Perceptions of the Islamic World*. Cambridge: Cambridge University Press, 2003.
Schacht, Joseph. *An Introduction to Islamic Law*. Oxford: Clarendon Press, 1964.
——. *The Origins of Muhammadan Jurisprudence*. Oxford: Clarendon Press, 1953.
Schäpers, Maria. *Lothar I. (795–855) und das Frankenreich*. Vienna: Böhlau Verlag, 2018.
Scheiner, Jens, and Damien Janos. "Baghdād: Political Metropolis and Intellectual Center." In *The Place to Go: Contexts of Learning in Baghdād, 750–1000 C.E.*, edited by Jens Scheiner and Damien Janos, 1–46. Princeton: Darwin Press, 2014.
Schick, Robert. *The Christian Communities of Palestine from Byzantine to Islamic Rule: A Historical and Archaeological Study*. Princeton: Darwin Press, 1995.
Schieffer, Rudolf. "Die Politik der Karolinger in Süditalien und im Mittelmeerraum." In *Southern Italy as Contact Area and Border Region during the Early Middle Ages: Religious-Cultural Heterogeneity and Competing Powers in Local, Transregional, and Universal Dimensions*, edited by Klaus Herbers and Kordula Wolf, 65–78. Cologne: Böhlau Verlag, 2018.
Schleifer, Joel. "Die Erzählung der Sibylle: Ein Apokryph nach den Karschunischen, Arabischen und Äthiopen Handschriften zu London, Oxford, Paris und Rom." *Denkschriften der Kaiserlichen Akademie der Wissenschaften, Phil.-hist* 53 (1910): 1–79.
Schmid, Karl. "Aachen und Jerusalem: Ein Beitrag zur historischen Personenfuhrung der Karolingerzeit." In *Das Einhardkreuz: Vorträge und Studien der Münsteraner*

*Diskussion zum arcus Einhardi*, edited by Karl Hauck, 122–142. Göttingen: Vandenhoeck & Ruprecht, 1974.

Schoeler, Gregor. "Die Frage der schriftlichen oder mündlichen Überlieferung der Wissenschaften in frühen Islam." *Der Islam* 62 (1985): 201–230. Translated by Uwe Vagelpohl as "The Transmission of the Sciences in Early Islam: Oral or Written?" In *The Oral and the Written in Early Islam*, edited by James E. Montgomery, 28–44. London: Routledge, 2006.

———. *The Genesis of Literature in Islam: From the Aural to the Read*. Translated by Shawkat M. Toorawa. Edinburgh: Edinburgh University Press, 2009.

Scior, Volker. "Stimme, Schrift und Performanz: 'Übertragungen' und 'Reproduktion' durch frühmittelalterliche Boten." In *Übertragungen: Formen und Konzepte von Reproduktion in Mittelalter und Früher Neuzeit*, edited by Britta Bußmann, Albrecht Hausmann, Annelie Kreft, and Cornelia Logemann, 77–99. Berlin: De Gruyter, 2005.

Screen, Elina. "Carolingian Fathers and Sons in Italy: Lothar I and Louis II's Successful Partnership." In *After Charlemagne: Carolingian Italy and Its Rulers*, edited by Clemens Gantner and Walter Pohl, 148–163. Cambridge: Cambridge University Press, 2020.

Searle, Eleanor. "Frankish Rivalries and Norse Warriors." *Anglo-Norman Studies* 8 (1986): 198–213.

———. *Predatory Kinship and the Creation of Norman Power, 840-1066*. Berkeley: University of California Press, 1988.

Segelken, Barbara, and Tim Urban. *Kaiser und Kalifen: Karl der Grosse und die Mächte am Mittelmeer um 800*. Darmstadt: Von Zabern, 2014.

Segoloni, Maria Paola. "Il prologus della *Medicina Plinii*." In *Prefazioni, prologhi, proemi di opere tecnico-scientifiche latine*. Vol. 1, edited by Carlo Santini, Nino Scivoletto, and Loriano Zurli, 361–366. Rome: Herder, 1990.

Semmler, Josef. "Renovatio regni Francorum: Die Herrschaft Ludwigs des Frommen im Frankenreich, 814–829/30." In *Charlemagne's Heir: New Perspectives on the Reign of Louis the Pious (814–840)*, edited by Peter Godman and Roger Collins, 125–146. Oxford: Clarendon Press, 1990.

Sénac, Philippe. "Estudio sobre los Primeros Condes Aragones." *Aragón en la Edad Media* 14 (1999): 1501–1506.

———. *Les Carolingiens et al-Andalus (VIII^e–IX^e siècles)*. Paris: Maisonneuve et Larose, 2002.

———. "Les Carolingiens et le califat Abbasside (VIII^e–IX^e siècles)." *Studia Islamica* 95 (2002): 37–56.

———. *L'image de l'autre: L'Occident medieval face à l'Islam*. Paris: Flammarion, 1983.

———. *Musulmans et Sarrasins dans le sud de la Gaule: VIII^e–XI^e siècle*. Paris: Sycomore, 1980.

———. "Note sur les Relations Diplomatiques entre les comtes de Barcelone et le Califat de Cordoue au X^e siècle." In *Histoire et Archéologie des Terres Catalanes au Moyen Age*, edited by Philippe Sénac, 87–101. Perpignan: Presses universitaires de Perpignan, 1995.

Sénac, Philippe, and Tawfiq Ibrahim. *Los precintos de la conquista omeya y la formación de al-Andalus (711–756)*. Granada: Editorial Universidad de Granada, 2017.

Shaban, Muḥammad ʿAbd al-Ḥayy. *The ʿAbbāsid Revolution*. Cambridge: Cambridge University Press, 1970.

——. *Islamic History: A New Interpretation*. Cambridge: Cambridge University Press, 1976.

Shalem, Avinoam. "Objects as Carriers of Real or Contrived Memories in a Cross-cultural Context." *Mitteilungen zur Spätantiken Archäologie und Byzantinischen Kunstgeschichte* 4 (2005): 101–117.

Sharon, Moshe. *Black Banners in the East*. Jerusalem: Magnes Press, 1983.

Shboul, Ahmad M. H. *Al-Mas'udi and His World: A Muslim Humanist and His Interest in Non-Muslims*. London: Ithaca Press, 1979.

Shepard, Jonathan. "The Rhos Guests of Louis the Pious: Whence and Wherefore?" *Early Medieval Europe* 4 (1995): 41–60.

——. "Trouble-Shooters and Men-on-the-Spot: The Emperor's Dealings with Outsiders." *Settimane di Studio* 58 (2011): 691–723.

Shepard, Jonathan, and Simon Franklin, eds. *Byzantine Diplomacy*. Aldershot: Variorum, 1992.

Shoshan, Boaz. *Poetics of Islamic Historiography: Deconstructing Ṭabarī's History*. Leiden: Brill, 2004.

Siegel, Ulrike. "Frühabbasidische Residenzbauten des Kalifen Hārūn ar-Rašīd in ar-Raqqa/ar-Rāfiqa (Syrien)." *Madrider Mitteilungen* 50 (2009): 482–502.

Signes Codoñer, Juan. *The Emperor Theophilos and the East, 829–842: Court and Frontier in Byzantium during the Last Phase of Iconoclasm*. Farnham: Ashgate, 2014.

Silverstein, Adam J. *Postal Systems in the Pre-Modern Islamic World*. Cambridge: Cambridge University Press, 2007.

Simms, Bernard. "The Return of the Primacy of Foreign Policy." *German History* 21 (2003): 275–291.

Smith, Julia M. H. "Fines Imperii: The Marches." In *The New Cambridge Medieval History*, vol. 2, edited by Rosamond McKitterick, 169–189. Cambridge: Cambridge University Press, 1995.

——. "Old Saints, New Cults: Roman Relics in Carolingian Francia." In *Early Medieval Rome and the Christian West*, edited by Julia M. H. Smith, 317–329. Leiden: Brill, 2000.

——. *Province and Empire: Brittany and the Carolingians*. Cambridge: Cambridge University Press, 1992.

Sode, Claudia. *Jerusalem, Konstantinopel, Rom: Die Viten des Michael Synkellos und der Brüder Theodoros und Theophanes*. Stuttgart: Steiner, 2001.

Sommar, Mary E. "Hincmar of Rheims and the Canon Law of Episcopal Translation." *Catholic Historical Review* 88 (2002): 429–445.

Soravia, Bruna. "Entre bureaucratie et *littérature*: La *kitāba* et les *kuttāb* dans l'administration de l'Espagne umayyade." *Studia Islamica* 7 (1994): 165–200.

Sorrell, Paul. "Alcuin's 'Comb' Riddle." *Neophilologus* 80 (1996): 311–318.

Sot, Michel. "Le palais d'Aix: Lieu de pouvoir et de culture." In *Le Monde Carolingien: Bilan, perspectives, champs de recherches*, edited by Wojciech Fałkowski and Yves Sassier, 243–261. Turnhout: Brepols, 2009.

Sotinel, Claire. "How Were Bishops Informed? Information Transmission across the Adriatic Sea in Late Antiquity." In *Travel Communication and Geography in Late*

*Antiquity: Sacred and Profane*, edited by Linda Ellis and Frank L. Kidner, 63–72. Aldershot: Ashgate, 2004.

Sourdel, Dominique. "Questions de cérémonial 'Abbaside." *Revue des Études Islamiques* 28 (1960): 121–148.

Southern, Richard W. *Western Views of Islam in the Middle Ages*. Cambridge, MA: Harvard University Press, 1962.

Spaulding, Jay. "Medieval Christian Nubia and the Islamic World: A Reconsideration of the *Baqt* Treaty." *International Journal of African Historical Studies* 28 (1995): 577–594.

Sperl, Stefan. "Islamic Kingship and Arabic Panegyric Poetry in the Early 9th Century." *Journal of Arabic Literature* 8 (1977): 20–35.

———. *Mannerism in Arabic Poetry: A Structural Analysis of Selected Texts (3rd century AH/9th century AD–5th century AH/11th century AD)*. Cambridge: Cambridge University Press, 1989.

Staubach, Nikolaus. "'Des großen Kaisers kleiner Sohn': Zum Bild Ludwigs des Frommen in der älteren deutschen Geschichtsforschung." In *Charlemagne's Heir: New Perspectives on the Reign of Louis the Pious (814–840)*, edited by Peter Godman and Roger Collins, 701–722. Oxford: Clarendon Press, 1990.

———. *Rex Christianus: Hofkultur und Herrschaftspropaganda im Reich Karls des Kahlen*. Cologne: Böhlau, 1993.

Steiger, Heinhard. *Die Ordnung der Welt: Eine Völkerrechtsgeschichte des karolingischen Zeitalters (741 bis 840)*. Cologne: Böhlau, 2010.

Steinmann, Marc. *Alexander der Grosse und die "nackten Weisen" Indiens: Der fiktive Briefwechsel zwischen Alexander und dem Brahmanenkönig Dindimus*. Berlin: Frank & Timme, 2012.

Štih, Peter. "Pribina Slawischer Furst oder Fränkischer Graf?" In *Ethnogenese und Überlieferung: Angewandte Methoden der Frühmittelalterforschung*, edited by Karl Brunner and Brigitte Merta, 209–222. Vienna: Oldenbourg, 1994.

Stone, Rachel. *Morality and Masculinity in the Carolingian Empire*. Cambridge: Cambridge University Press, 2012.

Story, Joanna. *Carolingian Connections: Anglo-Saxon England and Carolingian Francia, c. 750–870*. Aldershot: Ashgate, 2003.

Stuckey, Jace. "Charlemagne as Crusader? Memory, Propaganda and the Many Uses of Charlemagne's Legendary Expedition to Spain." In *The Legend of Charlemagne in the Middle Ages: Power, Faith and Crusade*, edited by Matthew Gabriele and Jace Stuckey, 137–152. New York: Palgrave Macmillan, 2008.

Takayama, Hiroshi. "Frederick II's Crusade: An Example of Christian-Muslim Diplomacy." *Mediterranean History Review* 25 (2010): 169–185.

Talbi, Mohamed. "Le Christianisme maghrébin de la conquête musulmane à sa disparition une tentative d'explication." In *Conversion and Continuity: Indigenous Christian Communities in Islamic Lands, Eighth to Eighteenth Centuries*, edited by Michael Gervers and Ramzi Jibran Bikhazi, 13–80. Toronto: Pontifical Institute of Mediaeval Studies, 1990.

———. *L'Émirat Aghlabide, 184–296, 800–909, histoire politique*. Paris: Librairie d'Amérique et d'Orient, 1966.

Tennyson, Alfred. "Recollections of the Arabian Nights." In *The Poems of Tennyson*, edited by Christopher B. Ricks. London: Oxford University Press, 1987.

Tibbetts, Gerald R. "The Beginnings of a Cartographic Tradition." In *The History of Cartography*. Vol. 2.1: *Cartography in the Traditional Islamic and South Asian Societies*, edited by John Brian Harley and David Woodward, 90–107. Chicago: University of Chicago Press, 1992.

Tieszen, Charles Lowell. *Christian Identity amid Islam in Medieval Spain*. Leiden: Brill, 2013.

——. "From Invitation to Provocation: 'Holy Cruelty' as Christian Mission in Ninth-Century Córdoba." *Al-Masāq* 24 (2012): 21–33.

Tillier, Mathieu. *Les Cadis d'Iraq et l'Etat abbasside (132/750–334/945)*. Damascus: IFPO, 2009.

Tischler, Matthias M. *Einharts "Vita Karoli": Studien zur Entstehung, Überlieferung und Rezeption*. Hannover: Hahn, 2001.

Toch, Michael. *The Economic History of European Jews: Late Antiquity and Early Middle Ages*. Leiden: Brill, 2013.

Tolan, John V. "Réactions chrétiennes aux conquêtes musulmanes: Etude compare des auteurs chrétiens de Syrie et d'Espagne (VII^e–IX^e siècles)." *Cahiers de Civilisation Médiévale* 44 (2001): 349–367.

——. *Saracens: Islam in the Medieval European Imagination*. New York: Columbia University Press, 2002.

——. "'A wild man, whose hand will be against all': Saracens and Ishmaelites in Latin Ethnographical Tradition from Jerome to Bede." In *Visions of Community in the Post-Roman World: The West, Byzantium and the Islamic World, 300–1100*, edited by Walter Pohl, Clemens Gantner, and Richard Payne, 513–530. Farnham: Ashgate, 2012.

Tonghi, Cristina. "Gli Arabi ad Amantea: Elementi di documentaziare material." *Annali dell'Instituto Universitario Orientale* 57 (1997): 203–230.

Tor, Deborah G. "The Long Shadow of Pre-Islamic Iranian Rulership: Antagonism or Assimilation?" In *Late Antiquity: Eastern Perspectives*, edited by Teresa Bernheimer and Adam Silverstein, 145–164. Warminster: Gibb Memorial Trust, 2012.

Touati, Houari. *Islam and Travel in the Middle Ages*. Translated by Lydia G. Cochrane. Chicago: University of Chicago Press, 2012.

Trautmann, Thomas R. *Elephants and Kings: An Environmental History*. Chicago: University of Chicago Press, 2015.

Tremp, Ernst. "Zwischen Paderborn und Barcelona: König Ludwig von Aquitanien und die Auseinandersetzung des Karlsreichs mit dem Islam." In *Am Vorabend der Kaiserkrönung: Das Epos "Karolus Magnus et Leo Papa" und der Papstbesuch in Paderborn 799*, edited by Peter Godman, Jörg Jarnut, and Peter Johanek, 283–299. Berlin: Berlin Akademie Verlag, 2002.

Tschacher, Werner. "Karl der Große: Aachens dienstbare Leiche." In *Die dienstbare Leiche: Der tote Körper als medizinische, soziokulturelle und ökonomische Ressource*, edited by Dominik Groß, 29–35. Kassel: Kassel University Press, 2009.

Turcan-Verkerk, Anne-Marie. "Faut-il rendre à Tertullien l'Ex libris Tertulliani de execrandis gentium diis du manuscrit Vatican latin 3852?" *Revue d'études augustiniennes et patristiques* 46 (2000): 205–234.

Turner, Bryan S. *Marx and the End of Orientalism*. London: Allen & Unwin, 1978.

——. *Weber and Islam: A Critical Study*. London: Routledge & Kegan Paul, 1974.

Udovitch, Abraham L. "Time, the Sea and Society: Duration of Commercial Voyages on the Southern Shores of the Mediterranean during the High Middle Ages." *Settimane di Studio* 25 (1978): 503–546.

Untermann, Matthias. "'*Opere mirabili constructa*': Die Aachener 'Residenz' Karls des Großen." In *799: Kunst und Kultur der Karolingerzeit: Karl der Grosse und Papst Leo III. in Paderborn*, edited by Christoph Stiegemann and Matthias Wemhoff, 152–164. Mainz: Von Zabern, 1999.

Vacca, Alison. *Non-Muslim Provinces under Early Islam: Islamic Rule and Iranian Legitimacy in Armenia and Caucasian Albania*. Cambridge: Cambridge University Press, 2017.

Valensi, Lucette. *The Birth of the Despot: Venice and the Sublime Porte*. Translated by Arthur Denner. Ithaca: Cornell University Press, 1993.

Valenzuela, Claudia. "The Faith of the Saracens: Forms of Knowledge of Islam in the Christian Kingdoms of the Iberian Peninsula until the 12th Century." *Millennium* 10 (2013): 314–330.

Valérian, Dominique. "La permanence du christianisme au Maghreb: L'apport problématique des sources latines." In *Islamisation et arabisation de l'Occident musulman médiéval (vii^e^–xii^e^ siècle)*, edited by Dominique Valérian, 131–149. Paris: Publications de la Sorbonne, 2011.

———. "The Medieval Mediterranean." In *A Companion to Mediterranean History*, edited by Peregrine Horden and Sharon Kinoshita, 77–90. Chichester: Wiley-Blackwell, 2014.

Vallejo Triano, Antonio. "Madīnat az-Zahrā': Transformation of a Caliphal City." In *Revisiting al-Andalus: Perspectives on the Material Culture of Islamic Iberia and Beyond*, edited by Glaire D. Anderson and Mariam Rosser-Owen, 2–26. Leiden: Brill, 2007.

van Donzel, E. J., and Andrea Schmidt. *Gog and Magog in Early Eastern Christian and Islamic Sources: Sallam's Quest for Alexander's Wall*. Leiden: Brill, 2010.

van Espelo, Dorine. "A Testimony of Carolingian Rule? The *Codex Epistolaris Carolinus*, Its Historical Context, and the Meaning of *Imperium*." *Early Medieval Europe* 21 (2013): 254–282.

van Koningsveld, P.Sj. "Christian Arabic Literature from Medieval Spain: An Attempt at Periodisation." In *Christian Arabic Apologetics during the Abbasid Period (750–1258)*, edited by Samir Khalil Samir and Jørgen S. Nielsen, 203–224. Leiden: Brill, 1994.

van Waard, Roelof. *Études sur l'Origine et la Formation de La Chanson d'Aspremont*. Groningen: J.-B. Wolters, 1937.

Vasiliev, Aleksandr Aleksandrovich. *Byzance et les Arabes*. Vol. 2: *La Dynastie Macédonienne (867–959)*. Brussels: Institut de philologie et d'histoire orientales et slaves, 1951.

Verhulst, Adriaan. "Economic Organisation." In *The New Cambridge Medieval History*, vol. 2, edited by Rosamond McKitterick, 481–509. Cambridge: Cambridge University Press, 1995.

Verlinden, Charles. "A propos de la place des Juifs dans l'économie de l'Europe occidentale aux IX^e^ et X^e^ siècles: Agobard de Lyon et l'historiographie." In *Storiografia et Storia: Studi in onore de Eugenio Dupré-Theseider*, 21–37. Rome: Bulzoni, 1974.

*Verzeichniss der Gemälde und Statuen des kgl. Maximilianeums*. Munich: Eigenverlag, 1878.

Viguera Molíns, María J. *Aragón musulmán*. Zaragoza: Librería General, 1981.

——. "The Muslim Settlement of Spain/Al-Andalus." In *The Formation of al-Andalus, Part 1: History and Sources*, edited by Manuela Marín, 13–38. Aldershot: Routledge, 1998.

Vollner, Franz. "Die Etichonen: Ein Beitrag zur Frage der Kontinuität früher Adels Familien." In *Studien und Vorarbeiten zur Geschichte des Grossfränkischen Frühdeutschens Adels*, edited by Gerd Tellenbach, 137–184. Freiburg: E. Albert, 1957.

Waardenburg, Jacques J. *Muslim Perceptions of Other Religions: A Historical Survey*. New York: Oxford University Press, 1999.

——. *Muslims and Others: Relations in Context*. New York: De Gruyter, 2003.

Waines, David. "The Pre-Būyid Amirate: Two Views from the Past." *International Journal of Middle East Studies* 8 (1977): 339–348.

Walker, R.B.J. *Inside/Outside: International Relations as Political Theory*. Cambridge: Cambridge University Press, 1992.

Wallace-Hadrill, John Michael. *Bede and His World*. Vol. 1. Aldershot: Variorum, 1994.

Waltz, James. "The Significance of the Voluntary Martyrs Movement of Ninth-Century Córdoba." *Muslim World* 60 (1970): 143–159, 226–236.

Wansbrough, John. "Diplomatica Siciliana." *Bulletin of the School of Oriental and African Studies* 47 (1984): 10–21.

Ward, Elizabeth. "Agobard of Lyons and Paschasius Radbertus as Critics of the Empress Judith." *Studies in Church History* 27 (1990): 15–25.

——. "Caesar's Wife: The Career of the Empress Judith, 819–829." In *Charlemagne's Heir: New Perspectives on the Reign of Louis the Pious (814–840)*, edited by Peter Godman and Roger Collins, 205–227. Oxford: Clarendon Press, 1990.

Wasserstein, David J. "Inventing Tradition and Constructing Identity: The Genealogy of Umar ibn Hafsūn between Christianity and Islam." *al-Qanṭara* 23 (2002): 269–297.

——. "The Language Situation in al-Andalus." In *The Formation of al-Andalus, Part 2: Language, Religion, Culture and the Sciences*, edited by Maribel Fierro and Julio Samsó, 1–15. Aldershot: Ashgate, 1998.

Watkins, John. "Toward a New Diplomatic History of Medieval and Early Modern Europe." *Journal of Medieval and Early Modern Studies* 38 (2008): 1–14.

Watt, W. Montgomery. *Muslim-Christian Encounters: Perceptions and Misperception*. London: Routledge, 1991.

Weber, Max. *The Theory of Social and Economic Organisation*. Edited and translated by A. M. Henderson and Talcott Parsons. New York: Free Press & Falcon's Wing Press, 1947.

Weigl, Michael. "Das Maximilianeum in München: Projekt des Königs, Symbol der Volksherrschaft." In *Die politische Architektur deutscher Parlamente: Von Häusern, Schlössern und Palästen*, edited by Julia Schwanholz and Patrick Theiner, 87–104. Wiesbaden: Springer VS, 2020.

Wendell, Charles. "Baghdâd: Imago Mundi, and Other Foundation-Lore." *International Journal of Middle East Studies* 2 (1971): 99–128.

Wendt, Alexander. "Anarchy Is What States Make of It: The Social Construction of Power Politics." *International Organization* 46 (1992): 391–425.

Werner, Karl Ferdinand. "*Hludovicus Augustus*: Gouverneur l'empire chrétien—Idées et réalités." In *Charlemagne's Heir: New Perspectives on the Reign of Louis the Pious (814–840)*, edited by Peter Godman and Roger Collins, 3–123. Oxford: Clarendon Press, 1990.

———. "Les principautés périphériques dans le monde franc du VIII^e siècle." In *Structures politiques du monde franc (VI^e–XII^e siècles): Etudes sur les origines de la France et de l'Allemagne*, 438–514. London: Variorum, 1979.

———. "Missus-Marchio-Comes: Entre l'administration central et l'administration locale de l'Empire carolingien." In *Histoire Comparée de l'administration (IV^e–XVIII^e siècles)*, edited by Werner Paravicini and Karl Ferdinand Werner, 191–239. Munich: Artemis, 1980.

West, Charles. *Reframing the Feudal Revolution: Political and Social Transformation between Marne and Moselle, c. 800–c. 1100*. Cambridge: Cambridge University Press, 2013.

West, G.V.B. "Charlemagne's Involvement in Central and Southern Italy: Power and the Limits of Authority." *Early Medieval Europe* 8 (1999): 341–367.

Whitby, Michael. "Byzantine Diplomacy: Good Faith, Trust and Co-operation in International Relations in Late Antiquity." In *War and Peace in Ancient and Medieval History*, edited by Philip de Souza and John France, 120–140. Cambridge: Cambridge University Press, 2008.

Wickham, Chris. *Framing the Early Middle Ages: Europe and the Mediterranean, 400–800*. Oxford: Oxford University Press, 2005.

———. "The Mediterranean around 800: On the Brink of the Second Trade Cycle." *Dumbarton Oaks Paper* 58 (2004): 161–174.

———. "Ninth-Century Byzantium through Western Eyes." In *Byzantium in the Ninth Century: Dead or Alive?* edited by Leslie Brubaker, 245–256. Aldershot: Ashgate, 1998.

Wilk, Mateusz. "Le malikisme et les Omeyyades en al-Andalus: Le droit et l'idéologie du pouvoir." *Annales Islamologiques* 45 (2011): 101–122.

Wink, André. *Al-Hind: The Making of the Indo-Islamic World*. Vol. 1. Leiden: Brill, 1990.

Wittfogel, Karl August. *Oriental Despotism: A Comparative Study of Total Power*. New Haven: Yale University Press, 1957.

Wolf, Kenneth Baxter. *Christian Martyrs in Muslim Spain*. Cambridge: Cambridge University Press, 1988.

———. "Christian Views of Islam in Early Medieval Spain." In *Medieval Christian Perceptions of Islam*, edited by John V. Tolan, 85–108. New York: Garland, 1996.

———. "The Earliest Latin Lives of Muḥammad." In *Conversion and Continuity: Indigenous Christian Communities in Islamic Lands, Eighth to Eighteenth Centuries*, edited by Michael Gervers and Ramzi Jibran Bikhazi, 89–101. Toronto: Pontifical Institute of Mediaeval Studies, 1990.

Wolf, Kordula. "Gli hypati di Gaeta, papa Giovanni VIII e i Saraceni: Tra dinamiche locali e transregionali." *Bullettino dell'Istituto Storico Italiano per il Medio Evo* 116 (2014): 25–59.

Wolff, Philippe. "Les Événements de Catalogne de 798–812 et la chronologie de l'Astronome." *Anuarios de Estudios Medievales* 2 (1965): 451–458.

Wolfram, Herwig. "The Creation of the Carolingian Frontier-System c. 800." In *The Transformation of Frontiers from Late Antiquity to the Carolingians*, edited by Walter Pohl, Ian Wood, and Helmut Reimitz, 233–245. Leiden: Brill, 2001.

Wolfthal, Diane. Introduction to *Peace and Negotiation: Strategies for Coexistence in the Middle Ages and Renaissance*, edited by Diane Wolfthal, xi–xviii. Turnhout: Brepols, 2000.

Wood, Ian. *The Merovingian Kingdoms, 450–751*. London: Longman, 1994.

——. *The Modern Origins of the Early Middle Ages*. Oxford: Oxford University Press, 2014.

Wright, Roger. "Language and Religion in Early Medieval Spain." In *Language of Religion, Language of the People: Medieval Judaism, Christianity and Islam*, edited by Ernst Bremer, Jörg Jarnut, Michael Richter, and David Wasserstein, 115–126. Munich: Wilhelm Fink Verlag, 2006.

Yücesoy, Hayrettin. *Messianic Beliefs and Imperial Politics in Medieval Islam: The ʿAbbāsid Caliphate in the Early Ninth Century*. Columbia: University of South Carolina Press, 2009.

Zakeri, Mohsen. "Al-Ṭabarī on Sasanian History: A Study in Sources." In *Al-Ṭabarī: A Medieval Muslim Historian and His Work*, edited by Hugh Kennedy, 27–40. Princeton: Princeton University Press, 2008.

Zichy, Étienne. "Le voyage de Sallām, l'interprète, à la muraille de Gog et Magog." *Körösi Csoma Archivum* 1 (1921–1925): 190–204.

Zimmermann, Michel. "Western Francia: The Southern Principalities." In *The New Cambridge Medieval History*, vol. 3, edited by Timothy Reuter, 420–455. Cambridge: Cambridge University Press, 1995.

Zotz, Thomas. "Pfalzen der Karolingerzeit: Neue Aspekte aus historischer Sicht." In *Deutsche Königspfalzen: Beiträge zu ihrer historischen und archäologischen Erforschung*. Vol. 8: *Places of Power, Orte der Herrschaft, Lieux du pouvoir*, edited by Lutz Fenske, Jörg Jarnut, and Matthias Wemhoff, 13–23. Göttingen: Vandenhoeck & Ruprecht, 2007.

# INDEX

## A NOTE ON THE TYPE

THIS BOOK has been composed in Miller, a Scotch Roman typeface designed by Matthew Carter and first released by Font Bureau in 1997. It resembles Monticello, the typeface developed for The Papers of Thomas Jefferson in the 1940s by C. H. Griffith and P. J. Conkwright and reinterpreted in digital form by Carter in 2003.

Pleasant Jefferson ("P. J.") Conkwright (1905–1986) was Typographer at Princeton University Press from 1939 to 1970. He was an acclaimed book designer and AIGA Medalist.